Clinical Neurophysiology, Neuroimaging, and Neuromodulation of Neuropsychiatric Disorders

Clinical Neurophysiology, Neuroimaging, and Neuromodulation of Neuropsychiatric Disorders

Editor

Yoshihiro Noda

MDPI • Basel • Beijing • Wuhan • Barcelona • Belgrade • Manchester • Tokyo • Cluj • Tianjin

Editor
Yoshihiro Noda
Neuropsychiatry
Keio University School of
Medicine
Tokyo
Japan

Editorial Office
MDPI
St. Alban-Anlage 66
4052 Basel, Switzerland

This is a reprint of articles from the Special Issue published online in the open access journal *Journal of Personalized Medicine* (ISSN 2075-4426) (available at: www.mdpi.com/journal/jpm/special_issues/Neuromodulation_Neuropsychiatric).

For citation purposes, cite each article independently as indicated on the article page online and as indicated below:

LastName, A.A.; LastName, B.B.; LastName, C.C. Article Title. *Journal Name* **Year**, *Volume Number*, Page Range.

ISBN 978-3-0365-3131-1 (Hbk)
ISBN 978-3-0365-3130-4 (PDF)

Contents

About the Editor

Yoshihiro Noda

Dr. Yoshihiro Noda, Associate Professor at the Department of Neuropsychiatry, Keio University School of Medicine, is a clinician–scientist who specializes in the development of novel TMS treatment technologies, such as rTMS, TBS, deep TMS, QPS, and MST, and combined TMS–EEG neurophysiology in psychiatry. Dr. Noda is one of the leading TMS researchers in Japan, and is currently promoting the TMS Database Registry Project (TMS Database Registry Consortium Research in Japan: TReC-J).

Preface to "Clinical Neurophysiology, Neuroimaging, and Neuromodulation of Neuropsychiatric Disorders"

Over 90 years have passed since Dr. Hans Berger first reported the electrical activity of the human brain in 1929, and, in recent years, as suggested by Dr. György Buzsáki, such ideas as the rhythm of the brain, the mind is not bornand brain is a device that predicts, and it is the rhythm of the brain that produces predictive abilityhave come to be accepted. Furthermore, recent advances in neuroimaging technology, including EEG, have made it possible to visualize various brain activities. In addition, research on neuromodulation, as an intervention for brain dynamics, the underlying neurophysiological basis of the brain, was rapidly accelerated by the development of TMS in 1985 by Dr. Anthony Barker. On the other hand, as a trend in the field of psychiatry in recent years, the concept of precision medicine has become important in elucidating mental disorders as well as for developing new therapeutic strategies. Research in these areas is progressing rapidly, and new knowledge is being accumulated every day. This Special Issue aims to present cutting-edge research in clinical neurophysiology, neuroimaging, and neuromodulation.

Yoshihiro Noda
Editor

Journal of
*Personalized
Medicine*

Editorial

Clinical Neurophysiology, Neuroimaging, and Neuromodulation of Neuropsychiatric Disorders

Yoshihiro Noda

Department of Neuropsychiatry, Keio University School of Medicine, Tokyo 160-8582, Japan; yoshi-tms@keio.jp;
Tel.: +81-3-3353-1211

The goal of this Special Issue is to introduce the cutting-edge research in clinical neurophysiology, neuroimaging, and neuromodulation. We were able to publish 11 original articles and 3 review papers that utilize the latest neuroscience approaches in the abovementioned fields. I would like to introduce these excellent works below.

1. EEG Related Research

First, Runnova and Selskii et al. conducted a long-term test in subjects where they maintain attention to sound stimuli, and the authors recorded EEGs and performed wavelet analysis to quantitatively evaluate how EEGs change during the daytime in patients with sleep disorders. In healthy subjects, alpha peak occurred around 9 Hz, but in patients with primary insomnia, the peak was found to increase to around 11 Hz. As for the changes in the dynamics of the alpha rhythm during the process of attention test, there was a significant difference between patients with sleep disorders and healthy controls in the frequency range of 7.5–10.5 Hz, supporting the concept of 24-h hyperarousal in primary insomnia [1].

Second, EEG activity in the brain at gamma frequencies reflects the process of encoding and transmitting information. A 40 Hz auditory steady-state response (40 Hz ASSR) has often been linked to cognitive processing changes in psychiatric disorders; however, the relationship between ASSR and cognitive function remains unclear. Most studies to date have assessed ASSR using a fixed 40 Hz gamma frequency, and less attention has been paid to studies using individual gamma resonance frequencies (IGFs), which are more reflective of individual network characteristics. Parciauskaite et al. focused on processing speeds in various types of cognitive tasks and examined the relationship between 40 Hz and IGF-induced ASSR to determine how IGF is related to certain aspects of cognitive function. The results showed that, when assessing ASSR with 40 Hz and IGF, gamma activity was associated with performance speed in both complex cognitive tasks, i.e., tapping planning and problem solving. However, in the individualized approach with IGF, the observed associations were stronger than with 40 Hz stimulation, and the associations mainly reflected individual differences in higher-order cognitive processing [2].

Third, in treatment-resistant schizophrenia (TRS), abnormal connectivity between the anterior cingulate cortex (ACC) and the default mode network (DMN) has been shown to potentially play an important role in its pathophysiology. Wada et al. aimed to evaluate the connectivity between the ACC and posterior cingulate cortex (PCC), the hub of the DMN, using iCoh, a causal connectivity index. The iCoh values between the PCC and ACC were calculated by sLORETA from 19-channel resting-state EEGs. The results showed that the iCoh ratio in the delta and theta bands with directionality from the left PCC to ACC was lower in the TRS group than in the non-TRS group, suggesting that it may reflect the neurophysiological basis of TRS [3].

Fourth, Shakeel et al. investigated whether forward prediction of time series using an adaptive least mean square (LMS)-based autoregressive (AR) model could be implemented in a real-time closed-loop system by applying state-dependent triggers to EEG alpha oscillation peaks and troughs. During the resting state and a visual task, the proposed

Citation: Noda, Y. Clinical Neurophysiology, Neuroimaging, and Neuromodulation of Neuropsychiatric Disorders. *J. Pers. Med.* **2021**, *11*, 1193. https://doi.org/10.3390/jpm11111193

Received: 9 November 2021
Accepted: 10 November 2021
Published: 12 November 2021

method successfully triggered at a specific phase of the EEG oscillations for all subjects. These results indicate that the LMS-based AR model is an adaptive approach that can be implemented in real-time closed-loop systems for specific phases of alpha oscillations, and can be used as an alternative to traditional or machine learning approaches with a lower computational load [4].

Fifth, EEG can be a powerful tool to assess the effects of substance use disorders (SUD) on cognitive functioning. Specifically, modulated gamma activity may be an indicator of the pathophysiology of SUDs. Ramlakhan et al. systematically reviewed the effects of alcohol, tobacco, cannabis, cocaine, and amphetamines on gamma activity of acute and chronic exposure and withdrawal states in preclinical and clinical populations. The results showed that all of the abovementioned substances were associated with modulation of gamma activity, in both preclinical and clinical populations, regardless of the state. However, the effect of alcohol on gamma activity is complex, indicating that it may affect differently from other substances. Thus, the modulation of gamma activity is involved in the pathophysiology of SUD, suggesting the possibility of novel therapies targeting this neurophysiological substrate [5].

2. Combined TMS and EMG/EEG Research

First, Noda administered 1 Hz-rTMS to the right DLPFC in healthy subjects and examined its acute neurophysiological effects using combined TMS-EEG. A 1 Hz-rTMS was administered at rest and during a verbal task, and TMS-related power and TMS-related coherence at the F4 and F3 electrode sites were calculated. The results showed that TMS-related power at rest was significantly increased by 1 Hz-rTMS at the stimulation site in alpha, beta, and gamma bands, and TMS-related power during verbal task was significantly increased in alpha and beta bands. On the other hand, TMS-related coherence was significantly increased by 1 Hz-rTMS to the right DLPFC in the resting state in alpha and beta bands, but not in gamma band. Therefore, 1 Hz-rTMS to the right DLPFC may rapidly neuromodulate EEG activity, which may be relevant to the treatment mechanism of depression [6].

Second, Noda et al. compared the amplitudes and latencies of each TMS-evoked potential (TEP) component evoked by single-pulse TMS (spTMS) to the left M1 and DLPFC between groups of healthy young subjects, older subjects, and schizophrenia patients to clarify the spatiotemporal characteristics of each group. Compared with healthy young, the amplitudes of N45 and P180 were decreased by M1-spTMS in the elderly and P180 in patients. On the other hand, N45 was reduced by DLPFC-spTMS in the elderly. Furthermore, in the elderly, P60 was delayed after M1-spTMS and N45-P60 was delayed in the right median after left DLPFC-spTMS, whereas in patients, N45-P60 was delayed in the right central area after DLPFC-spTMS. Our results suggest that the inhibitory and excitatory mechanisms, as indexed by TEP, may be altered in the elderly and in schizophrenia patients [7].

Third, Fisicaro et al. performed single-pulse TMS on patients with Parkinson's disease (PD) and progressive supranuclear palsy (PSP) to compare neurophysiological characteristics, including motor evoked potentials (MEPs) and cortical suppression periods (CSPs), and to determine whether these differences were related to cognitive function. The results showed that the amplitude of MEPs was higher in the patient groups than in healthy controls, and there was no difference between PD and PSP groups; CSPs were longer in both M1 in patient groups than in healthy controls, but were similar between patient groups. Furthermore, RMT was positively correlated with frontal lobe function in the PSP group, indicating that RMT may be an indicator reflecting cognitive decline in PSP [8].

Fourth, the glutamatergic hypothesis and excitatory/inhibitory (E/I) imbalance hypothesis have been proposed as new hypotheses for the pathophysiology of schizophrenia (SCZ). TMS-EEG is an attractive tool to study the neurophysiology of the human cortex. Li et al. systematically reviewed TMS-EEG studies that investigated cortical functions in SCZ to examine whether TMS-EEG is a suitable modality to account for the above hypotheses. The results suggested that TMS-EEG for SCZ patients showed E/I deficits in the prefrontal cortex, which may be related to cognitive impairment and clinical severity. Furthermore, TMS-induced gamma activity of the prefrontal cortex was associated with positive symptoms, while EEG activity in theta and delta bands was associated with negative symptoms. Thus, TMS-EEG neurophysiology may provide a physiological basis for the establishment of biomarkers for better diagnosis of SCZ and the development of novel treatment strategies [9].

3. Neuromodulation Intervention Research

First, rTMS for tinnitus has the advantage that effects can be assessed immediately after intervention, making it an excellent model for testing individualization of rTMS. In this context, Schoisswohl et al. aimed to investigate the reliability of test-retest in modifying tinnitus loudness and oscillatory brain activity with brief rTMS and to examine the feasibility of individualizing rTMS for tinnitus. Patients with tinnitus received brief active and sham stimulation, and EEG was measured before and after each protocol, as well as tinnitus loudness assessment. As a result, they could identify individual rTMS protocols characterized by reliable tinnitus loudness changes (55% of behavioral responders), increased alpha power with parieto-occipital dominance (91% of alpha responders), and decreased gamma power with frontal dominance (100% of gamma responders), respectively. This study demonstrates the potential for individualization using neurophysiological markers rather than behavioral responses, suggesting that individualization of stimulation protocols is possible despite the lack of group-level reliability [10].

Second, Kashyap et al. introduced the dose-target determination index (DTDI), the ratio of the average current density in the target ROI to the ROI with the maximum value (peak region), to quantify the focality of transcranial direct current stimulation (tDCS) and examined the dose-focality relationship in three populations: young adults, middle-aged adults, and older adults. Frontal montage was performed with the target ROI set to the left middle frontal gyrus. As a result, they found that nonlinearity was dominant and focality decreased in the older adults, and this decrease was stronger in males. Therefore, it is clear that increasing the current level can increase the focality of the stimulus in this population, and that DTDI can provide information on which tDCS current level optimizes the focality of the stimulus [11].

Third, vagal nerve stimulation (VNS) has been shown to be effective in the treatment of depression, but until recently VNS devices have required surgical implantation, which has limited their widespread use. However, a novel non-invasive VNS (nVNS) device that can externally stimulate the vagal nerve was developed, raising hopes for its clinical application in stress-related psychiatric disorders. Bremner et al. systematically reviewed the effects of nVNS on physiological functions of patients with stress-related psychiatric disorders in the perspectives of brain imaging, blood inflammation biomarkers, and wearable sensing devices. The results suggest that nVNS favorably affects central brain regions involved in the regulation of autonomic tone, cardiovascular function, inflammatory response, and emotion, and that dysregulation of these circuits and systems may constitute the pathological basis for stress-related psychiatric disorders such as post-traumatic stress disorder (PTSD) and depression. The application of nVNS to stress-related psychiatric disorders may lead to the prevention and treatment of these disorders [12].

Fourth, Noda et al. investigated the effects of gamma frequency violet light (VL) stimulation on human EEG in healthy subjects by comparing it with white light (WL) under the same conditions. Comparing the power spectral density (PSD) of 40 Hz-VL EEG with that of 40 Hz-WL EEG, 40 Hz-VL had significantly lower enhancement of delta and theta bands than 40 Hz-WL. In the occipital region, the negative peak of VEP of 40 Hz-VL was smaller than that of 40 Hz-WL. Furthermore, 40 Hz-VL showed increased alpha-phase and gamma-amplitude coupling compared to the baseline EEG at the F5 electrode site during stimulation and at the C4 electrode site immediately after stimulation. Therefore,

40 Hz-VL stimulation could induce a unique photobiological neuromodulation of human EEG activity [13].

4. MRI Neuroimaging Research

Lastly, Sato et al. measured the volumes of the amygdala, hippocampus, Heschl's gyrus, and temporal lobe in neuroanatomically defined regions of interest (ROIs) using high-resolution MRI in healthy subjects, patients with schizophrenia, and patients with bipolar disorder. The results showed that there was a difference in the right hippocampal volume between the groups (healthy control group > bipolar group > schizophrenia group), with the schizophrenia group showing the smallest value. The study suggested that the right hippocampal volume could be a biomarker for differentiating between schizophrenia and bipolar disorder [14].

As introduced above, I believe that translational and clinical research using state-of-the-art technologies in the field of neuropsychiatric disorders will continue to flourish and contribute to the health and well-being of people. Last but not least, we are currently working on a second part to this Special Issue (https://www.mdpi.com/journal/jpm/special_issues/Neuromodulation_Neuropsychiatric_Series_II) and are looking forward to receiving additional excellent submissions.

Funding: This research received no external funding.

Institutional Review Board Statement: Not applicable.

Informed Consent Statement: Not applicable.

Data Availability Statement: Not applicable.

Acknowledgments: I would like to thank all the authors who contributed to this Special Issue. I also appreciate *JPM* staff's excellent support throughout the editorial process.

Conflicts of Interest: There is no conflict of interest to declare in this Special Issue.

References

1. Runnova, A.; Selskii, A.; Kiselev, A.; Shamionov, R.; Parsamyan, R.; Zhuravlev, M. Changes in EEG Alpha Activity during Attention Control in Patients: Association with Sleep Disorders. *J. Pers. Med.* **2021**, *11*, 601. [CrossRef] [PubMed]
2. Parciauskaite, V.; Pipinis, E.; Voicikas, A.; Bjekic, J.; Potapovas, M.; Jurkuvenas, V.; Griskova-Bulanova, I. Individual Resonant Frequencies at Low-Gamma Range and Cognitive Processing Speed. *J. Pers. Med.* **2021**, *11*, 453. [CrossRef] [PubMed]
3. Wada, M.; Nakajima, S.; Tarumi, R.; Masuda, F.; Miyazaki, T.; Tsugawa, S.; Ogyu, K.; Honda, S.; Matsushita, K.; Kikuchi, Y.; et al. Resting-State Isolated Effective Connectivity of the Cingulate Cortex as a Neurophysiological Biomarker in Patients with Severe Treatment-Resistant Schizophrenia. *J. Pers. Med.* **2020**, *10*, 89. [CrossRef] [PubMed]
4. Shakeel, A.; Onojima, T.; Tanaka, T.; Kitajo, K. Real-Time Implementation of EEG Oscillatory Phase-Informed Visual Stimulation Using a Least Mean Square-Based AR Model. *J. Pers. Med.* **2021**, *11*, 38. [CrossRef] [PubMed]
5. Ramlakhan, J.U.; Ma, M.; Zomorrodi, R.; Blumberger, D.M.; Noda, Y.; Barr, M.S. The Role of Gamma Oscillations in the Pathophysiology of Substance Use Disorders. *J. Pers. Med.* **2021**, *11*, 17. [CrossRef] [PubMed]
6. Noda, Y. Potential Neurophysiological Mechanisms of 1Hz-TMS to the Right Prefrontal Cortex for Depression: An Exploratory TMS-EEG Study in Healthy Participants. *J. Pers. Med.* **2021**, *11*, 68. [CrossRef] [PubMed]
7. Noda, Y.; Barr, M.S.; Zomorrodi, R.; Cash, R.F.H.; Lioumis, P.; Chen, R.; Daskalakis, Z.J.; Blumberger, D.M. Single-Pulse Transcranial Magnetic Stimulation-Evoked Potential Amplitudes and Latencies in the Motor and Dorsolateral Prefrontal Cortex among Young, Older Healthy Participants, and Schizophrenia Patients. *J. Pers. Med.* **2021**, *11*, 54. [CrossRef] [PubMed]
8. Fisicaro, F.; Lanza, G.; Cantone, M.; Ferri, R.; Pennisi, G.; Nicoletti, A.; Zappia, M.; Bella, R.; Pennisi, M. Clinical and Electrophysiological Hints to TMS in De Novo Patients with Parkinson's Disease and Progressive Supranuclear Palsy. *J. Pers. Med.* **2020**, *10*, 274. [CrossRef] [PubMed]
9. Li, X.; Honda, S.; Nakajima, S.; Wada, M.; Yoshida, K.; Daskalakis, Z.J.; Mimura, M.; Noda, Y. TMS-EEG Research to Elucidate the Pathophysiological Neural Bases in Patients with Schizophrenia: A Systematic Review. *J. Pers. Med.* **2021**, *11*, 388. [CrossRef] [PubMed]
10. Schoisswohl, S.; Langguth, B.; Hebel, T.; Abdelnaim, M.A.; Volberg, G.; Schecklmann, M. Heading for Personalized rTMS in Tinnitus: Reliability of Individualized Stimulation Protocols in Behavioral and Electrophysiological Responses. *J. Pers. Med.* **2021**, *11*, 536. [CrossRef] [PubMed]

11. Kashyap, R.; Bhattacharjee, S.; Arumugam, R.; Bharath, R.D.; Udupa, K.; Oishi, K.; Desmond, J.E.; Chen, S.H.A.; Guan, C. Focality-Oriented Selection of Current Dose for Transcranial Direct Current Stimulation. *J. Pers. Med.* **2021**, *11*, 940. [CrossRef] [PubMed]
12. Bremner, J.D.; Gurel, N.Z.; Wittbrodt, M.T.; Shandhi, M.H.; Rapaport, M.H.; Nye, J.A.; Pearce, B.D.; Vaccarino, V.; Shah, A.J.; Park, J.; et al. Application of Noninvasive Vagal Nerve Stimulation to Stress-Related Psychiatric Disorders. *J. Pers. Med.* **2020**, *10*, 119. [CrossRef] [PubMed]
13. Noda, Y.; Takano, M.; Hayano, M.; Li, X.; Wada, M.; Nakajima, S.; Mimura, M.; Kondo, S.; Tsubota, K. Photobiological Neuromodulation of Resting-State EEG and Steady-State Visual-Evoked Potentials by 40 Hz Violet Light Optical Stimulation in Healthy Individuals. *J. Pers. Med.* **2021**, *11*, 557. [CrossRef] [PubMed]
14. Sato, J.; Hirano, Y.; Hirakawa, N.; Takahashi, J.; Oribe, N.; Kuga, H.; Nakamura, I.; Hirano, S.; Ueno, T.; Togao, O.; et al. Lower Hippocampal Volume in Patients with Schizophrenia and Bipolar Disorder: A Quantitative MRI Study. *J. Pers. Med.* **2021**, *11*, 121. [CrossRef] [PubMed]

Journal of *Personalized Medicine*

MDPI

Article

Changes in EEG Alpha Activity during Attention Control in Patients: Association with Sleep Disorders

Anastasiya Runnova [1,2,†], Anton Selskii [1,2,†], Anton Kiselev [1,3], Rail Shamionov [4], Ruzanna Parsamyan [1,†] and Maksim Zhuravlev [1,2,*,†]

1 Department of Basic Research in Neurocardiology, Institute of Cardiological Research, Saratov State Medical University Named after V.I. Razumovsky, B. Kazachaya Str., 112, 410012 Saratov, Russia; runnova.ae@staff.sgmu.ru (A.R.); selskiiao@gmail.com (A.S.); antonkis@list.ru (A.K.); kvl.PRR@mail.ru (R.P.)
2 Institute of Physics, Saratov State University, Astrakhanskaya Str., 83, 410012 Saratov, Russia
3 National Medical Research Center for Therapy and Preventive Medicine, 10, Petroverigsky per., 101953 Moscow, Russia
4 Faculty of Psychological, Pedagogical and Special Education, Saratov State University, Astrakhanskaya Str., 83, 410012 Saratov, Russia; shamionov@mail.ru
* Correspondence: zhuravlevmo@gmail.com
† These authors contributed equally to this work.

Abstract: We aimed to assess which quantitative EEG changes during daytime testing in patients with sleep disorder (primary insomnia and excessive daytime sleepiness groups). All experimental study participants were subjected to a long-term test for maintaining attention to sound stimuli, and their EEGs were recorded and then processed, using wavelet analysis, in order to estimate the power and frequency structure of alpha activity. In healthy subjects, the maximum increase in the alpha rhythm occurred near 9 Hz. Patients with primary insomnia were characterized by an increase in the amplitude of the alpha rhythm near 11 Hz. For subjects with sleep disorders, an increase in the amplitude of the alpha rhythm was observed in the entire frequency range (7.5–12.5 Hz), with a maximum increase at 9–10 Hz. Significant differences ($p \leq 0.001$) for changes in the alpha rhythm dynamics in the course of performing the attention test were observed in the frequency range of 7.5–10.5 Hz between the control group and patients with sleep disorders. The ratios of the alpha rhythm power values for passive stages with closed eyes before and after active stage were significantly different among the groups of healthy sleep volunteers, patients with primary insomnia, and patients with impaired sleep hygiene within the range of 9.5 to 12.5 Hz. The results of the current study supported the notion of a 24-h hyperarousal in primary insomnia.

Keywords: EEG; wavelet-analyse; alpha-activity; attention; sleep disorder; insomnia

Citation: Runnova, A.; Selskii, A.; Kiselev, A.; Shamionov, R.; Parsamyan, R.; Zhuravlev, M. Changes in EEG Alpha Activity during Attention Control in Patients: Association with Sleep Disorders. *J. Pers. Med.* **2021**, *11*, 601. https://doi.org/10.3390/jpm11070601

Academic Editor: Yoshihiro Noda

Received: 19 May 2021
Accepted: 23 June 2021
Published: 25 June 2021

1. Introduction

Although the prevalence of chronic primary insomnia in the general population is approximately 10%, transient symptoms of sleep disorders are detected much more often—in 30–35% of people [1,2]. Despite the effectiveness of contemporary psychotherapeutic and drug treatment contemporary psychotherapeutic and medicamentous treatment methods on many occasions, they are all associated with significant limitations [3–8]. A better understanding of the primary insomnia pathophysiology appears useful in assessing the potential of various treatment techniques, and also in developing novel approaches that specifically target neurophysiological characteristics correlating with primary insomnia symptoms. To date, the change in neurophysiological characteristics of patients with insomnia in the presleep period and during their sleep has been sufficiently studied [9–13]. Physiological markers may include an increase in high EEG frequencies in the peri-sleep onset period, as well as during non-rapid eye movement sleep and rapid eye movement phase [10,12,14], along with reduction in the slow-wave sleep [15,16] and power spectra decrease in delta and theta bands in some subjects [10,13,17].

At the same time, modern somnology suggests that primary insomnia is more a condition of 24-h hyperarousal than a purely nocturnal disorder [18]. In particular, it has been shown that patients with insomnia, in spite of their subjective complaints for daytime somnolence, as well as their significantly shorter nocturnal sleep, do not exhibit augmented somnolence, as compared with normal sleepers [19–21]. Recent evidence suggests that patients with primary insomnia show changes in neurophysiological activity during normal daytime wakefulness compared to those with normal sleep [22–24]. However, a very high individual variability of the brain electrical activity significantly reduces the ability to identify such traits across patients [25]. Currently, lower values of theta power and higher values of beta power in patients with primary insomnia were established [24]. However, the presented characteristics of EEG activity are weakly specific, since they can be observed in normal sleepers as well, for example, in conditions of visual fatigue accumulation [26,27] or with major depressive disorder [28].

In this study, we present a quantitative description of the change in the alpha rhythm (as electroencephalography biomarker) during the daytime in patients with primary insomnia. Despite the fact that the EEG activity parameters are extremely variable across the population [29,30], it is the alpha rhythm that is a very stable trait in subjects of different ages [31,32]. It is well known that the alpha rhythm activity increases with a decrease in the levels of sensory signals: e.g., when eyes are closed, the alpha rhythm power increases in the occipital brain lobe [33]. At the same time, it is known that the alpha rhythm amplitude changes in the course of cognitive activities, such as cognitive performance, visual attention, memory, and complex abstract tasks [26,34–38]. Besides, it has been shown that the alpha rhythm during sleep undergoes significant changes in patients with insomnia [39,40].

Hence, the main goal of our study was to identify objective quantitative changes in the electroencephalography occurring during the daytime activity of patients suffering from insomnia. For the first time, the comparison of patients with primary insomnia is conducted not only with a control group of apparently healthy subjects, but also with a group of patients suffering from insomnia caused by poor sleep hygiene.

2. Materials and Methods

2.1. Data and Materials

The participants volunteered in our experiments on a complimentary basis. All study subjects signed an informed medical consent to participate in the experimental work, received all necessary explanations about the research, and agreed to the subsequent publication of the study results. Collected experimental data were processed sensu the principles of confidentiality and anonymity of research participants. The design of experimental studies was approved by the local scientific research Ethics Committee. The experimental study subjects were recruited from the outpatients with sleep disorders at the Pain Management Clinic (Saratov, Russian Federation). The inclusion criteria for our study were as follows:

- Male gender, age <25 years;
- Complaints for insufficient and non-restorative sleep;
- Sleep onset disorder (>30 min to fall asleep) or sleep maintenance disorder (two or more awakenings per night of >15 min long or wake after sleep onset (WASO) time of >30 min);
- Problem incidence rate >3 nights per week;
- Problem duration >6 months.

Exclusion criteria were as follows:

- Beck Depression Inventory score (BDI) >13 [41];
- A score >7 on the Hospital Anxiety and Depression Scale [42];
- An apnea-hypopnea index (AHI) or periodic limb movements index (PLM) >5 or restless leg syndrome (RLS) during the polysomnography night;
- A medical or psychiatric disorder;
- Psychotropic medicine use over the last month.

A sleep diary was kept daily for a week by every participant. All patients underwent neuropsychological status assessment by means of the Schulte Table test, Digital Symbol Substitution Test (DSST), Hospital Anxiety and Depression Scale (HADS), somnolence and sleep quality test; as well as tests for semantic and phonemic awareness, and memory. A comparative assessment of the cognitive functions in study participants via DSST, did not reveal a significant difference in indicators; all patients successfully completed the task with no more than two errors in 90 s, which was acceptable. It was also noted that all participants were successful in their studies at various universities (Saratov, Russia). The sleep interviews and the medical examination were conducted by the physicians, certified in neurology and sleep medicine, whereas the psychiatric interviews were conducted by board certified psychiatrists. Chronic insomnia disorder was diagnosed sensu 2014 International Classification of Sleep Disorders-Third Edition.

The study included three groups of subjects. The control group comprised of 15 patients with healthy sleep (Group I, $n = 15$; age: 22.5 ± 1.5 years; BMI: 20.3 ± 1.2 kg/m^2; BDI: 6 ± 3; HADS: 5 ± 1.2). The primary insomnia group included 12 men with chronic insomnia (Group II, $n = 12$; age: 22.6 ± 1.4 years; BMI: 20 ± 1.5 kg/m^2; BDI: 7 ± 3; HADS: 6 ± 0.5). Test subjects in Group II complained of pre- and intrasomnic disorders. At the same time, according to their sleep diaries, they tried to provide themselves with adequate conditions for normal sleep. The daytime somnolence group consisted of 5 patients with chronic insomnia and regular impaired sleep hygiene (Group III, $n = 5$; age: 22.8 ± 1.2 years; BMI: 20 ± 1.1 kg/m^2; BDI: 7 ± 1; HADS: 5.2 ± 0.8). The main complaint in Group III was daytime sleepiness. An average age of the subjects was 21 years 3 months. The ailment duration averaged 1.5 years.

Analyzing anamneses, we discovered that 87% of patients in Groups II and III sleep less than 5–6 h a day. In Group II, 97% of patients experienced difficulty falling asleep; 85% of subjects were spending over an hour before falling asleep; shallow sleep with frequent nocturnal awakenings was observed in 73% of patients; and 86% of patients were dissatisfied with the quality of their sleep. In Group III, 100% of patients had unbearable somnolence during daytime hours, causing difficulties in performing their duties.

The experiments were carried out in the late afternoon hours at a specially equipped laboratory. The day before and on the day of the experiment, every test subject did not have any episodes of a daytime sleep. During the experiment, while the participants were lying comfortably in a relaxed mode, their brain activity was measured (via EEG) in three different states: (1) stage of passive wakefulness with closed eyes (CY, duration of about 6–7 min), (2) passive wakefulness with periodic sound stimuli (A, around 35 min), (3) repeated stage of passive wakefulness with closed eyes (RCY, approximately 6–7 min). During the A-stage, all test subjects were instructed to stay awake predominantly with eyes open. In order to estimate their state of awakening and sleep, they were instructed to press a specific button on the remote control after each sound signal. Beeping sound signals alternated with pauses, the duration of which was set randomly in the range 7 to 14 s. We automatically estimated the duration of time interval T_r between the sound signal and the test subject response (i.e., pressing the button). Time recordings for sound signals, pressing the button, and EEG data were conducted simultaneously.

The multichannel surface EEG data were collected using the Encephalan-EEGR-19/26 recorder (Medicom MTD Ltd, Russia). Data were recorded at 250 Hz sampling rate using the conventional monopolar method of registration with two referential points and $N = 31$ electrodes, as shown in Figure 1a. The adhesive Ag/AgCl electrodes in prewired head caps were used to obtain the EEG signals. Two reference electrodes, A1 and A2, were located on mastoids, while the ground electrode N was placed above the forehead. The EEG signals were filtered by a band-pass filter with cut-off points at 0.5 Hz (HP) and 70 Hz (LP) and a 50 Hz notch filter. Parts of EEG signals are presented in Figure 1b.

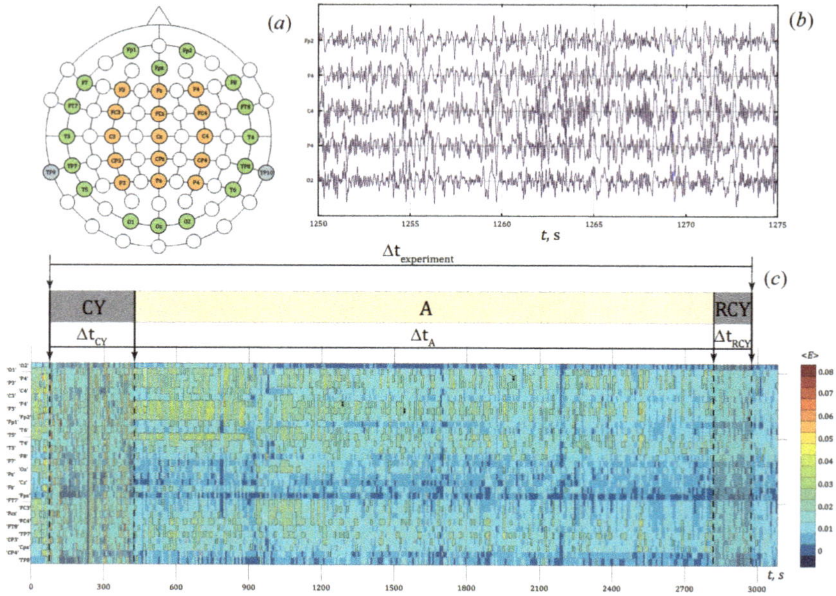

Figure 1. (**a**) The scheme of the "10–10" EEG electrode arrangement; (**b**) Fragments of EEG signals recorded during the experimental active stage; (**c**) The time dependence of the wavelet-energy in the band [8; 12] Hz by EEG.

2.2. Methods

EEG recordings were processed by using the method of spatio-temporal analysis of multichannel EEG signals, based upon continuous wavelet transform (CWT) [43,44]. Currently, CWT is considered one of the most effective tools for studying the signals of biological objects [44,45]. We denote CWT in the following form:

$$W(f,t_0) = \frac{1}{\sqrt{s}} \int_{-\infty}^{\infty} x(t)\psi^*_{f,t_0}\left(\frac{t-t_0}{f}\right)dt; \tag{1}$$

where $x(t)$ is the experimental signal, $\psi^*_{f,t_0}(t)$ is the wavelet base function, f is the analog of ordinary frequency in Fourier analysis, symbol "*" denotes the complex conjugation. We use the Morlet wavelet as the CWT base function:

$$\psi_0(\eta) = \frac{1}{\sqrt[4]{\pi}} e^{j2\pi\eta} e^{-\frac{\eta^2}{2}}; \tag{2}$$

Morlet wavelet is widely used for analyzing the signals of biological objects, allowing to maintain the optimal ratio between the frequency and time resolution achieved with CWT (1). Each one-dimensional signal $x(t)$ allows estimating a two-dimensional wavelet surface as:

$$W(f,t_0) = |W(f,t_0)| e^{j\phi_f(t_0)}; \tag{3}$$

This surface $W(f,t_0)$ characterizes the oscillatory activity for each frequency f at any time t_0 for the initial signal $x(t)$. Next, we define the integrated energy distribution $\langle E(t_0)\rangle$ for a certain frequency range $[f_{min}; f_{max}]$ as:

$$\langle E(t_0)\rangle = \int_{f_{min}}^{f_{max}} |W(f,t_0)|^2 df; \tag{4}$$

We consider the frequency range of the classic alpha rhythm, describing oscillatory activity in frequency range Δf_α, $f \in (8;12)$ Hz [45,46]. In the context of this study, we divided this frequency range into 1 Hz bands.

The function $\langle E(t_0)\rangle$ (4) is calculated for each of the EEG signal. To reduce the amount of data and the required time for numerical calculation, we averaged this function in a time window Δt = 5 s as

$$\langle E_k(n,t_0')\rangle = \int_{t_0}^{t_0+\Delta t} \langle E_k(n,t_0)\rangle dt; \tag{5}$$

where k denotes the range, n is the sequence number of EEG signal, t_0' is the discrete time for the function (5) and its step is the same as Δt. Thus, the two-dimensional function (5) allows performing a spatio-temporal analysis of oscillatory activity based on the estimates of the energy values in different frequency ranges. It also allows to conduct spatio-temporal analysis of EEG recordings from the estimates of the interrelation between the CWT energy values for different types of oscillation activity. In Figure 1c we show the results of the energy estimated in the band [8;12] Hz by each EEG channel with a time step Δt.

In order to estimate the total energy of the wavelet transformation per alpha wave range, we used $\langle E^{EEG}\rangle$, computed as:

$$\langle E\rangle = \sum_{k=1}^{5}\sum_{n=1}^{N}\langle E_k(n,t_0')\rangle. \tag{6}$$

where N represents the number of EEG channels.

Mean, median, and standard deviation were used in descriptive statistics of the data. The Mann-Whitney U test for independent samples was used for the comparison of quantitative data [47]. The results with a p-value ≤ 0.001 were considered to show statistical significance. Statistical analyses were performed in the SPSS version 22.0 program for Windows (IBM, Armonk, NY, USA).

3. Results

Response time, T_r, as a function of experimental time t were calculated for each subject. A typical pattern of such dependences is shown on the top panel in Figure 2. The bottom row in Figure 2 demonstrates the corresponding dependences of the total energy $\langle E\rangle$ for the entire frequency range Δf_α. Figure 2a–c demonstrate the characteristics for a participant of the group with a healthy sleep (Group I), insomnia (Group II), and daytime somnolence (Group III), correspondingly.

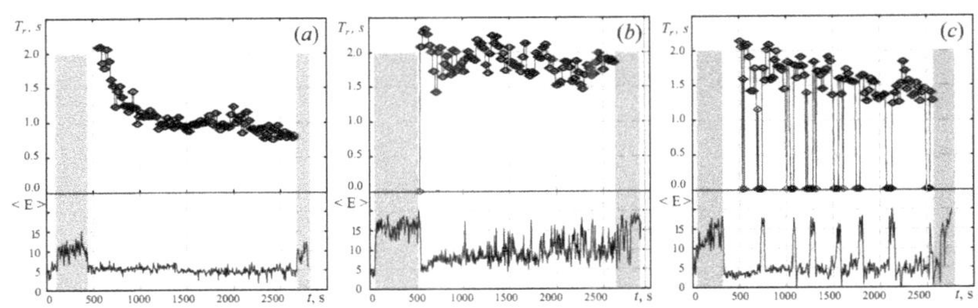

Figure 2. (**a**) The top panel: test subject response delays decreased with experimental time, over subsequent trials to the sound stimulus $T_r(t)$ on experimental time t; the bottom panel: the dependence of wavelet energy $\langle E(t)\rangle$ in the frequency interval of [8;12] Hz. These dependences were calculated for test subject #7 from Group I (control group with a healthy sleep); (**b**,**c**) represent similar dependences of $T_r(t)$ and $\langle E(t)\rangle$ for test subject #11 from experimental Group II (with primary insomnia) and for test subject #3 from Group III (with hypersomnia), respectively. Light gray rectangles indicate CY and RCY stages (passive wakefulness of test subjects with closed eyes–initial and repeated).

Passive wakefulness stages with closed eyes, CY and RCY, highlighted in gray in Figure 2, demonstrate the maximum values of $\langle E(t) \rangle$ for test subjects in all three groups. However, during the active stage A, alpha rhythm demonstrates different scenarios of its dynamics. In Group I (the control encompassing subjects with healthy sleep), we observe subject-to-subject variability in dependence of response time T_r. Among the subjects of this group, T_r varies 0.75–3.21 s with the $mean(T_r) \approx 1.25$ and the $median(T_r) \approx 1.21$. The overall dynamics of alpha rhythm energy $\langle E(t) \rangle$ is characterized by the wide range and variability during the active stage A. We can see some increase in the amplitude of the alpha rhythm at the end of this stage in the control group (see Figure 2a).

For patients with primary insomnia (Group II), we observe a minimum level of alpha rhythm energy during the active stage A, and fluctuations in the amplitude of $\langle E(t) \rangle$ are under 30–40% of the average (see Figure 2b). At the same time, test subjects from this group successfully maintain the state of wakefulness and a quick response to sound signals. The response time T_r after the short adaptation period decreases to a minimum, and then there is virtually no increase. In this group, the response time T_r is within 0.71–2.8 s range with the mean and the median of response time: $mean(T_r) \approx 1.02$; $median(T_r) \approx 0.99$. Thus, the Group II, shows an illustrative example of adaptation to the process of periodic responses to external stimuli, leading to a significant decrease in response time at the end of an active stage A.

As for the Group III, the dependences of $T_R(t)$ and $\langle E(t) \rangle$ for patients with poor sleep hygiene practices and daytime hypersomnia are characterized by the most complex dynamics during the active stage A. Test subjects in this group reveal the periods without responses to sound stimuli. Precise time intervals, at which the subject's responses are absent, are shown in the upper diagram in Figure 2c, using zero values of the $T_r(t)$ dependence. The duration of similar states without responses to the sounds for different subjects in the group varies from 38–437 s. The response time T_r in Group III ranges between 0.8 and 7.2 s, and its median and mean are quite similar: $mean(T_r) \approx 1.34$; $median(T_r) \approx 1.35$. On average, the total duration of stages without responses for subjects in this group is 397.98 ± 213.30 s.

It is worth noting that the subjects of the Groups I and II do not exhibit the long periods of "missed" sound stimuli (the largest amount of the latter is 4). During such periods without the subject's response, we observe a powerful increase in alpha activity, which, most likely, is associated with involuntary eye closure and the state of a micro-sleep [48]. We also observe that, at some stages, the energy level $\langle E(t) \rangle$ can exceed the value recorded during the passive wakefulness stages with closed eyes—CY and RCY.

Further on, we consider how the activity changes at each band $\Delta f = 1$ Hz within the alpha rhythm. For each group of subjects, we compare the change in energy $E_{RCY/CY}$ at the stages of passive wakefulness with closed eyes, CY and RCY, with the change in energy E_A during an active stage A. Hence, we estimate the value of $E_{RCY/CY}$ and E_A according to the following expressions:

$$E_{RCY/CY} = \frac{\sum_{RCY} \left\langle E_{\Delta f} \right\rangle}{\sum_{CY} \left\langle E_{\Delta f} \right\rangle}, \tag{7}$$

and also the value E_A:

$$E_A = \frac{\sum_{(A_{end-300})}^{A_{end}} \left\langle E_{\Delta f} \right\rangle}{\sum_{A_0}^{(A_{0+300})} \left\langle E_{\Delta f} \right\rangle}, \tag{8}$$

where RCY and CY are the registration durations for stages RCY and CY, respectively; A_{end} is the time of registration of the last sound stimulus during the stage A; $(A_{end-300})$ is a moment of time 300 s before the last sound stimulus during the stage A; (A_{0+300}) is a moment of time 300 s after the beginning of the stage A; A_0 is the registration time of the first sound stimulus during stage A.

Figure 3 illustrates the statistical assessment results of the distribution of these quantities in three groups of subjects. Figure 3a presents the data for Group I: it shows an increase in the alpha rhythm activity at all frequency intervals Δf during the repeated passive wakefulness stage RCY in comparison with the initial passive wakefulness stage CY. At the same time, the dynamics of alpha activity at the active stage A are less homogeneous. Frequency interval $\Delta f = [9; 10]$ shows the maximum increase in alpha rhythm energy in the EEG at the end of an active stage A; and with increase in frequency, the alpha rhythm level declines.

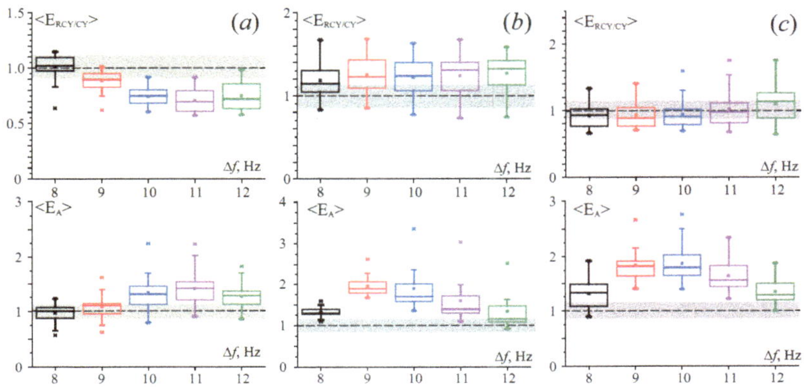

Figure 3. (**a**–**c**) The diagrams of energy ratio $E_{RCY/CY}$ (7) (top panel) and E_A (8) (bottom panel) by frequency interval $\Delta f \in \Delta f_\alpha$ for I, II, and III participant's groups, respectively. The diagrams depict the following statistical characteristics of energy ratios: the first and the third quartiles (25–75%, inside the box); the median and mean (dash line and point inside the box, accordingly); 1.5 interquartile range (shown by whiskers); and outliers represented by asterisks. Light gray rectangles delineate the ranges of values representing the ratios close to one.

For Group II, the energy variables, $E_{RCY/CY}$ and E_A, remain constant in the frequency interval $\Delta f = [8; 9]$, and as the frequency increases, these dependences are in antiphase, i.e., the energy E_{RCY} of alpha rhythm during second passive stage undergoes reduction, compared with the energy E_{CY} of first passive stage, and the energy E_A of the active stage A increases (see Figure 3b, top and bottom panels, accordingly). For test subjects in Group III, the ratio $E_{RCY/CY}$ does not change, whereas E_A rises dramatically to the maximum value at 10 Hz (see Figure 3c).

Table 1 presents the estimation results of the Wilcoxon test used for comparing independent data on the ratio of wavelet energies by channels. $p < 0.001$ is considered to confirm statistical significance. We used the stricter threshold of statistical significance to reduce the number of possible false detected differences [49,50]. All p-values below this threshold are marked in bold. Hence, for faster oscillatory activity in alpha rhythm (frequency range $f \in [9.5; 12.5]$ Hz) at passive wakefulness stages (CY and RCY), significant differences are observed for analyzed EEG results of all study groups.

At an active stage A, significant differences between the experimental groups shift to a lower frequency zone of the alpha rhythm (frequency range $f \in [7.5; 10.5]$ Hz). In the process of a cognitive activity, it is possible to distinguish between the subjects with a healthy sleep (Group I), insomnia (Group II), and daytime somnolence (Group III). However, the dynamics of alpha rhythm in patients with insomnia (Group II) and daytime sleepiness (Group III) during the cognitive processes does not show significant differences at any of investigated frequencies ($f \in [7.5; 12.5]$).

Table 1. Analysis of the energy ratio $ERCY/CY$ and EA for all groups in different frequency bands. m is a median; Δ is the standard deviation for each frequency interval for the corresponding group; $P1$ is the p value of the Group I (control) compared with the Group II (patients with primary insomnia); $P2$ is the p value of the Group II compared with the Group III (patients with daytime somnolence); $P3$ is the p value of the Group III compared with the Group I (control). All values of $p < 0.001$ characterize statistically significant differences and are highlighted in bold. Frequency bands are indicated as follows: Δf_1 = 7.5–8.5 Hz, Δf_2 = 8.5–9.5 Hz, Δf_3 = 9.5–10.5 Hz, Δf_4 = 10.5–11.5 Hz, Δf_5 = 11.5–12.5 Hz, Δf_α = 7.5–12.5 Hz.

Frequency Band	Group I		Group II		Groupe III		*P1*	*P2*	*P3*
	m	δ	m	δ	m	δ			
				$E_{RCY/CY}$					
Δf_1	1.14	0.211	1.02	0.105	0.929	0.168	0.001	**<0.001**	0.038
Δf_2	1.22	0.22	0.895	0.086	0.882	0.201	**<0.001**	**<0.001**	0.799
Δf_3	1.238	0.225	0.748	0.08	0.909	0.23	**<0.001**	**<0.001**	**<0.001**
Δf_4	1.31	0.235	0.694	0.1	0.978	0.246	**<0.001**	**<0.001**	**<0.001**
Δf_5	1.324	0.218	0.72	0.128	1.135	0.26	**<0.001**	**<0.001**	**<0.001**
Δf_α	1.274	0.211	0.837	0.084	0.953	0.207	**<0.001**	**<0.001**	**<0.001**
				E_A					
Δf_1	1.295	0.103	1.000	0.149	1.322	0.249	**<0.001**	0.531	**<0.001**
Δf_2	1.895	0.257	1.104	0.199	1.827	0.269	**<0.001**	0.068	**<0.001**
Δf_3	1.699	0.521	1.308	0.295	1.803	0.319	0.001	0.891	**<0.001**
Δf_4	1.389	0.509	1.413	0.278	1.562	0.300	0.378	0.17	0.011
Δf_5	1.159	0.422	1.28	0.207	1.278	0.237	0.953	0.493	0.256
Δf_α	7.42	1.635	6.15	1.1	7.864	1.177	0.001	0.891	**<0.001**

4. Discussion

Modern pathophysiological concepts of chronic insomnia link its development and transition into a chronic form with the central nervous system hyperarousal. Nonetheless, the manifestation mechanisms of such hyperarousal during the daytime hours, activation mechanisms in the evening, as well as its compensatory mechanisms under insomnia, still remain not fully known.

In this regard, studies of daytime activity in patients with insomnia attract substantial attention. The common feature of such projects involves a better understanding of the brain activity in subjects with insomnia, combined with their psychological traits. For example, a recent research by Losert et al. (2020) reported a daytime increase in the vigilance stability measured by the vigilance algorithm Leipzig (VIGALL) algorithm in patients with insomnia [51]. In earlier studies, it was quite successfully demonstrated that patients with insomnia exhibited a reduction in the power of a low-frequency activity, along with a rise in the power of a high-frequency activity [10,12,14]. At the same time, Kwan et al. showed that the indicated EEG changes in patients with insomnia were not specific and coincided with those in patients with depression [23]. In this article, we additionally studied structural changes of the alpha rhythm in the EEG of the study subjects during daytime psychophysiological tests.

Young people of similar ages with a normal BMI without cognitive and emotional impairments were selected to participate in our experimental work, distributed among the groups according to the nature of their sleep disorders, if any. Quantitative analysis of alpha activity during daytime studies showed significant differences in brain activity of patients with various types of insomnia, both among themselves and from the control group subjects. For the stage of the cognitive experiment, we discovered a steady increase in the alpha rhythm level in subjects with a healthy sleep during the stages of a passive rest. This increase was associated with a prolonged, gradual relaxation in a darkened room, which correlated with some previously published results [4,39]. Patients of Group III did not display significant differences from those with healthy sleep in the frequency interval of [7.5; 9.5] Hz. At the same time, in Group II subjects, the alpha rhythm dynamics was fundamentally different: it decreased at the end of the experiment, i.e., the ratio $E_{RCY/CY} \geq 1$ was true solely for patients with primary insomnia. In our opinion, this finding unequivocally demonstrates the difference between the psychophysiological insomnia, caused by the peculiarities of the central nervous system functioning, and acquired sleep disorders. Besides, it is interesting to note that the increase in alpha activity in patients with poor sleep hygiene is virtually unnoticeable. In other words, somnolence seems to lead to an initially high level of alpha activity, which stops increasing further on.

However, brain activity during the stage A in the course of the subject's reaction to monotonous sound signals shows less pronounced differences. In particular, patients with normal sleep cannot be reliably categorized by alpha activity scores versus those with poor sleep hygiene. Subjects of Group III demonstrated the maximum increase in the alpha rhythm with prolonged exposure to the cognitive function of attention, while patients of Group II even demonstrated a decrease in the intensity of the alpha rhythm for low-frequency components. It can be assumed that, in this case, different compensatory mechanisms for prolonged cognitive exposure in patients with sleep hygiene disorders vs. those with primary insomnia are clearly noticeable. In the former, long-term monotonous cognitive activity (e.g., responding to the sound stimuli) causes intolerable drowsiness and overall relaxation. According to [52] a similar effect could be caused by the paradoxical inhibition of the arousal in the nervous system during monotonous external stimulation. Simultaneously, the overall decrease in the concentration ability in such patients, manifested in augmented response time to stimuli, is consistent with the study by E. Tonnoli [53].

In patients with primary insomnia, activation and control of the cognitive function of attention appears just as effective (maybe, even more effective) as in people with healthy sleep. Thus, this characteristic state, generally known as alertness, automatically includes the states that occur in the course of falling asleep, which can be called anxious expectation. This condition increases tension, alertness and, as a consequence, the functional activity of the brain, leading to a decrease in the levels of such objective experimental criteria as reaction time and alpha rhythm.

Moreover, when analyzing the oscillatory structure of the alpha rhythm, it should be noted that significant differences among three groups of subjects during passive rest (CY and RCY stages) are observed in high-frequency alpha wave bands of [9.5; 12.5] Hz. For patients with acquired sleep disorders and subjects with primary insomnia, when comparing passive wakefulness stages, significant differences in the alpha rhythm parameters are observed for the entire frequency range. During the active stage of our experimental work, significant changes in the alpha rhythm unfold in the low frequency range of [7.5; 10.5] Hz, while poor sleep hygiene in Group III, relative to the control group, does not lead to changes in psychophysiological characteristics. It can be assumed, following the logic of some studies [18,23,51], that for subjects with primary insomnia, attempting to relax at passive wakefulness stages, we observe pronounced processes of increasing beta activity, which also leads to a rise in the power of the alpha rhythm at high frequencies, and upon activation of the cognitive function of attention, generates the processes of destroying low-frequency activity.

The limitation of the presented study involves the homogeneity of the studied subjects in terms of their young age and male gender. However, this was an unavoidable step towards an initial clear detection of the changing alpha activity characteristics. The further study should consider age and gender characteristics, and also analyze the stability of identified traits in the inevitably emerging comorbid conditions of the patients. In addition to these major limitations of participants population, local limitations of the study design also exist. They are associated with the difficulty of objective control of the subjects immediately before the experimental work. In this study design, we have not performed polysomnography of the subject's night-time sleep immediately before the day of the experiment. Additionally, the time spent awake prior testing could influence the results. At the same time, polysomnography and direct control of the time from awakening to experimental work are possible only if the participants stay in a clinical setting for 24 h, which is quite difficult to implement.

In our concluding remarks, we would like to emphasize that our results do not contradict earlier studies and support the hypothesis that insomnia is not just a sleep disorder, neither is it solely a nocturnal disorder of the central nervous system. Rather, it is a systemic condition, involving altered functioning of the central nervous system, and, in particular, the human brain. For subjects in this state, it is possible to objectively demonstrate an increase in the reaction speed to sound stimuli, an overall decrease in the power of the alpha rhythm and, at the same time, an increase in the frequency of oscillations within a EEG alpha-rhythm. Besides, the psychophysiological characteristics of patients with sleep hygiene disorders without primary insomnia demonstrate exceptional dynamics: a decrease in the reaction rate, the maximum increase in the alpha rhythm during cognitive exposure, and the absence of the alpha rhythm changes at the resting stages. Hence, we propose that the developed technique may be applied to clarify the impact level of poor sleep hygiene on insomnia in different groups of patients.

Today, digital and computerized methods of the cognitive behavioral therapy for insomnia (dCBT-I) have become increasingly important [54–56], caused by the expensive and difficult to obtain quality individual treatment, based on classic CBT-I. Such computer systems have great potential as a basis for the development of systems with biofeedback, including EEG neurofeedback [57]. In this case, the proposed detection of the power level of EEG oscillation on different frequency bands within the alpha-rhythm can be used as an objective control of the patient's state with sleep disorder complaints. In addition, it is possible that the relaxation training of the subject using the control of alpha-activity on the EEG to achieve the indicators characteristic of a normally sleeping person can also become an base on development of dCBT-I in the direction of the brain-computer interfaces (BCI). Today, the possibility of a quick study of the BCI-prospects can be implemented, for example, within the CRED checklist [58]. Additionally, we hypothesize that regular training alpha activity of the brain towards alpha rhythm in subjects with healthy sleep may be useful in general therapy for insomnia.

5. Conclusions

The results of the current study supported the notion of a 24-h hyperarousal in primary insomnia. Tracking the alpha rhythm activity by employing wavelet methods could be a pragmatic option for diagnostic purposes, as well as for BCI development in experimental studies on neuropsychological therapy of primary insomnia, using feedback, within the framework of cognitive attention tests.

Author Contributions: Conceptualization, A.R. and R.S.; methodology, R.S.; software, A.S. and M.Z.; validation, A.K.; formal analysis, A.S. and M.Z.; investigation, A.K. and R.P.; resources, R.P.; data curation, A.S. and M.Z.; writing—original draft preparation, A.R.; writing—review and editing, A.R., A.S., and M.Z.; visualization, A.S.; supervision, R.S.; project administration, A.R.; funding acquisition, A.R. and R.P. All authors have read and agreed to the published version of the manuscript.

Funding: Obtaining neurophysiological data from volunteers as experimental part of this study was financed by the Russian Foundation for Basic Research (Grant No. 20-02-00752). In the part of the clinical data interpretation study is carried out within the framework of the state task of the Russian Federation's Ministry of Health # 056-00030-21-01 dated 2 May 2021 "Theoretical and experimental study of the integrative activity of various physiological systems of patient under stress" (the State registration number 121030900357-3.

Institutional Review Board Statement: The study was conducted according to the guidelines of the Declaration of Helsinki, and approved by the local Research Ethics Committee of Saratov State Medical University.

Informed Consent Statement: Informed consent was obtained from all subjects involved in the study.

Data Availability Statement: The data that support the findings of this study are available from the corresponding author upon reasonable request.

Conflicts of Interest: The authors declare that they have no conflicts of interest. The results presented in this paper have not been presented previously in whole or part.

Abbreviations

The following abbreviations are used in this manuscript:

A-stage	Active experimental stage: wakefulness with periodic sound stimuli
CY	First experimental stage of passive wakefulness with closed eyes
RCY	Second experimental stage of passive wakefulness with closed eyes
CWT	Continuous wavelet transform

References

1. Diagnostic and Coding Manual. *International Classification of Sleep Disorders*, 3rd ed.; Diagnostic and Coding Manual: Westchester, NY, USA, 2014.
2. Riemann, D.; Nissen, C.; Palagini, L.; Otte, A.; Perlis, M.L.; Spiegelhalder, K. The neurobiology, investigation, and treatment of chronic insomnia. *Lancet Neurol.* **2015**, *14*, 547–558. [CrossRef]
3. Edinger, J.D.; Arnedt, J.T.; Bertisch, S.M.; Carney, C.E.; Harrington, J.J.; Lichstein, K.L.; Sateia, M.J.; Troxel, W.M.; Zhou, E.S.; Kazmi, U.; et al. Behavioral and psychological treatments for chronic insomnia disorder in adults: An American Academy of Sleep Medicine systematic review, meta-analysis and GRADE assessment. *J. Clin. Sleep Med.* **2021**, *17*, 263–298. [CrossRef]
4. van Straten, A.; van der Zweerde, T.; Kleiboer, A.; Cuijpers, P.; Morin, C.M.; Lancee, J. Cognitive and behavioral therapies in the treatment of insomnia: A meta-analysis. *Sleep Med. Rev.* **2018**, *38*, 3–16. [CrossRef]
5. Huedo-Medina, T.B.; Kirsch, I.; Middlemass, J.; Klonizakis, M.; Siriwardena, A.N. Effectiveness of non-benzodiazepine hypnotics in treatment of adult insomnia: Meta-analysis of data submitted to the Food and Drug Administration. *BMJ* **2012**, *345*, e8343. [CrossRef] [PubMed]
6. Cervena, K.; Dauvilliers, Y.; Espa, F.; Touchon, J.; Matousek, M.; Billiard, M.; Besset, A. Effect of cognitive behavioural therapy for insomnia on sleep architecture and sleep EEG power spectra in psychophysiological insomnia. *J. Sleep Res.* **2004**, *13*, 385–393. [CrossRef]
7. Krystal, A.D.; Edinger, J.D.; Wohlgemuth, W.K.; Marsh, G.R. NREM sleep EEG frequency spectral correlates of sleep complaints in primary insomnia subtypes. *Sleep* **2002**, *25*, 626–636.
8. Nowell, P.D.; Mazumdar, S.; Buysse, D.J.; Dew, M.A.; Reynolds, C.F.; Kupfer, D.J. Benzodiazepines and zolpidem for chronic insomnia: A meta-analysis of treatment efficacy. *JAMA* **1997**, *278*, 2170–2177. [CrossRef] [PubMed]
9. Buysse, D.J.; Germain, A.; Hall, M.L.; Moul, D.E.; Nofzinger, E.A.; Begley, A.; Ehlers, C.L.; Thompson, W.; Kupfer, D.J. EEG spectral analysis in primary insomnia: NREM period effects and sex differences. *Sleep* **2008**, *31*, 1673–1682. [CrossRef]
10. Perlis, M.L.; Smith, M.T.; Andrews, P.J.; Orff, H.; Giles, D.E. Beta/Gamma EEG activity in patients with primary and secondary insomnia and good sleeper controls. *Sleep* **2001**, *24*, 110–117. [CrossRef]
11. Bastien, C.H.; LeBlanc, M.; Carrier, J.; Morin, C.M. Sleep EEG Power Spectra, Insomnia, and Chronic Use of Benzodiazepines. *Sleep* **2003**, *26*, 313–317. [CrossRef]
12. Freedman, R.R. EEG power spectra in sleep-onset insomnia. *Electroencephalogr. Clin. Neurophysiol.* **1986**, *63*, 408–413. [CrossRef]
13. Merica, H.; Blois, R.; Gaillard, J.M. Spectral characteristics of sleep EEG in chronic insomnia. *Eur. J. Neurosci.* **1998**, *10*, 1826–1834. [CrossRef]
14. Svetnik, V.; Snyder, E.S.; Ma, J.; Tao, P.; Lines, C.; Herring, W.J. EEG spectral analysis of NREM sleep in a large sample of patients with insomnia and good sleepers: Effects of age, sex and part of the night. *J. Sleep Res.* **2017**, *26*, 92–104. [CrossRef] [PubMed]
15. Dijk, D.J. Slow-wave sleep deficiency and enhancement: Implications for insomnia and its management. *World J. Biol. Psychiatry* **2010**, *11*, 22–28. [CrossRef]
16. Gaillard, J.M. Chronic primary insomnia: Possible physiopathological involvement of slow wave sleep deficiency. *Sleep* **1978**, *1*, 133–147. [CrossRef] [PubMed]
17. Hogan, S.E.; Delgado, G.M.; Hall, M.H.; Nimgoankar, V.L.; Germain, A.; Buysse, D.J.; Wilckens, K.A. Slow-oscillation activity is reduced and high frequency activity is elevated in older adults with insomnia. *J. Clin. Sleep Med.* **2020**, *16*, 1445–1454. [CrossRef] [PubMed]
18. Basta, M.; Chrousos, G.P.; Vela-Bueno, A.; Vgontzas, A.N. Chronic insomnia and the stress system. *Sleep Med. Clin.* **2007**, *2*, 279–291. [CrossRef]

19. Stepanski, E.; Zorick, F.; Roehrs, T.; Young, D.; Roth, T. Daytime alertness in patients with chronic insomnia compared with asymptomatic control subjects. *Sleep* **1988**, *11*, 54–60. [CrossRef]
20. Edinger, J.D.; Glenn, D.M.; Bastian, L.A.; Marsh, G.R.; Daile, D.; Hope, T.V.; Young, M.; Shaw, E.; Meeks, G. Sleep in the laboratory and sleep at home II: Comparisons of middle-aged insomnia sufferers and normal sleepers. *Sleep* **2001**, *24*, 761–770. [CrossRef]
21. Bonnet, M.H.; Arand, D. 24-Hour metabolic rate in insomniacs and matched normal sleepers. *Sleep* **1995**, *18*, 581–588. [CrossRef]
22. Zhao, W.; Gao, D.; Yue, F.; Wang, Y.; Mao, D.; Liu, T.; Lei, X. Spontaneous Theta Rhythm Predicts Insomnia Duration: A Resting-State EEG Study. In *Advances in Cognitive Neurodynamics VI*; Springer: Berlin/Heidelberg, Germany, 2018; pp. 359–364.
23. Kwan, Y.; Baek, C.; Chung, S.; Kim, T.H.; Choi, S. Resting-state quantitative EEG characteristics of insomniac patients with depression. *Int. J. Psychophysiol.* **2018**, *124*, 26–32. [CrossRef]
24. Wołyńczyk-Gmaj, D.; Szelenberger, W. Waking EEG in primary insomnia. *Acta Neurobiol. Exp.* **2011**, *71*, 387–392.
25. Stastny, J.; Sovka, P.; Stancak, A. EEG signal classification. In Proceedings of the 23rd Annual International Conference of the IEEE Engineering in Medicine and Biology Society, Istanbul, Turkey, 25–28 October 2001; Volume 2, pp. 2020–2023.
26. Maksimenko, V.A.; Runnova, A.E.; Zhuravlev, M.O.; Makarov, V.V.; Nedayvozov, V.; Grubov, V.V.; Pchelintceva, S.V.; Hramov, A.E.; Pisarchik, A.N. Visual perception affected by motivation and alertness controlled by a noninvasive brain-computer interface. *PLoS ONE* **2017**, *12*, e0188700. [CrossRef]
27. Makarov, V.V.; Zhuravlev, M.O.; Runnova, A.E.; Protasov, P.; Maksimenko, V.A.; Frolov, N.S.; Pisarchik, A.N.; Hramov, A.E. Betweenness centrality in multiplex brain network during mental task evaluation. *Phys. Rev. E* **2018**, *98*, 062413. [CrossRef]
28. Iosifescu, D.V.; Greenwald, S.; Devlin, P.; Mischoulon, D.; Denninger, J.W.; Alpert, J.E.; Fava, M. Frontal EEG predictors of treatment outcome in major depressive disorder. *Eur. Neuropsychopharmacol.* **2009**, *19*, 772–777. [CrossRef] [PubMed]
29. Golz, M.; Schenka, A.; Haselbeck, F.; Pauli, M.P. Inter-individual variability of EEG features during microsleep events. *Curr. Dir. Biomed. Eng.* **2019**, *5*, 13–16. [CrossRef]
30. Valizadeh, S.A.; Riener, R.; Elmer, S.; Jäncke, L. Decrypting the electrophysiological individuality of the human brain: Identification of individuals based on resting-state EEG activity. *NeuroImage* **2019**, *197*, 470–481. [CrossRef] [PubMed]
31. Grandy, T.H.; Werkle-Bergner, M.; Chicherio, C.; Schmiedek, F.; Lövdén, M.; Lindenberger, U. Peak individual alpha frequency qualifies as a stable neurophysiological trait marker in healthy younger and older adults. *Psychophysiology* **2013**, *50*, 570–582. [CrossRef] [PubMed]
32. Niedermeyer, E. Alpha rhythms as physiological and abnormal phenomena. *Int. J. Psychophysiol.* **1997**, *26*, 31–49. [CrossRef]
33. Mulholland, T.B. Occurrence of the electroencephalographic alpha rhythm with eyes open. *Nature* **1965**, *206*, 746. [CrossRef]
34. Piantoni, G.; Romeijn, N.; Gomez-Herrero, G.; Van Der Werf, Y.D.; Van Someren, E.J. Alpha power predicts persistence of bistable perception. *Sci. Rep.* **2017**, *7*, 5208. [CrossRef]
35. Maksimenko, V.A.; Pavlov, A.; Runnova, A.E.; Nedaivozov, V.; Grubov, V.; Koronovslii, A.; Pchelintseva, S.V.; Pitsik, E.; Pisarchik, A.N.; Hramov, A.E. Nonlinear analysis of brain activity, associated with motor action and motor imaginary in untrained subjects. *Nonlinear Dyn.* **2018**, *91*, 2803–2817. [CrossRef]
36. Angelakis, E.; Lubar, J.F.; Stathopoulou, S. Electroencephalographic peak alpha frequency correlates of cognitive traits. *Neurosci. Lett.* **2004**, *371*, 60–63. [CrossRef] [PubMed]
37. Busch, N.; VanRullen, R. Pre-stimulus eeg oscillations reveal periodic sampling of visual attention. *J. Vis.* **2010**, *10*, 219. [CrossRef]
38. Klimesch, W. EEG alpha and theta oscillations reflect cognitive and memory performance: A review and analysis. *Brain Res. Rev.* **1999**, *29*, 169–195. [CrossRef]
39. Schwabedal, J.T.; Riedl, M.; Penzel, T.; Wessel, N. Alpha-wave frequency characteristics in health and insomnia during sleep. *J. Sleep Res.* **2016**, *25*, 278–286. [CrossRef]
40. Riedner, B.A.; Goldstein, M.R.; Plante, D.T.; Rumble, M.E.; Ferrarelli, F.; Tononi, G.; Benca, R.M. Regional patterns of elevated alpha and high-frequency electroencephalographic activity during nonrapid eye movement sleep in chronic insomnia: A pilot study. *Sleep* **2016**, *39*, 801–812. [CrossRef]
41. Beck, A.T.; Ward, C.H.; Mendelson, M.; Mock, J.; Erbaugh, J. An inventory for measuring depression. *Arch. Gen. Psychiatry* **1961**, *4*, 561–571. [CrossRef]
42. Snaith, R.P. The hospital anxiety and depression scale. *Health Qual. Life Outcomes* **2003**, *1*, 1–4. [CrossRef] [PubMed]
43. Torresani, B. *Continuous Wavelet Transform*; Savoire: Paris, France, 1995.
44. Hramov, A.E.; Koronovskii, A.A.; Makarov, V.A.; Pavlov, A.N.; Sitnikova, E. *Wavelets in Neuroscience*; Springer: Berlin/Heidelberg, Germany, 2015.
45. Aldroubi, A.; Unser, M.A. *Wavelets in Biology and Medicine*; CRC Press: Boca Raton, FL, USA, 1996.
46. Garcia-Losarcos, N.; Vuppala, A.; Loparo, K. *Continuous EEG Monitoring and Quantitative EEG Techniques*; Springer: Berlin/Heidelberg, Germany, 2020.
47. Mann, H.B.; Whitney, D.R. On a test of whether one of two random variables is stochastically larger than the other. *Ann. Math. Stat.* **1947**, *18*, 50–60. [CrossRef]
48. Djonlagic, I.; Mariani, S.; Fitzpatrick, A.L.; Van Der Klei, V.M.; Johnson, D.A.; Wood, A.C.; Seeman, T.; Nguyen, H.T.; Prerau, M.J.; Luchsinger, J.A.; et al. Macro and micro sleep architecture and cognitive performance in older adults. *Nat. Hum. Behav.* **2021**, *5*, 172–174. [CrossRef] [PubMed]
49. McShane, B.B.; Gal, D.; Gelman, A.; Robert, C.; Tackett, J.L. Abandon Statistical Significance. *Am. Stat.* **2019**, *73*, 235–245. [CrossRef]

50. Rougier, J. p-Values, Bayes Factors, and Sufficiency. *Am. Stat.* **2019**, *73*, 148–151. [CrossRef]
51. Losert, A.; Sander, C.; Schredl, M.; Heilmann-Etzbach, I.; Deuschle, M.; Hegerl, U.; Schilling, C. Enhanced Vigilance Stability during Daytime in Insomnia Disorder. *Brain Sci.* **2020**, *10*, 830. [CrossRef] [PubMed]
52. Zueva, E.Y.; Zuev, K.B. The concept of dominance by A.A. Ukhtomsky and Anticipation. In *Anticipation: Learning from the Past*; Springer: Berlin/Heidelberg, Germany, 2015; pp. 13–35.
53. Tognoli, E. More than Meets the Mind's Eye? Preliminary Observations Hint at Heterogeneous Alpha Neuromarkers for Visual Attention. *Brain Sci.* **2019**, *9*, 307. [CrossRef]
54. Cheng, S.K.; Dizon, J. Computerised cognitive behavioural therapy for insomnia: A systematic review and meta-analysis. *Psychother. Psychosom.* **2012**, *81*, 206–216. [CrossRef]
55. Sweetman, A.; Putland, S.; Lack, L.; McEvoy, R.D.; Adams, R.; Grunstein, R.; Stocks, N.; Kaambwa, B.; Van Ryswyk, E.; Gordon, C.; et al. The effect of cognitive behavioural therapy for insomnia on sedative-hypnotic use: A narrative review. *Sleep Med. Rev.* **2020**, 101404. [CrossRef]
56. Soh, H.L.; Ho, R.C.; Ho, C.S.; Tam, W.W. Efficacy of digital cognitive behavioural therapy for insomnia: A meta-analysis of randomised controlled trials. *Sleep Med.* **2020**, *75*, 315–325. [CrossRef] [PubMed]
57. Micoulaud-Franchi, J.A.; Mcgonigal, A.; Lopez, R.; Daudet, C.; Kotwas, I.; Bartolomei, F. Electroencephalographic neurofeedback: Level of evidence in mental and brain disorders and suggestions for good clinical practice. *Neurophysiol. Clin. Neurophysiol.* **2015**, *45*, 423–433. [CrossRef] [PubMed]
58. Ros, T.; Enriquez-Geppert, S.; Zotev, V.; Young, K.D.; Wood, G.; Whitfield-Gabrieli, S.; Wan, F.; Vuilleumier, P.; Vialatte, F.; Van De Ville, D.; et al. Consensus on the reporting and experimental design of clinical and cognitive-behavioural neurofeedback studies (CRED-nf checklist). *Brain* **2020**, *143*, 1674–1685. [CrossRef]

Journal of Personalized Medicine

Article

Individual Resonant Frequencies at Low-Gamma Range and Cognitive Processing Speed

Vykinta Parciauskaite [1,†], Evaldas Pipinis [1,†], Aleksandras Voicikas [1], Jovana Bjekic [2], Mindaugas Potapovas [1], Vytautas Jurkuvenas [3] and Inga Griskova-Bulanova [1,*]

1 Institute of Biosciences, Life Sciences Centre, Vilnius University, Sauletekio ave 7, LT-10257 Vilnius, Lithuania; vykinta.parciauskaite@stud.gmc.vu.lt (V.P.); evaldas.pipinis@gmc.vu.lt (E.P.); aleksandras.voicikas@gmc.vu.lt (A.V.); mindaugas.potapovas@gmail.com (M.P.)
2 Human Neuroscience Group, Institute for Medical Research, University of Belgrade, Dr Subotica 4, 11000 Belgrade, Serbia; jovana.bjekic@imi.bg.ac.rs
3 Department of General Psychology, Vilnius University, Universiteto 9/1, LT-01513 Vilnius, Lithuania; vytautas.jurkuvenas@fsf.vu.lt
* Correspondence: inga.griskova-bulanova@gf.vu.lt; Tel.: +37-0-6711-0954
† Equal contribution.

Abstract: Brain electrophysiological activity within the low gamma frequencies (30–80 Hz) has been proposed to reflect information encoding and transfer processes. The 40-Hz auditory steady-state response (40-Hz ASSR) is frequently discussed in relation to changed cognitive processing in neuropsychiatric disorders. However, the relationship between ASSRs and cognitive functioning still remains unclear. Most of the studies assessed the single frequency ASSR, while the individual resonance frequency in the gamma range (30–60 Hz), also called individual gamma frequency (IGF), has received limited attention thus far. Nevertheless, IGF potentially might better reflect individual network characteristics than standardly utilized 40-Hz ASSRs. Here, we focused on the processing speed across different types of cognitive tasks and explored its relationship with responses at 40 Hz and at IGFs in an attempt to uncover how IGFs relate to certain aspects of cognitive functioning. We show that gamma activity is related to the performance speed on complex cognitive task tapping planning and problem solving, both when responses at 40 Hz and at IGFs were evaluated. With the individualized approach, the observed associations were found to be somewhat stronger, and the association seemed to primarily reflect individual differences in higher-order cognitive processing. These findings have important implications for the interpretation of gamma activity in neuropsychiatric disorders.

Keywords: individual resonant frequency; gamma; cognitive performance; auditory steady-state response (ASSR); envelope following response (EFR)

Citation: Parciauskaite, V.; Pipinis, E.; Voicikas, A.; Bjekic, J.; Potapovas, M.; Jurkuvenas, V.; Griskova-Bulanova, I. Individual Resonant Frequencies at Low-Gamma Range and Cognitive Processing Speed. *J. Pers. Med.* **2021**, *11*, 453. https://doi.org/10.3390/jpm11060453

Academic Editor: Yoshihiro Noda

Received: 9 March 2021
Accepted: 21 May 2021
Published: 23 May 2021

1. Introduction

Brain electrophysiological activity within the low-gamma frequencies (30–80 Hz) has been proposed to reflect information encoding and transfer processes [1]. The gamma range oscillations have been linked to variety of perceptual processes [2,3] and cognitive functions [4–7]. Moreover, the impaired cognitive/perceptual processes, as observed in neuropsychiatric disorders, are often reflected in disturbed electrophysiological responses within the 30–80 Hz range [8,9]. It has therefore been proposed that the efficiency of neuronal information transfer in activated brain networks in the gamma range underlies the individual differences in cognitive performance [10].

One of the methods to explore the individual differences in neural synchronization in the gamma range is the auditory steady-state response (ASSR). The ASSR is an electrophysiological response of the brain that synchronizes to the frequency and phase of rapid, periodic auditory stimuli. The auditory stimulation evokes the greatest magnitude when stimuli are presented within the gamma range, especially around 40 Hz, and the evoked frequency is highly related to the frequency of stimulation [11,12].

Although the impairment of 40-Hz ASSRs is frequently put forward to reflect changed cognitive processing in neuropsychiatric disorders, especially schizophrenia [13–17], the relationship between ASSRs and cognitive functioning still remains unclear. In our recent critical review [18], we systematically analyzed existing findings on the associations between gamma-range ASSRs and cognitive functions in patients with neuropsychiatric or developmental disorders and healthy subjects. The evidence of the relationship between cognitive performance and ASSRs in pathological functioning was found across different studies (e.g., see [13–17,19–26]). However, there is not enough evidence in the literature to support this relationship in healthy participants.

One of the reasons why these effects have not been more prominent may lie in the resonance phenomena in the human auditory cortex. Namely, most of the previous studies assessed the single frequency ASSR, while the individual resonance frequency in the gamma range (30–60 Hz), also called individual gamma frequency (IGF [27–29]), has been mostly unexplored. In this respect, IGF represents the frequency at which the brain responds strongest in comparison to other frequencies when stimulated [30]. In other words, the key to the relationship between ASSR and cognitive performance may not necessarily be in the response to a single frequency such as 40 Hz, but in the response to person-dominant frequency within the gamma range.

This idea is especially compelling if the differences in cognitive performance are viewed as a continuum from "normal" to pathological [31], or more specifically, *superior-average-suboptimal/pre-clinical-pathological continuum*. The pathological conditions that display pronounced cognitive deficits are frequently accompanied by altered 40-Hz ASSRs [13]; however, the impairment is not limited to 40 Hz [21,24]. As the preferred oscillation frequencies of the networks are determined by the anatomical properties and the speed of neuronal communication [32], IGF potentially might better reflect individual network characteristics than standardly utilized 40-Hz ASSRs.

The responses at IGFs can be detected when multiple stimulation frequencies in the range under the interest are tested [30]. Alternatively, envelope following responses (EFRs, standing for a steady-state evoked response that follows the envelope of a stimulating waveform [33] to chirp stimulation covering the wide frequency window in one sweep [34]) show peak in the same frequency range as the individual preferred frequencies [34–36]. Although responses at IGFs and its individual variability have received limited attention thus far, recent research has provided evidence that frequency variation within the gamma range is related to certain functional aspects on the individual level in healthy subjects (i.e., the ability to detect small and sudden change in sound stimuli), [27,28,34] as well as in neuropsychiatric conditions (levels of psychopathology) [35,37].

However, the way responses at IGFs relate to certain aspects of cognitive functioning is not yet understood. Initial data on the gamma-range ASSRs in healthy participants showed that responses might be related to cognitive flexibility and reasoning (Tower of London task [38], Similarities [39], and the Mazes test [25]), as well as to behavioral indicators of processing speed (trial making test [25] and symbol coding [24]). Moreover, several studies showed a positive relationship between performance on gap detection task and the IGF in response to periodic stimulation [27,34]. Similarly, the individual resonant frequencies within the gamma range were negatively related to the speed on attentional control and executive tasks in patients with multiple sclerosis [19]. This suggests that the state of neural networks defining IGFs may reflect the temporal resolution, and thus may be related to the individual parameters of information processing speed. The information processing speed represents a fundamental capacity of the nervous system [40] that underlies higher-order cognitive functions such as learning, memory, and verbal and executive functions [41,42], and is often impaired in patients with neuropsychiatric and developmental disorders [43–46].

This study follows up on the idea that individual differences in the dominant gamma-band frequency may underlie the variability in the fundamental properties of cognitive functioning, even in the healthy population. Specifically, we focused on the processing speed across different types of cognitive tasks and explored its relationship with responses at 40 Hz and at IGFs.

2. Methods

2.1. Subjects

Thirty-seven healthy right-handed subjects (17 females) without reported history of psychiatric and neurological disorders participated in the study (mean age $\pm$ SD 23.8 $\pm$ 4.7). The hearing thresholds of all subjects were within the normal range (<25dB HL at octave frequencies). Subjects abstained from alcohol for 24 h prior to the testing and did not consume nicotine and caffeine-containing drinks at least one hour prior to the experiment. The study was approved by the Vilnius Regional Biomedical Research Ethics Committee (no. 2020/3-1213-701), and all participants gave their written informed consent.

2.2. Procedure

The study was conducted in two blocks—cognitive assessment block in which participants performed a computerized battery of cognitive tasks, and EEG recording block, in which participants were exposed to auditory stimulation while the EEG was recorded. Cognitive assessment always followed EEG recordings.

2.3. Cognitive Assessment

The cognitive testing was performed using the Psychology Experiment Building Language [47]-based task battery, consisting of:

1. Simple reaction time task, in which participants were as asked to detect the presence of a visual stimulus (A letter) as quickly and accurately as possible.
2. Two-choice response reaction time task, in which participants had to indicate the direction of the displayed arrow by pressing the left or right button on a keyboard.
3. Lexical decision task, in which participants were asked to indicate if the correct word was presented or it contained a mistake.
4. Arithmetic decision task, in which subjects were presented with simple arithmetic expressions (simple additions or subtractions) and were asked to indicate whether the displayed outcome was correct or incorrect.
5. Semantic categorization task, in which the participants were successively presented with words, and their task was to indicate if the word belonged to the specific category, e.g., furniture, animal, utensils, etc.
6. Object judgement task assessing the mental rotation speed by making a decision as to whether two presented abstract waveforms are identical or different.
7. Tower of London task (ToL), generally considering tapping at planning and execution speed. In this task, participants had to move the colored disks to achieve the goal configuration in as few moves as possible.

As in this study we focused on processing speed, we therefore used response times (RTs) as the outcome measures across all tasks.

2.4. Auditory Stimulation

Click-based chirps consisting of 22 white noise bursts spaced with changing inter-click periods to cover 35–55 Hz range in 1 Hz step were used for the auditory stimulation. Duration of the inter-click period corresponded to the stimulation frequency (e.g., for 40 Hz stimulation, inter-click period was 25 ms for 50 Hz-20 ms; Figure 1). The chirp stimulation train lasted 475.4 ms. The auditory stimuli were designed in the Matlab 2014 environment (The MathWorks, Inc., Natick, MA, USA) and presented binaurally through Sennheiser HD 280 PRO earphones with sound pressure level adjusted to 60 dB with a DVM 401 dB meter (Velleman, TX, USA).

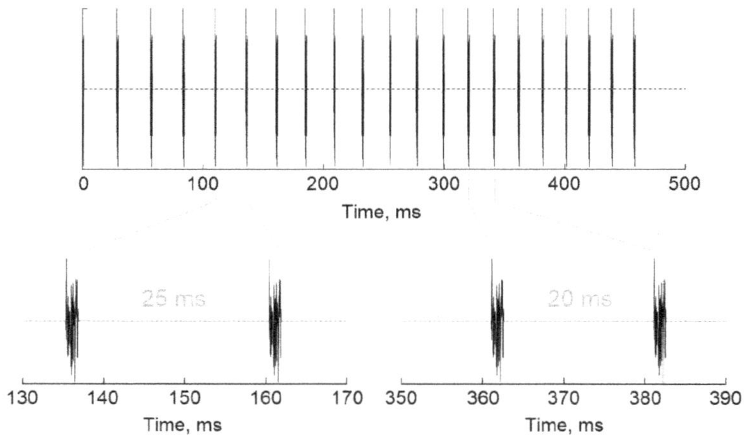

Figure 1. A schematic representation of chirp stimulus used in the study.

A total of 300 trains of chirps interspersed with single-frequency stimulation (not analyzed in the current work) were delivered with inter-stimulus intervals randomly set at 700–1000 ms. Subjects were asked to focus on stimulation and mentally count randomly presented single clicks interspersed within periodic sounds and to report the presented number after each of stimulation run in order to keep subjects' attention towards stimulation.

2.5. EEG Recording

EEG was recorded with an ANT device (ANT Neuro, Hengelo, the Netherlands) and a 64 channel WaveGuard EEG cap (International 10–20 System) with Ag/AgCl electrodes. Mastoids were used as a reference; the ground electrode was attached close to Fz. Impedance was kept below 20 kΩ, and the sampling rate was set at 1024 Hz. Simultaneously, vertical and horizontal electro-occulograms (VEOG and HEOG) were recorded from above and below the left eye and from the right and left outer canthi.

2.6. EEG Processing

The off-line pre-processing of EEG data was performed in EEGLAB for MatLab© 2014 [48,49]. The power-line noise was removed using multi-tapering and Thomas F-statistics, as implemented in CleanLine plugin for EEGLAB. Data were visually inspected, and channels with substantial noise (shift, movements) throughout the recording were manually rejected. An independent component analysis (ICA) was performed on the remaining channels with the ICA-implementation of EEGLAB ("runica" with default settings), and independent components related to eye movements were removed.

The further data analysis was based on the usage of custom written scripts based on EEGLAB [48] and Fieldtrip functions [50]. Epochs were created from −500 ms to 1100 ms post-stimulus onset. Data were baseline-corrected to the mean of the pre-stimulus period, and epochs were further visually inspected for the remaining artefacts. A wavelet transformation was performed utilizing complex Morlet wavelet from Matlab© Wavelet Toolbox with frequencies represented from 1 to 120 Hz, with 1 Hz intervals between each frequency.

The phase-locking index (PLI), corresponding to the phase consistency over the trials, and the event-related spectral perturbation (ERSP), indicating event-related changes in power relative to a pre-stimulus baseline, were calculated according to the following formulas [49]:

$$PLI(c,f,t) = \frac{1}{N}\sum_{n}^{N}\frac{X(c,f,t,n)}{|X(c,f,t,n)|}, \tag{1}$$

$$ERSP(c, f, t) = \frac{1}{N}\sum_{n}^{N}\left|X(c, f, t, n\right|_{2}, \tag{2}$$

where for every channel c, frequency f, and time point t, a measure is calculated by taking time frequency decomposition X of each trial n.

For the baseline correction, the signal during stimulation was divided by the signal averaged from −400 to 0 ms for each frequency. The topographical representation of the response resembled classical distribution observed for auditory-evoked gamma-range responses with a clear fronto-central distribution [38]; thus, the extracted PLIs and ERSPs at frequencies spanning 35–55 Hz were grouped for the fronto-central (Fz, Cz, FCz, C1, C2, F1, F2, FC1, FC2) region where responses were most pronounced (Figure 2).

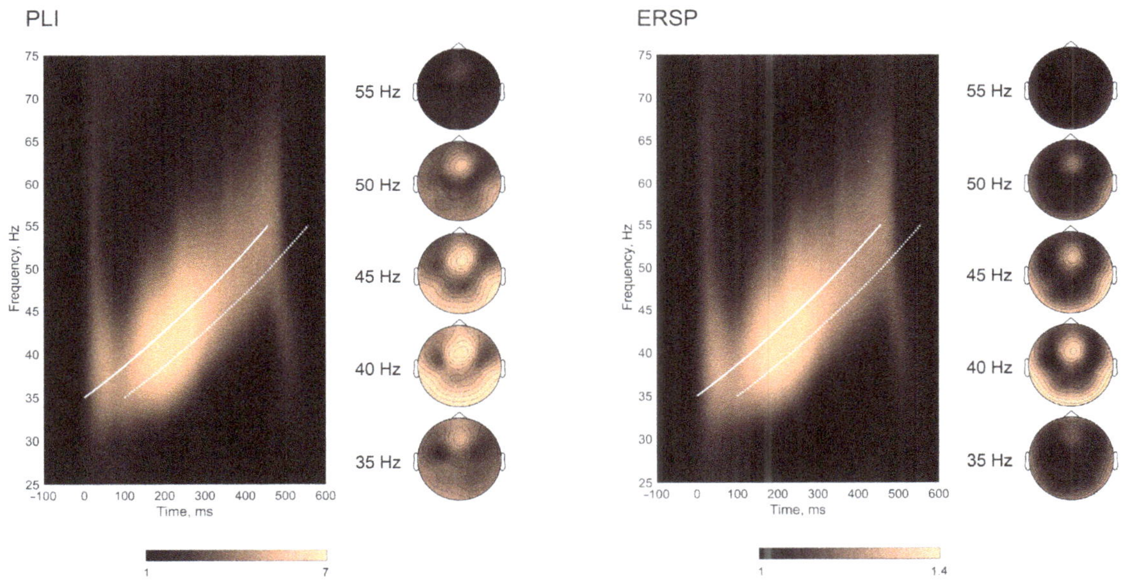

Figure 2. Time-frequency plots of PLIs and ERSPs for envelope following response. The white solid line corresponds to the course of auditory stimulation; the white dashed line denotes +100 ms window from the stimulation line. The grand-averaged topographies for envelope-following response at 35, 40, 45, 50, and 55 Hz stimulation are presented alongside the time-frequency plots.

For the responses to chirps, the curve representing time-frequency points of the stimulation (starting with the first click presented) was used to define the exact time points for each stimulation frequency (seen as a white bold line in the time-frequency plot in Figure 2). The average response to each stimulation frequency (from 35 to 55 Hz in 1 Hz steps) was calculated using a time window of +100 ms from the stimulation line (consistently with observed response windows in the time-frequency plots, seen as a white dashed line in Figure 2). The following measures were extracted: PLI/ERSP values at 40 Hz (40 Hz EFR), and PLI/ERSP values at the maximal response (further referred to as IGF-EFR).

2.7. Statistical Analysis

Descriptive statistics (means and standard deviations) were calculated for all variables in the study. PLI and ERSP values for 40 Hz and IGF were compared using paired sample t-test. For cognitive tasks, we performed principal component analysis to extract common latent dimension and assess the individual task loading. Pearson's correlation coefficients were calculated to assess the relationship between RTs from cognitive tasks and PLI/ERSP measures at 40 Hz, as well as at IGFs. To account for multiple comparisons, we Bonferroni-corrected the threshold for statistical significance, and the p-values less than 0.004 (0.05/13) were regarded as significant. Statistical analysis was performed using SPSSv20 (SPSS Inc., Chicago, IL, USA). In addition, we used JASP (version 0.14.1) [51] to conduct Bayesian analysis. To provide additional information on the level of evidence, we report Bayesian factors and credibility intervals for correlations between measures of cognitive processing speed and EEG measures.

3. Results

3.1. Cognitive Performance

The means and standard deviations of RTs on cognitive tasks are presented in Table 1. To assess the latent structure and verify common source of variance across all tasks, we conducted principal component analysis.

Table 1. Means, standard deviations and loadings of each task RT on all three components.

Task	RT (ms)		Principal Component Loadings		
	Mean	SD	Component 1	Component 2	Component 3
Simple reaction time task	294.38	50.75	0.65 *	0.59	−0.33
Two-choice response time task	378.16	61.19	0.76 *	0.51	-
Arithmetic decision task	1116.12	327.84	0.72 *	-	0.31
Lexical decision task	1248.64	357.79	0.63 *	−0.62	−0.40
Semantic categorization task	751.97	209.61	0.84 *	−0.44	-
Object judgement task	814.68	188.15	0.61 *	-	0.41
Tower of London task	1997.52	626.12	0.51	-	0.62 *

Note: For PCA the loadings <0.30 were suppressed; primary loadings marked with *.

As expected, the first principal component accounted for almost half of the variance of RTs across different tasks (46.4%); however, two additional components with eigenvalues >1 emerged. Table 1 shows loadings of RTs for each task on all three components. Notably, all cognitive tasks except ToL showed primary loading on the first principal component. This indicates that RTs on ToL had a significant amount of variance that was task-specific, i.e., which was not shared with other cognitive speed tasks.

3.2. Envelope Following Responses

The grand averaged time-frequency representation of PLIs and ERSPs is plotted in Figure 2, along with the topographical plots of EFRs at 35, 40, 45, 50, and 55 Hz. EFRs resembled classical fronto-central topographies. The extracted individual PLI and ERSP curves are plotted in Figure 3. IGFs spanned the frequency range of 36–53 Hz with mean maximums observed around 41–42 Hz. The PLI and ERSP values were extracted at 40 Hz and at IGFs. The means and standard deviations of PLIs, ERSPs, and IGFs are presented in Table 2.

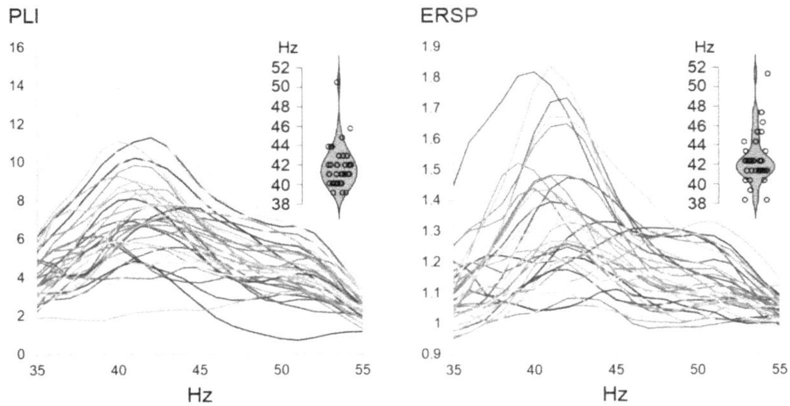

Figure 3. Individual phase-locking index (**PLI**) and event-related spectral perturbation (**ERSP**) curves with individual gamma frequency distributions.

Table 2. Means and standard deviations of PLIs and ERSPs at 40 Hz and at IGFs.

		40-Hz EFR	IGF-EFR	*t*-Test	IGF
PLI	Mean	7.07	7.63	−6.534,	41.89
	SD	2.39	2.20	$p < 0.001$	2.27
ERSP	Mean	1.29	1.35	−6.849,	42.19
	SD	0.20	0.20	$p < 0.001$	2.57

EFR—envelope following response; IGF—individual gamma frequency; IGF-EFR—envelope following response at individual gamma frequency.

3.3. The Relationship between EEG Measures and Cognitive Processing Speed

To explore the relationship between EFRs and cognitive functions, we first calculated the Pearson's correlation coefficients for all measures separately (Table 3). RTs from the ToL task showed significant associations to EEG measures: negative correlations were observed between RTs on ToL and PLIs, as well as ERSPs for responses at both 40 Hz and at IGFs. Of note, the correlations with cognitive speed measures at IGFs were very similar to those at 40 Hz, which was to be expected as both PLI and ERSP were highly correlated ($r > 0.95$); still, the associations appeared to be somewhat stronger for responses at IGFs (PLI: 40-Hz EFR $BF_{10} = 23.19$ vs. IGF-EFR $BF_{10} = 81.78$; ERSP: 40-Hz EFR $BF_{10} = 21.10$ vs. IGF-EFR $BF_{10} = 30.40$). Scatterplots of PLIs and ERSPs at IGFs against mean move times in the Tower of London task are presented in Figure 4. No correlations were observed for RTs on other tasks. The Bayesian factors and credibility intervals for all correlations are provided in the Supplementary Material.

To understand the nature of this association, we assessed whether EFR measures were related to general or unique processing speed variance form ToL. Namely, we correlated EFR measures with (a) first principal component (i.e., global processing speed variance that is shared across all cognitive tasks) and (b) unique variance of ToL (i.e., the residual variance of ToL when the global processing speed of other cognitive tasks is regressed out). The results showed zero correlations with the latent factor of global processing speed but showed stable correlations with ToL unique variance at 40 Hz ($r_{PLI} = -0.495$, $p = 0.002$; $r_{ERSP} = -0.491$, $p = 0.002$) as well as at IGFs ($r_{PLI} = -0.537$, $p = 0.001$; $r_{ERSP} = -0.483$, $p = 0.002$). Again, the correlation for PLI at IGFs was slightly higher than for 40 Hz when observed under the Bayesian model (PLI: 40-Hz EFR $BF_{10} = 13.96$ vs. IGF-EFR $BF_{10} = 30.09$; ERSP: 40-Hz EFR $BF_{10} = 20.03$ vs. IGF-EFR $BF_{10} = 19.82$). On the basis of the classification scheme for interpreting Bayesian factors [52], PLI at 40 Hz provides strong evidence, while the PLI at IGFs provides very strong evidence towards the hypothesis.

Table 3. Correlation coefficients and corresponding *p*-values for correlations between envelope following response measures and response times on cognitive tasks.

Task		PLI			ERSP		
		40-Hz EFR	IGF-EFR	IGF	40-Hz EFR	IGF-EFR	IGF
Simple reaction time task	r	0.05	0.04	−0.03	0.03	0.03	0.01
	p	0.79	0.83	0.86	0.86	0.85	0.94
Two-choice response time task	r	0.08	0.02	−0.18	0.09	0.03	−0.20
	p	0.62	0.93	0.29	0.60	0.87	0.23
Arithmetic decision task	r	−0.13	−0.15	−0.06	−0.12	−0.16	−0.12
	p	0.46	0.36	0.71	0.47	0.34	0.49
Lexical decision task	r	−0.10	−0.11	−0.02	−0.03	−0.07	−0.18
	p	0.58	0.52	0.90	0.87	0.70	0.28
Semantic categorization task	r	−0.20	−0.23	−0.04	−0.15	−0.18	−0.10
	p	0.23	0.18	0.80	0.39	0.28	0.55
Mental rotation task	r	−0.16	−0.16	0.21	−0.10	−0.12	0.10
	p	0.35	0.34	0.21	0.54	0.47	0.57
Tower of London task	r	*−0.50*	*−0.55*	0.08	*−0.49*	*−0.51*	0.09
	p	*0.002*	*<0.001*	0.65	*0.002*	*0.001*	0.60

EFR—envelope following response; IGF—individual gamma frequency; IGF-EFR—envelope following response at individual gamma frequency.

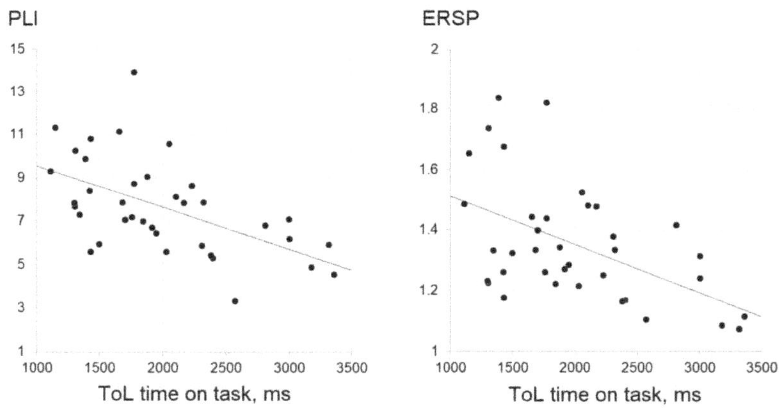

Figure 4. Scatterplots of PLIs and ERSPs at IGFs against the Tower of London task response times.

4. Discussion

ASSRs in the gamma range are frequently regarded as an index of impaired cognitive functioning in patients with schizophrenia [13,16,17]. Nevertheless, the association between ASSRs and cognitive domains is not that clear [18]. The 40-Hz ASSRs have received the most attention both from the clinical perspective [13,16,17,53] and as individual markers of the ability to generate synchronous gamma activity [54,55]. However, the individual resonant frequency phenomenon was observed [30], suggesting that responses assessed at IGFs might better reflect individual differences and more robustly translate into certain cognitive performance patterns.

We obtained the envelope following responses to click trains spaced in a logarithmic manner similar to chirps covering the frequency range within 35–55 Hz. IGFs were estimated as the stimulation frequencies producing the strongest and most synchronized responses [30]. A group mean maximum was observed at around 41–42 Hz with the individual peaks estimated within the 35–53 Hz range, being in line with previous reports [27,28,30,56]. We extracted phase-locking index and event-related spectral perturbation at 40 Hz (40-Hz EFR) and at IGFs (IGF-EFR) in order to be able to compare results to the existing 40-Hz ASSR literature. Both PLIs and ERSPs obtained at 40 Hz and IGFs were highly correlated, resembling topographical distribution corresponding to classical ASSRs [38,57] with a clear fronto-central locus (Figure 2). Although we did not assess 40-Hz ASSR, we believe that EFRs at 40 Hz capture similar brain activity, as can be seen from the topographical activation pattern.

We evaluated processing speed on different cognitive tasks that reveal simple and complex information processing, the later covering semantic, spatial, arithmetic, and lexical aspects. However, the only observed association to gamma-range responses was a negative correlation between mean response times on ToL task and measures at both 40 Hz and at IGFs. Interestingly, the results showed that the observed relationship was unique to the ToL speed variance. This negative association between response times and the level of synchronization showed that subjects with better synchronization properties in this study were faster when a planning/problem solving task was performed. This finding is in line with sparse earlier observations showing a positive correlation between the performance on the complex planning and reasoning tasks such as the Mazes test from MATRICS and Similarities and the phase-locking properties of 40-Hz ASSR in both patients with schizophrenia and controls [24,25], indicating better performance in subjects with more synchronized ASSRs. Additionally, gamma-range ASSRs in healthy subjects were positively related to behavioral indicators of processing speed on two other multifaceted tests—trial making test [25] and symbol coding [24]. In our previous work, we did not observe an association between parameters of 40-Hz ASSRs and response times on a set of cognitive tasks. However, we observed a positive association between parameters of 40-Hz ASSR and number of moves made on the Tower of London task [38]. Taken together, the relationship to measures of gamma activity suggests that synchronization properties of the brain shape individual potential to perform complex reasoning and planning tasks. Moreover, this type of response does not reflect simple motor or sensory processes but rather higher-order speed of cognitive performance. To this point, it was previously suggested that individual performance of ToL task depends on elaboration of diverse strategies [58], with different working memory [59,60] and abstract thinking [61,62] demands and distinct brain activation patterns [63]. Moreover, ToL is sensitive to trait variance in levels of impulsivity [60]. Thus, the finding that the lower number of moves in ToL [38] and higher response speed (current study) are related to higher synchronization level implies that these neurophysiological processes underline distinct cognitive subdomains.

In line with our expectations, responses at IGFs showed somewhat stronger association to behavioral measures than responses at 40 Hz. This trend was even more prominent when ToL unique variance was assessed. The fact that both responses at 40 Hz and at IGFs were related to the same cognitive domain measure was expected. We have previously shown that both 40-Hz ASSRs and responses to chirp stimulation within 38–43 Hz were related to clinical assessment scores in patients with disorders of consciousness [64,65]. Although the individual peaks estimated in this study were within the 35–53 Hz range, corresponding to the ranges reported in previous reports [27,28,30,56], the majority of subjects had their IGFs at 40–42 Hz. Gransier et al. suggested that the scalp-recorded ASSRs within the 30–60 Hz range originate from the same generators and the choice of stimulation frequency does not have a large effect on relative measures, even though peak frequencies differ across subjects [56]. This assumption is supported by similar topographies observed at different frequencies, as can be seen in Figure 2 and by our recent studies in clinical populations utilizing chirp stimulation where the significant associations with clinical symptoms spanned a certain frequency range: hallucination scores and PLIs in patients with schizophrenia were associated within the frequency range of 32–43 Hz [35], and a correlation between Coma Rating Scale—Revised total score in patients with disorder of consciousness was detected within the 38–42 Hz window [64,65]. However, individual peak frequencies of gamma oscillations were shown to determine temporal resolution, i.e., reflect the individual ability to detect small and sudden change in sound stimuli [27,28]. In patients with multiple sclerosis, IGFs were negatively related to the speed on attentional control and executive tasks [19]. We expected that the state of neural networks defining individual gamma frequencies would also reflect the temporal dynamics on more general cognitive tasks reflecting different aspects of simple and complex information processing. However, as shown by the lack of association between IGFs and processing speed in our sample, it is possible that connection can be observed in clinical populations with clearly impaired cognitive processing, or be highly modality-specific (i.e., auditory response is associated to the performance of auditory tasks). The latter assumption connects with a recent suggestion of Molina et al. [66] that evoked gamma may be an index of the brain's overall "adaptive integrity" of the lower-level perceptual networks. We tested healthy young participants, and all tasks utilized in the current research were based on visual domain assessment. Future research should combine visual and auditory domain-based processing in order to untangle the role that task modality plays in this relationship. Finally, it should be acknowledged that the sample size is not sufficient to reliably detect small-to-medium-sized correlations. Therefore, strength of evidence for the lack of the relationship between processing speed across different tasks and gamma oscillations needs to be replicated in a larger sample.

5. Conclusions

Gamma activity, as a response at 40 Hz and at IGFs, is related to the performance speed on complex cognitive task tapping planning and problem solving. With the individualized approach, the observed associations is somewhat stronger, and the association seem to primary reflect individual differences in higher-order cognitive processing. These findings are particularly important for the interpretation of gamma activity in neuropsychiatric disorders.

Supplementary Materials: The following are available online at https://www.mdpi.com/article/10.3390/jpm11060453/s1, Table S1: Bayesian correlation outcomes between EEG measures and cognitive measures.

Author Contributions: Conceptualization, M.P., V.J., and I.G.-B.; formal analysis, V.P., E.P., A.V., J.B., V.J., and I.G.-B.; funding acquisition, I.G.-B.; investigation, E.P. and M.P.; methodology, E.P. and A.V.; software, A.V.; supervision, I.G.-B.; validation, E.P. and I.G.-B.; writing—original draft, V.P., J.B., and I.G.-B.; writing—review and editing, J.B. and I.G.-B. All authors have read and agreed to the published version of the manuscript.

Funding: This study was supported by the Research Council of Lithuania (LMTLT agreement no. S-LJB-20-1). J.B. received institutional support from the Ministry of Education, Science and Technological Development of the Republic of Serbia (contract: 451-03-68/2020-14/200015).

Institutional Review Board Statement: The study was conducted according to the guidelines of the Declaration of Helsinki and approved by the Vilnius Regional Biomedical Research Ethics Committee (no. 2020/3-1213-701).

Informed Consent Statement: Informed consent was obtained from all subjects involved in the study.

Data Availability Statement: The data presented in this study are available on request from the corresponding author. The data are not publicly available due to privacy restrictions.

Acknowledgments: Authors would like to thank all the volunteers who participated in the experiment.

Conflicts of Interest: The authors declare no conflict of interest.

References

1. Legget, K.T.; Hild, A.K.; Steinmetz, S.E.; Simon, S.T.; Rojas, D.C. MEG and EEG Demonstrate Similar Test-Retest Reliability of the 40 Hz Auditory Steady-State Response. *Int. J. Psychophysiol.* **2017**, *114*, 16–23. [CrossRef] [PubMed]
2. Rodriguez, E.; George, N.; Lachaux, J.-P.; Martinerie, J.; Renault, B.; Varela, F.J. Perception's Shadow: Long-Distance Synchronization of Human Brain Activity. *Nature* **1999**, *397*, 430–433. [CrossRef]
3. Tallon-Baudry, C.; Bertrand, O.; Delpuech, C.; Pernier, J. Stimulus Specificity of Phase-Locked and Non-Phase-Locked 40 Hz Visual Responses in Human. *J. Neurosci.* **1996**, *16*, 4240–4249. [CrossRef] [PubMed]
4. Jensen, O.; Kaiser, J.; Lachaux, J.-P. Human Gamma-Frequency Oscillations Associated with Attention and Memory. *Trends Neurosci.* **2007**, *30*, 317–324. [CrossRef] [PubMed]

5. Keil, A.; Müller, M.M.; Ray, W.J.; Gruber, T.; Elbert, T. Human Gamma Band Activity and Perception of a Gestalt. *J. Neurosci.* **1999**, *19*, 7152–7161. [CrossRef] [PubMed]
6. Pulvermüller, F.; Lutzenberger, W.; Preißl, H.; Birbaumer, N. Spectral Responses in the Gamma-Band Physiological Signs of Higher Cognitive Processes? *Neurorep. Int. J. Rapid Commun. Res. Neurosci.* **1995**, *6*, 2059–2064. [CrossRef]
7. Tallon-Baudry, C.; Bertrand, O. Oscillatory Gamma Activity in Humans and Its Role in Object Representation. *Trends Cogn. Sci.* **1999**, *3*, 151–162. [CrossRef]
8. Herrmann, C.S.; Demiralp, T. Human EEG Gamma Oscillations in Neuropsychiatric Disorders. *Clin. Neurophysiol.* **2005**, *116*, 2719–2733. [CrossRef]
9. Mathalon, D.H.; Sohal, V.S. Neural Oscillations and Synchrony in Brain Dysfunction and Neuropsychiatric Disorders: It's About Time. *JAMA Psychiatry* **2015**, *72*, 840–844. [CrossRef]
10. van Es, M.W.J.; Schoffelen, J.-M. Stimulus-Induced Gamma Power Predicts the Amplitude of the Subsequent Visual Evoked Response. *NeuroImage* **2019**, *186*, 703–712. [CrossRef]
11. Picton, T.W.; John, M.S.; Dimitrijevic, A.; Purcell, D. Human Auditory Steady-State Responses: Respuestas Auditivas de Estado Estable En Humanos. *Int. J. Audiol.* **2003**, *42*, 177–219. [CrossRef] [PubMed]
12. Picton, T. Hearing in Time: Evoked Potential Studies of Temporal Processing. *Ear Hear.* **2013**, *34*, 385–401. [CrossRef] [PubMed]
13. Light, G.A.; Hsu, J.L.; Hsieh, M.H.; Meyer-Gomes, K.; Sprock, J.; Swerdlow, N.R.; Braff, D.L. Gamma Band Oscillations Reveal Neural Network Cortical Coherence Dysfunction in Schizophrenia Patients. *Biol. Psychiatry* **2006**, *60*, 1231–1240. [CrossRef] [PubMed]
14. Kim, S.; Jang, S.-K.; Kim, D.-W.; Shim, M.; Kim, Y.-W.; Im, C.-H.; Lee, S.-H. Cortical Volume and 40-Hz Auditory-Steady-State Responses in Patients with Schizophrenia and Healthy Controls. *NeuroImage Clin.* **2019**, *22*, 101732. [CrossRef] [PubMed]
15. Koshiyama, D.; Miyakoshi, M.; Joshi, Y.B.; Molina, J.L.; Tanaka-Koshiyama, K.; Sprock, J.; Braff, D.L.; Swerdlow, N.R.; Light, G.A. A Distributed Frontotemporal Network Underlies Gamma-Band Synchronization Impairments in Schizophrenia Patients. *Neuropsychopharmacology* **2020**, *45*, 2198–2206. [CrossRef] [PubMed]
16. Koshiyama, D.; Thomas, M.L.; Miyakoshi, M.; Joshi, Y.B.; Molina, J.L.; Tanaka-Koshiyama, K.; Sprock, J.; Braff, D.L.; Swerdlow, N.R.; Light, G.A. Hierarchical Pathways from Sensory Processing to Cognitive, Clinical, and Functional Impairments in Schizophrenia. *Schizophr. Bull.* **2020**, *47*. [CrossRef]
17. Koshiyama, D.; Miyakoshi, M.; Thomas, M.L.; Joshi, Y.B.; Molina, J.L.; Tanaka-Koshiyama, K.; Sprock, J.; Braff, D.L.; Swerdlow, N.R.; Light, G.A. Unique Contributions of Sensory Discrimination and Gamma Synchronization Deficits to Cognitive, Clinical, and Psychosocial Functional Impairments in Schizophrenia. *Schizophr. Res.* **2021**, *228*, 280–287. [CrossRef]
18. Parciauskaite, V.; Bjekic, J.; Griskova-Bulanova, I. Gamma-Range Auditory Steady-State Responses and Cognitive Performance: A Systematic Review. *Brain Sci.* **2021**, *11*, 217. [CrossRef]
19. Arrondo, G.; Alegre, M.; Sepulcre, J.; Iriarte, J.; Artieda, J.; Villoslada, P. Abnormalities in Brain Synchronization Are Correlated with Cognitive Impairment in Multiple Sclerosis. *Mult. Scler. Houndmills Basingstoke Engl.* **2009**, *15*, 509–516. [CrossRef]
20. van Deursen, J.A.; Vuurman, E.F.P.M.; van Kranen-Mastenbroek, V.H.J.M.; Verhey, F.R.J.; Riedel, W.J. 40-Hz Steady State Response in Alzheimer's Disease and Mild Cognitive Impairment. *Neurobiol. Aging* **2011**, *32*, 24–30. [CrossRef] [PubMed]
21. Lehongre, K.; Ramus, F.; Villiermet, N.; Schwartz, D.; Giraud, A.-L. Altered Low-Gamma Sampling in Auditory Cortex Accounts for the Three Main Facets of Dyslexia. *Neuron* **2011**, *72*, 1080–1090. [CrossRef]
22. Hirtum, T.V.; Ghesquière, P.; Wouters, J. Atypical Neural Processing of Rise Time by Adults with Dyslexia. *Cortex* **2019**, *113*, 128–140. [CrossRef]
23. Puvvada, K.C.; Summerfelt, A.; Du, X.; Krishna, N.; Kochunov, P.; Rowland, L.M.; Simon, J.Z.; Hong, L.E. Delta Vs. Gamma Auditory Steady State Synchrony in Schizophrenia. *Schizophr. Bull.* **2018**, *44*, 378–387. [CrossRef]
24. Rass, O.; Forsyth, J.; Krishnan, G.; Hetrick, W.P.; Klaunig, M.; Breier, A.; O'Donnell, B.F.; Brenner, C.A. Auditory Steady State Response in the Schizophrenia, First-Degree Relatives, and Schizotypal Personality Disorder. *Schizophr. Res.* **2012**, *136*, 143–149. [CrossRef] [PubMed]
25. Sun, C.; Zhou, P.; Wang, C.; Fan, Y.; Tian, Q.; Dong, F.; Zhou, F.; Wang, C. Defects of Gamma Oscillations in Auditory Steady-State Evoked Potential of Schizophrenia. *Shanghai Arch. Psychiatry* **2018**, *30*, 27.
26. Tada, M.; Nagai, T.; Kirihara, K.; Koike, S.; Suga, M.; Araki, T.; Kobayashi, T.; Kasai, K. Differential Alterations of Auditory Gamma Oscillatory Responses Between Pre-Onset High-Risk Individuals and First-Episode Schizophrenia. *Cereb. Cortex* **2016**, *26*, 1027–1035. [CrossRef]
27. Baltus, A.; Herrmann, C.S. Auditory Temporal Resolution Is Linked to Resonance Frequency of the Auditory Cortex. *Int. J. Psychophysiol.* **2015**, *98*, 1–7. [CrossRef] [PubMed]
28. Baltus, A.; Herrmann, C.S. The Importance of Individual Frequencies of Endogenous Brain Oscillations for Auditory Cognition—A Short Review. *Brain Res.* **2016**, *1640*, 243–250. [CrossRef] [PubMed]
29. Baltus, A.; Wagner, S.; Wolters, C.H.; Herrmann, C.S. Optimized Auditory Transcranial Alternating Current Stimulation Improves Individual Auditory Temporal Resolution. *Brain Stimulat.* **2018**, *11*, 118–124. [CrossRef]
30. Zaehle, T.; Lenz, D.; Ohl, F.W.; Herrmann, C.S. Resonance Phenomena in the Human Auditory Cortex: Individual Resonance Frequencies of the Cerebral Cortex Determine Electrophysiological Responses. *Exp. Brain Res.* **2010**, *203*, 629–635. [CrossRef] [PubMed]
31. Regier, D.A.; Kuhl, E.A.; Kupfer, D.J. The DSM-5: Classification and Criteria Changes. *World Psychiatry* **2013**, *12*, 92–98. [CrossRef]

32. Buzsáki, G.; Draguhn, A. Neuronal Oscillations in Cortical Networks. *Science* **2004**, *304*, 1926–1929. [CrossRef]
33. Dolphin, W.F. The Envelope Following Response to Multiple Tone Pair Stimuli. *Hear. Res.* **1997**, *110*, 1–14. [CrossRef]
34. Purcell, D.W.; John, S.M.; Schneider, B.A.; Picton, T.W. Human Temporal Auditory Acuity as Assessed by Envelope Following Responses. *J. Acoust. Soc. Am.* **2004**, *116*, 3581–3593. [CrossRef] [PubMed]
35. Griskova-Bulanova, I.; Voicikas, A.; Dapsys, K.; Melynyte, S.; Andruskevicius, S.; Pipinis, E. Envelope Following Response to 440 Hz Carrier Chirp-Modulated Tones Show Clinically Relevant Changes in Schizophrenia. *Brain Sci.* **2021**, *11*, 22. [CrossRef]
36. Artieda, J.; Valencia, M.; Alegre, M.; Olaziregi, O.; Urrestarazu, E.; Iriarte, J. Potentials Evoked by Chirp-Modulated Tones: A New Technique to Evaluate Oscillatory Activity in the Auditory Pathway. *Clin. Neurophysiol.* **2004**, *115*, 699–709. [CrossRef] [PubMed]
37. Arnfred, S.M.; Raballo, A.; Morup, M.; Parnas, J. Self-Disorder and Brain Processing of Proprioception in Schizophrenia Spectrum Patients: A Re-Analysis. *Psychopathology* **2015**, *48*, 60–64. [CrossRef] [PubMed]
38. Parciauskaite, V.; Voicikas, A.; Jurkuvenas, V.; Tarailis, P.; Kraulaidis, M.; Pipinis, E.; Griskova-Bulanova, I. 40-Hz Auditory Steady-State Responses and the Complex Information Processing: An Exploratory Study in Healthy Young Males. *PLoS ONE* **2019**, *14*, e0223127. [CrossRef]
39. Rass, O.; Krishnan, G.; Brenner, C.A.; Hetrick, W.P.; Merrill, C.C.; Shekhar, A.; O'Donnell, B.F. Auditory Steady State Response in Bipolar Disorder: Relation to Clinical State, Cognitive Performance, Medication Status, and Substance Disorders. *Bipolar Disord.* **2010**, *12*, 793–803. [CrossRef]
40. Deary, I.J.; Johnson, W.; Starr, J.M. Are Processing Speed Tasks Biomarkers of Cognitive Aging? *Psychol. Aging* **2010**, *25*, 219–228. [CrossRef]
41. Lu, P.H.; Lee, G.J.; Tishler, T.A.; Meghpara, M.; Thompson, P.M.; Bartzokis, G. Myelin Breakdown Mediates Age-Related Slowing in Cognitive Processing Speed in Healthy Elderly Men. *Brain Cogn.* **2013**, *81*, 131–138. [CrossRef]
42. Salthouse, T.A. The Processing-Speed Theory of Adult Age Differences in Cognition. *Psychol. Rev.* **1996**, *103*, 403–428. [CrossRef] [PubMed]
43. Friedova, L.; Rusz, J.; Motyl, J.; Srpova, B.; Vodehnalova, K.; Andelova, M.; Novotna, K.; Novotny, M.; Ruzickova, H.; Tykalova, T.; et al. Slowed Articulation Rate Is Associated with Information Processing Speed Decline in Multiple Sclerosis: A Pilot Study. *J. Clin. Neurosci.* **2019**, *65*, 28–33. [CrossRef] [PubMed]
44. Karbasforoushan, H.; Duffy, B.; Blackford, J.U.; Woodward, N.D. Processing Speed Impairment in Schizophrenia Is Mediated by White Matter Integrity. *Psychol. Med.* **2015**, *45*, 109–120. [CrossRef] [PubMed]
45. McKenna, B.S.; Theilmann, R.J.; Sutherland, A.N.; Eyler, L.T. Fusing Functional MRI and Diffusion Tensor Imaging Measures of Brain Function and Structure to Predict Working Memory and Processing Speed Performance among Inter-Episode Bipolar Patients. *J. Int. Neuropsychol. Soc.* **2015**, *21*, 330–341. [CrossRef]
46. Patrick, K.E.; Schultheis, M.T.; Agate, F.T.; McCurdy, M.D.; Daly, B.P.; Tarazi, R.A.; Chute, D.L.; Hurewitz, F. Executive Function "Drives" Differences in Simulated Driving Performance between Young Adults with and without Autism Spectrum Disorder. *Child Neuropsychol.* **2020**, *26*, 1–17. [CrossRef]
47. Mueller, S.T.; Piper, B.J. The Psychology Experiment Building Language (PEBL) and PEBL Test Battery. *J. Neurosci. Methods* **2014**, *222*, 250–259. [CrossRef]
48. Delorme, A.; Makeig, S. EEGLAB: An Open Source Toolbox for Analysis of Single-Trial EEG Dynamics Including Independent Component Analysis. *J. Neurosci. Methods* **2004**, *134*, 9–21. [CrossRef]
49. Mørup, M.; Hansen, L.K.; Arnfred, S.M. ERPWAVELAB: A Toolbox for Multi-Channel Analysis of Time-Frequency Transformed Event Related Potentials. *J. Neurosci. Methods* **2007**, *161*, 361–368. [CrossRef]
50. Oostenveld, R.; Fries, P.; Maris, E.; Schoffelen, J.-M. FieldTrip: Open Source Software for Advanced Analysis of MEG, EEG, and Invasive Electrophysiological Data. *Comput. Intell. Neurosci.* **2011**, *2011*, 156869. [CrossRef]
51. Love, J.; Selker, R.; Verhagen, J.; Marsman, M.; Gronau, Q.F.; Jamil, T.; Smira, M.; Epskamp, S.; Wild, A.; Ly, A.; et al. Software to Sharpen Your Stats. *APS Obs.* **2015**, *28*, 27–29.
52. Lee, M.D.; Wagenmakers, E.-J. *Bayesian Cognitive Modeling: A Practical Course*; Cambridge University Press: Cambridge, UK, 2014; ISBN 978-1-107-65391-7.
53. Oda, Y.; Onitsuka, T.; Tsuchimoto, R.; Hirano, S.; Oribe, N.; Ueno, T.; Hirano, Y.; Nakamura, I.; Miura, T.; Kanba, S. Gamma Band Neural Synchronization Deficits for Auditory Steady State Responses in Bipolar Disorder Patients. *PLoS ONE* **2012**, *7*, e39955. [CrossRef] [PubMed]
54. O'Donnell, B.F.; Vohs, J.L.; Krishnan, G.P.; Rass, O.; Hetrick, W.P.; Morzorati, S.L. The Auditory Steady-State Response (ASSR): A Translational Biomarker for Schizophrenia. *Suppl. Clin. Neurophysiol.* **2013**, *62*, 101–112. [PubMed]
55. Thuné, H.; Recasens, M.; Uhlhaas, P.J. The 40-Hz Auditory Steady-State Response in Patients With Schizophrenia: A Meta-Analysis. *JAMA Psychiatry* **2016**, *73*, 1145–1153. [CrossRef] [PubMed]
56. Gransier, R.; Hofmann, M.; van Wieringen, A.; Wouters, J. Stimulus-Evoked Phase-Locked Activity along the Human Auditory Pathway Strongly Varies across Individuals. *Sci. Rep.* **2021**, *11*, 143. [CrossRef]
57. Parker, D.A.; Hamm, J.P.; McDowell, J.E.; Keedy, S.K.; Gershon, E.S.; Ivleva, E.I.; Pearlson, G.D.; Keshavan, M.S.; Tamminga, C.A.; Sweeney, J.A.; et al. Auditory Steady-State EEG Response across the Schizo-Bipolar Spectrum. *Schizophr. Res.* **2019**, *209*, 218–226. [CrossRef]

58. Cazalis, F.; Valabrègue, R.; Pélégrini-Issac, M.; Asloun, S.; Robbins, T.W.; Granon, S. Individual Differences in Prefrontal Cortical Activation on the Tower of London Planning Task: Implication for Effortful Processing. *Eur. J. Neurosci.* **2003**, *17*, 2219–2225. [CrossRef]
59. Pulos, S.; Denzine, G. Individual Differences in Planning Behavior and Working Memory: A Study of the Tower of London. *Individ. Differ. Res.* **2005**, *3*, 99–104.
60. Luciana, M.; Collins, P.F.; Olson, E.A.; Schissel, A.M. Tower of London Performance in Healthy Adolescents: The Development of Planning Skills and Associations With Self-Reported Inattention and Impulsivity. *Dev. Neuropsychol.* **2009**, *34*, 461–475. [CrossRef]
61. Phillips, L.H. The Role of Memory in the Tower of London Task. *Memory* **1999**, *7*, 209–231. [CrossRef]
62. Unterrainer, J.M.; Rahm, B.; Kaller, C.P.; Leonhart, R.; Quiske, K.; Hoppe-Seyler, K.; Meier, C.; Müller, C.; Halsband, U. Planning Abilities and the Tower of London: Is This Task Measuring a Discrete Cognitive Function? *J. Clin. Exp. Neuropsychol.* **2004**, *26*, 846–856. [CrossRef] [PubMed]
63. Newman, S.D.; Carpenter, P.A.; Varma, S.; Just, M.A. Frontal and Parietal Participation in Problem Solving in the Tower of London: FMRI and Computational Modeling of Planning and High-Level Perception. *Neuropsychologia* **2003**, *41*, 1668–1682. [CrossRef]
64. Binder, M.; Górska, U.; Griskova-Bulanova, I. 40Hz Auditory Steady-State Responses in Patients with Disorders of Consciousness: Correlation between Phase-Locking Index and Coma Recovery Scale-Revised Score. *Clin. Neurophysiol.* **2017**, *128*, 799–806. [CrossRef] [PubMed]
65. Binder, M.; Górska, U.; Pipinis, E.; Voicikas, A.; Griskova-Bulanova, I. Auditory Steady-State Response to Chirp-Modulated Tones: A Pilot Study in Patients with Disorders of Consciousness. *NeuroImage Clin.* **2020**, *27*, 102261. [CrossRef] [PubMed]
66. Molina, J.L.; Thomas, M.L.; Joshi, Y.B.; Hochberger, W.C.; Koshiyama, D.; Nungaray, J.A.; Cardoso, L.; Sprock, J.; Braff, D.L.; Swerdlow, N.R.; et al. Gamma Oscillations Predict Pro-Cognitive and Clinical Response to Auditory-Based Cognitive Training in Schizophrenia. *Transl. Psychiatry* **2020**, *10*, 405. [CrossRef] [PubMed]

Journal of *Personalized Medicine*

MDPI

Article

Resting-State Isolated Effective Connectivity of the Cingulate Cortex as a Neurophysiological Biomarker in Patients with Severe Treatment-Resistant Schizophrenia

Masataka Wada [1], Shinichiro Nakajima [1,*], Ryosuke Tarumi [1,2], Fumi Masuda [1], Takahiro Miyazaki [1], Sakiko Tsugawa [1], Kamiyu Ogyu [1], Shiori Honda [3], Karin Matsushita [4], Yudai Kikuchi [4], Shinya Fujii [4], Daniel M. Blumberger [5], Zafiris J. Daskalakis [5], Masaru Mimura [1] and Yoshihiro Noda [1,*]

1 Department of Neuropsychiatry, Keio University School of Medicine, Tokyo 160-8582, Japan; m.wada@keio.jp (M.W.); ryousuke1114@gmail.com (R.T.); fumi_masuda@keio.jp (F.M.); takahime.miyazaki@nifty.com (T.M.); sakiko.tsugawa@gmail.com (S.T.); camille.1896@gmail.com (K.O.); mimura@a7.keio.jp (M.M.)

2 Department of Psychiatry, Komagino Hospital, Tokyo 193-8505, Japan

3 Graduate School of Media and Governance, Keio University, Kanagawa, Tokyo 252-0882, Japan; shiori.0913.honda@keio.jp

4 Faculty of Environment and Information Studies, Keio University, Kanagawa, Tokyo 252-0882, Japan; t17752km@sfc.keio.ac.jp (K.M.); yudai-kikuchi@keio.jp (Y.K.); fujii.shinya@gmail.com (S.F.)

5 Temerty Centre for Therapeutic Brain Intervention, Centre for Addiction and Mental Health, Department of Psychiatry, University of Toronto, Toronto, ON M6J 1H4, Canada; Daniel.Blumberger@camh.ca (D.M.B.); Jeff.Daskalakis@camh.ca (Z.J.D.)

* Correspondence: shinichiro_nakajima@hotmail.com (S.N.); yoshi-tms@keio.jp (Y.N.); Tel.: +81-3-3353-1211 (ext. 62454) (S.N.); +81-3-3353-1211 (ext. 61857) (Y.N.); Fax: +81-3-5379-0187 (S.N. & Y.N.)

Received: 21 June 2020; Accepted: 12 August 2020; Published: 14 August 2020

check for updates

Abstract: Background: The neural basis of treatment-resistant schizophrenia (TRS) remains unclear. Previous neuroimaging studies suggest that aberrant connectivity between the anterior cingulate cortex (ACC) and default mode network (DMN) may play a key role in the pathophysiology of TRS. Thus, we aimed to examine the connectivity between the ACC and posterior cingulate cortex (PCC), a hub of the DMN, computing isolated effective coherence (iCoh), which represents causal effective connectivity. **Methods**: Resting-state electroencephalogram with 19 channels was acquired from seventeen patients with TRS and thirty patients with non-TRS (nTRS). The iCoh values between the PCC and ACC were calculated using sLORETA software. We conducted four-way analyses of variance (ANOVAs) for iCoh values with group as a between-subject factor and frequency, directionality, and laterality as within-subject factors and post-hoc independent *t*-tests. **Results**: The ANOVA and post-hoc *t*-tests for the iCoh ratio of directionality from PCC to ACC showed significant findings in delta ($t_{45} = 7.659$, $p = 0.008$) and theta ($t_{45} = 8.066$, $p = 0.007$) bands in the left side (TRS < nTRS). **Conclusion**: Left delta and theta PCC and ACC iCoh ratio may represent a neurophysiological basis of TRS. Given the preliminary nature of this study, these results warrant further study to confirm the importance of iCoh as a clinical indicator for treatment-resistance.

Keywords: treatment-resistant schizophrenia; causal effective connectivity; isolated effective coherence; resting-state electroencephalography; anterior cingulate cortex; posterior cingulate cortex; default mode network

1. Introduction

Approximately one-third of patients with schizophrenia do not respond to antipsychotic treatment [1,2], which is considered as treatment-resistant schizophrenia (TRS). As the quality of life in patients with TRS is remarkably disturbed through their lifespan, understanding the pathophysiology of TRS is a priority for mental health research. However, the neural basis of TRS, especially the difference from non-treatment resistant schizophrenia (nTRS), remains unclear [3].

One brain region commonly reported to show abnormal structural and functional findings in patients with schizophrenia is the anterior cingulate cortex (ACC) [4–6]. The ACC is an area crucial for integrating emotional, cognitive/attentional, and nociceptive functioning, as well as motor processing [7]. Additionally, previous proton magnetic resonance spectroscopy studies demonstrated that patients with TRS showed increased levels of glutamatergic neurometabolites in the ACC compared with patients with nTRS [8] or healthy controls [9–11]. Thus, while dysfunction of the ACC is among pathological neural bases for schizophrenia, it may also be related to that for TRS.

Several resting-state functional magnetic resonance imaging (fMRI) studies have shown that connectivity within the default mode network (DMN) is increased in patients with schizophrenia compared with healthy controls [12–14]. The DMN correlates closely with the resting-state human brain activity and is thought to be involved in the monitoring of internal processes as well as internal and external cognition [15]. A number of studies suggested that impaired DMN may be related to various types of symptoms such as cognitive impairment and psychotic symptoms and be associated with long-term clinical outcomes in patients with schizophrenia [16–18]. In addition, previous fMRI studies have indicated that connectivity between the posterior cingulate cortex (PCC), one of the core nodes of the DMN, and ACC is associated with both positive and negative symptoms in patients with schizophrenia [19–21]. Notably, Alonso-Solís et al. reported that patients with TRS demonstrated decreased functional connectivity between the PCC and ACC compared with patients with nTRS [22]. Moreover, patients with schizophrenia who had higher severity of hallucination or delusions demonstrated reduced fractional anisotropy values of the cingulum bundle, as measured by diffusion tensor tractography [23], as well as a reduced magnetization transfer ratio, as measured by MRI [24]. These findings suggest that both functional and structural aberrant connectivity between the ACC and DMN may play a key role in the pathophysiology of TRS.

A recent development in computational techniques has enabled non-invasive measurements of scalp electroencephalography (EEG) to estimate not only local activities at arbitrary brain regions, but also functional connectivities between any two brain regions. Recently, in particular, a new method has been developed to calculate effective directional connectivities called "isolated effective coherence (iCoh)" [25]. The iCoh is considered to represent one of the causal effective connectivities that can specifically estimate the directionality of information flow along a specific path. Most of the brain nodes not only directly, but also indirectly affect one another. Distinguishing between them leads to more precise information. Although it is difficult to do so, the partial directed coherence (PDC) can be used to quantify direct connections that are not confounded by indirect paths, their directionality, and their spectral characteristics. However, this method is influenced by the sender nodes of interest and may decrease in the presence of many nodes, even if the relationship between a sender and receiver node of a particular interest remains unchanged [26]. Here, the iCoh is a novel method that overcomes the abovementioned limitations by estimating the partial coherence under a multivariate autoregressive model. Of note, the better accuracy of the iCoh method has been confirmed by several studies compared with the PDC [25–27].

For further investigation of the pathophysiology of TRS, it is indispensable to detect the direction of abnormality between the ACC and DMN. In this study, we hypothesized that the aberrant effective connectivity between the PCC and ACC may be associated with the pathophysiology of TRS. Therefore, we aimed to investigate the causal effective connectivities as indexed by iCoh of resting-state EEG, focusing on the path between the PCC and ACC between patients with TRS and nTRS.

2. Materials and Methods

2.1. Participants

This study was approved by the ethics committees at Komagino Hospital (IRB code: 20160504) on 22 October 2016 and Keio University School of Medicine (IRB code: 20160320) on 23 July 2018. All participants were included following the completion of an informed consent procedure. All patients were recruited from Komagino Hospital, Tokyo, Japan and had a diagnosis of schizophrenia or schizoaffective disorder based on the Diagnostic and Statistical Manual of Mental Disorders IV. Seventeen patients with TRS and thirty patients with nTRS were enrolled in this study. Treatment-resistance to antipsychotics was defined by the modified treatment response and resistance in psychosis (TRRIP) working group consensus criteria [28]. Specifically, TRS criteria included a history of treatment failure to optimal treatment with at least two previous non-clozapine antipsychotics, while nTRS criteria included the following: (i) current intake of a non-clozapine single antipsychotic and (ii) treatment response: every positive and negative syndrome scale (PANSS) [29] positive score less than 3 points, and clinical global impression score less than 3 points. We excluded patients who had (i) substance abuse/dependence within the past 6 months; (ii) history of head trauma resulting in loss of consciousness for more than 30 min; (iii) serious or unstable physical illness; or (iv) current administration of lamotrigine, topiramate, or memantine.

2.2. Clinical Assessments

The severity of clinical symptoms was assessed with the PANSS by experienced qualified psychiatrists (R.T. and S.N.).

2.3. Measurement and Preprocessing of Resting-State EEG

Resting-state EEG was acquired for approximately 5 min with a 19-channel EEG system (Neurofax EEG-1214, Nihon Kohden, Inc., Tokyo, Japan) according to the 10–20 international system using a linked earlobes reference. Subjects were instructed to keep their eyes closed while staying awake during the EEG recording. EEG data were recorded at the sampling rate of 500 Hz and electrode impedances were kept below 5 kΩ during the recording. EEG data were band-pass filtered off-line at 0.1–100 Hz. Blink and eye-movement related artifacts were removed using independent component analysis. After removing the periods contaminated with noise with a visual inspection, EEG data were concatenated and preprocessed with R software (2018). Subsequently, preprocessed EEG data was processed using standardized low-resolution brain electromagnetic tomography, which is implemented within sLORETA software [25,30].

2.4. iCoh Analysis

In the present study, we calculated the causal effective connectivity as indexed with the iCoh using sLORETA software [25] among the various functional connectivity indices. The iCoh is defined by the formula based on a multivariate autoregressive model, calculating the corresponding partial coherences after setting all irrelevant connections to zero other than the particular directional paths of interest. Here, a multivariate autoregressive model is a mathematical model of two-time series data that can be estimated using a linear sum of the history of the two-time series data. The partial coherence is a measure of connection between two complex-valued random variables after removing the effect of other measured variables. Again, technical details are described in a previously published article [25]. Information on effective connectivity provided by the iCoh method is supposed to represent "direct" paths of connections between the pairs of regions, excluding the influence of indirect connection paths [25]. Furthermore, iCoh provides two-directional estimators for the strength of oscillatory information flow between each pair of regions such as from region "A" to "B" and from region "B" to "A" [31].

The primary analysis of causal effective connectivity as indexed by iCoh was performed for region of interest (ROI) pairs between the PCC and ACC individually for each group. Subsequently, connectivity for each frequency band (i.e., delta: 1.5–3 Hz, theta: 4–7 Hz, alpha: 8–13 Hz, beta: 14–30 Hz, low-gamma: 30–45 Hz, and high-gamma: 55–70 Hz) was calculated. The ROI names, abbreviations, and the Montreal Neurological Institute (MNI)-coordinates are listed in Supplemental Table S1.

2.5. Statistical Analysis

Statistical analyses were performed using the SPSS software (version 25, SPSS Inc., Chicago, IL, USA). Clinico-demographic characteristics, including age, sex, years of education, age of onset, treatment duration, chlorpromazine (CPZ), and PANSS total scores were compared between the groups by χ^2-tests or independent t-tests for categorical or continuous variables, respectively. In this study, normal distributions of the iCoh data were confirmed with Shapiro–Wilk tests before performing the parametric statistical testing. The iCoh values were statistically analyzed by four-way repeated-measures analysis of variance (rm-ANOVA) using "group" (i.e., two groups: TRS and nTRS) as a between-subject factor and "frequency" (i.e., six frequency bands: delta, theta, alpha, beta, low-gamma, and high-gamma), "directionality" (two directions: e.g., PCC to ACC and ACC to PCC), and "laterality" (two lateralities: right and left) as within-subject factors. When significant differences were found in any interactions, subsequent post-hoc rm-ANOVAs (i.e., three-way and two-way ANOVAs) were conducted. Finally, we performed post-hoc independent t-tests for the ratio of bidirectionality of iCoh values. The ratio was calculated as follows: [(PCC to ACC) − (ACC to PCC)]/[(PCC to ACC) + (ACC to PCC)]. Here, the significance level of alpha was set as 0.05, however, only for post hoc analyses of four-way ANOVA, the alpha level was set as 0.01 depending on the number of frequency bands (0.05/5 = 0.01). Pearson's correlation coefficients between chlorpromazine (CPZ) equivalent daily doses and iCoh values were calculated in order to check the effect of antipsychotics on the iCoh as a confounding factor.

In addition, Pearson's correlation coefficients were calculated for the results showing significant findings in the above ANOVA model to examine the correlations among iCoh values within the ROIs and clinical symptoms as assessed with the PANSS total scores.

Moreover, we conducted a receiver operating characteristic (ROC) analysis to investigate the sensitivity and specificity of the iCoh index in discriminating between TRS and nTRS.

3. Results

3.1. Clinico-Demographics Data

Clinico-demographic data are summarized in Table 1. There were no significant group differences in age, sex, years of education, age of onset, and treatment duration other than CPZ equivalent daily doses and PANSS total scores, suggesting the nature of differences between TRS and nTRS.

Table 1. Clinico-demographics data.

	nTRS (n = 30)	TRS (n = 17)	t-Value (Chi-Squared Value for Sex), p-Value
Age, mean (SD), years	41.2 (12.6)	42.4 (13.4)	$t_{45} = 0.29, p = 0.78$
Sex (number of male) (%)	13 (43)	5 (29)	$\chi^2_{45} = 0.89, p = 0.34$
Education, mean (SD), years	13.3 (1.81)	13.3 (2.42)	$t_{45} = 0.06, p = 0.95$
Age of onset, mean (SD), years	26.0 (9.47)	26.6 (7.64)	$t_{45} = 0.23, p = 0.82$
Treatment duration, mean (SD), years	14.5 (12.0)	15.5 (11.3)	$t_{45} = 0.27, p = 0.79$
Chlorpromazine equivalents, mean (SD), mg	406 (233.5)	748 (319.0)	$t_{45} = 4.22, p < 0.001$ *
PANSS total, mean (SD)	48.8 (12.7)	114.6 (21.2)	$t_{45} = 13.4, p < 0.001$ *

TRS: treatment-resistant schizophrenia; nTRS: non treatment-resistant schizophrenia; SD: standard deviation; PANSS: positive and negative syndrome scale, * = $p < 0.05$.

3.2. Four-Way ANOVA for iCoh Values

Four-way ANOVAs for iCoh values between the PCC and ACC indicated the following results. There was a significant group × frequency × directionality × laterality interaction for iCoh values between the PCC and ACC connectivity among the four-way ANOVAs. Consequently, post-hoc independent *t*-tests for the iCoh ratio of directionality from PCC to ACC showed significant findings that the ratio was decreased in TRS compared with nTRS in delta ($t_{45} = 7.659$, $p = 0.008$; alpha = 0.01) and theta ($t_{45} = 8.066$, $p = 0.007$; alpha = 0.01) frequency bands in the left side (Figure 1). The results of ANOVAs and post-hoc independent *t*-tests are summarized in Supplemental Table S2.

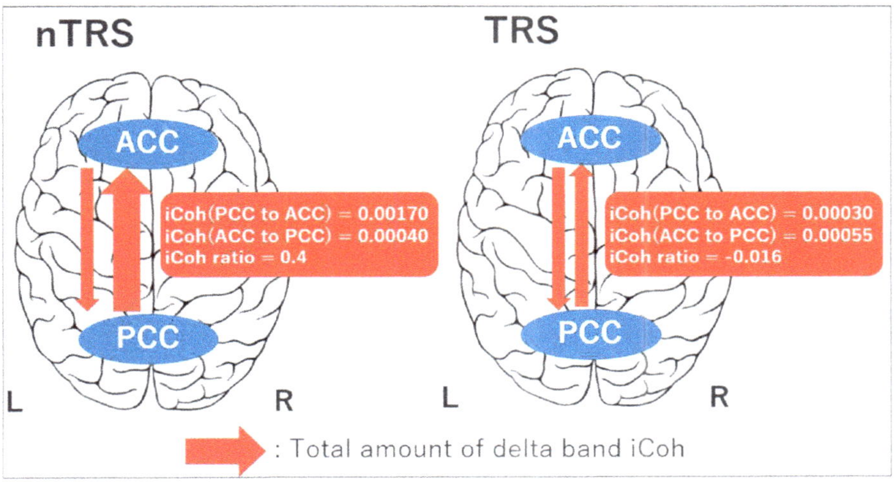

Figure 1. Schematics of the causal effective connectivity between the posterior cingulate cortex (PCC) and anterior cingulate cortex (ACC). In patients with treatment-resistant schizophrenia (TRS), the isolated effective coherence (iCoh) ratios [(PCC to ACC) − (ACC to PCC)]/[(PCC to ACC) + (ACC to PCC)] in delta and theta bands over the left side were significantly decreased compared with patients with non-TRS (nTRS).

Of note, there were no significant correlations between CPZ equivalent daily doses and iCoh values in either TRS group (r = −0.196, $p = 0.225$) or nTRS group (r = 0.064, $p = 0.368$).

3.3. Clinical Correlation with iCoh

Pearson's correlational analyses indicated a trend toward a significant correlation between the iCoh ratio for the left delta PCC–ACC connectivity and PANSS total score only for TRS group (r = 0.38, $p = 0.069$), but not for nTRS group (r = −0.18, $p = 0.17$) (Figure 2).

3.4. ROC Analysis of the iCoh Ratio between TRS and nTRS

Regarding the discrimination between TRS and nTRS groups, the ROC analysis that employed the iCoh ratio for the left delta PCC–ACC connectivity showed a significant asymptotic *p*-value ($p = 0.023$; confidence interval: 0.536–0.868) with an area under the curve of 0.70. Further, the sensitivity and specificity at the optimum point of the ROC curve were 0.64 and 0.70, respectively.

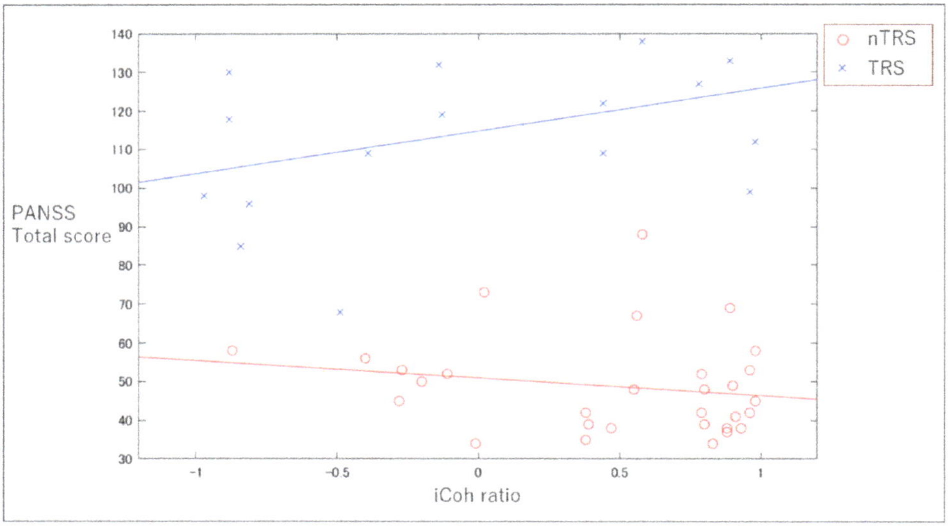

Figure 2. The relationship between the iCho ratio for the left delta PCC–ACC connectivity and positive and negative syndrome scale (PANSS) total score. In patients with TRS, there is trend toward a relationship (r = 0.38, p = 0.069), but not for the nTRS group (r = −0.18, p = 0.17).

4. Discussion

In the present study, we found that patients with TRS showed a significantly lower iCoh ratio between the PCC and ACC in delta and theta frequency bands over the left side than that of patients with nTRS. Furthermore, there was a trend toward a positive correlation between the PCC and ACC iCoh ratio in delta band over the left side and PANSS total scores in patients with TRS, but not in nTRS, suggesting that the higher iCoh ratio between the PCC and ACC in delta band over the left side was associated with greater psychotic symptoms severity in TRS group. These findings suggest that the absolute flow of information from the DMN to ACC was significantly attenuated in patients with TRS compared with patients with nTRS, while patients with TRS who had more severe psychiatric symptoms showed an increasing trend in relative information flow from the DMN to ACC.

Counterintuitively, we found a positive relationship between symptom severity and PCC–ACC iCoh ratio in the TRS group, while there was no association between them in the non-TRS group. These findings suggest that TRS may be accounted for by the hybrid model of categorical and continuous characteristics [32]. Although previous studies have shown consistent findings of the ACC abnormalities in patients with schizophrenia, no studies so far have examined the information flow in the cingulate bundle between the ACC and PCC in detail in this disorder. In addition, our result of a positive relationship between the PCC–ACC iCoh ratio and clinical severity may be related to impaired function of the ACC in patients with TRS.

The PCC is considered to play a crucial role in mediating spontaneous activity [33,34]. In addition, the PCC is thought to contribute to the essential functions such as emotional salience [35] and autobiographical memory [36]. Thus, dysfunction of the PCC may be related to clinical symptoms of schizophrenia such as hallucinations [37], delusions [38], or disorganized thinking [39]. Additionally, the PCC is also one of the core nodes of the theory of mind (ToM) network, which represents the cognitive ability to understand others as intentional agents by inferring their mental states [40,41]. Some studies showed that patients with schizophrenia had decreased activity of the ToM network including the PCC during the ToM task [5,42]. Thus, the PCC may be crucial as a pathological basis for this disorder. On the other hand, the ACC plays a role in mediating awareness and attention [43,44]. The ACC is thought to be a core region affected by schizophrenia [44] and dysfunction of the ACC may induce severity of symptoms or global impairment of cognitive function [45–47]. For example, a smaller volume of the ACC is significantly correlated with more severe positive symptoms of schizophrenia [45] and related to global cognitive impairment measured by the Brief Assessment of Cognition in Schizophrenia [47]. Notably, previous studies noted that patients with TRS had elevated levels of glutamatergic neurometabolites in the ACC [9–11]. These findings suggest that our results may explain the features of TRS including more severe positive symptoms, poorer cognitive function, and social function compared with nTRS. Additionally, impaired functional communication between the two regions might make them worse reciprocally. However, the ROC analysis using the iCoh ratio demonstrated a moderate accuracy to differentiate between patients with TRS and nTRS. While the iCoh ratio between the PCC and ACC may be a potential biomarker to distinguish between the two groups, future work is needed to disentangle the pathophysiology of TRS with a combination of multimodal biological measures.

Several studies have shown that the left cingulum is more related to positive symptoms of schizophrenia compared with the right cingulum. Reduced extracellular free-water as measured by diffusion MRI in the left cingulum was associated with delusions in patients with schizophrenia [48]. In addition, Palaniyappan et al. demonstrated that a reduced magnetization transfer ratio in the left cingulum was associated with a higher severity of delusions, while no such relationship was observed in the right cingulum [24]. Collectively, both functional and structural connectivities between the left PCC and ACC may be related to the severity of symptoms as represented by delusions. Additionally, Yuan et al. revealed that patients with schizophrenia who had never been treated for a long term showed more sever white matter abnormalities in the left cingulum-hippocampus pathway compared with patients with schizophrenia who had been treated [49]. This finding supports our hypothesis that the persistent symptoms observed in patients with TRS may be associated with functional abnormalities in the left cingulate cortex. Thus, these findings are in line with our result that the reduction of iCoh ratio was present only in the left side.

Unlike the neuroimaging studies, EEG enables the assessment of cortical network dynamics because of the high temporal resolution. Delta band oscillations are linked with learning, memory encoding and retrieval, and motivation and reward processes [50,51]. The activity of theta band oscillations has been linked to working memory, emotional arousal, and fear conditioning [51]. For example, Hlinka et al. reported that, in an inter-subject experimental design, a strong relationship was established between functional connectivity in delta band oscillations and the DMN [52]. Furthermore, Neuner et al. demonstrated a highly significant correlation between delta band oscillation and spontaneous blood-oxygen-level dependent (BOLD) signal within the DMN using simultaneous fMRI–EEG study [53]. Thus, delta band oscillations may represent the normal functioning of the DMN.

Our findings also suggest a new treatment option for TRS such as neuromodulation. Specifically, non-invasive novel neurostimulation techniques including transcranial magnetic stimulation (TMS) and deep brain stimulation (DBS) enable us to modulate the local neural connectivity [54,55]. Thus, the abnormal neural connectivity in the cingulate bundle can be one of the therapeutic targets. Given the limited treatment options for TRS, neurostimulation targeting the pathological neural basis as described above may be a promising therapeutic strategy.

There are several limitations to the present study. First, we did not include a healthy control group. Comparison between patients with schizophrenia and health control group may reveal comprehensive dysfunction in patients with schizophrenia, which will help to clarify the position of our current findings. Second, we did not include the potential covariates in the statistical analyses such as the dose of antipsychotics as indexed with CPZ equivalent daily doses. However, we did not see a correlation between the dose of antipsychotics and iCoh values or clinical severity. Third, the present study included relatively small sample sizes in both subdiagnostic groups (i.e., TRS and nTRS). Owing to Coronavirus disease 2019 (COVID-19), we could not continue to enroll subjects at this stage. Therefore, our findings warrant further studies with larger sample sizes in this illness using the TRRIP working group consensus criteria [28]. Forth, we focused only on the effective connectivity between the ACC and PCC as a hypothesis-based manner; however, there may be other potential network abnormalities in patients with schizophrenia. Further research is needed using multimodal imaging based on multifaceted perspectives. Fifth, we have only assessed psychiatric symptoms using the PANSS. Thus, there were no clinical measures for other symptoms like depression or anxiety. As schizophrenia is a multifaceted disorder, future research needs to include a variety of clinical measures. Lastly, in this study, we used the standard 10–20 EEG system using 19 electrodes, which could lead to incorrect localization. Because the number of source-level electrodes in the present study was small, we may not have been able to accurately estimate the source of the deep brain signals. Therefore, the present preliminary analyses warrant further studies to confirm the reproducibility and reliability of these results by, for example, using a higher resolution EEG system with 64 channel electrodes and combining them with more sophisticated signal source analysis techniques. However, several previous studies have performed the sLORETA analysis on 19-electrode EEGs [56–59].

5. Conclusions

In conclusion, we found significant differences in the iCoh ratio between the left PCC and ACC in delta and theta bands between patients with TRS and nTRS. Taken together, these findings may represent part of the underlying neural basis of TRS. The present findings warrant further research in larger sample sizes with multimodal examinations to elucidate underlying mechanisms of treatment-resistance in this illness.

Supplementary Materials: The following are available online at http://www.mdpi.com/2075-4426/10/3/89/s1. Table S1: MNI coordinates, Table S2: Summary of significant results of 4-way ANOVA.

Author Contributions: Conceptualization, Y.N.; methodology, Y.N. and T.M.; software, F.M.; validation, M.W.; formal analysis, M.W. and Y.N.; data curation, T.M., S.H., K.M., and Y.K.; writing: original draft preparation, M.W., F.M., and Y.N.; manuscript editing, Y.N., S.T., K.O., S.F., D.M.B., and Z.J.D.; visualization, M.W.; supervision, Y.N. and S.N.; project administration, R.T., S.H., K.M., Y.K., and S.N.; funding acquisition, S.N., M.M., and Y.N. All authors have read and agreed to the published version of the manuscript.

Funding: This work was supported by the Japan Society for the Promotion of Science and AMED to Y.N., S.N., and M.M. The funding agency did not contribute to the study design; in the data collection, analyses, and interpretation; in the writing of the manuscript; and in the decision to submit the manuscript for publication.

Acknowledgments: We thank Nishikata for his technical support. Furthermore, we appreciate all the patients who have participated in this study.

Conflicts of Interest: M.W., R.T., F.M., T.M., S.T., K.O., S.H., K.M., and Y.K. report no biomedical interests. S.N. has received fellowship grants from CIHR, Japan Research Foundation for Clinical Pharmacology, Naito Foundation, Takeda Science Foundation, Uehara Memorial Foundation, and Daiichi Sankyo Scholarship Donation Program within the past three years. S.N. has also received research supports, manuscript fees, or speaker's honoraria from Dainippon Sumitomo Pharma, Meiji-Seika Pharma, Otsuka Pharmaceutical, Shionogi, and Yoshitomi Yakuhin within the past three years. Z.J.D. has received research and equipment in-kind support for an investigator-initiated study through Brainsway Inc and Magventure Inc. His work was supported by the Ontario Mental Health Foundation (OMHF), the Canadian Institutes of Health Research (CIHR), the National Institutes of Mental Health (NIMH), and the Temerty Family and Grant Family and through the Centre for Addiction and Mental Health (CAMH) Foundation and the Campbell Institute. M.M. has received research support from Japan Society for the Promotion of Science and grants or speaker's honoraria from Daiichi Sankyo, Dainippon-Sumitomo Pharma, Eisai, Eli Lilly, Fuji Film RI Pharma, Janssen Pharmaceutical, Mochida Pharmaceutical, M.S.D., Nippon Chemipher, Novartis Pharma, Ono Yakuhin, Otsuka Pharmaceutical, Pfizer, Takeda Yakuhin, Tsumura, and Yoshitomi Yakuhin within the past three years. D.M.B. receives research support from the Canadian Institutes of Health Research (CIHR), National Institutes of Health—US (NIH), Weston Brain Institute, Brain Canada, and the Temerty Family through the CAMH Foundation and the Campbell Research Institute. He received research support and in-kind equipment support for an investigator-initiated study from Brainsway Ltd. and he is the site principal investigator for three sponsor-initiated studies for Brainsway Ltd. He received in-kind equipment support from Magventure for an investigator-initiated study. He received medication supplies for an investigator-initiated trial from Indivior. He has participated in an advisory board for Janssen. Y.N. has received a Grant-in-Aid for Young Scientists (KAKENHI), a research grant from Japan Agency for Medical Research and development (AMED), an investigator-initiated clinical study grant from TEIJIN PHARMA LIMITED. Y.N. also received research grants from Japan Health Foundation, Meiji Yasuda Mental Health Foundation, Mitsui Life Social Welfare Foundation, Takeda Science Foundation, SENSHIN Medical Research Foundation, Health Science Center Foundation, Mochida Memorial Foundation for Medical and Pharmaceutical Research, and Daiichi Sankyo Scholarship Donation Program. He has received research supports from Otsuka Pharmaceutical, Shionogi, and Meiji Seika Pharma. Y.N.

also received equipment-in-kind supports for an investigator-initiated study from Magventure Inc., Inter Reha Co., Ltd., Rogue Resolutions Ltd., and Miyuki Giken Co., Ltd.

Abbreviations

ACC	anterior cingulate cortex
CPZ	chlorpromazine
DMN	default mode network
DBS	deep brain stimulation
EEG	electroencephalography
fMRI	functional magnetic resonance imaging
iCoh	isolated effective coherence
IPL	inferior parietal lobe
ITL	inferior temporal lobe
mPFC	medial prefrontal cortex
MNI	Montreal Neurological Institute
PANSS	positive and negative syndrome scale
PCC	posterior cingulate cortex
rm-ANOVA	repeated-measures analysis of variance
ROC	receiver operating characteristic
ROIs	regions of interest
sLORETA	standardized low-resolution brain electromagnetic tomography
TRRIP	treatment response and resistance in psychosis
TMS	transcranial magnetic stimulation
TRS	treatment-resistant schizophrenia
nTRS	non treatment-resistant schizophrenia

References

1. Hasan, A.; Falkai, P.; Wobrock, T.; Lieberman, J.; Glenthoj, B.; Gattaz, W.F.; Thibaut, F.; Möller, H.-J. World Federation of Societies of Biological Psychiatry (WFSBP) Guidelines for Biological Treatment of Schizophrenia, Part 1: Update 2012 on the acute treatment of schizophrenia and the management of treatment resistance. *World J. Biol. Psychiatry* **2012**, *13*, 318–378. [CrossRef] [PubMed]
2. Samara, M.T.; Dold, M.; Gianatsi, M.; Nikolakopoulou, A.; Helfer, B.; Salanti, G.; Leucht, S. Efficacy, Acceptability, and Tolerability of Antipsychotics in Treatment-Resistant Schizophrenia: A network meta-analysis. *JAMA Psychiatry* **2016**, *73*, 199. [CrossRef]
3. Nakajima, S.; Takeuchi, H.; Plitman, E.; Fervaha, G.; Gerretsen, P.; Caravaggio, F.; Chung, J.K.; Iwata, Y.; Remington, G.; Graff-Guerrero, A. Neuroimaging findings in treatment-resistant schizophrenia: A systematic review: Lack of neuroimaging correlates of treatment-resistant schizophrenia. *Schizophr. Res.* **2015**, *164*, 164–175. [CrossRef] [PubMed]
4. Carter, C.S.; Macdonald, A.; Ross, L.L.; Stenger, V.A. Anterior Cingulate Cortex Activity and Impaired Self-Monitoring of Performance in Patients with Schizophrenia: An Event-Related fMRI Study. *Am. J. Psychiatry* **2001**, *158*, 1423–1428. [CrossRef]
5. Walter, H.; Ciaramidaro, A.; Adenzato, M.; Vasic, N.; Ardito, R.B.; Erk, S.; Bara, B.G. Dysfunction of the social brain in schizophrenia is modulated by intention type: An fMRI study. *Soc. Cogn. Affect. Neurosci.* **2009**, *4*, 166–176. [CrossRef] [PubMed]
6. Yan, H.; Tian, L.; Yan, J.; Sun, W.; Liu, Q.; Zhang, Y.-B.; Li, X.-M.; Zang, Y.-F.; Zhang, D. Functional and Anatomical Connectivity Abnormalities in Cognitive Division of Anterior Cingulate Cortex in Schizophrenia. *PLoS ONE* **2012**, *7*, e45659. [CrossRef]
7. Salgado-Pineda, P.; Landin-Romero, R.; Fakra, E.; Delaveau, P.; Amann, B.L.; Blin, O. Structural Abnormalities in Schizophrenia: Further Evidence on the Key Role of the Anterior Cingulate Cortex. *Neuropsychobiology* **2014**, *69*, 52–58. [CrossRef]

8. Mouchlianitis, E.; Bloomfield, M.A.P.; Law, V.; Beck, K.; Selvaraj, S.; Rasquinha, N.; Waldman, A.D.; Turkheimer, F.E.; Egerton, A.; Stone, J.; et al. Treatment-Resistant Schizophrenia Patients Show Elevated Anterior Cingulate Cortex Glutamate Compared to Treatment-Responsive. *Schizophr. Bull.* **2015**, *42*, 744–752. [CrossRef]
9. Iwata, Y.; Nakajima, S.; Plitman, E.; Caravaggio, F.; Kim, J.; Shah, P.; Mar, W.; Chavez, S.; De Luca, V.; Mimura, M.; et al. Glutamatergic Neurometabolite Levels in Patients With Ultra-Treatment-Resistant Schizophrenia: A Cross-Sectional 3T Proton Magnetic Resonance Spectroscopy Study. *Biol. Psychiatry* **2019**, *85*, 596–605. [CrossRef]
10. Demjaha, A.; Egerton, A.; Murray, R.M.; Kapur, S.; Howes, O.D.; Stone, J.; McGuire, P. Antipsychotic Treatment Resistance in Schizophrenia Associated with Elevated Glutamate Levels but Normal Dopamine Function. *Boil. Psychiatry* **2014**, *75*, e11–e13. [CrossRef]
11. Tarumi, R.; Tsugawa, S.; Noda, Y.; Plitman, E.; Honda, S.; Matshusita, K.; Chavez, S.; Sawada, K.; Wada, M.; Matsui, M.; et al. Levels of glutamatergic neurometabolites in patients with severe treatment-resistant schizophrenia: A proton magnetic resonance spectroscopy study. *Neuropsychopharmacology* **2020**, *46*, S313. [CrossRef] [PubMed]
12. Jafri, M.J.; Pearlson, G.D.; Stevens, M.C.; Calhoun, V.D. A method for functional network connectivity among spatially independent resting-state components in schizophrenia. *NeuroImage* **2008**, *39*, 1666–1681. [CrossRef] [PubMed]
13. Skudlarski, P.; Jagannathan, K.; Anderson, K.; Stevens, M.C.; Calhoun, V.D.; Skudlarska, B.A.; Pearlson, G. Brain Connectivity Is Not Only Lower but Different in Schizophrenia: A Combined Anatomical and Functional Approach. *Biol. Psychiatry* **2010**, *68*, 61–69. [CrossRef] [PubMed]
14. Zhou, C.; Yu, M.; Tang, X.; Wang, X.; Zhang, X.; Zhang, X.R.; Chen, J. Convergent and divergent altered patterns of default mode network in deficit and non-deficit schizophrenia. *Prog. Neuro Psychopharmacol. Biol. Psychiatry* **2019**, *89*, 427–434. [CrossRef] [PubMed]
15. Buckner, R.L.; Schacter, D.L.; Andrews-Hanna, J.R. The Brain's Default Network. *Ann. N. Y. Acad. Sci.* **2008**, *1124*, 1–38. [CrossRef] [PubMed]
16. Krukow, P.; Jonak, K.; Grochowski, C.; Plechawska-Wójcik, M.; Karakuła-Juchnowicz, H. Resting-state hyperconnectivity within the default mode network impedes the ability to initiate cognitive performance in first-episode schizophrenia patients. *Prog. Neuro Psychopharmacol. Biol. Psychiatry* **2020**, *102*, 109959. [CrossRef]
17. Lee, H.; Lee, D.-K.; Park, K.; Kim, C.-E.; Ryu, S. Default mode network connectivity is associated with long-term clinical outcome in patients with schizophrenia. *NeuroImage Clin.* **2019**, *22*, 101805. [CrossRef] [PubMed]
18. Fox, J.M.; Abram, S.V.; Reilly, J.L.; Eack, S.; Goldman, M.B.; Csernansky, J.G.; Wang, L.; Smith, M.J. Default mode functional connectivity is associated with social functioning in schizophrenia. *J. Abnorm. Psychol.* **2017**, *126*, 392–405. [CrossRef] [PubMed]
19. Bluhm, R.L.; Miller, J.; Lanius, R.A.; Osuch, E.A.; Boksman, K.; Neufeld, R.; Théberge, J.; Schaefer, B.; Williamson, P. Spontaneous Low-Frequency Fluctuations in the BOLD Signal in Schizophrenic Patients: Anomalies in the Default Network. *Schizophr. Bull.* **2007**, *33*, 1004–1012. [CrossRef]
20. Garrity, A.G.; Pearlson, G.D.; McKiernan, K.; Lloyd, D.; Kiehl, K.A.; Calhoun, V.D. Aberrant "default mode" functional connectivity in schizophrenia. *Am. J. Psychiatry* **2007**, *164*, 450–457. [CrossRef]
21. Hare, S.M.; Ford, J.M.; Mathalon, D.H.; Damaraju, E.; Bustillo, J.; Belger, A.; Lee, H.J.; A Mueller, B.; O Lim, K.; Brown, G.G.; et al. Salience–Default Mode Functional Network Connectivity Linked to Positive and Negative Symptoms of Schizophrenia. *Schizophr. Bull.* **2018**, *45*, 892–901. [CrossRef] [PubMed]
22. Alonso-Solís, A.; Vives-Gilabert, Y.; Grasa, E.; Portella, M.J.; Rabella, M.; Sauras, R.B.; Roldán, A.; Núñez-Marín, F.; Gomez-Anson, B.; Pérez, V.; et al. Resting-state functional connectivity alterations in the default network of schizophrenia patients with persistent auditory verbal hallucinations. *Schizophr. Res.* **2015**, *161*, 261–268. [CrossRef] [PubMed]
23. Whitford, T.J.; Lee, S.W.; Oh, J.S.; De Luis-García, R.; Savadjiev, P.; Alvarado, J.L.; Westin, C.-F.; Niznikiewicz, M.; Nestor, P.G.; McCarley, R.W.; et al. Localized abnormalities in the cingulum bundle in patients with schizophrenia: A Diffusion Tensor tractography study. *NeuroImage Clin.* **2014**, *5*, 93–99. [CrossRef] [PubMed]

24. Palaniyappan, L.; Al-Radaideh, A.; Mougin, O.; Das, T.; Gowland, P.A.; Liddle, P.F. Aberrant myelination of the cingulum and Schneiderian delusions in schizophrenia: A 7T magnetization transfer study. *Psychol. Med.* **2018**, *49*, 1890–1896. [CrossRef]
25. Pascual-Marqui, R.D.; Biscay, R.J.; Bosch-Bayard, J.; Lehmann, D.; Kochi, K.; Kinoshita, T.; Yamada, N.; Sadato, N. Assessing direct paths of intracortical causal information flow of oscillatory activity with the isolated effective coherence (iCoh). *Front. Hum. Neurosci.* **2014**, *8*, 448. [CrossRef]
26. Schelter, B.; Timmer, J.; Eichler, M. Assessing the strength of directed influences among neural signals using renormalized partial directed coherence. *J. Neurosci. Methods* **2009**, *179*, 121–130. [CrossRef] [PubMed]
27. Plomp, G.; Quairiaux, C.; Michel, C.M.; Astolfi, L. The physiological plausibility of time-varying Granger-causal modeling: Normalization and weighting by spectral power. *NeuroImage* **2014**, *97*, 206–216. [CrossRef]
28. Howes, O.D.; McCutcheon, R.A.; Agid, O.; De Bartolomeis, A.; Van Beveren, N.J.; Birnbaum, M.L.; Bloomfield, M.A.P.; Bressan, R.A.; Buchanan, R.W.; Carpenter, W.T.; et al. Treatment-Resistant Schizophrenia: Treatment Response and Resistance in Psychosis (TRRIP) Working Group Consensus Guidelines on Diagnosis and Terminology. *Am. J. Psychiatry* **2017**, *174*, 216–229. [CrossRef]
29. Kay, S.R.; Fiszbein, A.; Opler, L.A. The Positive and Negative Syndrome Scale (PANSS) for Schizophrenia. *Schizophr. Bull.* **1987**, *13*, 261–276. [CrossRef]
30. Pascual-Marqui, R.D.; Michel, C.; Lehmann, D. Low resolution electromagnetic tomography: A new method for localizing electrical activity in the brain. *Int. J. Psychophysiol.* **1994**, *18*, 49–65. [CrossRef]
31. Kitaura, Y.; Nishida, K.; Yoshimura, M.; Mii, H.; Katsura, K.; Ueda, S.; Ikeda, S.; Pascual-Marqui, R.D.; Ishii, R.; Kinoshita, T. Functional localization and effective connectivity of cortical theta and alpha oscillatory activity during an attention task. *Clin. Neurophysiol. Pr.* **2017**, *2*, 193–200. [CrossRef] [PubMed]
32. Mouchlianitis, E.; McCutcheon, R.A.; Howes, O.D. Brain-imaging studies of treatment-resistant schizophrenia: A systematic review. *Lancet Psychiatry* **2016**, *3*, 451–463. [CrossRef]
33. Coito, A.; Michel, C.M.; Vulliemoz, S.; Plomp, G. Directed functional connections underlying spontaneous brain activity. *Hum. Brain Mapp.* **2019**, *40*, 879–888. [CrossRef] [PubMed]
34. Fransson, P.; Marrelec, G. The precuneus/posterior cingulate cortex plays a pivotal role in the default mode network: Evidence from a partial correlation network analysis. *NeuroImage* **2008**, *42*, 1178–1184. [CrossRef]
35. Tao, Y.; Liu, B.; Zhang, X.; Li, J.; Qin, W.; Yu, C.; Jiang, T. The Structural Connectivity Pattern of the Default Mode Network and Its Association with Memory and Anxiety. *Front. Neuroanat.* **2015**, *9*, 152. [CrossRef]
36. Maddock, R.J.; Garrett, A.S.; Buonocore, M.H. Remembering familiar people: The posterior cingulate cortex and autobiographical memory retrieval. *Neuroscience* **2001**, *104*, 667–676. [CrossRef]
37. Lefebvre, S.; Demeulemeester, M.; Leroy, A.; Delmaire, C.; Lopes, R.; Pins, D.; Thomas, P.; Jardri, R. Network dynamics during the different stages of hallucinations in schizophrenia. *Hum. Brain Mapp.* **2016**, *37*, 2571–2586. [CrossRef]
38. Manoliu, A.; Riedl, V.; Zherdin, A.; Mühlau, M.; Schwerthöffer, D.; Scherr, M.; Peters, H.; Zimmer, C.; Förstl, H.; Bäuml, J.; et al. Aberrant dependence of default mode/central executive network interactions on anterior insular salience network activity in schizophrenia. *Schizophr. Bull.* **2014**, *40*, 428–437. [CrossRef]
39. Lagioia, A.; Van De Ville, D.; Debbané, M.; Lazeyras, F.; Eliez, S. Adolescent resting state networks and their associations with schizotypal trait expression. *Front. Syst. Neurosci.* **2010**, *4*, 4. [CrossRef]
40. Tettamanti, M.; Vaghi, M.M.; Bara, B.G.; Cappa, S.F.; Enrici, I.; Adenzato, M. Effective connectivity gateways to the Theory of Mind network in processing communicative intention. *NeuroImage* **2017**, *155*, 169–176. [CrossRef]
41. Quidé, Y.; Wilhelmi, C.; Green, M.J. Structural brain morphometry associated with theory of mind in bipolar disorder and schizophrenia. *PsyCh J.* **2020**, *9*, 234–246. [CrossRef]
42. Corcoran, R.; Mercer, G.; Frith, C.D. Schizophrenia, symptomatology and social inference: Investigating "theory of mind" in people with schizophrenia. *Schizophr. Res.* **1995**, *17*, 5–13. [CrossRef]
43. Hakamata, Y.; Iwase, M.; Kato, T.; Senda, K.; Inada, T. The Neural Correlates of Mindful Awareness: A Possible Buffering Effect on Anxiety-Related Reduction in Subgenual Anterior Cingulate Cortex Activity. *PLoS ONE* **2013**, *8*, e75526. [CrossRef] [PubMed]
44. Wu, D.; Deng, H.; Xiao, X.; Zuo, Y.; Sun, J.; Wang, Z. Persistent Neuronal Activity in Anterior Cingulate Cortex Correlates with Sustained Attention in Rats Regardless of Sensory Modality. *Sci. Rep.* **2017**, *7*, 43101. [CrossRef] [PubMed]

45. Choi, J.-S.; Kang, D.-H.; Kim, J.-J.; Ha, T.-H.; Roh, K.S.; Youn, T.; Kwon, J.S. Decreased caudal anterior cingulate gyrus volume and positive symptoms in schizophrenia. *Psychiatry Res. Neuroimaging* **2005**, *139*, 239–247. [CrossRef] [PubMed]
46. Nelson, B.D.; Bjorkquist, O.A.; Olsen, E.K.; Herbener, E.S. Schizophrenia symptom and functional correlates of anterior cingulate cortex activation to emotion stimuli: An fMRI investigation. *Psychiatry Res.* **2015**, *234*, 285–291. [CrossRef]
47. Ohi, K.; Shimada, T.; Nemoto, K.; Kataoka, Y.; Yasuyama, T.; Kimura, K.; Okubo, H.; Uehara, T.; Kawasaki, Y. Cognitive clustering in schizophrenia patients, their first-degree relatives and healthy subjects is associated with anterior cingulate cortex volume. *NeuroImage Clin.* **2017**, *16*, 248–256. [CrossRef]
48. Oestreich, L.K.; Pasternak, O.; Shenton, M.E.; Kubicki, M.; Gong, X.; Whitford, T.J.; Australian Schizophrenia Research Bank; McCarthy-Jones, S.; Whitford, T.J. Abnormal white matter microstructure and increased extracellular free-water in the cingulum bundle associated with delusions in chronic schizophrenia. *NeuroImage Clin.* **2016**, *12*, 405–414. [CrossRef]
49. Xiao, Y.; Sun, H.; Shi, S.; Jiang, D.; Tao, B.; Zhao, Y.; Zhang, W.; Gong, Q.; Sweeney, J.A.; Lui, S. White Matter Abnormalities in Never-Treated Patients With Long-Term Schizophrenia. *Am. J. Psychiatry* **2018**, *175*, 1129–1136. [CrossRef]
50. Ekstrom, A.; Watrous, A.J. Multifaceted roles for low-frequency oscillations in bottom-up and top-down processing during navigation and memory. *NeuroImage* **2014**, *85*, 667–677. [CrossRef]
51. Knyazev, G.G. Motivation, emotion, and their inhibitory control mirrored in brain oscillations. *Neurosci. Biobehav. Rev.* **2007**, *31*, 377–395. [CrossRef] [PubMed]
52. Hlinka, J.; Alexakis, C.; Diukova, A.; Liddle, P.F.; Auer, D.P. Slow EEG pattern predicts reduced intrinsic functional connectivity in the default mode network: An inter-subject analysis. *NeuroImage* **2010**, *53*, 239–246. [CrossRef] [PubMed]
53. Neuner, I.; Arrubla, J.; Werner, C.J.; Hitz, K.; Boers, F.; Kawohl, W.; Shah, N.J. The Default Mode Network and EEG Regional Spectral Power: A Simultaneous fMRI-EEG Study. *PLoS ONE* **2014**, *9*, e88214. [CrossRef] [PubMed]
54. Tik, M.; Hoffmann, A.; Sladky, R.; Tomova, L.; Hummer, A.; De Lara, L.I.N.; Bukowski, H.; Pripfl, J.; Biswal, B.B.; Lamm, C.; et al. Towards understanding rTMS mechanism of action: Stimulation of the DLPFC causes network-specific increase in functional connectivity. *Neuroimage* **2017**, *162*, 289–296. [CrossRef]
55. Chiken, S.; Nambu, A. Mechanism of Deep Brain Stimulation: Inhibition, Excitation, or Disruption? *Neuroscientist* **2016**, *22*, 313–322. [CrossRef]
56. Lehmann, D.; Faber, P.L.; Tei, S.; Pascual-Marqui, R.D.; Milz, P.; Kochi, K. Reduced functional connectivity between cortical sources in five meditation traditions detected with lagged coherence using EEG tomography. *NeuroImage* **2012**, *60*, 1574–1586. [CrossRef]
57. A Ponomarev, V.; Kropotov, I.D. Improving source localization of ERPs in the GO/NOGO task by modeling of their cross-covariance structure. *Fiziol. Cheloveka* **2013**, *39*, 36–50.
58. Coben, R.; Hammond, D.C.; Arns, M. 19 Channel Z-Score and LORETA Neurofeedback: Does the Evidence Support the Hype? *Appl. Psychophysiol. Biofeedback* **2019**, *44*, 1–8. [CrossRef]
59. Eugene, A.R.; Masiak, J. Identifying Treatment Response of Sertraline in a Teenager with Selective Mutism using Electrophysiological Neuroimaging. *Int. J. Clin. Pharmacol. Toxicol.* **2016**, *5*, 216–219. [CrossRef]

Journal of *Personalized Medicine*

MDPI

Article

Real-Time Implementation of EEG Oscillatory Phase-Informed Visual Stimulation Using a Least Mean Square-Based AR Model

Aqsa Shakeel [1,2], Takayuki Onojima [1], Toshihisa Tanaka [1,2] and Keiichi Kitajo [1,2,3,4,*]

1 CBS-TOYOTA Collaboration Center, RIKEN Center for Brain Science, Wako 351-0198, Japan; aqsashakeel@gmail.com (A.S.); takayuki.onojima@riken.jp (T.O.); tanakat@cc.tuat.ac.jp (T.T.)
2 Department of Electronic and Information Engineering, Tokyo University of Agriculture and Technology, Tokyo 184-8588, Japan
3 Division of Neural Dynamics, Department of System Neuroscience, National Institute for Physiological Sciences, National Institutes of Natural Sciences, Okazaki 444-8585, Japan
4 Department of Physiological Sciences, School of Life Science, The Graduate University for Advanced Studies (SOKENDAI), Okazaki 444-8585, Japan
* Correspondence: kkitajo@nips.ac.jp

Abstract: It is a technically challenging problem to assess the instantaneous brain state using electroencephalography (EEG) in a real-time closed-loop setup because the prediction of future signals is required to define the current state, such as the instantaneous phase and amplitude. To accomplish this in real-time, a conventional Yule–Walker (YW)-based autoregressive (AR) model has been used. However, the brain state-dependent real-time implementation of a closed-loop system employing an adaptive method has not yet been explored. Our primary purpose was to investigate whether time-series forward prediction using an adaptive least mean square (LMS)-based AR model would be implementable in a real-time closed-loop system or not. EEG state-dependent triggers synchronized with the EEG peaks and troughs of alpha oscillations in both an open-eyes resting state and a visual task. For the resting and visual conditions, statistical results showed that the proposed method succeeded in giving triggers at a specific phase of EEG oscillations for all participants. These individual results showed that the LMS-based AR model was successfully implemented in a real-time closed-loop system targeting specific phases of alpha oscillations and can be used as an adaptive alternative to the conventional and machine-learning approaches with a low computational load.

Keywords: electroencephalography (EEG); brain state-dependent stimulation; closed-loop; autoregressive (AR) model; Yule–Walker (YW) method; least mean square (LMS) method; alpha oscillation; Instantaneous phase

Citation: Shakeel, A.; Onojima, T.; Tanaka, T.; Kitajo, K. Real-Time Implementation of EEG Oscillatory Phase-Informed Visual Stimulation Using a Least Mean Square-Based AR Model. *J. Pers. Med.* **2021**, *11*, 38. https://doi.org/10.3390/jpm11010038

Received: 13 November 2020
Accepted: 6 January 2021
Published: 11 January 2021

1. Introduction

Closed-loop neuroscience is gaining more attention with ongoing technological and innovative advances that enable complex feedback loops to be executed with millisecond resolution on hardware. With regard to brain mechanics, much has been learned about stimulation in an open-loop manner using a pre-defined stimulus, such as the determination of input–output characteristics and how these are possibly modified. This open-loop approach has been quite productive in the field of non-invasive brain stimulation (NIBS), facilitating major developments in pharmacological understanding, as well as in the understanding of the functional basis of cortical dynamics [1,2].

An experiment may be viewed as a "closed-loop" when output from the brain becomes future input to the brain. By creating a causal relationship between the stimulus generator and the measured output, one can possibly "close the loop" [3] in laboratory settings. In reality, this can be achieved when a presented stimulus depends on the simultaneously measured instantaneous brain state. In this case, the neuronal output of the brain affects the input to the brain, thus closing the loop [3].

The combination of electroencephalography (EEG) and transcranial magnetic stimulation (TMS) [4] presents the potential for closed-loop NIBS, which is accentuated by the recent accessibility of cost-effective real-time processors. Although TMS has been around for several decades, it remains the most effective means to non-invasively excite a particular population of cortical neurons, with it being able to do this at a temporal resolution of microseconds and a spatial resolution of millimeters [2,5]. The EEG signal can be theoretically viewed as a lower-dimensional representation of the instantaneous brain state, and the application of TMS could be seen as a vector that results in a new trajectory by altering a spontaneously occurring brain state [6]. Notably, the new state achieved by the TMS pulse is heavily dependent on the precise state at the time of stimulation. This, therefore, leads to the motivation for developing closed-loop brain state-dependent stimulation paradigms.

In the current study, we focus on the most salient feature of the brain state, i.e., the spontaneous oscillatory activity of neuronal networks measured by EEG [7]. Spatially, the state of interest can be determined locally, i.e., the activity of a specific brain area [8], or on a large scale, such as a brain network's ensemble activity [9]. However, on a temporal scale, brain states can be observed by spectral power changes in a particular frequency band of interest (e.g., event-related desynchronization [ERD]) or perceiving the phase-state of an oscillating cycle. This former method has been effectively employed for both alpha (8–12 Hz) [10] and beta rhythms (16–22 Hz) [11] in brain-machine interfaces that allow stroke patients to perform robot-assisted motor tasks. Methodologically, closing the loop is challenging, not only for the spectral power but also for the instantaneous phase, because the requirement for real-time signal processing necessitates a time resolution of milliseconds; however, such a time resolution has become possible over the past decade [11–13]. The implementation of a closed-loop system requires several technically demanding steps: measurement of brain output, signal processing, and tuning/varying of the stimulus. This combination of procedures has become practicable with the latest advances in information technology, which permit intricate calculations to be implemented in real-time using low-cost standard hardware.

Previous benchmark studies [14–16] used a genetic algorithm to optimize parameters prior to algorithm deployment. The optimization process needed rigorous computational measures and could not therefore be implemented in real-time. The algorithm proposed in the aforementioned studies may be improved by adopting an online strategy [14] rather than implementing an offline optimization procedure before the actual execution. One alternative is to use the robust method, i.e., wavelet ridge extraction for instantaneous phase estimation [17]. Although this technique is quite useful for highly variable multiple oscillations presented simultaneously, it might be too computationally expensive for real-time implementation. It is possible that real-time implementation may also be restricted by edge effects due to the presence of data in the reverse direction only. Another alternative is the machine learning implemented by McIntosh and Sajda [18], who estimated the EEG phase for real-time applications. Their technique can be used as a substitute for non-causal filtering in offline analysis for phase estimation, but the major drawbacks include the need for preliminary data for training and the risk of unbiased phase estimation. Therefore, an adaptive method is needed to estimate the phase in real-time.

Our previous study [19] presented an adaptive approach for forward prediction of time-series by comparing a conventional Yule–Walker (YW)-based autoregressive model (AR) and a least mean square (LMS)-based AR model. The main aims of the study were to accurately estimate the instantaneous phase of alpha oscillations using the adaptive approach and to compare adaptive and conventional approaches. The present study is an extension of our previous work, i.e., real-time implementations of conventional YW-based AR and adaptive LMS-based AR models. For the current study, we constructed an EEG-triggered visual stimulus closed-loop setup that synchronized the visual stimulus with a specific phase of ongoing alpha oscillations from the occipital cortex. The previous benchmark study [14] used a YW-based AR model to estimate the instantaneous phase of intracranial EEG theta rhythms of only two patients in real-time, whereas a recent study [15] used the same conventional AR model combined with TMS for real-time mu rhythm phase estimation. The current study's main aim was to check and confirm whether an adaptive LMS-based AR model can be implemented in a real-time closed-loop system, along with a conventional one. Due to technical issues in the DC mode of EEG amplifiers, only data recorded in the AC mode were analyzed for a real-time closed-loop system, which led to a small number of participants. Therefore, this study did not confirm the advantage of the adaptive method over the conventional one.

2. Materials and Methods

2.1. Implementation of a Closed-Loop System

We propose an experimental setup that prolongs current approaches by closing the loop between EEG signals (representing the instantaneous brain state) and visual stimulation. The timing of visual stimulation is locked to the online-detected instantaneous phase of the EEG alpha-band signal (peak and trough phases). An implementation of a real-time closed-loop system is shown in Figure 1. EEG signals are acquired using an actiCAP slim (BrainProducts GmbH, Gilching, Germany) electrode system. Two 24-bit 32-channel Tesla EEG amplifiers (NeurOne; Bittium Biosignals Ltd., Kuopio, Finland) are used for the EEG recordings, with data recorded in the AC mode at a sample rate of 20 kHz for subsequent analysis. The amplifiers' analog output device is configured to recreate a filtered and an amplified analog signal from a user-selectable set of 16 amplifier channels covering the occipital cortex. Of the channel subset, O_z is analyzed by a real-time system. A MATLAB experimental control scripts PC is connected to the Performance real-time target machine (Speedgoat GmbH, Liebefeld, Switzerland), which receives input signals from a 24-bit analog input module (IO109) and sends TTL signal output to a digital output module (IO203 with 64 TTL channels). The digital output module further sends the TTL trigger signal from the Performance real-time target machine to the NeurOne model Black High (Bittium Biosignals Ltd., Kuopio, Finland), with it being referred to here as Trigger A. An additional 8-bit trigger is simultaneously sent from the Performance real-time target machine to the visual stimulus generating PC via serial port (RS232), which further sends it to the NeurOne model Black High for subsequent data analysis. A real-time data acquisition system (Figure 1b) utilizing a Performance real-time target machine runs in parallel on a dedicated target PC (SN4200, IO10; Speedgoat), digitally processing and archiving the raw EEG data through the implementation of a Simulink real-time model (MathWorks Inc., Natick, MA, USA, 2018a) for each scenario (YW peak and trough, LMS peak and trough). The time lag due to the Performance real-time target machine is approximately 10 ms, while the time lag due to the NeurOne is approximately 4 ms.

2.2. Algorithm

The ultimate goals of this study were the real-time phase estimation of alpha rhythms and phase-dependent triggering. The instantaneous phase prediction algorithm can be divided into four distinct parts: YW peak prediction, YW trough prediction, LMS peak prediction, and LMS trough prediction. Each part was further divided into the following sequential steps, except for step 4, which differs between the YW-based and LMS-based AR models. A distinct Simulink real-time model ("MATLAB experimental control scripts PC" block in Figure 1, part b) was designed for each one of the four methods and implemented in the Performance real-time target machine.

1. In each Simulink model, the raw EEG data are received as analog input via IO109 at a sample rate of 2 kHz and are downsampled to 500 Hz.
2. The data are then delayed by 500 samples, and the mean of the data is calculated and subtracted from the original data. The data are then sent to the next step for filtering.
3. The third step implements bandpass filtering. A two-pass finite impulse response (FIR) bandpass filter (filter order 128) with an 8–13 Hz frequency range is applied to the data, and the edges are removed.

4. The fourth step is forward prediction. After trimming 85 samples from both sides, the remaining 330 samples are then used for forward prediction (85 samples). The YW forward prediction algorithm predicts the future and computes coefficients using Yule–Walker equations, whereas the LMS forward prediction algorithm uses an adaptive method to compute coefficients and then uses them in the AR equation. This step results in a predicted signal as an output. The model order for both methods is 30.
5. The Hilbert transform is performed on resulting forward-predicted EEG data to determine the instantaneous phase at "time-zero".
6. The zero-phase crossing (a predetermined phase is crossed, with 0 and pi rad portraying positive and negative peaks, respectively) is monitored online, and a TTL signal is sent from the Performance real-time target machine via digital output module (IO203) and serial port (RS232). The Performance real-time target machine sends the TTL signal to the EEG recording PC via IO203, while at the same time, the TTL signal is sent via RS232 to the visual stimulus generating PC.

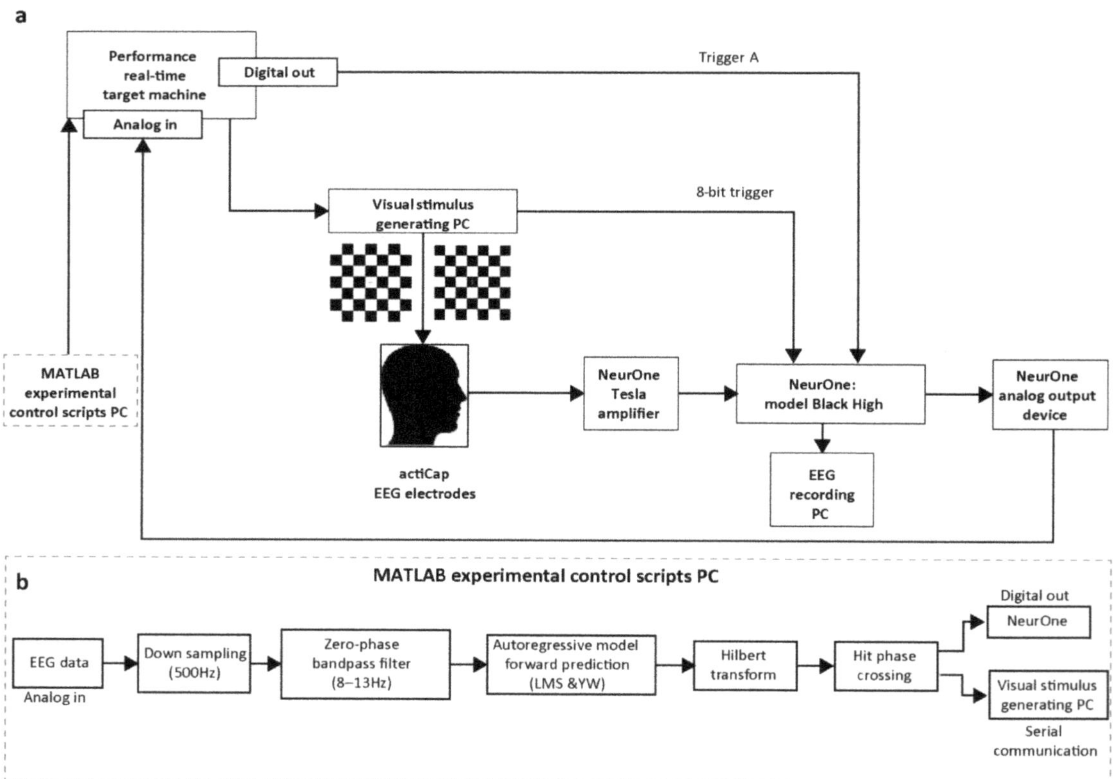

Figure 1. A schematic diagram of the real-time closed-loop system. (**a**) shows an implementation of a closed-loop brain state-dependent visual stimulation setup comprising electroencephalography (EEG), real-time signal processing, and triggered visual stimulation. The visual stimulation is locked to the instantaneous phase of the recorded EEG signal in the alpha band either at the peak or the trough. (**b**) shows sequential steps for time-series forward prediction implemented through MATLAB experimental control scripts PC via four distinct Simulink real-time models (Yule–Walker (YW) peak, YW trough, least mean square (LMS) peak, LMS trough). Raw EEG data were downsampled first, followed by finite impulse response (FIR) bandpass filtering. Coefficients of the autoregressive (AR) models were calculated, and the EEG signal was forward predicted. After time-series forward prediction based on YW/LMS methods, the instantaneous phase (at time-zero") was estimated using Hilbert transform. The visual stimulation was then triggered when a pre-set phase (peak or trough) condition was met.

The next subsections briefly explain the AR model, LMS, instantaneous phase, and phase-locking factor.

2.3. Autoregressive (AR) Model

AR modeling has been effectively utilized in various EEG analysis applications, such as forecasting [20,21], segmentation, and speech analysis [22]. AR modeling shows great results for the power spectrum estimation of short-duration EEG data because of its low vulnerability toward false results [20]. Numerous algorithms can be used to calculate the AR model coefficients, including the Yule–Walker and Burg lattice algorithms.

An AR model of order K is a random process defined as follows [14]:

$$x(t+1) = \sum_{k=0}^{K-1} \alpha_k \, x(t-k) + \varepsilon_t, \tag{1}$$

where $\alpha_0, \ldots, \alpha_{K-1}$ are the coefficients of the AR model; K is the model order; and ε_t is white noise.

2.4. Least Mean Square (LMS)

In 1960, Hoff and Widrow developed the LMS algorithm. LMS uses a stochastic gradient method to solve the least square issue. The equations that establish the adaptive LMS algorithm are defined as follows [23]:

$$\mathbf{X}(t) = [x(t),\ x(t-1),\ x(t-2), \ldots, x(t-K+1)]^T, \tag{2}$$

$$\boldsymbol{A}(t) = [a_0(t),\ a_1(t), \ldots, a_{K-1}\,(t)]^T, \tag{3}$$

$$y(t) = \boldsymbol{A}^T(t)\mathbf{X}(t), \tag{4}$$

$$e(t) = x(t+1) - y(t), \tag{5}$$

$$\boldsymbol{A}(t+1) = \boldsymbol{A}(t) + 2\mu e(t)\mathbf{X}(t), \tag{6}$$

where $\boldsymbol{x}(t)$ is an input signal at sample t, $y(t)$ is output, $e(t)$ is an error, $\boldsymbol{A}(t)$ is the filter weight, μ is the step size, and K is the filter order. The bold variables represent vectors.

For simplicity, in the remaining text, we will use YW to refer to the YW-based AR model and LMS to refer to the LMS-based AR model.

2.5. Instantaneous Frequency, Phase

To calculate the instantaneous phase, the analytic signal is created by joining the original data with its Hilbert transform [24]. The analytic signal $z_x(t)$, which is a complex signal of time t can be created as follows:

$$z_x(t) = x(t) + \mathrm{j}H\{x(t)\}, \tag{7}$$

where $x(t)$ is the real signal, and $H\{x(t)\}$ is the Hilbert transform of the real signal, which is defined as follows:

$$H\{x(t)\} = \frac{1}{\pi}\ \text{P.V.} \int_{-\infty}^{\infty} \frac{x(\tau)}{t-\tau}\, d\tau, \tag{8}$$

where P.V. indicates Cauchy's principal value. The instantaneous phase of the signal can be found from the complex analytic signal as follows:

$$\theta(t) = \arg z_x(t). \tag{9}$$

2.6. Participants

A total of nine volunteers (three males and six females; mean age 32.1 years ± 6.6 (standard deviation [SD])) with normal or corrected-to-normal vision were recruited to this study and provided informed consent for the EEG experiments. The study was approved by the ethics committee of RIKEN. Data from the first three participants were recorded using the DC mode of the Tesla amplifier, while data from the rest of the participants were recorded using the AC mode. The participant data recorded using the DC mode was noisier than that recorded using the AC mode, which resulted in quite low amplitude output signals. The AC mode has a higher signal-to-noise ratio than the DC mode and uses a low pass filter of 0.16 Hz, which leads to higher amplification of data for subsequent analysis. The prediction accuracy was highly affected by the signal-to-noise ratio, and therefore only the participant data collected using the AC mode were used for further analyses. A spectral analysis was performed on the remaining six participants to estimate the power in the alpha rhythm range (8–13 Hz).

2.7. Experiment

The experiment incorporated visual stimulation blocks and eyes-open resting blocks. Participants were asked to avoid eye blinks, eye movements, and jaw clenching. The whole experiment was divided into two sessions, each with ten blocks presented in random order, with these ten blocks consisting of five resting and five visual blocks. In both sessions, the ten blocks were linked with conditions, namely Resting, Visual Random, Resting YW (peak, trough), Resting LMS (peak, trough), Visual YW (peak, trough), and Visual LMS (peak, trough), as shown in Figure 2a. Results were analyzed from blocks 2–5 and blocks 7–10. The total experiment took 1 h and 10 min, including small breaks between blocks. There were 90 trials each block for the resting condition and 108 trials for the visual stimulation condition, as shown in part c of Figure 2. The visual experiment consisted of normal trials and response trials. Visual stimuli were shown on an LCD monitor (BenQ XL2420; BenQ Corporation, Taipei, Taiwan; refresh rate: 144 Hz; resolution: 1920 × 1080), with a chin rest placed 100 cm from the monitor being used to maintain head position. The checkerboard stimuli (visual angle of 8.8°) consisted of 49 black-and-white squares (7 by 7) with a fixation cross at the center. The color of the grids was temporally modulated between black and white (luminance of black: 9.18 cd/m^2; white: 152.2 cd/m^2). The fixation cross was colored gray in regular trials and red in response trials. Participants were instructed to press the left mouse button as soon as they saw a red fixation cross. The visual and resting tasks were implemented using NBS Presentation Version 20.0 (Neurobehavioral Systems Inc., Albany, CA, USA). In addition to the visual experiment, EEG signals were also measured for the resting scenario, while participants rested with their eyes open looking passively at the fixation cross displayed in the center of the screen part b Figure 2.

2.8. EEG Recording and Preprocessing

The 63-channel EEG signals were recorded at a sampling rate of 20 kHz using two Tesla amplifiers and an actiCAP slim EEG cap. Online low and high cutoff frequencies for the EEG amplifier were set to 0.16 Hz and 3500 Hz, respectively. Electrodes were positioned according to the 10/10 system, with electrode AF_z as the ground electrode and the left earlobe as the reference electrode. For offline analysis, EEG signals were re-referenced to the average of the right and left earlobe and downsampled to 500 Hz. Only the downsampled signal was used to calculate the phase-triggered response (PTR), whereas, for the phase-locking factor (PLF) and instantaneous phase calculation, a two-pass FIR bandpass filter (8–13 Hz) with a filter order of 128 was applied to the EEG signals. All analysis was performed in MATLAB R2018a (MathWorks Inc., Natick, MA, USA) using EEGLAB [25] and a personalized script.

2.9. Statistical Analysis

All statistical analyses were performed using MATLAB and the Statistics and Machine Learning Toolbox, with $p < 0.05$ being set as the level of statistical significance.

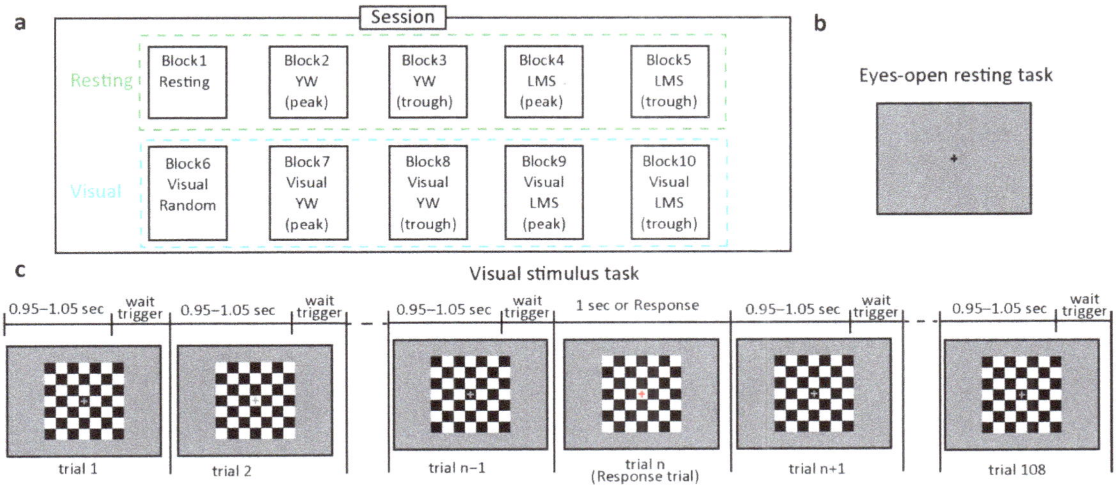

Figure 2. Overview of the experimental sessions and trials. (**a**) shows a session divided into resting (green) and visual (blue) tasks, each with five blocks. The instantaneous phase prediction algorithm was implemented utilizing four distinct models: YW peak, YW trough, LMS peak, and LMS trough. "Peak" means a positive peak or 0 rad, while "trough" depicts a negative peak or pi rad. (**b**) shows an eye-open resting condition. (**c**) shows trials of the visual stimulus condition. The visual stimulus task includes passive and response trials. The stimulus comprised of a checkerboard with a gray fixation cross at the center in passive trials. While response trials are shown with a red fixation cross at the center. Each trial took an average of 1.05 s.

3. Results

The main aim of the current study was to implement an adaptive LMS model in real-time as well as a conventional YW model for individual participants. We divided the results into two subsections: "resting" (focusing on resting with eyes open) and "visual" (based on the visual stimulus task). To check the performance of both YW and LMS methods, the PLF at time-zero was assessed.

3.1. Phase-Locking Factor

The PLF was defined as follows:

$$PLF = \frac{1}{N}\left|\sum_{n=1}^{N} e^{j\theta_n}\right|, \tag{10}$$

where θ_n is the instantaneous phase at time-zero for the nth trial, and N is the total number of trials. A *PLF* closer to zero indicates high phase variability across trials, while a *PLF* closer to 1 depicts all trials as having the same phase. It should be noted that the phase variance is 1-*PLF* [26].

The statistical significance of the *PLF* can be tested by a Rayleigh test to calculate *ZPLF* [26,27], which is Rayleigh's Z value computed using *PLF* as follows:

$$ZPLF = N(PLF)^2. \tag{11}$$

To assess the statistical significance of the participant-averaged *ZPLF* values, the value was corrected to $ZPLF_{all}$:

$$ZPLF_{all} = \frac{1}{\sqrt{M}}\sum_{m=1}^{M} ZPLF_m, \tag{12}$$

where M is the number of participants [28].

To evaluate the difference between YW and LMS within each participant, we also examined Watson's U^2 test for each of the two conditions (resting and visual), according to the method proposed by Persson [29]. If the calculated U^2 is larger than the critical value, the two sample circular distributions differ significantly from each other. For the current study, the critical value U^2 (∞, ∞; $p < 0.05$) = 0.187. As this test compares both the phase variance and the average of the phase angular data, the effects of the difference in average phase angles were removed by shifting the phase according to the following [30]:

$$\boldsymbol{\theta}_{new} = \boldsymbol{\theta} - \varphi, \tag{13}$$

$$C = \frac{1}{N}\sum_{n=1}^{N} \cos\theta_n, \tag{14}$$

$$S = \frac{1}{N}\sum_{n=1}^{N} \sin\theta_n, \tag{15}$$

where $\boldsymbol{\theta}$ is the vector of instantaneous phases at zero ms, and $[\theta_1, \cdots, \theta_N]$, $\varphi = tan^{-1}(S/C)$, and $\boldsymbol{\theta}_{new}$ are used in the calculation of Watson's U^2 test.

Using this transformation, we can compare the differences in phase variance between the two circular distributions.

3.2. Phase-Triggered Response (PTR)

PTR is defined as the grand-average of triggered EEG signals from distinct trials within each participant.

$$PTR(s) = \frac{1}{N}\sum_{n=1}^{N} S_n(s), \tag{16}$$

where S_n is the downsampled EEG signal for the nth trial as a function of the sample point s within each trial extracted based on the trigger at time zero, which are generated by the phase prediction methods. s ranges between 0 and 1000 centered around time-zero, N is the total number of trials for each participant.

PTR is calculated similarly to event-related potentials (ERP), but it does not depend on the external stimulus (such as visual or auditory stimuli) and uses a generated trigger based on the EEG phase. It is a measure for checking the prediction performance.

3.3. Resting Conditions

The results of ZPLF and PTR for the resting condition are shown in Figure 3. ZPLF and PTR are shown individually for the five participants. The bold black lines in Figure 3a–d indicate $ZPLF_{all}$. For a number of trials >60, a ZPLF > 2.995 (which is called the critical value) is considered statistically significant. $ZPLF_{all}$ is also statistically significant if it exceeds the critical value. The small square box on the $ZPLF_{all}$ line represents time-zero. In parts a–d, $ZPLF_{all}$ crosses the critical value indicated as a dotted red line. We found that ZPLF and $ZPLF_{all}$ were statistically significant for all participants except for the YW trough condition in participant P01. Our results are in accord with previous studies showing a ZPLF decrease when time increases [19,31]. Figure 3e–h shows the PTR for individual participants. In the PTR plots, the squares for time-zero are observed at the peak for the peak condition and the trough for the trough condition. The bold black lines show the mean PTR.

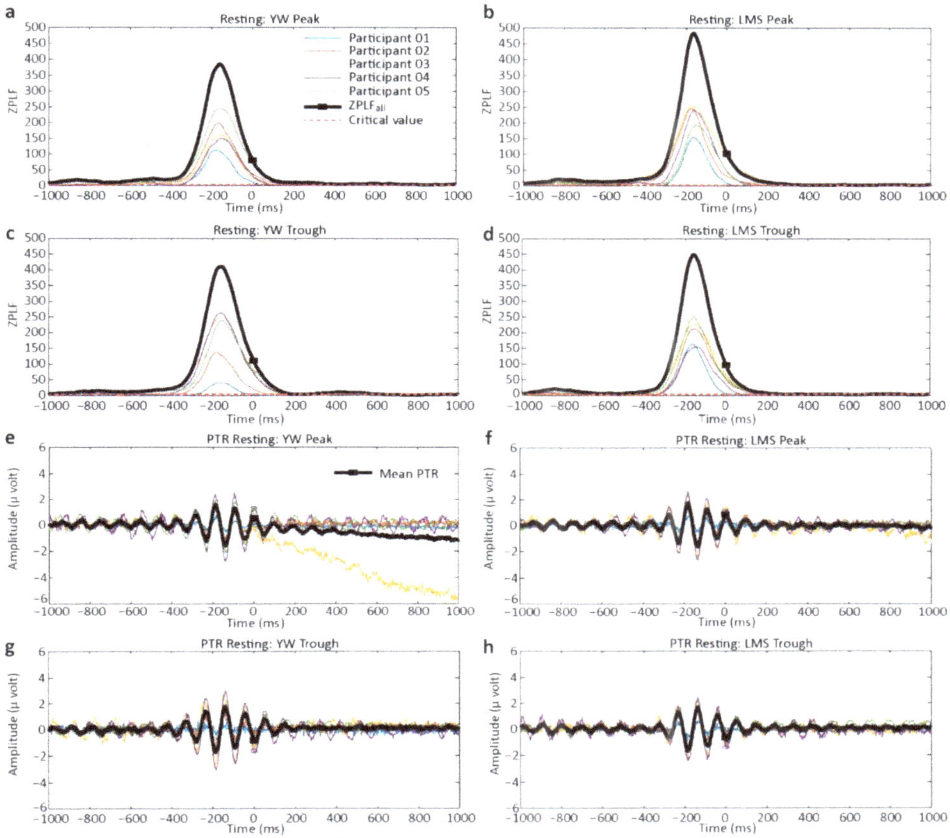

Figure 3. Rayleigh's Z value (ZPLF) and phase-triggered response (PTR) for the resting task for each participant. The bold lines depict $ZPLF_{all}$ or mean PTR. (**a**) ZPLF results for the individual participants for the YW method peak condition. (**b**) ZPLF results for the LMS method peak condition. (**c**) ZPLF results for the YW trough condition. (**d**) ZPLF for the LMS trough condition. (**e**) PTR for the YW peak condition. (**f**) PTR for the LMS peak condition. (**g**,**h**) PTR for the YW and LMS trough conditions, respectively. The red dashed lines in (**a**–**d**) shows the critical value of 2.995. ZPLF larger than this critical value is considered to be statistically significant. The black lines in e–h indicate the mean PTR averaged across five participants. The small black square depicts the time-zero.

Rose plots for each participant are shown in Figure 4. For the peak condition, these rose plots show an accumulation of values toward 0 rad, while for the trough condition, the rose plots show an accumulation toward pi rad. The summarized results of PLF and ZPLF and their mean ± SD are shown in Table 1. The bold values indicate significantly higher ZPLF compared to a critical value of 2.995. Moreover, the ZPLFs of all participants crossed the critical value at time-zero, except for the YW trough condition of participant P01, as shown in Figure 3c. The mean angle in radians and Watson's U^2 test results are shown in Table 2. The bold values indicate where the calculated U^2 values are greater than the critical value, and the differences in the two-phase variances are statistically significant. For participants P01 and P02, the LMS trough performed better than the YW trough. For participant P03, the LMS peak performed better than the YW peak condition. For participant P04, the YW trough surpassed the LMS trough. No significant difference was shown in the results of participant P05 indicating both methods YW and LMS performed equally at time-zero.

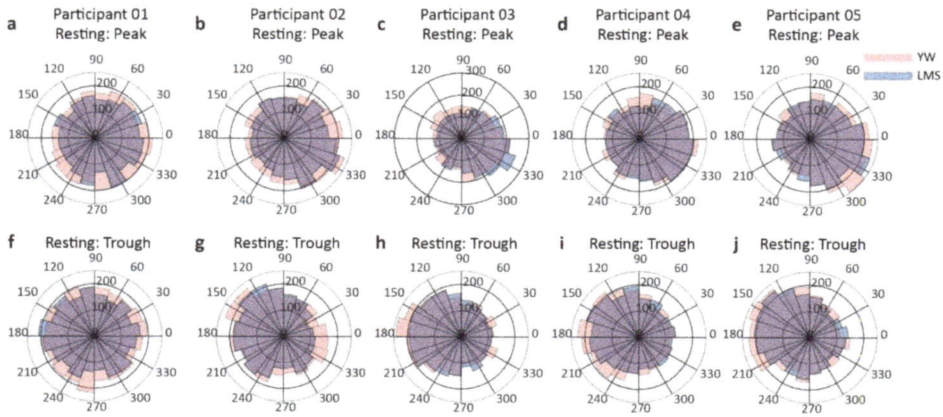

Figure 4. Rose plots for the resting conditions for each participant. The upper row (**a**–**e**) shows the rose plots for each participant's peak condition, while the lower row (**f**–**j**) depicts the rose plot for the trough condition for each participant. The peach color indicates the YW method, while purple indicates the LMS method. The violet color depicts the overlapping region. For the peak condition, the rose plots are inclined towards 0 rad and for the trough condition, the rose plots show an inclination towards pi rad.

Table 1. Summary of the results of the resting condition. The number of trials, PLF, and ZPLF at time-zero are shown.

	Resting											
ID	Number of Trials				PLF				ZPLF			
	YW Peak	LMS Peak	YW Trough	LMS Trough	YW Peak	LMS Peak	YW Trough	LMS Trough	YW Peak	LMS Peak	YW Trough	LMS Trough
P01	3598	3156	3710	3276	0.057	0.059	0.019	0.047	**11.872**	**11.102**	1.432	**7.378**
P02	3491	3093	3433	3075	0.104	0.103	0.075	0.126	**37.831**	**32.895**	**19.778**	**51.678**
P03	3192	3038	3099	2993	0.090	0.171	0.155	0.149	**26.283**	**89.706**	**74.474**	**66.55**
P04	3230	3089	3268	3053	0.101	0.125	0.146	0.107	**33.569**	**48.528**	**70.241**	**35.50**
P05	3326	3159	3340	3139	0.146	0.122	0.155	0.133	**71.307**	**47.381**	**80.566**	**55.752**
Mean	3367.4	3107	3370	3107.2	0.100	0.116	0.110	0.113	36.172	45.922	49.298	43.371
SD	173.068	50.955	226.005	107.843	0.031	0.040	0.060	0.039	21.978	28.758	36.099	23.005

Table 2. Mean angle and Watson U^2 test results at time-zero for the resting condition.

	Resting					
ID	Mean Angle (rad)				Watson U^2	
	YW Peak	LMS Peak	YW Trough	LMS Trough	YW vs. LMS Peak	YW vs. LMS Trough
P01	−0.475	−0.154	−3.009	2.580	0.059	**1.125**
P02	−0.228	−0.108	2.821	2.761	0.054	**0.273**
P03	−0.350	−0.369	2.923	2.956	**0.570**	0.099
P04	−0.271	−0.337	2.920	2.613	0.078	**0.207**
P05	−0.216	−0.333	2.872	2.827	0.887	0.064
Mean	−0.297	−0.260	2.961	2.747		

Taken together, the results suggest that we succeeded in outputting triggers targeting specific phases of alpha oscillations in a real-time implementation under resting conditions, doing this with both YW-based and LMS-based AR models.

3.4. Visual Condition

The results of ZPLF and PTR for the visual condition are shown in Figure 5. We observed two peaks in ZPLF for the visual condition, with the second peak corresponding to the visual response around 100 ms. The small black square in Figure 5 shows time-zero. Rose plots for the visual condition are presented in Figure 6. For the peak condition, the rose plots are somewhat inclined toward the right side (0 degrees), but for the trough condition, there is not a clear inclination toward the left side. For participant P01, the rose plots do not show any leaning toward the left side. The summarized PLF, ZPLF, mean angle, and Watson's U2 test results for the visual task are shown in Tables 3 and 4. All participants showed significant ZPLF values for each method and each condition. No significant difference was observed for any condition in participants P04 and P05. For participants P01 and P03, the LMS trough surpassed the YW trough, but for participant P02, the YW trough was better than the LMS trough, as shown by the bold Watson U2 test values.

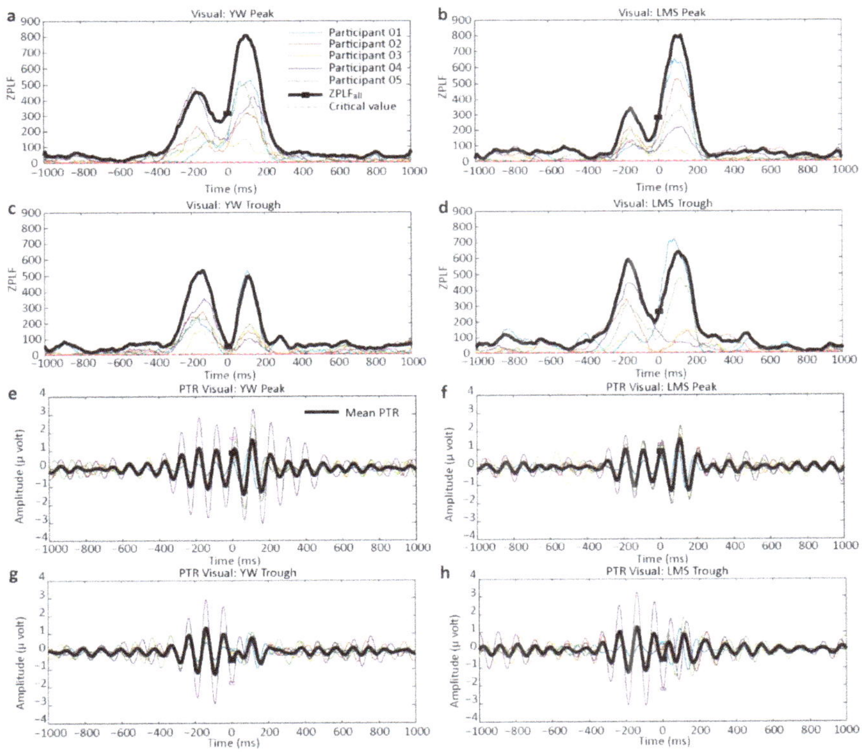

Figure 5. ZPLF and PTR for the visual task. (**a**–**d**) show ZPLF results for both YW and LMS methods with peak and trough conditions, while (**e**–**h**) show the phase-triggered response (PTR) for YW and LMS methods for the peak and trough conditions. ZPLF shows a second peak around 100 ms for the visual task. The small black square shows time-zero. The bold black signals in (**e**–**h**) show the mean PTR averaged across five participants. The red dashed lines in (**a**–**d**) shows the critical value of 2.995. ZPLF larger than this critical value is considered to be statistically significant.

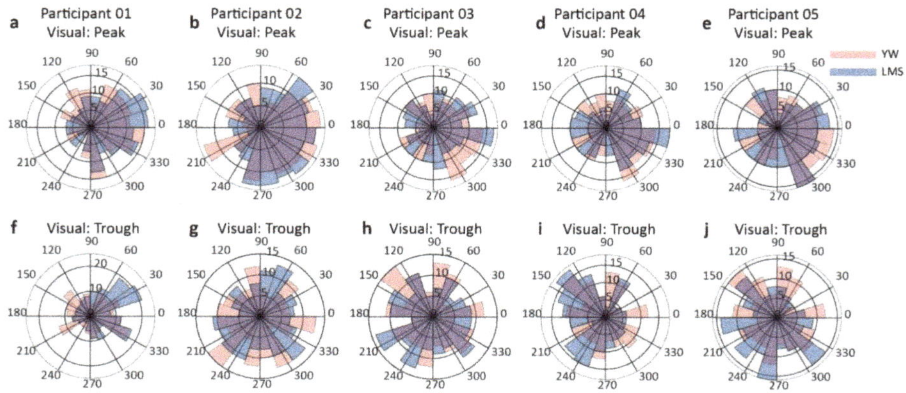

Figure 6. Rose plots for the visual condition. The peak conditions for each participant are shown in the first row (**a–e**), while the trough conditions are depicted in the second row (**f–j**). For the peak condition, the rose plots are inclined towards 0 rad and for the trough condition, the rose plots show an inclination towards pi rad. (**f**) shows no tendency towards any phase angle.

Table 3. Summary of the results of the visual condition. The number of trials, PLF, and ZPLF at time-zero are shown.

	Visual											
	Number of Trials				PLF				ZPLF			
ID	YW Peak	LMS Peak	YW Trough	LMS Trough	YW Peak	LMS Peak	YW Trough	LMS Trough	YW Peak	LMS Peak	YW Trough	LMS Trough
P01	3780	3671	3788	3646	0.204	0.264	0.062	0.302	**158.59**	**255.83**	**14.760**	**333.357**
P02	3772	3553	3776	3575	0.166	0.207	0.078	0.047	**105.10**	**153.43**	**23.016**	**8.146**
P03	3630	3420	3760	3385	0.176	0.107	0.037	0.071	**112.73**	**39.500**	**5.326**	**17.461**
P04	3745	3762	3472	3461	0.194	0.150	0.141	0.193	**142.02**	**85.397**	**69.912**	**128.927**
P05	3774	3549	3776	3588	0.224	0.162	0.035	0.170	**190.26**	**93.699**	**4.871**	**103.984**
Mean	3740.2	3591	3714.4	3531	0.193	0.178	0.071	0.157	141.74	125.57	23.577	118.384
SD	63.057	130.47	135.870	105.624	0.022	0.059	0.043	0.102	34.720	83.342	26.962	131.216

Table 4. Visual condition results. The mean angle and Watson U^2 test results for the visual condition at time-zero are shown.

	Visual					
ID	Mean Angle (rad)				Watson U^2	
	YW Peak	LMS Peak	YW Trough	LMS Trough	YW vs. LMS Peak	YW vs. LMS Trough
P01	0.478	0.158	0.708	0.449	0.054	**0.338**
P02	−0.481	−0.407	−2.030	−1.090	0.031	**0.951**
P03	−0.169	−0.117	2.643	−2.112	0.046	**0.554**
P04	−0.655	−0.603	−2.810	−3.067	0.064	0.069
P05	−0.883	−0.657	−2.673	−2.167	0.093	0.151
Mean	−0.355	−0.327	−2.918	−1.882		

The results suggest that we succeeded in giving visual stimulation targeting specific phases of alpha oscillations in a real-time implementation, doing this with both YW-based and LMS-based AR models and that we observed the stimulation-induced brain responses.

The results of both resting and visual tasks in terms of percentage and the total number of participants who showed the significant ZPLF are summarized in Table 5.

ZPLF value > 2.995 is considered to be significant. Significant ZPLF means that we achieved the desired result of outputting the triggers targeting a specific phase of alpha oscillations. For the resting peak condition, all participants showed significant ZPLF values for both methods. For the trough condition, all participants indicated the significant ZPLF for LMS and only one participant did not show the significant ZPLF value for the YW method. In the visual task, results indicate that all participants in both methods and all conditions crossed significant ZPLF value. Taken together, all the results indicate that we succeeded in outputting the triggers targeting specific phases of alpha oscillations in a real-time implementation, doing this with both YW-based and LMS-based AR models except for one participant in one condition.

Table 5. Overview of resting and visual task results. Percentage and the total number of participants showing a significant ZPLF value for each condition.

Total Participants = 5	Resting				Visual			
	YW Peak	LMS Peak	YW Trough	LMS Trough	YW Peak	LMS Peak	YW Trough	LMS Trough
Participants	5/5	5/5	4/5	5/5	5/5	5/5	5/5	5/5
Percentage	100%	100%	80%	100%	100%	100%	100%	100%

4. Discussion

Our study implemented, for the first time, real-time EEG phase-dependent triggers for visual stimulation using EEG signals from the human occipital cortex (channel Oz). These triggers were based on a novel adaptive LMS-based AR model as well as the conventional YW-based AR model. The primary purpose of our study was to investigate the possibility of a real-time implementation of a closed-loop system based on the adaptive LMS-based method, which we previously proposed and demonstrated by analyzing offline data [19]. Earlier studies employed the complex wavelet transform [32] or the Hilbert–Huang transform [33,34] to extract the frequency and phase information from EEG. However, the application of these methods is limited because of the future prediction of nonstationary data. Although the conventional YW-based AR model can resolve the EEG time-series' prediction, it presumes the stationarity of signals over a certain period and is, therefore, less appropriate for closed-loop and real-time applications for nonstationary time-series data such as EEG. By contrast, our previously proposed adaptive method depends on recurrent updates to cater for the non-stationarity of EEG signals, thereby making adjustments to dynamic changes while predicting the future signal. The results of this proof-of-concept study provide empirical evidence that the adaptive method is implementable in a real-time situation.

We found individual differences in the performance of the closed-loop system and results are presented individually at time-zero. In the resting condition, all participants showed significant ZPLF for both methods (peak and trough conditions), except for the trough condition in the YW-based method for participant P01. In the visual conditions, all participants showed significant ZPLF for each condition in both methods. Participant P05 showed no significant difference between any of the conditions, indicating that both methods performed equally for this participant. These results suggest that although there are individual differences in the predictability of EEG phases, the proposed method performed well in outputting the stimulation triggers for most participants.

In a previous study [19], we showed the advantage of our LMS-based method over the YW-based method in alpha-band EEG phase prediction using offline analyses. However, we could not provide evidence of the superiority of the adaptive LMS-based method at time-zero because of the small number of participants, which led to difficulty in making a clear comparison. Although the real-time implementation of the adaptive method was our aim, one limitation of this study is that technical issues in the DC mode of the EEG amplifiers meant that only data from five participants for whom the AC mode was used were analyzed for the real-time closed-loop system. Therefore, further studies will need to clarify whether the adaptive proposed method outperforms the conventional non-adaptive method in a real-time implementation. This is important because there can be technical issues that are specific to real-time implementation.

Our results show that we succeeded in measuring brain responses with respect to triggered visual stimulation. Although our study applied visual stimulation only, there is the possibility of using the adaptive method to trigger TMS and other NIBS techniques.

One advantage of our proposed method is the low computational cost. Some prior studies focused on using machine learning methods for phase estimation, and a variety of machine learning techniques, particularly deep learning, have been applied in brain-computer interface (BCI) systems [18,35,36]. The main drawback of such procedures is the demand for preliminary data for training prior to the principal experiment. Because of the absence of future information in real-time phase estimation, the trained filters rely on the properties and quality of the signal, and as a consequence, the technique does not perform unbiased phase estimation. Deep learning techniques, while being highly efficient, still need an abundant amount of data for training and a large amount of processing power, and are thus expensive to implement. By contrast, our proposed method does not require extensive training and computational cost.

We propose that our method can be applied not only to targeting in basic neuroscience (for example, the functional role of neural oscillations) but also to clinical fields. In the last decade, substantial progress has been made in invasive brain stimulation that dynamically responds to the presence of divergent neural activity [37,38]. For example, in a small group of Parkinson's disease patients, deep brain stimulation resulted in clinical improvements of approximately 30% compared to a standard open-loop system [39]. When required, a closed-loop stimulation device might deliver stimulation more proficiently by performing stimulation only when brain function is damaged or shows abnormal neural activity [40] and synchronizing each stimulus with the patient's instantaneous brain state. State-dependent brain stimulation has therapeutic potential for brain disorders like epilepsy, schizophrenia, Parkinson's disease, and stroke. Further studies will involve implementing the adaptive method in a TMS-EEG real-time scenario and exploring new prospects for alpha and other oscillations.

5. Conclusions

We have presented here a real-time closed-loop system that implements both an adaptive LMS-based AR model and a conventional YW-based AR model. This system consists of a time-series forward prediction and phase-locked visual stimulation. Brain state-dependent, EEG triggered visual stimulation was applied and synchronized with the EEG peaks and troughs of alpha oscillations in both a resting state (open eyes) and a visual task. Our results indicate that we succeeded in outputting triggers targeting specific phases of alpha oscillations in a real-time implementation, doing this with both YW-based and LMS-based AR models. Our adaptive approach for EEG phase estimation relies on predictions of instantaneous alpha oscillations, does not depend on the knowledge of the exact stochastic signal, and tracks the variation in the EEG signal by dynamically adjusting its coefficients. Although we have focused only on alpha oscillations, this system can also be employed to analyze oscillations in other frequency bands. This novel implementation may lead to EEG instantaneous phase prediction with low computational cost and provide versatile applications in basic and clinical neurosciences.

Author Contributions: Conceptualization, A.S., T.T., and K.K.; methodology, T.T. and K.K.; software, A.S., T.O.; validation, A.S., T.O., and K.K.; formal analysis, A.S.; investigation, A.S.; resources, K.K.; data curation, A.S., T.O., and K.K.; writing—original draft preparation, A.S.; writing—review and editing, A.S., T.O., T.T., and K.K.; visualization, A.S., T.O.; supervision, T.T. and K.K.; project administration, K.K.; funding acquisition, K.K. All authors have read and agreed to the published version of the manuscript.

Funding: The project was supported by a research grant from Toyota Motor Corporation and the Special Postdoctoral Research Program at RIKEN.

Institutional Review Board Statement: The study was conducted according to the guidelines of the Declaration of Helsinki, and approved by the Ethics Committee of RIKEN (protocol code: Wako3 30-8(3) approval on the 23 November 2019).

Informed Consent Statement: The informed consent was obtained from all subjects involved in the study.

Data Availability Statement: The data and code used to support the findings of this study are available from the corresponding author upon reasonable request.

Acknowledgments: We thank Kaori Maeda for supporting experiments.

Conflicts of Interest: K.K. has received a research grant from Toyota Motor Corporation. A.S., T.O., and T.T. declare no conflict of interest.

References

1. Ziemann, U.; Reis, J.; Schwenkreis, P.; Rosanova, M.; Strafella, A.; Badawy, R.; Müller-Dahlhaus, F. TMS and drugs revisited 2014. *Clin. Neurophysiol.* **2015**, *126*, 1847–1868. [CrossRef] [PubMed]
2. Hallett, M. Transcranial magnetic stimulation and the human brain. *Nature* **2000**, *406*, 147–150. [CrossRef] [PubMed]
3. Zrenner, C.; Belardinelli, P.; Müller-Dahlhaus, F.; Ziemann, U. Closed-loop neuroscience and non-invasive brain stimulation: A tale of two loops. *Front. Cell. Neurosci.* **2016**, *10*, 92. [CrossRef] [PubMed]
4. Ilmoniemi, R.J.; Kičić, D. Methodology for combined TMS and EEG. *Brain Topogr.* **2010**, *22*, 233–248. [CrossRef] [PubMed]
5. Müller-Dahlhaus, F.; Vlachos, A. Unraveling the cellular and molecular mechanisms of repetitive magnetic stimulation. *Front. Mol. Neurosci.* **2013**, *6*, 50. [CrossRef]
6. Mutanen, T.; Nieminen, J.O.; Ilmoniemi, R.J. TMS-evoked changes in brain-state dynamics quantified by using EEG data. *Front. Hum. Neurosci.* **2013**, *7*, 155. [CrossRef]
7. Buzsáki, G.; Draguhn, A. Neuronal oscillations in cortical networks. *Science* **2004**, *304*, 1926–1929. [CrossRef]
8. Gharabaghi, A.; Kraus, D.; Leao, M.T.; Spüler, M.; Walter, A.; Bogdan, M.; Rosenstiel, W.; Naros, G.; Ziemann, U. Coupling brain-machine interfaces with cortical stimulation for brain-state dependent stimulation: Enhancing motor cortex excitability for neurorehabilitation. *Front. Hum. Neurosci.* **2014**, *8*, 122. [CrossRef]
9. Bundy, D.T.; Wronkiewicz, M.; Sharma, M.; Moran, D.W.; Maurizio, C.; Eric, C.L. Using ipsilateral motor signals in the unaffected cerebral hemisphere as a signal platform for brain–computer interfaces in hemiplegic stroke survivors. *J. Neural. Eng.* **2012**, *9*, 036011. [CrossRef]
10. Pfurtscheller, G.; Neuper, C. Dynamics of sensorimotor oscillations in a motor task. In *Brain-Computer Interfaces*; Springer: Berlin/Heidelberg, Germany, 2009; pp. 47–64. [CrossRef]
11. Kraus, D.; Naros, G.; Bauer, R.; Maria Teresa, L.; Ziemann, U.; Gharabaghi, A. Brain–robot interface driven plasticity: Distributed modulation of corticospinal excitability. *Neuroimage* **2016**, *125*, 522–532. [CrossRef]
12. Ramos-Murguialday, A.; Broetz, D.; Rea, M.; Läer, L.; Yilmaz, O.; Brasil, F.L.; Liberati, G.; Curado, M.R.; Garcia-Cossio, E.; Vyziotis, A.; et al. Brain–machine interface in chronic stroke rehabilitation: A controlled study. *Ann. Neurol.* **2013**, *74*, 100–108. [CrossRef] [PubMed]
13. Buetefisch, C.; Heger, R.; Schicks, W.; Seitz, R.; Netz, J. Hebbian-type stimulation during robot-assisted training in patients with stroke. *Neurorehabil. Neural. Repair* **2011**, *25*, 645–655. [CrossRef] [PubMed]
14. Chen, L.L.; Madhavan, R.; Rapoport, B.I.; Anderson, W.S. Real-time brain oscillation detection and phase-locked stimulation using autoregressive spectral estimation and time-series forward prediction. *IEEE Trans. Biomed. Eng.* **2011**, *60*, 753–762. [CrossRef] [PubMed]
15. Zrenner, C.; Desideri, D.; Belardinelli, P.; Ziemann, U. Real-time EEG-defined excitability states determine efficacy of TMS-induced plasticity in human motor cortex. *Brain Stimul.* **2018**, *11*, 374–389. [CrossRef] [PubMed]
16. Zrenner, C.; Galevska, D.; Nieminen, J.O.; Baur, D.; Stefanou, M.I.; Ziemann, U. The shaky ground truth of real-time phase estimation. *Neuroimage* **2020**, *214*, 116761. [CrossRef] [PubMed]
17. Roux, S.G.; Cenier, T.; Garcia, S.; Litaudon, P.; Buonviso, N. A wavelet-based method for local phase extraction from a multi-frequency oscillatory signal. *J. Neurosci. Methods* **2007**, *160*, 135–143. [CrossRef]
18. McIntosh, J.R.; Sajda, P. Estimation of phase in EEG rhythms for real-time applications. *J. Neural. Eng.* **2020**, *17*, 034002. [CrossRef]
19. Shakeel, A.; Tanaka, T.; Kitajo, K. Time-series prediction of the oscillatory phase of EEG signals using the least mean square algorithm-based AR model. *Appl. Sci.* **2020**, *10*, 3616. [CrossRef]
20. Pardey, J.; Roberts, S.; Tarassenko, L. A review of parametric modelling techniques for EEG analysis. *Med. Eng. Phys.* **1996**, *18*, 2–11. [CrossRef]
21. Tseng, S.Y.; Chen, R.C.; Chong, F.C.; Kuo, T.S. Evaluation of parametric methods in EEG signal analysis. *Med. Eng. Phys.* **1995**, *17*, 71–78. [CrossRef]
22. Koo, B.; Gibson, J.D.; Gray, S.D. Filtering of colored noise for speech enhancement and coding. In Proceedings of the International Conference on Acoustics, Speech, and Signal Processing, Glasgow, UK, 23–26 May 1989; Volume 39, pp. 1732–1742. [CrossRef]

23. Poularikas, A.D.; Ramadan, Z.M. *Adaptive Filtering Primer with MATLAB*, 1st ed.; CRC Press: Boca Raton, FL, USA, 2006; pp. 101–135.
24. Boashash, B. Estimating and interpreting the instantaneous frequency of a signal. *Fundam. Proc. IEEE* **1992**, *80*, 520–538. [CrossRef]
25. Delorme, A.; Makeig, S. EEGLAB: An open source toolbox for analysis of single-trial EEG dynamics including independent component analysis. *J. Neurosci. Methods* **2004**, *134*, 9–21. [CrossRef] [PubMed]
26. Fisher, N.I. *Statistical Analysis of Circular Data*; Cambridge University Press: Cambridge, UK, 1995; pp. 69–70. [CrossRef]
27. Mathewson, K.E.; Gratton, G.; Fabiani, M.; Beck, D.M.; RO, T. To see or not to see: Prestimulus α phase predicts visual awareness. *Neurosci. Res.* **2009**, *29*, 2725–2732. [CrossRef] [PubMed]
28. Mazaheri, A.; Jensen, O. Posterior α activity is not phase-reset by visual stimuli. *Proc. Natl. Acad. Sci. USA* **2006**, *103*, 2948–2952. [CrossRef]
29. Persson, T. A new way to obtain Watson's U^2. *Scand. Stat. Theory Appl.* **1979**, *6*, 119–122.
30. Ueda, K.I.; Nishiura, Y.; Kitajo, K. Mathematical mechanism of state-dependent phase resetting properties of alpha rhythm in the human brain. *Neurosci. Res.* **2020**, *156*, 237–244. [CrossRef]
31. Zarubin, G.; Gundlach, C.; Nikulin, V.; Bogdan, M. Real-time phase detection for EEG-based tACS closed-loop system. In Proceedings of the 6th International Congress on Neurotechnology, Electronics and Informatics, Seville, Spain, 20–21 September 2018; Volume 1, pp. 13–20. [CrossRef]
32. Le Van Quyen, M.; Foucher, J.; Lachaux, J.P.; Rodriguez, E.; Lutz, A.; Martinerie, J.; Varela, F.J. Comparison of Hilbert transform and wavelet methods for the analysis of neuronal synchrony. *J. Neurosci. Methods* **2001**, *111*, 83–98. [CrossRef]
33. Bajaj, V.; Pachori, R.B. Separation of rhythms of EEG signals based on Hilbert-Huang transformation with application to seizure detection. In Proceedings of the International Conference on Hybrid Information Technology, Daejeon, Korea, 23–25 August 2012; Volume 7425, pp. 493–500. [CrossRef]
34. Lin, C.F.; Zhu, J.D. Hilbert–Huang transformation-based time-frequency analysis methods in biomedical signal applications. *Proc. Inst. Mech. Eng. Part H J. Eng. Med.* **2012**, *226*, 208–216. [CrossRef]
35. Oh, S.L.; Hagiwara, Y.; Raghavendra, U.; Yuvaraj, R.; Arunkumar, N.; Murugappan, M.; Acharya, U.R. A deep learning approach for Parkinson's disease diagnosis from EEG signals. *Neural. Comput. Appl.* **2018**, *32*, 10927–10933. [CrossRef]
36. Li, F.; Li, X.; Wang, F.; Zhang, D.; Xia, Y.; He, F. A novel P300 classification algorithm based on a principal component analysis-convolutional neural network. *Appli. Sci.* **2020**, *10*, 1546. [CrossRef]
37. Rosin, B.; Slovik, M.; Mitelman, R.; Rivlin-Etzion, M.; Haber, S.N.; Israel, Z.; Vaadia, E.; Bergman, H. Closed-loop deep brain stimulation is superior in ameliorating parkinsonism. *Neuron* **2011**, *72*, 370–384. [CrossRef] [PubMed]
38. Little, S.; Brown, P. What brain signals are suitable for feedback control of deep brain stimulation in Parkinson's disease? *Ann. N. Y. Acad. Sci.* **2012**, *1265*, 9–24. [CrossRef]
39. Little, S.; Pogosyan, A.; Neal, S.; Zavala, B.; Zrinzo, L.; Hariz, M.; Foltynie, T.; Limousin, P.; Ashkan, K.; Fitzgerald, J.; et al. Adaptive deep brain stimulation in advanced Parkinson disease. *Ann. Neurol.* **2013**, *74*, 449–457. [CrossRef] [PubMed]
40. Sun, F.T.; Morrell, M.J. Closed-loop neurostimulation: The clinical experience. *Neurotherapeutics* **2014**, *11*, 553–563. [CrossRef] [PubMed]

Journal of *Personalized Medicine*

MDPI

Review

The Role of Gamma Oscillations in the Pathophysiology of Substance Use Disorders

Jessica U. Ramlakhan [1], Ming Ma [1], Reza Zomorrodi [1], Daniel M. Blumberger [1,2,3], Yoshihiro Noda [4] and Mera S. Barr [1,2,3,*]

1 Temerty Centre for Therapeutic Brain Intervention, Division of Mood and Anxiety, Centre for Addiction and Mental Health, Toronto, ON M6J1H4, Canada; jessica.ramlakhan@gmail.com (J.U.R.); mingdonna.ma@mail.utoronto.ca (M.M.); Reza.Zomorrodi@camh.ca (R.Z.); Daniel.Blumberger@camh.ca (D.M.B.)
2 Institute of Medical Science, Faculty of Medicine, University of Toronto, Toronto, ON M5S1A8, Canada
3 Department of Psychiatry, Temerty Faculty of Medicine, University of Toronto, Toronto, ON M5S1A8, Canada
4 Multidisciplinary Translational Research Lab, Department of Neuropsychiatry, Keio University School of Medicine, Tokyo 160-8582, Japan; yoshi-tms@keio.jp
* Correspondence: Mera.Barr@gmail.com; Tel.: +416-535-8501 (ext. 33095)

Abstract: Substance use disorders (SUDs) are a major public health problem—with over 200 million people reporting drug use in 2016. Electroencephalography (EEG) is a powerful tool that can provide insights into the impact of SUDs on cognition. Specifically, modulated gamma activity may provide an index of the pathophysiology of SUDs. Thus, the purpose of this review was to investigate the impact of alcohol, tobacco, cannabis, cocaine, and amphetamine on gamma activity, among pre-clinical and clinical populations during acute and chronic exposure and withdrawal states. We searched multiple databases for key terms related to SUDs, EEG, and gamma and ensured rigorous methods by using a standardized review reporting tool. We included 30 studies in this review and found that all substances were associated with modulation of gamma activity, across states and in both preclinical and clinical populations. Gamma oscillations appeared to be differentially modulated in clinical versus preclinical populations and had the most complex relationship with alcohol, indicating that it may act differently than other substances. The findings of this review offer insights into the pathophysiology of SUDs, providing a potential window into novel treatments for SUDs via modulation of gamma activity.

Keywords: gamma oscillations; alcohol; tobacco; cannabis; cognition; co-morbidity

Citation: Ramlakhan, J.U.; Ma, M.; Zomorrodi, R.; Blumberger, D.M.; Noda, Y.; Barr, M.S. The Role of Gamma Oscillations in the Pathophysiology of Substance Use Disorders. *J. Pers. Med* **2021**, *11*, 17. https://dx.doi.org/10.3390/jpm11010017

Received: 10 November 2020
Accepted: 24 December 2020
Published: 28 December 2020

1. Introduction

Substance abuse represents a rapidly growing global public health concern. According to the United Nations Office on Drugs and Crime, 271 million people used at least one illicit drug in 2016 [1], of which 35 million have developed substance use disorders (SUDs) [1]. Approximately 2.3 billion people self-reported as current drinkers in 2016 [2], more than 1 billion people around the world smoked tobacco in 2019 [3] and 188 million people used cannabis in 2017 [1]. Furthermore, 35 million people worldwide have SUDs but less than 15% receive treatment [1].

Cognition has been shown to be modulated with acute and chronic substance use. For example, studies have found that working memory, the ability to maintain and manipulate information over short periods of time [4], has been impaired with alcohol and cannabis use disorders (AUDs and CUDs) [5,6]. Chronic alcohol use may cause pathological changes in the brain, such as ventricle enlargement [7] and reductions in grey and white matter volume [8,9], which have been linked to cognitive impairment [8]. Cognitive deficits have also been reported in individuals following acute alcohol intoxication, including disruptions in memory [10], divided attention [11], and information processing [12]. In addition, chronic non-psychiatric cannabis and cocaine users have demonstrated impaired learning [13,14], memory [14–17], attention [13,15,16,18], and executive function [19]. Interestingly, cognition has been shown to rebound with discontinuing substance use (e.g., cannabis [20]), thereby furthering support for the association between cognition and SUDs, possibly through shared pathophysiology [21]. Investigating different states (e.g., acute, chronic, and withdrawal) of substance use on such pathophysiology may help to optimize the treatment for SUDs and associated cognitive deficits.

Electroencephalography (EEG) is a powerful non-invasive neurophysiological imaging technique with high temporal resolution that can measure cortical neural activity through recording from scalp electrodes [22]. There are five conventional EEG frequency bands—delta (1–3.5 Hz), theta (4–7 Hz), alpha (8–12 Hz), beta (12–28 Hz), and gamma (30–120 Hz). Gamma oscillatory activity has been associated with higher-order perceptual and cognitive processes, including long-term memory [23], selective attention [24,25], visual search [26,27], learning [28], and working memory [29–31]. In fact, increases in gamma power have been associated with increases in working memory load in healthy subjects [29,30,32] and epileptic patients [31]. Patients with schizophrenia, however, lack this ability to modulate gamma activity [30,32]. Gamma oscillations therefore may provide a window into ongoing sensory-cognitive processes in the brain.

Gamma activity has been recorded in multiple brain regions, including the hippocampus [33], neocortex [34–37], entorhinal cortex [38], olfactory bulb [39], and amygdala [40]. Gamma-aminobutyric acid (GABA) is an inhibitory neurotransmitter present in large quantities in the mammalian brain. Networks of specialized GABAergic interneurons (in particular, basket and chandelier cells; [41]) and pyramidal cells are responsible for generating a large-scale gamma oscillatory activity [42,43]. Two types of GABAergic receptors—$GABA_A$ and $GABA_B$ receptors—are linked to the generation [43–45] and modulation [43] of gamma oscillations, respectively. Gamma activity can also be produced through activation of several other receptors [45], including the metabotropic glutamate receptor [43], the muscarinic-cholinergic receptor [46], and the kainate receptor [47]. The N-methyl-D-aspartic acid (NMDA) receptor has also been shown to influence gamma activity [48]. Given that gamma oscillations underlie several cognitive domains and are altered by substance use, deficits in gamma band activity may be a valuable index of the pathophysiology of SUDs.

The goal of this paper is to provide a comprehensive review of the existing body of literature on the effects of alcohol, tobacco, cannabis, cocaine, and amphetamine use on gamma oscillatory activity, among preclinical and clinical populations during acute, chronic, and withdrawal states.

2. Methods

A comprehensive literature search was conducted using the databases PubMed, MEDLINE, and PsycINFO on 3 September 2019 with no date restrictions. Search terms included "cannabi*", "marijuana", "THC" (tetra-hydrocannabinol), "delta-9-tetra-hydrocannabinol", "alcohol", "ethanol", "EtOH", "nicotine", "tobacco", "cigarette", "cocaine", "amphetamine", and "methamphetamine" with "EEG", "electroencephalography", "gamma oscillat*", "gamma activity", or "gamma power". Both relevant preclinical and clinical studies published in English were included. Studies were excluded if they investigated populations with psychiatric disorders other than alcohol, cannabis, tobacco, amphetamine, or cocaine use disorder; or schizophrenia. Studies were excluded if publication types were non-empirical research studies, editorials, opinion articles, protocols, abstracts, proceedings, conceptual analyses, case studies, patient resources, or reviews. Reference lists of reviews were manually searched for additional studies. The search produced 524 studies, and a total of 30 articles were included in the review. We complied with the Preferred Reporting Items for Systematic Reviews and Meta-Analyses (PRISMA) guideline, to ensure rigour (Figure 1) [49]. Given that oscillations in the gamma frequency are tightly linked to cognition, and that cognition is altered following substance use, gamma oscillations serves as a useful neurophysiological index for examining the underlying pathophysiology of SUDs for the development of novel treatment options.

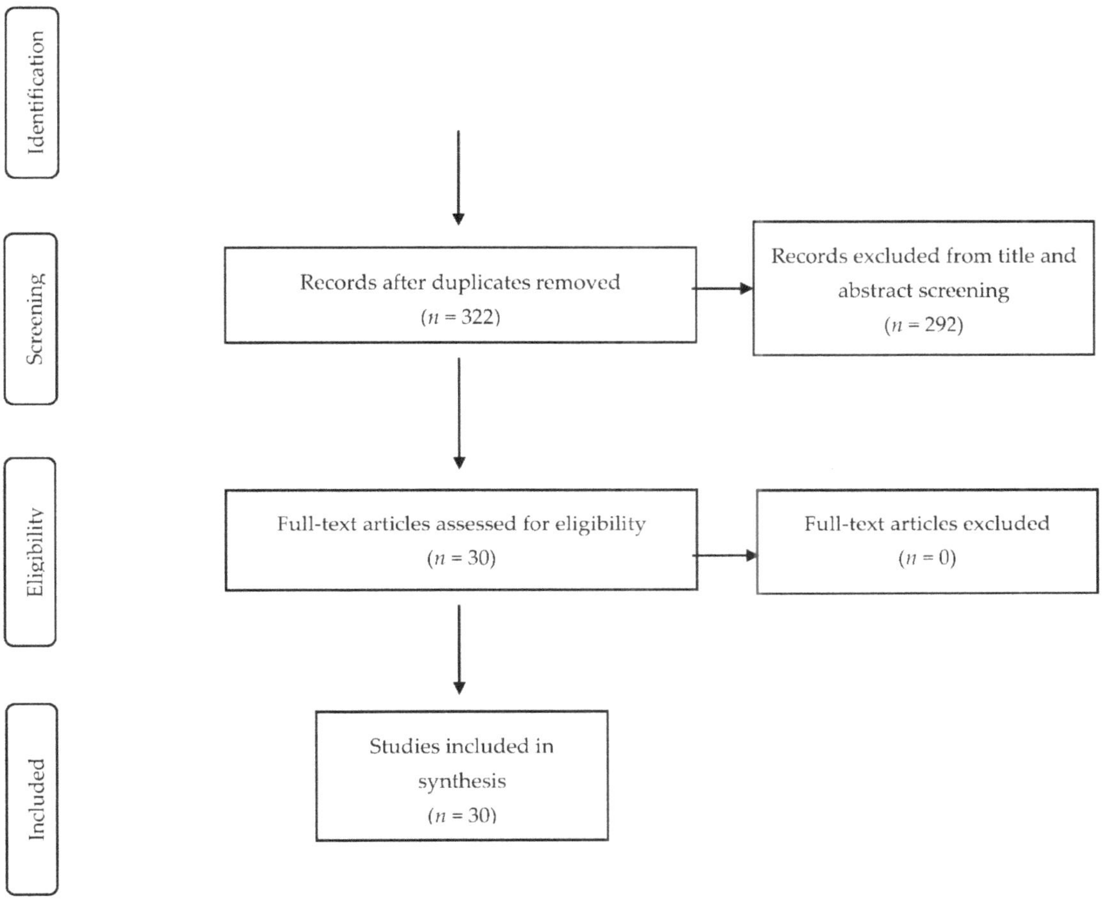

Figure 1. PRISMA flow diagram of the screening process.

3. Results

3.1. Preclinical Studies

Alcohol: There are a limited number of studies that examined gamma oscillatory activity following acute ethanol exposure (Table 1). Wang et al. reported a dose-dependent relationship between acute ethanol exposure and gamma activity in the rat hippocampal CA3 area [50]. At a low dose (10 mM), a minor increase in gamma power was observed. However, at higher doses (25–100 mM), alcohol significantly suppressed gamma activity, with the greatest reduction occurring at 100 mM (52.9 ± 8.5%). Peak gamma frequency was not altered with exposure [50]. In another study, Tsurugizawa and colleagues investigated the effects of alcohol on local field potential (LFP) oscillations in the nucleus accumbens of 34 male Wistar rats [51]. The animals were injected intraperitoneally with 0.4 g/kg of ethanol solution. Following ethanol exposure, alpha and beta power decreased while gamma power increased significantly [51].

Table 1. Preclinical Studies Examining the Effects of Alcohol on Gamma Oscillations.

Study	Gamma Frequency Range and Type	Subject Information	Method of Administration	Main Findings
Ehlers and Chaplin (1991)	32–64 Hz	38 Wistar rats	28-day continuous exposure to ethanol vapour (22–28 mg/L O_2)	Increased power in all frequency bands except 1–2 Hz and 16–32 Hz in the cortex 24 h after ethanol exposure. No differences in gamma power in both the cortex and dorsal hippocampus 10–30 min and 2 weeks following ethanol exposure.
Slawecki et al. (2006)	32–50 Hz	136 Male Sprague-Dawley rats (adolescents: 28–30 days; adults: 60–70 days)	14-day (12 h/day) continuous exposure to ethanol vapour (95% ethanol)	Increased parietal gamma and beta (16–32 Hz) power in adolescent rats during acute ethanol withdrawal (7–10 h post-exposure) on days 8 and 12. No change in frontal gamma power during withdrawal in both adolescent and adult rats.
Cheaha et al. (2013)	30.5–45 Hz	Male Wistar rats	Ethanol-containing modified liquid diet at steadily increasing concentrations for 28 days	Increased frontal and parietal gamma power during acute ethanol withdrawal (1–8 h after ethanol exposure).
Campbell et al. (2014)	30–80 Hz; Induced	16 Social drinkers (8 males, 8 females; mean age: 25.9 years) with average weekly alcohol consumption of 191.2 g for males and 132 g for females	40% (v/v) alcohol solution or placebo (males consumed 0.8 g/kg, females consumed 0.72 g/kg)	Increased peak gamma power in the visual and motor cortices. Decreased peak gamma frequency in the visual cortex. No change in peak gamma frequency in the motor cortex.
Tsurugizawa et al. (2016)	60–80 Hz; Induced	34 Male, alcohol-naïve Wistar rats (8–12 weeks)	Intraperitoneal injection of 0.4 g/kg of ethanol solution	Increased gamma power that peaks within 5 min after ethanol injection and returns to baseline at around 10 min post-injection.
Wang et al. (2016)	30–80 Hz; Induced (kainate)	Male Sprague Dawley rats (4–5 weeks)	5–100 mM ethanol added to artificial cerebrospinal fluid	No change in gamma power after 5 mM ethanol application. Increased gamma power after 10 mM ethanol application. Decreased gamma power following 25–100 mM ethanol application (dose-dependent). No change in peak gamma frequency following ethanol exposure.

Several studies to date have examined the effects of ethanol withdrawal on the EEG spectral profiles of mice and rats (Table 1). Ehlers and Chaplin found significant elevations in cortical EEG power across almost all frequency bands, including gamma, 24 h following termination of prolonged ethanol exposure [52]. This was also observed in a study by Slawecki et al., investigating the withdrawal responses of male adolescent and adult rats [53]. Following ethanol vapour exposure for 14 consecutive days, prepulse inhibition increased in both groups. Although changes in frontal gamma power were insignificant, beta and gamma power in the parietal cortex significantly increased in adolescent rats during withdrawal [53]. In addition to increases in parietal gamma power, Cheaha and colleagues also found enhanced gamma activity in the frontal region, as well as increased locomotor activity and decreased sleep time in mice experiencing ethanol withdrawal [54]. These preclinical studies demonstrate that ethanol withdrawal is associated with increased gamma band activity, indicating central nervous system hyperexcitability during withdrawal states.

Tobacco: Several animal studies have reported dose-dependent relationships between acute nicotine exposure and gamma band activity (Table 2). Phillips and colleagues administered nicotine (1.0 mg/kg), mecamylamine (2.0 mg/kg), saline, or nicotine combined with mecamylamine in 11 male mice [55]. It was found that nicotine significantly increased auditory evoked gamma power. Moreover, pretreatment with the nicotinic antagonist mecamylamine prevented this nicotine-induced increase [55]. Song et al. also reported an enhancement in gamma activity in the rat hippocampal slices following nicotine infusion under high doses [56]. In this study, administering 10 μM of nicotine did not significantly influence tetanically-induced gamma oscillations under both threshold stimulation intensity and double threshold stimulation intensity [56]. However, nicotine infusion at 100 μM significantly increased both tetanic gamma power and frequency [56]. Interestingly, a recent study found a significant increase in the amplitude of kainate-induced gamma activity after just 1 μM of nicotine application [57]. Furthermore, in a study conducted by Wang et al., nicotine at lower doses (0.1–10 μM) increased gamma power and slightly reduced peak gamma frequency [58]. The greatest increase in gamma power (83 ± 21%) was also achieved after 1 μM of nicotine application. However, contrary to Song et al.'s findings, Wang and colleagues reported that nicotine decreased gamma power at 100 μM [56,58].

Table 2. Preclinical Studies Examining the Effects of Tobacco on Gamma Oscillations.

Study	Gamma Frequency Range and Type	Subject Information	Method of Administration	Main Findings
Song et al. (2005)	30–80 Hz; Induced (tetanic stimulation)	Wistar rats (17–30 days)	(-) Nicotine dissolved in artificial cerebrospinal fluid	- No change in gamma power after 10 μM of nicotine perfusion at both threshold and double threshold stimulation intensity. - Increased gamma power and frequency after nicotine perfusion of 100 μM at both stimulation intensities.
Phillips et al. (2007)	31–61 Hz; Evoked (auditory)	11 Male C57BL/6 J mice (10–12 weeks)	Intraperitoneal injection of 0.1 mL of nicotine hydrogen tartrate salt (1.0 mg/kg) dissolved in saline (0.09%)	- Increased gamma power following nicotine administration.
Akkurt et al. (2010)	30–80 Hz; Induced (auditory)	Sprague-Dawley rats (23–36 days)	100 μM (-) Nicotine dissolved in artificial cerebrospinal fluid	- Decreased gamma oscillation complexity during nicotine exposure. - Decreased gamma oscillation complexity during nicotine washout.
Zhang et al. (2015)	20–80 Hz; Induced (kainate)	Male Wistar rats (3 weeks)	Nicotine sulfate	- Increased gamma power following 1 μM of nicotine administration versus control. - Increased gamma power during nicotine washout versus control.

Table 2. *Cont.*

Study	Gamma Frequency Range and Type	Subject Information	Method of Administration	Main Findings
Wang et al. (2015)	20–60 Hz; Induced (kainate)	Male Wistar rats (4–5 weeks)	0.1–100 μM nicotine sulfate dissolved in artificial cerebrospinal fluid	- Increased gamma power following 0.1–10 μM of nicotine administration. - Decreased peak gamma frequency following nicotine administration at concentrations 0.25–10 μM. - Decreased gamma power and no change in peak gamma frequency after 100 μM of nicotine administration.
Bueno-Junior et al. (2017)	40–130 Hz (low gamma: 40–60 Hz; high gamma: 60–130 Hz)	Male Long-Evans rats (85–90 days)	Daily intraperitoneal injection of 0.2 mg/kg of nicotine solution (dissolved nicotine hydrogen tartrate salt in saline) on days 1–5, followed by a 9-day washout, and a final nicotine injection after washout.	- Increased low gamma power following nicotine administration on days 1, 3, 5, and 15. - No change in high gamma power following nicotine exposure on day 1 but increased high gamma power on day 15.

One study explored the effects of acute nicotine exposure (100 μM) on the complexity of gamma oscillations in the mouse hippocampus ([59] Table 2). It was found that nicotine reduced gamma oscillation complexity compared to the control and washout conditions, indicating increased synchronization of hippocampal networks.

Recently, Bueno-Junior and colleagues examined the effects of acute versus chronic nicotine exposure on brain oscillatory activity in rats [60]. The authors implemented a daily dosing regimen of nicotine (0.2 mg/kg) in vivo and found that acute nicotine administration slightly increased gamma power and reduced theta and beta power. Daily nicotine exposure produced stronger and more robust gamma activity [60]. In the following experiment, a separate group of rats was treated with nicotine following the same daily dosing regimen. Nicotine-treated rats performed significantly better in a visual attention task compared to controls, verifying the cognitive enhancing effects of nicotine [60]. In sum, nicotine administration increases gamma band activity. According to most preclinical studies, this increase in gamma power can be achieved with doses as low as 0.1 μM.

Cannabis: Studies have shown that chronic exposure to THC-9 in adolescent rodents induces long-lasting deficits in neural oscillations during adulthood (Table 3). For example, Raver and colleagues [61,62] showed that repeated exposure to THC in adolescents, but not adults, suppresses pharmacologically evoked cortical oscillations and impairs working memory performance in adulthood. In vitro recording of local field potentials show reduced oscillatory activity across all frequencies, whereas in vivo electrocorticogram measured specific reductions in alpha and gamma oscillations. The areas with the most pronounced deficits in gamma oscillatory activity in adulthood are also regions that were least mature during THC exposure. These preclinical findings provide insight into how adolescent cannabis use may affect gamma oscillations in adulthood, potentially as a precursor of CUDs. Overall, preclinical studies demonstrate that cannabis exposure is associated with reduced gamma activity.

Table 3. Preclinical Studies Examining the Effects of Cannabis on Gamma Oscillations.

Study	Gamma Frequency Range and Type	Subject Information	Method of Administration	Main Findings
Raver et al. 2013	Gamma 30–80 Hz (Local Field Potentials and Power)	Male CD-1 Mice	THC (5 mg/kg) dissolved in 100% ethanol and injected in a 1:1:18 solution of ethanol castor oil: 0.9% saline (1 mL/kg)	Cannabis exposure suppresses evoked cortical oscillations (with marked reductions in gamma and alpha) and impairs working memory in adolescent but not adult mice.
Raver et al. 2014	Gamma 30–80 Hz (Local Field Potentials and Power)	Male CD-1 Mice	CB1R/CBR2 agonist WIN55, 212-2 (1 or 2 mg/kg), CB1R inverse agonist/antagonist AM251 (0.3, 0.5, 1 or 2 mg/kg), CB1R/CB2R agonist (THC 5 mg/kg) and putative CB1R-inactive enantiomer (WIN55, 212-3) dissolved in 100% ethanol and administered in a 1:1:18 solution of ethanol: 0.9% saline at final volume of 1 mL/kg	THC selectively suppresses oscillations in the medial prefrontal cortex mediated by CB1R and non-cannabinoid receptors.

Cocaine: Studies examining the effects of cocaine use on gamma oscillation are limited (Table 4). In a preclinical acute administration study, Dilgen and colleagues examined the effects of acute cocaine exposure on prefrontal cortex optogenetically evoked gamma oscillation in PV-Cre knock-in mice [63]. The results showed that acute cocaine administration resulted in a decrease in the spread of induced gamma oscillations, likely due to more synchronous principal neuron firing. The authors suggest that the increase in synchrony coupled with an increase in the entrainment of gamma oscillations may be a potential mechanism in which cocaine increases alertness in novice users.

Table 4. Preclinical Studies Examining the Effects of Cocaine on Gamma Oscillations.

Study	Gamma Frequency Range and Type	Subject Information	Method of Administration	Main Findings
Dilgen et al. 2013	Relative and peak power (1–100 Hz)	Male PV-Cre Mice (B6; 129P2-Pvalb)	Infusion (cocaine HCL, SCH 23390 15 mg/kg)	Acute cocaine administration increased the entrainment of gamma oscillations to the optogentically induced driving frequency.

Amphetamines: Studies investigating the role of amphetamines in neural oscillations are limited to rodent populations (Table 5). Janetsian and colleagues induced methamphetamine sensitization in rats as assessed temporal and recognition memory after 1 or 30 days of abstinence as well as recorded oscillatory activity in the medial prefrontal cortex [64]. Results showed that temporal memory was impaired after both 1 day and 30 days abstinence, while recognition memory was only impaired after 1 day of abstinence. Methamphetamine injections significantly decreased neuronal firing rates and pharmacologically induced slow gamma oscillations in both sensitized and control rats. Moreover, the number of neurons phase-locked gamma oscillations were reduced in methamphetamine sensitized rats compared to controls. Given that previous studies have demonstrated that gamma band activity is elevated during recognition tasks in both humans and rats, it has been suggested that deficits in memory following repeated methamphetamine exposure may be a result of altered gamma band activity [64]. A study by Morra and colleagues investigated the role of cannabinoid (CB) 1 receptor in methamphetamine-induced rodent stereotypies and disrupted gamma oscillations [65]. Prior to methamphetamine sensitization, rats were treated with either CB1 receptor antagonist rimonabant (0.3 mg/kg) or vehicle as control. Methamphetamine administration in control rats significantly increased high-frequency gamma oscillation power (70–94 Hz, ~80 Hz peak) in the nucleus accumbens. Interestingly, the methamphetamine mediated increase in high-frequency gamma oscillations was attenuated by CB1 receptor blockades in rimonabant treated rats. This finding suggests that CB1 receptor activity is implicated in the mechanism in which methamphetamines alter local gamma oscillations. Furthermore, motor stereotypy behaviours induced by methamphetamine were also diminished in CB1 antagonist treated rats, in line with previous findings that both CB1 KO mice and local CB1 receptor antagonist injections in Nucleus accumbens reduce amphetamine-induced stereotypies. Taken together, these studies provide evidence that acute methamphetamine administration disrupts normal gamma oscillation and that its ability to do so may be modulated by CB1 activity.

Table 5. Preclinical Studies Examining the Effects of Amphetamine on Gamma Oscillations.

Study	Gamma Frequency Range and Type	Subject Information	Method of Administration	Main Findings
Janetsian et al. 2015	Gamma power (30–50 Hz)	Male adult Sprague-Dawley rats	5.0 mg/kg of methamphetamine	Temporal memory was impaired after 1 and 30 days of abstinence. Injection of MA decreased neuronal firing rate and anesthesia-induced slow oscillation in both sensitized and control rats. Relationships were found between anesthesia-induced slow oscillation and gamma power. Decreased number of neurons phase-locked gamma frequency was observed in the sensitized rats.
Morra et al. 2012	Oscillatory Power 0–100 Hz)	Male adult Sprague-Dawley rats $n = 10$	Intravenous CB1 receptor antagonist rimonabant (0.3 mg/kg) or vehicle followed by an ascending dose regimen of methamphetamine (0.01, 0.1, 1 and 3 mg/kg)	Methamphetamine increased high frequency gamma oscillations (~80 Hz). Methamphetamine induced both stereotypy and high frequency gamma power that was later disrupted with CB1R blockade.

3.2. Clinical Studies

Alcohol: Two studies have examined gamma band activity following acute alcohol consumption in human subjects (Table 6). In an early study conducted by Jaaskelainen and colleagues, alcohol (10% (v/v)) administered at moderate doses (0.50 g/kg and 0.75 g/kg) significantly reduced gamma power [66]. In this randomized and double-blind study, 10 healthy young adults with a negative family history for alcoholism participated in a dichotic listening task after consuming 0.25, 0.50, or 0.75 g/kg of 10% alcohol beverage or placebo. The effect of alcohol on gamma power was insignificant at 0.25 g/kg, but doses 0.50 and 0.75 g/kg markedly suppressed gamma power in both the attended and non-attended task conditions, suggesting that blood alcohol concentrations of around 0.05% already begin to influence gamma activity in healthy humans [66]. However, Campbell et al. demonstrated that alcohol administered at a higher concentration (40% (v/v)) and dose (0.8 g/kg) increased peak gamma power in both the human visual and motor cortices and decreased peak gamma frequency in the visual cortex [67].

Table 6. Clinical Studies of Alcohol and Gamma Oscillations.

Study	Gamma Frequency Range and Type	Subject Information	Method of Administration	Main Findings
Jaaskelainen et al. (2000)	40-Hz; Evoked	10 Social drinkers FHNFA * (5 males and 5 females; age: 20–28 years)	0.25, 0.50, or 0.75 g/kg of 10% (v/v) ethanol solution or placebo	No differences in gamma power after consuming 0.25 g/kg. Decreased gamma power following ingestion of the 0.50 g/kg and 0.75 g/kg doses.
De Bruin et al. (2004)	30–45 Hz	22 Male social drinkers FHNFA (11 light drinkers: <360 g alcohol per week; 11 heavy drinkers: >360 g alcohol per week; age: 22–27 years)	—	Increased gamma and theta (4–8 Hz) synchronization in heavy drinkers compared to light drinkers. Insignificant between-group differences in relative gamma and theta power.
Padmanabhapillai et al. (2006a)	29–45 Hz; Evoked	122 people with alcoholism (male; age: 20–40 years), 72 social drinkers FHNFA (male; age: 19–36 years)	—	Decreased frontal gamma power in alcoholics compared to controls during target processing. Increased frontal gamma power in alcoholics compared to controls during non-target processing.
Padmanabhapillai et al. (2006b)	29–45 Hz; Evoked	68 Male adolescents with at least one alcohol-dependent parent (high-risk), 27 male adolescents from non-alcoholic families (low-risk)	—	Decreased frontal and parietal gamma band response in high-risk adolescents compared to controls during target processing. No change in gamma activity between target, non-target and novel stimuli conditions in the high-risk group.

* FHNFA: family-history negative for alcoholism.

Padmanabhapillai and colleagues investigated early evoked gamma oscillations in 122 alcohol-dependent individuals and 72 healthy controls during a visual oddball task [68]. In this study, alcoholic subjects reported an average of 10.07 drinks per drinking day. Controls were social drinkers with a mean of 1.68 drinks per drinking day. Gamma activity was found to be significantly lower in alcoholics during target stimuli processing compared to controls but significantly higher during non-target processing [68]. In addition to evoked gamma power, reductions in evoked delta and theta band activity during stimulus processing have also been previously reported in patients with chronic alcoholism [69]. Following a similar experimental design, the same group then investigated early evoked gamma oscillations in male adolescents at high risk for alcoholism [68]. Consistent with alcohol-dependent individuals, high-risk adolescents also exhibited lower evoked gamma power during target processing in both the frontal and parietal regions compared to controls [68]. Furthermore, while control subjects displayed higher evoked gamma band responses in target-present conditions compared to non-target and novel-stimuli conditions, high-risk subjects did not display this pattern [68]. Moreover, De Bruin and colleagues demonstrated that heavy alcohol drinkers may also undergo changes in hippocampal-neocortical connectivity [70]. In this study, 11 male heavy drinkers and 11 male light drinkers participated in two EEG recording sessions. Heavy drinkers were defined as consuming over 360 g of alcohol per week whereas light drinkers consumed less than 360 g per week. Heavy drinkers exhibited higher theta and gamma synchronization compared to light drinkers in both conditions [70].

To summarize, the relationship between alcohol and gamma band activity appears to be a dose-dependent and inverted U-shaped pattern—administration at a low dosage generally increases gamma power while gamma activity is suppressed by alcohol at intoxicating concentrations. In addition, chronic alcohol consumption may lead to reduced gamma power as well as altered brain connectivity, which may underlie impaired cognitive function observed with severe AUDs.

Tobacco: Gamma activity following acute nicotine exposure has also been studied in human tobacco smokers (Table 7). Crawford and colleagues examined sensory gating, P50, and auditory evoked gamma oscillations, among sex- and age-matched cigarette smokers and never-smokers [71]. In this study, smokers had smoked for more than 5 years and currently smoke at least 20 cigarettes per day. Both groups of participants were tested in two conditions—smokers tested after overnight abstinence and after smoking, while controls did not smoke. Sensory gating refers to the process of filtering stimuli, by separating irrelevant stimuli from meaningful stimuli [72]. Crawford et al. examined sensory gating using a paired-tone paradigm, where two identical auditory tones are played 50-milliseconds apart, and participant sensory gating levels are measured by calculating the ratio of P50 event-related potential amplitudes [71]. They found that smokers had significantly greater gamma power compared to never-smokers and also displayed greater sensory gating both before and after abstinence [71].

Table 7. Clinical Studies of Tobacco on Gamma Oscillations.

Study	Gamma Frequency Range and Type	Subject Information	Method of Administration	Main Findings
Crawford et al. (2002)	32–48 Hz; Evoked	13 Heavy cigarette smokers (>20 cigarettes per day) and 13 age- and sex-matched never-smokers (age: 20–40 years)	Smokers were assessed following overnight (9–15 h) abstinence and after smoking their usual brand of cigarettes	- Increased gamma power in smokers versus controls.
Wilbanks et al. (2016)	30–80 Hz	35 Smokers and 35 age- and demographically matched never-smokers three months postpartum	—	- No change in gamma, high alpha (10.5–13 Hz), and beta (13–30 Hz) power between smoking and non-smoking mothers. - Increased delta (1–4 Hz), theta (4–8 Hz) and low alpha (8–10.5 Hz) power in smokers compared to controls.

No study to date has yet examined changes in gamma band activity in human subjects following a prolonged nicotine administration paradigm. However, a study by Wilbanks et al. did examine the impact of tobacco smoking on resting neural oscillations in postpartum mothers [73]. Although delta, theta, and alpha power were found to be elevated in smokers, no significant difference in gamma oscillatory power was observed in smoking mothers compared to controls [73] (Table 7).

Generally, nicotine administration increases gamma band activity. In chronic tobacco smokers—compared to never-smokers, smokers have higher gamma power. The above findings support the hypothesis that nicotine may help improve neurocognitive dysfunction in individuals with schizophrenia [74] through the modulation of gamma oscillations [75].

Cannabis: Studies of acute THC administration in human populations suggest that cannabis disrupts gamma oscillatory activity (Table 8). Nottage and colleagues investigated the effects of intravenous THC on high-frequency EEG recordings compared to placebo in participants with prior exposure to cannabis use but who were not cannabis-dependent [76]. THC shifted oscillatory activities towards higher frequencies such that there was a decrease in high beta oscillation (21–27 Hz) and increased low gamma (27–45 Hz) at rest. Furthermore, reductions in the high beta range (21–27 Hz) were more prominent in anterior regions, while posterior regions generally showed increases in the low gamma range (27–45 Hz). The THC-induced shift to faster gamma oscillations resulting in a hyperactive cortex may be associated with saliency misattribution in delusional states observed with psychosis.

Table 8. Clinical Studies of Cannabis on Gamma Oscillations.

Study	Gamma Frequency Range and Type	Subject Information	Method of Administration	Main Findings
Nottage et al. 2015	Resting state low gamma (35–45 Hz ad event-related synchronization (ERS) during motor associated high gamma (65–85 Hz)	14 Human Subjects	Intravenous THC (1.25 mg)	THC induced a shift to faster gamma oscillations and may represent an over-activation of the cortex that was related to positive symptoms.
Cortes-Briones et al. 2015	Auditory steady-state at 20, 30, and 40 Hz evoked potentials (Inter-trial coherence and evoked power ~40 Hz)	Human Subjects $n = 20$	Intravenous THC (0.003 mg/kg)	THC reduced ITC in the 40 Hz condition and evoked gamma power compared to placebo Negative correlation was observed between 40 Hz ITC and PANSS subscales
Skosnik et al. 2006	Auditory steady-state evoked potentials (spectral power) during auditory click trains of 20, 30, and 40 Hz)	Human Subjects (Current cannabis users $n = 17$ and drug naïve $n = 16$)	—	Reduced power during the 20 Hz stimulation frequency among cannabis users that were correlated with schizotypal personality questionnaire scores.
Skosik et al. 2012	Auditory steady-state evoked potentials (spectral power) during auditory click trains at 9 different frequencies)	Human Subjects (Chronic cannabis users $n = 22$ and cannabis naïve controls $n = 24$)	—	Decreased spectral power was observed among cannabis users. Reduced gamma power was related to an earlier age of onset of cannabis use. No effects on phase-locking or the N100, suggesting that cannabis may selectively impair the ability to generate oscillations in the gamma frequency range.
Edwards et al. 2009	Gamma range (30–50 Hz) during event-related spectral perturbations (ERSP) and inter-trial coherence (ITC)	Human Subjects (Heavy cannabis users $n = 17$ and cannabis naïve $n = 16$)	—	Reduced P50 gating and attenuated ITC among heavy cannabis users compared to controls in the beta and gamma frequency ranges.
Skosnik et al. 2014	Gamma oscillations (40–59 Hz) during coherent motion perception	Human Subjects (Chronic cannabis users $n = 34$ and cannabis naïve $n = 23$)	—	Gamma power was reduced during coherent motion perception among cannabis users compared to controls. No differences were found between N100 or P200. Cannabis may interfere with the generation of gamma oscillations that may mediate perceptual alterations.

Another study by Cortes-Briones and colleagues also demonstrated the association between THC and effects on the positive and negative symptom scale (PANSS)—an index used among patients with schizophrenia. In this study, an auditory steady-state response paradigm to probe the effects of acute THC administration on broadband-frequency neural oscillations and its relation to psychosis-related effects in healthy, cannabis naïve, and recreational users [77]. Auditory steady-state evoked potentials were assessed in both cannabis using and cannabis naïve subjects at varying auditory stimulation frequencies. The study demonstrated for the first time that acute THC administration induces a dose-dependent reduction of intertrial coherence (ITC) at 40 Hz stimulation frequency, suggesting that exogenous THC disrupts time-locked gamma band activity. Moreover, there was an inverse relationship between ITC and positive symptoms as measured by the PANSS, implicating gamma activity in positive symptom presentation among a healthy population. These findings from acute administration trials thus provide evidence that cannabis use disrupts gamma band activity among the general population. Moreover, the effect of THC on gamma oscillations may represent the pathophysiological mechanism through which psychosis is mediated.

Clinical studies examining chronic cannabis use and its effects on EEG recordings provide further evidence that cannabinoid exposure contributes to positive symptoms in psychosis by disrupting gamma band activity. Researchers used the auditory steady-state response paradigm to examine the effects of chronic cannabis use on broadband-frequency neural oscillations in cannabis using and cannabis naïve controls [78]. Cannabis users showed reduced evoked 40 Hz harmonic during 20 Hz stimulation frequencies compared to controls. Evoked power values at 20 Hz stimulation frequency were also negatively correlated with scores of schizotypal personality characteristics. Cannabis using subjects demonstrated increased schizotypal characteristics compared to cannabis naïve subjects as assessed by the Schizotypal Personality Questionnaire. Total years of cannabis use were also positively correlated with higher measures of schizotypal characteristics. In a follow-up study, Skosnik again used the auditory steady-state response paradigm to investigate disruptions in broadband EEG neural oscillation associated with cannabis use in a larger sample with more variations in click-train frequencies [79]. Results showed a selective and significant decrease in Fourier-based mean trial power (MTP) at 40 Hz among cannabis users compared to cannabis naïve controls, while an earlier onset of cannabis use was associated with lower oscillatory power at 40 Hz. Edwards and colleagues investigated the effects of chronic cannabis use on auditory evoked neural oscillation and auditory P50 sensory gating [80]. Results from event-related spectral perturbations (ERSP) analysis showed abnormal high-frequency activity in gamma range (30–50Hz) in cannabis users following auditory stimulation. Cannabis users demonstrated a time-specific reduction in power in high-frequency gamma and beta bands following the first stimulus (S1) and reductions in just gamma power following the second stimulus (S2). P50 gating was reduced in the cannabis using population compared to cannabis naïve controls in a manner that is similar to gating disturbances found among patients with schizophrenia. Additionally, greater levels of cannabis use were associated with high P50 ratios and negatively correlated with ERSP gamma power [80]. In a study assessing gamma oscillation during a coherent motion task in chronic cannabis users and cannabis naïve controls, cannabis users demonstrated a significant decrease in induced gamma power in coherent conditions compared to controls [81]. Moreover, an increasing trend in the Perceptual Aberration Scale (PAS), with higher scores positively correlated with total years of cannabis use, was observed among chronic cannabis users [81] (Table 8).

Overall, these studies suggest that cannabis, and particularly THC, decreases gamma activity. Clinical studies indicate that the disruption of gamma activity resulting from both acute THC administration and chronic cannabis use is associated with central nervous system hyperexcitability and positive symptomatology typically observed in psychosis.

Cocaine: One human study examined attentional bias to drug related cues by measuring evoked and induced gamma reactivity measure in patients with cocaine use disorder before and following motivational interview-based neurofeedback treatment [82] (Table 9). It is interesting to note that out of 10 participants, 7 also tested positive for cannabis use. Following 12 sessions of treatment, cocaine use decreased marginally while cannabis use significantly decreased for all patients. EEG reactivity to drug related cues was decreased post-treatment and, specifically, both evoked and induced gamma power decreased globally for drug related cues and non-drug related cues. While it is difficult to correlate the decreased cocaine usage to changes in neurophysiology given the nature of the self-reporting method, the accidental finding of dramatic decreases in cannabis use further cofounds the investigation into cocaine effects on gamma oscillations.

Table 9. Clinical Studies of Cocaine on Gamma Oscillations.

Study	Gamma Frequency Range and Type	Subject Information	Method of Administration	Main Findings
Horrell et al. 2010	Evoked and induced gamma power (30–40 Hz)	Human Subjects (Current cocaine abusers n = 10)	—	Decreased regional evoked and induced gamma power to non-target and target cues. Induced gamma power to non-target and target cues was reduced globally.

Only two studies reported on cocaine and gamma activity (Table 9). Dilgen et al. found a decrease in gamma activity following acute administration of cocaine in a preclinical population [63]. Horrell et al. found decreased gamma activity among chronic cocaine users, persisting post-treatment [82]. These studies suggest that cocaine use may result in long-term decreases in gamma activity.

4. Discussion

In this paper, we provide a comprehensive review of current evidence on alcohol, tobacco, cannabis, cocaine, and amphetamine use on gamma oscillatory activity during acute, chronic, and withdrawal states, among preclinical and clinical populations. All substances were associated with modulated gamma activity, in both preclinical and clinical populations and across states. Moreover, gamma appeared to be differentially modulated by acute versus chronic exposure, which may be related to cognitive dysfunction associated with substance abuse.

Pre-clinical studies indicated that all five substances modulated gamma activity. Alcohol use displayed an inverted U-shaped pattern during exposure for gamma and an increase across all frequencies during withdrawal. Tobacco use resulted in increased gamma during both acute and chronic exposure. Acute cannabis and cocaine exposure resulted in a decrease in gamma. Amphetamine use had mixed effects on gamma activity.

Similarly, clinical studies demonstrated that alcohol, tobacco, and cannabis modulated gamma activity. Acute alcohol exposure resulted in a selective decrease in gamma among non-dependent individuals, while such decreases were observed across all frequency bands among dependent individuals. Chronic tobacco use led to an increase in gamma, whereas chronic cannabis use led to a decrease in gamma. Clinical studies of cocaine and amphetamine were limited, making it difficult to draw any patterns on their influence on gamma. Thus, it appears that alcohol may act differently than other substances.

Alcohol and gamma had the most complex relationship, with alcohol decreasing gamma during withdrawal and in non-dependent individuals but displaying an inverted U-shaped pattern during exposure. Findings were mixed, likely to do studies varying in tasks used, types of controls (e.g., social drinkers, light drinkers, never drinkers), participant state (i.e., exposure versus withdrawal), and whether alcohol exposure was acute or chronic. The preclinical evidence of increased gamma activity during periods of alcohol withdrawal may represent post alcohol withdrawal hyperexcitability, a phenomenon whereby alcohol inhibits NMDAR excitatory signalling and increases GABAR inhibitory signalling, leading to central nervous system suppression and resulting in hyperexcitability during withdrawal [83,84]. The clinical evidence of varying effects of alcohol on gamma based on the task used suggests that there may be differential effects of alcohol based on the brain area involved and the type of cognition involved, a finding previously noted in the literature [85–87]. These findings indicate that several brain areas may be involved in the neuropathology of AUDs.

This review contains several strengths and limitations. We searched multiple databases and followed the PRISMA reporting guidelines to ensure a rigorous standard of review and reporting. We also searched for a variety of terms in order to capture all potentially relevant studies. A limitation of this review was that we only reviewed the five most common SUDs (alcohol, tobacco, cannabis, cocaine, and amphetamine), potentially limiting the generalizability of findings to other substances. Next, we did not directly search for the term "schizophrenia" or "psychosis"; we instead focused on search terms related to gamma, EEG, and SUDs and then manually screened for studies including patients with schizophrenia. This may have led to unintended exclusion of relevant studies. Last, we excluded studies of gamma in other disease areas, such as the effects of gamma entrainment therapies on brain pathology and cognitive symptoms in Alzheimer's disease (e.g., [87–89]). This may have omitted potentially relevant studies; however, we intentionally focused on SUDs and schizophrenia, given the prevalence and lack of research on these disorders.

5. Conclusions and Implications

The findings of this review indicate that both acute and chronic substance use modulate gamma activity and do so across different states. These findings offer insights into the potential mechanism underlying the pathophysiology of SUDs. This review also contributes to the growing body of evidence indicating the potential for brain stimulation to address deficits associated with SUDs. Brain stimulation treatments, such as transcranial direct current stimulation and repetitive transcranial magnetic stimulation, that modulate gamma activity may offer a promising potential approach for targeting working memory. Further research is needed to fully understand the underlying pathophysiology of SUDs in order to advance treatment of these devastating disorders and reduce the global burden on healthcare systems.

Author Contributions: Conceptualization, M.S.B., R.Z. and Y.N.; methodology, M.S.B. and J.U.R.; software, M.S.B. and J.U.R.; validation, M.S.B.; formal analysis, M.S.B., J.U.R. and M.M.; investigation, M.S.B.; resources, M.S.B.; data curation, M.S.B., J.U.R. and M.M.; writing—original draft preparation, M.S.B., J.U.R. and M.M.; writing—review and editing, D.M.B., R.Z., Y.N. and M.S.B.; visualization, M.S.B. and J.U.R.; supervision, M.S.B.; project administration, M.S.B. and J.U.R.; funding acquisition, M.S.B. All authors have read and agreed to the published version of the manuscript.

Funding: M.S.B. has received support from Brain and Behavior Research Foundation (Formerly NARSAD). D.M.B. has received research support from the CIHR, NIH, Brain Canada and the Temerty Family through the CAMH Foundation and the Campbell Research Institute. He received research support and in-kind equipment support for an investigator-initiated study from Brainsway Ltd., and he is the principal site investigator for three sponsor-initiated studies for Brainsway Ltd. He receives in-kind equipment support from Magventure for investigator-initiated research. He received medication supplies for an investigator-initiated trial from Indivior. Y.N. has received a Grant-in-Aid for Young Scientists (KAKENHI) from the Promotion of Science, research grants from Japan Agency for Medical Research and Development (AMED), investigator-initiated clinical study grants from TEIJIN PHARMA LIMITED and Inter Reha Co., Ltd. Y.N. also receives research grants from Japan Health Foundation, Meiji Yasuda Mental Health Foundation, Mitsui Life Social Welfare Foundation, Takeda Science Foundation, SENSHIN Medical Research Foundation, Health Science Center Foundation, Mochida Memorial Foundation for Medical and Pharmaceutical Research, Taiju Life Social Welfare Foundation, and Daiichi Sankyo Scholarship Donation Program. Y.N. has received speaker's honoraria from Dainippon Sumitomo Pharma, MOCHIDA PHARMACEUTICAL Co., Ltd., and Yoshitomiyakuhin Corporation within the past three years. Y.N. also receives equipment-in-kind support for an investigator-initiated study from Magventure Inc., Inter Reha Co., Ltd., Rogue Resolutions Ltd., and Miyuki Giken Co., Ltd.

Acknowledgments: The authors acknowledge Mark X. Wan for his assistance with data collection for this review.

Conflicts of Interest: J.U.R., M.M. and R.Z. declare no conflict of interest.

References

1. United Nations Office on Drugs and Crime. *World Drug Report 2019 (Set of 5 Booklets)*; United Nations: New York, NY, USA, 2019; ISBN 978-92-1-004174-4.
2. World Health Organization. *Global Status Report on Alcohol and Health 2018*; World Health Organization: Geneva, Switzerland, 2018; ISBN 978-92-4-156563-9.
3. World Health Organization. *WHO Report on the Global Tobacco Epidemic, 2019: Offer Help to Quit Tobacco Use*; World Health Organization: Geneva, Switzerland, 2019; ISBN 978-92-4-151620-4.
4. Baddeley, A. Working Memory: Looking Back and Looking Forward. *Nat. Rev. Neurosci.* **2003**, *4*, 829–839. [CrossRef]
5. Brandt, J. Cognitive Loss and Recovery in Long-Term Alcohol Abusers. *Arch. Gen. Psychiatry* **1983**, *40*, 435. [CrossRef]
6. Smith, M.J.; Cobia, D.J.; Wang, L.; Alpert, K.I.; Cronenwett, W.J.; Goldman, M.B.; Mamah, D.; Barch, D.M.; Breiter, H.C.; Csernansky, J.G. Cannabis-Related Working Memory Deficits and Associated Subcortical Morphological Differences in Healthy Individuals and Schizophrenia Subjects. *Schizophr. Bull.* **2014**, *40*, 287–299. [CrossRef]
7. Pfefferbaum, A.; Rosenbloom, M.; Crusan, K.; Jernigan, T.L. Brain CT Changes in Alcoholics: Effects of Age and Alcohol Consumption. *Alcohol. Clin. Exp. Res.* **1988**, *12*, 81–87. [CrossRef]
8. Chanraud, S.; Martelli, C.; Delain, F.; Kostogianni, N.; Douaud, G.; Aubin, H.-J.; Reynaud, M.; Martinot, J.-L. Brain Morphometry and Cognitive Performance in Detoxified Alcohol-Dependents with Preserved Psychosocial Functioning. *Neuropsychopharmacology* **2007**, *32*, 429–438. [CrossRef]
9. Kril, J.J.; Halliday, G.M.; Svoboda, M.D.; Cartwright, H. The Cerebral Cortex Is Damaged in Chronic Alcoholics. *Neuroscience* **1997**, *79*, 983–998. [CrossRef]
10. Leitz, J.R.; Morgan, C.J.A.; Bisby, J.A.; Rendell, P.G.; Curran, H.V. Global Impairment of Prospective Memory Following Acute Alcohol. *Psychopharmacology* **2009**, *205*, 379–387. [CrossRef]
11. do Canto-Pereira, L.H.M.; de P A David, I.; Machado-Pinheiro, W.; Ranvaud, R.D. Effects of Acute Alcohol Intoxication on Visuospatial Attention. *Hum. Exp. Toxicol.* **2007**, *26*, 311–319. [CrossRef]
12. Schweizer, T.A.; Jolicoeur, P.; Vogel-Sprott, M.; Dixon, M.J. Fast, but Error-Prone, Responses during Acute Alcohol Intoxication: Effects of Stimulus-Response Mapping Complexity. *Alcohol. Clin. Exp. Res.* **2004**, *28*, 643–649. [CrossRef]
13. Harvey, M.A.; Sellman, J.D.; Porter, R.J.; Frampton, C.M. The Relationship between Non-Acute Adolescent Cannabis Use and Cognition. *Drug Alcohol Rev.* **2007**, *26*, 309–319. [CrossRef] [PubMed]
14. Solowij, N.; Stephens, R.S.; Roffman, R.A.; Babor, T.; Kadden, R.; Miller, M.; Christiansen, K.; McRee, B.; Vendetti, J. Marijuana Treatment Project Research Group Cognitive Functioning of Long-Term Heavy Cannabis Users Seeking Treatment. *JAMA* **2002**, *287*, 1123–1131. [CrossRef]
15. Ardila, A.; Rosselli, M.; Strumwasser, S. Neuropsychological Deficits in Chronic Cocaine Abusers. *Int. J. Neurosci.* **1991**, *57*, 73–79. [CrossRef]
16. O'Malley, S.; Adamse, M.; Heaton, R.K.; Gawin, F.H. Neuropsychological Impairment in Chronic Cocaine Abusers. *Am. J. Drug Alcohol Abus.* **1992**, *18*, 131–144. [CrossRef]
17. Ranganathan, M.; D'Souza, D.C. The Acute Effects of Cannabinoids on Memory in Humans: A Review. *Psychopharmacology* **2006**, *188*, 425–444. [CrossRef]
18. Rentzsch, J.; Stadtmann, A.; Montag, C.; Kunte, H.; Plöckl, D.; Hellweg, R.; Gallinat, J.; Kronenberg, G.; Jockers-Scherübl, M.C. Attentional Dysfunction in Abstinent Long-Term Cannabis Users with and without Schizophrenia. *Eur. Arch. Psychiatry Clin. Neurosci.* **2016**, *266*, 409–421. [CrossRef]
19. Ramaekers, J.G.; Kauert, G.; van Ruitenbeek, P.; Theunissen, E.L.; Schneider, E.; Moeller, M.R. High-Potency Marijuana Impairs Executive Function and Inhibitory Motor Control. *Neuropsychopharmacology* **2006**, *31*, 2296–2303. [CrossRef]
20. Pope, H.G.; Gruber, A.J.; Hudson, J.I.; Huestis, M.A.; Yurgelun-Todd, D. Neuropsychological Performance in Long-Term Cannabis Users. *Arch. Gen. Psychiatry* **2001**, *58*, 909. [CrossRef]
21. Chambers, R.A.; Krystal, J.H.; Self, D.W. A Neurobiological Basis for Substance Abuse Comorbidity in Schizophrenia. *Biol. Psychiatry* **2001**, *50*, 71–83. [CrossRef]
22. Berger, H. Über das Elektrenkephalogramm des Menschen. *Arch. Psychiatr. Nervenkrankh.* **1929**, *87*, 527–570. [CrossRef]
23. Sederberg, P.B.; Kahana, M.J.; Howard, M.W.; Donner, E.J.; Madsen, J.R. Theta and Gamma Oscillations during Encoding Predict Subsequent Recall. *J. Neurosci.* **2003**, *23*, 10809–10814. [CrossRef]
24. Gruber, T.; Müller, M.M.; Keil, A.; Elbert, T. Selective Visual-Spatial Attention Alters Induced Gamma Band Responses in the Human EEG. *Clin. Neurophysiol.* **1999**, *110*, 2074–2085. [CrossRef]
25. Tiitinen, H.; Sinkkonen, J.; Reinikainen, K.; Alho, K.; Lavikainen, J.; Näätänen, R. Selective Attention Enhances the Auditory 40-Hz Transient Response in Humans. *Nature* **1993**, *364*, 59–60. [CrossRef] [PubMed]
26. Bichot, N.P.; Rossi, A.F.; Desimone, R. Parallel and Serial Neural Mechanisms for Visual Search in Macaque Area V4. *Science* **2005**, *308*, 529–534. [CrossRef] [PubMed]
27. Ossandón, T.; Vidal, J.R.; Ciumas, C.; Jerbi, K.; Hamamé, C.M.; Dalal, S.S.; Bertrand, O.; Minotti, L.; Kahane, P.; Lachaux, J.-P. Efficient "Pop-out" Visual Search Elicits Sustained Broadband γ Activity in the Dorsal Attention Network. *J. Neurosci.* **2012**, *32*, 3414–3421. [CrossRef] [PubMed]
28. Miltner, W.H.; Braun, C.; Arnold, M.; Witte, H.; Taub, E. Coherence of Gamma-Band EEG Activity as a Basis for Associative Learning. *Nature* **1999**, *397*, 434–436. [CrossRef] [PubMed]

29. Barr, M.S.; Farzan, F.; Rusjan, P.M.; Chen, R.; Fitzgerald, P.B.; Daskalakis, Z.J. Potentiation of Gamma Oscillatory Activity through Repetitive Transcranial Magnetic Stimulation of the Dorsolateral Prefrontal Cortex. *Neuropsychopharmacology* **2009**, *34*, 2359–2367. [CrossRef] [PubMed]
30. Basar-Eroglu, C.; Brand, A.; Hildebrandt, H.; Karolina Kedzior, K.; Mathes, B.; Schmiedt, C. Working Memory Related Gamma Oscillations in Schizophrenia Patients. *Int. J. Psychophysiol.* **2007**, *64*, 39–45. [CrossRef]
31. Howard, M.W.; Rizzuto, D.S.; Caplan, J.B.; Madsen, J.R.; Lisman, J.; Aschenbrenner-Scheibe, R.; Schulze-Bonhage, A.; Kahana, M.J. Gamma Oscillations Correlate with Working Memory Load in Humans. *Cereb. Cortex* **2003**, *13*, 1369–1374. [CrossRef]
32. Barr, M.S.; Farzan, F.; Tran, L.C.; Chen, R.; Fitzgerald, P.B.; Daskalakis, Z.J. Evidence for Excessive Frontal Evoked Gamma Oscillatory Activity in Schizophrenia during Working Memory. *Schizophr. Res.* **2010**, *121*, 146–152. [CrossRef]
33. Bragin, A.; Jandó, G.; Nádasdy, Z.; Hetke, J.; Wise, K.; Buzsáki, G. Gamma (40–100 Hz) Oscillation in the Hippocampus of the Behaving Rat. *J. Neurosci.* **1995**, *15*, 47–60. [CrossRef]
34. Brosch, M.; Budinger, E.; Scheich, H. Stimulus-Related Gamma Oscillations in Primate Auditory Cortex. *J. Neurophysiol.* **2002**, *87*, 2715–2725. [CrossRef] [PubMed]
35. Buhl, E.H.; Tamás, G.; Fisahn, A. Cholinergic Activation and Tonic Excitation Induce Persistent Gamma Oscillations in Mouse Somatosensory Cortex In Vitro. *J. Physiol.* **1998**, *513*, 117–126. [CrossRef] [PubMed]
36. Fries, P.; Reynolds, J.H.; Rorie, A.E.; Desimone, R. Modulation of Oscillatory Neuronal Synchronization by Selective Visual Attention. *Science* **2001**, *291*, 1560–1563. [CrossRef] [PubMed]
37. Gray, C.M.; Singer, W. Stimulus-Specific Neuronal Oscillations in Orientation Columns of Cat Visual Cortex. *Proc. Natl. Acad. Sci. USA* **1989**, *86*, 1698–1702. [CrossRef]
38. Cunningham, M.O.; Davies, C.H.; Buhl, E.H.; Kopell, N.; Whittington, M.A. Gamma Oscillations Induced by Kainate Receptor Activation in the Entorhinal Cortex In Vitro. *J. Neurosci.* **2003**, *23*, 9761–9769. [CrossRef] [PubMed]
39. Beshel, J.; Kopell, N.; Kay, L.M. Olfactory Bulb Gamma Oscillations Are Enhanced with Task Demands. *J. Neurosci.* **2007**, *27*, 8358–8365. [CrossRef]
40. Sato, W.; Kochiyama, T.; Uono, S.; Matsuda, K.; Usui, K.; Inoue, Y.; Toichi, M. Temporal Profile of Amygdala γ Oscillations in Response to Faces. *J. Cogn. Neurosci.* **2012**, *24*, 1420–1433. [CrossRef]
41. Lewis, D.A.; Hashimoto, T.; Volk, D.W. Cortical Inhibitory Neurons and Schizophrenia. *Nat. Rev. Neurosci.* **2005**, *6*, 312–324. [CrossRef]
42. Gray, C.M.; McCormick, D.A. Chattering Cells: Superficial Pyramidal Neurons Contributing to the Generation of Synchronous Oscillations in the Visual Cortex. *Science* **1996**, *274*, 109–113. [CrossRef]
43. Whittington, M.A.; Traub, R.D.; Jefferys, J.G.R. Synchronized Oscillations in Interneuron Networks Driven by Metabotropic Glutamate Receptor Activation. *Nature* **1995**, *373*, 612–615. [CrossRef]
44. Bartos, M.; Vida, I.; Jonas, P. Synaptic Mechanisms of Synchronized Gamma Oscillations in Inhibitory Interneuron Networks. *Nat. Rev. Neurosci.* **2007**, *8*, 45–56. [CrossRef] [PubMed]
45. Wang, X.-J.; Buzsáki, G. Gamma Oscillation by Synaptic Inhibition in a Hippocampal Interneuronal Network Model. *J. Neurosci.* **1996**, *16*, 6402–6413. [CrossRef] [PubMed]
46. Fisahn, A.; Pike, F.G.; Buhl, E.H.; Paulsen, O. Cholinergic Induction of Network Oscillations at 40 Hz in the Hippocampus In Vitro. *Nature* **1998**, *394*, 186–189. [CrossRef] [PubMed]
47. Fisahn, A.; Contractor, A.; Traub, R.D.; Buhl, E.H.; Heinemann, S.F.; McBain, C.J. Distinct Roles for the Kainate Receptor Subunits GluR5 and GluR6 in Kainate-Induced Hippocampal Gamma Oscillations. *J. Neurosci.* **2004**, *24*, 9658–9668. [CrossRef]
48. Faulkner, H.J.; Traub, R.D.; Whittington, M.A. Anaesthetic/Amnesic Agents Disrupt Beta Frequency Oscillations Associated with Potentiation of Excitatory Synaptic Potentials in the Rat Hippocampal Slice. *Br. J. Pharm.* **1999**, *128*, 1813–1825. [CrossRef]
49. Moher, D.; Liberati, A.; Tetzlaff, J.; Altman, D.G. PRISMA Group Preferred Reporting Items for Systematic Reviews and Meta-Analyses: The PRISMA Statement. *PLoS Med.* **2009**, *6*, e1000097. [CrossRef]
50. Wang, J.; Zhao, J.; Liu, Z.; Guo, F.; Wang, Y.; Wang, X.; Zhang, R.; Vreugdenhil, M.; Lu, C. Acute Ethanol Inhibition of γ Oscillations Is Mediated by Akt and GSK3β. *Front. Cell. Neurosci.* **2016**, *10*. [CrossRef]
51. Tsurugizawa, T.; Abe, Y.; Le Bihan, D. Water Apparent Diffusion Coefficient Correlates with Gamma Oscillation of Local Field Potentials in the Rat Brain Nucleus Accumbens Following Alcohol Injection. *J. Cereb. Blood Flow Metab.* **2017**, *37*, 3193–3202. [CrossRef]
52. Ehlers, C.L.; Chaplin, R.I. EEG and ERP Response to Chronic Ethanol Exposure in Rats. *Psychopharmacology* **1991**, *104*, 67–74. [CrossRef]
53. Slawecki, C.J. Altered EEG Responses to Ethanol in Adult Rats Exposed to Ethanol During Adolescence. *Alcohol. Clin. Exp. Res.* **2002**, *26*, 246–254. [CrossRef]
54. Cheaha, D.; Sawangjaroen, K.; Kumarnsit, E. Characterization of Fluoxetine Effects on Ethanol Withdrawal-Induced Cortical Hyperexcitability by EEG Spectral Power in Rats. *Neuropharmacology* **2014**, *77*, 49–56. [CrossRef] [PubMed]
55. Phillips, J.M.; Ehrlichman, R.S.; Siegel, S.J. Mecamylamine Blocks Nicotine-Induced Enhancement of the P20 Auditory Event Related Potential and Evoked Gamma. *Neuroscience* **2007**, *144*, 1314–1323. [CrossRef] [PubMed]
56. Song, C.; Murray, T.A.; Kimura, R.; Wakui, M.; Ellsworth, K.; Javedan, S.P.; Marxer-Miller, S.; Lukas, R.J.; Wu, J. Role of A7-Nicotinic Acetylcholine Receptors in Tetanic Stimulation-Induced γ Oscillations in Rat Hippocampal Slices. *Neuropharmacology* **2005**, *48*, 869–880. [CrossRef] [PubMed]

57. Zhang, X.; Ge, X.Y.; Wang, J.G.; Wang, Y.L.; Wang, Y.; Yu, Y.; Li, P.P.; Lu, C.B. Induction of Long-Term Oscillations in the γ Frequency Band by NAChR Activation in Rat Hippocampal CA3 Area. *Neuroscience* **2015**, *301*, 49–60. [CrossRef]
58. Wang, Y.; Wang, Z.; Wang, J.; Wang, Y.; Henderson, Z.; Wang, X.; Zhang, X.; Song, J.; Lu, C. The Modulation of Nicotinic Acetylcholine Receptors on the Neuronal Network Oscillations in Rat Hippocampal CA3 Area. *Sci. Rep.* **2015**, *5*, 9493. [CrossRef]
59. Akkurt, D.; Akay, Y.M.; Akay, M. Investigating the Synchronization of Hippocampal Neural Network in Response to Acute Nicotine Exposure. *J. Neuroeng. Rehabil.* **2010**, *7*, 31. [CrossRef]
60. Bueno-Junior, L.S.; Simon, N.W.; Wegener, M.A.; Moghaddam, B. Repeated Nicotine Strengthens Gamma Oscillations in the Prefrontal Cortex and Improves Visual Attention. *Neuropsychopharmacology* **2017**, *42*, 1590–1598. [CrossRef]
61. Raver, S.M.; Haughwout, S.P.; Keller, A. Adolescent Cannabinoid Exposure Permanently Suppresses Cortical Oscillations in Adult Mice. *Neuropsychopharmacology* **2013**, *38*, 2338–2347. [CrossRef]
62. Raver, S.M.; Keller, A. Permanent Suppression of Cortical Oscillations in Mice after Adolescent Exposure to Cannabinoids: Receptor Mechanisms. *Neuropharmacology* **2014**, *86*, 161–173. [CrossRef]
63. Dilgen, J.E.; Tompa, T.; Saggu, S.; Naselaris, T.; Lavin, A. Optogenetically Evoked Gamma Oscillations Are Disturbed by Cocaine Administration. *Front. Cell. Neurosci.* **2013**, *7*. [CrossRef]
64. Janetsian, S.S.; Linsenbardt, D.N.; Lapish, C.C. Memory Impairment and Alterations in Prefrontal Cortex Gamma Band Activity Following Methamphetamine Sensitization. *Psychopharmacology* **2015**, *232*, 2083–2095. [CrossRef] [PubMed]
65. Morra, J.T.; Glick, S.D.; Cheer, J.F. Cannabinoid Receptors Mediate Methamphetamine Induction of High Frequency Gamma Oscillations in the Nucleus Accumbens. *Neuropharmacology* **2012**, *63*, 565–574. [CrossRef] [PubMed]
66. Jääskeläinen, I.P.; Hirvonen, J.; Saher, M.; Pekkonen, E.; Sillanaukee, P.; Näätänen, R.; Tiitinen, H. Dose-Dependent Suppression by Ethanol of Transient Auditory 40-Hz Response. *Psychopharmacology* **2000**, *148*, 132–135. [CrossRef] [PubMed]
67. Campbell, A.E.; Sumner, P.; Singh, K.D.; Muthukumaraswamy, S.D. Acute Effects of Alcohol on Stimulus-Induced Gamma Oscillations in Human Primary Visual and Motor Cortices. *Neuropsychopharmacology* **2014**, *39*, 2104–2113. [CrossRef]
68. Padmanabhapillai, A.; Tang, Y.; Ranganathan, M.; Rangaswamy, M.; Jones, K.A.; Chorlian, D.B.; Kamarajan, C.; Stimus, A.; Kuperman, S.; Rohrbaugh, J.; et al. Evoked Gamma Band Response in Male Adolescent Subjects at High Risk for Alcoholism during a Visual Oddball Task. *Int. J. Psychophysiol.* **2006**, *62*, 262–271. [CrossRef]
69. Porjesz, B.; Begleiter, H. Alcoholism and Human Electrophysiology. *Alcohol Res. Health* **2003**, *27*, 153–160.
70. de Bruin, E.A.; Bijl, S.; Stam, C.J.; Böcker, K.B.E.; Kenemans, J.L.; Verbaten, M.N. Abnormal EEG Synchronisation in Heavily Drinking Students. *Clin. Neurophysiol.* **2004**, *115*, 2048–2055. [CrossRef]
71. Crawford, H.J.; McClain-Furmanski, D.; Castagnoli, N.; Castagnoli, K. Enhancement of Auditory Sensory Gating and Stimulus-Bound Gamma Band (40 Hz) Oscillations in Heavy Tobacco Smokers. *Neurosci. Lett.* **2002**, *317*, 151–155. [CrossRef]
72. Cromwell, H.C.; Mears, R.P.; Wan, L.; Boutros, N.N. Sensory Gating: A Translational Effort from Basic to Clinical Science. *Clin. EEG Neurosci.* **2008**, *39*, 69–72. [CrossRef]
73. Wilbanks, H.E.; Von Mohr, M.; Potenza, M.N.; Mayes, L.C.; Rutherford, H.J.V. Tobacco Smoking and the Resting Maternal Brain: A Preliminary Study of Frontal EEG. *Yale J. Biol. Med.* **2016**, *89*, 115–122.
74. Freedman, R. A7-Nicotinic Acetylcholine Receptor Agonists for Cognitive Enhancement in Schizophrenia. *Annu. Rev. Med.* **2014**, *65*, 245–261. [CrossRef] [PubMed]
75. Uhlhaas, P.J.; Singer, W. High-Frequency Oscillations and the Neurobiology of Schizophrenia. *Dialogues Clin. Neurosci.* **2013**, *15*, 301–313. [PubMed]
76. Nottage, J.F.; Stone, J.; Murray, R.M.; Sumich, A.; Bramon-Bosch, E.; ffytche, D.; Morrison, P.D. Delta-9-Tetrahydrocannabinol, Neural Oscillations above 20 Hz and Induced Acute Psychosis. *Psychopharmacology* **2015**, *232*, 519–528. [CrossRef] [PubMed]
77. Cortes-Briones, J.; Skosnik, P.D.; Mathalon, D.; Cahill, J.; Pittman, B.; Williams, A.; Sewell, R.A.; Ranganathan, M.; Roach, B.; Ford, J.; et al. Δ9-THC Disrupts Gamma (γ)-Band Neural Oscillations in Humans. *Neuropsychopharmacol* **2015**, *40*, 2124–2134. [CrossRef]
78. Skosnik, P.D.; Krishnan, G.P.; Aydt, E.E.; Kuhlenshmidt, H.A.; O'Donnell, B.F. Psychophysiological Evidence of Altered Neural Synchronization in Cannabis Use: Relationship to Schizotypy. *AJP* **2006**, *163*, 1798–1805. [CrossRef]
79. Skosnik, P.D.; D'Souza, D.C.; Steinmetz, A.B.; Edwards, C.R.; Vollmer, J.M.; Hetrick, W.P.; O'Donnell, B.F. The Effect of Chronic Cannabinoids on Broadband EEG Neural Oscillations in Humans. *Neuropsychopharmacology* **2012**, *37*, 2184–2193. [CrossRef]
80. Edwards, C.R.; Skosnik, P.D.; Steinmetz, A.B.; O'Donnell, B.F.; Hetrick, W.P. Sensory Gating Impairments in Heavy Cannabis Users Are Associated with Altered Neural Oscillations. *Behav. Neurosci.* **2009**, *123*, 894–904. [CrossRef]
81. Skosnik, P.D.; Krishnan, G.P.; D'Souza, D.C.; Hetrick, W.P.; O'Donnell, B.F. Disrupted Gamma-Band Neural Oscillations During Coherent Motion Perception in Heavy Cannabis Users. *Neuropsychopharmacology* **2014**, *39*, 3087–3099. [CrossRef]
82. Horrell, T.; El-Baz, A.; Baruth, J.; Tasman, A.; Sokhadze, G.; Stewart, C.; Sokhadze, E. Neurofeedback Effects on Evoked and Induced EEG Gamma Band Reactivity to Drug-Related Cues in Cocaine Addiction. *J. Neurother.* **2010**, *14*, 195–216. [CrossRef]
83. Begleiter, H.; Porjesz, B. Persistence of Brain Hyperexcitability Following Chronic Alcohol Exposure in Rats. In *Alcohol Intoxication and Withdrawal—IIIb: Studies in Alcohol Dependence*; Gross, M.M., Ed.; Advances in Experimental Medicine and Biology; Springer: Boston, MA, USA, 1977; pp. 209–222. ISBN 978-1-4615-9038-5.
84. Ahveninen, J.; Escera, C.; Polo, M.D.; Grau, C.; Jääskeläinen, I.P. Acute and Chronic Effects of Alcohol on Preattentive Auditory Processing as Reflected by Mismatch Negativity. *Audiol. Neurootol.* **2000**, *5*, 303–311. [CrossRef]
85. Loheswaran, G.; Barr, M.S.; Rajji, T.K.; Blumberger, D.M.; Le Foll, B.; Daskalakis, Z.J. Alcohol Intoxication by Binge Drinking Impairs Neuroplasticity. *Brain Stimul.* **2016**, *9*, 27–32. [CrossRef] [PubMed]

86. Ramlakhan, J.U.; Zomorrodi, R.; Downar, J.; Blumberger, D.M.; Daskalakis, Z.J.; George, T.P.; Kiang, M.; Barr, M.S. Using Mismatch Negativity to Investigate the Pathophysiology of Substance Use Disorders and Comorbid Psychosis. *Clin. EEG Neurosci.* **2018**, *49*, 226–237. [CrossRef] [PubMed]
87. Martorell, A.J.; Paulson, A.L.; Suk, H.-J.; Abdurrob, F.; Drummond, G.T.; Guan, W.; Young, J.Z.; Kim, D.N.-W.; Kritskiy, O.; Barker, S.J.; et al. Multi-Sensory Gamma Stimulation Ameliorates Alzheimer's-Associated Pathology and Improves Cognition. *Cell* **2019**, *177*, 256–271.e22. [CrossRef] [PubMed]
88. Clements-Cortes, A.; Ahonen, H.; Evans, M.; Freedman, M.; Bartel, L. Short-Term Effects of Rhythmic Sensory Stimulation in Alzheimer's Disease: An Exploratory Pilot Study. *JAD* **2016**, *52*, 651–660. [CrossRef]
89. Adaikkan, C.; Middleton, S.J.; Marco, A.; Pao, P.-C.; Mathys, H.; Kim, D.N.-W.; Gao, F.; Young, J.Z.; Suk, H.-J.; Boyden, E.S.; et al. Gamma Entrainment Binds Higher-Order Brain Regions and Offers Neuroprotection. *Neuron* **2019**, *102*, 929–943.e8. [CrossRef]

Journal of *Personalized Medicine*

MDPI

Article

Potential Neurophysiological Mechanisms of 1Hz-TMS to the Right Prefrontal Cortex for Depression: An Exploratory TMS-EEG Study in Healthy Participants

Yoshihiro Noda

Department of Neuropsychiatry, Graduate School of Medicine, Keio University School of Medicine, 35 Shinanomachi, Shinjuku-ku, Tokyo 160-8582, Japan; yoshi-tms@keio.jp; Tel.: +81-3-3353-1211 (ext. 61857)

Abstract: Background: The present study aimed to examine the acute neurophysiological effects of 1Hz transcranial magnetic stimulation (TMS) administered to the right dorsolateral prefrontal cortex (DLPFC) in healthy participants. Methods: TMS combined with simultaneous electroencephalography (EEG) recording was conducted for 21 healthy participants. For the right DLPFC, 1Hz-TMS (100 pulses/block × 17 sessions) was applied in the resting-state, while for the left DLPFC, 1Hz-TMS (100 pulses/block × 2 sessions) was administered during the verbal fluency tasks (VFTs). For TMS-EEG data, independent component analysis (ICA) was applied to extract TMS-evoked EEG potentials to calculate TMS-related power as well as TMS-related coherence from the F4 and F3 electrode sites during the resting-state and VFTs. Results: TMS-related power was significantly increased in alpha, beta, and gamma bands by 1Hz-TMS at the stimulation site during the resting-state, while TMS-related power was significantly increased in alpha and beta bands but not in the gamma band during the VFTs. On the other hand, TMS-related coherence in alpha and beta bands significantly increased but not in gamma band by 1Hz-TMS that was administered to the right DLPFC in resting-state, whereas there were no significant changes in coherence for all frequency bands by 1Hz-TMS that applied to the left DLPFC during the VFTs. Conclusions: Collectively, 1Hz-repetitive TMS (rTMS) to the right DLPFC may rapidly neuromodulate EEG activity, which might be associated with a therapeutic mechanism for depression.

Keywords: dorsolateral prefrontal cortex (DLPFC); electroencephalography (EEG); neuromodulation; neurophysiology; transcranial magnetic stimulation (TMS); TMS-EEG; TMS-evoked potential (TEP); TMS-related coherence; TMS-related power

Citation: Noda, Y. Potential Neurophysiological Mechanisms of 1Hz-TMS to the Right Prefrontal Cortex for Depression: An Exploratory TMS-EEG Study in Healthy Participants. *J. Pers. Med.* **2021**, *11*, 68. https://doi.org/10.3390/jpm11020068

Academic Editor: Sabata Martino
Received: 31 December 2020
Accepted: 22 January 2021
Published: 24 January 2021

Highlights

- Low-frequency 1Hz-TMS to the right DLPFC in healthy participants resulted in a significant increase in spectral power in alpha, beta, and gamma bands.
- The same 1Hz-TMS induced a significant increase in alpha and beta coherences between the right and left DLPFC in healthy participants.
- These findings suggest parts of the therapeutic mechanisms of 1Hz-rTMS to the right DLPFC which may exert in patients with depression.

1. Introduction

Repetitive transcranial magnetic stimulation (rTMS) to the dorsolateral prefrontal cortex (DLPFC) in major depression can improve clinical symptoms and cognitive function as shown in previous clinical studies [1–3]. However, the neurophysiological therapeutic mechanisms are not fully understood [4–6]. On the other hand, most previous studies that examined the neurophysiology of healthy subjects focused on the motor cortex and demonstrated changes in electroencephalography (EEG) power and EEG coherence in the motor cortex [7–11], but few studies have examined the EEG changes induced by rTMS administered to the prefrontal cortex [12], which also implies that the therapeutic mechanism induced by rTMS in depression has not been fully elucidated.

Specifically, previous studies have shown that patients with depression have lower activity in the left prefrontal cortex and relatively higher activity in the right prefrontal cortex, suggesting that an imbalance between the activity of the left and right prefrontal cortex may be associated with the pathophysiology of depression [13–15]. Given the clinical effects of low-frequency rTMS of the right DLPFC on depression, it may have the effect of normalizing the imbalance of right and left prefrontal activity. Here, the present study aimed to investigate the prefrontal EEG activity changes induced by low-frequency rTMS over the right DLPFC as indexed by the functional connectivity between right and left DLPFC as well as the EEG power changes in the prefrontal cortex in healthy participants, using TMS-compatible EEG equipment [16–21].

Thereupon, it was speculated that the EEG aftereffects of low-frequency rTMS to the right DLPFC [22] may be detected as changes in EEG power in the prefrontal cortex and changes in EEG coherence between the left and right DLPFC [23]. The present study aimed to explore such neurophysiological therapeutic mechanisms, assuming that 1Hz-rTMS for the right DLPFC would cause EEG changes in healthy participants that would be partially similar to the effects on depressed patients [24,25].

2. Material and Methods

2.1. Participants

Twenty-one healthy young adults (11 males and 10 females; mean age ± S.D = 34 ± 6 years) participated in the study. Participants reported no neurological, psychiatric, or other excluding medical conditions. A trained psychiatrist administered a short structured diagnostic interview using the Mini-international Neuropsychiatric Interview (M.N.N.I.) [26,27] to confirm that they did not have a lifetime diagnosis of affective, anxiety or psychotic disorders based on the criteria of the Diagnostic and Statistical Manual of Mental Disorders, 4th edition (DSM-IV). The study was approved by the local ethics committee of Kanagawa Psychiatric Center and was conducted under the principles laid down in the Declaration of Helsinki. All participants provided written informed consent.

2.2. TMS and EEG System

TMS was conducted with a Magstim Rapid system (The Magstim Company Ltd., Spring Gardens, Whitland, UK). TMS was delivered through a figure-of-8-shaped coil (70 mm diameter; Magstim). TMS-compatible EEG system (NEURO PRAX, neuroConn Gmbh, Ilmenau, Germany) which can record the EEG data at a sampling rate of 4096Hz. The EEGs were continuously acquired from 19 recording electrode sites (i.e., Fp1, Fp2, F7, F3, Fz, F4, F8, T3, C3, Cz, C4, T4, T5, P3, Pz, P4, T6, O1, and O2) according to the International 10–20 System. An elastic cap with small Ag/AgCl pellet electrodes was used to avoid overheats due to TMS. The ground electrode was positioned at Fpz, and linked earlobes (A1 and A2) served as the active reference for all the electrodes. Skin–electrode impedance was maintained below 5 kΩ during the EEG recording.

2.3. TMS Experimental Procedure

First, each participant's resting motor threshold (RMT) was measured. RMT was defined as the lowest stimulus intensity produced in the relaxed right abductor digiti minimi (ADM) muscle at least 5 motor-evoked potentials (MEPs) over 50 μV in 10 consecutive trials [28]. Next, TMS stimulation was applied to the F4 electrode site on the right DLPFC during the resting-state (17 blocks as described below) at various stimulus intensities, while TMS stimulation was administered to the F3 electrode site on the left DLPFC during the verbal fluency task (VFT) (two blocks as described below) at the RMT intensity in all participants. Specifically, the protocol for TMS in the resting-state consisted of a set of 100 s of 1Hz stimulation (i.e., 100 pulses per block) for F4 electrodes in 5% increments from 10% to 90% maximum stimulus output (MSO) (10%, 15%,..., 90%), for a total of 17 blocks of 1700 pulses to obtain the recruitment curve (i.e., input–output curve) of TMS-evoked potentials (TEPs). On the other hand, the TMS protocol during VFTs (VFT-1 and VFT-2) was performed as a set of 1Hz stimulation for 100 s (i.e., a total of 200 pulses in two blocks). During the TMS-EEG measurement experiment, the participants were instructed to remain in a resting-state as in the standard EEG experiment, not to move or talk, and to remain awake and close their eyes lightly.

2.4. TMS-EEG Experiment during the Verbal Fluency Task (VFT)

The VFT was conducted after the recruitment curve experiment to examine the synergy effect between VFT and TMS. The VFT-1 was the task that participants were instructed to vocalize *hiragana* in order such as "a, i, u, e, o, ka, ki, ku, ke, ko, ..." during the 1Hz TMS for 100 s over the left DLPFC. The VFT-2 task was that participants were instructed to say as many common nouns as they could think of beginning with "a" (e.g., asa, aka, ao, aki, and so on), next with "i" (e.g., ike, isi, ika, and so on), then "u", in *hiragana* order, during 1Hz-TMS for 100 s. In this study, the number of words were not counted, because these tasks were intended to apply a verbal cognitive load to the participants during TMS stimulation over the left DLPFC.

2.5. EEG Signal Processing

EEG data were exported from the EEG device as European data format (EDF) files and processed offline using the EEGLAB toolbox [29] running in MATLAB software (Mathworks, Natic, MA, USA). The EEG signal was processed in accordance with the published methodology [30,31]. All EEG data were epoched from −500 ms to 500 ms relative to the TMS pulse and further baseline correction was performed for the pre-stimulus interval −300 ms to −110 ms. Then, EEG data were visually double-checked to exclude bad channels and trials. Next, independent component analysis (ICA) was applied to minimize and remove the typical TMS–related decay artifacts and eye-related and muscle activity-related components [32–35]. Afterwards, a notch filter was applied to avoid the power-line noise of 50Hz. Further, the processed data were down-sampled to 500Hz and then bandpass filtered between 1 and 100Hz. The number of ICA components that were removed from the original 19 IC was no greater than 20% in each participant. Finally, the data were re-referenced to an average of both earlobes' electrodes (A1 and A2).

2.6. ICA Technique to Remove TMS-Related Artifacts

The ICA method was applied to remove TMS-related artifacts, which can separate statistically independent sources from a mixed signal. ICA is ideally suited to separate the electrical artifacts from physiological data in the EEG recordings and this technique has already been successfully applied to remove other non-neurophysiological EEG artifacts in previous studies [33–36]. Residual TMS artifacts such as eye-blinks and some muscle activity contractions were identified and removed with ICA as implemented in EEGLAB [29]. Two rounds of ICAs were conducted on the EEG data according to the previous study [34]. TMS-related artifact components were identified based on the following characteristics. First, the power spectrum of ICs that shows an extremely strong power, above 50 µV, presumably due to muscle activity contractions. Second, the power spectrum of ICs that shows peaks at over 100Hz (e.g., mechanical-like shaped peaks), potentially due to muscle activities as well, and do not usually have a peak at around 10Hz (the α-band peak). A third criterion concerned the component activity as follows. If the TMS-related artifact is present, it is limited to the first 15 ms (~30 ms at most) after the TMS pulse with the TMS-compatible EEG system [16,36,37]. Therefore, ideally, the ICs reflecting the TMS-related decay artifacts should peak within a few milliseconds of the start of TMS pulse [34].

2.7. Data Analysis

First, the amplitudes of N100 TEP for each intensity from 10% to 90% MSO were analyzed to obtain the recruitment curve. Then, the event-locked analysis was conducted by averaging 100 times for each intensity to obtain TEPs. EEG powers at the stimulation site (F4 site for the recruitment curve experiment and F3 site for the VFTs) were calculated before and after 1Hz-TMS during the resting-state. Here, since the time window after TMS stimulation was short (~500 ms), the event-related power was analyzed at an intensity close to the RMT (approximately 70% MSO intensity on average) of each patient from alpha (8–14Hz) to gamma (30–70Hz) bands considering a reliable margin. In other words, the spectral power of the delta and theta bands could not be calculated in the present analysis because of the narrow time window after TMS.

Next, the coherence analyses were conducted using the EEGLAB toolbox for both the baseline and after the TMS stimulation of each block. In the coherence analysis, the functional connectivity between the F4 and F3 electrode sites during the TMS was calculated to explore the neurophysiological and potential therapeutic mechanism for depression, since 1Hz-rTMS over the right DLPFC is often applied for this disorder as therapeutic neuromodulation. Specifically, the average coherence values in the alpha (8–14Hz), beta (15–30Hz), and gamma (30–50Hz) bands between the F4–F3 electrodes in the RMT of each subject were calculated.

2.8. Statistical Analysis

A one-way repeated measure analysis of variance (ANOVA) with time was performed using SPSS Statistics 19 (IBM, Armonk, NY, USA) for the changes in power and coherence before and after TMS according to each frequency band. Of note, Bonferroni correction was applied in this study and thus the significance level α was set to 0.0083 (=0.05/6: three frequency bands by two VFTs).

3. Results

3.1. Recruitment Curve of TEPs

The mean RMT in this study was 68 $\pm$ 11%. TMS-evoked potentials from the F4 electrode site during the resting-state were calculated and the recruitment (input–output) curve was created (Figure 1). The input–output (I–O) curve increased nonlinearly with intensity, reaching a plateau at approximately 80% MSO intensity in the present study of healthy participants.

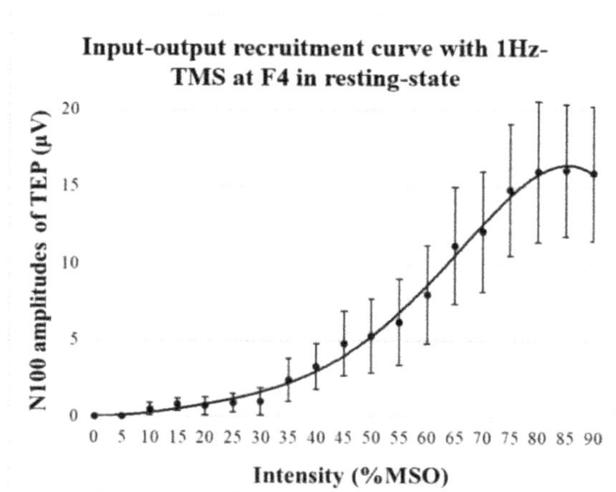

Figure 1. Recruitment curve of N100 component of TMS-evoked potentials (TEPs) at the stimulation site. The graph shows the recruitment curve at the F4 electrode site where 1Hz-TMS was administered. It shows that the input-output (I-O) curve increases nonlinearly with intensity and plateaus at an intensity of 80% maximum stimulus output (MSO).

3.2. TMS-Related Power Changes at the F4 Electrode Site

3.2.1. Results in Resting-State

One-way ANOVA with time before and after the TMS for each frequency band indicated the following results. The spectral power at the F4 site indicated 10.2% increase in alpha band ($F_{1,20}$ = 132.4, $p < 0.0001$), 2.2% increase in beta band ($F_{1,20}$ = 1824.7, $p < 0.0001$), and 51% increase in gamma band ($F_{1,20}$ = 1028.5, $p < 0.0001$) after 100 times 1Hz-TMS to the right DLPFC (F4 electrode site). Figure 2 shows the results of EEG power changes at F4 electrode site induced by 1Hz-TMS (100 pulses/block).

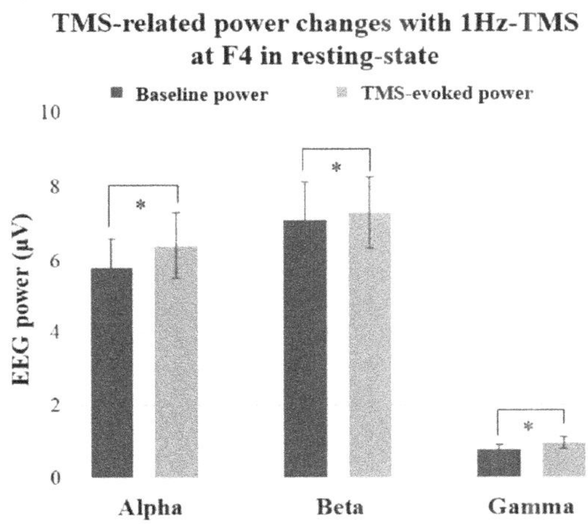

Figure 2. TMS-related power changes at F3 in the resting-state. The spectral power changes at the F4 electrode site after 100 pulses of 1Hz-TMS to the right dorsolateral prefrontal cortex (DLPFC) showed 10.2% increase in the alpha band ($F_{1,20}$ = 132.4, $p < 0.0001$), 2.2% increase in the beta band ($F_{1,20}$ = 1824.7, $p < 0.0001$), and 51% increase in the gamma band ($F_{1,20}$ = 1028.5, $p < 0.0001$). *: significant findings ($p < 0.0083$).

3.2.2. Results during VFTs

One-way ANOVA with time for each band demonstrated significant power changes in alpha band during the VFT-1 ($F_{1,20}$ = 54.0, $p < 0.0001$) as well as VFT-2 ($F_{1,20}$ = 76.7, $p < 0.0001$) by 1Hz-TMS (100 pulses/block) over the left DLPFC (F3 electrode site). Further, the ANOVA also indicated significant power changes by 1Hz-TMS (100 pulses/block) in beta band during the VFT-1 ($F_{1,20}$ = 20.8, p = 0.0001) as well as VFT-2 ($F_{1,20}$ = 13.0, p = 0.004). However, no significant changes were observed in gamma band during VFT-1 ($F_{1,20}$ = 0.039, p = 0.847) or VFT-2 ($F_{1,20}$ = 0.369, p = 0.555). Furthermore, no significant difference was found between TMS-related power in each frequency band during VFT-1 and VFT-2 administrations. Figure 3 shows the results of TMS-related power changes at F3 electrode site during the resting-state and VFTs.

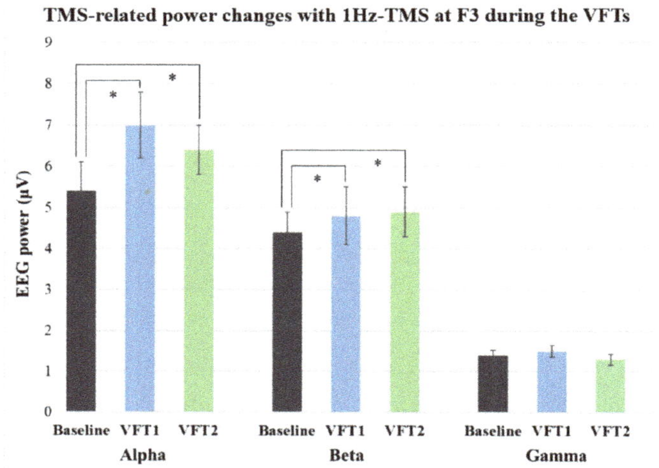

Figure 3. TMS-related power changes during the verbal fluency tasks (VFTs). One-way ANOVA with time for each band demonstrated significant power changes with 1Hz-TMS administered to the left DLPFC in alpha band during the VFT-1 ($F_{1,20} = 53.96$, $p < 0.0001$) as well as during the VFT-2 ($F_{1,20} = 76.68$, $p < 0.0001$). Furthermore, the ANOVA indicated significant power changes with 1Hz-TMS for the left DLPFC in beta band during the VFT-1 ($F_{1,20} = 20.79$, $p = 0.0001$) as well as during the VFT-2 ($F_{1,20} = 13.00$, $p = 0.004$). However, no significant changes were observed in gamma power during the VFT-1 or VFT-2. *: significant findings ($p < 0.0083$).

3.3. *TMS-Related Coherence Changes between F4 and F3 Electrode Sites*

3.3.1. Results in Resting-State

Figure 4 shows the coherence-frequency curves and coherence changes induced by 1Hz-TMS applied to the right DLPFC (F4 electrode site).

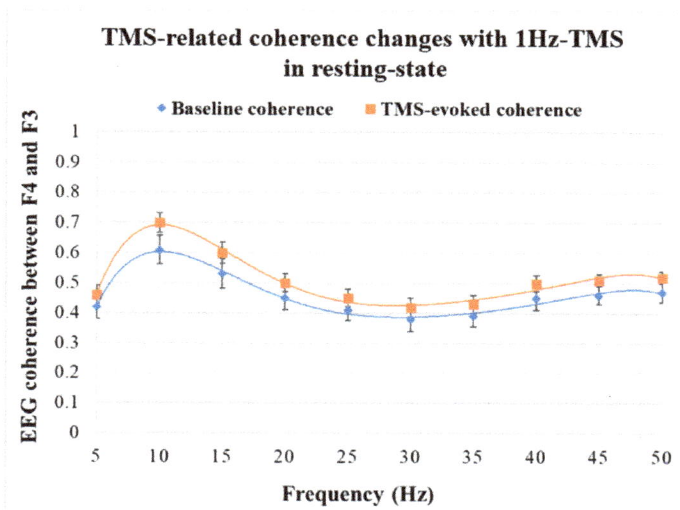

Figure 4. TMS-related coherence changes between F4 and F3 with 1Hz-TMS in resting-state.

Figure 4 depicts the EEG coherence-frequency curves before and after 1Hz-TMS stimulation. In this experiment, TMS was applied to the right DLPFC (i.e., F4 electrode site) and the coherences between F4 and F3 electrodes was calculated.

One-way ANOVA with time for each band revealed significant coherence changes in alpha ($F_{1,20} = 78.8$, $p < 0.0001$), and beta band ($F_{1,20} = 26.2$, $p < 0.0001$). However, the ANOVA did not show a significant coherence change in gamma band ($F_{1,20} = 11.6$, $p = 0.003$). The descriptive data showed a significant increase in alpha and beta coherences and an increasing trend in gamma coherence. Figure 5 shows the results of TMS-related coherence changes between F4 and F3 electrode sites with 1Hz-TMS that applied to the right DLPFC (i.e., F4 electrode site) in the resting-state.

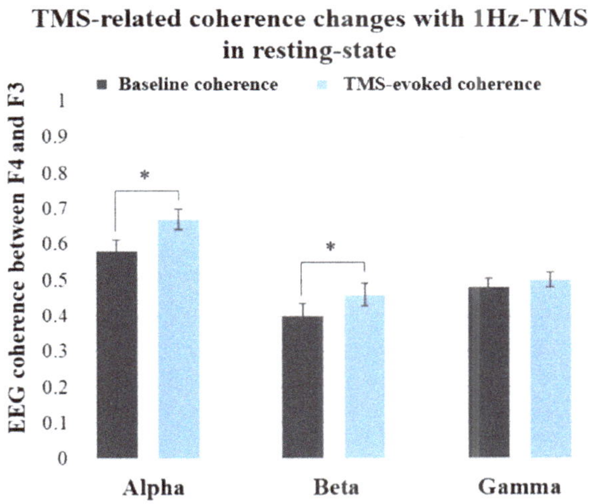

Figure 5. TMS-related coherence changes in the resting-state. The ANOVA showed significant changes of coherence in alpha band ($F_{1,20} = 78.8$, $p < 0.0001$) and beta band ($F_{1,20} = 26.2$, $p < 0.0001$) but not in gamma band ($F_{1,20} = 11.6$, $p = 0.003$) in resting-state. *: significant findings ($p < 0.0083$).

3.3.2. Results during VFTs

A one-way ANOVA with time showed no significant coherence changes by 1Hz-TMS for the left DLPFC (F3 electrode site) in all frequency bands as follows: coherence changes in alpha band (Baseline vs. VFT-1: $F_{1,20} = 3.16$, $p = 0.101$; Baseline vs. VFT-2: $F_{1,20} = 1.41$, $p = 0.26$); beta band (Baseline vs. VFT-1: $F_{1,20} = 3.73$, $p = 0.077$; Baseline vs. VFT-2: $F_{1,20} = 1.69$, $p = 0.22$), gamma band (Baseline vs. VFT-1: $F_{1,20} = 3.23$, $p = 0.098$; Baseline vs. VFT-2: $F_{1,20} = 0.50$, $p = 0.49$). Furthermore, there were no significant coherence changes between VFT-1 and VFT-2 in each frequency band. Figure 6 shows coherence changes induced by 1Hz-TMS over the left DLPFC during the VFTs for each frequency band.

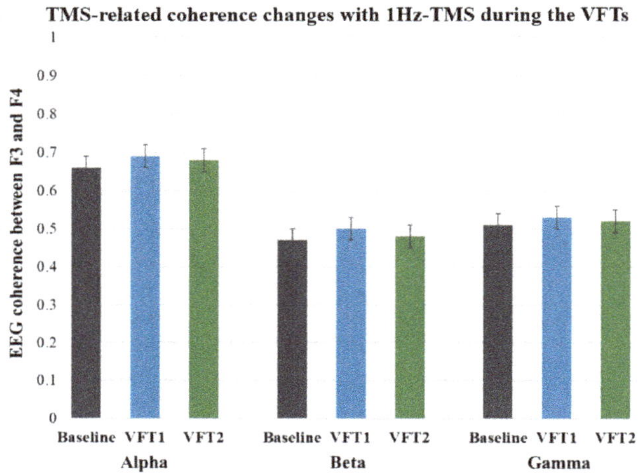

Figure 6. TMS-related coherence changes during the VFTs. The ANOVA showed no significant changes in coherence for all frequency bands during the VFT-1 (alpha: $F_{1,20} = 3.16$, $p = 0.101$; beta: $F_{1,20} = 3.73$, $p = 0.077$; gamma: $F_{1,20} = 3.23$, $p = 0.098$) or VFT-2 (alpha: $F_{1,20} = 1.41$, $p = 0.258$; beta: $F_{1,20} = 1.69$, $p = 0.217$; gamma: $F_{1,20} = 0.497$, $p = 0.494$).

4. Discussion

In the present study, the neurophysiological effects of 1Hz-TMS administered to the right DLPFC were investigated in healthy participants. First, the recruitment curve of N100 component of TEPs by 1Hz-right DLPFC stimulation showed sigmoidal nonlinear changes. Second, 1Hz-TMS to the right DLPFC in the resting-state transiently and significantly increased the TEPs in the alpha, beta, and gamma bands at the stimulation site. Third, 1Hz-TMS to the left DLPFC during VFT was found to increase the TMS-evoked EEG powers transiently and significantly in the alpha and beta bands at the stimulation site. Fourth, 1Hz-TMS to the right DLPFC in the resting-state was found to increase the alpha and beta band coherences transiently and significantly between the right and left DLPFC with TMS stimulation. Fifth, 1Hz-TMS to the left DLPFC during VFTs did not show any specific coherence changes between the left and right DLPFC with TMS stimulation.

4.1. Recruitment Curve of TEPs

The recruitment curve obtained in the present experiment changed nonlinearly with stimulus intensity, and the change plateaued at 80% MSO. This result is a positive finding suggesting that the responsivity in TEP detects neurobiological responses rather than artificial changes caused by TMS stimulation.

4.2. TMS-Related Power Changes

In previous studies, Valiulis et al. reported that the right prefrontal 1Hz-rTMS induced significant increases of EEG power in alpha, theta, and beta bands in the patients with depression [38], while Noda et al. demonstrated that the left prefrontal 20Hz-rTMS induced a significant increase of EEG gamma power in patients with depression at the stimulation site, which was also associated with an improvement in depressive symptoms [39]. Thus, it may be possible that increases of EEG power in alpha, beta, and gamma bands might reflect the therapeutic mechanism of rTMS for depression regardless of the left or right side of the DLPFC stimulation.

On the other hand, previous studies that examined EEG changes induced by verbal cognitive tasks have shown that alpha power increases in a wide range of brain regions [40], and alpha and beta power increases in the frontal and occipital regions [41]. In the present study, 1Hz-TMS (100 pulses/block) to the left DLPFC during VFTs significantly increased alpha- and beta-band powers, suggesting that TMS stimulation with this protocol does not have a particularly antagonistic interference effect on EEG power changes induced by VFT per se, but may have a synergistic effect. However, in this study, EEG changes due to the VFT itself were not measured as a control condition, and thus further research is needed.

Besides, previous studies that evaluated EEG power changes immediately after high-frequency rTMS to the left M1 of healthy subjects have shown increases in alpha and beta powers in the prefrontal cortex [10,42]. Thus, TMS stimulation of the cortex may induce ubiquitous alpha, beta, and, possibly, gamma-band power changes, independent of the stimulation site. However, Rosanova et al. have also shown that natural frequency responses were observed in the cortex depending on the stimulation site [43], thus further research is needed.

In addition, although the physiological role of gamma-band activity is still not fully understood, previous studies have reported that the generation of gamma-band activity, which is involved in cognitive processes and information processing, is impaired in neuropsychiatric disorders such as schizophrenia and Alzheimer's disease [44–46]. In this context, the present transient increase in gamma power by 1Hz-TMS to the right DLPFC may indicate a physiological mechanism that contributes to cognitive enhancement in healthy subjects and procognitive effects in patients with psychiatric disorders, including depression [47].

4.3. TMS-Related Coherence Changes

In the present study, alpha and beta coherences were significantly increased with 1Hz-TMS between both DLPFCs (the F4 and F3 electrode sites) in the resting-state. However, gamma coherence was not significantly changed with 1Hz-TMS. In contrast, there were no significant coherence changes in all frequency bands during the VFTs.

Several studies have examined EEG alpha coherence in healthy subjects and reported that alpha coherence was directly involved in internal information processing and the mechanisms of attention and consciousness [48,49]. Furthermore, these studies have shown an association between the enhancement of these functions and increases in the frontal alpha coherence. These findings suggest that the significant increase in alpha coherence in the prefrontal cortex with 1Hz-rTMS for the right DLPFC may be related to the therapeutic mechanism of depression with TMS therapy.

Previous studies have reported that the frontal intra-hemispheric interdependence in beta band was significantly decreased in patients with depression [50] while the frontal inter-hemispheric coherence in all bands was significantly decreased in patients with depression during emotional face processing [51], compared with healthy controls. Therefore, the present finding that 1Hz-TMS to the right DLPFC significantly increased alpha and beta coherence, albeit transiently, may reflect part of the therapeutic mechanism of 1Hz-rTMS to the right DLPFC for depression. However, since the present study only evaluated the temporary aftereffects of a single session of TMS in healthy subjects, the longer-term neurophysiological effects of 1Hz-rTMS on the right DLPFC in patients with depression should be investigated in the future.

For gamma coherence, Li et al. reported that the global EEG gamma coherence in patients with depression was significantly higher than that of healthy controls during emotional face processing [52]. However, since no study has reported the gamma coherence differences between patients with depression and healthy controls in resting-state, further studies are awaited.

On the other hand, there was no significant change in coherence in the experiments combining VFT and TMS stimulation. It is possible that the combination of VFT and left prefrontal 1Hz-TMS did not produce significant changes in coherence because the effects of the two stimuli interfered with each other, since VFT or 1Hz-TMS stimulation itself has a distinct effect on increasing frontal coherence [53,54]. Further studies are needed to verify this finding by measuring the EEG in the VFT as a control condition.

4.4. Limitations

This study has several limitations. First, since the study subjects in this study were healthy subjects, there was a limitation in examining the treatment mechanism of depression itself. Second, since a sham coil was not used, it was not possible to establish a strict control condition. However, these limitations can be justified, as it is common practice to develop new therapies and explore their therapeutic mechanisms on healthy subjects first in an exploratory way as an open-label pilot study. Third, the analysis of regions of interest in this study was limited to the F3 and F4 electrode sites from the beginning, thus it was not possible to examine TMS-related effects in other areas. Finally, because this study examined aftereffects as acute effects after TMS stimulation, it was not possible to evaluate the long-term effects associated with the entire rTMS treatment for depression.

4.5. Conclusions

The present study demonstrated that low-frequency 1Hz TMS to the right DLPFC in healthy participants resulted in a significant increase in spectral power in the alpha and beta bands.

Likewise, 1Hz-TMS to the right DLPFC induced a significant increase in alpha and beta coherences between the right and left DLPFC in healthy participants. Collectively, these findings suggest parts of the therapeutic mechanisms of 1Hz-rTMS to the right DLPFC for depression. Lastly, the present study warrants future research that investigates the neurophysiological effects of various types of TMS treatment, providing unique and informative perspectives on the pathophysiology underlying neuropsychiatric disorders as represented by major depressive disorders and schizophrenia [55].

Funding: This research received no external funding.

Institutional Review Board Statement: The study was conducted according to the guidelines of the Declaration of Helsinki, and approved by the Ethics Committee of Kanagawa Psychiatric Center (protocol code: 2011-1; date of approval: 2011/1/27).

Informed Consent Statement: Informed consent was obtained from all subjects involved in the study.

Data Availability Statement: Data sharing not applicable. No new data were created or analyzed in this study. Data sharing is not applicable to this article.

Acknowledgments: I would like to express my gratitude to the staff of Miyuki Giken Co., Ltd. for their technical support of the TMS-EEG system and valuable advice on EEG analysis during my graduate school days, especially to Makoto Sawano, Atsushi Shirasawa, and Kenji Uehara. Further, I am grateful to Reza Zomorrodi for teaching me the basics of TMS-EEG analysis during my postdoctoral fellowship. Finally, I would like to thank all the people who willingly participated in this study as healthy volunteers, including many of my good friends, especially to Takashi Saeki and Yoshinori Mikami.

Conflicts of Interest: Y.N. has received a Grant-in-Aid for Young Scientists (KAKENHI) from the Japan Society for the Promotion of Science (JSPS), research grants from Japan Agency for Medical Research and Development (AMED), investigator-initiated clinical study grants from TEIJIN PHARMA LIMITED and Inter Reha Co., Ltd. Y.N. has also received research grants from Japan Health Foundation, Meiji Yasuda Mental Health Foundation, Mitsui Life Social Welfare Foundation, Takeda Science Foundation, SENSHIN Medical Research Foundation, Health Science Center Foundation, Mochida Memorial Foundation for Medical and Pharmaceutical Research, Taiju Life Social Welfare Foundation, and Daiichi Sankyo Scholarship Donation Program. Y.N. has received speaker's honoraria from Dainippon Sumitomo Pharma, MOCHIDA PHARMACEUTICAL CO., LTD., and Yoshitomiyakuhin Corporation within the past three years. Y.N. also receives equipment-in-kind support for an investigator-initiated study from Magventure Inc, Inter Reha Co., Ltd., Brainbox Ltd., and Miyuki Giken Co., Ltd.

References

1. George, M.S.; Lisanby, S.H.; Avery, D.; McDonald, W.M.; Durkalski, V.; Pavlicova, M.; Anderson, B.; Nahas, Z.; Bulow, P.; Zarkowski, P.; et al. Daily Left Prefrontal Transcranial Magnetic Stimulation Therapy for Major Depressive Disorder: A Sham-Controlled Randomized Trial. *Arch. Gen. Psychiatry* **2010**, *67*, 507–516. [CrossRef]
2. McDonald, W.M.; Durkalski, V.; Ball, E.R.; Holtzheimer, P.E.; Pavlicova, M.; Lisanby, S.H.; George, M.S. Improving the antidepressant efficacy of transcranial magnetic stimulation: Maximizing the number of stimulations and treatment location in treatment-resistant depression. *Depress. Anxiety* **2011**, *28*, 973–980. [CrossRef]
3. Pallanti, S.; Di Rollo, A.; Antonini, S.; Cauli, G.; Hollander, E.; Quercioli, L. Low-frequency rTMS over right dorsolateral prefrontal cortex in the treatment of resistant depression: Cognitive improvement is independent from clinical response, resting motor threshold is related to clinical response. *Neuropsychobiology* **2012**, *65*, 227–235. [CrossRef] [PubMed]
4. Li, C.T.; Wang, S.J.; Hirvonen, J.; Hsieh, J.C.; Bai, Y.M.; Hong, C.J.; Su, T.P. Antidepressant mechanism of add-on repetitive transcranial magnetic stimulation in medication-resistant depression using cerebral glucose metabolism. *J. Affect. Disord.* **2010**, *127*, 219–229. [CrossRef] [PubMed]
5. Pell, G.S.; Roth, Y.; Zangen, A. Modulation of cortical excitability induced by repetitive transcranial magnetic stimulation: Influence of timing and geometrical parameters and underlying mechanisms. *Prog. Neurobiol.* **2011**, *93*, 59–98. [CrossRef] [PubMed]
6. Fuggetta, G.; Noh, N.A. A neurophysiological insight into the potential link between transcranial magnetic stimulation, thalamocortical dysrhythmia and neuropsychiatric disorders. *Exp. Neurol.* **2013**, *245*, 87–95. [CrossRef]
7. Strens, L.H.; Oliviero, A.; Bloem, B.R.; Gerschlager, W.; Rothwell, J.C.; Brown, P. The effects of subthreshold 1Hz repetitive TMS on cortico-cortical and interhemispheric coherence. *Clin. Neurophysiol.* **2002**, *113*, 1279–1285. [CrossRef]
8. Oliviero, A.; Strens, L.H.; Di Lazzaro, V.; Tonali, P.A.; Brown, P. Persistent effects of high frequency repetitive TMS on the coupling between motor areas in the human. *Exp. Brain Res.* **2003**, *149*, 107–113. [CrossRef]
9. Chen, W.H.; Mima, T.; Siebner, H.R.; Oga, T.; Hara, H.; Satow, T.; Begum, T.; Nagamine, T.; Shibasaki, H. Low-frequency rTMS over lateral premotor cortex induces lasting changes in regional activation and functional coupling of cortical motor areas. *Clin. Neurophysiol.* **2003**, *114*, 1628–1637. [CrossRef]
10. Fuggetta, G.; Pavone, E.F.; Fiaschi, A.; Manganotti, P. Acute modulation of cortical oscillatory activities during short trains of high-frequency repetitive transcranial magnetic stimulation of the human motor cortex: A combined EEG and TMS study. *Hum. Brain Mapp.* **2008**, *29*, 1–13. [CrossRef]
11. Azila Noh, N.; Fuggetta, G. Human cortical theta reactivity to high-frequency repetitive transcranial magnetic stimulation. *Hum. Brain Mapp.* **2012**, *33*, 2224–2237. [CrossRef] [PubMed]
12. Jing, H.; Takigawa, M. Observation of EEG coherence after repetitive transcranial magnetic stimulation. *Clin. Neurophysiol.* **2000**, *111*, 1620–1631. [CrossRef]
13. Grimm, S.; Beck, J.; Schuepbach, D.; Hell, D.; Boesiger, P.; Bermpohl, F.; Niehaus, L.; Boeker, H.; Northoff, G. Imbalance between left and right dorsolateral prefrontal cortex in major depression is linked to negative emotional judgment: An fMRI study in severe major depressive disorder. *Biol. Psychiatry* **2008**, *63*, 369–376. [CrossRef] [PubMed]
14. Bajwa, S.; Bermpohl, F.; Rigonatti, S.P.; Pascual-Leone, A.; Paulo S Boggio, P.; Fregni, F. Impaired interhemispheric interactions in patients with major depression. *J. Nerv. Ment. Dis.* **2008**, *196*, 671–677. [CrossRef] [PubMed]
15. Hecht, D. Depression and the hyperactive right-hemisphere. *Neurosci. Res.* **2010**, *68*, 77–87. [CrossRef] [PubMed]
16. Virtanen, J.; Ruohonen, J.; Näätänen, R.; Ilmoniemi, R.J. Instrumentation for the measurement of electric brain responses to transcranial magnetic stimulation. *Med. Biol. Eng. Comput.* **1999**, *37*, 322–326. [CrossRef] [PubMed]
17. Thut, G.; Ives, J.R.; Kampmann, F.; Pastor, M.A.; Pascual-Leone, A. A new device and protocol for combining TMS and online recordings of EEG and evoked potentials. *J. Neurosci. Methods* **2005**, *141*, 207–217. [CrossRef]
18. Bonato, C.; Miniussi, C.; Rossini, P.M. Transcranial magnetic stimulation and cortical evoked potentials: A TMS/EEG co-registration study. *Clin. Neurophysiol.* **2006**, *117*, 1699–1707. [CrossRef]
19. Komssi, S.; Kahkonen, S. The novelty value of the combined use of electroencephalography and transcranial magnetic stimulation for neuroscience research. *Brain Res. Rev.* **2006**, *52*, 183–192. [CrossRef]
20. Veniero, D.; Bortoletto, M.; Miniussi, C. TMS-EEG co-registration: On TMS-induced artifact. *Clin. Neurophysiol.* **2009**, *120*, 1392–1399. [CrossRef]
21. Ilmoniemi, R.J.; Kicic, D. Methodology for combined TMS and EEG. *Brain Topogr.* **2010**, *22*, 233–248. [CrossRef] [PubMed]
22. Chaieb, L.; Paulus, W.; Antal, A. Evaluating aftereffects of short-duration transcranial random noise stimulation on cortical excitability. *Neural. Plast* **2011**, *2011*, 105927. [CrossRef] [PubMed]
23. Thut, G.; Pascual-Leone, A. A review of combined TMS-EEG studies to characterize lasting effects of repetitive TMS and assess their usefulness in cognitive and clinical neuroscience. *Brain Topogr.* **2010**, *22*, 219–232. [CrossRef] [PubMed]
24. George, M.S.; Ketter, T.A.; Parekh, P.I.; Horwitz, B.; Herscovitch, P.; Post, R.M. Brain activity during transient sadness and happiness in healthy women. *Am. J. Psychiatry* **1995**, *152*, 341–351. [PubMed]
25. Liotti, M.; Mayberg, H.S.; Brannan, S.K.; McGinnis, S.; Jerabek, P.; Fox, P.T. Differential limbic–cortical correlates of sadness and anxiety in healthy subjects: Implications for affective disorders. *Biol. Psychiatry* **2000**, *48*, 30–42. [CrossRef]

26. Sheehan, D.V.; Lecrubier, Y.; Sheehan, K.H.; Amorim, P.; Janavs, J.; Weiller, E.; Hergueta, T.; Baker, R.; Dunbar, G.C. The Mini-International Neuropsychiatric Interview (M.I.N.I.): The development and validation of a structured diagnostic psychiatric interview for DSM-IV and ICD-10. *J. Clin. Psychiatry* **1998**, *59* (Suppl. 20), 224–231.
27. Otsubo, T.; Tanaka, K.; Koda, R.; Shinoda, J.; Sano, N.; Tanaka, S.; Aoyama, H.; Mimura, M.; Kamijima, K. Reliability and validity of Japanese version of the Mini-International Neuropsychiatric Interview. *Psychiatry Clin. Neurosci.* **2005**, *59*, 517–526. [CrossRef]
28. Rossini, P.M.; Barker, A.T.; Berardelli, A.; Caramia, M.D.; Caruso, G.; Cracco, R.Q.; Dimitrijević, M.R.; Hallett, M.; Katayama, Y.; Lücking, C.H.; et al. Non-invasive electrical and magnetic stimulation of the brain, spinal cord and roots: Basic principles and procedures for routine clinical application. *Electroencephalogr. Clin. Neurophysiol.* **1994**, *91*, 79–92. [CrossRef]
29. Delorme, A.; Makeig, S. EEGLAB: An open source toolbox for analysis of single-trial EEG dynamics including independent component analysis. *J. Neurosci. Methods* **2004**, *134*, 9–21. [CrossRef]
30. Noda, Y.; Cash, R.F.H.; Zomorrodi, R.; Garcia Dominguez, L.; Farzan, F.; Rajji, T.K.; Barr, M.S.; Chen, R.; Daskalakis, Z.J.; Blumberger, D.M. A combined TMS-EEG study of short-latency afferent inhibition in the motor and dorsolateral prefrontal cortex. *J. Neurophysiol.* **2016**, *116*, 938–948. [CrossRef]
31. Cash, R.F.H.; Noda, Y.; Zomorrodi, R.; Radhu, N.; Farzan, F.; Rajji, T.K.; Fitzgerald, P.B.; Chen, R.; Daskalakis, Z.J.; Blumberger, D.M. Characterization of Glutamatergic and GABAA-Mediated Neurotransmission in Motor and Dorsolateral Prefrontal Cortex Using Paired-Pulse TMS-EEG. *Neuropsychopharmacology* **2017**, *42*, 502–511. [CrossRef] [PubMed]
32. Jung, T.P.; Makeig, S.; Humphries, C.; Lee, T.W.; McKeown, M.J.; Iragui, V.; Sejnowski, T.J. Removing electroencephalographic artifacts by blind source separation. *Psychophysiology* **2000**, *37*, 163–178. [CrossRef] [PubMed]
33. Crespo-Garcia, M.; Atienza, M.; Cantero, J.L. Muscle artifact removal from human sleep EEG by using independent component analysis. *Ann. Biomed. Eng.* **2008**, *36*, 467–475. [CrossRef] [PubMed]
34. Hamidi, M.; Slagter, H.A.; Tononi, G.; Postle, B.R. Brain responses evoked by high-frequency repetitive transcranial magnetic stimulation: An event-related potential study. *Brain Stimul.* **2010**, *3*, 2–14. [CrossRef]
35. Hernandez-Pavon, J.C.; Metsomaa, J.; Mutanen, T.; Stenroos, M.; Mäki, H.; Ilmoniemi, R.J.; Sarvas, J. Uncovering neural independent components from highly artifactual TMS-evoked EEG data. *J. Neurosci. Methods* **2012**, *209*, 144–157. [CrossRef]
36. Iwahashi, M.; Arimatsu, T.; Ueno, S.; Iramina, K. Differences in evoked EEG by transcranial magnetic stimulation at various stimulus points on the head. In Proceedings of the 2008 30th Annual International Conference of the IEEE Engineering in Medicine and Biology Society, Vancouver, BC, Canada, 20–25 August 2008; pp. 2570–2573.
37. Ilmoniemi, R.J.; Virtanen, J.; Ruohonen, J.; Karhu, J.; Aronen, H.J.; Näätänen, R.; Katila, T. Neuronal responses to magnetic stimulation reveal cortical reactivity and connectivity. *Neuroreport* **1997**, *8*, 3537–3540. [CrossRef]
38. Valiulis, V.; Gerulskis, G.; Dapšys, K.; Vištartaite, G.; Šiurkute, A.; Mačiulis, V. Electrophysiological differences between high and low frequency rTMS protocols in depression treatment. *Acta Neurobiol. Exp.* **2012**, *72*, 283–295.
39. Noda, Y.; Zomorrodi, R.; Saeki, T.; Rajji, T.K.; Blumberger, D.M.; Daskalakis, Z.J.; Nakamura, M. Resting-state EEG gamma power and theta-gamma coupling enhancement following high-frequency left dorsolateral prefrontal rTMS in patients with depression. *Clin. Neurophysiol.* **2017**, *128*, 424–432. [CrossRef]
40. Fink, A.; Neubauer, A.C. EEG alpha oscillations during the performance of verbal creativity tasks: Differential effects of sex and verbal intelligence. *Int. J. Psychophysiol.* **2006**, *62*, 46–53. [CrossRef]
41. Hwang, G.; Jacobs, J.; Geller, A.; Danker, J.; Sekuler, R.; Kahana, M.J. EEG correlates of verbal and nonverbal working memory. *Behav. Brain Funct.* **2005**, *1*, 20. [CrossRef]
42. Veniero, D.; Brignani, D.; Thut, G.; Miniussi, C. Alpha-generation as basic response-signature to transcranial magnetic stimulation (TMS) targeting the human resting motor cortex: A TMS/EEG co-registration study. *Psychophysiology* **2011**, *48*, 1381–1389. [CrossRef] [PubMed]
43. Rosanova, M.; Casali, A.; Bellina, V.; Resta, F.; Mariotti, M.; Massimini, M. Natural frequencies of human corticothalamic circuits. *J. Neurosci.* **2009**, *29*, 7679–7685. [CrossRef] [PubMed]
44. Uhlhaas, P.J.; Haenschel, C.; Nikolić, D.; Singer, W. The role of oscillations and synchrony in cortical networks and their putative relevance for the pathophysiology of schizophrenia. *Schizophr. Bull.* **2008**, *34*, 927–943. [CrossRef] [PubMed]
45. Uhlhaas, P.J.; Pipa, G.; Neuenschwander, S.; Wibral, M.; Singer, W. A new look at gamma? High- (>60Hz) gamma-band activity in cortical networks: Function, mechanisms and impairment. *Prog. Biophys. Mol. Biol.* **2011**, *105*, 14–28. [CrossRef] [PubMed]
46. Uhlhaas, P.J.; Singer, W. The development of neural synchrony and large-scale cortical networks during adolescence: Relevance for the pathophysiology of schizophrenia and neurodevelopmental hypothesis. *Schizophr. Bull.* **2011**, *37*, 514–523. [CrossRef] [PubMed]
47. Fitzgerald, P.J.; Watson, B.O. Gamma oscillations as a biomarker for major depression: An emerging topic. *Transl. Psychiatry* **2018**, *8*, 177. [CrossRef] [PubMed]
48. Palva, S.; Palva, J.M. New vistas for alpha-frequency band oscillations. *Trends. Neurosci.* **2007**, *30*, 150–158. [CrossRef] [PubMed]
49. Benedek, M. EEG alpha synchronization is related to top-down processing in convergent and divergent thinking. *Neuropsychologia* **2011**, *49*, 3505–3511. [CrossRef]
50. Sun, Y. Electroencephalographic differences between depressed and control subjects: An aspect of interdependence analysis. *Brain Res. Bull.* **2008**, *76*, 559–564. [CrossRef]
51. Wei, L. Brain functional connectivity in depression during emotion processing. *J. Biomed. Eng.* **2010**, *27*, 961–967.

52. Li, Y. Abnormal functional connectivity of EEG gamma band in patients with depression during emotional face processing. *Clin. Neurophysiol.* **2015**, *126*, 2078–2089. [CrossRef]
53. Harris, J.A.; Clifford, C.W.; Miniussi, C. The functional effect of transcranial magnetic stimulation: Signal suppression or neural noise generation? *J. Cogn. Neurosci.* **2008**, *20*, 734–740. [CrossRef] [PubMed]
54. Siebner, H.R. How does transcranial magnetic stimulation modify neuronal activity in the brain? *Implications for studies of cognition. Cortex* **2009**, *45*, 1035–1042. [PubMed]
55. Noda, Y. Toward the establishment of neurophysiological indicators for neuropsychiatric disorders using transcranial magnetic stimulation-evoked potentials: A systematic review. *Psychiatry Clin. Neurosci.* **2020**, *74*, 12–34. [CrossRef] [PubMed]

Journal of *Personalized Medicine*

MDPI

Article

Single-Pulse Transcranial Magnetic Stimulation-Evoked Potential Amplitudes and Latencies in the Motor and Dorsolateral Prefrontal Cortex among Young, Older Healthy Participants, and Schizophrenia Patients

Yoshihiro Noda [1,*], Mera S. Barr [2], Reza Zomorrodi [3], Robin F. H. Cash [4], Pantelis Lioumis [5], Robert Chen [6], Zafiris J. Daskalakis [7] and Daniel M. Blumberger [2,3,8]

1 Department of Neuropsychiatry, Graduate School of Medicine, Keio University School of Medicine, Tokyo 160-8582, Japan
2 Department of Psychiatry, University of Toronto, Toronto, ON M5T 1R8, Canada; mera.barr@gmail.com (M.S.B.); Daniel.Blumberger@camh.ca (D.M.B.)
3 Temerty Centre for Therapeutic Brain Intervention, Centre for Addiction and Mental Health, Toronto, ON M6J 1H4, Canada; Reza.Zomorrodi@camh.ca
4 Monash Alfred Psychiatry Research Centre, Monash University Central Clinical School and the Alfred, Melbourne 3004, Australia; robin.cash2@gmail.com
5 Department of Neuroscience and Biomedical Engineering, Aalto University School of Science, FI-00076 Espoo, Finland; plioumis@gmail.com
6 Division of Neurology, Department of Medicine, University of Toronto, Division of Brain, Imaging and Behaviour—Systems Neuroscience, Krembil Research Institute, University Health Network, Toronto, ON M5T 2S8, Canada; robert.chen@uhn.ca
7 Department of Psychiatry, UC San Diego Health, San Diego, CA 92093, USA; zdaskalakis@health.ucsd.edu
8 Campbell Family Mental Health Research Institute, Centre for Addiction and Mental Health, Toronto, ON M5T 1R8, Canada
* Correspondence: yoshi-tms@keio.jp; Tel.: +81-3-3353-1211 (ext. 61857)

Citation: Noda, Y.; Barr, M.S.; Zomorrodi, R.; Cash, R.F.H.; Lioumis, P.; Chen, R.; Daskalakis, Z.J.; Blumberger, D.M. Single-Pulse Transcranial Magnetic Stimulation-Evoked Potential Amplitudes and Latencies in the Motor and Dorsolateral Prefrontal Cortex among Young, Older Healthy Participants, and Schizophrenia Patients. *J. Pers. Med.* **2021**, *11*, 54. https://doi.org/10.3390/jpm11010054

Received: 19 December 2020
Accepted: 15 January 2021
Published: 17 January 2021

Abstract: Background: The combination of transcranial magnetic stimulation (TMS) with electroencephalography (EEG) allows for non-invasive investigation of cortical response and connectivity in human cortex. This study aimed to examine the amplitudes and latencies of each TMS-evoked potential (TEP) component induced by single-pulse TMS (spTMS) to the left motor (M1) and dorsolateral prefrontal cortex (DLPFC) among healthy young participants (YNG), older participants (OLD), and patients with schizophrenia (SCZ). Methods: We compared the spatiotemporal characteristics of TEPs induced by spTMS among the groups. Results: Compared to YNG, M1-spTMS induced lower amplitudes of N45 and P180 in OLD and a lower amplitude of P180 in SCZ, whereas the DLPFC-spTMS induced a lower N45 in OLD. Further, OLD demonstrated latency delays in P60 after M1-spTMS and in N45-P60 over the right central region after left DLPFC-spTMS, whereas SCZ demonstrated latency delays in N45-P60 over the midline and right central regions after DLPFC-spTMS. Conclusions: These findings suggest that inhibitory and excitatory mechanisms mediating TEPs may be altered in OLD and SCZ. The amplitude and latency changes of TEPs with spTMS may reflect underlying neurophysiological changes in OLD and SCZ, respectively. The spTMS administered to M1 and the DLPFC can probe cortical functions by examining TEPs. Thus, TMS-EEG can be used to study changes in cortical connectivity and signal propagation from healthy to pathological brains.

Keywords: TMS-EEG; TMS-evoked potentials; dorsolateral prefrontal cortex; motor cortex; schizophrenia

Highlights

- The single-pulse transcranial magnetic stimulation (TMS) (spTMS) allows probing and visualization of the spatiotemporal characteristics of each young (YNG), older (OLD), and schizophrenia (SCZ) group.

- Different TMS-evoked potential (TEP) characteristics induced by spTMS were observed in the OLD and SCZ compared with YNG.
- Specifically, changes in P30 and N45 deflections of TEPs by spTMS were important in classifying these groups across the motor cortex (M1) and dorsolateral prefrontal cortex (DLPFC).

1. Introduction

Electroencephalography (EEG) studies probed by transcranial magnetic stimulation (TMS) have become feasible since Ilmoniemi et al. initially developed the technology of the TMS-compatible EEG system [1]. One advantage of the TMS-EEG paradigm is that it allows for the investigation and mapping of cortical regions without the need to administer perception stimuli (e.g., visual, auditory, sensory stimuli) or specific cognitive tasks as in event-related potential studies. The TMS-EEG technique has been applied in several research labs worldwide mainly for healthy participants [2–8], and previous studies using TMS-EEG have demonstrated the typical pattern of TMS-evoked potentials (TEPs) and their topographical distribution [9–12]. Specifically, single-pulse TMS (spTMS) to the primary motor cortex (M1) as well as the dorsolateral prefrontal cortex (DLPFC) induces a well-characterized series of TEP components of P30, N45, P60, N100, and P180 [9,10,13], that are highly reproducible [10] and the amplitudes of these TEP components vary depending on the intensity of TMS [14,15]. Individual TEP components are thought to be mediated by distinct inhibitory and excitatory processes. Moreover, it has been reported that amplitudes of TEPs elicited by spTMS vary depending on the stimulated area [16], notable being reduced at the DLPFC compared to M1-spTMS [17,18].

A previous spTMS-EEG study investigated the topographical distribution pattern and amplitude power of TEPs after left superior frontal cortex stimulation between healthy young (YNG) and older (OLD) participants compared to patients with Alzheimer's disease [19]. The study demonstrated no significant difference in the topographical distribution of TEPs or amplitude power of early TEP components (N45 to N100) between healthy YNG and OLD participants. However, significantly smaller distribution area and power of the early TEPs were observed among patients with Alzheimer's disease compared to healthy young participants. The other spTMS-EEG studies examined spectrum power and time-frequency analyses of TEPs after premotor cortex stimulation between patients with schizophrenia (SCZ) and healthy participants, which demonstrated a significantly smaller early TEP power [20] and reduced amplitude of TMS-induced gamma oscillations and its effective connectivity [21] in patients with SCZ compared to the healthy participants.

In OLD adults as well as in patients with SCZ, it is known that atrophy of the cerebral cortex is associated with aging [22] or disease progression [23]. Further, age and neuropathological changes may contribute to decreased nerve conduction velocity [24–26]. Therefore, it is speculated that TEP responses by spTMS, especially in latency, may be reduced in these populations compared to younger healthy adults. Thus, it may be possible to probe these physiological and pathological alterations using spTMS-EEG [27].

To our knowledge, there are a limited number of studies [19–21,28] examining the spatiotemporal patterns of TEP components by spTMS in OLD adults and patients with SCZ compared to YNG adults, specifically investigating the TEPs with stimulation of the DLPFC, which is an area more directly associated with the changes that occur during healthy aging as well as the pathophysiology of SCZ [29,30]. It is therefore important to identify the neurophysiological profile of TEPs by spTMS among healthy and pathological brains to better understand the pathophysiology of neuropsychiatric disorders [31,32]. Based on the previous findings that showed reduced TEP amplitude with age [19–21,28], we hypothesized that the OLD group and SCZ group would have significantly lower amplitudes of TEPs and more delayed latencies of TEPs compared to those of the YNG group. Thus, we aimed to investigate the amplitudes and latencies of TEPs by spTMS to M1 as well as the DLPFC in an exploratory fashion from both the stimulated region (i.e., M1 and DLPFC) and other connected regions of interest (ROI: contralateral M1, DLPFC, and midline central area) among the groups (YNG, OLD, and SCZ).

2. Materials and Methods

2.1. Participants

Twelve right-handed YNG (6 female, mean age: 39 ± 12 yrs), 12 right-handed OLD (6 female, mean age: 72 ± 9 yrs), and 12 right-handed patients with SCZ (4 female, mean age: 41 ± 10 yrs) participated in this study. Participants of all groups were eligible to participate in this study if they met the following criteria: (i) between ages 18 and 59 for the YNG and SCZ, or ages above 60 for the OLD; (ii) no history of neurological disorders including seizure or stroke; (iii) no history of alcohol or other drug abuse/dependence; and (iv) not being a smoker.

In addition, the YNG and OLD also satisfied with the following criteria: (v) no history of neuropsychiatric disorders; (vi) normal cognitive function assessed by neurocognitive battery; (vii) no prescription medications; while patients with SCZ met the following criteria; (viii) not taking benzodiazepines and anticholinergics. All participants were screened with the Structured Clinical Interview for DSM–IV Axis I Disorders or the Mini-International Neuropsychiatric Interview prior to study participation. The present study was performed according to the Declaration of Helsinki and was reviewed and approved by the Research Ethics Board of the Centre for Addiction and Mental Health.

2.2. TMS Procedure

Monophasic TMS pulses were administered to the left M1 using a 70 mm figure-of-eight coil, and a Magstim 200 stimulator (Magstim Company Ltd., Whitland, UK). During the TMS testing, the participants sat in a chair with their eyes open, and their bodies relaxed throughout the study. First, the M1 hotspot site for the right first dorsal interosseous muscle to evoke the largest motor evoked potential (MEP) with the lowest intensity was determined. Second, the individual intensity to induce 1 mV peak-to-peak MEP amplitude of the same muscle was determined. The intensity to induce 1 mV peak-to-peak MEP amplitude was used for the spTMS in this study. At each stimulation site of M1 and DLPFC, 100 TMS pulses were applied per session, respectively. In addition, the stimulation site of the left DLPFC was identified using the EEG cap method. Specifically, the F5 electrode site was used as the target site of the left DLPFC according to our other studies (Noda et al., 2017a, Noda et al., 2017b).

2.3. EEG Recording and Pre-Processing

EEG was recorded through a 64-channel Neuroscan Synamps 2 with a TMS-compatible EEG cap (Compumedics Neuroscan, Victoria, Australia). Recording electrodes impedance was kept below 5 kΩ during the experiment. All electrodes were referenced to an electrode placed on the vertex. EEG signals were recorded at DC with a sampling rate of 20 kHz and then an online lowpass filter of 200 Hz was applied. EEG data were processed offline using the MATLAB software (R2014a, The MathWorks, Natick, MA, USA).

2.4. EEG Signal Processing

EEG signal processing was performed in accordance to already published methodology (Noda et al., 2016). All EEG data were epoched from −1000 ms to 2000 ms relative to the TMS pulse. Baseline correction was performed with respect to the pre-stimulus interval −500 ms to −110 ms. The epoched EEG data was re-segmented from 10 ms to 2000 ms post-TMS to limit the TMS-induced artifact. Then, EEG data were visually inspected to exclude trials and channels that were highly contaminated with noise. Subsequently, independent component analysis (ICA) was applied to minimize and remove the typical TMS-related decay artifacts as well as eye-related and muscle activity related components. Next, the Butterworth, zero-phase shift 1–55 Hz bandpass filter (24 dB/Oct) and notch filter were applied. Then, the processed data were downsampled to 1000 Hz. In each subject, the number of ICA components that were removed from the original 62 ICA components was no greater than 20%. Finally, data were re-referenced to the average reference for further analyses.

2.5. Single-Pulses TMS-Evoked Potential (TEP) Analyses

The TEP was analyzed individually focusing on the amplitude and latency of each TEP component (P30, N45, P60, N100, and P180) at the 5 ROIs (left frontal: AF3, F3, F5; right frontal: AF4, F4, F6; left central: C3, C5, CP5; right central: C4, C6, CP6; midline central: Fz, FCz, Cz; see Figure 1), which were obtained from M1-spTMS and DLPFC-spTMS experiments.

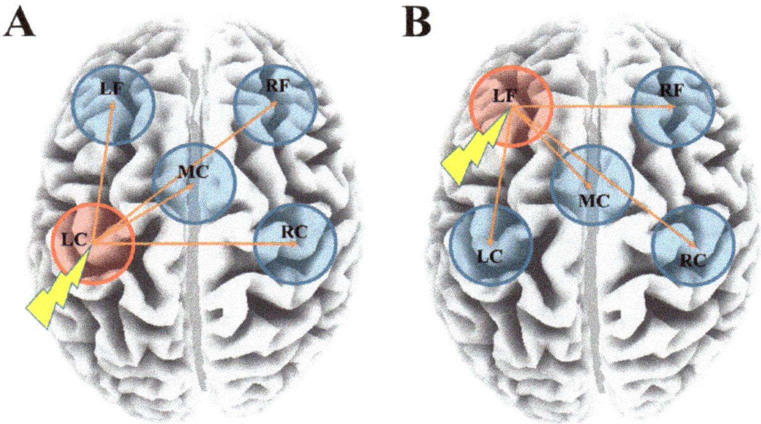

Figure 1. Schematic diagram of the transcranial magnetic stimulation (TMS) stimulation site and analysis site. (**A**) depicts single-pulse TMS (spTMS) administered to the left motor cortex (M1), while (**B**) shows spTMS applied to the left dorsolateral prefrontal cortex (DLPFC).

2.6. Statistical Analyses

The SPSS Statistics 19 (IBM, Armonk, New York, USA) was used for statistical analysis. In this study, normal distributions of the TEP data were confirmed with the Shapiro-Wilk test before performing the parametric statistical testing. For the analyses of TEP amplitudes, the analysis of variance (ANOVA) with TEP components (i.e., P30, N45, P60, N100, and P180) as a within-subject factor and groups (i.e., YNG, OLD, or SCZ) as a between-subject factor was applied for each M1-spTMS and the DLPFC-spTMS paradigm, separately. Here, we analyzed TEP data of M1-spTMS focusing on the left central (LC) ROI (i.e., left M1) while we analyzed TEP data of the DLPFC-spTMS focusing on the left frontal (LF) ROI (i.e., left DLPFC). When there was a significant interaction between the TEP component and group, post-hoc independent t-tests were applied to examine group differences of TEP amplitudes. Next, we conducted the multiple regression analysis with the group (i.e., YNG, OLD, or SCZ) as a dependent variable and the site of stimulation (i.e., M1 or DLPFC) and TEP component (i.e., P30, N45, P60, N100, and P180) as independent variables to explore the predictive factors to identify the groups using an enter method. In this regression analysis, we set a significant level of $\alpha = 0.05/10$ (site of stimulations*TEP components) with Bonferroni correction.

For the analyses of TEP latencies, one-way ANOVAs and post-hoc paired t-tests were applied to explore the group difference of each TEP component for the same ROIs. Further, within-group level, the differences of TEP latencies between the LC ROI (i.e., the stimulated region of M1-spTMS) and other ROIs for M1-spTMS as well as between the

LF ROI (i.e., the stimulated region of the DLPFC-spTMS) and other ROIs for the DLPFC-spTMS. A significant level of $\alpha = 0.05/25$ (site of ROIs*TEP components) with Bonferroni correction was applied here.

3. Results

3.1. TEP Amplitude Differences between the YNG, OLD, and SCZ Groups

With M1-spTMS, at the LC ROI (i.e., left M1), the ANOVA indicated a significant TEP-by-group interaction ($F_{8,132} = 4.504$, $p < 0.0001$). Subsequently, compared to the YNG group, post-hoc independent t-tests revealed that the OLD group had significantly lower amplitudes of N45 ($t_{22} = -2.872$, $p = 0.009$; amplitude N45 at the LC in YNG > amplitude N45 at the LC in OLD) and P180 ($t_{22} = 5.283$, $p < 0.0001$; amplitude P180 at the LC in YNG > amplitude P180 at the LC in OLD) TEPs, whereas the SCZ group had a significantly lower amplitude of P180 ($t_{22} = 4.394$, $p = 0.0002$; amplitude P180 at the LC in HC > amplitude P180 at the LC in SCZ). The results of TEPs after M1-spTMS are depicted in Figure 2A.

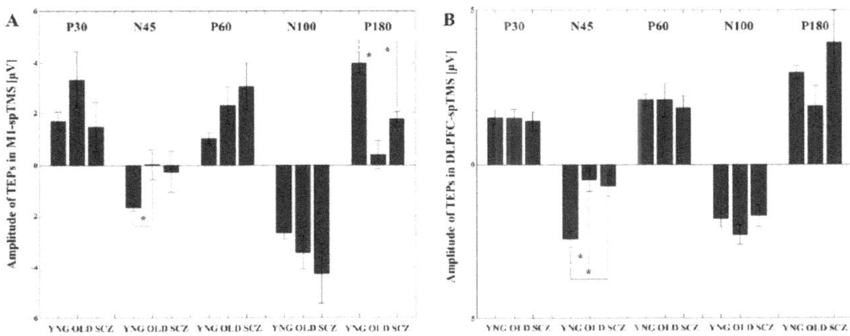

Figure 2. Amplitude differences for each TMS-evoked potential (TEP) component among healthy young (YNG), older (OLD), and patients with schizophrenia (SCZ) at the left central (LC) ROI (left M1). TEP amplitude differences among the groups at the left M1 induced by M1-spTMS were demonstrated in (**A**), while TEP amplitude differences among the groups over the left DLPFC induced by the DLPFC-spTMS are shown in (**B**). Compared to the YNG group, the OLD group had a significantly lower amplitude of the N45 TEP, while the OLD group and SCZ group had significantly lower amplitudes on the P180 TEP over the LC ROI (left M1) in M1-spTMS paradigm. In the DLPFC-spTMS, compared to the YNG group, the OLD group and SCZ group had significantly lower amplitudes on N45 TEP over the left frontal ROI (left DLPFC). * Significant differences.

On the other hand, at the LF ROI (i.e., left DLPFC) by the DLPFC-spTMS, the ANOVA showed a significant TEP-by-group interaction ($F_{8,132} = 2.599$, $p = 0.011$). Post-hoc independent t-tests indicated that the OLD group had a significantly lower amplitude of N45 ($t_{22} = -4.200$, $p = 0.0004$; amplitude N45 at the LF in YNG > amplitude N45 at the LF in OLD), while the SCZ group also had a significantly lower amplitude of N45 ($t_{22} = -4.047$, $p = 0.001$; amplitude N45 at the LF in HC > amplitude N45 at the LF in SCZ), compared to the YNG group. The results of TEPs by the DLPFC-spTMS are described in Figure 2B.

Regarding P30 and N100 TEP amplitudes, no significant differences were observed among the three groups both in M1-spTMS or DLPFC-spTMS paradigm

Representative TEP waveforms from the left DLPFC obtained by spTMS for the YNG, OLD, and SCZ groups in this study are shown in the Supplementary Figure S1.

3.2. Predictive Factors to Classify the Groups Based on the Multiple Regression Analysis

The multiple regression analysis revealed that P30 and N45 components were significant factors (P30: $\beta = -0.410$, $p = 0.004$; N45: $\beta = 6.22$, $p < 0.001$; F6, 65 = 4.825, adjusted $R^2 = 0.244$) to identify the difference between these groups.

3.3. Latency Differences for Each TEP between the YNG, OLD, and SCZ Groups

With M1-spTMS, when we compared each TEP latency over all 5 ROIs between the YNG and OLD groups, the OLD group had a significantly longer P60 latency ($t_{22} = -4.275$, $p = 0.0003$; latency P60 at the LC in YNG < latency P60 at the LC in OLD) over the LC ROI compared to the YNG group (see Figure 3A).

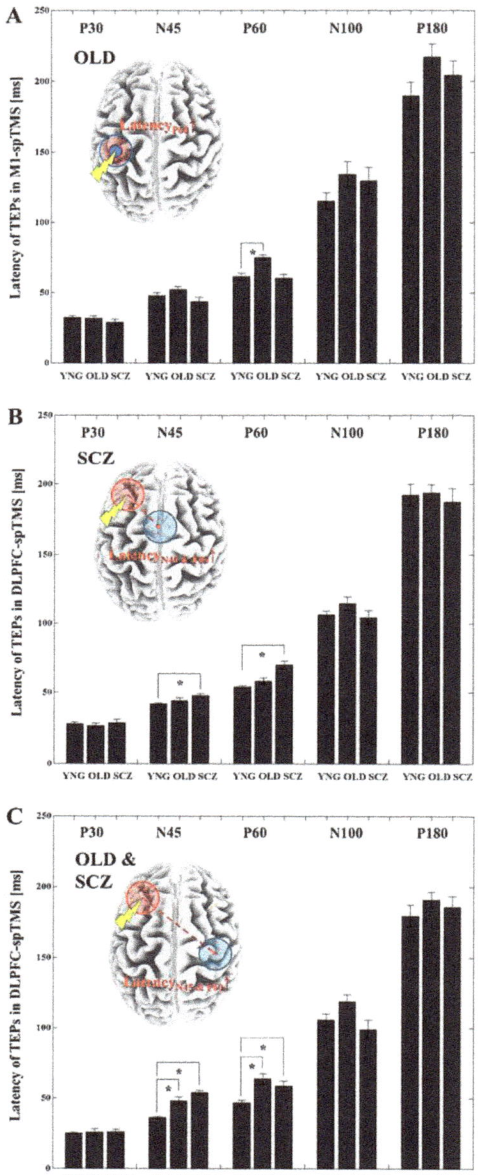

Figure 3. Latency differences for each TEP component among healthy young (YNG) participants, older (OLD) participants, and patients with schizophrenia (SCZ). TEP latency differences among groups at the LC ROI (left M1) induced by M1-spTMS

were demonstrated in (**A**), while TEP latency differences among the groups induced by the DLPFC-spTMS are shown in (**B**) (over the midline central ROI) and (**C**) (over the right central ROI). In M1-spTMS, compared to the YNG group, the OLD group showed a significantly longer latency of the N45 TEP over the left M1 in M1-spTMS paradigm, whereas in the DLPFC-spTMS, the SCZ group showed significantly longer latencies of the N45 and P60 TEPs over the midline central ROI. Furthermore, after DLPFC-spTMS, the OLD group and SCZ group demonstrated significantly longer latencies of N45 and P60 TEPs over the right M1. In (**A**–**C**), a schematic diagram of a group showing significant findings is shown in the box. * Significant differences.

Likewise, when we looked at the DLPFC-spTMS paradigm, the OLD group showed significantly longer N45 ($t_{22} = -4.255$, $p = 0.0003$) and P60 ($t_{22} = -4.033$, $p = 0.0006$) TEP latencies (latencies N45-P60 at the RC in YNG < latencies N45-P60 at the RC in OLD) from the right central ROI compared to the YNG group. The SCZ group indicated significantly longer N45 ($t_{22} = -3.622$, $p = 0.0015$) and P60 ($t_{22} = -5.095$, $p < 0.0001$) TEP latencies (latencies N45-P60 at the MC in HC < latencies N45-P60 at the MC in SCZ) at the midline central ROI (Figure 3B) as well as longer N45 (t22 = −9.207, $p < 0.0001$) and P60 (P60: $t_{22} = -2.945$, $p = 0.007$) TEP latencies (latencies N45-P60 at the RC in HC < latency N45-P60 at the RC in SCZ) at the right central ROI (Figure 3C). For P30 and N100 TEP latencies, there were no significant differences among groups both in M1-spTMS or DLPFC-spTMS paradigm.

3.4. Latency Differences between the Stimulated ROI and Other ROIs within the YNG, OLD, and SCZ Groups

With M1-spTMS, there was no significant latency difference between the LC ROI (i.e., left M1) and other ROIs within groups. After DLPFC-spTMS, there was no significant difference in latencies between the LF ROI (i.e., left DLPFC) and other ROIs within the YNG or OLD group. However, within the SCZ group, there was a significant latency difference on N45 ($t_{11} = -4.326$, $p = 0.0012$; latency N45 at the LF in SCZ < latency N45 at the RC in SCZ) between the LF (i.e., left DLPFC) and right central ROIs (i.e., right M1), showing that the latency of N45 was significantly longer from the right central ROI compared to that of the left DLPFC (see Figure 4).

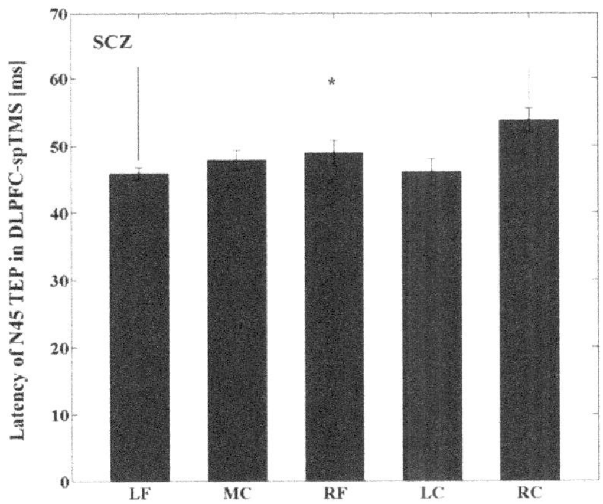

Figure 4. Latency differences between the left DLPFC and other ROIs within a schizophrenia (SCZ) group in the DLPFC-spTMS paradigm. There were no significant TEP latency differences between the left DLPFC and other ROIs within the young (YNG) and older (OLD) groups. However, within the SCZ group, the latency of N45 TEP was significantly longer over the right M1 compared to the left DLPFC. * Significant differences.

4. Discussion

The present study demonstrated unique spatiotemporal profiles of TEPs induced by spTMS of M1 and DLPFC. First, the OLD group demonstrated an attenuated response in the amplitude of N45 after M1-spTMS, which is in line with previous studies showing that there was a TEP amplitude reduction with age in healthy subjects [21,28], compared to the YNG group. Further, both the OLD and SCZ groups had attenuated responses in the amplitude of P180 after M1-spTMS, which is, at least in part, consistent with a previous study showing that SCZ had reduced spTMS-evoked gamma oscillations [21], as well as the amplitude of N45 by the DLPFC-spTMS, compared to those of the YNG group. Second, the OLD group showed a delayed response in the latency of P60 at the stimulated ROI after M1-spTMS compared to the YNG group. The SCZ group demonstrated a delayed response in the latency of N45 over the right central ROI within-subjects level as well as delayed responses in the latency of N45-P60 at the midline central ROI between-subjects level by the DLPFC-spTMS. In addition, the OLD and SCZ groups demonstrated a delayed response in the latency of N45-P60 over the right central ROI after DLPFC-spTMS compared to the YNG group.

To date, the origin and mechanisms of N45 and P180 have not been fully elucidated. However, previous studies demonstrated that N45 may be associated with gamma-aminobutyric acid receptor A ($GABA_A$) mediated inhibition [7,33–35]. In the healthy YNG group, the amplitude of N45 component was relatively increased consistently across M1 and DLPFC by spTMS in our study (Figure 2). In contrast, P180 has been proposed to relate either to a late excitatory potential or cortical disinhibition. The latter interpretation may be more consistent with the GABAergic deficits shown in both aging and SCZ [29,30]. Thus, it seems that N45 may represent $GABA_A$ergic inhibitory function and P180 may reflect more $GABA_A$ergic disinhibition rather than just an excitatory potential itself.

In addition, several lines of evidence have shown that $GABA_A$ receptor-mediated inhibition in M1 as indexed by motor-evoked potentials decreases with age [36–38]. Further, magnetic resonance spectroscopic (MRS) studies have demonstrated that OLD participants have a significantly lower level of GABA compared to the young participants [39,40]. Therefore, these MRS findings appear at least partially consistent with TMS neurophysiological studies in OLD participants [29].

On the other hand, in patients with SCZ, GABAergic deficit is supported by neuropathological findings that demonstrate substantial reductions in GABAergic interneurons, GABA-synthesizing enzyme glutamic acid decarboxylase, and GABA-related gene expression in the cortex [41–46]. Further, there are several lines of evidence that patients with SCZ had reduced $GABA_A$ receptor-mediated inhibition [30,47,48] compared to healthy YNG group.

Again, as shown in Figure 2A, the amplitude of N45 component of spTMS was smaller in the OLD group and SCZ group (especially significantly lower in the OLD group) than in the YNG group, suggesting a relative decrease in $GABA_A$ receptor-mediated neurophysiological function. Thus, the decline in inhibitory neurophysiological function due to age-related changes as well as the pathophysiology of schizophrenia may affect the impairment of coordinated motor skills among motor control [49].

In addition, the multiple regression analysis demonstrated that P30 and N45 components are the significant factors to classify the groups. Interestingly, since P30 and N45 TEP components are supposed to be generated by $GABA_A$ receptor-mediated function [7,11,35,50], it is likely that $GABA_A$ergic inhibition in the cortex is essential to maintain normal brain function.

Moreover, in terms of the response of TEP latencies after spTMS, since N45 and P60 are thought to be linked to $GABA_A$ and $GABA_B$ receptor-mediated functions as well as its excitatory function, respectively [13,35], our finding of delayed response of P60 latency at the LC ROI by M1-spTMS in the OLD group may be related to the $GABA_B$ergic inhibitory and/or its excitatory dysfunctions due to aging [39,40], whereas the findings of delayed responses of N45 and P60 latencies at the midline central and right central ROIs after DLPFC-spTMS in the SCZ group may be associated with $GABA_A$ (i.e., N45) and $GABA_B$ (i.e., P60) receptor-mediated inhibitory and/or its excitatory (i.e., P60) dysfunctions [13,35]. Thus, these results might reflect conduction delays in both inhibitory and excitatory circuits, and that together these delayed responses of N45 and P60 might contribute to disrupted network connectivity in SCZ. Specifically, recent studies also suggest that a latency of P60 may be a correlate of neuronal excitability in M1 [13] and the DLPFC [51,52]. This reflects a larger distribution of cortical areas possibly due to more widespread neuropathological involvement related to the illness [43–46]. Indeed, we observed significantly delayed responses of N45-P60 latencies over the right central ROI even in the OLD group. However, the SCZ group demonstrated abnormal TEP latencies across short cortical distances compared to the OLD group (Figure 3), which may represent greater GABAergic inhibition deficits in the SCZ group.

Further, only the SCZ group showed a significantly delayed response of N45 latency over the right central ROI after DLPFC-spTMS. This finding may indicate more widespread $GABA_A$ergic inhibitory dysfunction possibly due to the functional disconnection between the left DLPFC and right central ROI in the SCZ [53]. Consistent with this contention, a previous functional magnetic resonance imaging study in SCZ demonstrated the functional hypoconnectivity in the somatomotor network [53], which may support our above finding of the delayed response of N45 in the SCZ group.

There are some limitations in the present study. First, the number of participants for each group was relatively small, although comparable to that of many previous TMS studies [7,35]. Thus, the findings warrant further research with larger sample sizes. Second, since we did not apply the auditory masking system during the experiments, the effect of auditory evoked potentials due to the conduction of the TMS click sounds on TEPs cannot be completely excluded [54]. Therefore, for future TMS-EEG studies, auditory white noise should be used during TMS stimulation as masking of the TMS click sound. Third, since patients with schizophrenia took medications when they participated in this study, there may be some medication effects on TEPs. Therefore, it would be necessary to more strictly control the influence of medications in the future study.

5. Conclusions

The present study demonstrated that TEP responses on amplitude and latency induced by spTMS have potential clinical application as a feasible neurophysiological probe to examine cortical functions in healthy people and patients with neuropsychiatric disorders such as SCZ and to assess the therapeutic effects of various interventions on TEP responses. Further, between the OLD and the SCZ groups, there were similarities in TEP responses in amplitude while there was a difference in TEP latency when looking at the propagation after the DLPFC-spTMS. To this end, our findings warrant further research in a larger sample size as well as in other neuropsychiatric disorders.

Supplementary Materials: The following are available online at https://www.mdpi.com/2075-4426/11/1/54/s1, Figure S1: Representative TEP waveforms at the left DLPFC obtained by spTMS for the YNG, OLD, and SCZ groups.

Author Contributions: Conceptualization, Y.N.; methodology, Y.N., R.Z., and P.L.; software, R.Z.; validation, Y.N., Z.J.D., and D.M.B.; formal analysis, Y.N. and R.Z.; investigation, Y.N., M.S.B., and R.F.H.C.; writing: original draft preparation, Y.N.; writing: review and editing, M.S.B., D.M.B., and P.L.; visualization, Y.N.; supervision, D.M.B., Z.J.D., and R.C.; project administration, Y.N., R.F.H.C., and M.S.B.; funding acquisition, D.M.B. All authors have read and agreed to the published version of the manuscript.

Funding: Temerty Centre for Therapeutic Brain Intervention and the Campbell Family Research Institute through the CAMH Foundation, and the Canada Foundation for Innovation.

Institutional Review Board Statement: The study was conducted according to the guidelines of the Declaration of Helsinki, and approved by the Institutional Review Board of the Centre for Addiction and Mental Health (protocol code: 003-2009; date of approval: 1 April 2014).

Informed Consent Statement: Informed consent was obtained from all subjects involved in the study.

Data Availability Statement: Data sharing not applicable. No new data were created or analyzed in this study. Data sharing is not applicable to this article.

Acknowledgments: This research was supported by the Temerty Centre for Therapeutic Brain Intervention, the Campbell Family Research Institute through the CAMH Foundation, and the Canada Foundation for Innovation.

Conflicts of Interest: None of the authors declare any conflicts of interest. Y.N. has received a Grant-in-Aid for Young Scientists (KAKENHI) from the Japan Society for the Promotion of Science (JSPS), research grants from Japan Agency for Medical Research and Development (AMED), investigator-initiated clinical study grants from TEIJIN PHARMA LIMITED and Inter Reha Co., Ltd. Y.N. also receives research grants from Japan Health Foundation, Meiji Yasuda Mental Health Foundation, Mitsui Life Social Welfare Foundation, Takeda Science Foundation, SENSHIN Medical Research Foundation, Health Science Center Foundation, Mochida Memorial Foundation for Medical and Pharmaceutical Research, Taiju Life Social Welfare Foundation, and Daiichi Sankyo Scholarship Donation Program. Y.N. has received speaker's honoraria from Dainippon Sumitomo Pharma, MOCHIDA PHARMACEUTICAL CO., Ltd., and Yoshitomiyakuhin Corporation within the past three years. Y.N. also receives equipment-in-kind support for an investigator-initiated study from Magventure Inc, Inter Reha Co., Ltd., Rogue Resolutions Ltd., and Miyuki Giken Co., Ltd. R.F.H.C. was supported by a Canadian Institutes of Health Research (CIHR)—Dystonia Medical Research Foundation Fellowship award. M.S.B. receives research support from the Brain and Behavior Research Foundation (Formerly NARSAD) Young Investigator Grant, Schizophrenia Junior Faculty Grant from the CAMH Foundation, and funding through the Excellence Fund, Department of Psychiatry, University of Toronto. R.C. received research support from the Canadian Institutes of Health Research (FDN 154292) and the National Institutes of Health (NS106822). Z.J.D. has received research support from the Ontario Mental Health (OMH) Foundation, the CIHR, the Brain and Behaviour Research Foundation (Formerly NARSAD), and the Temerty family and Grant family through the CAMH Foundation and the Campbell Institute. In the last 3 years, Z.J.D. has received research and equipment in-kind support for an investigator-initiated study through Brainsway Inc and Magventure Inc. His work was supported by the Ontario Mental Health Foundation (OMHF), the Canadian Institutes of Health Research (CIHR), the National Institutes of Mental Health and the Temerty Family and Grant Family and through the Centre for Addiction and Mental Health (CAMH) Foundation and the Campbell Institute. D.M.B. has received research support from the CIHR, NIH, Brain Canada and the Temerty Family through the CAMH Foundation and the Campbell Research Institute. He receives research support and in-kind equipment support for an investigator-initiated study from Brainsway Ltd. and he is the site principal investigator for three sponsor-initiated studies for Brainsway Ltd. He receives in-kind equipment support from Magventure for an investigator-initiated study. He receives medication supplies for an investigator-initiated trial from Indivior.

Abbreviations

SpTMS	single-pulse transcranial magnetic stimulation
M1	primary motor cortex
DLPFC	dorsolateral prefrontal cortex
TEP	TMS-evoked potential

References

1. Ilmoniemi, R.J.; Virtanen, J.; Ruohonen, J.; Karhu, J.; Aronen, H.J.; Näätänen, R.; Katila, T. Neuronal responses to magnetic stimulation reveal cortical reactivity and connectivity. *Neuroreport* **1997**, *8*, 3537–3540. [CrossRef] [PubMed]
2. Daskalakis, Z.J.; Farzan, F.; Barr, M.S.; Maller, J.J.; Chen, R.; Fitzgerald, P.B. Long-interval cortical inhibition from the dorsolateral prefrontal cortex: A TMS-EEG study. *Neuropsychopharmacology* **2008**, *33*, 2860–2869. [CrossRef] [PubMed]
3. Farzan, F.; Barr, M.S.; Wong, W.; Chen, R.; Fitzgerald, P.B.; Daskalakis, Z.J. Suppression of gamma-oscillations in the dorsolateral prefrontal cortex following long interval cortical inhibition: A TMS-EEG study. *Neuropsychopharmacology* **2009**, *34*, 1543–1551. [CrossRef] [PubMed]
4. Fitzgerald, P.B.; Maller, J.J.; Hoy, K.; Farzan, F.; Daskalakis, Z.J. GABA and cortical inhibition in motor and non-motor regions using combined TMS-EEG: A time analysis. *Clin. Neurophysiol.* **2009**, *120*, 1706–1710. [CrossRef]
5. Fuggetta, G.; Fiaschi, A.; Manganotti, P. Modulation of cortical oscillatory activities induced by varying single-pulse transcranial magnetic stimulation intensity over the left primary motor area: A combined EEG and TMS study. *Neuroimage* **2005**, *27*, 896–908. [CrossRef]
6. Paus, T.; Sipila, P.K.; Strafella, A.P. Synchronization of neuronal activity in the human primary motor cortex by transcranial magnetic stimulation: An EEG study. *J. Neurophysiol.* **2001**, *86*, 1983–1990. [CrossRef]
7. Premoli, I.; Castellanos, N.; Rivolta, D.; Belardinelli, P.; Bajo, R.; Zipser, C.; Espenhahn, S.; Heidegger, T.; Müller-Dahlhaus, F.; Ziemann, U. TMS-EEG signatures of GABAergic neurotransmission in the human cortex. *J. Neurosci.* **2014**, *34*, 5603–5612. [CrossRef]
8. Rogasch, N.C.; Daskalakis, Y.J.; Fitzgerald, P.B. Cortical inhibition of distinct mechanisms in the dorsolateral prefrontal cortex is related to working memory performance: A TMS-EEG study. *Cortex* **2015**, *64*, 68–77. [CrossRef]
9. Bonato, C.; Miniussi, C.; Rossini, P.M. Transcranial magnetic stimulation and cortical evoked potentials: A TMS/EEG co-registration study. *Clin. Neurophysiol.* **2006**, *117*, 1699–1707. [CrossRef]
10. Lioumis, P.; Kičić, D.; Savolainen, P.; Mäkelä, J.P.; Kähkönen, S. Reproducibility of TMS-evoked EEG responses. *Hum. Brain Mapp.* **2009**, *30*, 1387–1396. [CrossRef]
11. Ferreri, F.; Rossini, P.M. TMS and TMS-EEG techniques in the study of the excitability, connectivity, and plasticity of the human motor cortex. *Rev. Neurosci.* **2013**, *24*, 431–442. [CrossRef] [PubMed]
12. Komssi, S.; Kahkonen, S. The novelty value of the combined use of electroencephalography and transcranial magnetic stimulation for neuroscience research. *Brain. Res. Rev.* **2006**, *52*, 183–192. [CrossRef] [PubMed]
13. Cash, R.F.; Noda, Y.; Zomorrodi, R.; Radhu, N.; Farzan, F.; Rajji, T.K.; Fitzgerald, P.B.; Chen, R.; Daskalakis, Z.J.; Blumberger, D.M. Characterization of glutamatergic and GABAA-Mediated neurotransmission in motor and dorsolateral prefrontal cortex using paired-pulse TMS-EEG. *Neuropsychopharmacology* **2017**, *42*, 502–511. [CrossRef] [PubMed]
14. Komssi, S.; Kahkonen, S.; Ilmoniemi, R.J. The effect of stimulus intensity on brain responses evoked by transcranial magnetic stimulation. *Hum. Brain Mapp.* **2004**, *21*, 154–164. [CrossRef]
15. Kahkonen, S.; Komssi, S.; Wilenius, J.; Ilmoniemi, R.J. Prefrontal transcranial magnetic stimulation produces intensity-dependent EEG responses in humans. *Neuroimage* **2005**, *24*, 955–960. [CrossRef]
16. Rosanova, M.; Casali, A.; Bellina, V.; Resta, F.; Mariotti, M.; Massimini, M. Natural frequencies of human corticothalamic circuits. *J. Neurosci.* **2009**, *29*, 7679–7685. [CrossRef]
17. Kahkonen, S.; Wilenius, J.; Komssi, S.; Ilmoniemi, R.J. Distinct differences in cortical reactivity of motor and prefrontal cortices to magnetic stimulation. *Clin. Neurophysiol.* **2004**, *115*, 583–588. [CrossRef]

18. Kahkonen, S.; Komssi, S.; Wilenius, J.; Ilmoniemi, R.J. Prefrontal TMS produces smaller EEG responses than motor-cortex TMS: Implications for rTMS treatment in depression. *Psychopharmacology* **2005**, *181*, 16–20. [CrossRef]
19. Casarotto, S.; Herukka, S.; Pigorini, A.; Napolitani, M.; Gosseries, O.; Niskanen, E.; Könönen, M.; Mervaala, E.; Rosanova, M.; Soininen, H.; et al. Transcranial magnetic stimulation-evoked EEG/cortical potentials in physiological and pathological aging. *Neuroreport* **2011**, *22*, 592–597. [CrossRef]
20. Levit-Binnun, N.; Litvak, V.; Pratt, H.; Moses, E.; Zaroor, M.; Peled, A. Differences in TMS-evoked responses between schizophrenia patients and healthy controls can be observed without a dedicated EEG system. *Clin. Neurophysiol.* **2010**, *121*, 332–339. [CrossRef]
21. Ferrarelli, F.; Massimini, M.; Peterson, M.J.; Riedner, B.A.; Lazar, M.; Murphy, M.J.; Huber, R.; Rosanova, M.; Alexander, A.L.; Kalin, N.; et al. Reduced evoked gamma oscillations in the frontal cortex in schizophrenia patients: A TMS/EEG study. *Am. J. Psychiatry* **2008**, *165*, 996–1005. [CrossRef] [PubMed]
22. Bagarinao, E.; Watanabe, H.; Maesawa, S.; Mori, D.; Hara, K.; Kawabata, K.; Yoneyama, N.; Ohdake, R.; Imai, K.; Masuda, M.; et al. An unbiased data-driven age-related structural brain parcellation for the identification of intrinsic brain volume changes over the adult lifespan. *Neuroimage* **2018**, *169*, 134–144. [CrossRef] [PubMed]
23. Konopaske, G.T.; Lange, N.; Coyle, J.T.; Benes, F.M. Prefrontal cortical dendritic spine pathology in schizophrenia and bipolar disorder. *JAMA Psychiatry* **2014**, *71*, 1323–1331. [CrossRef] [PubMed]
24. Wang, S.; Young, K.M. White matter plasticity in adulthood. *Neuroscience* **2014**, *276*, 148–160. [CrossRef] [PubMed]
25. Peters, A. The effects of normal aging on myelin and nerve fibers: A review. *J. Neurocytol.* **2002**, *31*, 581–593. [CrossRef]
26. Pajevic, S.; Basser, P.J.; Fields, R.D. Role of myelin plasticity in oscillations and synchrony of neuronal activity. *Neuroscience* **2014**, *276*, 135–147. [CrossRef]
27. Noda, Y. Toward the establishment of neurophysiological indicators for neuropsychiatric disorders using transcranial magnetic stimulation-evoked potentials: A systematic review. *Psychiatry Clin. Neurosci.* **2020**, *74*, 12–34. [CrossRef]
28. Maatta, S.; Könönen, M.; Kallioniemi, E.; Lakka, T.; Lintu, N.; Lindi, V.; Ferreri, F.; Ponzo, D.; Säisänen, L. Development of cortical motor circuits between childhood and adulthood: A navigated TMS-HdEEG study. *Hum. Brain Mapp.* **2017**, *38*, 2599–2615. [CrossRef]
29. Noda, Y.; Zomorrodi, R.; Cash, R.F.H.; Barr, M.S.; Farzan, F.; Rajji, T.K.; Chen, R.; Daskalakis, Z.J.; Blumberger, D.M. Characterization of the influence of age on GABAA and glutamatergic mediated functions in the dorsolateral prefrontal cortex using paired-pulse TMS-EEG. *Aging* **2017**, *9*, 556–572. [CrossRef]
30. Noda, Y.; Barr, M.S.; Zomorrodi, R.; Cash, R.F.H.; Farzan, F.; Rajji, T.K.; Chen, R.; Daskalakis, Z.J.; Blumberger, D.M. Evaluation of short interval cortical inhibition and intracortical facilitation from the dorsolateral prefrontal cortex in patients with schizophrenia. *Sci. Rep.* **2017**, *7*, 17106. [CrossRef]
31. Chung, S.W.; Rogasch, N.C.; Hoy, K.E.; Fitzgerald, P.B. Measuring brain stimulation induced changes in cortical properties using TMS-EEG. *Brain Stimul.* **2015**, *8*, 1010–1020. [CrossRef] [PubMed]
32. McClintock, S.M.; Freitas, C.; Oberman, L.; Lisanby, S.H.; Pascual-Leone, A. Transcranial magnetic stimulation: A neuroscientific probe of cortical function in schizophrenia. *Biol. Psychiatry* **2011**, *70*, 19–27. [CrossRef] [PubMed]
33. Davies, C.H.; Davies, S.N.; Collingridge, G.L. Paired-pulse depression of monosynaptic GABA-mediated inhibitory postsynaptic responses in rat hippocampus. *J. Physiol.* **1990**, *424*, 513–531. [CrossRef] [PubMed]
34. Deisz, R.A. GABA(B) receptor-mediated effects in human and rat neocortical neurones In Vitro. *Neuropharmacology* **1999**, *38*, 1755–1766. [CrossRef]
35. Ferreri, F.; Pasqualetti, P.; Määttä, S.; Ponzo, D.; Ferrarelli, F.; Tononi, G.; Mervaala, E.; Miniussi, C.; Rossini, P.M. Human brain connectivity during single and paired pulse transcranial magnetic stimulation. *Neuroimage* **2011**, *54*, 90–102. [CrossRef]
36. Peinemann, A.; Lehner, C.; Conrad, B.; Siebner, H.R. Age-related decrease in paired-pulse intracortical inhibition in the human primary motor cortex. *Neurosci. Lett.* **2001**, *313*, 33–36. [CrossRef]
37. Marneweck, M.; Loftus, A.; Hammond, G. Short-interval intracortical inhibition and manual dexterity in healthy aging. *Neurosci. Res.* **2011**, *70*, 408–414. [CrossRef]
38. Heise, K.F.; Zimerman, M.; Hoppe, J.; Gerloff, C.; Wegscheider, K.; Hummel, F.C. The aging motor system as a model for plastic changes of GABA-mediated intracortical inhibition and their behavioral relevance. *J. Neurosci.* **2013**, *33*, 9039–9049. [CrossRef]
39. Grachev, I.D.; Apkarian, A.V. Aging alters regional multichemical profile of the human brain: An. in vivo 1H-MRS study of young versus middle-aged subjects. *J. Neurochem.* **2001**, *76*, 582–593. [CrossRef]
40. Grachev, I.D.; Swarnkar, A.; Szeverenyi, N.M.; Ramachandran, T.S.; Apkarian, A.V. Aging alters the multichemical networking profile of the human brain: An. In Vivo (1)H-MRS study of young versus middle-aged subjects. *J. Neurochem.* **2001**, *77*, 292–303. [CrossRef]
41. Benes, F.M.; McSparren, J.; Bird, E.D.; SanGiovanni, J.P.; Vincent, S.L.B. Deficits in small interneurons in prefrontal and cingulate cortices of schizophrenic and schizoaffective patients. *Arch. Gen. Psychiatry* **1991**, *48*, 996–1001. [CrossRef] [PubMed]
42. Benes, F.M.; Kwok, E.W.; Vincent, S.L.; Todtenkopf, M.S. A reduction of nonpyramidal cells in sector CA_2 of schizophrenics and manic depressives. *Biol. Psychiatry* **1998**, *44*, 88–97. [CrossRef]
43. Woo, T.U.; Walsh, J.P.; Benes, F.M. Density of glutamic acid decarboxylase 67 messenger RNA-containing neurons that express the N-methyl-D-aspartate receptor subunit NR2A in the anterior cingulate cortex in schizophrenia and bipolar disorder. *Arch. Gen. Psychiatry* **2004**, *61*, 649–657. [CrossRef] [PubMed]

44. Lewis, D.A.; Hashimoto, T.; Volk, D.W. Cortical inhibitory neurons and schizophrenia. *Nat. Rev. Neurosci.* **2005**, *6*, 312–324. [CrossRef] [PubMed]
45. Akbarian, S.; Huang, H.S. Molecular and cellular mechanisms of altered GAD1/GAD67 expression in schizophrenia and related disorders. *Brain Res. Rev.* **2006**, *52*, 293–304. [CrossRef]
46. Benes, F.M.; Lim, B.; Matzilevich, D.; Walsh, J.P.; Subburaju, S.; Minns, M. Regulation of the GABA cell phenotype in hippocampus of schizophrenics and bipolars. *Proc. Natl. Acad. Sci. USA* **2007**, *104*, 10164–10169. [CrossRef] [PubMed]
47. Takahashi, S.; Ukai, S.; Kose, A.; Hashimoto, T.; Iwatani, J.; Okumura, M.; Tsuji, T.; Shinosaki, K. Reduction of cortical GABAergic inhibition correlates with working memory impairment in recent onset schizophrenia. *Schizophr. Res.* **2013**, *146*, 238–243. [CrossRef]
48. Bridgman, A.C.; Barr, M.S.; Goodman, M.S.; Chen, R.; Rajji, T.K.; Daskalakis, Z.J.; George, T.P. Deficits in GABAA receptor function and working memory in non-smokers with schizophrenia. *Schizophr. Res.* **2016**, *171*, 125–130. [CrossRef]
49. Umesawa, Y.; Matsushima, K.; Atsumi, T.; Kato, T.; Fukatsu, R.; Wada, M.; Ide, M. Altered GABA concentration in brain motor area is associated with the severity of motor disabilities in individuals with autism spectrum disorder. *J. Autism Dev. Disord.* **2020**, *50*, 2710–2722. [CrossRef]
50. Gray, D.T.; Engle, J.R.; Rudolph, M.L.; Recanzone, G.H. Regional and age-related differences in GAD67 expression of parvalbumin- and calbindin-expressing neurons in the rhesus macaque auditory midbrain and brainstem. *J. Comp. Neurol.* **2014**, *522*, 4074–4084. [CrossRef]
51. Hill, A.T.; Rogasch, N.C.; Fitzgerald, P.B.; Hoy, K.E. TMS-EEG: TMS-EEG: A window into the neurophysiological effects of transcranial electrical stimulation in non-motor brain regions. *Neurosci. Biobehav. Rev.* **2016**, *64*, 175–184. [CrossRef] [PubMed]
52. Chung, S.W.; Sullivan, C.M.; Rogasch, N.C.; Hoy, K.E.; Bailey, N.W.; Cash, R.F.H.; Fitzgerald, P.B. The effects of individualised intermittent theta burst stimulation in the prefrontal cortex: A TMS-EEG study. *Hum. Brain Mapp.* **2019**, *40*, 608–627. [CrossRef] [PubMed]
53. Li, M.; Deng, W.; He, Z.; Wang, Q.; Huang, C.; Jiang, L.; Gong, O.; Ziedonis, D.M.; King, J.A.; Ma, X.; et al. A splitting brain: Imbalanced neural networks in schizophrenia. *Psychiatry Res.* **2015**, *232*, 145–153. [CrossRef] [PubMed]
54. Rocchi, L.; Di Santo, A.; Brown, K.; Ibáñez, J.; Casula, E.; Rawji, V.; Di Lazzaro, V.; Koch, G.; Rothwell, J. Disentangling EEG responses to TMS due to cortical and peripheral activations. *Brain Stimul.* **2020**, *14*, 4–18. [CrossRef]

Journal of *Personalized Medicine*

MDPI

Article

Photobiological Neuromodulation of Resting-State EEG and Steady-State Visual-Evoked Potentials by 40 Hz Violet Light Optical Stimulation in Healthy Individuals

Yoshihiro Noda [1,*], Mayuko Takano [1], Motoshi Hayano [1,2,3], Xuemei Li [1], Masataka Wada [1], Shinichiro Nakajima [1], Masaru Mimura [1], Shinichiro Kondo [4] and Kazuo Tsubota [2,4]

1 Department of Neuropsychiatry, Keio University School of Medicine, Tokyo 160-8582, Japan; mayuko.takano@keio.jp (M.T.); mhayano@keio.jp (M.H.); lixmovo@gmail.com (X.L.); masa.wada0622@gmail.com (M.W.); shinichiro.l.nakajima@gmail.com (S.N.); mimura@a7.keio.jp (M.M.)
2 Department of Ophthalmology, Keio University School of Medicine, Tokyo 160-8582, Japan; tsubota@z3.keio.jp
3 Faculty of Science and Technology, Keio University, Yokohama 223-0061, Japan
4 Tsubota Laboratory, Inc., Tokyo 160-0016, Japan; kondo@tsubota-lab.com
* Correspondence: yoshi-tms@keio.jp; +81-3-3353-1211 (ext. 61857)

Citation: Noda, Y.; Takano, M.; Hayano, M.; Li, X.; Wada, M.; Nakajima, S.; Mimura, M.; Kondo, S.; Tsubota, K. Photobiological Neuromodulation of Resting-State EEG and Steady-State Visual-Evoked Potentials by 40 Hz Violet Light Optical Stimulation in Healthy Individuals. *J. Pers. Med.* **2021**, *11*, 557. https://doi.org/10.3390/jpm11060557

Academic Editor: Toshiaki Onitsuka

Received: 10 April 2021
Accepted: 11 June 2021
Published: 15 June 2021

Abstract: Photobiological neuromodulation and its clinical application has been investigated in recent years. The response of the gamma-oscillation to human visual stimuli is known to be both burst and resonant in nature, and the coupling between alpha and gamma oscillations may play a functional role in visual processing. To date, there is no study that examined the effects of gamma-frequency violet light (VL) stimulation on human electroencephalography (EEG). In this study, we investigated the neurophysiological changes induced by light stimulation using EEG. The purpose of this study was to evaluate the specific effects of 40 Hz gamma-frequency VL stimulation on EEG activity by comparing the effects of white light (WL) with the same condition. Twenty healthy participants (10 females: 37.5 ± 14.3 years; 10 males: 38.0 ± 13.3 years) participated in this study and the following results were observed. First, when compared with the power spectrum density (PSD) of baseline EEG, 40 Hz-WL induced significant increase of PSD in theta band. Second, compared the PSDs between EEG with 40 Hz-VL and EEG with 40 Hz-WL, 40 Hz-VL induced significantly lower enhancement in delta and theta bands than 40 Hz-WL. Third, when focused on the occipital area, negative peak of VEP with 40 Hz-VL was smaller than that of 40 Hz-WL. Fourth, 40 Hz-VL induced an increase of alpha-gamma coupling during the VEP at the F5 electrode site as well as post-EEG at the C4 electrode site, compared with baseline EEG. Thus, the present study suggested that 40 Hz-VL stimulation may induce unique photobiological neuromodulations on human EEG activity.

Keywords: photobiological neuromodulation; violet light; steady-state gamma-frequency stimulation; resting-state electroencephalography (EEG); visual-evoked potential; alpha-phase and gamma-amplitude coupling

1. Introduction

1.1. Photobiological Neuromodulation

Vision is based on the interaction of light with photosensitive receptors in the retina. Once light is absorbed by these receptors, it causes photochemical reactions, and the light energy is converted into electrical signals. Photobiological neuromodulation is a concept that describes the comprehensive biophysical modifying effects of light energy. Furthermore, clinical applications using the light sources in non-ionizing forms, such as lasers, LEDs, and broadband light, have been investigated in recent years. Photobiological neuromodulation is a non-thermal process that induces photophysical and photochemical events at various biological scales. Indeed, since light is a powerful stimulus for regulating circadian rhythms, hormones, and behavioral systems, a conventional light therapy is effective in treating seasonal affective disorders, and sleep disorders including circadian rhythm sleep disorder. Moreover, light induces a complex chain of physiological reactions in tissues through its photophysical and photochemical effects, which in turn helps to restore normal cellular functions by promoting blood circulation and reducing inflammation [1] by way of distinct photoreceptors in the retina such as melanopsin or neuropsin expressed in retinal ganglion cells other than the traditional rods and cones [2]. As such, photobiological neuromodulation therapy for brain has potential to enhance the metabolic capacity of neurons and stimulate anti-inflammatory, anti-apoptotic, and antioxidant responses, neurogenesis, and synapse formation, and thus it is expected to have therapeutic applications for central nervous system diseases including depression and dementia [3].

1.2. Melanopsin/Neuropsin Expressed in Retinal Ganglion Cells and Violet Light (VL)

The signals from retinal ganglion cells project both into the retina and the brain [4] and contain membrane receptors for the neurotransmitters such as glutamate, glycine, and GABA [5]. Of note, photosensitive ganglion cells depolarize on sensing light, thus increasing the rate of neural firings, which is the opposite of other photoreceptor cells that hyperpolarize in response to light [6]. For example, melanopsin acts as an excitable photopigment as well as photoisomerase, which isomerizes all-trans-retinal into 11-cis-retinal by itself when stimulated with light [6]. In contrast, neuropsin is the other photoreceptor protein in neural tissues encoded by the OPN5 gene [7,8] and it is sensitive to VL. Human neuropsin, which is expressed in the eyes, brain, and spinal cord, can activate the heterotrimeric G protein Gi-mediated pathway [9,10]. Furthermore, there are more than five types of retinal ganglion cells in the brain, and their different processing in the central nervous system may result in the diversity of brain functioning [11]. In addition, since each of these various types of retinal ganglion cells has a different central projection pattern, their diversity may result in complex regulatory mechanisms for circadian and neurophysiological responses [12–14]. In mice, OPN5 is also expressed in the hypothalamic preoptic area (POA) as a violet light-sensitive deep brain photoreceptor other than in the retina and skin. Indeed, direct measurements of intracellular cAMP showed that OPN5 POA neurons increase cAMP when stimulated with VL [15]. In addition, VL exposure leads to up-regulate EGR-1, which is a transcriptional regulator, expression in the chick model [16]. For example, the induction of EGR-1 is associated with neuronal activity such as neuronal plasticity and memory formation [17]. More specifically, EGR-1 is used in programming the distribution of methylation sites on brain DNA during brain development, in learning and in long-term neuronal plasticity. Furthermore, VL exposure induces significantly higher up-regulation of EGR1 than blue light and EGR1 mRNA expression varies according to the strength of VL. VL has a wavelength between approximately 360 and 400 nm, referring to the color of any different single wavelength of light on the short-wavelength end of the visible spectrum (see Figure 1). Since human vision is relatively insensitive to these wavelengths, violet colors often appear dark. In recent years, in addition to the lack of ultraviolet (UV) light from light sources such as fluorescent lamps and LEDs, exposure to VL has become relatively low in modern society because many windows, glasses, and contact lenses are now UV protected. Furthermore, especially at this time of the year when the COVID-19 pandemic is forcing people to limit their outings, VL exposure is currently overwhelmingly inadequate.

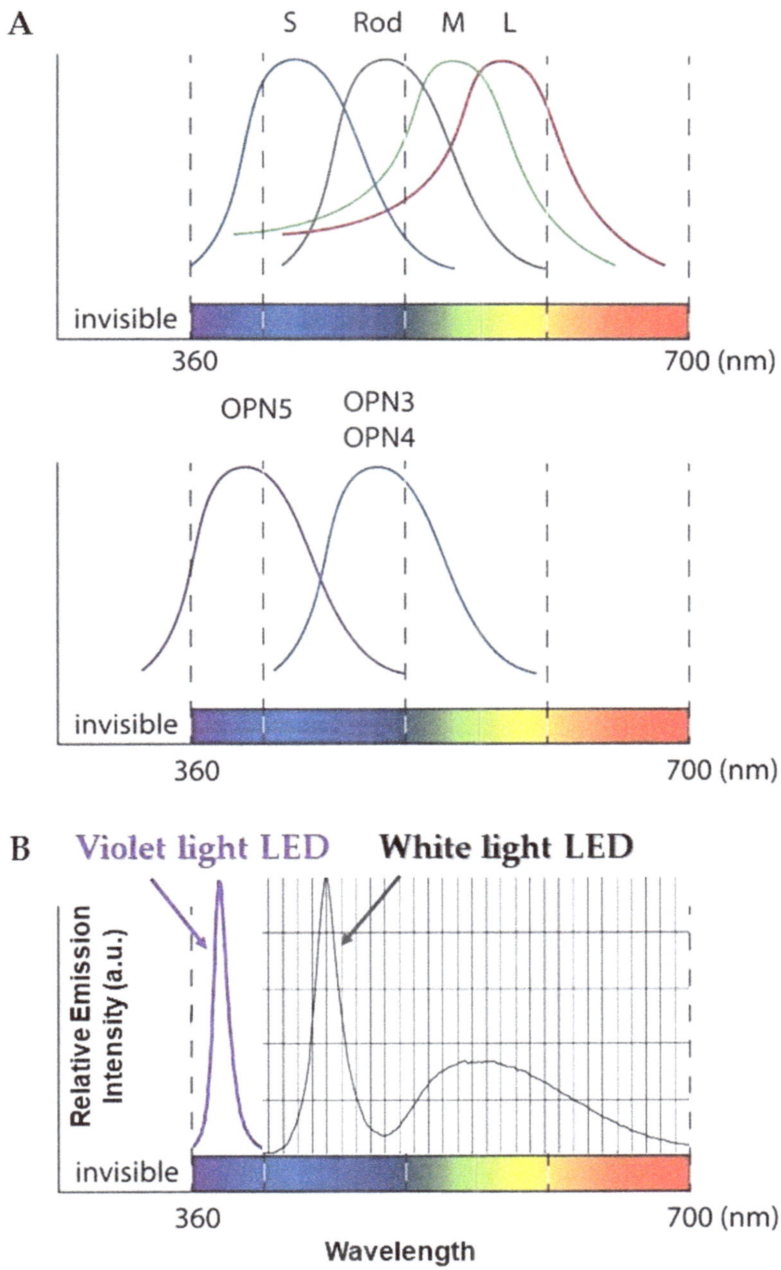

Figure 1. A diagram showing the relationships between the emission spectrum of the LEDs (VL and WL) and the absorption spectrum of the opsins (OPN5, OPN3, and OPN4). (**A**) shows the biological absorption spectrum of opsins; (**B**) represents the emission wavelength of the VL-LED and WL-LED. As shown in Figure 1, the emission wavelength of the VL-LED and the absorption spectrum of OPN5 correspond to each other. VL: violet light; WL: white light; OPN: opsin; S: short-wavelength cone; M: middle-wavelength cone; L: long-wavelength cone.

1.3. Clinical Applicability of Non-Visual Stimulation of Light

Again, the most influential aspect of the non-visual stimulation is light-induced phase resetting of endogenous circadian clocks. Because circadian rhythmicity is a feature of nearly every physiological, metabolic, and behavioral system, this phenomenon brings a wide array of biological processes under indirect retinal control. Thus, light acts as a neurophysiological stimulant, increasing subjective and objective measures of alertness and psychomotor reaction time, and reducing lapses of attention [2]. Light has been shown to have antidepressant properties, especially in the treatment of seasonal affective disorder. Furthermore, appropriately timed light exposure can be a non-invasive treatment for circadian rhythm sleep disorders and circadian rhythm disturbances associated with jet lag, shift work, and space flight. In recent years, light therapy has shown promise as a treatment for non-seasonal depression, problems associated with the menstrual cycle, bulimia nervosa, and cognitive problems associated with dementia [18]. More surprisingly, a recent basic study showed that driving fast-spiking parvalbumin-positive interneurons with a gamma-rhythm (40 Hz) reduced the levels of amyloid beta Aβ1-40 and Aβ1-42 [19]. Furthermore, the study showed that non-invasive 40 Hz light-flickering stimulation reduced the accumulation of Aβ1-40 and Aβ1-42 in the visual cortex of the mouse model of Alzheimer's disease (AD) before the onset of symptoms, and reduced plaque burden in the mouse model of AD even after the onset of symptoms, which suggested that gamma-rhythm stimulation may induce both neuronal and glial responses and alleviate the pathology of AD [19].

1.4. Potential Roles of Gamma Oscillations in Visual Stimulation and Visual Pathways

Gamma oscillations consist of interactions between excitatory and inhibitory neurons, resulting in rhythmic inhibition capable of entraining firing within local cortical circuits. Several mechanisms have been reported in which gamma oscillations could act on cortical circuits to modulate their responses to inputs, alter their patterns of activity, and enhance the efficacy of their outputs to downstream targets. Recently, it has been confirmed that optogenetic manipulation of gamma oscillations in the neocortex of animals can alter their behavior. Thus, since gamma oscillations are thought to modulate cortical circuit function, it is necessary to clarify the physiological correlates associated with their specific gamma mechanism in the future. Therefore, it is important to elucidate the role of gamma oscillations on cortical circuit functions in normal and pathological conditions through EEG measurements [20]. Furthermore, gamma-rhythm has been associated with high-level cognitive functions such as attention and feature binding and has been reported to be abnormal in brain disorders such as autism and schizophrenia [21]. On the other hand, long-range gamma-band EEG oscillations are known to mediate information transfer between distant brain regions. Gamma-band-based coupling may be used not only for intercortical communication but also in non-cortical areas related to visual pathways. Evoked potentials associated with retinal inputs and the visual cortex show temporally synchronized gamma coherence, which suggests gamma oscillatory coupling between the retina and the visual cortex [22]. Moreover, gamma-band response to visual stimulation exhibits both burst and resonant properties. For example, the photic driving stimulation with alpha-frequency band often produces not only strong alpha entrainment but also significant amplitude modulation of gamma-frequency activity. Conversely, alpha amplitude modulation may occur when gamma-rhythm photic stimulation induces transient alpha rhythm activity and subsequent its suppression. Thus, alpha- and gamma-band activity may be neuromodulated in response to visual stimuli, and it is known that there is a mutual interaction between alpha- and gamma-rhythm generating systems [23].

1.5. EEG as a Means of Detecting Representations in the Brain

Since Hans Berger first measured the bioelectrical activity of the human brain non-invasively in 1929, EEG has been developed and established as a tool to monitor brain dynamics and brain functions. In particular, EEG is a modality that can directly evaluate brain activity and has high temporal resolution, making it suitable for neurophysiological assessment that reflects representations in the brain. In recent years, high-density EEG system with multiple channels has become common and both spontaneous and evoked activities have been of interest. In EEG recordings, undesired signals or artifacts other than EEG can be divided into two main categories: physiological and non-physiological. Physiological artifacts are electrical signals generated by the heart, muscles, especially eye and facial muscles, and retina. These artifacts, which can be several orders of magnitude larger than the EEG signal of interest, usually have a characteristic topography and can be reduced by sophisticated spatial artifact removal techniques such as ICA [24].

1.6. Visual-Evoked Potentials (VEPs) and Cross-Frequency Coupling (CFC) of Alpha-Phase and Gamma-Amplitude

Visual-evoked potentials (VEPs) are the brain's response to repetitive visual stimuli, and their high signal-to-noise ratio and ability to entrain oscillatory brain activity are useful for investigating the neural processes underlying rhythmic activity in the brain, and for elucidating the causal role of brain rhythms in cognition and emotion. A previous study examined oscillatory EEG dynamics in the time-frequency domain of VEP induced by visual stimulation with gamma-frequency (40–60 Hz). Gamma-frequency visual stimulation induced VEPs at the parieto-occipital region, and transient responses were accompanied by increases in frontal and occipital delta and theta power between 0 and 300 ms after stimulus onset, returning to baseline after about 500 ms. Furthermore, occipital beta/gamma-band power enhanced during the visual stimulation period, which may have been due to increased power at the sub-harmonic frequency of the stimulus [25]. Thus, cross-frequency coupling (CFC) has been suggested to be a highly flexible mechanism for information gating and processing in the cerebral cortex, giving rise to a wide range of higher-order cognitive functions in humans. Specifically, CFC may be an elegant mechanism for integrating information across multiple spatiotemporal scales in coupled neuronal networks. Indeed, a previous study has demonstrated that selective entrainment of alpha/gamma oscillations induced specific neuromodulation on CFC, which indicated that entrainment of low-frequency components (e.g., alpha band activity) increased phase-amplitude coupling, especially gamma-band power, which became preferentially locked to alpha oscillations, whereas entrainment of the gamma-band resulted in a decrease in alpha power. These reciprocal influencing results indicate that the coupling between alpha and gamma oscillations may play a functionally important role in visual processing [26].

1.7. Objectives and Hypotheses of the Present Study

To date, no study has evaluated the effects of combined 40 Hz gamma-frequency violet light (VL) stimulation on human EEG. Thus, in the present study, we aimed to investigate the neurophysiological effects of 40 Hz gamma-frequency VL stimulation on human resting EEG activity as well as steady-state visual-evoked potentials (VEPs) by comparing the effects of wavelengths of white light (WL). Specifically, we hypothesized that 40 Hz gamma-frequency VL stimulation would cause photobiological neuromodulation specific to the alpha and gamma activity generating systems, as represented by the coupling between alpha-phase and gamma-amplitude.

2. Materials and Methods

2.1. Participants

Twenty healthy individuals participated in this study. Participants were eligible to participate in this study if they met the following criteria: (i) over 20 years old; (ii) no current or history of cardiovascular, hepatic, endocrine, cerebral/neurological, or psychiatric diseases that may affect the study results; (iii) no prescription medications; (iv) no history of alcohol or other drug abuse/dependence; and (v) no history of photosensitive seizures or family history of photosensitive seizures. Participants were screened by the research group to ensure that they met the above inclusion criteria. The present study was conducted according to the Declaration of Helsinki and was reviewed and approved by the Ethics Committee of Keio University School of Medicine (Shinjuku-ku, Tokyo, Japan; ID: 20190096). In this experiment, the investigators also interviewed the participants to confirm the safety and adverse events during and after the light stimulation.

2.2. Experimental Design

This experiment was conducted in a crossover design. Specifically, we measured resting-state EEG for 5 min as baseline, 7 min of EEG during light stimulation (violet light (VL) or white light (WL)), 5 min of resting-state EEG after light stimulation, then 7 min of EEG during light stimulation by switching the light stimulation condition (VL or WL), and 5 min of resting EEG after the light stimulation, for a total of approximately 30 min. The order of WL and VL stimulation to the participants was completely randomized based on a random number table to avoid bias. A schematic diagram of the experiment is shown in Figure 2.

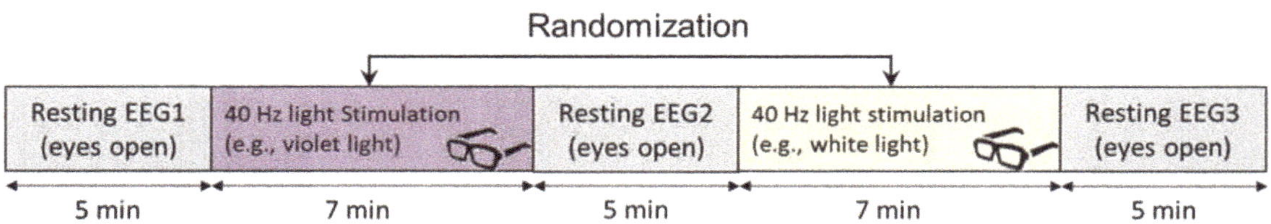

Figure 2. A schematic diagram of the experiment in this study.

2.3. Violet Light (VL) and White Light (WL) Stimulation

EEG was measured before, during, and after exposure to different light conditions, using steady-state 40 Hz-VL (375 nm) and steady-state 40 Hz-WL with 2-s interval flicker stimulation in healthy adults. For the VL used for optical stimulation, we use goggles with a commercially available LED light source module (VL-LED: NSSU123; Nichia Corporation, Anan, Tokushima, Japan; peak wavelength 375 nm) with a circuit for pulse width modulation (PWM; modulation frequency kHz). The UV radiation from this LED is 310 $\mu W/cm^2$. For the WL, we used separate goggles equipped with a commercial LED light source module with a circuit for PWM (WL-LED: NSSW157T; Nichia Corporation, Anan, Tokushima, Japan). Regarding the intensity of VL and WL conditions, we did not make them identical in terms of physical intensity but adjusted them to be as equivalent as possible in brightness at the perceptual level seen by the human eyes. Specifically, in the preparation stage of this research protocol, three scientists (Y.N., X.L., and M.H.) in our research group adjusted the brightness of the VL and WL multiple times so that the perception of the brightness of both conditions would be almost identical. Furthermore, the reason we matched the brightness of VL and WL at the perceptual level in this way was that if we unified the brightness at the physical intensity, the energy of VL becomes relatively higher than that of WL due to the wavelength and frequency of each light. In addition, if we match the brightness with the physical intensity, the brightness of the light sources in VL and WL will be obviously different, which may eliminate the blindness of the participants regarding the type of light and may introduce psychological placebo effect into the light stimulation experiment. See Figure 3 for photos of these goggles.

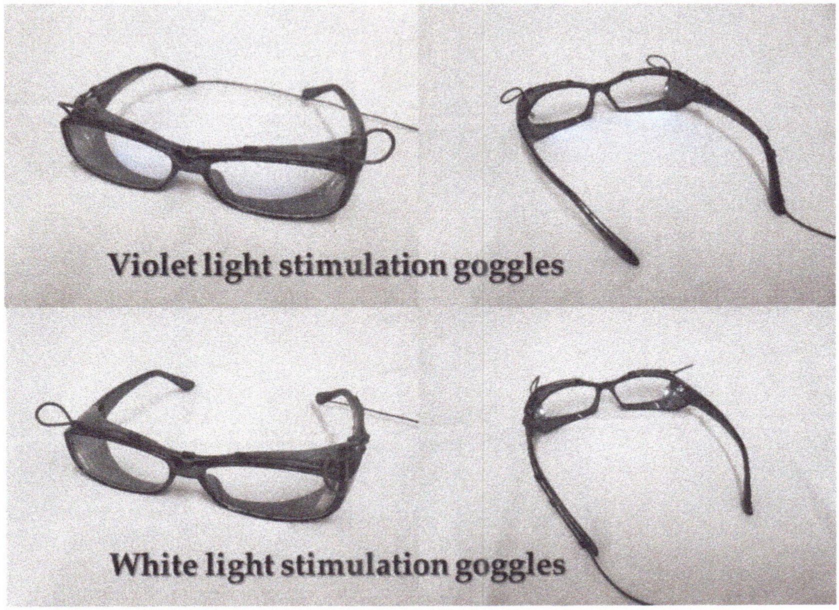

Figure 3. Goggles for violet light (VL) stimulation and goggles for white light (WL) stimulation used in this experiment.

2.4. EEG Recording

EEG was recorded through a 62-channel TruScan LT with an EEG cap (DEYMED Diagnostic s.r.o., Hronov, Czech Republic). During the EEG recording, electrodes impedance was kept below 5 kΩ. All electrodes were referenced to an average of both earlobes' electrodes (A1 and A2). EEG signals were recorded at a sampling rate of 3000 Hz. Since the main purpose of this study was to precisely investigate the neurophysiological effects induced by violet light stimulation through the retina on EEG, we used a high-resolution EEG system.

2.5. EEG Signal Preprocessing

EEG data were processed offline using the MATLAB software (R2020a, The MathWorks, Natick, MA, USA) and EEGLAB toolbox (Swartz Center for Computational Neuroscience, University of California at San Diego, CA, USA). First, continuous EEG data were segmented every 2-s, and then the EEG data during visual light stimulation were epoched from −1000 ms to 2000 ms based on the trigger signal of the first light stimulus (see Supplementary Materials). Furthermore, the baseline correction was performed using the pre-stimulus interval between −500 ms and −100 ms. Then, these EEG data were referenced to the average reference. Next, the Butterworth 0.5–70 Hz bandpass filter and notch filter (48–52 Hz: this is because in eastern Japan, the frequency of power line noise is 50 Hz) were applied. Afterwards, the preprocessed data were downsampled to 1000 Hz. Furthermore, the preprocessed EEG data were visually inspected to exclude segments that were highly contaminated with artifacts. Here, there was no need to remove the bad channels because the quality of the EEG data was maintained in this study. Subsequently, independent component analysis (ICA) was applied to minimize and remove the eye-related and muscle activity related components. In each participant, the number of ICA components that were removed from the original 62 components was no greater than 20%.

2.6. Power Spectrum Density (PSD) Analysis

The power spectrum of a time series describes the distribution of power to the frequency components that comprise the signal. The PSD refers to the spectral energy distribution found per unit time. Fourier transform was applied to the preprocessed EEG data to compute the PSD. In the present analysis, the average PSDs of all electrodes (62 channels), frontal region (Fp1, Fp2, Fpz, AF7, AF3, AFz, AF4, and AF8), and occipital region (O1, O2, Oz, PO7, PO3, POz, PO4, and PO8) were calculated for each delta (1–3 Hz), theta (4–7 Hz), alpha (8–13 Hz), beta (14–30 Hz), and gamma (30–70 Hz) frequency bands.

2.7. Visual-Evoked Potential (VEP) Analysis

VEP is an evoked potential elicited by presenting light flash which can be clinically used to examine some visual pathway damage including retina, optic nerve, optic chiasm, optic radiations, and occipital cortex. As with other evoked potential tests, VEP is conducted in the event-related potential (ERP) paradigm. The 40 Hz photo-stimulation with a time duration of 1 s was flashed at 2-s intervals, and a total of 200 flashes were presented in one condition of photo-stimulation experiment, and then the steady-state VEP was analyzed by summing and averaging those 200 epochs for the first 500 ms during light stimulation.

2.8. Phase-Amplitude Coupling (PAC) Analysis during the VEP

First, EEG signal was filtered into separate delta, theta, alpha, and beta band waveforms for phase and theta, alpha, beta, and gamma waveforms for amplitude with a zero-phase shift filter for all electrodes for 500 ms time windows. Subsequently, the Hilbert transform was applied to the processed EEG data and then time series data of phase and amplitude were calculated. The modulation index (MI) of phase-amplitude coupling was computed as possible relationships between the delta, theta, alpha, and beta band phases and the theta, alpha, beta, and gamma amplitudes based on the previously published method [27]. The specific-amplitudes corresponding to the specific-phase were sorted into 18 bins and then they were averaged. To quantify the coupling, the relative amplitude distribution for each participant was calculated, dividing the amplitude of each phase by the sum of all amplitudes across bins. In other words, the MI was obtained by measuring the divergence of the amplitude group from a uniform distribution.

2.9. Statistical Analysis

Statistical analysis was conducted by the MATLAB software (R2020a, The MathWorks, Natick, MA, USA). For demographic data, an independent t-test was applied to compare age difference between female and male participants. For the EEG analysis data, permutation tests with 10,000 permutation samples were applied to compare the difference in PSDs among the conditions. In addition, exploratory correlation analyses were performed between the VEP peak and PSD of each frequency band as well as the MI values for significant changes of phase-amplitude couplings and PSD of each frequency band. In the present study, we set the significance level at 0.05 and did not correct for multiple comparisons, since these were preliminary hypothesis-testing analyses as described in the introduction.

3. Results

3.1. Demographic Data of the Participants

In the present study, 20 healthy individuals (10 females and 10 males) were participated. The mean age (±S.D.) of the participants was 37.8 ± 13.4 years (females: 37.5 ± 14.3 years; males: 38.0 ± 13.3 years). There was no significant difference in age between females and males ($t_{18} = -0.081$, $p = 0.936$). The breakdown of participants who were preceded by 40 Hz-WL stimulation and followed by 40 Hz-VL stimulation was as follows: the number of participants was 10 (4 females and 6 males) with a mean age (±S.D.) of 37.9 ± 11.7 years. In contrast, the number of participants who were preceded by 40 Hz-VL stimulation and followed by 40 Hz-WL stimulation was 10 (6 females and

4 males) with a mean age (±S.D.) of 37.6 ± 15.6 years. There was no significant difference in sex (χ^2 = 0.800, p = 0.371) and age (t_{18} = −0.049, p = 0.962) between the above-mentioned attributes for the different order of light stimulation. Of note, no obvious adverse events were reported during or after the light stimulation experiments in this study, such as eye or skin damage, visual abnormalities, headache, discomfort, or nausea.

3.2. PSD Analysis

3.2.1. Averaged PSDs over All Electrodes for Baseline EEG, during, and after the Light Stimulations

Compared with the averaged PSD over the all electrodes of baseline EEG, the averaged PSD for all electrodes with 40 Hz-WL stimulation showed a significant increase in theta band. Furthermore, when compared the averaged PSDs for all electrodes between VEP with 40 Hz-VL and VEP with 40 Hz-WL, there were significant differences in delta and theta bands, indicating that the averaged PSDs for 40 Hz-WL in these bands showed significantly higher powers compared with the averaged PSDs for 40 Hz-VL. In addition, the averaged PSD over the all electrodes for post-EEG with 40 Hz-VL demonstrated a marginally significant increase in gamma-band compared with the averaged PSD of baseline EEG (Figure 4A; Table 1).

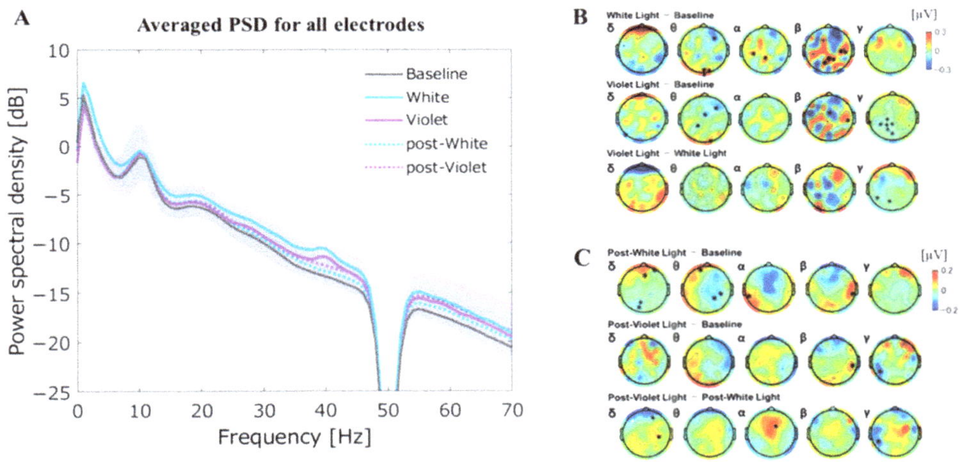

Figure 4. Averaged PSDs for all electrodes during and after the light stimulation and their topographical plots. (**A**) shows the averaged power spectrum density (PSD) over all electrodes for each condition; (**B**) depicts topographical plots of PSDs during the light stimulation; (**C**) demonstrated topographical plots of PSDs after the light stimulation. Of note, black asterisks indicate significant findings at the 0.05 level of significance, while white asterisks indicate significant findings at the 0.01 level of significance. The graph is shown with ±S.D. shadows to the mean PSD for each condition.

3.2.2. Topographical Plots of PSDs during the Light Stimulation

Topographical plots of PSD during the light stimulation are depicted in Figure 4B.

PSD of Baseline EEG vs. PSD of VEP with 40 Hz-WL Stimulation

When the topological plots for the PSDs of baseline EEG and VEP paradigm with 40 Hz-WL stimulation are viewed at the electrode level, the PSDs were neuromodulated from theta to beta bands. Specifically, in theta band, 40 Hz-WL stimulation induced reduced PSD over the right prefrontal area and increased PSD over the occipital area; in alpha band, increased PSD at the left central and midline parietal areas; and in beta band, increased PSD at the right temporal and midline parietal areas, compared with baseline EEG (Figure 4B, upper row).

PSD of Baseline EEG vs. PSD of VEP with 40 Hz-VL Stimulation

Likewise, in the VEP paradigm with 40 Hz-VL stimulation, PSDs at the electrode level were neuromodulated over the theta, beta, and gamma bands. Specifically, 40 Hz-VL stimulation induced reduced PSD in theta band over the right frontal and midline central areas; reduced PSD at the midline central area and increased PSD at the right temporal area in beta band; and reduced PSD in gamma-band over the midline and left parietal areas (Figure 4B, middle row).

Table 1. Summary of statistical analysis results comparing all electrode averaged PSD between each condition for each frequency band (* $p < 0.05$).

Frequency Band	Baseline vs. 40 Hz-WL		Baseline vs. 40 Hz-VL		40 Hz-WL vs. 40 Hz-VL		Baseline vs. Post-WL		Baseline vs. Post-VL		Post-WL vs. Post-VL	
	t_{38}	P	t_{38}	p	t_{38}	P	t_{38}	p	t_{38}	p	t_{38}	p
Delta	1.92	0.07	0.74	0.47	2.40	0.02 *	0.23	0.81	0.67	0.51	0.47	0.64
Theta	2.15	0.04 *	0.11	0.91	2.05	0.05 *	0.21	0.83	0.07	0.94	0.27	0.78
Alpha	0.91	0.37	0.28	0.78	0.62	0.53	0.52	0.60	0.34	0.73	0.19	0.86
Beta	1.56	0.14	0.69	0.51	0.83	0.41	0.96	0.35	1.08	0.29	0.19	0.86
Gamma	1.34	0.20	0.99	0.34	0.45	0.66	0.93	0.36	1.87	0.06	0.94	0.35

PSD of VEP with 40 Hz-WL vs. PSD of VEP with 40 Hz-VL

At the electrode level, the analyses between the PSDs of VEP with 40 Hz-WL and 40 Hz-VL revealed that there was a difference in the PSD in gamma-band at the left parieto-occipital area, indicating that 40 Hz-VL showed a lower gamma modulation on PSD compared with 40 Hz-WL (Figure 4B, lower row).

3.2.3. Topographical Plots of PSD after the Light Stimulation

Topographical plots of PSD after the light stimulation are shown in Figure 4C.

PSD of Baseline EEG vs. PSD of Post-EEG with 40 Hz-WL

Compared with PSD of baseline EEG, PSD for post-EEG with 40 Hz-WL stimulation showed partial EEG neuromodulations from the delta to beta bands at the electrode level. Specifically, PSD for post-EEG with 40 Hz-WL increased at the mid-prefrontal while it was reduced at the mid-parieto-occipital areas in delta band; PSD was reduced at the right parietal area in theta band; PSD increased at the left temporal area in alpha band; and PSD increased at the right temporal area in beta band (Figure 4C, upper row).

PSD of Baseline EEG vs. PSD of Post-EEG with 40 Hz-VL

Compared with baseline EEG, 40 Hz-VL stimulation induced enhanced PSD in beta band at the right parietal area and reduced PSD in gamma-band at the left parietal area (Figure 4C, middle row).

PSD of Post-EEG with 40 Hz-WL vs. PSD of Post-EEG with 40 Hz-VL

When compared the PSDs between VEP with 40 Hz-WL and VEP with 40 Hz-VL at the electrode level, 40 Hz-VL stimulation induced reduced PSD for post-EEG in delta band over the left and right prefrontal areas and increased PSD at the right parietal area; increased PSD in alpha band over the midline central area; and reduced PSD in gamma-band at the left parietal area, compared with 40 Hz-WL stimulation (Figure 4C, lower row).

3.2.4. Averaged PSD for the Prefrontal and Occipital Cortex during the Light Stimulation

Averaged PSDs for the prefrontal and occipital cortex during the light stimulation are shown in Figure 5. In addition, statistical results are summarized in Table 2.

Averaged PSDs for the Prefrontal ROI during the Light Stimulation

For the PSDs focused on the prefrontal area, the PSD in theta band during the 40 Hz-WL stimulation showed an increase compared with PSDs of baseline EEG and post-EEG with 40 Hz-VL. Additionally, for both the PSDs with 40 Hz-VL and 40 Hz-WL, 40 Hz frequency peaks on PSDs were non-significantly enhanced probably due to the entrainment of this specific gamma-frequency (Figure 5A).

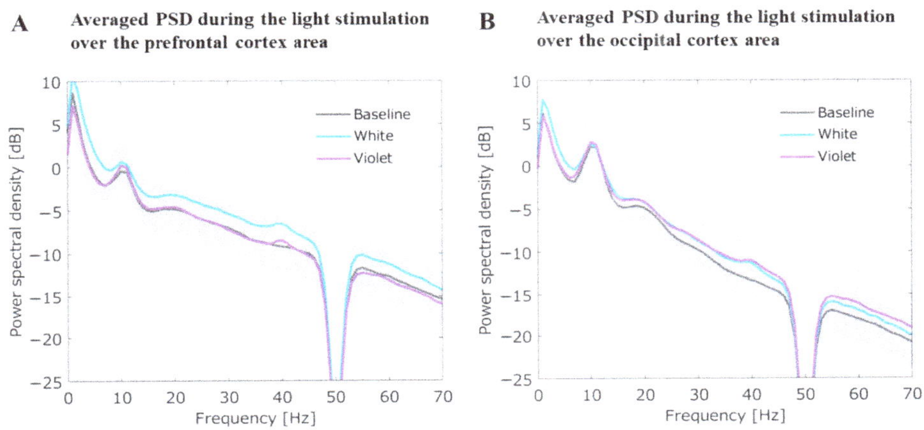

Figure 5. Averaged PSDs for the prefrontal and occipital cortex during the light stimulation. (**A**) shows averaged PSDs for the prefrontal region of interest (ROI) during the light stimulation. Compared with the PSD of baseline EEG, the prefrontal PSD for post-EEG with 40 Hz-WL was significantly increased in theta band (t_{38} = 2.03, p = 0.04); (**B**) shows averaged PSDs for the occipital ROI during the light stimulation. Compared with the PSD of baseline EEG, the occipital PSD for post-EEG with 40 Hz-WL was significantly increased in delta band (t_{38} = 1.98, p = 0.04). The graphs are presented with ±S.D. shadows to the mean PSD for each condition.

Table 2. Summary of statistical analysis results comparing averaged PSD for the prefrontal and occipital ROIs between 40 Hz-WL and 40 Hz-VL condition for each frequency band (* $p < 0.05$).

Frequency Band	**Prefrontal Cortex 40 Hz-WL vs. 40 Hz-VL**		**Occipital Cortex 40 Hz-WL vs. 40 Hz-VL**	
	t_{38}	p	t_{38}	p
Delta	1.89	0.07	1.87	0.04 *
Theta	2.03	0.04 *	1.34	0.18
Alpha	0.99	0.32	0.06	0.95
Beta	1.22	0.24	0.08	0.94
Gamma	1.18	0.24	0.30	0.77

Averaged PSDs for the Occipital ROI during the Light Stimulation

The PSD in delta band during the 40 Hz-WL stimulation showed an increase compared with PSDs of baseline EEG and post-EEG with 40 Hz-VL. Likewise, for both the PSDs with 40 Hz-VL and 40 Hz-WL, 40 Hz frequency peaks on PSDs were non-significantly enhanced probably due to the entrainment of this specific gamma-frequency (Figure 5B).

3.2.5. Averaged PSDs for the Prefrontal and Occipital ROIs for Post-EEG with the Light Stimulation

Averaged PSDs for the prefrontal and occipital cortex for post-EEG with the light stimulation are shown in Figure 6. Furthermore, statistical results are summarized in Table 3.

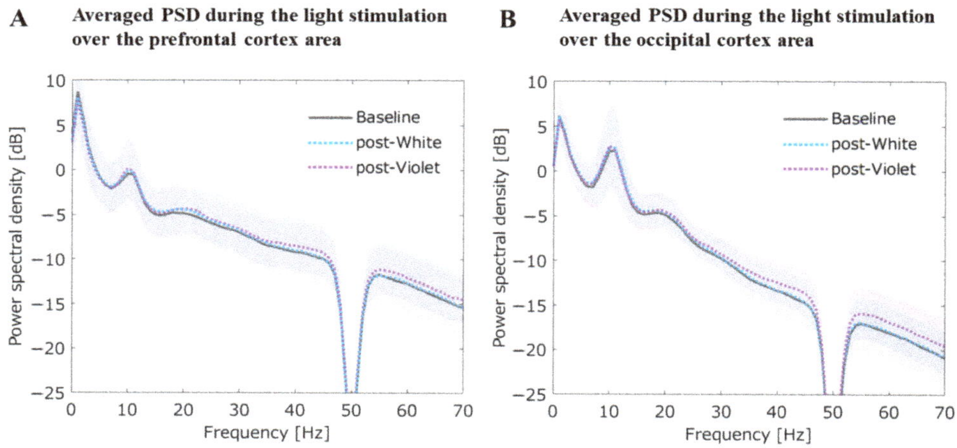

Figure 6. Averaged PSDs for the prefrontal and occipital cortex after the light stimulation. (**A**) shows averaged PSDs for the prefrontal ROI after the light stimulation. When comparing the PSD in the baseline EEG, EEG after 40 Hz-WL, and EEG after 40 Hz-VL conditions, there was no significant difference in any of the frequency bands; (**B**) shows averaged PSDs for the occipital ROI after the light stimulation. There was no significant difference in any of the frequency bands among the three conditions (i.e., baseline EEG, post-EEG with 40 Hz-WL, and post-EEG with 40 Hz-VL). The graphs are presented with ±S.D. shadows to the mean PSD for each condition.

Table 3. Summary of statistical analysis results comparing averaged PSD for the prefrontal and occipital ROIs between post-EEG with 40 Hz-WL and post-EEG with 40 Hz-VL for each frequency band (* $p < 0.05$).

Figure	Prefrontal Cortex		Occipital Cortex	
	t_{38}	p	t_{38}	p
Delta	0.34	0.73	0.45	0.66
Theta	0.25	0.81	0.23	0.81
Alpha	−0.03	0.98	0.15	0.87
Beta	−0.04	0.96	−0.22	0.82
Gamma	−0.53	0.60	−1.00	0.27

Averaged PSDs for the Prefrontal ROI after the Light Stimulation

When compared the PSDs of baseline EEG, post-EEG with 40 Hz-WL, and post-EEG with 40 Hz-VL conditions, there was no significant difference in any of the frequency bands (Figure 6A).

Averaged PSDs for the Occipital ROI after the Light Stimulation

In contrast, the analysis focused on the occipital area showed no significant differences in any of the frequency bands among the three conditions (i.e., baseline EEG, post-EEG with 40 Hz-WL, and post-EEG with 40 Hz-VL) (Figure 6B).

3.2.6. VEP at the Occipital Area

For the VEP at the occipital area (Oz electrode site), the negative peak of VEP appeared around 100 ms with 40 Hz-WL stimulation, whereas the corresponding negative peak of VEP with 40 Hz-VL was significantly smaller ($t_{38} = 2.04$, $p = 0.032$) than that of 40 Hz-WL (Figure 7). However, there was no significant difference in the negative peak latencies between the VEP with 40 Hz-VL and the VEP with 40 Hz-WL. Interestingly, there were significant correlations between VEP peak and PSD of gamma-band during 40 Hz-WL stimulation as well as between VEP peak and PSD of gamma-band during 40 Hz-VL stimulation over the occipital area.

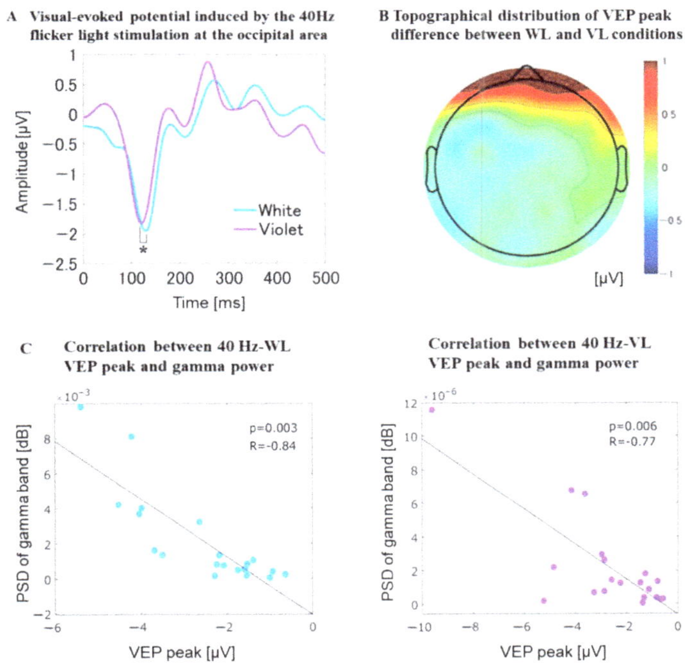

Figure 7. Visual-evoked potential at the occipital area. (**A**) represents the VEP at the occipital area (Oz electrode site). The negative peak of VEP appeared around 100 ms with 40 Hz-WL stimulation, whereas the corresponding negative peak of VEP with 40 Hz-VL was significantly smaller (t_{38} = 2.04, p = 0.032) than that of 40 Hz-WL. However, there was no significant difference in the negative peak latencies between the VEPs with 40 Hz-VL and the VEP with 40 Hz-WL; (**B**) depicts topographical distribution of VEP peak difference between 40 Hz-WL and 40 Hz-VL stimulation conditions; (**C**) shows significant correlations between VEP peak and PSD of gamma-band during 40 Hz-WL stimulation as well as between VEP peak and PSD of gamma-band during 40 Hz-VL stimulation.

3.2.7. Phase-Amplitude Coupling Analysis during VEP

Differences in Phase-Amplitude Coupling between EEG with 40 Hz-WL Stimulation and Baseline EEG as Well as between Post-EEG for 40 Hz-WL Stimulation and Baseline EEG

There were no significant impacts on phase-amplitude coupling by 40 Hz-WL stimulation for all electrodes and for both conditions (VEP during 40 Hz-WL and post-EEG with 40 Hz-WL stimulation).

Differences in Phase-Amplitude Coupling between EEG with 40 Hz-VL Stimulation and Baseline EEG as Well as between Post-EEG for 40 Hz-VL Stimulation and Baseline EEG

The 40 Hz-VL stimulation induced a significant increase of alpha-phase and gamma-amplitude coupling at the left prefrontal area (F5 electrode site: t_{38} = 2.08, p = 0.029) among the possible phase and amplitude coupling combinations (Figure 8A). Furthermore, there was a significant increase of alpha-phase and gamma-amplitude coupling at the right central area (C4 electrode site: t_{38} = 2.07, p = 0.033) after the 40 Hz-VL stimulation as well (Figure 8B).

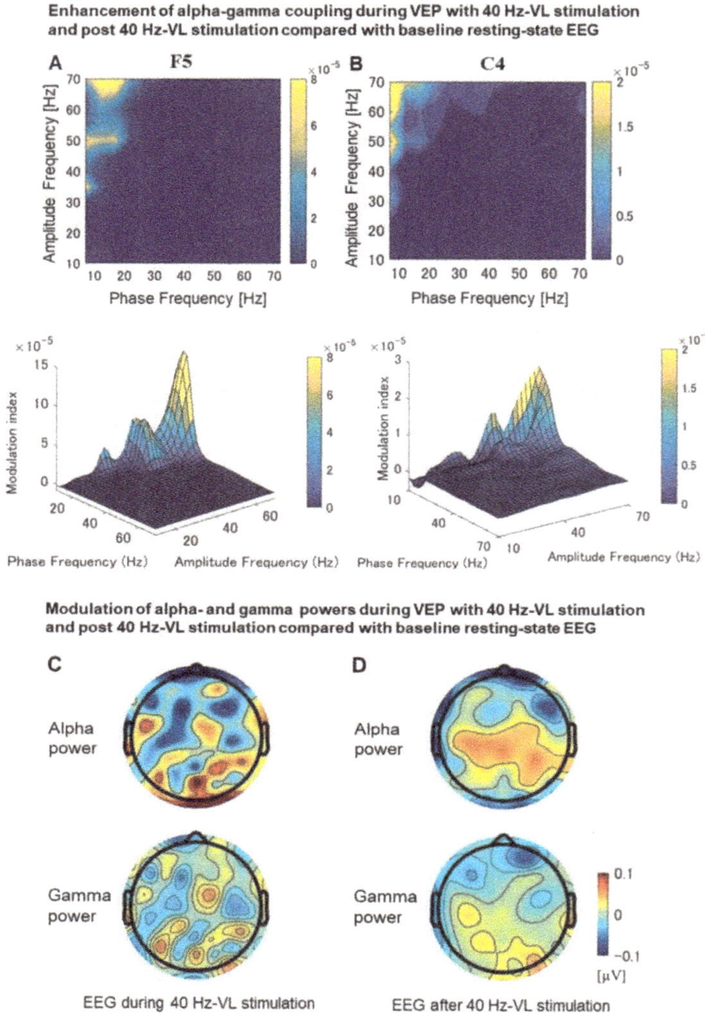

Figure 8. Enhanced alpha-phase and gamma-amplitude coupling and modulation of alpha and gamma power during and after 40 Hz-VL stimulation. (**A**, **B**) show the comodulogram, where the vertical axis represents the amplitude frequency, and the horizontal axis represents the phase frequency. The alpha-phase and gamma-amplitude coupling, which was significant during and after 40 Hz-VL stimulation, corresponds to the area shown in yellow in the color map display on the comodulogram. The upper row are 2-dimensional display graphs, and the lower row are 3-dimensional display graphs (Z-axis is the modulation index value). (**A**) demonstrated a significant increase of alpha-phase and gamma-amplitude coupling at the left prefrontal area (F5 electrode site: $t_{38} = 2.08$, $p = 0.029$) during the 40 Hz-VL stimulation (i.e., VEP with 40 Hz-VL minus baseline EEG); (**B**) indicated a significant increase of alpha-phase and gamma-amplitude coupling at the right central area (C4 electrode site: $t_{38} = 2.07$, $p = 0.033$) after the 40 Hz-VL stimulation (i.e., post-EEG with 40 Hz-VL minus baseline EEG); (**C**) displays EEG topological plots illustrating the changes in alpha- and gamma-band PSDs (0–1000 ms) during 40 Hz-VL stimulation compared to baseline resting-state EEG; (**D**) represents EEG topological plots depicting the changes in alpha- and gamma-band PSDs (0–1000 ms) after 40 Hz-VL stimulation compared to baseline resting-state EEG.

4. Discussion

4.1. Summary of Findings

The present study yielded several important findings as follows: (1) compared with averaged PSD of baseline EEG, averaged PSD of 40 Hz-WL in theta band was significantly increased; (2) when compared averaged PSDs between EEG with 40 Hz-VL and EEG with 40 Hz-WL, averaged PSDs for 40 Hz-WL in delta and theta bands showed significantly higher powers compared with averaged PSDs for 40 Hz-VL; (3) when focused on the prefrontal area, the PSD with 40 Hz-VL was significantly lower than PSD with 40 Hz-WL in theta band; (4) when focused on the occipital area, the PSD with 40 Hz-VL was significantly lower than PSD with 40 Hz-WL in delta band; (5) the VEP with 40 Hz-WL showed the negative peak around 100 ms at the Oz electrode site, whereas the VEP with 40 Hz-VL showed a significantly smaller negative peak than that of the VEP with 40 Hz-WL; (6) 40 Hz-VL induced significant increases of alpha-gamma coupling during the VEP at the F5 electrode site as well as for post-EEG with 40 Hz-VL at the C4 electrode site, compared with the coupling of baseline EEG.

4.2. Photobiological Neuromodulation of EEG during the 40 Hz-VL Stimulation Compared with 40 Hz-WL Stimulation

During the stimulation, averaged PSD over the all electrodes for EEG with 40 Hz-VL showed significantly lower neuromodulation in delta and theta bands compared with the PSD of EEG with 40 Hz-WL. In addition, averaged PSD over the all electrodes for post-EEG with 40 Hz-VL demonstrated a marginally significant increase in gamma-band compared with the PSD of baseline EEG. Here, since there is a phenomenon in the nervous system called "neural entrainment" in which neural activity is synchronized to the frequency of repetitive external stimuli, it is possible that the whole brain EEG power spectrum at the driving frequency, corresponding to 40 Hz in this study, increased as a steady-state response regardless of the stimulation wavelength of WL or VL [25,28]. Furthermore, when focused on the prefrontal ROI and occipital ROI, the PSD for EEG with 40 Hz-VL over the prefrontal ROI indicated significantly lower neuromodulation in theta band compared with the PSD of EEG with 40 Hz-WL, while the PSD of EEG with 40 Hz-VL over the occipital ROI revealed significantly lower neuromodulation in delta band compared with the PSD of EEG with 40 Hz-WL. Moreover, at the electrode level, when compared with the PSD of baseline EEG, 40 Hz-VL stimulation induced reduced neuromodulations in theta band at the right frontal and midline central areas; reduced neuromodulation in alpha band at the midline central area; reduced neuromodulation at the midline central area and increased neuromodulation at the right temporal area in beta band; and reduced neuromodulation at the midline and left parietal areas in gamma-band. Furthermore, when compared the PSDs between VEP with 40 Hz-WL and VEP with 40 Hz-VL, 40 Hz-VL stimulation induced lower neuromodulations in gamma-band at the left parieto-occipital area, compared with 40 Hz-WL stimulation. In the whole cortex level, both 40 Hz-WL and 40 Hz-VL stimulation tended to induce enhancement of theta oscillation system compared with baseline EEG. Furthermore, 40 Hz-VL stimulation induced a weaker enhancement of PSD in delta and theta bands compared with 40 Hz-WL stimulation. In other words, 40 Hz-VL stimulation may be causing activation of a distinct pathway from the activation of the delta/theta system in the usual visual pathway [29,30]. In addition, 40 Hz-VL stimulation caused local PSD changes compared to the baseline at the electrode level, including broadband neuromodulation from theta to gamma bands. In particular, the attenuative neuromodulation by 40 Hz-VL in the theta, alpha, and gamma bands may reflect unique responses mediated by special pathways, such as OPN5 receptors, that differ from the usual visual pathways. Notably, it is known that there is an interaction between the alpha- and gamma-oscillation generating systems; specifically, activity in the gamma-band induces activity in the alpha band, and furthermore, amplitude modulation occurs by suppressing activity in the alpha system [23]. Taken together, 40 Hz-VL stimulation may be involved in the activation of transient cognitive functions in humans.

4.3. Significant Difference in the Negative Peak of the VEPs between 40 Hz-VL and 40 Hz-WL

Both 40 Hz-WL and 40 Hz-VL stimulation evoked a typical VEP pattern in the occipital region. Indeed, it is known that gamma-frequency visual stimulation with WL can induce the typical VEPs at the parieto-occipital region [25]. However, in the present results, the VEP by 40 Hz-VL stimulation was significantly lower than VEP induced by 40 Hz-WL stimulation. This finding suggests that 40 Hz-VL stimulation, unlike 40 Hz-WL, may activate different circuits such as non-visual processing circuits via VL stimulus-OPN5 receptor system. In addition, since there were significant correlations between the VEP peak and PSD of gamma-band in both conditions, during 40 Hz-WL and 40 Hz-VL stimulation, light stimulation at 40 Hz can induce entrainment of the gamma-frequency band in the EEG activity at the occipital region.

4.4. Significant Enhancement of Alpha-Gamma Coupling during and after 40 Hz-VL Stimulation

The present study demonstrated that 40 Hz-VL stimulation induced significant increase of alpha-gamma coupling at the left prefrontal area during the stimulation period while it induced the alpha-gamma coupling over the right central area after the stimulation compared to resting-state EEG. Brain oscillations are one of the core mechanisms underlying cognitive functions, including episodic memory, which have also been considered to be important for long-term memory since they induce synchronized firing between cell assemblies that form synaptic plasticity. Indeed, several previous studies have focused on the role of synchronization in episodic memory, as reflected in increases in theta rhythm (~5 Hz) and gamma-rhythm (>40 Hz) power. However, recent studies have also focused not only on changes in theta and gamma power, but also on the importance of coupling between desynchronization of basic rhythms in the neocortex as represented by alpha rhythm power and synchronization in the gamma-rhythm in the process of cognitive functioning [31,32]. For example, successful encoding and recall of episodic memories requires the ability to (1) represent detailed multisensory information and (2) combine that information into a coherent episode. Previous studies suggest that these two cognitive processes are achieved by desynchronization of alpha rhythms in the neocortex (i.e., decrease in alpha power) and synchronization of gamma rhythms in the hippocampus (i.e., increase in gamma power), respectively. In other words, it has been shown that the co-existence and interaction of these two processes may be important for cognitive processing [33]. As such, the present findings regarding the alpha-gamma coupling during and following the 40 Hz-VL stimulation may represent a potential neurophysiological enhancement of cognitive function.

4.5. Limitations of This Study

There are some limitations in this study. First, due to the nature of the study, which was primarily intended for a preliminary hypothesis-based analysis, the sample size of the participants was relatively small, and the significance level was set at 0.05 in this study. Therefore, the results of this study need further validation in the future. Second, since this was a non-interventional experiment with healthy participants, we did not evaluate the effects of 40 Hz-VL light stimulation on cognitive functions and clinical symptoms. Future interventional studies in patient groups compared to controls are needed. Third, since we examined the neurophysiological changes of EEG during and immediately after the light stimulation, the long-term effects after the light stimulation were not assessed. Therefore, future studies need to include long-term follow-up examinations after the light stimulation.

5. Conclusions

Collectively, the present study demonstrated that 40 Hz-VL stimulation induced unique photobiological neuromodulations of resting EEG activity as well as the steady-state VEP in healthy participants as represented by alpha-gamma coupling. These neurophysiological modulations suggest that the 40 Hz-VL with stimulation may have some potential proactive effects on cognitive processes in humans. In the future, clinical trials using 40 Hz-VL stimulation in patients with major depression and mild cognitive impairment should be conducted to rigorously confirm whether this 40 Hz-VL optical neuromodulation is actually safe and has beneficial effects on clinical symptoms and cognitive function. Indeed, we are planning to start those clinical trials by the end of 2021.

Supplementary Materials: Page: 18. The following are available online at https://www.mdpi.com/article/10.3390/jpm11060557/s1, Figure S1: Schematic diagram of time of interest for PSD and VEP analyses. In the photo-stimulation experiment, 40 Hz light stimulation with a time width of 1 s was performed at 2-s intervals (i.e., 0.5 Hz) as shown in the figure above, and the EEG analysis was performed after epoching the continuous EEG data in the −1000 to 2000 ms segment. Specifically, the calculation of PSD was performed for the section indicated by the blue band, while the calculation of VEP was performed for the section indicated by the red band.

Author Contributions: Conceptualization, Y.N., M.H., S.K. and K.T.; methodology, Y.N. and S.K.; validation, Y.N.; investigation, X.L.; formal analysis, M.T.; writing: original draft preparation, Y.N.; writing: review and editing, Y.N., M.H., M.W., S.N., M.M. and K.T.; visualization, M.T.; supervision, Y.N., M.H. and K.T.; project administration, Y.N. and M.H. All authors have read and agreed to the published version of the manuscript.

Funding: This research received no external funding.

Institutional Review Board Statement: The study was conducted according to the guidelines of the Declaration of Helsinki, and approved by the Ethics Committee of Keio University School of Medicine (protocol code ID: 20190096 and date of approval: 2019-10-29).

Informed Consent Statement: Informed consent was obtained from all subjects involved in the study.

Data Availability Statement: Data sharing not applicable.

Acknowledgments: We would like to thank all the participants in this study and the research assistants who helped with the experiments. We would like to thank Tatsumi Furukawa and Makoto Sawano of Miyuki Giken Co., Ltd. (Tokyo, Japan) for their full support in setting up the experimental system for light stimulation. Y.N. has received a Grant-in-Aid for Young Scientists (18K15375) and a Grant-in-Aid for Scientific Research (B) (21H02813) from the Japan Society for the Promotion of Science (JSPS), research grants from Japan Agency for Medical Research and Development (AMED), investigator-initiated clinical study grants from TEIJIN PHARMA LIMITED (Tokyo, Japan) and Inter Reha Co., Ltd.(Tokyo, Japan) Y.N. also receives research grants from Japan Health Foundation, Meiji Yasuda Mental Health Foundation, Mitsui Life Social Welfare Foundation, Takeda Science Foundation, SENSHIN Medical Research Foundation, Health Science Center Foundation, Mochida Memorial Foundation for Medical and Pharmaceutical Research, Taiju Life Social Welfare Foundation, and Daiichi Sankyo Scholarship Donation Program. Y.N. has received speaker's honoraria from Dainippon Sumitomo Pharma, MOCHIDA PHARMACEUTICAL CO., LTD. (Tokyo, Japan), and Yoshitomiyakuhin Corporation within the past three years. Y.N. also receives equipment-in-kind support for an investigator-initiated study from Magventure Inc. (Farum, Denmark), Inter Reha Co., Ltd., BrainBox Ltd. (Cardiff, United Kingdom), and Miyuki Giken Co., Ltd. M.H. has received a Grant-in-Aid for Young Scientists (19K16619) and a Grant-in-Aid for Scientific Research on Innovative Areas (19H05269). S.N. has received a Grant-in-Aid for Young Scientists A and Grants-in-Aid for Scientific Research B and C from JSPS, and research grants from Japan Research Foundation for Clinical Pharmacology, Naito Foundation, Takeda Science Foundation, Uehara Memorial Foundation, and Daiichi Sankyo Scholarship Donation Program within the past three years. S.N. has also received research support, manuscript fees or speaker's honoraria from Dainippon Sumitomo Pharma, Meiji-Seika Pharma, Otsuka Pharmaceutical, Shionogi, and Yoshitomi Yakuhin within the past three years. M.M. received grants and/or speaker's honoraria from Asahi Kasei Pharma, Astellas Pharma, Daiichi Sankyo, Sumitomo Dainippon Pharma, Eisai, Eli Lilly, Fuji Film RI Pharma, Janssen Pharmaceutical, Kracie, Meiji-Seika Pharma, Mochida Pharmaceutical, Merck Sharp and Dohme, Novartis Pharma, Ono Pharmaceutical, Otsuka Pharmaceutical, Pfizer, Shionogi, Takeda Pharmaceutical, Mitsubishi Tanabe Pharma, and Yoshitomi Yakuhin.

Conflicts of Interest: None of the authors declare any conflict of interest.

References

1. Salehpour, F.; Mahmoudi, J.; Kamari, F.; Sadigh-Eteghad, S.; Rasta, S.H.; Hamblin, M.R. Brain Photobiomodulation Therapy: A Narrative Review. *Mol. Neurobiol.* **2018**, *55*, 6601–6636. [CrossRef]
2. Lucas, R.J.; Peirson, S.N.; Berson, D.M.; Brown, T.M.; Cooper, H.M.; Czeisler, C.A.; Figueiro, M.G.; Gamlin, P.D.; Lockley, S.W.; O'Hagan, J.B.; et al. Measuring and using light in the melanopsin age. *Trends Neurosci.* **2014**, *37*, 1–9. [CrossRef] [PubMed]
3. Cassano, P.; Petrie, S.R.; Hamblin, M.R.; Henderson, T.A.; Iosifescu, D.V. Review of transcranial photobiomodulation for major depressive disorder: Targeting brain metabolism, inflammation, oxidative stress, and neurogenesis. *Neurophotonics* **2016**, *3*, 031404. [CrossRef] [PubMed]
4. Do, M.T.H.; Yau, K.-W. Intrinsically Photosensitive Retinal Ganglion Cells. *Physiol. Rev.* **2010**, *90*, 1547–1581. [CrossRef] [PubMed]
5. Kolb, H.; Fernandez, E.; Nelson, R. *Webvision: The Organization of the Retina and Visual System*; Kolb, H., Fernandez, E., Nelson, R., Eds.; University of Utah Health Sciences Center: Salt Lake City, UT, USA, 1995.
6. Do, M.T.H.; Kang, S.H.; Xue, T.; Zhong, H.; Liao, H.-W.; Bergles, D.; Yau, K.-W. Photon capture and signalling by melanopsin retinal ganglion cells. *Nat. Cell Biol.* **2008**, *457*, 281–287. [CrossRef]
7. Tarttelin, E.E.; Bellingham, J.; Hankins, M.W.; Foster, R.G.; Lucas, R. Neuropsin (Opn5): A novel opsin identified in mammalian neural tissue1. *FEBS Lett.* **2003**, *554*, 410–416. [CrossRef]
8. Fredriksson, R.; Höglund, P.J.; Gloriam, D.E.; Lagerström, M.C.; Schiöth, H.B. Seven evolutionarily conserved human rhodopsin G protein-coupled receptors lacking close relatives. *FEBS Lett.* **2003**, *554*, 381–388. [CrossRef]
9. Kojima, D.; Mori, S.; Torii, M.; Wada, A.; Morishita, R.; Fukada, Y. UV-Sensitive Photoreceptor Protein OPN5 in Humans and Mice. *PLoS ONE* **2011**, *6*, e26388. [CrossRef] [PubMed]
10. Yamashita, T.; Ohuchi, H.; Tomonari, S.; Ikeda, K.; Sakai, K.; Shichida, Y. Opn5 is a UV-sensitive bistable pigment that couples with Gi subtype of G protein. *Proc. Natl. Acad. Sci. USA* **2010**, *107*, 22084–22089. [CrossRef]
11. Ecker, J.L.; Dumitrescu, O.N.; Wong, K.Y.; Alam, N.M.; Chen, S.-K.; LeGates, T.; Renna, J.M.; Prusky, G.T.; Berson, D.M.; Hattar, S. Melanopsin-Expressing Retinal Ganglion-Cell Photoreceptors: Cellular Diversity and Role in Pattern Vision. *Neuron* **2010**, *67*, 49–60. [CrossRef]
12. Estevez, M.E.; Fogerson, P.M.; Ilardi, M.C.; Borghuis, B.G.; Chan, E.; Weng, S.; Auferkorte, O.N.; Demb, J.; Berson, D.M. Form and Function of the M4 Cell, an Intrinsically Photosensitive Retinal Ganglion Cell Type Contributing to Geniculocortical Vision. *J. Neurosci.* **2012**, *32*, 13608–13620. [CrossRef]
13. Schmidt, T.M.; Kofuji, P. Functional and morphological differences among intrinsically photosensitive retinal ganglion cells. *J. Neurosci.* **2009**, *29*, 476–482. [CrossRef]
14. Schmidt, T.M.; Kofuji, P. Differential cone pathway influence on intrinsically photosensitive retinal ganglion cell subtypes. *J. Neurosci.* **2010**, *30*, 16262–16271. [CrossRef] [PubMed]
15. Zhang, K.X.; D'Souza, S.; Upton, B.A.; Kernodle, S.; Vemaraju, S.; Nayak, G.; Gaitonde, K.D.; Holt, A.L.; Linne, C.D.; Smith, A.N.; et al. Violet-light suppression of thermogenesis by opsin 5 hypothalamic neurons. *Nat. Cell Biol.* **2020**, *585*, 420–425. [CrossRef]
16. Torii, H.; Kurihara, T.; Seko, Y.; Negishi, K.; Ohnuma, K.; Inaba, T.; Kawashima, M.; Jiang, X.; Kondo, S.; Miyauchi, M.; et al. Violet Light Exposure Can Be a Preventive Strategy Against Myopia Progression. *EBioMedicine* **2017**, *15*, 210–219. [CrossRef] [PubMed]
17. Knapska, E.; Kaczmarek, L. A gene for neuronal plasticity in the mammalian brain: Zif268/Egr-1/NGFI-A/Krox-24/TIS8/ZENK? *Prog. Neurobiol.* **2004**, *74*, 183–211. [CrossRef] [PubMed]
18. Dijk, D.J.; von Schantz, M. Timing and consolidation of human sleep, wakefulness, and performance by a symphony of oscillators. *J. Biol. Rhythms* **2005**, *20*, 279–290. [CrossRef] [PubMed]
19. Iaccarino, H.F.; Singer, A.C.; Martorell, A.J.; Rudenko, A.; Gao, F.; Gillingham, T.Z.; Mathys, H.; Seo, J.; Kritskiy, O.; Abdurrob, F.; et al. Gamma frequency entrainment attenuates amyloid load and modifies microglia. *Nat. Cell Biol.* **2016**, *540*, 230–235. [CrossRef] [PubMed]
20. Sohal, V.S. How Close Are We to Understanding What (if Anything) gamma Oscillations Do in Cortical Circuits? *J. Neurosci.* **2016**, *36*, 10489–10495. [CrossRef]
21. Murty, D.V.; Shirhatti, V.; Ravishankar, P.; Ray, S. Large Visual Stimuli Induce Two Distinct Gamma Oscillations in Primate Visual Cortex. *J. Neurosci.* **2018**, *38*, 2730–2744. [CrossRef]
22. Todorov, M.I.; Kékesi, K.A.; Borhegyi, Z.; Galambos, R.; Juhász, G.; Hudetz, A.G. Retino-cortical stimulus frequency-dependent gamma coupling: Evidence and functional implications of oscillatory potentials. *Physiol. Rep.* **2016**, *4*, e12986. [CrossRef]
23. Chorlian, D.B.; Porjesz, B.; Begleiter, H. Amplitude modulation of gamma band oscillations at alpha frequency produced by photic driving. *Int. J. Psychophysiol.* **2006**, *61*, 262–278. [CrossRef]
24. Paszkiel, S. Data Acquisition Methods for Human Brain Activity. In *Analysis and Classification of EEG Signals for Brain–Computer Interfaces*; Studies in Computational Intelligence; Springer: Cham, Switzerland, 2020; Volume 852.
25. Tsoneva, T.; Garcia-Molina, G.; Desain, P. Neural dynamics during repetitive visual stimulation. *J. Neural Eng.* **2015**, *12*, 66017. [CrossRef]
26. Helfrich, R.F.; Herrmann, C.; Engel, A.K.; Schneider, T.R. Different coupling modes mediate cortical cross-frequency interactions. *NeuroImage* **2016**, *140*, 76–82. [CrossRef]
27. Tort, A.B.L.; Komorowski, R.; Eichenbaum, H.; Kopell, N. Measuring Phase-Amplitude Coupling Between Neuronal Oscillations of Different Frequencies. *J. Neurophysiol.* **2010**, *104*, 1195–1210. [CrossRef]

28. Otero, M.; Prado-Gutiérrez, P.; Weinstein, A.; Escobar, M.-J.; El-Deredy, W. Persistence of EEG Alpha Entrainment Depends on Stimulus Phase at Offset. *Front. Hum. Neurosci.* **2020**, *14*, 139. [CrossRef]
29. Köster, M.; Finger, H.; Graetz, S.; Kater, M.; Gruber, T. Theta-gamma coupling binds visual perceptual features in an associative memory task. *Sci. Rep.* **2018**, *8*, 17688. [CrossRef] [PubMed]
30. Köster, M.; Martens, U.; Gruber, T. Memory entrainment by visually evoked theta-gamma coupling. *NeuroImage* **2019**, *188*, 181–187. [CrossRef] [PubMed]
31. Hanslmayr, S.; Staudigl, T.; Fellner, M.C. Oscillatory power decreases and long-term memory: The information via desynchronization hypothesis. *Front. Hum. Neurosci.* **2012**, *6*, 74. [CrossRef] [PubMed]
32. Hanslmayr, S.; Staresina, B.P.; Bowman, H. Oscillations and Episodic Memory: Addressing the Synchronization/Desynchronization Conundrum. *Trends Neurosci.* **2016**, *39*, 16–25. [CrossRef]
33. Griffiths, B.J.; Parish, G.; Roux, F.; Michelmann, S.; van der Plas, M.; Kolibius, L.D.; Chelvarajah, R.; Rollings, D.T.; Sawlani, V.; Hamer, H.; et al. Directional coupling of slow and fast hippocampal gamma with neocortical alpha/beta oscillations in human episodic memory. *Proc. Natl. Acad. Sci. USA* **2019**, *116*, 21834–21842. [CrossRef] [PubMed]

Journal of *Personalized Medicine*

MDPI

Article

Clinical and Electrophysiological Hints to TMS in de novo Patients with Parkinson's Disease and Progressive Supranuclear Palsy

Francesco Fisicaro [1,†], Giuseppe Lanza [2,3,*,†], Mariagiovanna Cantone [4], Raffaele Ferri [3], Giovanni Pennisi [2], Alessandra Nicoletti [5], Mario Zappia [5], Rita Bella [5] and Manuela Pennisi [1]

1 Department of Biomedical and Biotechnological Sciences, University of Catania, Via Santa Sofia, 97-95123 Catania, Italy; drfrancescofisicaro@gmail.com (F.F.); manuela.pennisi@unict.it (M.P.)
2 Department of Surgery and Medical-Surgical Specialties, University of Catania, Via Santa Sofia, 78-95123 Catania, Italy; pennigi@unict.it
3 Department of Neurology IC, Oasi Research Institute-IRCCS, Via Conte Ruggero, 73-94018 Troina, Italy; rferri@oasi.en.it
4 Department of Neurology, Sant'Elia Hospital, ASP Caltanissetta, Via Luigi Russo, 6-93100 Caltanissetta, Italy; m.cantone@asp.cl.it
5 Department of Medical and Surgical Sciences and Advanced Technologies, University of Catania, Via Santa Sofia, 87-95123 Catania, Italy; anicolet@unict.it (A.N.); m.zappia@unict.it (M.Z.); rbella@unict.it (R.B.)
* Correspondence: glanza@oasi.en.it; Tel.: +39-095-3782448
† These authors contributed equally to this work.

Received: 30 September 2020; Accepted: 10 December 2020; Published: 12 December 2020

check for updates

Abstract: Background: Transcranial magnetic stimulation (TMS) can non-invasively probe cortical excitability in movement disorders, although clinical significance is still controversial, especially at early stages. We compare single-pulse TMS in two prototypic synucleinopathy and tauopathy—i.e., Parkinson's disease (PD) and Progressive Supranuclear Palsy (PSP), respectively—to find neurophysiological differences and identify early measures associated with cognitive impairment. Methods: 28 PD and 23 PSP de novo patients were age-matched with 28 healthy controls, all right-handed and drug-free. Amplitude and latency of motor evoked potentials (MEP), central motor conduction time, resting motor threshold (rMT), and cortical silent period (CSP) were recorded through a figure-of-eight coil from the First Dorsal Interosseous muscle (FDI), bilaterally. Results: Mini Mental Examination and Frontal Assessment Battery (FAB) scored worse in PSP; PD had worse FAB than controls. Higher MEP amplitude from right FDI in PD and PSP than controls was found, without difference between them. CSP was bilaterally longer in patients than controls, but similar between patient groups. A positive correlation between FAB and rMT was observed in PSP, bilaterally. Conclusions: Despite the small sample size, PD and PSP might share, at early stage, a similar global electrocortical asset. rMT might detect and possibly predict cognitive deterioration in PSP.

Keywords: transcranial magnetic stimulation; cortical excitability; electrophysiology; neurodegeneration; parkinsonian syndrome; atypical parkinsonism

1. Introduction

Among movement disorders, an accurate and early diagnosis of the most common tauopathy—i.e., Progressive Supranuclear Palsy (PSP)—and the differential diagnosis from the prototypic α-synucleinopathy—i.e., Parkinson's disease (PD)—is often challenging, particularly at their early stages [1–3]. In addition to the typical histopathological lesion observed in PD (i.e., degeneration of the substantia nigra pars compacta), the thinning of the medial frontal (premotor and supplementary motor) and posterior cingulate cortex has been described [4]. Furthermore, dopamine depletion can induce a functional reorganization of the motor maps [5]. In PSP, argyrophilic and tau-positive tufted astrocytes, neurofibrillary tangles, coiled bodies, and thread-like processes are found not only in the basal ganglia and brainstem nuclei, but also in the primary motor cortex (M1) [6]. The different histological substrates of these diseases might be associated with specific neurophysiological characteristics. In this context, the role of non-invasive brain stimulation techniques, such as transcranial magnetic stimulation (TMS), may help in disentangling this complex pathophysiology.

TMS is a non-invasive electrophysiological technique able to assess the intracortical excitability and the cortico-spinal conductivity in vivo and in "real time", thus being used in clinical practice [7–11], research settings [12–15], and experimental treatments [16,17]. Single-pulse stimulation is routinely used to assess basic features of motor evoked potentials (MEPs), including MEP latency and amplitude, central motor conduction time (CMCT), and some global measures of excitability, such as the resting motor threshold (rMT) and the cortical silent period (CSP). rMT and MEP reflect not only the conductivity of the cortico-spinal tract, but also the excitability of the M1 and nerve roots, as well as the conduction along the peripheral motor pathway till the muscles [8]. While CSP is believed to be due to inhibitory mechanisms at the M1 level, spinal components (such as the Renshaw inhibition) are thought to contribute, although only to the first 50–60 ms of this suppression [18].

Since the early studies [19], indeed, TMS has been used to explore the inhibitory and excitatory interactions of both motor and non-motor cortical regions, within and across cerebral hemispheres, thus providing insights into the intracortical and intercortical mechanisms underlying the role of different brain regions in cognitive processes, motor control, and plastic changes after a brain lesion or during the course of a neurodegenerative process [20]. Used in combination with neuroimaging, TMS also provides information on the functional connectivity between different motor and non-motor regions and on the relationship between pathophysiological processes and specific brain areas [20]. Although the abnormalities revealed by TMS are not disease-specific [18], there may be distinct neurophysiological changes that co-segregate in each dementing illness, consistent with the involvement of specific neurobiological substrates [19,21–24]. These indexes have also been proposed for the early detection of cognitive impairment, the monitoring of disease progression, and the evaluation of treatment response [25,26].

A new concept of the M1 has also emerged, in which motor cortical output is influenced also by non-primary motor areas, including ventral and dorsal premotor cortex, and supplementary motor area, and even by non-motor regions (such as the cingulate cortex) [20]. Accordingly, although not always clinically evident, the involvement of motor areas in dementia has been demonstrated, with changes in motor areas that may be secondary to direct structural alterations caused by the disease process or, more often, to indirect plastic remodeling mechanisms [19]. Finally, by evaluating the effects of agonists or antagonists for specific neurotransmitters, TMS can selectively and non-invasively probe the functioning of glutamatergic, gamma-aminobutyric acid (GABA)-ergic and cholinergic cortical circuits [27], which are all implicated in cognitive and movement disorders.

When applied to movement disorders, TMS can characterize the cortical excitability at the final motor output stage and its modulation by altered basal ganglia activity [28]. Histology [29] and functional imaging in vivo studies [30] demonstrated that the direct dopaminergic innervation of M1 degenerates relatively early in PD patients, a finding which is in line with a local reduction in its metabolism [31]. Furthermore, electrophysiological effects of dopaminergic degeneration also on subcortical motor structures are well documented, as well as the evidence that M1 activity is influenced by existing PD therapies, including not only l-3,4-dihydroxyphenylalanine (l-DOPA) but also deep brain stimulation of the subthalamic nucleus, as very recently reviewed [32].

Overall, in PD patients, the majority of TMS studies suggests an imbalance of M1 excitability towards a state of reduced inhibition. Specifically, a marked reduction in the short-interval intracortical inhibition (SICI), which is a measure of the GABA-A receptor transmission, has been reported, suggesting an impaired intracortical inhibitory activity which partially reverted after dopaminergic therapy [33–36]. Shortening of CSP duration has been reported in PD patients, particularly in the early untreated stages, and correlated with limb rigidity [37]. Regarding the short-latency afferent inhibition (SAI), which is thought to reflect the central cholinergic functioning, evidence is conflicting, with researchers reporting reduced [38,39], normal [40], or increased values [41]. Finally, most studies have reported that rMT is normal in PD [34,36,42], whereas increased MEP amplitude at rest has been found [43,44].

In PSP, earlier studies revealed CMCT abnormality, although only in a subgroup of patients with a long disease duration [37,45,46]. Reduced SICI, changes in CSP duration, and increased MEP amplitude have been reported and appeared to correlate with the disease progression [46–48]. More recent work also showed changes in cortical excitability and synaptic plasticity [47,49–51]. Regarding CSP, a longer duration has been reported in PSP, whereas the opposite has been observed in PD patients [52]. However, CSP is highly variable depending on several factors (e.g., TMS intensity, selection of target muscle, coil shape, and position) [53], and its significance in clinical practice is still controversial.

As TMS can detect early electrophysiological changes of movement disorders, we examined and compared single-pulse TMS in de novo patients with PD and PSP with a relatively short disease duration. As mentioned, indeed, studies directly comparing PD and PSP at their early stages are scarce and rather conflicting, whereas those correlating clinical-cognitive data with TMS findings in early non-demented patients are lacking. We hypothesized that the two groups of patients may show different neurophysiological patterns and that specific TMS measures might be associated with cognitive impairment, which is known to be more prominent in PSP than in PD.

2. Materials and Methods

2.1. Subjects and Assessment

We consecutively recruited 28 de novo patients with idiopathic PD (median age 63.5 years, range 59.0–69.5; 18 males) and 23 de novo patients with PSP (median age 67 years, range 63.0–72.0; 11 males) from the Neurology Department of the "Azienda Ospedaliera Universitaria Policlinico Gaspare Rodolico-San Marco" of Catania (Italy), from November 2018 to September 2020. The control group consisted of 28 age-matched healthy subjects (median age 65 years, range 58.5–69.0; 16 males), recruited from the TMS Lab of the above-mentioned Institution. All participants were right-handed, as assessed by the Edinburgh Handedness Inventory [54]. Controls were drug-free, did not have any history of neurological or psychiatric disorders, and their neurological examination and brain magnetic resonance imaging (MRI) were both normal.

All patients had a diagnosis of probable PD based on the clinical diagnostic criteria of the Movement Disorder Society [55], or PSP following the criteria of the National Institute of Neurological Disorders and Stroke—Society for PSP [56]. The median disease duration was 2 years (range 2–4) in the PD group and 3 years (range 2–4) in the PSP group. DaTscan single-photon emission computed tomography and magnetic resonance parkinsonism index, performed in all patients, were compatible with an early stage of the diseases [57,58]. Among PD patients, 22 had an akinetic-rigid form, whereas the other 6 exhibited a mixed presentation, with a predominant akinetic-rigid phenotype; brain MRI was normal in all of them. The majority of PD patients (25 out of 28) presented an asymmetry of their motor manifestations, being the right side more clinically affected than the left side; the remaining three exhibited a bilateral presentation. All PSP patients had a bilateral akinetic-rigid syndrome with predominant symptoms in the right limbs, which poorly responded to l-DOPA; brain MRI showed varying degrees of brainstem, basal ganglia, and frontal lobe atrophy. All patients were clinically evaluated by using the Unified Parkinson's Disease Rating Scale (UPDRS)—part III (motor examination) [59] and the Hoehn and Yahr (H-Y) scale [60].

None of the participants had major neurocognitive disorder (dementia) on the basis of the latest diagnostic criteria of the Diagnostic and Statistical Manual of Mental Disorders, Fifth Edition [61]. The Mini Mental State Examination (MMSE) [62] was administered to all subjects in order to screen cognitive functioning, as well as the Frontal Assessment Battery (FAB) [63] to assess the frontal lobe abilities, and the Hamilton Depression Rating Scale [64] to quantify any symptom of depression. Both MMSE and FAB scores were adjusted for age and educational level for each subject. Clinical and neuropsychological variables were evaluated independently by different investigators (AN and RB), and the TMS operators (GL and MP) were blinded to the clinical scores. Patients were drug-naïve and no other medication able to affect cortical excitability was assumed before TMS [27,65,66].

Exclusion criteria were: other neurological diseases (e.g., traumatic head or back injury, stroke or chronic cerebrovascular disease, spinal cord injury or any other spinal cord disease, any other movement disorder, any inflammatory or demyelinating disease, tumors, etc.); peripheral neuropathies, radiculopathies, or neuromuscular disorders; previous cranial or spinal surgery; major psychiatric diseases; acute, advanced, or chronic not compensated medical illnesses (including diabetes, hypothyroidism, and neoplasm); history or presence of seizures, implanted biomedical devices (i.e., pacemaker, prosthesis, intracranial clips), pregnancy at the time of testing, or any other contraindication to TMS [7]. Although evidence of cervical disc protrusions was present in some patients, none had any clinical or radiological sign of cervical cord or spinal root compression. A conventional electroencephalography was preliminary performed prior to TMS to exclude predisposition to seizures.

The study was carried out by trained operators in accordance with the latest recommendations of the International Federation of Clinical Neurophysiology (IFCN) for the diagnostic use of TMS [8]. All the experimental procedures were approved by the Ethics Committee of the "Azienda Ospedaliera Universitaria Policlinico Gaspare Rodolico-San Marco" (approval number: 9/2018/PO) and carried out following the rules of the Declaration of Helsinki of 1975, revised in 2013. All subjects gave their signed informed consent for inclusion before they participated in the study.

2.2. Transcranial Magnetic Stimulation

TMS was performed using a high-power Magstim 220 mono-pulse magnetic stimulator (Magstim Co., Whitland, Dyfed, UK). A figure-of-eight coil (external loop diameter 90 mm) was held tangentially over the M1 of each hemisphere, at the optimum scalp position ("hot spot") to elicit MEPs in the contralateral First Dorsal Interosseous (FDI) muscle of each hand, with the induced current flowing in a posterior–anterior direction, as recommended [8]. Once located, the hot spot was marked on the scalp with a soft-tip pen.

Electromyographic (EMG) activity was recorded with silver/silver-chloride disposable self-adhesive and self-conductive surface electrodes. The active electrode was placed over the muscular belly of the target muscle, the reference was positioned distally at the metacarpal-phalangeal joint of the index finger, and the ground was on the dorsal face of the wrist. MEPs were amplified and filtered (bandwidth 3–3000 Hz), and recorded by using a 2-channel Medelec Synergy system (Oxford Instruments Medical, Inc, Surrey, UK).

The rMT was defined as the lowest stimulus intensity able to elicit MEP at rest of an amplitude >50 μV in at least 5 of 10 trials, according to the above-mentioned guidelines [8]. Five reproducible MEPs during moderate active muscle contraction (about 10–20% of the subject's maximum voluntary contraction, by using a strain gauge) were elicited. Among them, the MEP with the shortest latency was considered for CMCT calculation, according to the IFCN guidelines [8]. CMCT was calculated by subtracting the conduction time in peripheral nerves obtained by magnetic stimulation of the cervical root, from the shortest MEP cortical latency obtained with a stimulus intensity set at 130% of the rMT. To ensure reproducibility, three peripheral motor responses were recorded at rest and averaged. Peak-to-peak MEP amplitude during active contraction level was also calculated.

The CSP was determined with an approximately 50% of maximum tonic voluntary contraction of the FDI muscle, induced by single TMS pulses delivered at 130% of rMT. As recommended [8], the mean CSP duration of 7 rectified trials was calculated. Namely, in a single trial, the CSP was measured as the time elapsing from the onset of the MEP until the recurrence of voluntary tonic EMG activity.

Since PD and, to a lesser extent, PSP are characterized by an asymmetry of the motor manifestations, side-to-side difference was also considered for each TMS index, with "right" and "left" referred to the recording side of the target muscle. To avoid motor fatigue and inter-trial variability, a pause of 20 s was taken after every stimulus. A continuous EMG audio–visual feedback at high gain assisted the participants in maintaining a complete muscle relaxation. Trials containing any type of artifact were removed. Similarly, we excluded trials contaminated by EMG activity at rest (indicating a non-relaxed muscle), as well as those "active" trials (during contraction) with excessive EMG voluntary activity that made a reliable recognition of the onset of MEP cortical latency difficult or doubtful.

In sum, the following TMS measurements and repetitions were obtained for each participant:

- rMT (%): at least 5 of 10 trials with a MEP amplitude >50 μV at rest;
- MEP latency (ms): 5 reproducible recordings during active contraction;
- MEP amplitude (mV): 5 reproducible recordings during active contraction;
- peripheral motor latency (ms): 3 reproducible recordings at rest;
- CSP (ms): 7 reproducible rectified trials during active contraction.

All measurements were conducted while subjects were seated in a comfortable armchair, with their arms maintained relaxed in the same position throughout the procedure. All recordings were performed in the same laboratory, equipment, and experimental conditions, by the same operators and at the same time of the day (09:30–11:30 a.m.), in order to exclude possible confounding due to the circadian rhythm. All data were collected on a dedicated PC and stored with an ad hoc software for off-line analysis [67].

2.3. Statistical Analysis

Because of the non-normal distribution of some variables, the differences between the continuous variables obtained in the different groups of subjects (patients and controls) were evaluated by means of the non-parametric Kruskal–Wallis ANOVA, followed by the Mann–Whitney test for independent datasets, used as a post hoc test for the comparison of each pair of groups, when appropriate. Within-group comparisons were carried out by means of the Wilcoxon test, and correlations were evaluated by means of the Spearman's rho. P values were considered statistically significant when <0.05.

Because of the relatively low number of subjects and in order to limit the possibility to miss significant differences, we computed the effect size for all comparisons by calculating the Cohen's d and checked for instances in which a "large" effect size was present, which is commonly accepted to be indicated by a Cohen's d value >0.8 [68].

3. Results

All participants underwent TMS without any discomfort or undesired effect. The clinical and demographic features of participants are summarized in Table 1. As shown, the three groups were similar in terms of age, height, disease duration and severity, motor impairment, and mood status. MMSE and FAB scored worse in PSP patients than controls, but they did not significantly differ from the scores of PD subjects. PD patients exhibited a significantly lower FAB score than controls.

As shown in Table 2, single-pulse TMS revealed a significantly higher MEP amplitude from the right FDI muscle in both PD and PSP patients compared to controls, but not between the two groups of patients. Similarly, CSP duration was significantly and bilaterally longer in patients than controls, but it was similar between PD and PSP. No other difference was observed.

Table 3 shows the right-to-left differences within the patients' groups. In the PSP group, MEP amplitude from the right FDI was significantly higher and MEP latency was significantly prolonged compared to the contralateral side, although these differences did not have a large effect size.

Table 1. Clinical-demographic and neuropsychological features of the three groups.

Variable	Group 1 (Controls; $n = 28$)			Group 2 (PD; $n = 28$)			Group 3 (PSP; $n = 23$)			Kruskal–Wallis ANOVA			*post hoc*		
	Median	Lower	Upper	Median	Lower	Upper	Median	Lower	Upper	$H_{(2,79)}$	p	Effect Size Cohen's d	1 vs. 2 p	1 vs. 3 p	2 vs. 3 p
Age, years	65.0	58.5	69.0	63.5	59.0	69.5	67.0	63.0	72.0	3.113	NS	0.244	-	-	-
Height, cm	162.0	160.0	170.0	163.5	160.0	170.0	163.0	155.0	170.0	0.105	NS	-	-	-	-
Disease duration, years	-	-	-	2.0	2.0	4.0	3.0	2.0	4.0	-	-	-	-	-	NS
Hoehn-Yahr	-	-	-	2.0	2.0	2.5	2.5	2.0	3.0	-	-	-	-	-	NS
UPDRS-ME	-	-	-	31.0	25.5	38.5	32.0	25.0	45.0	-	-	-	-	-	NS
MMSE	28.6	27.0	30.0	27.5	25.9	28.9	27.2	25.4	28.3	6.263	**0.044**	0.488	NS	**0.022**	NS
FAB	16.9	14.3	18.0	15.0	11.4	16.4	12.6	9.6	14.9	18.657	**0.0001**	**1.060**	**0.04**	**0.00005**	NS
HDRS	4.0	2.0	6.5	5.0	3.0	8.5	5.0	2.0	7.0	3.409	NS	0.275	-	-	-

Legend (in alphabetical order): FAB: Frontal Assessment Battery; HDRS: Hamilton Depression Rating Scale; MMSE: Mini Mental State Examination; NS: not significant; PD: Parkinson's disease; PSP: Progressive Supranuclear Palsy; UPDRS-ME: Unified Parkinson's Disease Rating Scale–part III (motor examination); numbers in bold: statistically significant p values and large (>0.8) effect sizes.

Table 2. Single-pulse transcranial magnetic stimulation (TMS) data obtained from all participants.

Variable	Group 1 (Controls; $n = 28$)			Group 2 (PD; $n = 28$)			Group 3 (PSP; $n = 23$)			Kruskal–Wallis ANOVA			*post hoc*		
	Median	Lower	Upper	Median	Lower	Upper	Median	Lower	Upper	$H_{(2,37)}$	p	Effect Size Cohen's d	1 vs. 2 p	1 vs. 3 p	2 vs. 3 p
Right FDI MEP amplitude, mV	3.9	2.3	5.1	7.9	6.4	10.2	7.9	5.6	11.1	23.879	**0.00001**	**1.272**	**0.00001**	**0.00015**	NS
Right FDI MEP latency, ms	20.7	19.9	21.9	20.4	19.3	21.3	19.7	18.6	21.2	4.407	NS	0.362	-	-	-
Right FDI CMCT, ms	6.5	6.0	7.3	5.9	5.3	6.3	5.9	5.2	6.8	8.063	NS	0.589	-	-	-
Right FDI rMT, %	43.0	39.0	45.5	37.5	35.0	45.5	39.0	34.0	49.0	3.178	NS	0.251	-	-	-
Right FDI CSP, ms	69.4	58.5	87.2	125.4	95.0	135.2	131.8	92.8	162.0	23.131	**0.0001**	**1.241**	**0.00007**	**0.00004**	NS
Left FDI MEP amplitude, mV	4.6	4.0	6.0	6.1	4.2	8.2	6.4	4.0	9.2	3.234	NS	0.257	-	-	-
Left FDI MEP latency, ms	19.2	18.4	20.6	20.1	19.5	21.1	19.3	18.1	21.1	5.262	NS	0.424	-	-	-
Left FDI CMCT, ms	5.5	5.1	6.5	5.9	5.1	6.5	5.8	4.9	6.8	0.406	NS	-	-	-	-
Left FDI rMT, %	40.0	38.0	43.5	38.0	35.0	41.5	41.0	36.0	44.0	3.247	NS	0.258	-	-	-
Left FDI CSP, ms	74.5	60.5	117.0	131.5	79.3	139.0	146.3	101.0	151.0	12.807	**0.0017**	**0.814**	**0.035**	**0.00062**	NS

Legend (in alphabetical order): CMCT: central motor conduction time; CSP: cortical silent period; FDI: First Dorsal Interosseous muscle; K–W: Kruskal–Wallis; MEP: motor evoked potential; NS: not significant; PD: Parkinson's disease; PSP: Progressive Supranuclear Palsy; rMT: resting motor threshold; TMS: transcranial magnetic stimulation; numbers in bold: statistically significant p value sand large (>0.8) effect sizes.

Table 3. Right-to-left difference of TMS parameters within the PD and PSP group.

Variable	PD Group				PSP Group			
	Wilcoxon's Test			Effect Size Cohen's *d*	Wilcoxon's Test			Effect Size Cohen's *d*
	Valid	Z	*p*		Valid	Z	*p*	
Right versus left FDI MEP amplitude	27	1.670	0.095	0.321	22	2.581	**0.001**	0.550
Right versus left FDI MEP latency	25	0.740	0.459	0.148	21	2.468	**0.0135**	0.539
Right versus left FDI CMCT	28	0.079	0.936	0.015	20	0.317	0.751	0.071
Right versus left FDI rMT	25	0.673	0.501	0.135	23	0.395	0.693	0.082
Right versus left FDI CSP	28	0.285	0.776	0.054	23	0.426	0.670	0.089

Legend (in alphabetical order): CMCT: central motor conduction time; CSP: cortical silent period; FDI: First Dorsal Interosseous muscle; MEP: motor evoked potential; PD: Parkinson's disease; PSP: Progressive Supranuclear Palsy; rMT: resting motor threshold; TMS: transcranial magnetic stimulation; NS: not significant; numbers in bold: statistically significant *p* values.

Finally, the correlation analysis between clinical-cognitive and TMS data in the three groups disclosed a significant positive correlation between FAB score and rMT from both hemispheres in PSP patients (Figure 1).

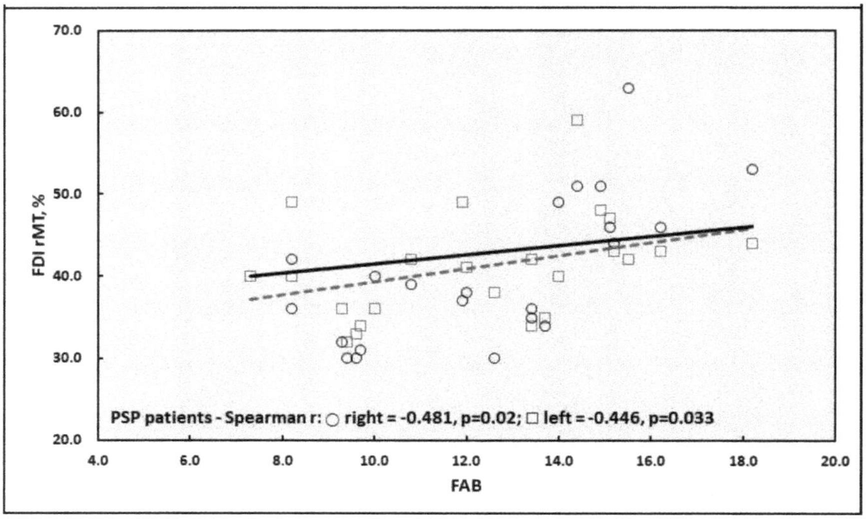

Figure 1. Correlation between FAB score and rMT from the left and right FDI muscles in PSP patients. Legend (in alphabetical order): FAB: Frontal Assessment Battery; FDI: First Dorsal Interosseous; PSP: Progressive Supranuclear Palsy; rMT: resting motor threshold; lines: linear regression lines.

4. Discussion

4.1. Main Findings

Compared to the existing literature, we first documented a similar global electrocortical asset in PD and PSP patients at their early stage and proposed the potential role of the rMT in the early detection and possibly prediction of cognitive deterioration in PSP subjects. We also confirm that the excitability of specific cortical networks is abnormal in both PD and PSP patients, although they did not exhibit distinctive electrocortical patterns to single-pulse TMS. In this scenario, a previous study suggested that some global measures of motor cortex inhibition (i.e., CSP) differed between the two conditions, the CSP being longer in PSP and shorter in PD with respect to healthy controls [52]. However, our findings support the hypothesis that, at their early stages, a similar level of impairment of motor cortex inhibition might occur. Interestingly, patients' MEP latency and CMCT were similar to those of healthy controls, suggesting a normal cortico-spinal conductivity. This finding might help the differential diagnosis with other atypical parkinsonisms (APs)—i.e., Multiple Systemic Atrophy, which typically exhibits prolonged CMCT [52].

A role was previously proposed for neurophysiological testing in the differential diagnosis between PD and APs and between the various APs [37,46,69]. However, owing to the relatively low sensitivity of the majority of findings and the lack of post mortem diagnostic confirmation in most of the studies, it is not yet possible to conclude that neurophysiological techniques can reliably differentiate between these disorders [52]. The inconsistencies may be in part due to the heterogeneity of the patients studied, the high inter-individual variability of parameters, the differences in disease severity, the pre-activation of target muscles, and the dopaminergic state. Conversely, some follow-up studies indicate that longitudinal assessments using neurophysiological techniques may provide useful surrogate biomarkers [52], although further evidences are needed. Based on the results of the present study, we would suggest that PD and PSP could not be early differentiated on the basis of single-pulse TMS alone and that more advanced protocols (e.g., paired-pulse TMS, SAI, paired-associative stimulation) should be considered.

The significant increase in MEP amplitude in both groups of patients compared to controls, along with the previous finding of abnormally enhanced MEP amplitude after theta-burst stimulation in PSP patients [47], may be interpreted as a status of M1 hyperexcitability, likely through the basal ganglia-motor cortex loop [51,70], similarly to that posited in PD patients [42,71]. A possible explanation is that the enhanced excitability may reflect an increased glutamatergic excitatory interneuronal activity. The excessive glutamate release, indeed, is a key feature in the excitotoxicity model in cultured cortical neurons, as reported in several neurodegenerative diseases [72–74]. Therefore, an imbalanced glutamatergic activity may take place in both synucleinopathy and tauopathy [47]. Translationally, the increased MEP amplitude in both PD and PSP might suggest that the motor output neurons and the cortico-spinal tract are not severely affected [46], as also confirmed by the lack of any clinical motor deficit in our patients. In this context, the fact that both groups of patients had higher MEP amplitude from the right FDI compared to controls can be ascribed to the right handedness of these subjects, as previously reported in normal subjects [75,76], and possibly to the clinical asymmetry of their motor manifestations.

The same factors might explain the higher MEP amplitude obtained from the right side compared to the contralateral side within patients' groups, although with a statistically significant difference in the PSP group only. In this context, pioneer neuroanatomical studies showed that the dominant hemisphere may have higher corticospinal tract density [77,78], although the neurophysiology underlying brain asymmetries is still controversial, with some authors suggesting that the dominant hemisphere exhibits larger cortical representation areas with lower excitability [79], while others report the opposite [80,81], or even no difference [82–84]. It has been recently demonstrated that a laterality asymmetry possibly leads to a more pronounced MEP distribution on the dominant hemisphere compared to the non-dominant side in healthy right-handers [85], and that patients with motor and movement disorders exhibit disruptions of motor unit recruitment and discharge patterns [86–89], which may affect dominant and non-dominant sides differently [90]. However, the lack of similar data in PSP precludes a better understanding of laterality asymmetries in these patients and stimulates further studies on this intriguing topic.

However, these observations do not fully explain why a markedly prolonged CSP in both PD and PSP patients with respect to controls was also found. Regarding the inhibitory components of the cortical excitability, one should keep in mind that, although these measures are known to reflect the activity of a main transmission pathway, they are actually influenced by different neurotransmitters, since they are sensitive to the global weight of several neurochemical pathways and circuitries from both cortical and subcortical inputs [66]. Therefore, the significant prolongation of CSP observed in PD and PSP patients, but without differences between them, might suggest that unbalanced excitatory and inhibitory cortical activity in M1 would occur similarly in these patients. Accordingly, a reduced SICI has been reported in both PD [33–36] and PSP [47], adding further support the hypothesis of an unbalanced cortical facilitatory and inhibitory circuitry within the M1 of both disorders. Translationally, this would imply the involvement of both glutamatergic and GABAergic systems in the cortical pathology of PD and PSP.

Regarding cognition, although not demented, a lower MMSE was detected in PSP subjects and a lower FAB in both groups of patients compared to controls. This finding is in line with the evidence of a worse global cognitive status and executive performance in PSP than PD and other APs, thus supporting a neuropsychological profile at higher risk for progression into dementia in these patients [91]. Accordingly, a novel finding of our study is the significant correlation between FAB and rMT in PSP patients. In particular, with worse FAB scores, PSP patients tended to exhibit a reduced rMT bilaterally, thus suggesting a global higher excitability from both hemispheres. Given that a reduced rMT, although not disease-specific, is a finding stably observed in degenerative dementias [19] and that, unlike MMSE, FAB has been considered a reliable test to assess cognitive impairment in these patients [91], the correlation we found might possibly disclose early cognitive and TMS markers of cognitive deterioration in PSP.

On the other hand, earlier independent investigations have demonstrated that different neurological diseases may exhibit similar TMS profiles. For instance, among cognitive disorders, it has been shown that patients with Alzheimer's disease and subcortical ischemic vascular dementia can share common TMS features [92]. This suggests the existence of mechanisms that partially overlap and probably act in the same neurophysiological way, although they are, at least in principle, different in both localization (cortical versus subcortical) and origin (degenerative versus vascular) [93]. This alteration might promote a functional neuroplastic rearrangement allowing the preservation of motor programming and execution despite disease progression [92,94,95]. Conversely, the lack of correlation between clinical and MEP features in both PD and PSP patients can be explained by considering that TMS basically explores the M1, whereas the UPDRS–part III and the H-Y scale evaluate several aspects of motor and functional status, respectively. Since there is as yet little evidence of the clinical-neurophysiological correlations in PD and APs [46,96], the present study provides further insights, although further research is warranted.

4.2. Limitations

Some limitations should be mentioned. First, as usual in TMS studies, the sample size was small, although the patients were carefully screened, thus making the samples very homogeneous. Accordingly, in order to examine comparable groups, patients were selected to be as homogeneous as possible in terms of clinical features, disease duration, and severity. Additionally, control subjects were matched for age, sex, and height to both groups of patients. Furthermore, in order to limit the possibility of missing significant differences, we included a careful evaluation of the effect size by calculating the Cohen's d. Indeed, the statistical analysis indicated a significant difference in all instances in which a "large" effect size was present, which is commonly accepted to be indicated by a Cohen's d value >0.8. Nevertheless, further stratifications could not be performed—e.g., based on clinical phenotype or on the clinically affected side. Therefore, since the low population size remains a major limitation of the study, this should be considered as a pilot study needing further validation.

Second, a more precise estimation of the MEP size was obtained through the amplitude ratio—i.e., the ratio between the maximal transcranially evoked MEP amplitude and the maximal distally evoked compound motor action potential. Similarly, CMCT was not calculated by eliciting the F-waves. Additionally, a peripheral nerve conduction velocity study was not performed, although all subjects recruited did not have any sign or history of peripheral nerve pathology.

Another caveat is that only de novo patients with non-severe clinical phenotypes were enrolled and, therefore, longitudinal clinical, cognitive, and TMS investigations are needed. As a consequence, the present results should be considered as descriptive and the monitoring with serial MEP recordings will clarify the role and the pathophysiological weight of our findings over time.

Given that the right side was more clinically affected, we cannot exclude that the evaluation of the rMT from the right FDI muscle might have been influenced by the difficulty to obtain a complete muscle relaxation. However, in addition to the continuous EMG audio-visual feedback at high gain, we checked continuously that subjects remained relaxed as much as possible during the exam. Moreover, as stated, all the trials containing any type of artifact, as well as those trials contaminated by EMG activity at rest, were removed.

Finally, this study used basic MEP features, which represent a routine diagnostic application of TMS. As known, TMS can evaluate different parameters, such as the paired-pulse-derived measures, SAI, and indexes of interhemispheric functioning, although that was beyond the primary target of this clinically-oriented study. Overall, we acknowledge that errors in the study design might still have been present, although all possible measures to prevent them have been adopted.

5. Conclusions

Notwithstanding the limitations of the study (especially the small sample size), PD and PSP might share, at their early stage, a similar global electrocortical asset. Specific TMS metrics may be useful for monitoring PSP subjects at risk for cognitive deterioration. Advanced TMS, together with clinical-cognitive and structural-functional neuroimaging data, may lead to the detection of abnormalities more closely related to the specific pathological substrate of these diseases. Future translational applications will include the identification of markers of disease progression and response to pharmacological treatment in a wide range of movement disorders.

Author Contributions: Conceptualization, F.F. and M.Z.; methodology, A.N. and R.B.; validation, M.C. and M.P.; formal analysis, R.F.; investigation, F.F. and G.L.; resources, G.P.; data curation, M.C.; writing—original draft preparation, G.L. and M.P.; writing—review and editing, A.N. and M.Z.; visualization, R.F.; supervision, R.B.; project administration, G.P. All authors have contributed substantially to the work. All authors have read and agreed to the published version of the manuscript.

Funding: This research received no external funding.

Conflicts of Interest: The authors declare no conflict of interest.

References

1. Osaki, Y.; Ben-Shlomo, Y.; Lees, A.J.; Daniel, S.E.; Colosimo, C.; Wenning, G.; Quinn, N. Accuracy of clinical diagnosis of progressive supranuclear palsy. *Mov. Disord. Off. J. Mov. Disord. Soc.* **2004**, *19*, 181–189. [CrossRef] [PubMed]
2. Lanza, G.; Papotto, M.; Pennisi, G.; Bella, R.; Ferri, R. Epileptic seizure as a precipitating factor of vascular progressive supranuclear palsy: A case report. *J. Stroke Cerebrovasc. Dis. Off. J. Natl. Stroke Assoc.* **2014**, *23*, e379–e381. [CrossRef] [PubMed]
3. Lanza, G.; Papotto, M.; Pennisi, G.; Bella, R.; Ferri, R. Unusual presentation of atypical akinetic-rigid syndrome after liver transplantation: A case report and review of the literature. *Acta Med. Mediterr.* **2015**, *31*, 647–650.
4. Zarei, M.; Ibarretxe-Bilbao, N.; Compta, Y.; Hough, M.; Junque, C.; Bargallo, N.; Tolosa, E.; Martí, M.J. Cortical thinning is associated with disease stages and dementia in Parkinson's disease. *J. Neurol. Neurosurg. Psychiatry* **2013**, *84*, 875–881. [CrossRef] [PubMed]
5. Lindenbach, D.; Bishop, C. Critical involvement of the motor cortex in the pathophysiology and treatment of Parkinson's disease. *Neurosci. Biobehav. Rev.* **2013**, *37*, 2737–2750. [CrossRef] [PubMed]
6. Nagao, S.; Yokota, O.; Nanba, R.; Takata, H.; Haraguchi, T.; Ishizu, H.; Ikeda, C.; Takeda, N.; Oshima, E.; Sakane, K.; et al. Progressive supranuclear palsy presenting as primary lateral sclerosis but lacking parkinsonism, gaze palsy, aphasia, or dementia. *J. Neurol. Sci.* **2012**, *323*, 147–153. [CrossRef] [PubMed]
7. Rossi, S.; Hallett, M.; Rossini, P.M.; Pascual-Leone, A. Safety, ethical considerations, and application guidelines for the use of transcranial magnetic stimulation in clinical practice and research. *Clin. Neurophysiol.* **2009**, *120*, 2008–2039. [CrossRef]
8. Rossini, P.M.; Burke, D.; Chen, R.; Cohen, L.G.; Daskalakis, Z.; Di Iorio, R.; Di Lazzaro, V.; Ferreri, F.; Fitzgerald, P.B.; George, M.S.; et al. Non-invasive electrical and magnetic stimulation of the brain, spinal cord, roots and peripheral nerves: Basic principles and procedures for routine clinical and research application. An updated report from an I.F.C.N. Committee. *Clin. Neurophysiol. Off. J. Int. Fed. Clin. Neurophysiol.* **2015**, *126*, 1071–1107. [CrossRef]
9. Cantone, M.; Lanza, G.; Le Pira, A.; Barone, R.; Pennisi, G.; Bella, R.; Pennisi, M.; Fiumara, A. Adjunct Diagnostic Value of Transcranial Magnetic Stimulation in Mucopolysaccharidosis-Related Cervical Myelopathy: A Pilot Study. *Brain Sci.* **2019**, *9*, 200. [CrossRef]
10. Cantone, M.; Lanza, G.; Vinciguerra, L.; Puglisi, V.; Ricceri, R.; Fisicaro, F.; Vagli, C.; Bella, R.; Ferri, R.; Pennisi, G.; et al. Age, Height, and Sex on Motor Evoked Potentials: Translational Data from a Large Italian Cohort in a Clinical Environment. *Front. Hum. Neurosci.* **2019**, *13*. [CrossRef]

11. Lanza, G.; Cantone, M.; Puglisi, V.; Vinciguerra, L.; Fisicaro, F.; Vagli, C.; Bella, R.; Pennisi, G.; Di Lazzaro, V.; Pennisi, M. "Mute" plantar response: Does the cortico-spinal tract "speak"? *Brain Stimul.* **2019**, *12*, S1935861X1930292X. [CrossRef] [PubMed]
12. Lanza, G.; Bella, R.; Giuffrida, S.; Cantone, M.; Pennisi, G.; Spampinato, C.; Giordano, D.; Malaguarnera, G.; Raggi, A.; Pennisi, M. Preserved transcallosal inhibition to transcranial magnetic stimulation in nondemented elderly patients with leukoaraiosis. *BioMed Res. Int.* **2013**, *2013*, 351680. [CrossRef] [PubMed]
13. Bella, R.; Cantone, M.; Lanza, G.; Ferri, R.; Vinciguerra, L.; Puglisi, V.; Pennisi, M.; Ricceri, R.; Di Lazzaro, V.; Pennisi, G. Cholinergic circuitry functioning in patients with vascular cognitive impairment—No dementia. *Brain Stimul.* **2016**, *9*, 225–233. [CrossRef] [PubMed]
14. Lanza, G.; Bella, R.; Cantone, M.; Pennisi, G.; Ferri, R.; Pennisi, M. Cognitive Impairment and Celiac Disease: Is Transcranial Magnetic Stimulation a Trait d'Union between Gut and Brain? *Int. J. Mol. Sci.* **2018**, *19*, 2243. [CrossRef] [PubMed]
15. Lanza, G.; Lanuzza, B.; Aricò, D.; Cantone, M.; Cosentino, F.I.I.; Bella, R.; Pennisi, G.; Ferri, R.; Pennisi, M. Impaired short-term plasticity in restless legs syndrome: A pilot rTMS study. *Sleep Med.* **2018**, *46*, 1–4. [CrossRef]
16. Fisicaro, F.; Lanza, G.; Grasso, A.A.; Pennisi, G.; Bella, R.; Paulus, W.; Pennisi, M. Repetitive transcranial magnetic stimulation in stroke rehabilitation: Review of the current evidence and pitfalls. *Ther. Adv. Neurol. Disord.* **2019**, *12*, 175628641987831. [CrossRef]
17. Fisicaro, F.; Lanza, G.; Bella, R.; Pennisi, M. "Self-Neuroenhancement": The Last Frontier of Noninvasive Brain Stimulation? *J. Clin. Neurol.* **2020**, *16*, 158–159. [CrossRef]
18. Kobayashi, M.; Pascual-Leone, A. Transcranial magnetic stimulation in neurology. *Lancet Neurol.* **2003**, *2*, 145–156. [CrossRef]
19. Cantone, M.; Di Pino, G.; Capone, F.; Piombo, M.; Chiarello, D.; Cheeran, B.; Pennisi, G.; Di Lazzaro, V. The contribution of transcranial magnetic stimulation in the diagnosis and in the management of dementia. *Clin. Neurophysiol.* **2014**, *125*, 1509–1532. [CrossRef]
20. Reis, J.; Swayne, O.B.; Vandermeeren, Y.; Camus, M.; Dimyan, M.A.; Harris-Love, M.; Perez, M.A.; Ragert, P.; Rothwell, J.C.; Cohen, L.G. Contribution of transcranial magnetic stimulation to the understanding of cortical mechanisms involved in motor control. *J. Physiol.* **2008**, *586*, 325–351. [CrossRef]
21. Bella, R.; Ferri, R.; Lanza, G.; Cantone, M.; Pennisi, M.; Puglisi, V.; Vinciguerra, L.; Spampinato, C.; Mazza, T.; Malaguarnera, G.; et al. TMS follow-up study in patients with vascular cognitive impairment-no dementia. *Neurosci. Lett.* **2013**, *534*, 155–159. [CrossRef] [PubMed]
22. Bella, R.; Lanza, G.; Cantone, M.; Giuffrida, S.; Puglisi, V.; Vinciguerra, L.; Pennisi, M.; Ricceri, R.; D'Agate, C.C.; Malaguarnera, G.; et al. Effect of a Gluten-Free Diet on Cortical Excitability in Adults with Celiac Disease. *PLoS ONE* **2015**, *10*, e0129218. [CrossRef] [PubMed]
23. Pennisi, M.; Lanza, G.; Cantone, M.; Ricceri, R.; Spampinato, C.; Pennisi, G.; Di Lazzaro, V.; Bella, R. Correlation between Motor Cortex Excitability Changes and Cognitive Impairment in Vascular Depression: Pathophysiological Insights from a Longitudinal TMS Study. *Neural Plast.* **2016**, *2016*, 8154969. [CrossRef] [PubMed]
24. Pennisi, M.; Lanza, G.; Cantone, M.; Ricceri, R.; Ferri, R.; D'Agate, C.C.; Pennisi, G.; Di Lazzaro, V.; Bella, R. Cortical involvement in celiac disease before and after long-term gluten-free diet: A Transcranial Magnetic Stimulation study. *PLoS ONE* **2017**, *12*, e0177560. [CrossRef] [PubMed]
25. Pierantozzi, M.; Panella, M.; Palmieri, M.G.; Koch, G.; Giordano, A.; Marciani, M.G.; Bernardi, G.; Stanzione, P.; Stefani, A. Different TMS patterns of intracortical inhibition in early onset Alzheimer dementia and frontotemporal dementia. *Clin. Neurophysiol. Off. J. Int. Fed. Clin. Neurophysiol.* **2004**, *115*, 2410–2418. [CrossRef]
26. Rossini, P.M.; Rossi, S.; Babiloni, C.; Polich, J. Clinical neurophysiology of aging brain: From normal aging to neurodegeneration. *Prog. Neurobiol.* **2007**, *83*, 375–400. [CrossRef]
27. Paulus, W.; Classen, J.; Cohen, L.G.; Large, C.H.; Di Lazzaro, V.; Nitsche, M.; Pascual-Leone, A.; Rosenow, F.; Rothwell, J.C.; Ziemann, U. State of the art: Pharmacologic effects on cortical excitability measures tested by transcranial magnetic stimulation. *Brain Stimulat.* **2008**, *1*, 151–163. [CrossRef]
28. Cantello, R. Applications of transcranial magnetic stimulation in movement disorders. *J. Clin. Neurophysiol. Off. Publ. Am. Electroencephalogr. Soc.* **2002**, *19*, 272–293. [CrossRef]

29. Gaspar, P.; Duyckaerts, C.; Alvarez, C.; Javoy-Agid, F.; Berger, B. Alterations of dopaminergic and noradrenergic innervations in motor cortex in Parkinson's disease. *Ann. Neurol.* **1991**, *30*, 365–374. [CrossRef]
30. Moore, R.Y.; Whone, A.L.; Brooks, D.J. Extrastriatal monoamine neuron function in Parkinson's disease: An 18F-dopa PET study. *Neurobiol. Dis.* **2008**, *29*, 381–390. [CrossRef]
31. Nagano-Saito, A.; Kato, T.; Arahata, Y.; Washimi, Y.; Nakamura, A.; Abe, Y.; Yamada, T.; Iwai, K.; Hatano, K.; Kawasumi, Y.; et al. Cognitive- and motor-related regions in Parkinson's disease: FDOPA and FDG PET studies. *NeuroImage* **2004**, *22*, 553–561. [CrossRef] [PubMed]
32. Underwood, C.F.; Parr-Brownlie, L.C. Primary motor cortex in Parkinson's disease: Functional changes and opportunities for neurostimulation. *Neurobiol. Dis.* **2021**, *147*, 105159. [CrossRef] [PubMed]
33. Leon-Sarmiento, F.E.; Rizzo-Sierra, C.V.; Bayona, E.A.; Bayona-Prieto, J.; Doty, R.L.; Bara-Jimenez, W. Novel mechanisms underlying inhibitory and facilitatory transcranial magnetic stimulation abnormalities in Parkinson's disease. *Arch. Med. Res.* **2013**, *44*, 221–228. [CrossRef] [PubMed]
34. Ni, Z.; Bahl, N.; Gunraj, C.A.; Mazzella, F.; Chen, R. Increased motor cortical facilitation and decreased inhibition in Parkinson disease. *Neurology* **2013**, *80*, 1746–1753. [CrossRef] [PubMed]
35. Barbin, L.; Leux, C.; Sauleau, P.; Meyniel, C.; Nguyen, J.-M.; Pereon, Y.; Damier, P. Non-homogeneous effect of levodopa on inhibitory circuits in Parkinson's disease and dyskinesia. *Parkinsonism Relat. Disord.* **2013**, *19*, 165–170. [CrossRef] [PubMed]
36. MacKinnon, C.D.; Gilley, E.A.; Weis-McNulty, A.; Simuni, T. Pathways mediating abnormal intracortical inhibition in Parkinson's disease. *Ann. Neurol.* **2005**, *58*, 516–524. [CrossRef]
37. Morita, Y.; Osaki, Y.; Doi, Y. Transcranial magnetic stimulation for differential diagnostics in patients with parkinsonism. *Acta Neurol. Scand.* **2008**, *118*, 159–163. [CrossRef]
38. Sailer, A.; Molnar, G.F.; Paradiso, G.; Gunraj, C.A.; Lang, A.E.; Chen, R. Short and long latency afferent inhibition in Parkinson's disease. *Brain J. Neurol.* **2003**, *126*, 1883–1894. [CrossRef]
39. Manganelli, F.; Vitale, C.; Santangelo, G.; Pisciotta, C.; Iodice, R.; Cozzolino, A.; Dubbioso, R.; Picillo, M.; Barone, P.; Santoro, L. Functional involvement of central cholinergic circuits and visual hallucinations in Parkinson's disease. *Brain J. Neurol.* **2009**, *132*, 2350–2355. [CrossRef]
40. Celebi, O.; Temuçin, C.M.; Elibol, B.; Saka, E. Short latency afferent inhibition in Parkinson's disease patients with dementia. *Mov. Disord. Off. J. Mov. Disord. Soc.* **2012**, *27*, 1052–1055. [CrossRef]
41. Nardone, R.; Florio, I.; Lochner, P.; Tezzon, F. Cholinergic cortical circuits in Parkinson's disease and in progressive supranuclear palsy: A transcranial magnetic stimulation study. *Exp. Brain Res.* **2005**, *163*, 128–131. [CrossRef] [PubMed]
42. Ridding, M.C.; Inzelberg, R.; Rothwell, J.C. Changes in excitability of motor cortical circuitry in patients with Parkinson's disease. *Ann. Neurol.* **1995**, *37*, 181–188. [CrossRef] [PubMed]
43. Cantello, R.; Gianelli, M.; Bettucci, D.; Civardi, C.; De Angelis, M.S.; Mutani, R. Parkinson's disease rigidity: Magnetic motor evoked potentials in a small hand muscle. *Neurology* **1991**, *41*, 1449–1456. [CrossRef] [PubMed]
44. Valls-Solé, J.; Pascual-Leone, A.; Brasil-Neto, J.P.; Cammarota, A.; McShane, L.; Hallett, M. Abnormal facilitation of the response to transcranial magnetic stimulation in patients with Parkinson's disease. *Neurology* **1994**, *44*, 735–741. [CrossRef] [PubMed]
45. Abbruzzese, G.; Tabaton, M.; Morena, M.; Dall'Agata, D.; Favale, E. Motor and sensory evoked potentials in progressive supranuclear palsy. *Mov. Disord. Off. J. Mov. Disord. Soc.* **1991**, *6*, 49–54. [CrossRef]
46. Kühn, A.A.; Grosse, P.; Holtz, K.; Brown, P.; Meyer, B.-U.; Kupsch, A. Patterns of abnormal motor cortex excitability in atypical parkinsonian syndromes. *Clin. Neurophysiol.* **2004**, *115*, 1786–1795. [CrossRef]
47. Conte, A.; Belvisi, D.; Bologna, M.; Ottaviani, D.; Fabbrini, G.; Colosimo, C.; Williams, D.R.; Berardelli, A. Abnormal cortical synaptic plasticity in primary motor area in progressive supranuclear palsy. *Cereb. Cortex* **2012**, *22*, 693–700. [CrossRef]
48. Wittstock, M.; Pohley, I.; Walter, U.; Grossmann, A.; Benecke, R.; Wolters, A. Interhemispheric inhibition in different phenotypes of progressive supranuclear palsy. *J. Neural Transm.* **2013**, *120*, 453–461. [CrossRef]
49. Udupa, K.; Chen, R. Motor cortical circuits in Parkinson disease and dystonia. *Handb. Clin. Neurol.* **2019**, *161*, 167–186. [CrossRef]
50. Brusa, L.; Ponzo, V.; Mastropasqua, C.; Picazio, S.; Bonnì, S.; Di Lorenzo, F.; Iani, C.; Stefani, A.; Stanzione, P.; Caltagirone, C.; et al. Theta burst stimulation modulates cerebellar-cortical connectivity in patients with progressive supranuclear palsy. *Brain Stimulat.* **2014**, *7*, 29–35. [CrossRef]

51. Bologna, M.; Bertram, K.; Paparella, G.; Papi, C.; Belvisi, D.; Conte, A.; Suppa, A.; Williams, D.R.; Berardelli, A. Reversal of long term potentiation-like plasticity in primary motor cortex in patients with progressive supranuclear palsy. *Clin. Neurophysiol. Off. J. Int. Fed. Clin. Neurophysiol.* **2017**, *128*, 1547–1552. [CrossRef] [PubMed]
52. Bologna, M.; Suppa, A.; Stasio, F.D.; Conte, A.; Fabbrini, G.; Berardelli, A. Neurophysiological studies on atypical parkinsonian syndromes. *Parkinsonism Relat. Disord.* **2017**, *42*, 12–21. [CrossRef] [PubMed]
53. Cantello, R.; Tarletti, R.; Civardi, C. Transcranial magnetic stimulation and Parkinson's disease. *Brain Res. Brain Res. Rev.* **2002**, *38*, 309–327. [CrossRef]
54. Oldfield, R.C. The assessment and analysis of handedness: The Edinburgh inventory. *Neuropsychologia* **1971**, *9*, 97–113. [CrossRef]
55. Postuma, R.B.; Berg, D.; Stern, M.; Poewe, W.; Olanow, C.W.; Oertel, W.; Obeso, J.; Marek, K.; Litvan, I.; Lang, A.E.; et al. MDS clinical diagnostic criteria for Parkinson's disease. *Mov. Disord. Off. J. Mov. Disord. Soc.* **2015**, *30*, 1591–1601. [CrossRef] [PubMed]
56. Höglinger, G.U.; Respondek, G.; Stamelou, M.; Kurz, C.; Josephs, K.A.; Lang, A.E.; Mollenhauer, B.; Müller, U.; Nilsson, C.; Whitwell, J.L.; et al. Clinical diagnosis of progressive supranuclear palsy: The movement disorder society criteria. *Mov. Disord. Off. J. Mov. Disord. Soc.* **2017**, *32*, 853–864. [CrossRef] [PubMed]
57. Cummings, J.L.; Henchcliffe, C.; Schaier, S.; Simuni, T.; Waxman, A.; Kemp, P. The role of dopaminergic imaging in patients with symptoms of dopaminergic system neurodegeneration. *Brain J. Neurol.* **2011**, *134*, 3146–3166. [CrossRef]
58. Nigro, S.; Arabia, G.; Antonini, A.; Weis, L.; Marcante, A.; Tessitore, A.; Cirillo, M.; Tedeschi, G.; Zanigni, S.; Calandra-Buonaura, G.; et al. Magnetic Resonance Parkinsonism Index: Diagnostic accuracy of a fully automated algorithm in comparison with the manual measurement in a large Italian multicentre study in patients with progressive supranuclear palsy. *Eur. Radiol.* **2017**, *27*, 2665–2675. [CrossRef]
59. Fahn, S. Unified Parkinson's Disease Rating Scale. In *Recent Development in Parkinson's Disease*; Macmillan Health Care Information: Florham Park, NJ, USA, 1987; Volume 2, pp. 153–164.
60. Hoehn, M.M.; Yahr, M.D. Parkinsonism: Onset, progression and mortality. *Neurology* **1967**, *17*, 427–442. [CrossRef]
61. American Psychiatric Association. *Diagnostic and Statistical Manual of Mental Disorders*, 5th ed.; American Psychiatric Association: Washington, DC, USA, 2013; ISBN 978-0-89042-555-8.
62. Folstein, M.F.; Folstein, S.E.; McHugh, P.R. "Mini-mental state". A practical method for grading the cognitive state of patients for the clinician. *J. Psychiatr. Res.* **1975**, *12*, 189–198. [CrossRef]
63. Dubois, B.; Slachevsky, A.; Litvan, I.; Pillon, B. The FAB: A Frontal Assessment Battery at bedside. *Neurology* **2000**, *55*, 1621–1626. [CrossRef] [PubMed]
64. Hamilton, M. A rating scale for depression. *J. Neurol. Neurosurg. Psychiatry* **1960**, *23*, 56–62. [CrossRef] [PubMed]
65. Ziemann, U. Pharmaco-transcranial magnetic stimulation studies of motor excitability. *Handb. Clin. Neurol.* **2013**, *116*, 387–397. [CrossRef] [PubMed]
66. Ziemann, U.; Reis, J.; Schwenkreis, P.; Rosanova, M.; Strafella, A.; Badawy, R.; Müller-Dahlhaus, F. TMS and drugs revisited 2014. *Clin. Neurophysiol. Off. J. Int. Fed. Clin. Neurophysiol.* **2015**, *126*, 1847–1868. [CrossRef] [PubMed]
67. Faro, A.; Giordano, D.; Kavasidis, I.; Pino, C.; Spampinato, C.; Cantone, M.G.; Lanza, G.; Pennisi, M. An Interactive Tool for Customizing Clinical Transacranial Magnetic Stimulation (TMS) Experiments. In *IFMBE Proceedings, Proceedings of the XII Mediterranean Conference on Medical and Biological Engineering and Computing 2010, Chalkidiki, Greece, 27–30 May 2010*; Bamidis, P.D., Pallikarakis, N., Eds.; Springer: Berlin/Heidelberg, Germany, 2010; pp. 200–203.
68. Cohen, J. *Statistical Power Analysis for the Behavioral Sciences*, 2nd ed.; Lawrence Erlbaum Associates: Hillsdale, NJ, USA, 1988; ISBN 978-0-8058-0283-2.
69. Lanza, G.; Kosac, A.; Trajkovic, G.; Whittaker, R.G. Nerve Conduction Studies as a Measure of Disease Progression: Objectivity or Illusion? *J. Neuromuscul. Dis.* **2017**, *4*, 209–215. [CrossRef] [PubMed]
70. Halliday, G.M.; Macdonald, V.; Henderson, J.M. A comparison of degeneration in motor thalamus and cortex between progressive supranuclear palsy and Parkinson's disease. *Brain J. Neurol.* **2005**, *128*, 2272–2280. [CrossRef] [PubMed]

71. Priori, A.; Berardelli, A.; Inghilleri, M.; Accornero, N.; Manfredi, M. Motor cortical inhibition and the dopaminergic system. Pharmacological changes in the silent period after transcranial brain stimulation in normal subjects, patients with Parkinson's disease and drug-induced parkinsonism. *Brain J. Neurol.* **1994**, *117 Pt 2*, 317–323. [CrossRef] [PubMed]
72. Sasaki, K.; Shimura, H.; Itaya, M.; Tanaka, R.; Mori, H.; Mizuno, Y.; Kosik, K.S.; Tanaka, S.; Hattori, N. Excitatory amino acid transporter 2 associates with phosphorylated tau and is localized in neurofibrillary tangles of tauopathic brains. *FEBS Lett.* **2009**, *583*, 2194–2200. [CrossRef] [PubMed]
73. Fan, J.; Vasuta, O.C.; Zhang, L.Y.J.; Wang, L.; George, A.; Raymond, L.A. N-Methyl-d-aspartate receptor subunit- and neuronal-type dependence of excitotoxic signaling through post-synaptic density 95. *J. Neurochem.* **2010**, *115*, 1045–1056. [CrossRef]
74. Nutini, M.; Frazzini, V.; Marini, C.; Spalloni, A.; Sensi, S.L.; Longone, P. Zinc pre-treatment enhances NMDAR-mediated excitotoxicity in cultured cortical neurons from SOD1(G93A) mouse, a model of amyotrophic lateral sclerosis. *Neuropharmacology* **2011**, *60*, 1200–1208. [CrossRef]
75. Yahagi, S.; Kasai, T. Motor evoked potentials induced by motor imagery reveal a functional asymmetry of cortical motor control in left- and right-handed human subjects. *Neurosci. Lett.* **1999**, *276*, 185–188. [CrossRef]
76. De Gennaro, L.; Cristiani, R.; Bertini, M.; Curcio, G.; Ferrara, M.; Fratello, F.; Romei, V.; Rossini, P.M. Handedness is mainly associated with an asymmetry of corticospinal excitability and not of transcallosal inhibition. *Clin. Neurophysiol.* **2004**, *115*, 1305–1312. [CrossRef] [PubMed]
77. Kertesz, A.; Geschwind, N. Patterns of pyramidal decussation and their relationship to handedness. *Arch. Neurol.* **1971**, *24*, 326–332. [CrossRef] [PubMed]
78. Nathan, P.W.; Smith, M.C.; Deacon, P. The corticospinal tracts in man. Course and location of fibres at different segmental levels. *Brain J. Neurol.* **1990**, *113 Pt 2*, 303–324. [CrossRef] [PubMed]
79. Wassermann, E.M.; McShane, L.M.; Hallett, M.; Cohen, L.G. Noninvasive mapping of muscle representations in human motor cortex. *Electroencephalogr. Clin. Neurophysiol.* **1992**, *85*, 1–8. [CrossRef]
80. Macdonell, R.A.; Shapiro, B.E.; Chiappa, K.H.; Helmers, S.L.; Cros, D.; Day, B.J.; Shahani, B.T. Hemispheric threshold differences for motor evoked potentials produced by magnetic coil stimulation. *Neurology* **1991**, *41*, 1441–1444. [CrossRef] [PubMed]
81. Triggs, W.J.; Calvanio, R.; Macdonell, R.A.; Cros, D.; Chiappa, K.H. Physiological motor asymmetry in human handedness: Evidence from transcranial magnetic stimulation. *Brain Res.* **1994**, *636*, 270–276. [CrossRef]
82. Davidson, T.; Tremblay, F. Hemispheric differences in corticospinal excitability and in transcallosal inhibition in relation to degree of handedness. *PLoS ONE* **2013**, *8*, e70286. [CrossRef]
83. Ferron, L.; Tremblay, F. (Lack of) Corticospinal facilitation in association with hand laterality judgments. *Exp. Brain Res.* **2017**, *235*, 2317–2326. [CrossRef]
84. Shibuya, K.; Park, S.B.; Howells, J.; Huynh, W.; Noto, Y.-I.; Shahrizaila, N.; Matamala, J.M.; Vucic, S.; Kiernan, M.C. Laterality of motor cortical function measured by transcranial magnetic stimulation threshold tracking. *Muscle Nerve* **2017**, *55*, 424–427. [CrossRef]
85. Souza, V.H.; Baffa, O.; Garcia, M.A.C. Lateralized asymmetries in distribution of muscular evoked responses: An evidence of specialized motor control over an intrinsic hand muscle. *Brain Res.* **2018**, *1684*, 60–66. [CrossRef] [PubMed]
86. Christakos, C.N.; Erimaki, S.; Anagnostou, E.; Anastasopoulos, D. Tremor-related motor unit firing in Parkinson's disease: Implications for tremor genesis. *J. Physiol.* **2009**, *587*, 4811–4827. [CrossRef] [PubMed]
87. de Carvalho, M. Testing upper motor neuron function in amyotrophic lateral sclerosis: The most difficult task of neurophysiology. *Brain J. Neurol.* **2012**, *135*, 2581–2582. [CrossRef] [PubMed]
88. Hu, X.; Suresh, A.K.; Rymer, W.Z.; Suresh, N.L. Assessing altered motor unit recruitment patterns in paretic muscles of stroke survivors using surface electromyography. *J. Neural Eng.* **2015**, *12*, 066001. [CrossRef] [PubMed]
89. Issa, N.P.; Frank, S.; Roos, R.P.; Soliven, B.; Towle, V.L.; Rezania, K. Intermuscular coherence in amyotrophic lateral sclerosis: A preliminary assessment. *Muscle Nerve* **2017**, *55*, 862–868. [CrossRef] [PubMed]
90. Mitchell, M.; Martin, B.J.; Adamo, D.E. Upper Limb Asymmetry in the Sense of Effort Is Dependent on Force Level. *Front. Psychol.* **2017**, *8*, 643. [CrossRef]
91. Sulena; Gupta, D.; Sharma, A.K.; Kumar, N. Clinical Profile of Cognitive Decline in Patients with Parkinson's Disease, Progressive Supranuclear Palsy, and Multiple System Atrophy. *J. Neurosci. Rural Pract.* **2017**, *8*, 562–568. [CrossRef]

92. Guerra, A.; Petrichella, S.; Vollero, L.; Ponzo, D.; Pasqualetti, P.; Määttä, S.; Mervaala, E.; Könönen, M.; Bressi, F.; Iannello, G.; et al. Neurophysiological features of motor cortex excitability and plasticity in Subcortical Ischemic Vascular Dementia: A TMS mapping study. *Clin. Neurophysiol.* **2015**, *126*, 906–913. [CrossRef]
93. Pennisi, G.; Bella, R.; Lanza, G. Motor cortex plasticity in subcortical ischemic vascular dementia: What can TMS say? *Clin. Neurophysiol. Off. J. Int. Fed. Clin. Neurophysiol.* **2015**, *126*, 851–852. [CrossRef]
94. List, J.; Duning, T.; Kürten, J.; Deppe, M.; Wilbers, E.; Flöel, A. Cortical plasticity is preserved in nondemented older individuals with severe ischemic small vessel disease. *Hum. Brain Mapp.* **2013**, *34*, 1464–1476. [CrossRef]
95. Lanza, G.; Bramanti, P.; Cantone, M.; Pennisi, M.; Pennisi, G.; Bella, R. Vascular Cognitive Impairment through the Looking Glass of Transcranial Magnetic Stimulation. *Behav. Neurol.* **2017**, *2017*. [CrossRef] [PubMed]
96. Marchese, R.; Trompetto, C.; Buccolieri, A.; Abbruzzese, G. Abnormalities of motor cortical excitability are not correlated with clinical features in atypical parkinsonism. *Mov. Disord.* **2000**, *15*, 1210–1214. [CrossRef]

Journal of *Personalized Medicine*

MDPI

Review

TMS-EEG Research to Elucidate the Pathophysiological Neural Bases in Patients with Schizophrenia: A Systematic Review

Xuemei Li [1], Shiori Honda [1], Shinichiro Nakajima [1,*], Masataka Wada [1], Kazunari Yoshida [2], Zafiris J. Daskalakis [3], Masaru Mimura [1] and Yoshihiro Noda [1,*]

1 Department of Neuropsychiatry, Keio University School of Medicine, Tokyo 160-8582, Japan; lixmovo@gmail.com (X.L.); shiori.0913.honda@keio.jp (S.H.); masa.wada0622@gmail.com (M.W.); mimura@a7.keio.jp (M.M.)
2 Pharmacogenetics Research Clinic, Centre for Addiction and Mental Health, Toronto, ON M5T 1R8, Canada; kadu.yoshida@gmail.com
3 Department of Psychiatry, UC San Diego Health, San Diego, CA 92093, USA; zdaskalakis@health.ucsd.edu
* Correspondence: shinichiro_nakajima@hotmail.com (S.N.); yoshi-tms@keio.jp (Y.N.); Tel.: +81-3-3353-1211 (ext. 62454) (S.N.); +81-3-3353-1211 (ext. 61857) (Y.N.); Fax: +81-3-5379-0187 (S.N.)

Abstract: Schizophrenia (SCZ) is a serious mental disorder, and its pathogenesis is complex. Recently, the glutamate hypothesis and the excitatory/inhibitory (E/I) imbalance hypothesis have been proposed as new pathological hypotheses for SCZ. Combined transcranial magnetic stimulation (TMS) and electroencephalography (EEG) is a non-invasive novel method that enables us to investigate the cortical activity in humans, and this modality is a suitable approach to evaluate these hypotheses. In this study, we systematically reviewed TMS-EEG studies that investigated the cortical dysfunction of SCZ to examine the emerging hypotheses for SCZ. The following search terms were set in this systematic review: (TMS or 'transcranial magnetic stimulation') and (EEG or electroencephalog*) and (schizophrenia). We inspected the articles written in English that examined humans and were published by March 2020 via MEDLINE, Embase, PsycINFO, and PubMed. The initial search generated 379 studies, and 14 articles were finally identified. The current review noted that patients with SCZ demonstrated the E/I deficits in the prefrontal cortex, whose dysfunctions were also associated with cognitive impairment and clinical severity. Moreover, TMS-induced gamma activity in the prefrontal cortex was related to positive symptoms, while theta/delta band activities were associated with negative symptoms in SCZ. Thus, this systematic review discusses aspects of the pathophysiological neural basis of SCZ that are not explained by the traditional dopamine hypothesis exclusively, based on the findings of previous TMS-EEG research, mainly in terms of the E/I imbalance hypothesis. In conclusion, TMS-EEG neurophysiology can be applied to establish objective biomarkers for better diagnosis as well as to develop new therapeutic strategies for patients with SCZ.

Keywords: cortical excitation; cortical inhibition; electroencephalography; schizophrenia; transcranial magnetic stimulation; TMS-evoked potentials

Citation: Li, X.; Honda, S.; Nakajima, S.; Wada, M.; Yoshida, K.; Daskalakis, Z.J.; Mimura, M.; Noda, Y. TMS-EEG Research to Elucidate the Pathophysiological Neural Bases in Patients with Schizophrenia: A Systematic Review. *J. Pers. Med.* **2021**, *11*, 388. https://doi.org/10.3390/jpm11050388

Academic Editor: Sabata Martino

Received: 17 March 2021
Accepted: 6 May 2021
Published: 10 May 2021

1. Introduction

1.1. Overview of Schizophrenia

Schizophrenia (SCZ) is a serious mental disorder that affects approximately 1% of the population worldwide. SCZ is characterized by positive symptoms such as hallucinations/delusions, negative symptoms such as reduced motivation and blunted affect, and cognitive symptoms, which are considered core features of the illness [1–3]. As one of hypotheses to explain the pathophysiology of SCZ, the dopamine hypothesis has been classically proposed [4]; however, the glutamate hypothesis, gamma-aminobutyric acid (GABA) hypothesis, cholinergic hypothesis, and especially the excitatory/inhibitory (E/I) imbalance hypothesis have also been attracting attention in recent years because some pathologies in this disorder cannot be explained by the dopamine hypotheses alone [3,5,6].

Ketamine and phencyclidine, which were developed as dissociative anesthetics in the 1970s, are known to cause schizophrenia-like symptoms such as negative symptoms and cognitive symptoms as well as psychotic symptoms and thought disorder in healthy subjects. In this context, the dysfunction of glutamate receptors is thought to be particularly relevant to negative symptoms and cognitive impairment in schizophrenia. Thus, dysfunction of N-methyl-D-aspartate (NMDA) receptors has recently been proposed as one of hypotheses to explain the pathogenesis of schizophrenia. The glutamate hypothesis in SCZ suggests that the hypofunction of NMDA receptors on interneurons would cause hyperexcitability of the cerebral cortex, leading to symptoms of the disease [7].

Neural computation, the basis for the expression of mental functions, is through balanced E/I, primarily by the glutamatergic system and GABAergic input. Excitation allows neurons to respond to stimuli, while inhibition regulates neuronal selectivity and allows for accurate neural representation [8,9]. Indeed, the E/I balance is necessary for optimal neural signal formation, synchrony, and transmission, which in turn support information processing that drives both simple and complex behaviors. Thus, the E/I imbalance hypothesis has been conceptualized as a pathology caused by an imbalance between glutamatergic and GABAergic inputs and is thought to underlie brain dysfunction in neuropsychiatric disorders, including SCZ [10,11]. Here, a common assumption throughout this hypothesis is that an increase in the E/I ratio, that is, an increase in excitation or a decrease in inhibition, is involved in the expression of psychiatric symptoms. In this context, several lines of evidence indicate that patients with SCZ showed decreased glutamate and GABA levels in the prefrontal cortex (PFC) as measured by proton magnetic resonance spectroscopy (^{1}H-MRS) [12–14]. However, on the other hand, recent meta-analysis studies have shown inconsistencies in the findings of these MRS findings [15,16]. One way to address these limitations is the development of a combined transcranial magnetic stimulation (TMS) and electroencephalography (EEG) technique that can non-invasively assess the neurophysiological properties of the human cerebral cortex [2,3,17].

1.2. Technical Advance of Combined TMS-EEG

TMS was first introduced by Barker et al. in 1985 to investigate the corticospinal circuits applying to the primary motor cortex (M1) in humans [18]. When a single-pulse TMS is administered to M1, motor-evoked potential (MEP) is elicited, and its amplitude is thought to reflect corticospinal excitability. In addition, TMS neurophysiology has recently been combined with EEG to assess E/I profiles in specific cortical areas outside of the motor cortex as well [19,20]. Although most previous TMS studies in patients with SCZ have examined cortical excitability and inhibition in M1, it has been assumed that neurophysiological dysfunction in the PFC, rather than M1, may be relevant in patients with SCZ.

EEG is able to provide a direct measure of the electrical signals generated by neuronal activity and allow us to detect the E/I profiles of network connections [20]. Specifically, high-density electroencephalography (EEG) has a high-temporal resolution as well as better spatial resolution compared to the conventional EEG system due to the increased number of channels such as EEG electrodes with 64 or more channels. Hence, the combination of TMS with EEG recording (TMS-EEG) can be applied to probe and investigate the cortical responses and propagation of TMS-evoked EEG between some specific brain areas [21–23]. In particular, since TMS-evoked potentials propagate to brain regions that are anatomically and functionally connected [21,24], simultaneous measurement with EEG, which has high temporal resolution, can accurately detect the temporal pattern of TMS-evoked responses and is likely to identify causal relationships of connectivity between brain regions. In other words, the spatial and temporal patterns of brain responses to TMS can contribute to defining causal relationships in the connections across brain areas.

1.3. TMS-EEG Neurophysiology

1.3.1. GABAergic (Short-Interval Intracortical Inhibition: SICI and Long-Interval Intracortical Inhibition: LICI) and Glutamatergic (Intracortical Facilitation: ICF) Neurophysiological Functions

GABA is a critical inhibitory neurotransmitter to modulate cortical excitability and neuroplasticity of the brain. There are two main types of GABA receptors, $GABA_A$ and $GABA_B$ receptors for mediating cortical inhibition. Specifically, $GABA_A$ receptor-mediated cortical inhibitory function can be measured with short-interval intracortical inhibition [25,26], which is a paired-pulse paradigm of TMS that consists of one subthreshold preceding stimulus (conditioning stimulus) and one suprathreshold following stimulus (test stimulus) with an interstimulus interval (ISI) of 1 to 5 ms [27]. The conditioning stimulus activates a low threshold inhibitory network, causing inhibitory postsynaptic potentials to hyperpolarize the neurons when the following test pulse is applied [25,27,28]. In addition, pharmacological studies combined with TMS neurophysiology demonstrated that benzodiazepines (i.e., agonists for the $GABA_A$ receptors) increased the SICI [25,29–34], suggesting that SICI may be closely related to $GABA_A$ receptor-mediated inhibition. Further, other pharmaco-TMS studies indicated that baclofen, specific $GABA_B$ receptor agonists, increased the LICI [35,36], suggesting that LICI is mediated through the $GABA_B$ receptors. LICI comprises two suprathreshold stimuli with an ISI of 50 to 150 ms. In both SICI and LICI, final outputs of MEP amplitudes or TMS-evoked potential (TEP), which can be measured with EEG, are reduced by the test stimulus. On the other hand, glutamatergic acid is a main excitatory neurotransmitter in the brain and glutamatergic N-methyl-D-aspartate (NMDA) receptor-mediated cortical facilitation can be measured with intracortical facilitation (ICF) paradigm [33]. ICF is a paired-pulse TMS paradigm that uses the same conditioning and test stimulus intensities as SICI while the ISI of ICF is 10 to 15 ms. Other studies also revealed that NMDA receptor antagonists decreased the ICF [36,37], suggesting that ICF may be closely associated with facilitation mediated through glutamatergic NMDA receptors.

1.3.2. Cholinergic (Short-Latency Afferent Inhibition: SAI) Neurophysiological Function

SAI is mainly considered to reflect cholinergic function and is partially mediated by $GABA_A$ receptor function [30–32]. Regarding SAI, it was increased by donepezil, an acetylcholinesterase inhibitor, while it was reduced by scopolamine, muscarinic acetylcholine receptor antagonists. SAI was also increased by diazepam, the $GABA_A$ receptor agonists [32,38,39]. Moreover, previous studies have demonstrated that the SAI is associated with cognitive function, which is mediated through cholinergic function [40,41]. Previous studies have explained that the SAI is associated with cholinergically modulated cognitive function [40,41]. The SAI paradigm consists of a preceding peripheral median nerve stimulus and a subsequent single-pulse TMS. Median nerve stimulation is set at the intensity of three times the sensory thresholds, while TMS is set at the intensity of suprathreshold. The sensory afferent stimulation inhibits MEP or TEP. For the SAI paradigm applied to M1, the latency of somatosensory evoked potential N20 plus 2 ms induced by peripheral median nerve stimulation is used for the ISI between median nerve stimulation and TMS. In contrast, when the SAI is applied to the dorsolateral prefrontal cortex (DLPFC), the ISI of N20 plus 4 ms is used to evaluate the optimal SAI change from the DLPFC [42].

1.3.3. Other Neurophysiological Measures in TMS-EEG (Power, ERSP, Coherence, and Natural Frequency)

EEG power indicates the time-averaged value of wave energy, and it can be calculated according to the frequency bands, from the slow wave delta component to the fast wave gamma component. In SCZ, a decrease in EEG power of theta and gamma bands is indicated, especially in relation to cognitive impairment. Event-related spectral perturbation (ERSP), a generalization of event-related desynchronization, is a measure of the average dynamic change in the amplitude of the broadband EEG frequency spectrum as a function of time relative to an experimental event. In other words, ERSP measures the average time course of relative changes in the spontaneous EEG amplitude spectrum evoked by a series of similar experimental events, in this case TMS stimulation. EEG coherence is a linear synchronization measure between two signals over time recorded at different electrode sites, which is specifically a statistical measure of the average agreement in phase difference weighted by amplitude and is frequency dependent, showing a value from 0 (completely random phase difference) to 1 (perfectly matched phase difference) [43]. Furthermore, natural frequency is obtained by measuring the main frequency associated with direct TMS perturbations to the brain, which is mainly related to frequency tuning in the corticothalamic system. Indeed, the measurement of natural frequencies may provide important information about the properties and state of a particular brain system [44].

1.4. Objectives of This Systematic Review

In previous reviews, GABAergic dysfunction as well as gamma oscillatory abnormalities in SCZ have been well described [2,3,45–48]. However, these reviews did not discuss in detail the neurophysiological indices, including glutamatergic and cholinergic functions in SCZ, from the perspective of neurotransmitters. Thus, the current systematic review aimed to comprehensively assess and summarize the previous TMS-EEG studies on neurophysiological dysfunctions in patients with SCZ, including glutamatergic and cholinergic functions, and to discuss the useful role of combined TMS-EEG that can contribute to elucidating the pathophysiology of SCZ. To this end, we systematically reviewed TMS-EEG studies that compared neurophysiological findings of TMS-EEG studies, such as TMS-evoked potentials, oscillatory activities, and functional connectivity, in the various cortical areas between patients with SCZ and healthy controls (HC). Furthermore, we discussed the importance of TMS-EEG neurophysiology that may lead to a better understanding of the underlying pathophysiology of SCZ as well as the clinical application of this special modality.

2. Materials and Methods

2.1. Study Search and Selection Strategy

The search was conducted on PubMed, MEDLINE, Embase, and PsycINFO (May 2000 to March 2020) with the following search items: "(Schizophrenia) and (TMS or (transcranial magnetic stimulation)) and (EEG or electroencephalog*) not ((tDCS) or (transcranial direct current stimulation)) not ((ECT) or (electroconvulsive therapy)) not ((DBS) or (deep brain stimulation)) not ((MST) or (magnetic seizure therapy))". Studies were included if (i) they were written in English; (ii) they compared participants diagnosed with SCZ and HC; and (iii) they measured TMS neurophysiology using combined TMS-EEG. In addition, the following articles were excluded if they were (i) animal model studies; (ii) review articles; or (iii) conference reports. We also excluded clinical studies applying repetitive TMS for treatment, since this review focused primarily on TMS-EEG neurophysiology in patients with SCZ. Then, we reviewed the titles and abstracts of the remaining studies and selected those that utilized TMS-EEG measures to characterize cortical excitability, inhibition, oscillatory activity, or connectivity in patients with SCZ. Next, we read through the full text of the included studies to identify the relevant data.

2.2. Data Extraction

Two investigators (X.L. and S.H.) assessed the studies based on the eligibility criteria independently. The following data were extracted from each study: (1) characteristics of participants; (2) parameters and areas of TMS; (3) cognitive/clinical measures; (4) outcome measures; (5) neurophysiological findings; and (6) clinical/cognitive correlations. Then, we summarized the neurophysiological findings from the studies that included HC as a control. Any discrepancies in data extraction were discussed and resolved with the senior author, Y.N.

2.3. Outcome Measures

The outcome measures focused on TMS neurophysiology regarding TMS-evoked potentials, functional connectivity, and time-frequency analysis. In this review, M1 and DLPFC were the main areas of interest; however, where TMS neurophysiology studies in other areas have been reported, those areas were also included.

2.4. Risk of Bias Assessment

Risk of bias for the included studies was assessed with the Risk of Bias Assessment for Non-randomized Studies tool. The following items were evaluated: participant selection, confounding variables, intervention measurement, blinding of outcome assessment, incomplete outcome data, and selective outcome reporting.

3. Results

3.1. Characteristics of the Included Studies

The initial search generated a total of 376 articles from MEDLINE, Embase, PsycINFO, and PubMed. Additionally, we found another three articles by manual search. Finally, we identified 14 articles. The Preferred Reporting Items for Systematic Reviews and Meta-Analyses (PRISMA) flow diagram is shown in Figure 1.

Figure 1 depicts the flow diagram regarding the information on the different phases in this systematic review, mapping out the number of records identified, included and excluded, and the reasons for exclusions.

In the included studies, regarding the stimulation site, eight studies examined TMS neurophysiology in M1 [41,49–55], five studies in the premotor cortex [41,49,50,56,57], two studies in the parietal cortex [49,50], eight studies in the DLPFC [41,49,50,54,55,58–60], and one study in the other cortical regions [61], respectively. Six studies examined two or more cortical areas in the same study [41,49,50,54,55,60]. In addition, for the stimulation paradigm, nine studies investigated single-pulse TMS including SAI paradigm [41,49–53,56,57,61]. However, there was no study on paired associative stimulation paradigm in patients with SCZ. In contrast, five studies examined paired-pulse TMS including SICI, ICF, and LICI [54,55,58–60]. Furthermore, as for the analysis method, 5 studies analyzed TMS-evoked potentials [41,49,57,58,61], 10 studies conducted time-frequency analysis [50–56,58–60], and 4 studies explored functional connectivity [49,54,55,57] from the TMS-EEG data.

3.2. Schematic Summary of the TMS-EEG Findings from the DLPFC in Patients with SCZ

We summarized the schematics of the TMS-EEG neurophysiology from the DLPFC in Figure 2.

Figure 2A: Prefrontal inhibition for each frequency band power. Patients with SCZ have significantly reduced activity in the inhibitory gamma band of the prefrontal cortex compared to HC, indicating that it can be associated with cognitive dysfunction. Figure 2B: ERSP of the natural frequency. In patients with SCZ, the natural frequency of the prefrontal cortex is significantly reduced compared to HC, and this reduction can be associated with impaired working memory. Figure 2C: TEP changes induced by each TMS paradigm. These waveforms schematically illustrate the changes in TEP induced by each TMS paradigm (SICI, LICI, and ICF). Figure 2D: Paired pulse/Single pulse ratio in each paradigm. This bar graph is a schematic illustration of the group differences between HC and SCZ in each TMS paradigm. Specifically, based on the results of previous studies, compared with HC, patients with SCZ showed significantly reduced SICI ($GABA_A$ receptor-mediated neurophysiological activity), which may be associated with executive dysfunction, as well as significantly reduced LICI ($GABA_B$ receptor-mediated neurophysiological activity), which also may be related to working memory deficit. In addition, patients with SCZ had significantly reduced ICF (glutamatergic NMDA receptor-mediated neurophysiological activity) compared with HC, which may be associated with the clinical severity in this disorder. Collectively, it is assumed that excitatory and inhibitory imbalance could be caused by neurophysiological dysfunction, mainly in the prefrontal cortex, as indexed by SICI, LICI, and ICF in patients with SCZ.

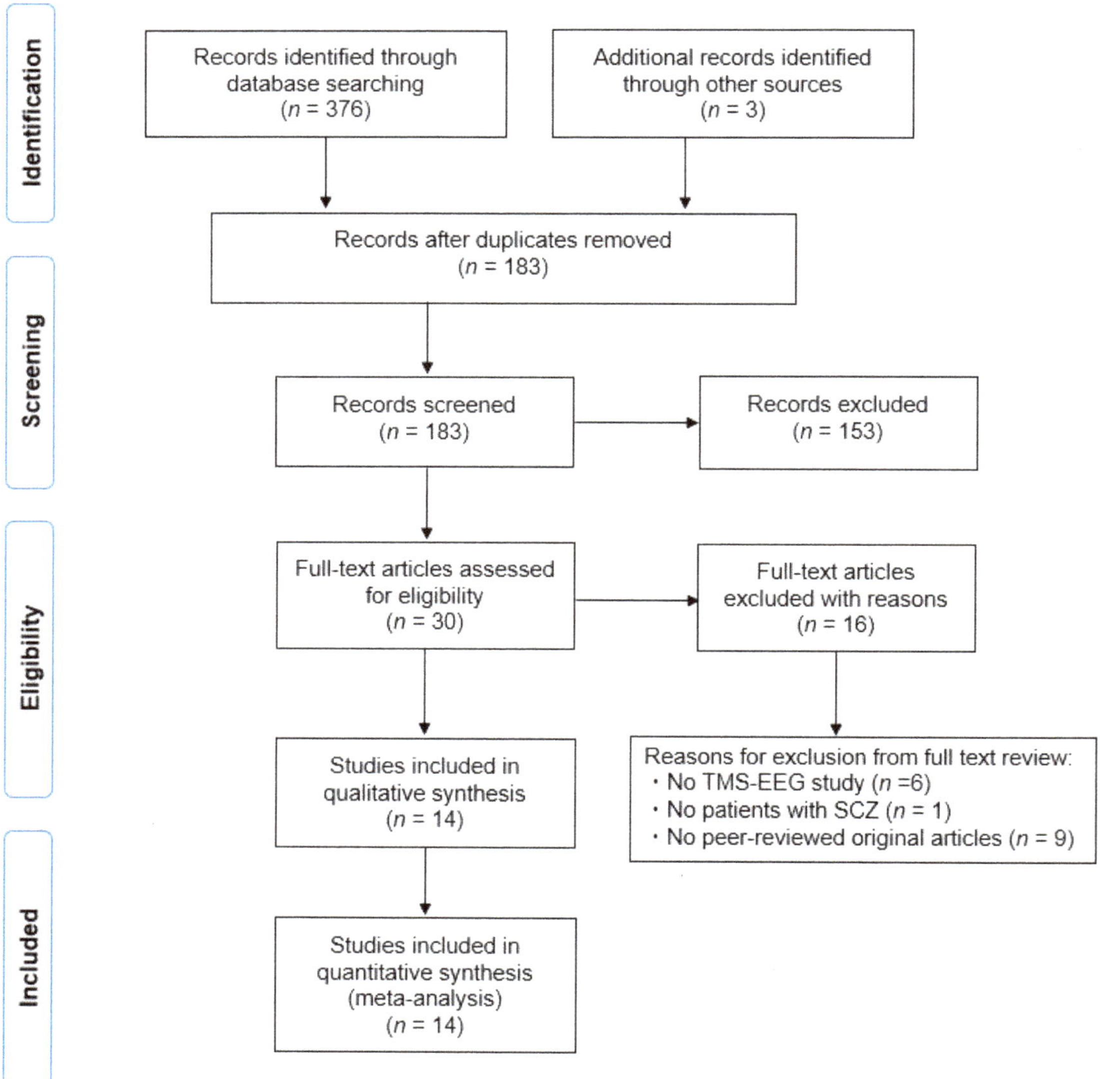

Figure 1. The PRISMA flow diagram.

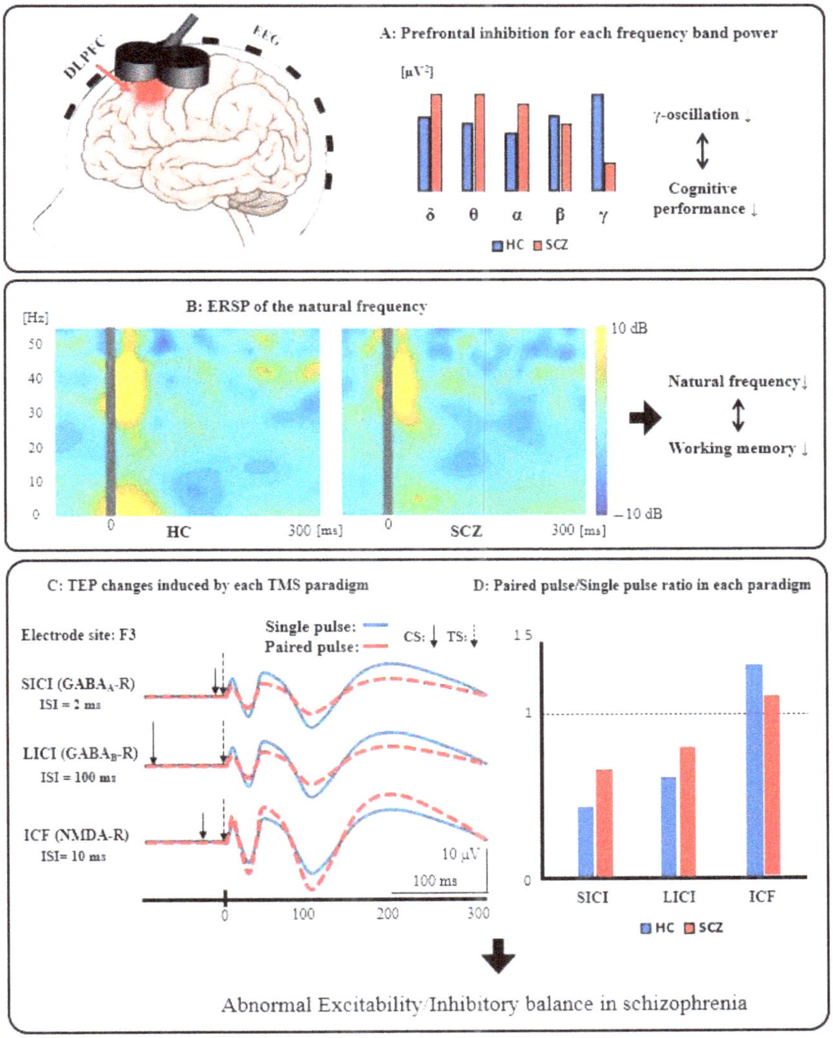

Figure 2. Schematics of combined TMS-EEG neurophysiology from the DLPFC.

3.3. TMS-Evoked Potentials (TEP) Analyses

3.3.1. Single-Pulse TMS Paradigm

The results are summarized in Table 1. SCZ had altered functional connectivity [61] and cholinergic dysfunction in the DLPFC compared with HC [41]. Levit-Binnun et al. administered single-pulse TMS over the Cz electrode site and compared the amplitude and latency of TEP between patients with SCZ and HC [61]. After TMS pulse, as a short latency EEG response, HC showed frontal negativity and parietal positivity, while patients with SCZ showed no frontal negativity or greatly reduced parietal positivity. These different patterns of the amplitude and latency of TEPs on topological plots indicate that patients with SCZ have altered functional connectivity between distributed brain areas, which may also cause abnormal cognitive functioning.

Table 1. TMS-evoked potentials (TEP) analyses.

(A)	*Single-Pulse TMS Paradigm*												
Authors, Year	**Patient Group**	**Age (Mean ± SD)**	**Number of Subjects (Female)**	**Clinical Severity (Mean ± SD)**	**Medication**	**Control Group**	**Age (Mean ± SD)**	**Number of Subjects (Female)**	**Stimulation Parameters**	**Areas of Stimulation**	**Cognitive Measures**	**Analyses**	**Neurophysiological Findings**
Levit-Binnun et al., 2009	SCZ	38 ± 8	8(0)	PANSS	Five patients were on atypical antipsychotics (ziprasidone) and two were on typical antipsychotics (haloperidol and fluphenazine: mean dose equivalent of 415 mg chlorpromazine).	HC	29 ± 10	6(3)	Single-pulse TMS Sham	Over the Cz electrode	N/A	TMS-evoked potential (TEP) analysis Amplitude Latency	In HCs, clear frontal negativity and parietal positivity were observed at 29 ms after TMS stimulation, but in SCZ, there was no frontal negativity and parietal positivity was greatly reduced.
Noda et al., 2018	Chronic SCZ	41 ± 10	12(4)	PANSS total: 50 ± 6.2 PANSS negative: 12 ± 3.4 PANSS positive: 11 ± 3.0 PANSS general: 24 ± 2.8	Patients were taking chlorpromazine equivalent dose (330 ± 290 mg/day) of antipsychotics.	HC	39 ± 12	12(6)	Short-latency afferent inhibition (SAI)	Left primary motor cortex (M1) Dorsolateral prefrontal cortex (DLPFC)	Wechsler Test of Adult Reading Letter-Number Span Test Hopkins Verbal Learning Test Trail Making Test	TMS-evoked potential (TEP) analysis Amplitude of components	Patients with SCZ had significantly smaller modulation of N100 by DLPFC-SAI compared to HC, suggesting impaired cholinergic neurophysiological function in DLPFC. Furthermore, reduced DLPFC-SAI correlated with executive dysfunction as measured by TMT.
(B)	*Paired-Pulse TMS Paradigm*												
Authors, Year	**Patient Group**	**Age (Mean ± SD)**	**Number of Subjects (Female)**	**Clinical Severity (Mean ± SD)**	**Medication**	**Control Group**	**Age (Mean ± SD)**	**Number of Subjects (Female)**	**Stimulation Parameters**	**Areas of Stimulation**	**Cognitive/Clinical Measures**	**Analyses**	**Neurophysiological Findings**
Noda et al., 2017	SCZ	41 ± 10	12(4)	PANSS total: 50 ± 6.2 PANSS negative: 12 ± 3.4 PANSS positive: 11 ± 3.0 PANSS general: 24 ± 2.8	Patients were taking chlorpromazine equivalent dose (330 ± 290 mg/day) of antipsychotics.	HC	39 ± 12	12(6)	Short interval intracortical inhibition (SICI) Intracortical facilitation (ICF)	Left dorsolateral prefrontal cortex (DLPFC)	Wechsler Test of Adult Reading Letter-Number Span Test Trail Making Test Hopkins Verbal Learning Test	TMS-evoked potential (TEP) analysis Amplitude of components Frequency band powers Time-frequency analysis	Patients with SCZ showed reduced inhibition in TEP P60 by DLPFC-SICI compared with HC, which was correlated with the longest span of the LNST. Further, patients with SCZ showed reduced facilitation in TEP P60 and N100 by DLPFC-ICF compared with HC, which were correlated with the total score of the PANSS.

SAI: Noda et al. compared SAI in the left M1 and DLPFC between patients with SCZ and HC [41]. They analyzed major TEP components such as N100 and P180 in each condition. They found that patients with SCZ had a significantly smaller modulation of N100 by DLPFC-SAI compared with HC, which was also correlated with executive function as measured by the Trail Making Test. These findings suggest that patients with SCZ may have cholinergic dysfunction in the DLPFC and that this may cause their executive dysfunction.

3.3.2. Paired-Pulse TMS Paradigm

SICI and ICF: The results are shown in Table 1. SCZ showed $GABA_A$ receptor-mediated and glutamatergic NMDA receptor-mediated neurophysiological dysfunctions in the DLPFC [58]. Noda et al. investigated SICI and ICF from the DLPFC in patients with SCZ and HC [58]. Amplitudes for each TEP component (i.e., P30, N45, P60, N100, and P180), frequency band powers of TEP, and time-frequency of TEP were separately analyzed for each condition. They found that patients with SCZ showed reduced inhibition in TEP P60 by SICI compared with HC, which was correlated with the longest span of the Letter-Number Span Test in patients with SCZ. On the other hand, compared with HC, patients with SCZ showed reduced facilitation in TEP P60 and N100 by ICF, which correlated with the total score of the Positive and Negative Syndrome Scale (PANSS). This study suggests that $GABA_A$ receptor-mediated and glutamatergic NMDA receptor-mediated neurophysiological dysfunctions in the DLPFC may be associated with the underlying pathophysiology of cognitive and clinical symptoms in patients with SCZ.

3.4. *Time-Frequency Analyses*

3.4.1. Single-Pulse TMS Paradigm

The results are summarized in Table 2. Natural frequencies are the major endogenous frequencies that are caused by external perturbations. The human cerebral cortex tends to maintain a natural frequency in each cortical region. Therefore, TMS-EEG can be used to directly stimulate the cerebral cortex and measure its natural frequencies [44]. SCZ showed the remarkable pathophysiological changes in natural frequency [50]. That is, excessive gamma and theta/delta activations by single-pulse TMS over the M1 were observed, which were also associated with clinical symptoms [53]. Ferrarelli et al. applied single-pulse TMS over the M1, DLPFC, and premotor and posterior parietal areas in patients with SCZ and HC [50]. They assessed cognitive function by measuring the accuracy and reaction time for the word memory and facial memory tasks. Intertrial coherence and event-related spectral perturbation (ERSP) were analyzed for the time-frequency domain. When single-pulse TMS was applied to each cortex, natural frequency induced by TMS became faster in the order of the parietal cortex, M1, premotor cortex, and DLPFC in HC. However, in patients with SCZ, since the natural frequency response itself was generally attenuated, there was no clear induction of site-specific natural frequencies by single-pulse TMS as in HC. Furthermore, lowered natural frequency in the prefrontal areas was related to the PANSS positive subscale scores as well as reaction time in the word memory task in patients with SCZ. Frantseva et al. administered single-pulse TMS and sham TMS over the left M1 in patients with SCZ and schizoaffective disorders and HC to analyze the time-domain, frequency-domain, and time-frequency-domain of TEP, separately [53]. The study demonstrated that the TMS-induced cortical activation in the gamma frequency band between 400 and 700 ms over the M1 was positively correlated with positive symptom severity in patients with SCZ. In contrast, the activation in theta and delta frequency bands at 200 ms after TMS was positively correlated with negative symptom severity in patients with SCZ. These results suggest that excessive gamma and theta/delta activations over the M1 may account for the underlying pathophysiology of positive and negative symptoms in SCZ. Moreover, it is proposed that excessive cortical activation can abnormally propagate to the remote areas of the cognitive domain, which may result in cognitive deficits due to impaired information processing in patients with SCZ. To test this, Canali et al. applied single-pulse TMS to the premotor cortex to investigate the natural frequency and its ERSP among patients with SCZ, bipolar disorder, major depressive disorder, and HC [56]. Specifically, ERSP was computed to quantify the response in the time-frequency domain. Natural frequency in the frontal area was significantly slower in each patient group compared with HC, while frontal natural frequencies were not significantly different among the patient groups. In addition, there was no correlation between natural frequency in the frontal area, PANSS scores, and medication dose in these patients. Similar to the natural frequency results, TMS-induced gamma oscillations were significantly slower in all the three diagnostic groups compared to HC, while there was no significant difference in the frequency of gamma oscillations over the PFC between the patient groups.

Ferrarelli et al. investigated the time-domain and frequency-domain of TEP in M1 applying single-pulse TMS over the left M1 in patients with first-episode psychosis (FEP) and HC [51]. Specifically, the global mean field power for the time domain was not significantly different between patients with FEP and HC. For the relative spectral power assessed for the frequency domain, patients with FEP showed a significantly decreased beta/low-gamma activities on TEP at the fronto-central area compared to HC. Furthermore, the lower cumulative spectral power was associated with worse scores on the scales of positive symptoms as well as negative symptoms in the PANSS. These results suggest that TMS-evoked fast oscillations over the fronto-central areas may be impaired from the time of onset. Andrews et al. applied single-pulse TMS to M1 when participants observed the other's hand movements, which were designed to elicit mirror neuron system activity [52] and for which the facial affect recognition and theory of mind tasks were administered. The mu rhythm (8–13 Hz) was measured from the C3, Cz, and C4 EEG electrodes over the sensorimotor cortex. They found that patients with SCZ showed lower accuracy on the facial affect recognition and theory of mind tasks compared to HC. However, there were no significant differences in the degree of mu suppression and motor resonance between patients with SCZ and HC. These findings suggest that patients with SCZ may have an intact mirror neuron system.

3.4.2. Paired-Pulse TMS Paradigm

LICI: The results are summarized in Table 2. SCZ showed significantly reduced LICI in the DLPFC [60], and it was correlated with working memory dysfunction [59]. Thus, the prefrontal aberrant $GABA_B$ receptor-mediated dysfunction in SCZ may be part of the cause of working memory deficit in this disorder. Radhu et al. investigated LICI in the M1 and DLPFC in patients with SCZ, patients with bipolar disorder, and HC [60]. They assessed overall cortical inhibition in the frequency band from 1 to 50 Hz through the cluster mass tests between the groups. The LICI was significantly reduced in patients with SCZ compared with the other groups in the DLPFC not in M1, suggesting that LICI deficits in the DLPFC may be specific to the pathophysiology of SCZ. Lett et al. investigated the relationship between LICI in the DLPFC and glutamic acid decarboxylase I gene, a major determinant of GABA, in patients with SCZ [59]. They found that the variation in the glutamic acid decarboxylase I gene might play a pivotal role in the GABAergic inhibitory neurotransmission in the DLPFC and working memory performance in SCZ. In other words, working memory dysfunction may be attributable to the prefrontal aberrant $GABA_B$ receptor-mediated function in patients with SCZ.

Table 2. Time-frequency analyses.

Authors, Year	Patient Group	Age (Mean ± SD)	Number of Subjects (Female)	Clinical Severity (Mean ± SD)	Medication	Control Group	Age (Mean ± SD)	Number of Subjects (Female)	Stimulation Parameters	Areas of Stimulation	Cognitive Measures	Analyses	Neurophysiological Findings
(A)	*Single-Pulse TMS Paradigm*												
Ferrarelli et al., 2012	SCZ	33 ± 6.2	20(7)	PANSS general: 39 ± 11 PANSS negative: 22 ± 6.0 PANSS positive: 18 ± 6.3	Eighteen patients were taking second-generation antipsychotics while two were on first-generation antipsychotics.	HC	32 ± 7.8	20(4)	Single-pulse	Posterior parietal cortex Motor cortex Premotor cortex Prefrontal cortex	The word memory Penn Word Recognition Test The facial memory Penn Facial Memory Test	Time-Frequency Analysis Event-related spectra perturbation (ERSP) Intertrial coherence (ITC)	In patients with SCZ, the natural frequency response was generally attenuated compared with HC when single-pulse TMS was applied to the prefrontal cortex. Further, the lowered natural frequency in the prefrontal areas in SCZ was related to the PANSS positive scores and reaction time in the word memory task.
Frantseva et al., 2014	SCZ or schizoaffective disorder	37 ± 10	16(4)	PANSS total: 65 ± 18 PANSS negative: 18 ± 6.1 PANSS positive: 16 ± 4.3 PANSS global: 30 ± 8.6	Fourteen patients with schizophrenia were treated with antipsychotic medications (clozapine: n = 6, mean dose 400 ± 55 mg/day; risperidone: n = 3, mean dose 3.2 ± 2.5 mg; haloperidol: n = 2, mean dose 2.0 ± 1.4 mg; quetiapine: n = 1, 100 mg; perphenazine: n = 1, 16 mg; olanzapine: n = 1, 7.5 mg) and two patients did not take any psychotropic medications.	HC	36 ± 7.9	16(5)	Single-pulse (single monophasic TMS pulse) Sham	Left motor cortex	N/A	Time-domain Analysis Frequency-domain Analysis Time-Frequency Analysis	TMS-induced cortical activation in the gamma band between 400 and 700 ms at the M1 was positively correlated with positive symptoms in patients with SCZ. In contrast, the activation in theta and delta bands at 200 ms after TMS was positively correlated with negative symptoms in patients with SCZ.

Table 2. *Cont.*

(A)	*Single-Pulse TMS Paradigm*												
Authors, Year	**Patient Group**	**Age (Mean ± SD)**	**Number of Subjects (Female)**	**Clinical Severity (Mean ± SD)**	**Medication**	**Control Group**	**Age (Mean ± SD)**	**Number of Subjects (Female)**	**Stimulation Parameters**	**Areas of Stimulation**	**Cognitive Measures**	**Analyses**	**Neurophysiological Findings**
Canali et al., 2015	Chronic undifferentiated SCZ	38 ± 9	12(3)	PANSS general: 37 ± 5 PANSS negative: 18 ± 4 PANSS positive: 18 ± 4	All patients were taking antipsychotics (typical antipsychotics: n = 5; atypical antipsychotics: n = 7).	HC	39 ± 15	12(7)	Single-pulse	Premotor cortex	N/A	Time-Frequency analysis Event-related spectral perturbation (ERSP)	Natural frequency in the frontal cortex was significantly slower in patients with bipolar disorder (20 ± 3.7 Hz), major depressive disorder (19 ± 5.0 Hz), and SCZ (20 ± 4.2 Hz) than HC (27 ± 3.2 Hz). However, frontal natural frequencies among the patient groups (i.e., bipolar disorder, major depressive disorder, and SCZ) were not significantly different. There was no correlation among natural frequency in the frontal area, PANSS scores, and medication dose in these populations.
Ferrarelli et al., 2019	First-episode psychosis(FEP)	23 ± 5.2	16(4)	Scale for the assessment of positive symptoms (SAPS): 18 ± 13 Scale for the assessment of negative symptoms scores (SANS): 31 ± 12	Nine FEP patients were antipsychotic naïve and seven patients were taking antipsychotics less than 1 month.	HC	23 ± 6.3	11(3)	Single-pulse	Left primary motor cortex (M1)	N/A	Time-Frequency analysis Time domain: The global mean field power (GMFP) Frequency domain: Relative spectral power (RSP)/Cumulated RSP (cRSP)	GMFP for the time domain was not significantly different between patients with FEP and HC. When RSP was assessed for the frequency domain, patients with FEP showed a significantly decreased beta/low-gamma TEP activities at the fronto-central area relative to HC. The lower RSP was associated with both worse scores on the SAPS and the SANS. TMS-evoked fast oscillations over the fronto-central areas were impaired from the time of onset, suggesting that these deficits may be related to the clinical symptoms.
Andrews et al., 2015	SCZ or schizoaffective disorder	44 ± 11	19	PANSS general: 34 ± 8.1 PANSS negative: 16 ± 5.5 PANSS positive: 15 ± 6.1	Patients were taking chlorpromazine equivalent dose (67~1307 mg/day) of antipsychotics.	HC	38 ± 13	19	Single-pulse TMS during the observation of hand movements designed to elicit mirror system activity	Primary motor cortex (M1)	NimStim Static Face Task Cognitive and Affective Mental Inference Task (Inference Task)	Frequency analysis mu rhythm (8–13 Hz) TMS induced motor-evoked potentials (MEPs)	Patients with SCZ showed lower accuracy on the facial affect recognition and theory of mind tasks than HC. No significant differences in the degree of mu suppression and motor resonance between the patients with SCZ and HC.

Table 2. *Cont.*

(B)	*Paired-Pulse TMS Paradigm*												
Authors, Year	**Patient group**	**Age (Mean ± SD)**	**Number of Subjects (Female)**	**Clinical Severity (Mean ± SD)**	**Medication**	**Control Group**	**Age (Mean ± SD)**	**Number of Subjects (Female)**	**Stimulation Parameters**	**Areas of Stimulation**	**Cognitive Measures**	**Analyses**	**Neurophysiological Findings**
Radhu et al., 2015	SCZ	36	38(13)	Brief Psychiatric Rating Scale (BPRS)	All patients were treated with antipsychotics.	HC	34	46(23)	Long-Interval Cortical Inhibition (LICI)	Left motor cortex Dorsolateral prefrontal cortex (DLPFC)	N/A	Time-Frequency analysis	LICI was significantly reduced in patients with SCZ compared with other groups in the DLPFC not in M1.
Lett et al., 2016	SCZ or schizoaffective disorder	35 ± 10	23(5)	N/A	Not reported	HC	35 ± 11	33(18)	Long-Interval Cortical Inhibition (LICI)	Dorsolateral prefrontal cortex (DLPFC)	IQ Wechsler Test of Adult ReadingWorking memory Letter-number sequencing task Digit-span forward taskSelective attention Stroop Neuropsychological Screening Test	Time-Frequency analysis Cluster-Based analysis	Variation of the GAD1 gene in patients with SCZ may play a pivotal role in GABA(B)ergic inhibitory neurotransmission and working memory performance in the DLPFC.

3.5. Connectivity Analyses

3.5.1. Single-Pulse TMS Paradigm

The results are shown in Table 3. SCZ showed the defects in gamma cortical activity and connectivity over the frontal region [49,57]. Ferrarelli et al. applied single-pulse TMS to the parietal, M1, premotor, and DLPFC in patients with SCZ and HC [49]. They analyzed the significant current density (SCD) [62], which captures the amplitude of TMS-evoked cortical currents, indexing the cortical activity, as well as the significant current scattering (SCS) [62], which reflects the average distance of TMS-activated cortical sources, representing the cortical connectivity. They found that both SCD and SCS were most impaired in the DLPFC after single-pulse TMS in patients with SCZ compared with HC, but there was no difference in SCD or SCS over the parietal cortex and M1 after single-pulse TMS. There was a negative correlation between SCD and performance in episodic memory by the Penn Word memory delayed task, whereas higher SCS values were associated with a lower executive function assessed by the Penn Conditional Exclusion test. Those findings indicate that the defects in cortical activity and connectivity of the DLPFC may underlie the pathophysiology of cognitive impairments in patients with SCZ.

One study administered single-pulse TMS to the premotor cortex to analyze amplitude measures using global mean field power and ERSP as well as synchronization measures using intertrial coherence of TEP and source localization in patients with SCZ and HC [57]. Patients with SCZ showed significantly decreased amplitude and synchronization of TMS-evoked gamma oscillations particularly in the frontocentral area during the 100 ms after TMS pulse compared with HC. In the source modeling analysis, patients with SCZ presented with a slow propagation of TMS-evoked gamma oscillations from the bilateral premotor cortex to the bilateral M1 along with the midline, whereas HC showed the gamma propagation from the bilateral premotor cortex to the right sensorimotor, left anterior premotor, and left sensorimotor areas. Given the findings in previous studies that gamma oscillations occur in the corticothalamic loop [63,64], the above findings suggest that there may be intrinsic dysfunctions in the frontal thalamocortical circuits in patients with SCZ [50].

3.5.2. Paired-Pulse TMS Paradigm

LICI: The results are summarized in Table 3. SCZ showed significant deficits in cortical inhibition as well as inhibitory gamma modulation in the DLPFC during the LICI paradigm [54,55]. Farzan et al. conducted the LICI paradigm over the left M1 and DLPFC in patients with SCZ and major depressive disorder, and HC using active and sham stimulation conditions [54]. They analyzed the modulatory effect of LICI on cortical oscillations across the five frequency bands as follows: δ (1–3 Hz), θ (4–7 Hz), α (8–12 Hz), β (12.5–28 Hz), and γ (30–50 Hz). They found that patients with SCZ had significantly reduced cortical inhibition and induction of gamma oscillations by TMS-EEG neurophysiology in the DLPFC but not in M1 compared with the other groups. Radhu et al. measured LICI from the DLPFC in patients with SCZ or schizoaffective disorder, patients with obsessive-compulsive disorder, unaffected first-degree relatives of these patients, and HC [55]. They analyzed time-frequency decomposition to compare the cortical inhibitory function among these groups. As a result, they found that the degree of cortical inhibition was significantly decreased in patients with SCZ compared to HC. In addition, there was no significant difference in the degree of cortical inhibition between HC and first-degree relatives of patients with SCZ. Therefore, the deficits of LICI in the DLPFC may represent one of the diagnostic biomarkers of SCZ.

Table 3. Connectivity analyses.

(A)	*Single-Pulse TMS Paradigm*												
Authors, Year	**Patient Group**	**Age (Mean ± SD)**	**Number of Subjects (Female)**	**Clinical Severity (Mean ± SD)**	**Medication**	**Control Group**	**Age (Mean ± SD)**	**Number of Subjects (Female)**	**Stimulation Parameters**	**Areas of Stimulation**	**Cognitive Measures**	**Analyses**	**Neurophysiological Findings**
Ferrarelli et al., 2015	SCZ	33 ± 6.2	20(7)	PANSS general: 39 ± 11 PANSS negative: 22 ± 5.8 PANSS positive: 18 ± 6.3	Patients were taking chlorpromazine equivalent dose (314 ± 129 mg/day) of antipsychotics.	HC	32 ± 7.8	20(4)	Single-pulse TMS	Prefrontal cortex (PFC) Premotor cortex Motor cortex Parietal cortex	Episodic Memory Word Memory Delayed Executive Function Penn Conditional Exclusion Test	TMS-evoked potential (TEP) analysis Significant current density (SCD) Connectivity analysis Significant current scattering (SCS)	Both SCD and SCS were most impaired in the DLPFC after single-pulse TMS in patients with SCZ compared with HC. No difference in SCD and SCS were observed in the parietal cortex and M1 after single-pulse TMS. SCD and performance in episodic memory were negatively correlated, whereas higher SCS values were associated with a lower executive function.
Ferrarelli et al., 2008	SCZ	34 ± 8.0	16(3)	PANSS	N/A	HC	35 ± 7.0	14(3)	Single-pulse TMS	Right premotor cortex	N/A	TMS-evoked potential (TEP) analysis Amplitude The global mean field power (GMFP) Event-related spectral perturbation phase Connectivity analysis	Patients with SCZ indicated significantly decreased amplitude and synchronization of TMS-evoked gamma oscillations particularly in the frontocentral region during the 100 ms after TMS pulse compared with HC. In the source modeling analysis, cortical propagation of TMS-evoked gamma oscillations was more localized compared with HC.

Table 3. *Cont.*

(B)	*Paired-Pulse TMS Paradigm*												
Authors, Year	**Patient Group**	**Age (Mean ± SD)**	**Number of Subjects (Female)**	**Clinical Severity (Mean ± SD)**	**Medication**	**Control Group**	**Age (Mean ± SD)**	**Number of Subjects (Female)**	**Stimulation Parameters**	**Areas of Stimulation**	**Cognitive Measures**	**Analyses**	**Neurophysiological Findings**
Farzan et al., 2010	SCZ	38 ± 10	14(4)	PANSS total: 66 ± 18 PANSS negative: 18 ± 6.3 PANSS positive: 17 ± 4.4 PANSS global: 31 ± 9.2	Two patients were unmedicated (one medication-naive; one medication-free for 6 months) and 12 patients were on medication (n = 5, 390.0 ± 54.8 mg clozapine; n = 3, 3.2 ± 2.5 mg risperidone; n = 2, 2 ± 1.4 mg haloperidol; n-1, 100 mg of quetiapine; n = 1, 16 mg perphenazine)	HC	37 ± 7.6	14(5)	Long-Interval Cortical Inhibition (LICI) Sham	Left motor cortex Dorsolateral prefrontal cortex (DLPFC)	N/A	Time-Frequency analysis	Patients with SCZ had significant deficits of cortical inhibition and inhibitory modulation of gamma oscillations in the DLPFC but not in M1 compared with the other groups.
Radhu et al., 2017	(a) SCZ or schizoaffective disorder (b) First-degree relatives of patients with SCZ	(a) 30 (b) 54	(a) 19(9) (b) 30(17)	Schizotypal Personality Questionnaire The 24-construct Brief Psychiatric Rating Scale	Patients were taking clozapine (150–475 mg/day).	HC	33	49(25)	Long-Interval Cortical Inhibition (LICI)	Motor cortex Dorsolateral prefrontal cortex (DLPFC)	N/A	Time-Frequency analysis	The degree of cortical inhibition as indexed by LICI was significantly decreased in patients with SCZ compared to HC. Further, no significant difference in the degree of cortical inhibition between HC and first-degree relatives of patients with SCZ.

3.6. Risk of Bias

Out of 14 studies, 11 (79%) showed a low risk of bias for the participant selection, 10 (71%) showed a low risk of bias for the confounding variables, and all of the included studies showed a low risk of bias for the measurement of exposure, blinding of outcome assessment, and incomplete outcome data. On the other hand, 10 studies (71%) were judged to be unclear for the selective outcome reporting because the details of most research protocols were not specified in the articles.

4. Discussion

4.1. Summary of This Review

The present systematic review found that patients with SCZ had oscillatory abnormalities, especially in the prefrontal cortex. Indeed, for the DLPFC, patients with SCZ showed inhibitory (i.e., SICI and LICI) and facilitatory (i.e., ICF) dysfunctions [55,58,60]; however, for M1, there was no significant dysfunction in cortical inhibition (i.e., LICI) or TMS-induced gamma oscillations [54,60]. On the other hand, a previous study assessing I-wave facilitation of SCZ with TMS-EMG reported that there may be some deficit in cortical inhibition in M1 [65]. Furthermore, the other study reported that single-pulse TMS to M1 in patients with SCZ showed excessive gamma oscillations in the M1 region in the 400–700 ms post-stimulus interval [53]. Thus, further studies are needed to confirm whether the impairment of cortical inhibition of SCZ also extends to M1. Moreover, this review found reduced connectivity between the premotor cortex and prefrontal cortex [49] and reduced TMS-induced gamma oscillations in the fronto-central regions [57] in patients with SCZ. In addition, TMS-induced functional cortical conductivity in the gamma band was positively related to positive symptoms, while the functional cortical conductivity in the theta and delta bands was positively related to negative symptoms in SCZ [53]. Moreover, cholinergic dysfunction in the DLPFC, as indexed by SAI, was associated with cognitive impairment in SCZ [41].

4.2. Evidence to Support the E/I Imbalance Hypothesis in SCZ

The E/I imbalance hypothesis in SCZ postulates that an imbalance between excitation and inhibition in neural circuits would be involved in the pathophysiology of SCZ, which may be related to clinical symptoms and cognitive deficits in patients with SCZ. Numerous studies have reported abnormalities in the excitatory function of the glutamatergic system and the inhibitory function of the GABAergic system in patients with SCZ [66–69]. Based on the E/I imbalance hypothesis, it would be anticipated that patients with SCZ may have altered GABAergic function as indexed by SICI and LICI paradigms as well as increased or decreased glutamatergic function as indexed by ICF paradigm depending on the clinical condition and stage of this disorder.

4.3. Evidence to Support the GABA Hypothesis in SCZ

Previous studies have reported decreased SICI and LICI in the DLPFC of SCZ, suggesting that $GABA_A$ receptor- and $GABA_B$ receptor-mediated dysfunctions in the DLPFC are pathological features of SCZ [58,60]. Furthermore, previous studies showed that clozapine, an atypical antipsychotic medication, has the binding potential to the $GABA_B$ receptor and acts as a modulator for the receptor [70,71]. Indeed, Daskalakis et al. reported that clozapine treatment was associated with increased cortical inhibition in patients with SCZ, which might be exerted by the potentiation of cortical $GABA_B$ receptor-mediated inhibitory neurotransmission [20,72]. Likewise, other studies that examined the TMS-EMG on patients with SCZ indicated that SCZ had significantly decreased SICI compared with HC even after controlling for age and medications [45]. In addition, postmortem studies noted that there was decreased GABA levels in patients with SCZ [73].

4.4. Evidence to Support the Glutamate Hypothesis in SCZ

On the other hand, one study has shown that patients with SCZ have reduced ICF on the DLPFC, suggesting reduced function via glutamatergic NMDA receptors [58], supporting the glutamate hypothesis. For example, phencyclidine, a prototype of noncompetitive NMDA receptor antagonist, induces psychotic symptoms, thought disorder, blunted affect, and cognitive impairments in healthy individuals [74]. However, for the ICF, a previous meta-analysis study revealed that there was no significant difference in ICF between patients with SCZ and HC after controlling for age and medications [45]. A recent meta-analysis of ^{1}H-MRS studies noted that there were no significant changes in glutamate levels in the DLPFC in patients with SCZ [13,75]. However, the present study showed decreased ICF in patients with SCZ as measured by TMS-EEG that come from one study [58]. Thus, our finding warrants further studies to confirm the present study.

4.5. Potential Evidence to Support the Cholinergic Hypothesis in SCZ

In addition, the decrease in SAI in the DLPFC of SCZ reported by Noda et al. indicates that the cholinergic function of the region may be reduced in SCZ [41], supporting the cholinergic hypothesis [76]. However, in the TMS-EEG experiments of Noda et al. at that time, noise masking methods such as white noise were not used to suppress the auditory evoked potential (AEP) to TMS clicks. Therefore, it is possible that there was contamination of the AEP by the TMS click sounds in the N100-P180 complex of TEP [77]. Therefore, it is necessary to confirm the reproducibility of the results of this study using a more accurate experimental method in the future. In addition, cholinergic receptors (α7-nicotinic acetylcholine receptors, α7-nAChRs) have recently been considered a potential therapeutic target for SCZ as well as other cognitive disorders without causing adverse effects [78]. Indeed, this notion is supported by multiple lines of evidence, ranging from genetic studies to behavioral studies. For example, a postmortem brain study has indicated deficits of α7-nAChRs in the DLPFC and hippocampus of patients with SCZ [79]. Furthermore, such deficits are thought to contribute to abnormalities in smooth pursuit eye movements, sustained attention, and other cognitive domains in patients with SCZ [80].

4.6. Abnormalities of TMS-Induced Gamma Oscillations in SCZ

The present review also noted that TMS-evoked gamma oscillations in the frontocentral area were significantly reduced in patients with SCZ, which was also associated with reduced effective connectivity in related regions. Furthermore, since GABAergic function in the cerebral cortex is reduced in SCZ, the E/I balance is also likely to be naturally impaired [81], which may result in reduced natural frequency, especially in the prefrontal cortex [50]. However, on the other hand, studies that assessed frontal natural frequency by TMS-EEG in patients with major depressive disorder and bipolar disorder have also shown a decreased natural frequency, suggesting that this finding may be a pathophysiology that is at least in part shared among the major psychiatric disorders [56]. Specifically, since gamma band activity in the DLPFC is supposed to be related to higher-order cortical processing [82,83], these findings may represent neural bases that contribute to the pathophysiology of SCZ [84,85]. Taken together, these findings suggest that patients with SCZ may involve dysfunction of the frontal-thalamocortical circuits necessary to execute appropriate information processing [50,57]. Moreover, the similar abnormal findings observed in the PFC can also be found in M1 in patients with SCZ, which may be due to the effects of the corresponding abnormal network resonance properties on M1 [53]. Moreover, Ferrarelli et al. measured cortical oscillatory responses with single-pulse TMS targeting the left frontal, parietal, and occipital cortices at rest, and they showed that different cortical networks could be characterized by different oscillatory activities [57]. Specifically, they showed that each cortical region may respond at a characteristic frequency, termed the natural frequency, described above. In addition, the study by Ferrarelli et al. also showed that the topography of TMS-evoked oscillatory activity was changed corresponding to the site of stimulation. Moreover, the pattern of topography corresponding to each stimulation site hardly overlaps between target sites, suggesting that functionally separated networks in HC oscillate at different frequencies at rest [86,87]. On the other hand, Andrew et al. first investigated the activity of the mirror system in response to behavioral observations in SCZ using TMS-EEG and found that mu-suppression and motor resonance were related. In addition, the study demonstrated that the mirror system was intact in the stable SCZ, suggesting that other neural substrates may be involved in the social cognitive deficits in SCZ [52].

4.7. Insights from This Systematic Review

Ferrarelli et al. showed that TMS-evoked gamma oscillations in the fronto-central areas occurring within 100 ms after single-pulse TMS were significantly reduced in SCZ, and amplitude and phase synchronization in the same gamma oscillations were also significantly reduced, and source modeling analysis showed that TMS-evoked EEG propagation was found to be restricted to the TMS stimulation site compared to HC [57]. On the other hand, a study by Frantseva et al. observed excessive gamma oscillations at the M1 400–700 ms after single-pulse TMS over the M1 in patients with SCZ [53]. In the same study, functional cortical conductivity of TMS-induced gamma activity was positively correlated with positive symptoms, while functional cortical conductivity of theta and delta bands was positively correlated with negative symptoms in patients with SCZ [53]. In addition, a SICI study by Noda et al. [58] and LICI studies by Radhu et al. [55,60] have shown that patients with SCZ had decreased GABA receptor-mediated function as indexed by SICI and LICI paradigms as well as decreased glutamatergic NMDA receptor-mediated function as indexed by ICF paradigm in the DLPFC. Furthermore, studies by Farzan et al. [54] and Radhu et al. [55] have shown that LICI paradigm that applied to the DLPFC in patients with SCZ induced significantly lower power of gamma oscillations at the same region within 100 ms after TMS when compared with HC, whereas those studies have shown that there was no significant reduction of GABAergic inhibitory function or gamma oscillation activity in patients with SCZ when applying the LICI paradigm to M1 [54,60]. Although several studies using measurement modalities other than TMS neurophysiology [66–69] have already reported abnormalities in glutamatergic excitatory function and GABAergic inhibitory function in patients with SCZ, the present systematic review of TMS-EEG neurophysiology indicates that GABAergic function, mainly in the frontal region, could be decreased in patients with SCZ [81], and E/I balance in the prefrontal and frontal-thalamic cortical responses is likely to be impaired [50]. In particular, since reduced TMS-evoked gamma oscillations in the DLPFC of patients with SCZ are associated with higher-order information processing deficits [82,83], these findings may explain the pathophysiology and neural basis of cognitive dysfunction in SCZ [57,84,85]. Therefore, exactly as the E/I imbalance hypothesis proposes, the imbalance between excitation and inhibition in neural circuits may be involved in the pathophysiology of SCZ, which may be related to the clinical symptoms and cognitive deficits of this disorder.

4.8. Limitations of This Review and TMS-EEG Study in General

Fourteen research papers were extracted for this review, all of which are TMS-EEG studies in schizophrenia. However, the research objectives and methodologies of each paper are different, and it is currently difficult to discuss, interpret, and integrate the results of each study in a truly systematic way. Therefore, it is necessary to verify the reproducibility of the results of each study and establish a more reliable methodology through further research in this area.

Combined TMS-EEG is a non-invasive and useful evaluation method for neuropsychiatric disorders; however, there is a limitation on the principle to this modality that it cannot directly measure the neuron activity itself. Since there were only 14 studies in the current review that met the inclusion criteria, it must be said that at present, we can report preliminarily results in this discipline. For example, there is only one TMS-EEG study that examined the cholinergic system in schizophrenic [41], and more studies with larger sample sizes are needed to establish sufficient evidence. Other common problems of TMS-EEG are as follows: muscle activities, TMS-induced cranial reflexes, and somatosensory and auditory evoked potentials can easily contaminate TMS-EEG responses as artifacts [2]. In particular, the detection of EEG gamma rhythm can be affected by various artifacts derived from TMS [88]. In addition, since the effects of psychotropic medications on EEG activities cannot be ignored, a study design that controls medication in patients with SCZ is also important in TMS-EEG research [89]. Alternatively, at least, elaborated analyses that control the effect of the medication is required. Furthermore, most of the previous TMS-EEG studies have been conducted by various recording systems, different experimental methods, and unique analysis methods. Thus, these methodological differences in the included studies make it difficult to interpret the results. Hence, future research applying more standardized experimental methods with larger sample sizes in a transdiagnostic approach will help improve the quality of TMS-EEG study [89] and further such sophisticated TMS-EEG research will be important to replicate and confirm the currently available findings of this special modality [17]. In addition, previous TMS-EEG studies have reported TMS neurophysiological findings in patients with SCZ at various clinical stages, but it remains unclear at which clinical stage of SCZ these abnormal neurophysiological findings occur and how they progress. Therefore, to address the above issues, future TMS-EEG studies must use standardized experimental and analytical methods to evaluate longitudinal changes in neurophysiological findings from the pre-onset, prodromal, acute, and chronic stages of SCZ.

5. Conclusions

The findings of this systematic review support, at least in part, several hypotheses that explain the pathophysiological bases of SCZ, including the E/I imbalance hypothesis discussed in the introduction. Furthermore, the present systematic review demonstrated the usefulness of combined TMS-EEG to identify the neurophysiological biomarkers to better understand the neural bases of this disorder. Moreover, this modality can be applied to develop objective diagnostics of this disorder, facilitate the prognostication of clinical symptoms, and improve therapeutic strategies for patients with SCZ.

Author Contributions: Conceptualization, Y.N.; methodology, K.Y. and X.L.; validation, Y.N.; investigation, X.L. and S.H.; writing: original draft preparation, X.L.; writing: review and editing, S.N., M.W., K.Y., Z.J.D., M.M. and Y.N.; visualization, X.L.; supervision, Y.N.; project administration, X.L. and Y.N. All authors have read and agreed to the published version of the manuscript.

Funding: This research received no external funding.

Institutional Review Board Statement: Not applicable.

Informed Consent Statement: Not applicable.

Data Availability Statement: Data sharing not applicable.

Acknowledgments: Y.N. has received a Grant-in-Aid for Young Scientists and Grant-in-Aid for Scientific Research (B) from the Japan Society for the Promotion of Science (JSPS), research grants from Japan Agency for Medical Research and Development (AMED), investigator-initiated clinical study grants from TEIJIN PHARMA LIMITED and Inter Reha Co., Ltd. Y.N. also receives research grants from Japan Health Foundation, Meiji Yasuda Mental Health Foundation, Mitsui Life Social Welfare Foundation, Takeda Science Foundation, SENSHIN Medical Research Foundation, Health Science Center Foundation, Mochida Memorial Foundation for Medical and Pharmaceutical Research, Taiju Life Social Welfare Foundation, and Daiichi Sankyo Scholarship Donation Program. Y.N. has received speaker's honoraria from Dainippon Sumitomo Pharma, MOCHIDA PHARMACEUTICAL CO., LTD., and Yoshitomiyakuhin Corporation within the past three years. Y.N. also receives equipment-in-kind support for an investigator-initiated study from Magventure Inc, Inter Reha Co., Ltd., BrainBox Ltd., and Miyuki Giken Co., Ltd. S.N. has received a Grant-in-Aid for Young Scientists A and Grants-in-Aid for Scientific Research B and C from JSPS, and research grants from Japan Research Foundation for Clinical Pharmacology, Naito Foundation, Takeda Science Foundation, Uehara Memorial Foundation, and Daiichi Sankyo Scholarship Donation Program within the past three years. S.N. has also received research support, manuscript fees, or speaker's honoraria from Dainippon Sumitomo Pharma, Meiji-Seika Pharma, Otsuka Pharmaceutical, Shionogi, and Yoshitomi Yakuhin within the past three years. Z.J.D has received research support from the Ontario Mental Health (OMH) Foundation, the CIHR, the Brain and Behaviour Research Foundation (Formerly NARSAD), and the Temerty family and Grant family through the CAMH Foundation and the Campbell Institute. In the last 3 years, Z.J.D has received research and equipment in-kind support for an investigator-initiated study through Brainsway Inc and Magventure Inc. His work was supported by the Ontario Mental Health Foundation (OMHF), the Canadian Institutes of Health Research (CIHR), the National Institutes of Mental Health and the Temerty Family and Grant Family and through the Centre for Addiction and Mental Health (CAMH) Foundation and the Campbell Institute. M.M. received grants and/or speaker's honoraria from Asahi Kasei Pharma, Astellas Pharma, Daiichi Sankyo, Sumitomo Dainippon Pharma, Eisai, Eli Lilly, Fuji Film RI Pharma, Janssen Pharmaceutical, Kracie, Meiji-Seika Pharma, Mochida Pharmaceutical, Merck Sharp and Dohme, Novartis Pharma, Ono Pharmaceutical, Otsuka Pharmaceutical, Pfizer, Shionogi, Takeda Pharmaceutical, Mitsubishi Tanabe Pharma, and Yoshitomi Yakuhin. All other authors declare that they have no conflicts of interest.

Conflicts of Interest: None of the authors declare any conflict of interest.

Abbreviations

DLPFC: dorsolateral prefrontal cortex; EEG: electroencephalograph; E/I: excitatory and inhibitory; ERSP: event-related spectral perturbation; FEP: first-episode psychosis; GABA: gamma-aminobutyric acid; HC: healthy control; ^{1}H-MRS: proton magnetic resonance spectroscopy; ICF: intracortical facilitation; ISI: interstimulus interval; LICI: long-interval cortical inhibition; MEP: motor-evoked potential; M1: primary motor cortex; NMDA: N-methyl-d-aspartate; PANSS: positive and negative syndrome scale; PFC: prefrontal cortex; SAI: short-latency afferent inhibition; SCD: significant current density; SCS: significant current scattering; SCZ: schizophrenia; SICI: short-interval intracortical inhibition; TEP: TMS-evoked potential; TMS: transcranial magnetic stimulation; Preferred Reporting Items for Systematic Reviews and Meta-Analyses: PRISMA.

References

1. Saha, S.; Chant, D.; Welham, J.; McGrath, J. A Systematic Review of the Prevalence of Schizophrenia. *PLoS Med.* **2005**, *2*, e141. [CrossRef]
2. Radhu, N.; Ravindran, L.N.; Levinson, A.J.; Daskalakis, Z.J. Inhibition of the cortex using transcranial magnetic stimulation in psychiatric populations: Current and future directions. *J. Psychiatry Neurosci.* **2012**, *37*, 369–378. [CrossRef] [PubMed]
3. Rogasch, N.C.; Daskalakis, Z.J.; Fitzgerald, P.B. Cortical Inhibition, Excitation, and Connectivity in Schizophrenia: A Review of Insights from Transcranial Magnetic Stimulation. *Schizophr. Bull.* **2013**, *40*, 685–696. [CrossRef]
4. Van Os, J.; Kapur, S. Schizophrenia. *Lancet* **2009**, *374*, 635–645. [CrossRef]
5. Coyle, J.T. Substance use disorders and schizophrenia: A question of shared glutamatergic mechanisms. *Neurotox. Res.* **2006**, *10*, 221–233. [CrossRef]
6. Lewis, D.A.; Hashimoto, T.; Volk, D.W. Cortical inhibitory neurons and schizophrenia. *Nat. Rev. Neurosci.* **2005**, *6*, 312–324. [CrossRef] [PubMed]
7. Uno, Y.; Coyle, J.T. Glutamate hypothesis in schizophrenia. *Psychiatry Clin. Neurosci.* **2019**, *73*, 204–215. [CrossRef] [PubMed]
8. Murray, J.D.; Anticevic, A.; Gancsos, M.; Ichinose, M.; Corlett, P.R.; Krystal, J.H.; Wang, X.-J. Linking Microcircuit Dysfunction to Cognitive Impairment: Effects of Disinhibition Associated with Schizophrenia in a Cortical Working Memory Model. *Cereb. Cortex* **2012**, *24*, 859–872. [CrossRef]
9. Rao, S.G.; Williams, G.V.; Goldman-Rakic, P.S. Destruction and creation of spatial tuning by disinhibition: GABA(A) blockade of prefrontal cortical neurons engaged by working memory. *J. Neurosci.* **2000**, *20*, 485–494. [CrossRef] [PubMed]
10. Foss-Feig, J.H.; Adkinson, B.D.; Ji, J.L.; Yang, G.; Srihari, V.H.; McPartland, J.C.; Krystal, J.H.; Murray, J.D.; Anticevic, A. Searching for Cross-Diagnostic Convergence: Neural Mechanisms Governing Excitation and Inhibition Balance in Schizophrenia and Autism Spectrum Disorders. *Biol. Psychiatry* **2017**, *81*, 848–861. [CrossRef]
11. Canitano, R.; Pallagrosi, M. Autism Spectrum Disorders and Schizophrenia Spectrum Disorders: Excitation/Inhibition Imbalance and Developmental Trajectories. *Front. Psychiatry* **2017**, *8*, 69. [CrossRef]
12. Marsman, A.; Mandl, R.C.; Klomp, D.W.; Bohlken, M.M.; Boer, V.O.; Andreychenko, A.; Cahn, W.; Kahn, R.S.; Luijten, P.R.; Pol, H.E.H. GABA and glutamate in schizophrenia: A 7 T 1H-MRS study. *NeuroImage Clin.* **2014**, *6*, 398–407. [CrossRef]
13. Kumar, V.; Vajawat, B.; Rao, N.P. Frontal GABA in schizophrenia: A meta-analysis of 1H-MRS studies. *World J. Biol. Psychiatry* **2020**, 1–13. [CrossRef]

14. Rowland, L.M.; Kontson, K.; West, J.; Edden, R.A.; Zhu, H.; Wijtenburg, S.A.; Holcomb, H.H.; Barker, P.B. In Vivo Measurements of Glutamate, GABA, and NAAG in Schizophrenia. *Schizophr. Bull.* **2012**, *39*, 1096–1104. [CrossRef] [PubMed]
15. Schür, R.R.; Draisma, L.W.; Wijnen, J.P.; Boks, M.P.; Koevoets, M.G.; Joëls, M.; Klomp, D.W.; Kahn, R.S.; Vinkers, C.H. Brain GABA levels across psychiatric disorders: A systematic literature review and meta-analysis of1H-MRS studies. *Hum. Brain Mapp.* **2016**, *37*, 3337–3352. [CrossRef] [PubMed]
16. Egerton, A.; Modinos, G.; Ferrera, D.; McGuire, P. Neuroimaging studies of GABA in schizophrenia: A systematic review with meta-analysis. *Transl. Psychiatry* **2017**, *7*, e1147. [CrossRef] [PubMed]
17. Noda, Y. Toward the establishment of neurophysiological indicators for neuropsychiatric disorders using transcranial magnetic stimulation-evoked potentials: A systematic review. *Psychiatry Clin. Neurosci.* **2020**, *74*, 12–34. [CrossRef] [PubMed]
18. Barker, A.; Jalinous, R.; Freeston, I. Non-invasive magnetic stimulation of human motor cortex. *Lancet* **1985**, *325*, 1106–1107. [CrossRef]
19. McClintock, S.M.; Freitas, C.; Oberman, L.; Lisanby, S.H.; Pascual-Leone, A. Transcranial Magnetic Stimulation: A Neuroscientific Probe of Cortical Function in Schizophrenia. *Biol. Psychiatry* **2011**, *70*, 19–27. [CrossRef]
20. Daskalakis, Z.J.; Farzan, F.; Radhu, N.; Fitzgerald, P.B. Combined transcranial magnetic stimulation and electroencephalography: Its past, present and future. *Brain Res.* **2012**, *1463*, 93–107. [CrossRef]
21. Siebner, H.R.; Hartwigsen, G.; Kassuba, T.; Rothwell, J.C. How does transcranial magnetic stimulation modify neuronal activity in the brain? Implications for studies of cognition. *Cortex* **2009**, *45*, 1035–1042. [CrossRef] [PubMed]
22. Shafi, M.M.; Westover, M.B.; Fox, M.D.; Pascual-Leone, A. Exploration and modulation of brain network interactions with noninvasive brain stimulation in combination with neuroimaging. *Eur. J. Neurosci.* **2012**, *35*, 805–825. [CrossRef]
23. Shafi, M.M.; Westover, M.B.; Oberman, L.; Cash, S.S.; Pascual-Leone, A. Modulation of EEG Functional Connectivity Networks in Subjects Undergoing Repetitive Transcranial Magnetic Stimulation. *Brain Topogr.* **2014**, *27*, 172–191. [CrossRef] [PubMed]
24. O'Shea, J.; Taylor, P.C.; Rushworth, M.F. Imaging causal interactions during sensorimotor processing. *Cortex* **2008**, *44*, 598–608. [CrossRef] [PubMed]
25. Ilić, T.V.; Meintzschel, F.; Cleff, U.; Ruge, D.; Kessler, K.R.; Ziemann, U. Short-interval paired-pulse inhibition and facilitation of human motor cortex: The dimension of stimulus intensity. *J. Physiol.* **2002**, *545*, 153–167. [CrossRef]
26. Tamburin, S.; Fiaschi, A.; Marani, S.; Andreoli, A.; Manganotti, P.; Zanette, G. Enhanced intracortical inhibition in cerebellar patients. *J. Neurol. Sci.* **2004**, *217*, 205–210. [CrossRef] [PubMed]
27. Kujirai, T.; Caramia, M.D.; Rothwell, J.C.; Day, B.L.; Thompson, P.D.; Ferbert, A.; Wroe, S.; Asselman, P.; Marsden, C.D. Corticocortical inhibition in human motor cortex. *J. Physiol.* **1993**, *471*, 501–519. [CrossRef]
28. Cash, R.F.H.; Noda, Y.; Zomorrodi, R.; Radhu, N.; Farzan, F.; Rajji, T.K.; Fitzgerald, P.B.; Chen, R.; Daskalakis, Z.J.; Blumberger, D.M. Characterization of Glutamatergic and GABAA-Mediated Neurotransmission in Motor and Dorsolateral Prefrontal Cortex Using Paired-Pulse TMS–EEG. *Neuropsychopharmacology* **2016**, *42*, 502–511. [CrossRef]
29. Di Lazzaro, V.; Oliviero, A.; Meglio, M.; Cioni, B.; Tamburrini, G.; Tonali, P.; Rothwell, J. Direct demonstration of the effect of lorazepam on the excitability of the human motor cortex. *Clin. Neurophysiol.* **2000**, *111*, 794–799. [CrossRef]
30. Di Lazzaro, V.; Oliviero, A.; Tonali, P.A.; Marra, C.; Daniele, A.; Profice, P.; Saturno, E.; Pilato, F.; Masullo, C.; Rothwell, J.C. Noninvasive in vivo assessment of cholinergic cortical circuits in AD using transcranial magnetic stimulation. *Neurology* **2002**, *59*, 392–397. [CrossRef]
31. Di Lazzaro, V.; Oliviero, A.; Saturno, E.; Dileone, M.; Pilato, F.; Nardone, R.; Ranieri, F.; Musumeci, G.; Fiorilla, T.; Tonali, P. Effects of lorazepam on short latency afferent inhibition and short latency intracortical inhibition in humans. *J. Physiol.* **2005**, *564 Pt 2*, 661–668. [CrossRef]
32. Di Lazzaro, V.; Pilato, F.; Dileone, M.; Tonali, P.A.; Ziemann, U. Dissociated effects of diazepam and lorazepam on short-latency afferent inhibition. *J. Physiol.* **2005**, *569 Pt 1*, 315–323. [CrossRef] [PubMed]
33. Ziemann, U.; Corwell, B.; Cohen, L.G. Modulation of Plasticity in Human Motor Cortex after Forearm Ischemic Nerve Block. *J. Neurosci.* **1998**, *18*, 1115–1123. [CrossRef] [PubMed]
34. Peurala, S.H.; Müller-Dahlhaus, J.F.M.; Arai, N.; Ziemann, U. Interference of short-interval intracortical inhibition (SICI) and short-interval intracortical facilitation (SICF). *Clin. Neurophysiol.* **2008**, *119*, 2291–2297. [CrossRef]
35. McDonnell, M.N.; Orekhov, Y.; Ziemann, U. The role of GABA(B) receptors in intracortical inhibition in the human motor cortex. *Exp. Brain Res.* **2006**, *173*, 86–93. [CrossRef]
36. Ziemann, U.; Reis, J.; Schwenkreis, P.; Rosanova, M.; Strafella, A.; Badawy, R.; Müller-Dahlhaus, F. TMS and drugs revisited 2014. *Clin. Neurophysiol.* **2015**, *126*, 1847–1868. [CrossRef] [PubMed]
37. Schwenkreis, P.; Witscher, K.; Janssen, F.; Addo, A.; Dertwinkel, R.; Zenz, M.; Malin, J.-P.; Tegenthoff, M. Influence of the N-methyl-d-aspartate antagonist memantine on human motor cortex excitability. *Neurosci. Lett.* **1999**, *270*, 137–140. [CrossRef]
38. Fujiki, M.; Hikawa, T.; Abe, T.; Ishii, K.; Kobayashi, H. Reduced short latency afferent inhibition in diffuse axonal injury patients with memory impairment. *Neurosci. Lett.* **2006**, *405*, 226–230. [CrossRef]
39. Nardone, R.; Golaszewski, S.; Ladurner, G.; Tezzon, F.; Trinka, E. A Review of Transcranial Magnetic Stimulation in the in vivo Functional Evaluation of Central Cholinergic Circuits in Dementia. *Dement. Geriatr. Cogn. Disord.* **2011**, *32*, 18–25. [CrossRef]
40. Cucurachi, L.; Immovilli, P.; Granella, F.; Pavesi, G.; Cattaneo, L. Short-latency afferent inhibition predicts verbal memory performance in patients with multiple sclerosis. *J. Neurol.* **2008**, *255*, 1949. [CrossRef]

41. Noda, Y.; Barr, M.S.; Zomorrodi, R.; Cash, R.F.H.; Rajji, T.K.; Farzan, F.; Chen, R.; George, T.P.; Daskalakis, Z.J.; Blumberger, D.M. Reduced Short-Latency Afferent Inhibition in Prefrontal but not Motor Cortex and Its Association With Executive Function in Schizophrenia: A Combined TMS-EEG Study. *Schizophr. Bull.* **2017**, *44*, 193–202. [CrossRef]
42. Noda, Y.; Cash, R.F.H.; Zomorrodi, R.; Dominguez, L.G.; Farzan, F.; Rajji, T.K.; Barr, M.S.; Chen, R.; Daskalakis, Z.J.; Blumberger, D.M. A combined TMS-EEG study of short-latency afferent inhibition in the motor and dorsolateral prefrontal cortex. *J. Neurophysiol.* **2016**, *116*, 938–948. [CrossRef]
43. Chorlian, D.B.; Rangaswamy, M.; Porjesz, B. EEG coherence: Topography and frequency structure. *Exp. Brain Res.* **2009**, *198*, 59–83. [CrossRef] [PubMed]
44. Rosanova, M.; Casali, A.; Bellina, V.; Resta, F.; Mariotti, M.; Massimini, M. Natural frequencies of human corticothalamic circuits. *J. Neurosci.* **2009**, *29*, 7679–7685. [CrossRef] [PubMed]
45. Radhu, N.; de Jesus, D.R.; Ravindran, L.N.; Zanjani, A.; Fitzgerald, P.B.; Daskalakis, Z.J. A meta-analysis of cortical inhibition and excitability using transcranial magnetic stimulation in psychiatric disorders. *Clin. Neurophysiol.* **2013**, *124*, 1309–1320. [CrossRef] [PubMed]
46. Başar, E.; Güntekin, B. Review of delta, theta, alpha, beta, and gamma response oscillations in neuropsychiatric disorders. *Suppl. Clin. Neurophysiol.* **2013**, *62*, 303–341.
47. Schmitt, A.; Hasan, A.; Gruber, O.; Falkai, P. Schizophrenia as a disorder of disconnectivity. *Eur. Arch. Psychiatry Clin. Neurosci.* **2011**, *261* (Suppl. 2), 150–154. [CrossRef] [PubMed]
48. Vittala, A.; Murphy, N.; Maheshwari, A.; Krishnan, V. Understanding Cortical Dysfunction in Schizophrenia with TMS/EEG. *Front. Neurosci.* **2020**, *14*, 554. [CrossRef]
49. Ferrarelli, F.; Riedner, B.A.; Peterson, M.J.; Tononi, G. Altered prefrontal activity and connectivity predict different cognitive deficits in schizophrenia. *Hum. Brain Mapp.* **2015**, *36*, 4539–4552. [CrossRef]
50. Ferrarelli, F.; Sarasso, S.; Guller, Y.; Riedner, B.A.; Peterson, M.J.; Bellesi, M.; Massimini, M.; Postle, B.R.; Tononi, G. Reduced Natural Oscillatory Frequency of Frontal Thalamocortical Circuits in Schizophrenia. *Arch. Gen. Psychiatry* **2012**, *69*, 766–774. [CrossRef]
51. Ferrarelli, F.; Kaskie, R.E.; Graziano, B.; Reis, C.C.; Casali, A.G. Abnormalities in the evoked frontal oscillatory activity of first-episode psychosis: A TMS/EEG study. *Schizophr. Res.* **2019**, *206*, 436–439. [CrossRef]
52. Andrews, S.C.; Enticott, P.G.; Hoy, K.E.; Thomson, R.H.; Fitzgerald, P.B. No evidence for mirror system dysfunction in schizophrenia from a multimodal TMS/EEG study. *Psychiatry Res.* **2015**, *228*, 431–440. [CrossRef] [PubMed]
53. Frantseva, M.; Cui, J.; Farzan, F.; Chinta, L.V.; Velazquez, J.L.P.; Daskalakis, Z.J. Disrupted Cortical Conductivity in Schizophrenia: TMS-EEG Study. *Cereb. Cortex* **2012**, *24*, 211–221. [CrossRef] [PubMed]
54. Farzan, F.; Barr, M.S.; Levinson, A.J.; Chen, R.; Wong, W.; Fitzgerald, P.B.; Daskalakis, Z.J. Evidence for gamma inhibition deficits in the dorsolateral prefrontal cortex of patients with schizophrenia. *Brain* **2010**, *133 Pt 5*, 1505–1514. [CrossRef] [PubMed]
55. Radhu, N.; Dominguez, L.G.; Greenwood, T.A.; Farzan, F.; Semeralul, M.O.; Richter, M.A.; Kennedy, J.L.; Blumberger, D.M.; Chen, R.; Fitzgerald, P.B.; et al. Investigating Cortical Inhibition in First-Degree Relatives and Probands in Schizophrenia. *Sci. Rep.* **2017**, *7*, 43629. [CrossRef] [PubMed]
56. Canali, P.; Sarasso, S.; Rosanova, M.; Casarotto, S.; Sferrazza-Papa, G.; Gosseries, O.; Fecchio, M.; Massimini, M.; Mariotti, M.; Cavallaro, R.; et al. Shared reduction of oscillatory natural frequencies in bipolar disorder, major depressive disorder and schizophrenia. *J. Affect. Disord.* **2015**, *184*, 111–115. [CrossRef]
57. Ferrarelli, F.; Massimini, M.; Peterson, M.J.; Riedner, B.A.; Lazar, M.; Murphy, M.J.; Huber, R.; Rosanova, M.; Alexander, A.L.; Kalin, N.; et al. Reduced Evoked Gamma Oscillations in the Frontal Cortex in Schizophrenia Patients: A TMS/EEG Study. *Am. J. Psychiatry* **2008**, *165*, 996–1005. [CrossRef]
58. Noda, Y.; Barr, M.S.; Zomorrodi, R.; Cash, R.F.H.; Farzan, F.; Rajji, T.K.; Chen, R.; Daskalakis, Z.J.; Blumberger, D.M. Evaluation of short interval cortical inhibition and intracortical facilitation from the dorsolateral prefrontal cortex in patients with schizophrenia. *Sci. Rep.* **2017**, *7*, 17106. [CrossRef]
59. Lett, T.A.; Kennedy, J.L.; Radhu, N.; Dominguez, L.G.; Chakravarty, M.M.; Nazeri, A.; Farzan, F.; Walter, H.; Heinz, A.; Mulsant, B.H.; et al. Prefrontal White Matter Structure Mediates the Influence of GAD1 on Working Memory. *Neuropsychopharmacology* **2016**, *41*, 2224–2231. [CrossRef] [PubMed]
60. Radhu, N.; Dominguez, L.G.; Farzan, F.; Richter, M.A.; Semeralul, M.O.; Chen, R.; Fitzgerald, P.B.; Daskalakis, Z.J. Evidence for inhibitory deficits in the prefrontal cortex in schizophrenia. *Brain* **2015**, *138 Pt 2*, 483–497. [CrossRef] [PubMed]
61. Levit-Binnun, N.; Litvak, V.; Pratt, H.; Moses, E.; Zaroor, M.; Peled, A. Differences in TMS-evoked responses between schizophrenia patients and healthy controls can be observed without a dedicated EEG system. *Clin. Neurophysiol.* **2010**, *121*, 332–339. [CrossRef]
62. Casali, A.G.; Casarotto, S.; Rosanova, M.; Mariotti, M.; Massimini, M. General indices to characterize the electrical response of the cerebral cortex to TMS. *NeuroImage* **2010**, *49*, 1459–1468. [CrossRef] [PubMed]
63. Steriade, M. Grouping of brain rhythms in corticothalamic systems. *Neuroscience* **2006**, *137*, 1087–1106. [CrossRef] [PubMed]
64. Steriade, M.; Timofeev, I.; Dürmüller, N.; Grenier, F. Dynamic Properties of Corticothalamic Neurons and Local Cortical Interneurons Generating Fast Rhythmic (30–40 Hz) Spike Bursts. *J. Neurophysiol.* **1998**, *79*, 483–490. [CrossRef] [PubMed]
65. Fitzgerald, P.B.; Brown, T.L.; Marston, N.A.; Oxley, T.J.; De Castella, A.; Daskalakis, Z.J.; Kulkarni, J. A transcranial magnetic stimulation study of abnormal cortical inhibition in schizophrenia. *Psychiatry Res.* **2003**, *118*, 197–207. [CrossRef]

66. Tarumi, R.; Tsugawa, S.; Noda, Y.; Plitman, E.; Honda, S.; Matsushita, K.; Chavez, S.; Sawada, K.; Wada, M.; Matsui, M.; et al. Levels of glutamatergic neurometabolites in patients with severe treatment-resistant schizophrenia: A proton magnetic resonance spectroscopy study. *Neuropsychopharmacology* **2020**, *45*, 632–640. [CrossRef]
67. Iwata, M.; Ota, K.T.; Li, X.-Y.; Sakaue, F.; Li, N.; Dutheil, S.; Banasr, M.; Duric, V.; Yamanashi, T.; Kaneko, K.; et al. Psychological Stress Activates the Inflammasome via Release of Adenosine Triphosphate and Stimulation of the Purinergic Type 2X7 Receptor. *Biol. Psychiatry* **2016**, *80*, 12–22. [CrossRef]
68. Davenport, E.C.; Szulc, B.R.; Drew, J.; Taylor, J.; Morgan, T.; Higgs, N.F.; López-Doménech, G.; Kittler, J.T. Autism and Schizophrenia-Associated CYFIP1 Regulates the Balance of Synaptic Excitation and Inhibition. *Cell Rep.* **2019**, *26*, 2037–2051.e6. [CrossRef]
69. Gao, R.; Penzes, P. Common mechanisms of excitatory and inhibitory imbalance in schizophrenia and autism spectrum disorders. *Curr. Mol. Med.* **2015**, *15*, 146–167. [CrossRef]
70. Nair, P.C.; McKinnon, R.A.; Miners, J.O.; Bastiampillai, T. Binding of clozapine to the GABAB receptor: Clinical and structural insights. *Mol. Psychiatry* **2020**, *25*, 1910–1919. [CrossRef]
71. Wu, Y.; Blichowski, M.; Daskalakis, Z.J.; Wu, Z.; Liu, C.C.; Cortez, M.A.; Snead, O.C. Evidence that clozapine directly interacts on the GABAB receptor. *NeuroReport* **2011**, *22*, 637–641. [CrossRef] [PubMed]
72. Kaster, T.S.; de Jesus, D.; Radhu, N.; Farzan, F.; Blumberger, D.M.; Rajji, T.K.; Fitzgerald, P.B.; Daskalakis, Z.J. Clozapine potentiation of GABA mediated cortical inhibition in treatment resistant schizophrenia. *Schizophr. Res.* **2015**, *165*, 157–162. [CrossRef] [PubMed]
73. Benes, F.M.; Berretta, S. GABAergic interneurons: Implications for understanding schizophrenia and bipolar disorder. *Neuropsychopharmacology* **2001**, *25*, 1–27. [CrossRef]
74. Krystal, J.H.; D'Souza, D.C.; Mathalon, D.; Perry, E.; Belger, A.; Hoffman, R. NMDA receptor antagonist effects, cortical glutamatergic function, and schizophrenia: Toward a paradigm shift in medication development. *Psychopharmacology* **2003**, *169*, 215–233. [CrossRef] [PubMed]
75. Kegeles, L.S.; Mao, X.; Stanford, A.D.; Girgis, R.; Ojeil, N.; Xu, X.; Gil, R.; Slifstein, M.; Abi-Dargham, A.; Lisanby, S.H.; et al. Elevated prefrontal cortex gamma-aminobutyric acid and glutamate-glutamine levels in schizophrenia measured in vivo with proton magnetic resonance spectroscopy. *Arch. Gen. Psychiatry* **2012**, *69*, 449–459. [PubMed]
76. Tani, M.; Akashi, N.; Hori, K.; Konishi, K.; Kitajima, Y.; Tomioka, H.; Inamoto, A.; Hirata, A.; Tomita, A.; Koganemaru, T.; et al. Anticholinergic Activity and Schizophrenia. *Neurodegener. Dis.* **2015**, *15*, 168–174. [CrossRef]
77. Ter Braack, E.M.; de Vos, C.C.; van Putten, M.J. Masking the Auditory Evoked Potential in TMS-EEG: A Comparison of Various Methods. *Brain Topogr.* **2015**, *28*, 520–528. [CrossRef]
78. Terry, A.V.; Callahan, P.M. α7 nicotinic acetylcholine receptors as therapeutic targets in schizophrenia: Update on animal and clinical studies and strategies for the future. *Neuropharmacology* **2020**, *170*, 108053. [CrossRef]
79. Guan, Z.-Z.; Zhang, X.; Blennow, K.; Nordberg, A. Decreased protein level of nicotinic receptor α7 subunit in the frontal cortex from schizophrenic brain. *Neuroreport* **1999**, *10*, 1779–1782. [CrossRef] [PubMed]
80. Martin, L.F.; Kem, W.R.; Freedman, R. Alpha-7 nicotinic receptor agonists: Potential new candidates for the treatment of schizophrenia. *Psychopharmacology* **2004**, *174*, 54–64. [CrossRef]
81. Volman, V.; Behrens, M.M.; Sejnowski, T.J. Downregulation of Parvalbumin at Cortical GABA Synapses Reduces Network Gamma Oscillatory Activity. *J. Neurosci.* **2011**, *31*, 18137–18148. [CrossRef] [PubMed]
82. Farzan, F.; Barr, M.S.; Wong, W.; Chen, R.; Fitzgerald, P.B.; Daskalakis, Z.J. Suppression of gamma-oscillations in the dorsolateral prefrontal cortex following long interval cortical inhibition: A TMS-EEG study. *Neuropsychopharmacology* **2009**, *34*, 1543–1551. [CrossRef] [PubMed]
83. Farzan, F.; Barr, M.S.; Sun, Y.; Fitzgerald, P.B.; Daskalakis, Z.J. Transcranial magnetic stimulation on the modulation of gamma oscillations in schizophrenia. *Ann. N. Y. Acad. Sci.* **2012**, *1265*, 25–35. [CrossRef] [PubMed]
84. McNally, J.M.; McCarley, R.W. Gamma band oscillations: A key to understanding schizophrenia symptoms and neural circuit abnormalities. *Curr. Opin. Psychiatry* **2016**, *29*, 202–210. [CrossRef]
85. Senkowski, D.; Gallinat, J. Dysfunctional Prefrontal Gamma-Band Oscillations Reflect Working Memory and Other Cognitive Deficits in Schizophrenia. *Biol. Psychiatry* **2015**, *77*, 1010–1019. [CrossRef]
86. Brignani, D.; Manganotti, P.; Rossini, P.M.; Miniussi, C. Modulation of cortical oscillatory activity during transcranial magnetic stimulation. *Hum. Brain Mapp.* **2008**, *29*, 603–612. [CrossRef]
87. Veniero, D.; Brignani, D.; Thut, G.; Miniussi, C. Alpha-generation as basic response-signature to transcranial magnetic stimulation (TMS) targeting the human resting motor cortex: A TMS/EEG co-registration study. *Psychophysiology* **2011**, *48*, 1381–1389. [CrossRef]
88. Whitham, E.M.; Pope, K.J.; Fitzgibbon, S.P.; Lewis, T.; Clark, C.R.; Loveless, S.; Broberg, M.; Wallace, A.; DeLosAngeles, D.; Lillie, P.; et al. Scalp electrical recording during paralysis: Quantitative evidence that EEG frequencies above 20Hz are contaminated by EMG. *Clin. Neurophysiol.* **2007**, *118*, 1877–1888. [CrossRef]
89. Kaskie, R.E.; Ferrarelli, F. Investigating the neurobiology of schizophrenia and other major psychiatric disorders with Transcranial Magnetic Stimulation. *Schizophr. Res.* **2018**, *192*, 30–38. [CrossRef]

Journal of *Personalized Medicine*

MDPI

Article

Heading for Personalized rTMS in Tinnitus: Reliability of Individualized Stimulation Protocols in Behavioral and Electrophysiological Responses

Stefan Schoisswohl [1,*], Berthold Langguth [1], Tobias Hebel [1], Mohamed A. Abdelnaim [1], Gregor Volberg [2] and Martin Schecklmann [1]

1 Department of Psychiatry and Psychotherapy, University of Regensburg, 93053 Regensburg, Germany; berthold.langguth@medbo.de (B.L.); tobias.hebel@medbo.de (T.H.); Mohamed.Abdelnaim@medbo.de (M.A.A.); martin.schecklmann@medbo.de (M.S.)

2 Institute of Psychology, University of Regensburg, 93053 Regensburg, Germany; gregor.volberg@psychologie.uni-regensburg.de

* Correspondence: stefanschoisswohl@yahoo.de; Tel.: +49-941-941-2054

Abstract: Background: Repetitive transcranial magnetic stimulation (rTMS) is a non-invasive brain stimulation tool potentially modulating pathological brain activity. Its clinical effectiveness is hampered by varying results and characterized by inter-individual variability in treatment responses. RTMS individualization might constitute a useful strategy to overcome this variability. A precondition for this approach would be that repeatedly applied protocols result in reliable effects. The condition tinnitus provides the advantage of immediate behavioral consequences (tinnitus loudness changes) after interventions and thus offers an excellent model to exemplify TMS personalization. Objective: The aim was to investigate the test–retest reliability of short rTMS stimulations in modifying tinnitus loudness and oscillatory brain activity as well as to examine the feasibility of rTMS individualization in tinnitus. Methods: Three short verum (1, 10, 20 Hz; 200 pulses) and one sham (0.1 Hz; 20 pulses) rTMS protocol were administered on two different days in 22 tinnitus patients. Before and after each protocol, oscillatory brain activity was recorded with electroencephalography (EEG), together with behavioral tinnitus loudness ratings. RTMS individualization was executed on the basis of behavioral and electrophysiological responses. Stimulation responders were identified via consistent sham-superior increases in tinnitus loudness (behavioral responders) and alpha power increases or gamma power decreases (alpha responders/gamma responders) in accordance with the prevalent neurophysiological models for tinnitus. Results: It was feasible to identify individualized rTMS protocols featuring reliable tinnitus loudness changes (55% behavioral responder), alpha increases (91% alpha responder) and gamma decreases (100% gamma responder), respectively. Alpha responses primary occurred over parieto-occipital areas, whereas gamma responses mainly appeared over frontal regions. On the contrary, test–retest correlation analyses per protocol at a group level were not significant neither for behavioral nor for electrophysiological effects. No associations between behavioral and EEG responses were found. Conclusion: RTMS individualization via behavioral and electrophysiological data in tinnitus can be considered as a feasible approach to overcome low reliability at the group level. The present results open the discussion favoring personalization utilizing neurophysiological markers rather than behavioral responses. These insights are not only useful for the rTMS treatment of tinnitus but also for neuromodulation interventions in other pathologies, as our results suggest that the individualization of stimulation protocols is feasible despite absent group-level reliability.

Keywords: repetitive transcranial magnetic stimulation; tinnitus; neuro-navigation; electroencephalography; reliability; rTMS personalization

Citation: Schoisswohl, S.; Langguth, B.; Hebel, T.; Abdelnaim, M.A.; Volberg, G.; Schecklmann, M. Heading for Personalized rTMS in Tinnitus: Reliability of Individualized Stimulation Protocols in Behavioral and Electrophysiological Responses. *J. Pers. Med.* **2021**, *11*, 536. https://doi.org/10.3390/jpm11060536

Academic Editor: Yoshihiro Noda

Received: 19 May 2021
Accepted: 5 June 2021
Published: 9 June 2021

1. Introduction

With a prevalence of about 10% of the population, tinnitus is a rather common condition. It is characterized by the perception of ringing or hissing in the absence of a corresponding external stimulus. The majority of tinnitus cases are caused by cochlear damage leading to hearing loss [1–3], whereby the absence of auditory input from the periphery provokes maladaptive neural changes, which ultimately manifest in hyperactivity of auditory and non-auditory cortical regions. These pathological alterations of the central nervous system are assumed to underly the perception of tinnitus [4–8].

Recent neuromodulation techniques attempt to reverse or modulate these pathological alterations (for a recent overview, see Langguth et al. [9]). One of these is repetitive transcranial magnetic stimulation (rTMS), a non-invasive brain stimulation tool with the capability to evoke neuroplastic changes by a rhythmic administration of brief electromagnetic pulses [10–12]. By means of low-frequency rTMS, it is possible to inhibit cortical excitability, whereas high-frequency protocols are assumed to increase cortical excitability. These statements should be seen as a rule of thumb, as several findings show high inter- and intra-individual variability of rTMS, with a lot of subjects not behaving accordingly [13–16].

On account of this, temporal 1 Hz rTMS was applied in order to inhibit tinnitus-associated hyperactivity of the auditory cortex and consequently suppress the tinnitus percept [17,18].

For many years, various treatment trials deployed left-temporal low-frequency rTMS, showing greatly varying findings and high inter-individual variability in responses (for an overview, see Schoisswohl et al. [19]). Given this backdrop, additional studies also examined the consequences of other rTMS approaches such as multi-site stimulation protocols [20,21], prefrontal cortex stimulation [22–24] or high-frequency rTMS [25–27], as well as continuous theta-burst stimulations [25,28,29] as a treatment option for tinnitus. Nevertheless, its clinical effectiveness is still not obvious. Recent reviews and meta-analyses conclude that there is no clear indication for an effect [9,30,31], while others report potential effectiveness for its clinical administration [32,33], especially over the auditory cortex [34]. This lack of evidence may be explained by the fact that there is still a certain ambiguity concerning the correct rTMS parameters (e.g., frequency or position) for the application in tinnitus. Admittedly, the effects of non-invasive brain stimulation methods in general are subject to rigorous intra- and inter-individual variability, conceivably caused by a complex interplay of technical and physiological parameters [35–38].

A personalization of stimulation protocols might provide a remedy and further enhance efficacy. Individualization of magnetic stimulation might be capable of resolving the issue of effect variability within the same type of pathology. Its implementation in neuropsychiatric research is highly dependent on phenotypes as well as the identification of appropriate and valid clinical or physiological outcome measures [39,40]. However, tinnitus provides the tremendous benefit of direct reactions from the patients' side by virtue of changes in tinnitus perception and can therefore function as a kind of role model in rTMS personalization.

Test sessions (i.e., short stimulations with recording of immediate responses) and an administration of different protocols offer the opportunity to examine the ability of the different protocols to suppress tinnitus loudness in an individual. In several studies, it has been demonstrated that tinnitus loudness can be suppressed by means of a single rTMS sessions for some minutes [41–45], and that suppression patterns vary among patients [46]. The concept of rTMS personalization in the clinical context of tinnitus was first introduced by Kreuzer et al. [47]. By means of rTMS test sessions with different types of frequencies and positions, individualized protocols for brief tinnitus suppression were identified and further used in the course of a daily treatment. These findings emphasize the feasibility of rTMS individualization and imply superiority over a standard treatment protocol by means of a higher number of treatment responders, even if no statistical differences between the standard and the individualized treatment were detected in this relatively small pilot study. In another preliminary work from our group, using an e-field guided system, we were able to demonstrate reliable tinnitus loudness decreases for certain stimulation parameters as well as the possibility to individualize rTMS characterized by a consistent and sham-controlled tinnitus loudness suppression in five out of five individuals [48]. Nonetheless, behavioral responses are governed by certain limitations, such as their highly subjective matter and the difficulty to accurately evaluate minor changes in the tinnitus percept in many cases, which might constitute an additional reason for variability in responses.

It is widely established that tinnitus is accompanied by pathologically altered oscillatory brain activity patterns. According to the "Thalamo-cortical Dysrhythmia Model" (TCD), the assumed mechanism behind these changes is peripheral deafferentation causing thalamic low-frequency activity, which in turn provokes a boost in neural synchrony and increased gamma activity in auditory regions of the cortex [49–51]. An expansion of the TCD model, termed "Synchronization-by-Loss-of-Inhibition-Model" (SLIM), presumes that an ancillary suppression of neurons relevant for inhibition additionally causes diminished activity in the alpha frequency range. Moreover, pathological gamma in tinnitus is prompted by this alpha decrease and the concomitant loss of inhibition [52].

Several neurophysiological investigations using electro- or magneto-encephalographic measurements revealed decreased activity in the alpha band and increased activity in the delta and gamma frequency ranges [53–58]. In particular, gamma is suggested to be closely related to the actual tinnitus perception [57,59,60]. These altered spontaneous brain activities might provide a potential indicator to examine the effect of rTMS in tinnitus.

TMS-EEG investigations have already demonstrated that rTMS successfully modulates evoked and ongoing brain activity, with effects exceeding the stimulation offset (neuroplastic consequences) [61–63]. In the clinical context, TMS-EEG approaches are already used for several neuropsychiatric conditions, such as schizophrenia, depression or Alzheimer's disease, in order to identify and investigate the relevance of neurophysiological markers as well as to provide a more profound insight into the neuroplastic consequences of rTMS [64,65]. In case of tinnitus, a combination of rTMS and EEG might not only help to improve our understanding of the pathophysiology and altered ongoing brain activity patterns behind tinnitus, but also shed light on neurophysiological markers for tinnitus suppression. As of yet, only a handful of studies have investigated the consequences of single rTMS sessions on spontaneous brain activity in tinnitus. Müller et al. [46] applied different stimulation types (1 Hz, continuous theta burst, intermittent theta burst and individual alpha frequency rTMS) over the temporal cortex and aimed to detect the most efficient protocol for transient tinnitus suppression per subject. By using magnetencephalography (MEG), they could detect a significant increase of alpha power (8–12 Hz) in the auditory cortex associated with tinnitus suppression. Due to the absence of clear effects on a whole-group level, the authors emphasize the relevance of analysis on an individual subject level to unveil the key mechanisms behind tinnitus suppression. In this context, especially modulations in the alpha frequency band might provide a potential marker for future attempts in individualizing rTMS. Schecklmann et al. [66] compared the neuroplastic consequences of rTMS in tinnitus patients with healthy controls and observed rTMS-specific modulations almost entirely for the group of tinnitus patients. A left-temporal 1 Hz stimulation with 200 pulses decreased power spectra in the delta (2–3.5 Hz) and theta (4–7.5 Hz) frequency ranges, as well as increased beta2 (18.5–21 Hz) frequency band power over frontal areas in tinnitus patients. Right prefrontal cortex 1 Hz stimulation reduced beta3 (21.5–30 Hz) and gamma (30.5–44 Hz) band activity in tinnitus patients in temporal areas. In contrast, the control group exhibited enhanced beta3 and gamma power. Results emphasize the ability to modulate tinnitus-related ongoing brain activity, or rather, to induce neuroplastic changes in tinnitus by rTMS in accordance with the TCD model. However, on a behavioral level, reliable sham-controlled decreases in tinnitus loudness were solely present in two out of 20 tinnitus patients (one after right-prefrontal, one after left-temporal rTMS).

Considering past findings, in particular the ability of certain rTMS protocols to transiently decrease tinnitus loudness plus modulate tinnitus-associated oscillatory brain activity, up to now, there is no convincing data on test–retest reliability of the effects of single-session rTMS. A test–retest design has the potential to yield essential details about effect-consistency, more specifically, if rTMS produces reliable and valid modulations. Findings may promote decisions in choosing appropriate rTMS protocols for daily treatments. Due to the overall high variability of non-invasive brain stimulation effects, it is of utmost importance to identify reliable brain stimulation techniques to cope with this variability. Hence, one of the objectives of the current experiment was to scrutinize the test–retest reliability of different rTMS protocols in short-term tinnitus suppression and modifying resting state EEG activity. For this purpose, the study design used in Schoisswohl et al. [48] with pre–post-rTMS tinnitus loudness ratings was expanded by electrophysiological measures before and after each rTMS. Furthermore, it was reduced by the factor stimulation position since the majority of patients (three out of five) responded to a stimulation over temporo-parietal regions. An e-field guided stimulation over the left and right temporo-parietal junction allows for a more precise investigation of the parameter frequency, since past studies show inconsistent results in this regard.

Beyond that, we wanted to undertake further research on the personalization of rTMS by means of the model tinnitus. The aim was to assess the feasibility of identifying an rTMS protocol for consistent and sham-superior brief tinnitus suppression per patient (behavioral response). In light of previous work from Müller et al. [46], together with the current prevalent neurophysiological models in tinnitus, we wanted to go one step beyond and strive for a rTMS personalization based on electrophysiological responses. The specific objective was to ascertain a protocol per patient, which is able to produce consistent and sham-superior increases in alpha or decreases in the gamma frequency band (EEG response), respectively. Based on past research, we hypothesize that for the majority of subjects, it is feasible to identify a personalized rTMS protocol by means of behavioral or EEG responses. Additionally, we were interested if an EEG response in the alpha or gamma band is related to a behavioral response, and vice versa.

2. Materials and Methods

2.1. Participants

N = 22 patients (5 female) with chronic subjective tinnitus, recruited from the Interdisciplinary Tinnitus Centre in Regensburg, Germany, participated in this experiment. Participants had to comply with the following inclusion criteria: age between 18 and 75 years, German-speaking, no or stable treatment with psychoactive drugs, absence of severe somatic, neurological or psychiatric conditions (e.g., acute psychosis, severe depression, alcohol and/or substance abuse or known brain tumor) and no simultaneous participation in other tinnitus-related experiments or treatments. Further, participants had to exhibit no contraindications with respect to TMS (e.g., epilepsy or state after traumatic brain injuries; cf. [67,68]) as well as magnetic resonance imaging (MRI) (e.g., heart pacemaker, vascular clamp, implanted insulin pump or severe claustrophobia). Each participant received detailed clarification about the study aim, procedure and applied methods as well as potential adverse effects related to TMS, and provided written informed consent before the study start. The study was approved by the ethics committee of the University of Regensburg, Germany (ethical approval number: 17-820-101).

2.2. Test Session Procedure

Ahead of the rTMS tests sessions, participants' hearing thresholds for the frequency range of 125 Hz to 8 kHz were determined by the use of a clinical audiometer (Madsen Midimate, 622D; GN Otometrics, Taustrus, Denmark). In addition, structural MRI brain scans (T1) were undertaken with a MAGNETOM 1.5 Tesla scanner (Siemens, Munich, Germany) for neuro-navigated rTMS and participants were requested to complete German versions of the Tinnitus Handicap Inventory (THI; [69,70]), the Tinnitus Sample Case History Questionnaire (TSCHQ; [71]) and the European School for Interdisciplinary Tinnitus Research Screening Questionnaire (ESIT-SQ; [72]).

The actual rTMS test sessions lasted approximately three hours and took place on two different days, with a maximum inter-session interval of two days, whereby daytime was always the same (±1 h). Both test session days followed the same procedure. On each day, subjects were stimulated with four different rTMS protocols over the left temporo-parietal junction (TPJ) and with the same four protocols over the right TPJ (see Section 2.3 Repetitive Transcranial Magnetic Stimulation). Thus, a total number of 8 different rTMS protocols was applied on each test session day. Magnetic stimulation protocols were administered in a randomized sequence on each day, with the exception that the order of hemisphere was inverted (if the stimulation sequence on the first day started over the left hemisphere, it began with a stimulation over the right hemisphere on the second day). During three minutes before and after each stimulation, patients were requested to focus on their tinnitus and verbally rate the current loudness of their tinnitus perception on a numeric rating scale ranging from 0% to 110% at seven different points in time, with an inter-rating interval of 30 s (T0, T30, T60, T90, T120, T150 and T180). The numeric rating scale was anchored at 0% (absence of tinnitus) and at 110% (tinnitus loudness increase of 10%), whereby 100% corresponds to the patients' usual perceived tinnitus loudness. Concurrent to these ratings, resting state oscillatory brain activity was recorded for three minutes each by means of EEG. For this purpose, participants were instructed to sit calmly, focus on a certain point in the room and avoid unnecessary eye blinks or muscle movements. Subsequent to each post-stimulation loudness rating/EEG recording, participants had to evaluate the level of discomfort caused by the applied rTMS protocol on a numeric rating scale from 0 to 10, where 10 corresponds to utmost discomfort, or rather intolerability. Figure 1 provides an illustration of the entire test session proceeding.

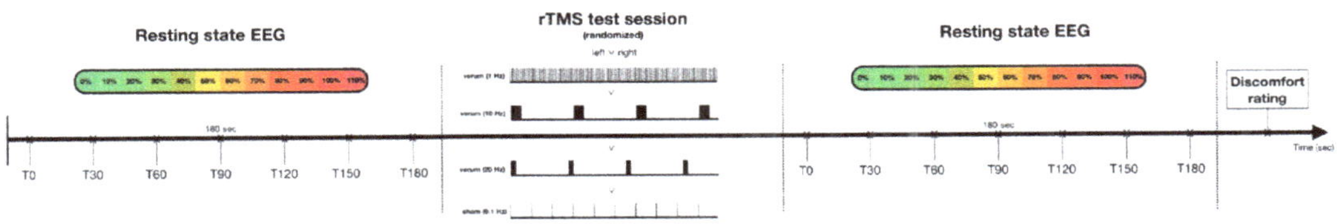

Figure 1. Test session procedure. Test sessions were conducted on two different days according to the same procedure. Three different verum rTMS protocols (1, 10, 20 Hz) with 200 pulses each and one sham protocol (0.1 Hz) with 20 pulses were administered over the left and right temporo-parietal junction in a randomized order. Thus, a total of 8 different rTMS protocols were applied on each test session day. Before and after each magnetic stimulation, participants were requested to rate the subjective loudness of their tinnitus on a numeric rating scale from 0% to 110% (0%—complete absence of tinnitus; 100%—no change; 110%—10% loudness increase) at seven points in time (30 s inter-rating interval). In parallel to these ratings, resting state brain activity was recorded with electroencephalography (EEG) for three minutes. At the end of each rTMS protocol (pre-rating/recording–stimulation–post-rating/recording), patients had to rate the induced level of discomfort on a numeric rating scale from 0 to 10 (10—utmost discomfort).

2.3. *Repetitive Transcranial Magnetic Stimulation (rTMS)*

An e-field guided rTMS system (NBT System 2; Nexstim Plc., Helsinki, Finland) together with individual structural MRI scans (T1) was utilized for the test sessions. Prior to the first session, participants' resting motor threshold (RMT) was determined according to the same procedure as already described in Schoisswohl et al. [48]. Thereby, various positions over the left primary motor cortex were stimulated until several motor-evoked potentials (MEP) derived from the thenar muscles of the right hand with a peak-to-peak amplitude of >50 µV were visible. The stimulation position with the highest MEP amplitude was repeated via the neuro-navigation system and single pulses with intensity shifts were applied. The lowest stimulation intensity which produced MEPs with an amplitude of at least 50 µV in half of the administered pulses was defined as subjects' RMT. Additionally, the RMT determination was repeated with a mounted EEG cap using the same motor hotspot. Magnetic stimulation consisted of 1, 10 and 20 Hz protocols with 200 pulses each at 110% RMT, whereas a series of 20 pulses at 0.1 Hz was deployed as an active control condition (sham) with no assumed neuroplastic consequences [73,74]. Each protocol was administered over the left and right TPJ, resulting in a total number of eight different rTMS protocols with approximately six minutes of inter-protocol intervals (3 min of pre- and post-rTMS EEG recordings; if applicable, there was a waiting period until the subject's tinnitus loudness returned to the initial level). An uncooled coil was used for the test sessions, as the cooled coil produces additional noise, and we aimed at minimizing the stimulation noise since it could confound both behavioral and neurophysiological effects. Stimulation positions were localized according to the electrode positions CP5 and CP6 (10–20 System). By virtue of the application of an e-field guided neuro-navigation system and the opportunity for online visualization of strength and direction of the TMS-induced e-field on subjects' anatomical scans, each stimulation was administered with the induced e-field perpendicular to the sulcus of the brain area of interest. In order to ensure that the stimulation positions, respectively the induced e-field, remained the same over the two test sessions, both electrode positions were tagged with a digitization pen and marked on the individual anatomical images. Next, the coil was placed accordingly, a single pulse with an intensity of 10% RMT was administered and the corresponding position of the coil was saved in the neuro-navigation system. With the aid of a system-intern aiming tool, the exact position of the coil could be repeated with respect to centering, rotation and tilting. After each protocol, the position was verified and adjusted if necessary. For safety reasons, all participants were wearing in-ear plugs during the whole stimulation procedure.

2.4. *Electroencephalography*

2.4.1. Data Acquisition and Preprocessing

Participants' electrophysiological resting state brain activity was recorded for three minutes before and after each of the eight rTMS protocols by means of EEG with a BrainAmp DC system (Brain Products GmbH, Gilching, Germany), in combination with an Easycap elastic electrode cap (Easycap GmbH, Herrsching, Germany) consisting of 64 electrodes placed according to the 10–20 System (GND: AFz) and the software Brain Vision Recorder 1.20 (Brain Products GmbH, Germany). EEG measurements were online referenced to FCz and recorded at a sampling rate of 500 Hz. Impedances were kept lower than 10 kΩ during the whole recording.

Preprocessing of raw EEG data was conducted with a custom-built pipeline in Matlab (Matlab R2018b; Mathworks, Natick, MA, USA) by employing functions implemented in the EEGLAB toolbox [75]. In a first step, EEG data were filtered between 1 and 45 Hz and segmented into 2 s epochs. Afterwards, the data were visually inspected and single epochs featuring artifacts or verbal tinnitus loudness ratings were removed from the signal. For each dataset, the first and last two epochs were rejected as well, and noisy or deviant sensors were identified for subsequent interpolation. In order to identify and reject vertical and horizontal eye movements, an independent component analysis (ICA; fastICA toolbox http://research.ics.aalto.fi/ica/fastica/) was executed. In a next step, datasets were re-referenced using an average reference and the online reference electrode FCz was reconstructed and added as a data channel. Previously identified channels with high signal-to-noise ratio were interpolated using the spherical spline method [76]. As a last step, preprocessed datasets underwent a final visual inspection.

2.4.2. Power Spectra

Power spectra analysis was performed with the Fieldtrip toolbox [77] in Matlab. Fast Fourier Transformation (FFT, "mtmfft") and a hanning window with 1 Hz spectral smoothing was used for the calculation of pre- and post-stimulation power spectra for each channel per rTMS protocol. Obtained power spectra underwent a normalization through a division of the spectral power of every single frequency by the average spectral power of the whole frequency spectrum. Grand averages were calculated for every pre- and post-stimulation dataset per channel and the following frequency bands: delta (2–3.5 Hz), theta (4–7.5 Hz), alpha (8–12.5 Hz), beta (13–32.5 Hz) and gamma (33–44 Hz) [66,78]. RTMS protocol-specific pre-to-post-power changes in the respective frequency bands were obtained by subtracting the pre-stimulation from the post-stimulation power for each channel (Δpower = post − pre). Channels Iz, TP9 and TP10, which usually contain noisy signal, were excluded, resulting in 60 channels for further statistical analysis.

2.5. Statistical Analysis

All subsequent statistical analyses were performed with the statistics software R (R version 4.0.3; R Foundation for Statistical Analysis, Vienna, Austria) using the packages "psych" and "ggstatsplot".

Assumptions for parametric testing were examined with Shapiro–Wilk tests (normal distribution) and F-Tests (sphericity), and if violated, non-parametric tests were performed. Significance levels were set to ≤ 0.05 for all analysis, whereby < 0.10 was considered as a statistical trend. Differences between left and right hearing level, RMT as well as induced e-field strength with and without mounted EEG cap were analyzed with paired-sample *t*-tests and Wilcoxon signed-rank tests, respectively.

2.5.1. Reliability Analysis of TMS-Induced Tinnitus Loudness Changes and Discomfort Evaluation

Pre-stimulation ratings were averaged (T0–T180) to receive a stable tinnitus loudness baseline for each protocol per subject. TMS-induced tinnitus loudness changes were calculated via a subtraction of the mean baseline loudness level from the mean post-stimulation loudness level (Δloudness = post − baseline). Test–retest reliability of TMS-induced mean tinnitus suppression as well as discomfort evaluation over both test session days was analyzed by means of Spearman correlations for each protocol. *p*-values were adjusted for multiple comparisons using the Holm–Bonferroni method [79].

2.5.2. Reliability Analysis of TMS-Induced Changes in Oscillatory Brain Activity

Test–retest reliability of protocol-specific pre–post-power spectra changes were analyzed with Spearman correlations. Therefore, the obtained changes were correlated between the first and second test sessions on a single sensor level per rTMS protocol and frequency band. Thus, 300 correlations were calculated per rTMS protocol (5 frequency bands x 60 sensors). Obtained *p*-values of sensor correlations were adjusted according to the number of sensors separated per frequency band and protocol using the Holm–Bonferroni method [79]. In case of significant results, *p*-values were further corrected for the number of applied protocols akin to an adjustment for multiple comparisons of behavioral results. We were exclusively interested in positive correlation outcomes, representing reliability of TMS effects. Significant positive correlations of channel pairs were identified via correlation matrices and projected on a 60-channel topographical scalp map, applying color-coding for received correlation coefficients (r_s). A minimum number of two neighboring electrodes featuring significant positive correlations (electrode cluster) was considered as a reliable TMS-induced change in power spectra. Triangulation of 2D sensors was utilized for neighboring sensor identification.

2.5.3. rTMS Individualization via Responder Identification Using Behavioral and Electrophysiological Data

Additional to test–retest reliability analysis, rTMS individualization was examined based on single-subject responses concerning loudness evaluation and electrophysiological consequences. Behavioral response to one of the verum interventions was defined as a mean tinnitus loudness suppression (compare Section 2.5.1 Reliability Analysis of TMS-Induced Tinnitus Loudness Changes and Discomfort Evaluation) superior to sham stimulation (Δloudness verum > Δloudness sham) on both test session days for the same rTMS protocol and stimulated hemisphere. EEG responders were defined for the alpha (8–12.5 Hz) and gamma (33–44 Hz) frequency bands separately. In particular, we were interested in alpha power increases and gamma power decreases from pre- to post-stimulation. As indicated in the Introduction Section, alpha increases and gamma decreases are the most valid biomarkers for tinnitus reductions, as indicated by literature reviews and expert knowledge. For each subject and protocol, the top 20% of channels exhibiting alpha increases/gamma decreases were detected and scrutinized with regards to sham-superiority per day.

If a sham-superior alpha increase, respectively gamma decrease, was observed in the same sensor on both days, plus the corresponding pattern occurred in a minimum number of two adjacent channels, the subject was designated as either an alpha or gamma responder. Associations of a behavioral response to any of the eight protocols with an electrophysiological response in the alpha or gamma frequency band and vice versa were examined with Fisher's exact tests due to cell frequencies less than five.

3. Results

3.1. Sample Characteristics

Participants were aged from 43 to 69 years (M = 57.05, SD = 6.79) and had an average tinnitus duration of 131.64 months (SD = 116.76). The majority reported a bilateral tinnitus perception as well as loudness fluctuations. No difference in hearing loss between the left and the right ear was observed, $t_{(13)} = -1.36$, $p = 0.198$. THI severity grades ranged from mild (grade 2) to catastrophic (grade 5) and manifested on average as severe (grade 4) for the whole sample (M = 58.49, SD = 19.55). As expected, the RMTs were significantly higher with a mounted EEG cap, $p < 0.001$. Unexpectedly, the corresponding strength of the induced e-field was similarly higher, with an EEG-cap $t_{(21)} = -6.07$, $p < 0.001$. Although the motor hotspot for RMT determination was identical, as well as coil centering and rotation, differences in the e-field might derive from difficulties in the adjustment of coil tilting due to distances to the scalp, as well as the concomitant stimulation at higher intensities.

Information about participant characteristics can be seen in Table 1.

Table 1. Participant characteristics.

N (female)	22 (5)			
Handedness (left/right/both) (4 missing)	0/14/4			
Tinnitus laterality (left/right/both/inside head) (4 missing)	1/1/14/2			
Tinnitus loudness fluctuation (yes/no) (4 missing)	14/4			
	M ± SD	**Md**	**Min**	**Max**
Age (years)	57.05 ± 6.79	57.50	43.00	69.00
Tinnitus duration (months) (2 missing)	131.65 ± 116.79	102.00	5.00	420.00
Hearing loss left (dB) (8 missing)	23.42 ± 9.72	22.22	7.22	41.67
Hearing loss right (dB) (8 missing)	27.87 ± 14.29	23.06	7.78	61.88
THI score (0–100)	58.49 ± 19.55	58.00	30.00	90.00
Tinnitus loudness (%) (6 missing)	70.31 ± 19.87	80.00	30.00	90.00
RMT (%)	33.95 ± 5.33	33.00	25.00	46.00
RMT (%) + EEG cap	41.91 ± 9.65	41.00	30.00	66.00
Electrical field (V/m)	54.47 ± 13.90	52.50	27.00	86.00
Electrical field (V/m) + EEG cap	66.66 ± 15.38	66.25	44.00	99.00

M = mean; SD = standard deviation; Md = median; Min = minimum; Max = maximum; THI = Tinnitus Handicap Inventory; RMT = resting motor threshold; EEG = electroencephalography.

Besides anticipated side effects such as discomfort during rTMS (in particular by rapid muscle contraction caused by high-frequency protocols) or temporary tinnitus loudness increases after stimulation, no additional side effects could be observed in the current sample. Spearman correlations showed significant positive correlations for discomfort evaluations of each applied rTMS protocol between the two test sessions (see Figure S1 in the Supplemental Materials).

3.2. Test–Retest Reliability of TMS-Induced Changes in Tinnitus Loudness and Oscillatory Brain Activity

No significant correlations were observed for the two test session days with regards to mean tinnitus loudness changes for any of the protocols (Figure 2). It should be noted that without considering corrections for multiple comparisons, a significant test–retest reliability was found for left hemispheric stimulation with 10 Hz and right hemispheric stimulation with 20 Hz.

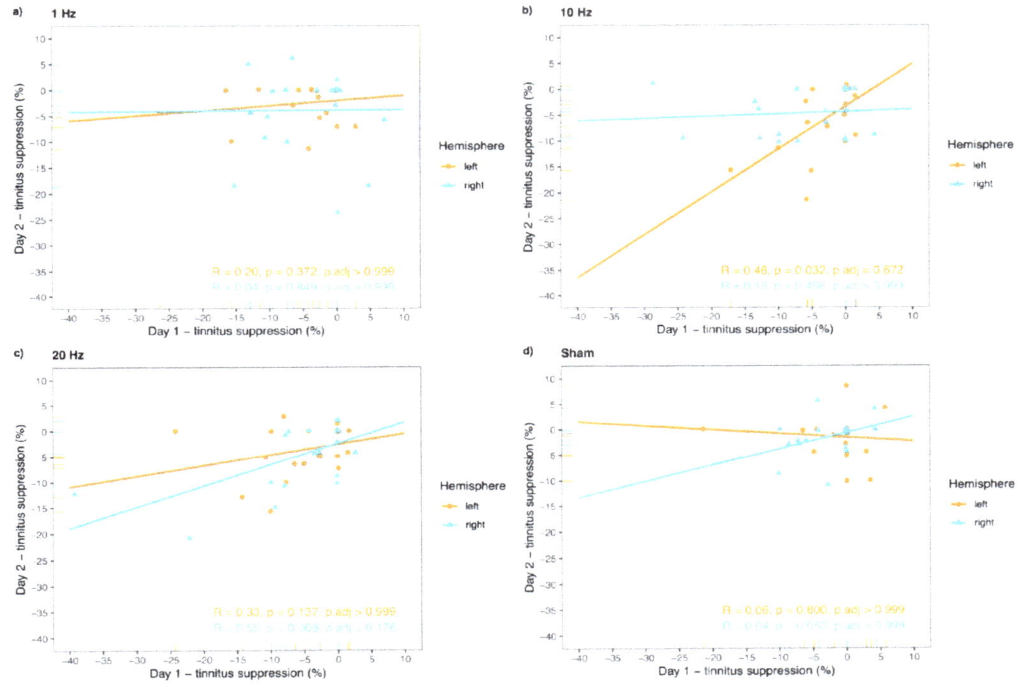

Figure 2. Reliability of TMS-induced changes in tinnitus loudness. Spearman correlations of rated tinnitus suppression (%) per rTMS protocol (1 Hz (**a**), 10 Hz (**b**), 20 Hz (**c**), sham (**d**)) between the first and the second test session days are illustrated in Figure 2. Colored ribbons represent confidence intervals (95%). Reliable changes were observed for a (**b**) 10 Hz stimulation over the left temporo-parietal junction and a (**c**) 20 Hz stimulation over the right temporo-parietal junction. Both correlations do not withstand a correction for multiple comparison and should therefore not be overrated and interpreted only exploratively.

On the basis of our predefined reliability criteria, reliable changes in oscillatory brain activity were solely present for 1 Hz stimulation of the right TPJ, exclusively for the gamma frequency band. As can be seen from Figure 3, these reliable changes were primarily observed over parieto-occipital regions, whereby neighboring channels PO7 and O1 constitute a significant reliable cluster. If corrected for multiple comparisons, this effect disappears and is therefore only conditionally interpretable.

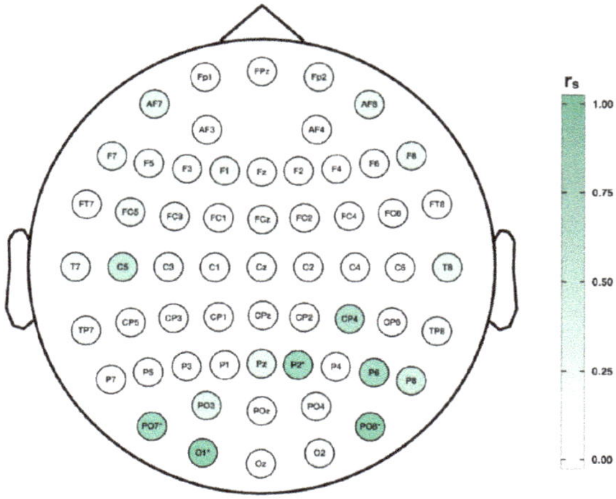

Figure 3. Reliability of TMS-induced changes in oscillatory brain activity. Spearman correlations coefficients (r_S) of right hemispheric 1 Hz rTMS-induced changes in the gamma frequency band (33–44 Hz) for the two test session days are projected on a topographical map per electrode in Figure 3. Significant reliable electrodes are highlighted with asterisks. Separate reliable changes are primarily present over parieto-occipital electrodes, whereby neighboring channels PO7 and O1 form a significant reliable cluster. However, this effect disappears after a correction for multiple comparisons and is therefore only conditionally interpretable.

3.3. *rTMS Individualization Using Behavioral and Electrophysiological Data*

In 12 out of 22 (55%) participants, it was possible to identify an individualized rTMS protocol for short-term tinnitus suppression characterized by sham-superiority on both test session days. From those 12 patients, 10 (83.33%) responded to more than one stimulation type. Detailed information about individual responses together with the induced mean tinnitus suppression (averaged over both test session days) can be found in Table 2. As presented in Table 3, the majority of subjects responded to a stimulation over the left TPJ with 20 Hz (n = 7) and 10 Hz (n = 6), and over the right TPJ with 20 Hz (n = 5).

EEG responders were defined by sham-superior alpha power increase or gamma power decrease in a minimum of two neighboring electrodes in both test sessions. Using this criterion, 20 alpha responders (90.91%) were identified, showing alpha power increases for at least one of the six used verum protocols. Left TPJ stimulation with 10 Hz (n = 10) or 1 Hz (n = 9), and right TPJ stimulation with 10 Hz (n = 7) produced the most alpha responders (Table 3). Electrophysiological responses in the gamma band were present in each investigated subject (100%) for at least one protocol. Subjects responded mainly to left TPJ stimulation with 10 Hz (n = 13) or 1 Hz (n = 10) and right TPJ stimulation with 10 Hz (n = 8) or 1 Hz (n = 8) (Table 2). Interestingly, 75% of alpha and gamma responders showed consistent power increases/decreases for more than one protocol. Table 3 presents an overview of alpha increases and gamma decreases per rTMS protocol on a single subject level. Fisher's exact tests showed no significant association neither for behavioral responders with alpha or gamma responders nor the other way around.

Electrodes featuring sham-superior alpha/gamma modifications on both days are presented in Figures 4 and 5 by means of topographical maps displaying the quantity of electrodes within alpha and gamma responders per rTMS protocol. It is apparent from Figure 4 that alpha responses primarily appeared in parieto-occipital regions on both hemispheres, whereas responses in the gamma range were especially present over frontal regions bilaterally and to some extent over parieto-occipital parts, as outlined in Figure 5. Detailed electrode information per subject and rTMS protocol can be found in the Supplementary Materials for alpha (Table S1) and gamma responders (Table S2).

Table 2. Individual test session responses per protocol—behavioral and EEG responder.

Subject	Behavioral Responder				Alpha (8–12.5 Hz)/Gamma (30.5–44 Hz)			
		1 Hz	10 Hz	20 Hz		1 Hz	10 Hz	20 Hz
1	Left	12.86	-	-	Left	-	$\downarrow\gamma$	$\uparrow\alpha\downarrow\gamma$
	Right	17.15	-	-	Right	-	$\downarrow\gamma$	-
2			-		Left	$\uparrow\alpha\downarrow\gamma$	$\uparrow\alpha\downarrow\gamma$	-
					Right	-	-	-
3	Left	3.98	-	3.71	Left	$\uparrow\alpha\downarrow\gamma$	$\uparrow\alpha$	-
	Right	-	-	-	Right	$\downarrow\gamma$	-	-
4	Left	-	10.35	-	Left	$\uparrow\alpha\downarrow\gamma$	-	-
	Right	-	9.28	25.71	Right	-	-	-
5	Left	-	16.42	-	Left	$\uparrow\alpha$	$\downarrow\gamma$	$\uparrow\alpha$
	Right	10	16.79	21.42	Right	-	-	-
6	Left	-	10.71	-	Left	$\uparrow\alpha$	-	$\uparrow\alpha$
	Right	-	-	-	Right	-	$\uparrow\alpha\downarrow\gamma$	-
7			-		Left	-	$\uparrow\alpha$	-
					Right	-	$\uparrow\alpha$	$\uparrow\alpha\downarrow\gamma$
8	Left	-	6.07	8.93	Left	-	$\uparrow\alpha\downarrow\gamma$	$\downarrow\gamma$
	Right	-	4.64	9.28	Right	-	$\uparrow\alpha$	-
9	Left	-	-	3.93	Left	$\uparrow\alpha\downarrow\gamma$	$\uparrow\alpha\downarrow\gamma$	$\uparrow\alpha\downarrow\gamma$
	Right	7.55	-	-	Right	$\downarrow\gamma$	-	-
10	Left	15.36	-	5.71	Left	$\downarrow\gamma$	$\uparrow\alpha$	$\downarrow\gamma$
	Right	-	-	-	Right	-	$\downarrow\gamma$	$\uparrow\alpha\downarrow\gamma$
11			-		Left	$\uparrow\alpha$	-	-
					Right	$\downarrow\gamma$	$\uparrow\alpha\downarrow\gamma$	$\uparrow\alpha$
12			-		Left	-	-	-
					Right	-	$\uparrow\alpha$	$\downarrow\gamma$
13			-		Left	$\downarrow\gamma$	$\uparrow\alpha\downarrow\gamma$	-
					Right	$\uparrow\alpha\downarrow\gamma$	$\downarrow\gamma$	-
14			-		Left	$\uparrow\alpha$	$\downarrow\gamma$	$\uparrow\alpha\downarrow\gamma$
					Right	$\downarrow\gamma$	-	$\uparrow\alpha$
15			-		Left	$\downarrow\gamma$	$\uparrow\alpha$	-
					Right	$\downarrow\gamma$	-	-
16	Left	-	5	12.85	Left	-	$\uparrow\alpha\downarrow\gamma$	-
	Right	-	-	10	Right	-	$\uparrow\alpha$	$\downarrow\gamma$
17			-		Left	-	$\downarrow\gamma$	-
					Right	$\uparrow\alpha$	$\downarrow\gamma$	$\uparrow\alpha\downarrow\gamma$
18			-		Left	$\downarrow\gamma$	$\downarrow\gamma$	$\uparrow\alpha\downarrow\gamma$
					Right	$\uparrow\alpha\downarrow\gamma$	$\uparrow\alpha$	-
19	Left	-	13.57	13.57	Left	$\uparrow\alpha$	$\downarrow\gamma$	-
	Right	-	-	-	Right	$\uparrow\alpha$	$\downarrow\gamma$	$\uparrow\alpha$
20			-		Left	$\downarrow\gamma$	$\downarrow\gamma$	-
					Right	-	-	-
21	Left	-	-	-	Left	-	-	$\downarrow\gamma$
	Right	7.14	-	3.93	Right	$\downarrow\gamma$	$\downarrow\gamma$	$\downarrow\gamma$
22	Left	-	-	7.85	Left	$\downarrow\gamma$	$\uparrow\alpha\downarrow\gamma$	-
	Right	-	-	-	Right	-	-	-

Note: Behavioral response was defined via a sham-superior tinnitus suppression on both test session days in at least one of the verum protocols. EEG response was defined as sham-superior alpha increases, respectively gamma decreases, in a minimum number of two neighboring electrodes on both test session days in at least one verum protocol. For behavioral responders, the mean tinnitus suppression (averaged over both test session days) is presented per rTMS protocol. Alpha increases ($\uparrow\alpha$) and gamma decreases ($\downarrow\gamma$) are equally presented per subject and protocol. Dashes indicate no response.

Table 3. Summary of behavioral and electrophysiological responder per rTMS protocol.

	Behavioral Responder	↑ Alpha	↓ Gamma
Total number of responders (N)	12	20	22
Number of responders per protocol (N)			
Left 1 Hz	3	9	10
Right 1 Hz	4	4	8
Left 10 Hz	6	10	13
Right 10 Hz	3	7	8
Left 20 Hz	7	6	7
Right 20 Hz	5	6	6

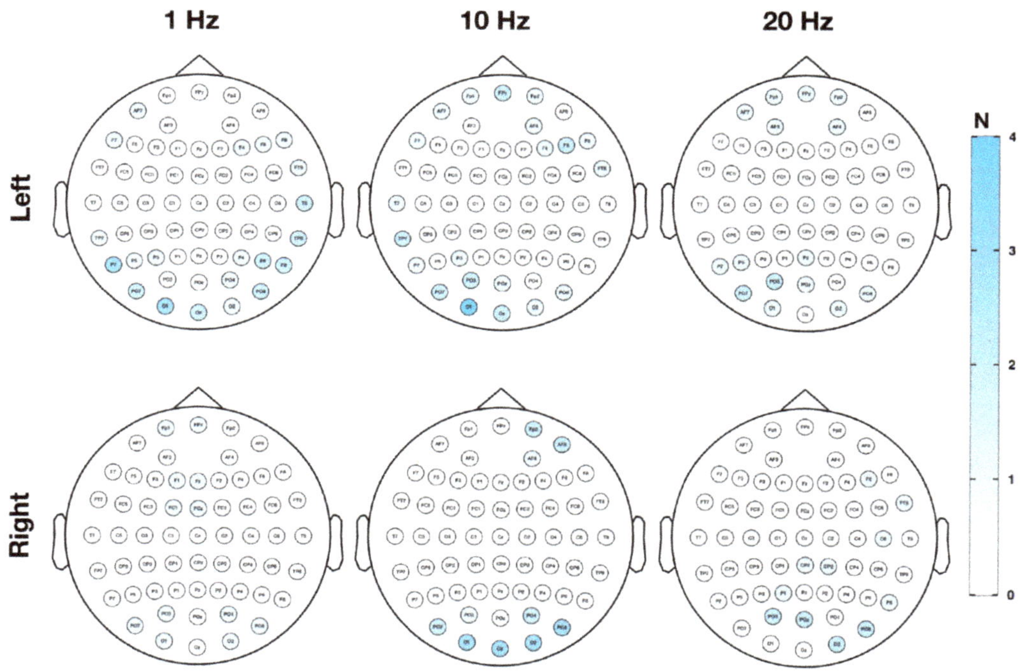

Figure 4. Topography of electrophysiological response—alpha responder. In Figure 4, topography and quantity of sensors showing sham-superior increases in the alpha frequency band in a minimum number of two neighboring channels on both test session days are illustrated per rTMS protocol. Responses in the alpha frequency band (8–12.5 Hz) to one of the verum protocols primarily occurred over parieto-occipital electrodes.

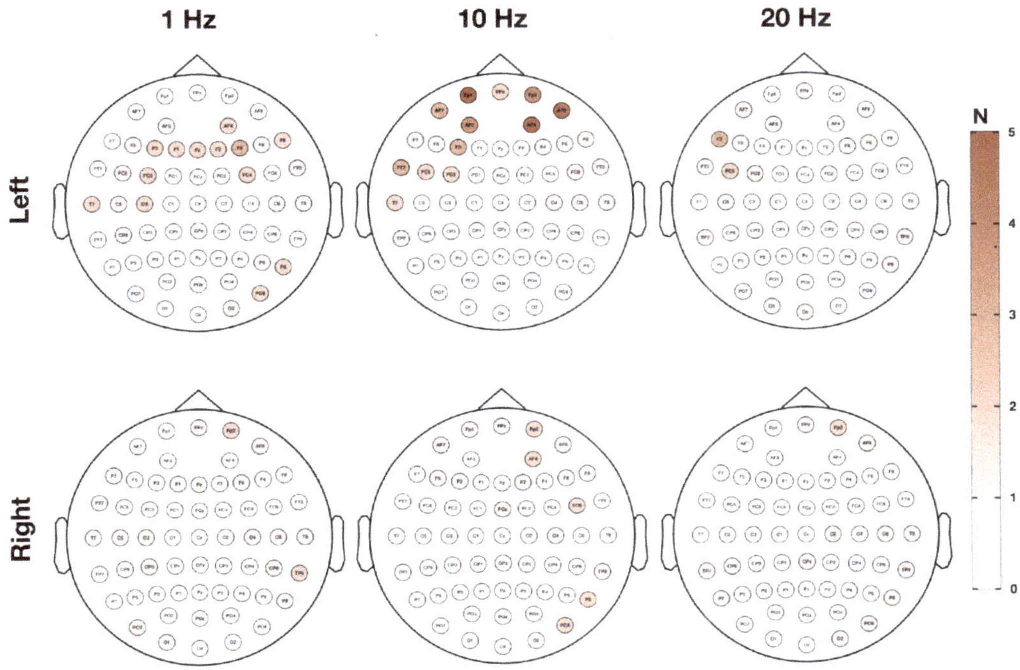

Figure 5. Topography of electrophysiological response—gamma responder. In Figure 5, topography and quantity of sensors showing sham-superior decreases in the gamma frequency band in a minimum number of two neighboring channels on both test session days are illustrated per rTMS protocol. Responses in the gamma frequency band (33–44 Hz) to one of the verum protocols mostly appeared over frontal electrodes on both hemispheres and partially over parieto-occipital sensors.

4. Discussion

The goals of this experiment were to ascertain whether it is possible to identify treatment protocols that provide reliable effects both on the behavioral and on the electrophysiological level, as this is a precondition for individualizing treatment. We performed two test sessions, at which six active and two sham protocols were administered. We evaluated reliability by comparing tinnitus suppression effects and electrophysiological effects on an individual level by responder identification. Moreover, we performed whole-group analysis, in which we correlated the behavioral and electrophysiological effects of all stimulation protocols between both test sessions.

The main finding of our study was that in 55% of patients, we could identify a stimulation protocol that reduced tinnitus loudness transiently in both sessions, reliably more than sham stimulation. When we defined response by the effects on oscillatory brain activity, the number was even higher, with 20 out of 22 patients in which a specific rTMS protocol increased alpha more than sham, and with 22 out of 22 in which a specific rTMS protocol decreased gamma more than sham. These observations are in accordance with our a priori assumptions of rTMS personalization in the majority of subjects as well as findings from previous studies.

Correlation analysis for the whole group revealed reliable changes in tinnitus loudness after left TPJ stimulation with 10 Hz and right TPJ stimulation with 20 Hz. With respect to modulatory effects of rTMS on oscillatory brain activity, reliable changes could be obtained after right TPJ stimulation with 1 Hz in the gamma frequency band over parieto-occipital regions. However, these findings do not withstand a correction for multiple comparison and should therefore not be overrated and interpreted only exploratively. Nevertheless, the observed effect of rTMS on gamma activity fits well with a previous TMS-EEG study, where right frontal 1 Hz rTMS decreased gamma band activity over right temporal regions in tinnitus patients, whereas it increased gamma activity in healthy controls [66]. Gamma activity is supposed to be strongly connected with tinnitus perception [57,59,60]. However, as mentioned above, the effects of the first and the second session were not significantly correlated when statistical corrections for multiple comparisons were performed.

Taking our findings together, we can conclude that it is possible to identify responders for specific rTMS protocols, who demonstrate a reliable behavioral or electrophysiologic response on a specific rTMS protocol. However, if we investigate the effects of a given protocol for the whole sample, the variability of the effect is relatively large from session to session.

Presumably, the effects depend on the brain state before or during rTMS [80], and this brain state might vary from session to session. In the current study, the experimental design with six active and two sham protocols per session might have increased this variability, as after-effects from preceding protocols cannot be excluded as confounding factors.

The limited test–retest reliability corroborates the claim that effects of rTMS in general [37,38,81–83] but also treatment effects in tinnitus [9,84] are subject to high variability. Thus, it is most likely that single-subject impacts simply do not transfer to statistical analysis on a group level, highlighting the need and importance of personalized rTMS approaches.

On the other hand, it has been demonstrated that patients who benefit once from rTMS have a high chance to benefit from repeated rTMS treatment [85,86].

This clinical observation fits with our finding to identify treatment responders to specific rTMS protocols.

Our results also corroborate findings from several previous studies in which the feasibility of a customization of rTMS for tinnitus via test sessions has been demonstrated [47,48]. The responder rate of 55% in our study (12 out of 22) is in a similar range as in two previous studies (Kreuzer et al., 50% responder [47], and Schoisswohl et al., 100% responder [48]). However, both studies deployed magnetic stimulations over either prefrontal cortical regions or different positions over the superior temporal gyrus, whereas the current study targeted only a single region of the temporal cortex. The present goal was to examine the parameter frequency in more detail. Interestingly, the vast majority of participants responded to high-frequency stimulations over the left TPJ. It is assumed that high-frequency protocols produce increases of cortical excitability [15]. Consequently, high-frequency rTMS is most likely not able to reduce tinnitus-associated temporal hyperactivity. However, it has been suggested that the induced effects can vary or shift across different targets of the cortex [43] and are dependent on the intrinsic state of the brain region prior to stimulation [80,87–89]. Based on this, it could be the case that pathological auditory cortex hyperactivity as an intrinsic state of the "tinnitus brain" might cause a reversal of supposed high-frequency effects (shift from excitatory to inhibitory). In accordance with the present results, previous studies have demonstrated responder rates between 40% and 57% in single-session experiments with high-frequency stimulation protocols [41,42,45,90]. Likewise, treatment studies with high-frequency rTMS over the temporo-parietal cortex were able to show significant reductions in tinnitus distress [26,27].

In addition to an rTMS individualization based on behavioral responses, the current investigation has striven for a novel attempt in rTMS individualization with objective measures. By the use of TMS-EEG combinatory measurements, we wanted to overcome the limitations of subjective tinnitus loudness ratings and identify personalized rTMS protocols via sham-superior increases in alpha, respectively decreases in gamma, frequency band power in at least two neighboring EEG electrodes in both test sessions. The utilization of especially these frequency bands as an electrophysiological response indicator is based on current neurophysiological models. In tinnitus, pathological diminished alpha band activity was observed in contrast to healthy controls [57,58], whereby during states of brief tinnitus suppression either after sound stimulation [91] or after rTMS [46], increases in alpha power were detected, while gamma band activity is assumed to underly the actual tinnitus perception [57,59] by associations with tinnitus loudness [54,60]. Interestingly, we were able to identify a substantially higher number of EEG responders than behavioral responders. For a total number of 20 participants, it was possible to detect an alpha response for at least one rTMS protocol, whereas the entire sample featured responses in the gamma frequency band. It is noteworthy that the quantity of alpha or gamma responders was almost twice as much as for behavioral responders. In line with our behavioral observations, a left 10 Hz stimulation resulted in the highest quantity of alpha and gamma responders. It has been shown that this type of stimulation can modulate alpha oscillations [92] and that alpha and gamma oscillations show a strong interplay not only in tinnitus [52,93].

Since neurophysiological investigations were able to demonstrate relationships of the alpha and gamma band with tinnitus loudness [46,54,60,91], we addressed the question of whether a response in the alpha or gamma band is associated with a behavioral response, and vice versa. Our analysis did not reveal any relationship of EEG and behavioral responders, hampering the interpretability of our alpha and gamma findings as relevant for tinnitus loudness decreases in the current sample. A potential explanation for this lack of association could derive from the possibility that rTMS-specific modulations/neuroplastic consequences as measured with EEG simply do not instantly translate into behavioral responses. Consequently, longer periods of stimulation with an individualized rTMS protocol based on patients' EEG response (protocol with strongest alpha increase/gamma decrease), for example within the course of a daily treatment, might accumulate over time into behavioral effects and could tackle the deficiency of effectiveness in current rTMS treatment trials for tinnitus.

Future studies should strive for a systematic implementation of test session approaches and investigate the therapeutic consequences of personalized rTMS in more detail. The present experiment underscores the feasibility of rTMS individualization via behavioral or electrophysiological responses. The results and methodology described in this sample of tinnitus patients might encourage neuromodulation attempts in other pathologies to personalize rTMS in order to account for inter-subject variability in rTMS response.

5. Conclusions

The aim of this investigation was to examine the feasibility of rTMS individualization in tinnitus. This involved the identification of responders to specific rTMS protocols and the assessment of test–retest reliability of rTMS effects in tinnitus suppression and ongoing brain activity. We were able to demonstrate the feasibility of rTMS individualization by using test sessions with different rTMS protocols. Responses to specific protocols based on electrophysiological signatures could be identified in all patients, and responses based on behavioral effects in the majority of patients. In contrast, test–retest reliability, as assessed with correlation analyses for the various rTMS protocols, was rather low both for behavioral and electrophysiological effects.

Taken together, these findings are highly encouraging for efforts to enhance the efficacy of rTMS by personalizing stimulation protocols.

Supplementary Materials: The following are available online at https://www.mdpi.com/article/10.3390/jpm11060536/s1, Figure S1: Reliability of TMS-induced discomfort. Table S1: Alpha responder—overview of electrodes per subject and protocol. Table S2: Gamma responder—overview of electrodes per subject and protocol.

Author Contributions: Conceptualization, S.S., M.S. and B.L.; methodology, S.S., M.S.; software, S.S.; validation, S.S. and M.S.; formal analysis, S.S.; investigation, S.S., M.S., T.H. and M.A.A.; data curation, S.S.; writing—original draft preparation, S.S.; writing—review and editing, M.S., B.L., T.H., M.A.A. and G.V.; visualization, S.S.; supervision, M.S.; project administration, S.S. and M.S. All authors have read and agreed to the published version of the manuscript.

Funding: The project was conducted as part of the European School for Interdisciplinary Tinnitus Research (ESIT) and was partially funded by the European Union's Horizon 2020 Marie Sklodowska-Curie Actions (grant agreement number 722046, ESIT project) and the European Union's Horizon 2020 Framework Programme (grant agreement number 848261, UNITI project).

Institutional Review Board Statement: Not applied.

Informed Consent Statement: Not applied.

Acknowledgments: We want to thank Nexstim Plc. for providing the electric-field guided neuro-navigation rTMS system to perform this feasibility trial.

Conflicts of Interest: The authors declare that they have no conflict of interest associated with this publication and there has been no significant financial support that could have influenced the outcomes. Author T.H. received a one-time travel cost coverage by Nexstim Plc. for an oral presentation.

References

1. Baguley, D.; McFerran, D.; Hall, D. Tinnitus. *Lancet* **2013**, *382*, 1600–1607. [CrossRef]
2. Langguth, B.; Kreuzer, P.M.; Kleinjung, T.; De Ridder, D. Tinnitus: Causes and clinical management. *Lancet Neurol.* **2013**, *12*, 920–930. [CrossRef]
3. McCormack, A.; Edmondson-Jones, M.; Somerset, S.; Hall, D. A systematic review of the reporting of tinnitus prevalence and severity. *Hear. Res.* **2016**, *337*, 70–79. [CrossRef] [PubMed]
4. Eggermont, J.J. Pathophysiology of tinnitus. *Prog. Brain Res.* **2007**, *166*, 19–543. [CrossRef]
5. Eggermont, J.J.; Roberts, L.E. The Neuroscience of Tinnitus: Understanding Abnormal and Normal Auditory Perception. *Front. Syst. Neurosci.* **2012**, *6*, 53. [CrossRef]
6. Eggermont, J.J.; Tass, P. Maladaptive Neural Synchrony in Tinnitus: Origin and Restoration. *Front. Neurol.* **2015**, *6*, 29. [CrossRef] [PubMed]
7. Henry, J.A.; Roberts, L.E.; Caspary, D.M.; Theodoroff, S.M.; Salvi, R.J. Underlying Mechanisms of Tinnitus: Review and Clinical Implications. *J. Am. Acad. Audiol.* **2014**, *25*, 005–022. [CrossRef]
8. Roberts, L.E.; Eggermont, J.J.; Caspary, D.M.; Shore, S.E.; Melcher, J.R.; Kaltenbach, J.A. Ringing Ears: The Neuroscience of Tinnitus. *J. Neurosci.* **2010**, *30*, 14972–14979. [CrossRef] [PubMed]
9. Langguth, B. Non-Invasive Neuromodulation for Tinnitus. *J. Audiol. Otol.* **2020**, *24*, 113–118. [CrossRef]
10. Hallett, M. Transcranial Magnetic Stimulation: A Primer. *Neuron* **2007**, *55*, 187–199. [CrossRef]
11. Hoogendam, J.M.; Ramakers, G.M.; Di Lazzaro, V. Physiology of repetitive transcranial magnetic stimulation of the human brain. *Brain Stimul.* **2010**, *3*, 95–118. [CrossRef]
12. Siebner, H.R.; Rothwell, J. Transcranial magnetic stimulation: New insights into representational cortical plasticity. *Exp. Brain Res.* **2003**, *148*, 1–16. [CrossRef] [PubMed]
13. Fitzgerald, P.B. Intensity-dependent effects of 1 Hz rTMS on human corticospinal excitability. *Clin. Neurophysiol.* **2002**, *113*, 1136–1141. [CrossRef]
14. Fitzgerald, P.B.; Fountain, S.; Daskalakis, Z.J. A comprehensive review of the effects of rTMS on motor cortical excitability and inhibition. *Clin. Neurophysiol.* **2006**, *117*, 2584–2596. [CrossRef]
15. Klomjai, W.; Katz, R.; Lackmy-Vallée, A. Basic principles of transcranial magnetic stimulation (TMS) and repetitive TMS (rTMS). *Ann. Phys. Rehabilitation Med.* **2015**, *58*, 208–213. [CrossRef] [PubMed]
16. Rossini, P.; Burke, D.; Chen, R.; Cohen, L.; Daskalakis, Z.; Di Iorio, R.; Di Lazzaro, V.; Ferreri, F.; Fitzgerald, P.; George, M.; et al. Non-invasive electrical and magnetic stimulation of the brain, spinal cord, roots and peripheral nerves: Basic principles and procedures for routine clinical and research application. An updated report from an I.F.C.N. Committee. *Clin. Neurophysiol.* **2015**, *126*, 1071–1107. [CrossRef]
17. Eichhammer, P.; Langguth, B.; Marienhagen, J.; Kleinjung, T.; Hajak, G. Neuronavigated repetitive transcranial magnetic stimulation in patients with tinnitus: A short case series. *Biol. Psychiatry* **2003**, *54*, 862–865. [CrossRef]
18. Langguth, B.; Eichhammer, P.; Wiegand, R.; Marienhegen, J.; Maenner, P.; Jacob, P.; Hajak, G. Neuronavigated rTMS in a patient with chronic tinnitus. Effects of 4 weeks treatment. *NeuroReport* **2003**, *14*, 980–997. [CrossRef]
19. Schoisswohl, S.; Agrawal, K.; Simoes, J.; Neff, P.; Schlee, W.; Langguth, B.; Schecklmann, M. RTMS parameters in tinnitus trials: A systematic review. *Sci. Rep.* **2019**, *9*, 1–11. [CrossRef]
20. Lehner, A.; Schecklmann, M.; Greenlee, M.W.; Rupprecht, R.; Langguth, B. Triple-site rTMS for the treatment of chronic tinnitus: A randomized controlled trial. *Sci. Rep.* **2016**, *6*, 22302. [CrossRef]
21. Lehner, A.; Schecklmann, M.; Poeppl, T.B.; Kreuzer, P.M.; Vielsmeier, V.; Rupprecht, R.; Landgrebe, M.; Langguth, B. Multisite rTMS for the Treatment of Chronic Tinnitus: Stimulation of the Cortical Tinnitus Network—A Pilot Study. *Brain Topogr.* **2012**, *26*, 501–510. [CrossRef]
22. De Ridder, D.; Song, J.-J.; Vanneste, S. Frontal Cortex TMS for Tinnitus. *Brain Stimul.* **2013**, *6*, 355–362. [CrossRef]

23. Noh, T.S.; Kyong, J.S.; Chang, M.Y.; Park, M.K.; Lee, J.H.; Oh, S.H.; Kim, J.S.; Chung, C.K.; Suh, M.W. Comparison of Treatment Outcomes Following Either Prefrontal Cortical-only or Dual-site Repetitive Transcranial Magnetic Stimulation in Chronic Tinnitus Patients: A Double-blind Randomized Study. *Otol. Neurotol.* **2017**, *38*, 296–303.
24. Vanneste, S.; De Ridder, D. Differences between a single session and repeated sessions of 1 Hz TMS by double-cone coil prefrontal stimulation for the improvement of tinnitus. *Brain Stimul.* **2013**, *6*, 155–159. [CrossRef] [PubMed]
25. Forogh, B.; Yazdi-Bahri, S.-M.; Ahadi, T.; Fereshtehnejad, S.-M.; Raissi, G.R. Comparison of two protocols of transcranial magnetic stimulation for treatment of chronic tinnitus: A randomized controlled clinical trial of burst repetitive versus high-frequency repetitive transcranial magnetic stimulation. *Neurol. Sci.* **2014**, *35*, 227–232. [CrossRef] [PubMed]
26. Khedr, E.M.; Abo-Elfetoh, N.; Rothwell, J.C.; El-Atar, A.; Sayed, E.; Khalifa, H. Contralateral versus ipsilateral rTMS of temporoparietal cortex for the treatment of chronic unilateral tinnitus: Comparative study. *Eur. J. Neurol.* **2010**, *17*, 976–983. [CrossRef]
27. Khedr, E.M.; Rothwell, J.C.; Ahmed, M.A.; El-Atar, A. Effect of daily repetitive transcranial magnetic stimulation for treatment of tinnitus: Comparison of different stimulus frequencies. *J. Neurol. Neurosurg. Psychiatry* **2008**, *79*, 212–215. [CrossRef] [PubMed]
28. Plewnia, C.; Vonthein, R.; Wasserka, B.; Arfeller, C.; Naumann, A.; Schraven, S.P.; Plontke, S.K. Treatment of chronic tinnitus with theta burst stimulation: A randomized controlled trial. *Neurology* **2012**, *78*, 1628–1634. [CrossRef]
29. Schecklmann, M.; Giani, A.; Tupak, S.; Langguth, B.; Raab, V.; Polak, T.; Várallyay, C.; Großmann, W.; Herrmann, M.J.; Fallgatter, A.J. Neuronavigated left temporal continuous theta burst stimulation in chronic tinnitus. *Restor. Neurol. Neurosci.* **2016**, *34*, 165–175. [CrossRef]
30. Dong, C.; Chen, C.; Wang, T.; Gao, C.; Wang, Y.; Guan, X.; Dong, X. Low-Frequency Repetitive Transcranial Magnetic Stimulation for the Treatment of Chronic Tinnitus: A Systematic Review and Meta-Analysis of Randomized Controlled Trials. *BioMed. Res. Int.* **2020**, *2020*, 1–9. [CrossRef]
31. Zenner, H.-P.; Delb, W.; Kröner-Herwig, B.; Jäger, B.; Peroz, I.; Hesse, G.; Mazurek, B.; Goebel, G.; Gerloff, C.; Trollmann, R.; et al. A multidisciplinary systematic review of the treatment for chronic idiopathic tinnitus. *Eur. Arch. Otorhinolaryngol.* **2017**, *274*, 2079–2091. [CrossRef]
32. Lefaucheur, J.-P.; André-Obadia, N.; Antal, A.; Ayache, S.S.; Baeken, C.; Benninger, D.H.; Cantello, R.M.; Cincotta, M.; De Carvalho, M.; De Ridder, D.; et al. Evidence-based guidelines on the therapeutic use of repetitive transcranial magnetic stimulation (rTMS). *Clin. Neurophysiol.* **2014**, *125*, 2150–2206. [CrossRef] [PubMed]
33. Londero, A.; Bonfils, P.; Lefaucheur, J. Transcranial magnetic stimulation and subjective tinnitus. A review of the literature, 2014–2016. *Eur. Ann. Otorhinolaryngol. Head Neck Dis.* **2018**, *135*, 51–58. [CrossRef]
34. Lefebvre-Demers, M.; Doyon, N.; Fecteau, S. Non-invasive neuromodulation for tinnitus: A meta-analysis and modeling studies. *Brain Stimul.* **2021**, *14*, 113–128. [CrossRef] [PubMed]
35. Guerra, A.; López-Alonso, V.; Cheeran, B.; Suppa, A. Variability in non-invasive brain stimulation studies: Reasons and results. *Neurosci. Lett.* **2020**, *719*, 133330. [CrossRef] [PubMed]
36. López-Alonso, V.; Cheeran, B.; Río-Rodríguez, D.; Fernández-Del-Olmo, M. Inter-individual Variability in Response to Non-invasive Brain Stimulation Paradigms. *Brain Stimul.* **2014**, *7*, 372–380. [CrossRef] [PubMed]
37. Polanía, R.; Nitsche, M.A.; Ruff, C.C. Studying and modifying brain function with non-invasive brain stimulation. *Nat. Neurosci.* **2018**, *21*, 174–187. [CrossRef]
38. Terranova, C.; Rizzo, V.; Cacciola, A.; Chillemi, G.; Calamuneri, A.; Milardi, D.; Quartarone, A. Is There a Future for Non-invasive Brain Stimulation as a Therapeutic Tool? *Front. Neurol.* **2019**, *9*, 1146. [CrossRef] [PubMed]
39. Cocchi, L.; Zalesky, A. Personalized Transcranial Magnetic Stimulation in Psychiatry. *Biol. Psychiatry Cogn. Neurosci. Neuroimaging* **2018**, *3*, 731–741. [CrossRef] [PubMed]
40. Garnaat, S.L.; Fukuda, A.M.; Yuan, S.; Carpenter, L.L. Identification of clinical features and biomarkers that may inform a personalized approach to rTMS for depression. *Pers. Med. Psychiatry* **2019**, *17–18*, 4–16. [CrossRef] [PubMed]
41. Folmer, R.L.; Carroll, J.R.; Rahim, A.; Shi, Y.; Martin, W.H. Effects of repetitive transcranial magnetic stimulation (rTMS) on chronic tinnitus. *Acta Otolaryngol.* **2006**, *126*, 96–101. [CrossRef]
42. Fregni, F.; Marcondes, R.; Boggio, P.; Marcolin, M.A.; Rigonatti, S.P.; Sanchez, T.G.; Nitsche, M.A.; Pascual-Leone, A. Transient tinnitus suppression induced by repetitive transcranial magnetic stimulation and transcranial direct current stimulation. *Eur. J. Neurol.* **2006**, *13*, 996–1001. [CrossRef]
43. Lorenz, I.; Müller, N.; Schlee, W.; Langguth, B.; Weisz, N. Short-Term Effects of Single Repetitive TMS Sessions on Auditory Evoked Activity in Patients With Chronic Tinnitus. *J. Neurophysiol.* **2010**, *104*, 1497–1505. [CrossRef] [PubMed]
44. Meeus, O.; Blaivie, C.; Ost, J.; De Ridder, D.; Van de Heyning, P. Influence of Tonic and Burst Transcranial Magnetic Stimulation Characteristics on Acute Inhibition of Subjective Tinnitus. *Otol. Neurotol.* **2009**, *30*, 697–703. [CrossRef] [PubMed]
45. Plewnia, C.; Bartels, M.; Gerloff, C. Transient suppression of tinnitus by transcranial magnetic stimulation. *Ann. Neurol.* **2003**, *53*, 263–266. [CrossRef] [PubMed]
46. Müller, N.; Lorenz, I.; Langguth, B.; Weisz, N. rTMS Induced Tinnitus Relief Is Related to an Increase in Auditory Cortical Alpha Activity. *PLoS ONE* **2013**, *8*, e55557. [CrossRef] [PubMed]
47. Kreuzer, P.M.; Poeppl, T.B.; Rupprecht, R.; Vielsmeier, V.; Lehner, A.; Langguth, B.; Schecklmann, M. Individualized Repetitive Transcranial Magnetic Stimulation Treatment in Chronic Tinnitus? *Front. Neurol.* **2017**, *8*. [CrossRef] [PubMed]

48. Schoisswohl, S.; Langguth, B.; Schecklmann, M. Short-Term Tinnitus Suppression With Electric-Field Guided rTMS for Individualizing rTMS Treatment: A Technical Feasibility Report. *Front. Neurol.* **2020**, *11*. [CrossRef]
49. Ridder, D.E.; Evanneste, S.; Elangguth, B.; Ellinas, R. Thalamocortical Dysrhythmia: A Theoretical Update in Tinnitus. *Front. Neurol.* **2015**, *6*, 124. [CrossRef]
50. Llinás, R.; Urbano, F.J.; Leznik, E.; Ramírez, R.R.; van Marle, H.J. Rhythmic and dysrhythmic thalamocortical dynamics: GABA systems and the edge effect. *Trends Neurosci.* **2005**, *28*, 325–333. [CrossRef]
51. Llinás, R.R.; Ribary, U.; Jeanmonod, D.; Kronberg, E.; Mitra, P.P. Thalamocortical dysrhythmia: A neurological and neuropsychiatric syndrome characterized by magnetoencephalography. *Proc. Natl. Acad. Sci. USA* **1999**, *96*, 15222–15227. [CrossRef] [PubMed]
52. Weisz, N.; Dohrmann, K.; Elbert, T. The relevance of spontaneous activity for the coding of the tinnitus sensation. *Prog. Brain Res.* **2007**, *166*, 61–70. [CrossRef]
53. Adjamian, P.; Sereda, M.; Zobay, O.; Hall, D.A.; Palmer, A.R. Neuromagnetic Indicators of Tinnitus and Tinnitus Masking in Patients with and without Hearing Loss. *J. Assoc. Res. Otolaryngol.* **2012**, *13*, 715–731. [CrossRef] [PubMed]
54. Balkenhol, T.; Wallhäusser-Franke, E.; Delb, W. Psychoacoustic Tinnitus Loudness and Tinnitus-Related Distress Show Different Associations with Oscillatory Brain Activity. *PLoS ONE* **2013**, *8*, e53180. [CrossRef] [PubMed]
55. Moazami-Goudarzi, M.; Michels, L.; Weisz, N.; Jeanmonod, D. Temporo-insular enhancement of EEG low and high frequencies in patients with chronic tinnitus. QEEG study of chronic tinnitus patients. *BMC Neurosci.* **2010**, *11*, 40. [CrossRef] [PubMed]
56. Schlee, W.; Schecklmann, M.; Lehner, A.; Kreuzer, P.M.; Vielsmeier, V.; Poeppl, T.B.; Langguth, B. Reduced Variability of Auditory Alpha Activity in Chronic Tinnitus. *Neural Plast.* **2014**, *2014*, 1–9. [CrossRef]
57. Weisz, N.; Müller, S.; Schlee, W.; Dohrmann, K.; Hartmann, T.; Elbert, T. The Neural Code of Auditory Phantom Perception. *J. Neurosci.* **2007**, *27*, 1479–1484. [CrossRef] [PubMed]
58. Weisz, N.; Moratti, S.; Meinzer, M.; Dohrmann, K.; Elbert, T. Tinnitus Perception and Distress Is Related to Abnormal Spontaneous Brain Activity as Measured by Magnetoencephalography. *PLoS Med.* **2005**, *2*, e153. [CrossRef]
59. De Ridder, D.; Congedo, M.; Vanneste, S. The neural correlates of subjectively perceived and passively matched loudness perception in auditory phantom perception. *Brain Behav.* **2015**, *5*, e00331. [CrossRef]
60. Van Der Loo, E.; Gais, S.; Congedo, M.; Vanneste, S.; Plazier, M.; Menovsky, T.; Van De Heyning, P.; De Ridder, D. Tinnitus Intensity Dependent Gamma Oscillations of the Contralateral Auditory Cortex. *PLoS ONE* **2009**, *4*, e7396. [CrossRef]
61. Noda, Y. Toward the establishment of neurophysiological indicators for neuropsychiatric disorders using transcranial magnetic stimulation-evoked potentials: A systematic review. *Psychiatry Clin. Neurosci.* **2020**, *74*, 12–34. [CrossRef] [PubMed]
62. Qiu, S.; Wang, S.; Yi, W.; Zhang, C.; He, H. The lasting effects of 1Hz repetitive transcranial magnetic stimulation on resting state EEG in healthy subjects. In Proceedings of the 2019 41st Annual International Conference of the IEEE Engineering in Medicine and Biology Society (EMBC), Berlin, Germany, 23–27 July 2019; Volume 2019, pp. 5918–5922.
63. Thut, G.; Pascual-Leone, A. A Review of Combined TMS-EEG Studies to Characterize Lasting Effects of Repetitive TMS and Assess Their Usefulness in Cognitive and Clinical Neuroscience. *Brain Topogr.* **2009**, *22*, 219–232. [CrossRef] [PubMed]
64. Hui, J.; Tremblay, S.; Daskalakis, Z.J. The Current and Future Potential of Transcranial Magnetic Stimulation with Electroencephalography in Psychiatry. *Clin. Pharmacol. Ther.* **2019**, *106*, 734–746. [CrossRef] [PubMed]
65. Tremblay, S.; Rogasch, N.C.; Premoli, I.; Blumberger, D.M.; Casarotto, S.; Chen, R.; Di Lazzaro, V.; Farzan, F.; Ferrarelli, F.; Fitzgerald, P.B.; et al. Clinical utility and prospective of TMS–EEG. *Clin. Neurophysiol.* **2019**, *130*, 802–844. [CrossRef]
66. Eschecklmann, M.; Elehner, A.; Egollmitzer, J.; Eschmidt, E.; Eschlee, W.; Elangguth, B. Repetitive transcranial magnetic stimulation induces oscillatory power changes in chronic tinnitus. *Front. Cell. Neurosci.* **2015**, *9*, 421. [CrossRef]
67. Langguth, B.; Landgrebe, M.; Frank, E.; Schecklmann, M.; Sand, P.; Vielsmeier, V.; Hajak, G.; Kleinjung, T. Efficacy of different protocols of transcranial magnetic stimulation for the treatment of tinnitus: Pooled analysis of two randomized controlled studies. *World J. Biol. Psychiatry* **2012**, *15*, 276–285. [CrossRef] [PubMed]
68. Schecklmann, M.; Landgrebe, M.; Kleinjung, T.; Frank, E.; Sand, P.G.; Rupprecht, R.; Eichhammer, P.; Hajak, G.; Langguth, B. Changes in motor cortex excitability associated with temporal repetitive transcranial magnetic stimulation in tinnitus: Hints for cross-modal plasticity? *BMC Neurosci.* **2014**, *15*, 71. [CrossRef]
69. Kleinjung, T.; Fischer, B.; Langguth, B.; Sand, P.; Hajak, G.; Dvořáková, J.; Eichhammer, P. Validierung einer deutschsprachigen Version des "Tinnitus Handicap Inventory". *Psychiatr. Prax.* **2007**, *34*, 140–142. [CrossRef]
70. Newman, C.W.; Jacobson, G.P.; Spitzer, J.B. Development of the Tinnitus Handicap Inventory. *Arch. Otolaryngol. Head Neck Surg.* **1996**, *122*, 143–148. [CrossRef]
71. Langguth, B.; Goodey, R.; Azevedo, A.; Bjorne, A.; Cacace, A.; Crocetti, A.; Del Bo, L.; De Ridder, D.; Diges, I.; Elbert, T.; et al. Consensus for tinnitus patient assessment and treatment outcome measurement: Tinnitus Research Initiative meeting, Regensburg, July 2006. *Neural Regen.* **2007**, *166*, 525–536. [CrossRef]
72. Genitsaridi, E.; Partyka, M.; Gallus, S.; Lopez-Escamez, J.A.; Schecklmann, M.; Mielczarek, M.; Trpchevska, N.; Santacruz, J.L.; Schoisswohl, S.; Riha, C.; et al. Standardised profiling for tinnitus research: The European School for Interdisciplinary Tinnitus Research Screening Questionnaire (ESIT-SQ). *Hear. Res.* **2019**, *377*, 353–359. [CrossRef]
73. Chen, R.; Classen, J.; Gerloff, C.; Celnik, P.; Wassermann, E.M.; Hallett, M.; Cohen, L.G. Depression of motor cortex excitability by low-frequency transcranial magnetic stimulation. *Neurology* **1997**, *48*, 1398–1403. [CrossRef] [PubMed]

74. Kumru, H.; Albu, S.; Rothwell, J.; Leon, D.; Flores, C.; Opisso, E.; Tormos, J.M.; Valls-Sole, J. Modulation of motor cortex excitability by paired peripheral and transcranial magnetic stimulation. *Clin. Neurophysiol.* **2017**, *128*, 2043–2047. [CrossRef]
75. Delorme, A.; Makeig, S. EEGLAB: An Open Source Toolbox for Analysis of Single-Trial EEG Dynamics Including Independent Component Analysis. *J. Neurosci. Methods* **2004**, *134*, 9–21. [CrossRef]
76. Perrin, F.; Pernier, J.; Bertrand, O.; Echallier, J. Spherical splines for scalp potential and current density mapping. *Electroencephalogr. Clin. Neurophysiol.* **1989**, *72*, 184–187. [CrossRef]
77. Oostenveld, R.; Fries, P.; Maris, E.; Schoffelen, J.-M. FieldTrip: Open Source Software for Advanced Analysis of MEG, EEG, and Invasive Electrophysiological Data. *Comput. Intell. Neurosci.* **2010**, *2011*, 1–9. [CrossRef]
78. Vanneste, S.; Van De Heyning, P.; De Ridder, D. The neural network of phantom sound changes over time: A comparison between recent-onset and chronic tinnitus patients. *Eur. J. Neurosci.* **2011**, *34*, 718–731. [CrossRef]
79. Holm, S. A Simple Sequentially Rejective Multiple Test Procedure. *Scand. J. Stat.* **1979**, *6*, 65–70.
80. Siebner, H.R.; Lang, N.; Rizzo, V.; Nitsche, M.A.; Paulus, W.; Lemon, R.N.; Rothwell, J.C. Preconditioning of Low-Frequency Repetitive Transcranial Magnetic Stimulation with Transcranial Direct Current Stimulation: Evidence for Homeostatic Plasticity in the Human Motor Cortex. *J. Neurosci.* **2004**, *24*, 3379–3385. [CrossRef] [PubMed]
81. Maeda, F.; Keenan, J.P.; Tormos, J.M.; Topka, H.; Pascual-Leone, A. Interindividual variability of the modulatory effects of repetitive transcranial magnetic stimulation on cortical excitability. *Exp. Brain Res.* **2000**, *133*, 425–430. [CrossRef] [PubMed]
82. Nettekoven, C.; Volz, L.J.; Leimbach, M.; Pool, E.-M.; Rehme, A.K.; Eickhoff, S.B.; Fink, G.R.; Grefkes, C. Inter-individual variability in cortical excitability and motor network connectivity following multiple blocks of rTMS. *NeuroImage* **2015**, *118*, 209–218. [CrossRef] [PubMed]
83. Sommer, M.; Wu, T.; Tergau, F.; Paulus, W. Intra- and interindividual variability of motor responses to repetitive transcranial magnetic stimulation. *Clin. Neurophysiol.* **2002**, *113*, 265–269. [CrossRef]
84. Soleimani, R.; Jalali, M.M.; Hasandokht, T. Therapeutic impact of repetitive transcranial magnetic stimulation (rTMS) on tinnitus: A systematic review and meta-analysis. *Eur. Arch. Otorhinolaryngol.* **2015**, *273*, 1663–1675. [CrossRef] [PubMed]
85. Lehner, A.; Schecklmann, M.; Poeppl, T.B.; Kreuzer, P.M.; Peytard, J.; Frank, E.; Langguth, B. Efficacy and Safety of Repeated Courses of rTMS Treatment in Patients with Chronic Subjective Tinnitus. *BioMed. Res. Int.* **2015**, *2015*, 1–7. [CrossRef] [PubMed]
86. Rachid, F. Maintenance repetitive transcranial magnetic stimulation (rTMS) for relapse prevention in with depression: A review. *Psychiatry Res.* **2018**, *262*, 363–372. [CrossRef] [PubMed]
87. Silvanto, J.; Pascual-Leone, A. State-Dependency of Transcranial Magnetic Stimulation. *Brain Topogr.* **2008**, *21*, 1–10. [CrossRef]
88. Weisz, N.; Lüchinger, C.; Thut, G.; Müller, N. Effects of individual alpha rTMS applied to the auditory cortex and its implications for the treatment of chronic tinnitus. *Hum. Brain Mapp.* **2014**, *35*, 14–29. [CrossRef] [PubMed]
89. Weisz, N.; Steidle, L.; Lorenz, I. Formerly known as inhibitory: Effects of 1-Hz rTMS on auditory cortex are state-dependent: Formerly known as inhibitory. *Eur. J. Neurosci.* **2012**, *36*, 2077–2087. [CrossRef] [PubMed]
90. De Ridder, D.; Verstraeten, E.; Van der Kelen, K.; De Mulder, G.; Sunaert, S.; Verlooy, J.; Van de Heyning, P.; Moller, A. Transcranial Magnetic Stimulation for Tinnitus: Influence of Tinnitus Duration on Stimulation Parameter Choice and Maximal Tinnitus Suppression. *Otol. Neurotol.* **2005**, *26*, 616–619. [CrossRef]
91. King, R.O.C.; Shekhawat, G.S.; King, C.; Chan, E.; Kobayashi, K.; Searchfield, G.D. The Effect of Auditory Residual Inhibition on Tinnitus and the Electroencephalogram. *Ear Hear.* **2021**, *42*, 130–141. [CrossRef] [PubMed]
92. Thut, G.; Veniero, D.; Romei, V.; Miniussi, C.; Schyns, P.; Gross, J. Rhythmic TMS Causes Local Entrainment of Natural Oscillatory Signatures. *Curr. Biol.* **2011**, *21*, 1176–1185. [CrossRef] [PubMed]
93. Wagner, J.; Makeig, S.; Hoopes, D.; Gola, M. Can Oscillatory Alpha-Gamma Phase-Amplitude Coupling be Used to Understand and Enhance TMS Effects? *Front. Hum. Neurosci.* **2019**, *13*, 263. [CrossRef] [PubMed]

Journal of *Personalized Medicine*

MDPI

Article

Focality-Oriented Selection of Current Dose for Transcranial Direct Current Stimulation

Rajan Kashyap [1,*], Sagarika Bhattacharjee [2], Ramaswamy Arumugam [1,3], Rose Dawn Bharath [4], Kaviraja Udupa [5], Kenichi Oishi [6], John E. Desmond [6,†], S. H. Annabel Chen [2,3,7,8,‡] and Cuntai Guan [1,*,‡]

1 School of Computer Science and Engineering, Nanyang Technological University, 50 Nanyang Avenue, Singapore 639798, Singapore; ARUMUGAM004@e.ntu.edu.sg
2 School of Social Sciences (SSS), Nanyang Technological University, Singapore 639818, Singapore; bhattacharya.sagarika7@gmail.com (S.B.); annabelchen@ntu.edu.sg (S.H.A.C.)
3 Centre for Research and Development in Learning (CRADLE), Nanyang Technological University, Singapore 637460, Singapore
4 Department of Neuroimaging and Interventional Radiology, National Institute of Mental Health and Neurosciences, Hosur Road, Bangalore 560029, India; drrosedawn@nimhans.kar.nic.in
5 Department of Neurophysiology, National Institute of Mental Health and Neurosciences, Hosur Road, Bangalore 560029, India; kaviudupa.nimhans@nic.in
6 The Johns Hopkins University School of Medicine, Baltimore, MD 21205, USA; koishi@mri.jhu.edu (K.O.); jdesmon2@jhmi.edu (J.E.D.)
7 Lee Kong Chian School of Medicine (LKC Medicine), Nanyang Technological University, Singapore 637553, Singapore
8 National Institute of Education, Nanyang Technological University, Singapore 637553, Singapore
* Correspondence: rajankashyap6@gmail.com (R.K.); ctguan@ntu.edu.sg (C.G.)
† Senior author.
‡ Equal contribution.

Citation: Kashyap, R.; Bhattacharjee, S.; Arumugam, R.; Bharath, R.D.; Udupa, K.; Oishi, K.; Desmond, J.E.; Chen, S.H.A.; Guan, C. Focality-Oriented Selection of Current Dose for Transcranial Direct Current Stimulation. *J. Pers. Med.* **2021**, *11*, 940. https://doi.org/10.3390/jpm11090940

Academic Editors: Yoshihiro Noda and Chiara Villa

Received: 22 June 2021
Accepted: 18 September 2021
Published: 21 September 2021

Abstract: Background: In transcranial direct current stimulation (tDCS), the injected current becomes distributed across the brain areas. The objective is to stimulate the target region of interest (ROI) while minimizing the current in non-target ROIs (the 'focality' of tDCS). For this purpose, determining the appropriate current dose for an individual is difficult. **Aim:** To introduce a dose–target determination index (DTDI) to quantify the focality of tDCS and examine the dose–focality relationship in three different populations. **Method:** Here, we extended our previous toolbox i-SATA to the MNI reference space. After a tDCS montage is simulated for a current dose, the i-SATA(MNI) computes the average (over voxels) current density for every region in the brain. DTDI is the ratio of the average current density at the target ROI to the ROI with a maximum value (the peak region). Ideally, target ROI should be the peak region, so DTDI shall range from 0 to 1. The higher the value, the better the dose. We estimated the variation of DTDI within and across individuals using T1-weighted brain images of 45 males and females distributed equally across three age groups: (a) young adults ($20 \leq x < 40$ years), (b) mid adults ($40 \leq x < 60$ years), and (c) older adults ($60 \leq x < 80$ years). DTDI's were evaluated for the frontal montage with electrodes at F3 and the right supraorbital for three current doses of 1 mA, 2 mA, and 3 mA, with the target ROI at the left middle frontal gyrus. **Result:** As the dose is incremented, DTDI may show (a) increase, (b) decrease, and (c) no change across the individuals depending on the relationship (nonlinear or linear) between the injected tDCS current and the distribution of current density in the target ROI. The nonlinearity is predominant in older adults with a decrease in focality. The decline is stronger in males. Higher current dose at older age can enhance the focality of stimulation. **Conclusion:** DTDI provides information on which tDCS current dose will optimize the focality of stimulation. The recommended DTDI dose should be prioritized based on the age (>40 years) and sex (especially for males) of an individual. The toolbox i-SATA(MNI) is freely available.

Keywords: transcranial direct current stimulation (tDCS); realistic volumetric approach-based simulator for transcranial electric stimulation (ROAST); systematic approach for tDCS analysis (SATA); current dose; individualized tDCS; age and sex difference

1. Introduction

Transcranial direct current stimulation (tDCS) is a noninvasive brain stimulation technique that could alleviate symptoms of several neurological and psychiatric brain disorders [1–3]. A conventional tDCS setup consists of an anode and cathode placed over the scalp (referred to as a 'montage') with a low intensity of current (~1–3 mA) being injected to stimulate the target region of interest (ROI) [4,5]. However, the injected current becomes diffused in the intermediary regions of the brain and might not effectively stimulate the target ROI with the desired intensity [6,7]. Computational models that predict the pattern of current flow across the brain of an individual are used to optimize the tDCS stimulation parameters [8–14]. The amount of injected current (referred as the 'current dose') plays an important role in the dispersal of the stimulation's intensity across the brain regions [15,16]. The distribution may vary from person to person and within a person based on the quantity of the dose [17–19]. Therefore, the selection of the optimal current dose for an individual's brain that could sufficiently stimulate the target ROI while minimizing the current in non-target ROIs is important.

In recent years, there has been a growing interest in the individualization of the current dose [15,16,20]. It has been reported that varying the current intensity on the scalp for each individual can reduce the interindividual variability in the electric field intensity (or current density) at the target ROI [20]. The current dose calculated through inverse modelling of the tDCS-induced electric field at the target ROI correlates with the motor thresholds generated by transcranial magnetic stimulation [15]. In a recent tDCS experiment using a frontal montage and a 2 mA (fixed) current dose, individuals with a high current density at the target ROI (left dorsolateral prefrontal cortex) were found to have stronger improvements in working memory compared to those with a low current density [21]. They also showed that individualizing the current dose by fixing the desired current density at the target region can maximize the benefits of tDCS [21]. Though the models are a step towards individualizing the current dose, they do not consider the spread of the field to intermediary (non-target) regions. The current flow in the intermediary regions have a vital role to play in determining the outcome of tDCS [6,12,22–25]. It has been found that some brain regions may act as conduits, clustering most of the current to a specific location that can deter the intensity of the stimulation expected at the target ROI [6,26]. At this point, it is important to mention that other stimulation techniques (like peripheral nerve stimulation) are also intended to increase the stimulation intensity at target region while minimizing the stimulation received at non-target regions [27–30]. With tDCS, poor focality in stimulating the target region has constrained its efficacy. Therefore, the approaches to individualize the current dose [31–34] should consider the focality of stimulation in order to recommend the optimal intensity of input current.

In our previous work, we developed an individual-Systematic-Approach-for-tDCS-Analysis (i-SATA) toolbox [35] that estimates the average current density received by target ROIs and intermediary regions of an individual's brain after a montage has been simulated in a realistic volumetric approach-based simulator for transcranial electric stimulation (ROAST) toolbox [10]. The ROAST-simulated current density in the ROIs has been found to be strongly correlated with electrophysiological measurements performed in vivo [9]. Integrated with ROAST, the i-SATA toolbox can be applied on an individual brain to reverse-calculate the current dose that can be used to stimulate the target ROI with the desired intensity [35]. This was performed based on the assumption that electric field intensity at the target ROI increases linearly with increase in the current dose by following the procedure laid down by Evans et al. [20]. Since we will be using it throughout the study, it will be helpful to familiarize our readers with an example. Suppose the calculated current density at the target ROI is 0.25 mA/m^2 when 1 mA of current is applied on the scalp. To achieve a desired density of 0.5 mA/m^2 at the target ROI, the required dosage (individualized) can be reverse-calculated as $Individualised\ dose = \left(\frac{Desired\ Current\ Density}{Actual\ Current\ Density}\right) \times Fixed\ dose$ [i.e., $\left(\frac{0.5}{0.25}\right) \times 1 = 2$ mA].

In i-SATA, we used the Talairach client toolbox [36] to map an individual brain to the Talairach atlas space [37]. Another widely used brain template that provides detailed stereotaxic information on the location and variability of cortical areas is provided by the Montreal Neurological Institute (MNI) reference space [38–42]. Simon et al. [43–45] had developed the SPM anatomy toolbox that integrates the cytoarchitectonic maps in the MNI space. Here, we leveraged the potential of the SPM anatomy toolbox to extend i-SATA to the MNI space. The extended i-SATA(MNI) toolbox, which integrates the SPM anatomy toolbox with i-SATA, will enable researchers to visualize the comprehensive overview of the current density distribution across the cortex (target and intermediary regions) in the MNI space.

With i-SATA(MNI), we introduce the *dose–target determination index* (DTDI), a simple estimate that will quantify the focality of stimulation and facilitate the selection of optimal current dose required to stimulate the target ROI in an individual's brain. A similar metric defined as the 'selectivity index' that measures the recruitment of the targeted region compared to other non-targeted regions is used to quantify the effectiveness of peripheral nerve stimulation [27–30]. For tDCS, the DTDI will aim to provide a comprehensive overview of the intensity of the stimulation received by the target ROI and intermediary regions after a montage has been postprocessed in i-SATA(MNI). To explain DTDI, we will use the montage with an anode positioned at F3 and a cathode at the right supraorbital (RSO) (referred to as F3-RSO). The montage has been shown to stimulate the left middle frontal gyrus [22,25] and is effective for depression [3,22,46] and working memory [47]. To make it easy for our readers to interpret how DTDI facilitates selection of the current dose, we will show the interindividual as well as the intraindividual variation in the index by uniformly increasing the current dose. Finally, we will evaluate the variation in DTDI by the age and sex of individuals. The purpose will be to explore if dose selection should be prioritised for any category (age and sex) of individuals.

2. Methods

2.1. Data

We obtained the T1-weighted (T1WI) magnetic resonance image (MRI) of the brain of 90 age–sex matched healthy individuals (45 male) from Cambridge Centre for Ageing and Neuroscience (Cam-CAN) study (available at http://www.mrc-cbu.cam.ac.uk/datasets/camcan/, accessed on 21 October 2020 [48,49]). This study was approved by the local ethics committee, Cambridgeshire 2, Research Ethics Committee (reference: 10/H0308/50). In this study, the Cam-CAN team recruited adult participants (aged 18–87 years old) in three stages that comprised of a home-based interview (stage one), followed by an evaluation of their health status (stage two). Subjects that were cognitively healthy (determined by a mini-mental state exam (MMSE) score ≥ 27), who met hearing, vision, and English language ability criteria, and who were free of MRI contraindications and neurologic or psychiatric conditions were recruited for stage three. In stage three, multimodal data (functional and structural MRI, magnetoencephalography, and behavioural) were collected from each participant. The T1WIs were collected from a 3T Siemens TIM Trio scanner with a 32-channel head coil using an MPRAGE sequence, TR = 2250 milliseconds (ms), TE = 2.99 ms, flip angle = 9°, Voxel size = $1 \times 1 \times 1$ mm^3, FOV = $256 \times 240 \times 192$ mm^3, GRAPPA: 2; TI: 900 ms. We selected 90 T1WIs from the following three age groups with 30 individuals (15 right-handed males and females) in each group:(a) young adults ($20 \leq x < 40$ years), (b) mid adults ($40 \leq x < 60$ years), and (c) older adults ($60 \leq x < 80$ years) were selected. The equal grouping across the three groups would allow an evaluation of the relationship of tDCS current dosage with sex and age.

2.2. Preprocessing with ROAST

We simulated the montage F3-RSO with the electrode size 5×5 cm^2 (Figure 1A). For each individual MRI, the montages were simulated for three current doses of 1 mA, 2 mA, and 3 mA. In total, 270 simulations were performed in ROAST (Total = 90 MRI × 3 current doses = 270) [10]. Default conductivity values of the tissues (white matter (default 0.126 S/m); grey matter (default 0.276 S/m); cerebrospinal fluid (default 1.65 S/m); bone (default 0.01 S/m); skin (default 0.465 S/m); air (default 2.5 × 10^{-14} S/m); gel (default 0.3 S/m); electrode (default 5.9 × 10^7 S/m)) were used for each MRI that we simulated in ROAST. The ROAST simulation outputs the locations (x, y, and z coordinates) of the brain regions and the current density (mA/m^2) value at each location in the native space.

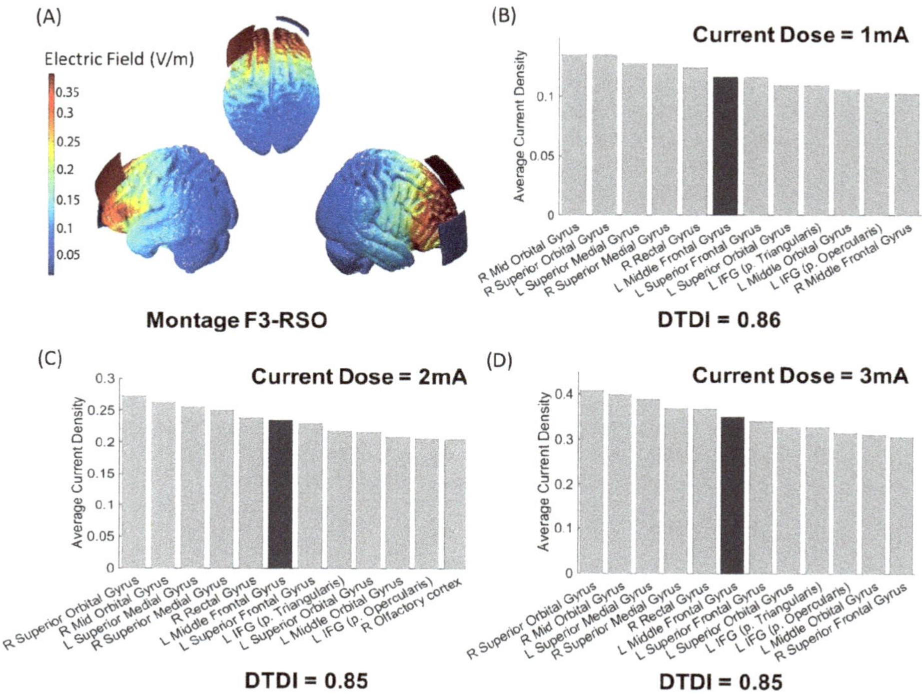

Figure 1. Illustration of the applied montage F3-RSO (shown in (**A**)) and output of i-SATA(MNI) for the MNI152 standard head image across the three current doses: (**B**) 1 mA; (**C**) 2 mA; and (**D**) 3 mA. The average current density at the target ROI (left middle frontal gyrus) is shown in the dark-gray colored bar. The DTDI index (~0.85) remains fairly constant across the three current doses, indicating a linear relationship between the injected current and induced electric field. For the standard head, tDCS users can choose any current dose, and their choice depends on the intensity of the desired stimulation in the target ROI. Note that the i-SATA(MNI) outputs shown in the figure highlight only the ROIs that received the highest current density (top 10%) amongst all other areas. A user can use the i-SATA(MNI) toolbox to obtain the average current density across all the brain regions.

2.3. *i-SATA(MNI)*

The i-SATA(MNI) is similar to i-SATA (available for download at https://doi.org/10.21979/N9/5W3RIM, [35]) except for the atlas space. In short, for each montage simulated in ROAST, i-SATA extracts the location (x, y, and z coordinates) of all the points in the cortex to detect the location of three anatomical landmarks (anterior commissure, posterior commissure, and mid-sagittal) using the acpcdetect toolbox [35,50]. With these landmarks, the individual's native space was mapped to the reference space (i.e., the Talairach atlas space) using the fieldtrip toolbox [51] followed by the Talairach client toolbox [36]. Details on the methodology and application can be obtained from previous works [11,35,52]. For i-SATA(MNI), instead of the Talairach atlas space, we mapped the outputs (x, y, and z coordinates) to the MNI reference space using the SPM anatomy toolbox [43–45]. The SPM anatomy toolbox has an option for using the gyri/sulci-based labelling system wherein the automated anatomical labeling atlas with 116 regions outlined on the Colin27 brain template is implemented (for details, see [53]). The i-SATA(MNI) extracts and uses the labels provided by this atlas for assigning the cortical and subcortical region corresponding to each location. A detailed explanation on the nomenclature of the delineated regions can be found at [53]. We developed i-SATA(MNI) using SPM12 (revision 6470, available at https://www.fil.ion.ucl.ac.uk/spm/software/spm12/) that has the SPM Anatomy toolbox (version 2.2b) inbuilt into the framework. The magnitude of current density corresponding to each location (voxel) was then used to obtain the average magnitude of the current density received by each cortical region of the brain. This will provide an estimate of the current density induced in the target and intermediary region due to tDCS. As an example, we will postprocess the standard MNI 152 averaged head in i-SATA(MNI) for the three current doses (1 mA, 2 mA, and 3 mA) using the F3-RSO montage to show the distribution of the average current density across the cortical regions (Figure 1B–D).

2.4. Dose–Target Determination Index (DTDI)

The output of i-SATA(MNI) (i.e., the average current density in the target ROI and the non-target regions) is used to calculate the DTDI for a montage simulated at a current dose. For this, we will find the ROI that has the maximum value of average current density (peak region) amongst all the ROIs. DTDI is then calculated as

$$DTDI = \frac{Average\ Current\ density\ at\ the\ Target\ ROI}{Maximum\ value\ of\ average\ current\ density\ formed\ at\ any\ ROI}$$

DTDI will lie within the range of 0 to 1. An ideal tDCS setup will deliver the maximum intensity of stimulation (average current density) to the target ROI, thereby generating a DTDI value equal to 1. However, the peak intensity may be received at non-targeted ROI. A DTDI value = 0 will indicate no stimulation of the target ROI. For an individual, the current dose for which DTDI is higher should be preferred over other doses. To make this clear, we will estimate the DTDI of three individuals across three current doses. Hypothetically, the value of the DTDI should remain constant across doses, since it is assumed that the current flow in the brain increases linearly with an increase in current intensity [15,16,20,23,54].

2.5. Statistical Analysis of Variation in DTDI

All individual MRIs were post-processed in i-SATA(MNI) for the three current doses using the F3-RSO montage to estimate the DTDI's (Total = 90 MRI × 3 current doses = 270). We show the interindividual and intraindividual variation in the DTDI for both sexes across the three age groups. We performed a three-way mixed ANOVA with age and sex as between subject and dose as within subject factor. Post hoc analyses were performed to further characterize the nature of the main effects and interactions.

2.6. Code Availability

The i-SATA(MNI) is a Linux-based MATLAB toolbox integrating acpcdetect v2.0, fieldtrip, and SPM12 (version 6470) with the integrated SPM Anatomy toolbox (version 2.2b). The package can be downloaded at (https://doi.org/10.21979/N9/KWTCWK). A reference manual is also provided to help users run each step with ease.

3. Results

3.1. Output of i-SATA(MNI) on the Standard Head Model

The montage F3-RSO that we applied to the MNI 152 averaged head model and simulated in ROAST is shown in Figure 1A. The output of i-SATA(MNI), i.e., the distribution of the average current density across the cortical regions, are shown in Figure 1B–D for the three current doses (1 mA, 2 mA, and 3 mA). The average current density in the target ROI (the left middle frontal gyrus) varies linearly with the current dose. Therefore, the DTDI remains constant (at approximately ~ 0.85) across the doses. Of note, similarly to i-SATA [35] and SATA (the standard head model with a graphical user interface is available for download at https://doi.org/10.21979/N9/DMWPZK [11,52,55]), users can visualize the i-SATA(MNI) outputs on the brain surface as well (Figure not shown).

3.2. Interpretation of DTDI for Appropriate Selection of Current Dose

For any individual, DTDI can guide the selection of the appropriate current dose that will sufficiently stimulate the target ROI with minimal spread of current to other regions. For interpretation, we have shown the variation of DTDI for three individuals across the three current doses (Figure 2). For the first individual, the current intensity at the target region increases with the increase in dose, and the DTDI remains fairly constant (Figure 2A). This implies that the target ROI will be sufficiently stimulated by any current dose, and that the user can tune it according to the extent of stimulation desired. For the second individual, a low DTDI (0.43) is seen at lower dose (1 mA) suggesting that target ROI is receiving minimal current and non-target regions are receiving most of the current. With the increase in dose, it can be seen that the current intensity at the target ROI is increasing, but fewer regions are receiving a current higher than the target ROI. As a result, the DTDI is increasing with increase in the dose, suggesting that higher current dose should be beneficial (Figure 2B). Finally for the third individual, a decrease in DTDI is seen with the increase in dose (Figure 2C). The drop in DTDI from 1 mA to 2 and 3 mA seems to be due to an increase in current in the right superior parietal lobule at 2 mA and 3 mA only. Although the current intensity at the target ROI increases with the increases in the dose, the maximal amount of current also becomes dissipated to other brain regions. Thus, the conventional way of increasing the current dose to attain the desired stimulation intensity at the target ROI might result in the stimulation of unwanted brain regions (as seen for the superior parietal lobule). For this individual, a lower dose showing higher DTDI can maximize the advantages of stimulation.

3.3. Statistical Analysis of Variance in DTDI

The change in DTDI as a function of the dose for males and females across three age groups is shown in Figure 3. The mixed ANOVA revealed a significant main effect of age (F(2, 84) = 43.98, $p = 8.51 \times 10^{-14}$, effect size = 0.405 (generalised eta squared)), with DTDI significantly decreasing in older adults compared to young adults ($p = 0.0008$). The main effect of sex (F(1, 84) = 12.14, $p < 7.85 \times 10^{-4}$, effect size = 0.086) and its interaction with age (F(2, 84) = 3.78, $p = 2.70 \times 10^{-2}$, effect size = 0.05) was also found to be significant. The post hoc analysis shows that females had higher DTDI values than males for both mid ($p = 2.89 \times 10^{-6}$) and older adults ($p = 3.18 \times 10^{-3}$). The interaction effect of age and dose was also found to be significant (F(3.34, 140.48) = 7.269, $p = 7.65 \times 10^{-5}$, effect size = 0.05). In older adults only, the post hoc analysis revealed that there is a significant increase in the DTDI values at 3 mA compared to 1 mA for both males ($p = 0.01$) and females ($p = 0.02$). All the post hoc pairwise comparisons were Bonferroni-corrected. This shows that the focality of stimulation could be enhanced in older adults by increasing the dose.

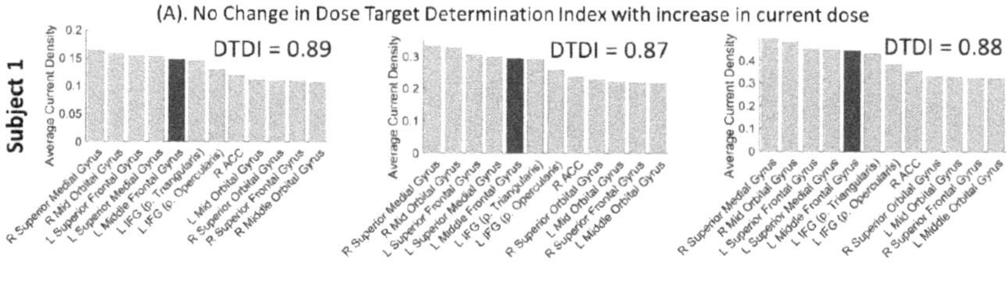

Figure 2. *Cont.*

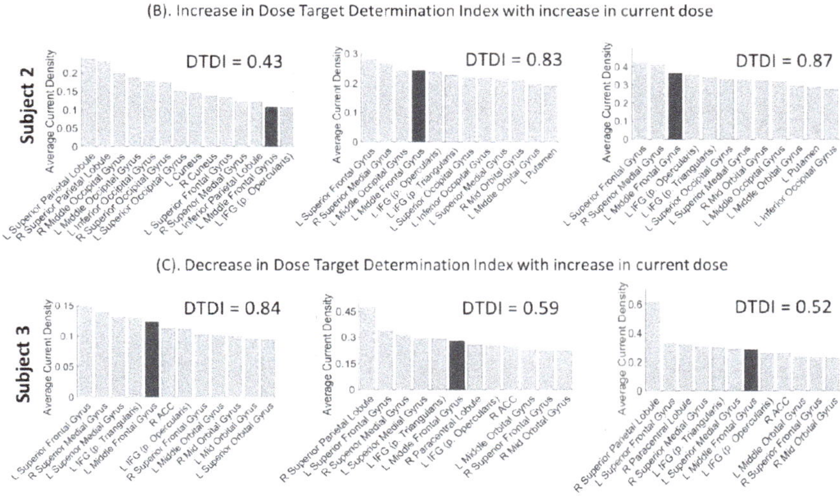

Figure 2. Illustration of the variation in DTDI for three current doses (1 mA, 2 mA, and 3 mA) with F3-RSO montage applied over three individuals showing: (**A**) no change in DTDI with an increase in current dose; (**B**) increase in DTDI with an increase in current dose; and (**C**) decrease in DTDI with an increase in current dose. Subject 1, with no change in DTDI, is neutral to variation in current dose, and the dose can be adjusted based on the intensity of the stimulation desired at the target ROI. Subject 2, showing increase in DTDI, would receive adequate stimulation from a higher dose (above 1 mA), whereas subject 3, showing a decrease, will most likely benefit from the lower dose (1 mA).

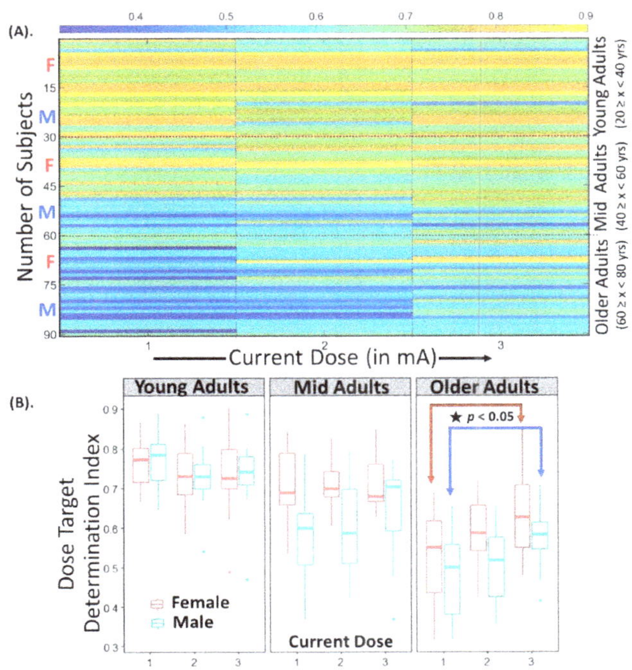

Figure 3. Illustration of the variation in DTDI at individual and group level with: (**A**) The individual variation of DTDI values (0 to 1) in the females (font in red 'F') and males (font in blue 'M') distributed

equally across the three age groups ((i) young adults ($20 \leq x < 40$ years), (ii) mid adults ($40 \leq x < 60$ years), and (iii) older adults ($60 \leq x < 80$ years)) for the three current doses (1 mA, 2 mA, and 3 mA). The interindividual and intraindividual variation in DTDI clearly shows the current dose that could be appropriate for an individual to stimulate the target ROI after a montage has been fixed; (**B**) The variation of DTDI for both sexes across the three age groups using a three-way mixed ANOVA. The DTDI decreases with an increase in age. In mid and older adults, females show higher focality compared to males for the three current doses (1 mA, 2 mA, and 3 mA). In older adults only, the significant ($p < 0.05$, Bonferroni-corrected) difference between DTDI at 1 mA and 3 mA for both sexes conveys that higher current doses are required to appropriately stimulate the target ROI.

4. Discussion

In this paper, we extended the toolbox i-SATA [35] to the MNI reference space to enable users to obtain the average current density induced at each cortical region of an individual's brain during tDCS. We then used these values to estimate the DTDI as an objective measure to quantify the focality of stimulation and aid the selection of appropriate current dose for an individual. We demonstrated the utility of DTDI across three subjects and doses (Figure 2). The optimal stimulation of the target ROI was experienced differently across the three subjects: (a) subject 1 was neutral to changes in current dose, and the electric field intensity remained proportional to the injected current; (b) subject 2 had better focality from a dose of 2 mA or more (but not from 1 mA); and (c) subject 3 gained better stimulation from 1 mA compared to 2 or 3 mA of current dose. Such interindividual inconsistency in tDCS due to the current dose has been widely reported in previous studies [17–19,56–62]. With this i-SATA(MNI) framework post-processing the structural scans simulated in ROAST, tDCS users can configure personalized protocols for montage selection (refer to [11,35]) and identify the optimal current dose for cortical targeting (guided by DTDI). We applied the framework on a wide age range (20 to 80 years) of individuals from both sexes to highlight the importance of DTDI and the need for a focality-based selection of the current dose.

Previous tDCS based studies have combined electroencephalography, functional MRI, or transcranial magnetic stimulation to determine the current dose for optimal targeting [63–66]. Recently, a computational study has put forward the model to reverse calculate the current dose from the simulated electric field [16] based on the assumption that the intensity of current flow increases linearly with current dose [54]. A similar prototype was also put forward by Evans et al. [20]. All these studies used young, healthy subjects to delineate the model. On one hand, we see this linearity (constant value of DTDI) being followed in the MNI standard head model (Figure 1) and to an extent in young and middle-aged individuals (Figures 2A and 3A). However, on the other hand, linearity appears to diminish with advancement in age (Figures 2B,C and 3A), suggesting a potential nonlinear relationship.

The different values of DTDI as a function of current dose across different subjects could be because the injected current might become clustered in brain areas (referred to as hotspots), a phenomenon that has been widely reported in tDCS studies [6,25,26,67–69]. Hotspots cause shunting of the current towards the surrounding brain tissue and a surge in the electric field strength at localised areas [70]. Areas that form hotspots can be away from the electrode site as well [70]. In the two cases presented in Figure 2 (Subject 2 and 3), the superior parietal lobule appears to be a hotspot. Here, it is difficult to comprehend the neuroanatomical factors that contribute to the formation of such hotspots. It has been found that tissue heterogeneities and pathological alterations (like neurodegeneration and cerebral infarcts) are the primary contributors [26,70]. As we age, atrophy in the neural configuration escalates the nonlinearities in the spatial distribution of induced electric fields [71,72]. Care must be taken to limit the possibilities of such hotspots forming for clinical application of tDCS [73]. DTDI that considers the current density in target and non-target areas incorporates an understanding of the effect of hotspots to provide a rigorous estimate of the optimal current dose.

Since maximum stimulation might not be received at the target ROI, nor in a consistent location [6,17,18,74], the interindividual and intraindividual variation in DTDI can provide insights for the appropriate determination of current dose based on the age and sex of a healthy individual. In young adults, the focality of stimulation remains intact (approximately) across the doses, indicating that there is flexibility in choosing (individualizing) a dose depending on the extent of current density desired at the target ROI. However, the focality declines with advancing age (middle age onwards, see Figure 3). This decline is higher for males compared to females. Such sexual dimorphism in tDCS-related effects have been reported in previous studies [75] and several factors related to cortical anatomy like volume [76], bone density [77], hormonal levels [77], and electrode location have been postulated to account for it. We also found that higher current doses can enhance the focality in older adults. This is in support of a recent study [78] which reported that cerebral atrophy in older adults was causing the reduction in the amount of current reaching the target ROI. With that being said, we feel that it is important to guide our readers on how to use DTDI in their tDCS study (at an individual or group level), wherein their interest may lie in stimulating single or multiple target ROIs. We will discuss this in the next section.

How to Use DTDI

(A). DTDI for Group-level Study

We have shown how DTDI can be used to titrate the current dose at the individual level. This can be performed at the group level also. Evans et al. [20] have suggested that the input current should be varied across individuals to maintain a constant current density at the target ROI. While we agree with them, we also suggest that the focality of the stimulation needs to be considered, especially when older individuals are recruited for the study. For primary clinical/therapeutic applications of tDCS, the focality, as revealed by DTDI, could be especially useful for setting tDCS dosage. Although the compatibility of the patient with the computationally recommended dose is always important [79], recent studies have indicated that participants readily tolerate tDCS current up to 4 mA [80,81].

In group studies in which researchers do not want to vary the current from subject to subject, DTDI values may still be used in two different ways to improve the efficacy of the study. The first would be to include a threshold for DTDI (e.g., DTDI ≥ 0.75) as a precautionary measure when individualizing the current dose. We recommend this value because studies pertaining to peripheral nerve stimulation have also found that such a threshold value (≥ 0.75) for the 'selectivity index' could ensure that the targeted region of the nerve is well activated [28,30]. While this may narrow down the suitability of subjects, such inclusion criteria could reduce the variability of tDCS. The second would be to use DTDI analyses for the populations under study to determine, at the start of the study, the optimal value of the tDCS current dose to be used on all subjects that will produce the greatest focality and the least amount of subject–subject variability in DTDI. For example, the current study suggests that for the F3-RSO montage, if you are including older and younger subjects, a higher current value (for the study overall) might produce the least variability in terms of focality of tDCS.

(B). DTDI for Multiple Target ROIs

We have shown how DTDI can be used for a target ROI. However, a user may be interested in stimulating multiple target ROIs, or a network of ROIs specific to a particular functionality [82–88]. This may be because studies have shown that more than one brain area can be involved in neuropsychiatric disorders like depression [89,90]. Alternatively (in an unexpected scenario), it may also happen that two or more ROIs receive the same current density after a montage is simulated for an individual's brain. In such scenarios, the DTDI can be averaged across all the target ROIs ($\frac{DTDI\ for\ first\ TargetROI + DTDI\ for\ second\ TargetROI + \ldots + DTDI\ for\ nth\ targetROI}{Number\ of\ areas\ (n)}$). The averaged DTDI will also lie in between 0 and 1. The optimal dose should focus on determining the current at which the value of the averaged DTDI exhibits an increasing trend.

5. Limitations

Here, we show how DTDI aids selection of focality-based current dose in tDCS. Although the findings on the relationship between tDCS dose, sex, and age could be limited by the small sample size, they reveal that, while brains which have a linear relationship between the electric field intensity and the tDCS current are flexible to the selection of current dose, brains that have a nonlinear relationship are dose sensitive. Therefore, biomarkers that could identify brains that can behave nonlinearly prior to the onset of an experiment could improve the precision of tDCS. However, this will require large datasets for validation of the biomarker. We leave it for future studies to investigate the exact nature of such nonlinearities and to determine the factors (structural, functional, and behavioural) that contribute to them.

Finally, we would like to highlight that DTDI can be estimated from i-SATA as well. The Talairach atlas space has several benefits [36], and similarly the i-SATA(MNI) that was developed for users who prefer the MNI space has its own advantages [43]. However, simulation in i-SATA(MNI) is considerably faster than in i-SATA. This is because both i-SATA(MNI) and the integrated SPM anatomy toolbox for cortical labelling are MATLAB-based and automated. This makes i-SATA(MNI) efficient at post-processing large data sets, a trend that is emerging in neuroscientific research.

6. Conclusions

The study extends the i-SATA framework to the MNI atlas space. With i-SATA(MNI), it will be easier to calculate the individualized dose as suggested in previous studies [15,16,20,21]. Here, we introduce the DTDI as a measure to titrate the individualized current doses and select the optimum dose that has high focality and could appropriately stimulate the target ROI in an individual. This will facilitate the personalized application of tDCS so that the desired stimulation benefits are achieved. Using a montage that has been found to be optimal for a DLPFC stimulation, DTDI analysis across a broad spectrum of men and women of different age groups has revealed that focality decreases with advancing age, especially in males with more than 40 years of age. Finally, the study reveals that the selection of a current dose that increases the focality is strictly necessary for older (>60 years) individuals irrespective of sex.

Author Contributions: Conceptualization, R.K. and S.B.; methodology, R.K. and R.A.; software, R.A. and R.K.; validation, R.A., S.B. and R.K.; formal analysis, R.K. and S.B.; investigation, R.K.; resources, S.H.A.C. and C.G.; data curation, S.B.; writing—original draft preparation, R.K.; writing—review and editing, J.E.D., S.H.A.C., K.O., R.D.B., K.U. and C.G.; visualization, K.O. and J.E.D.; supervision, S.H.A.C. and C.G.; project administration, R.K. and C.G.; funding acquisition, C.G. All authors have read and agreed to the published version of the manuscript.

Funding: The work is funded by the grant RIE2020 AME Programmatic Fund, Singapore (No. A20G8b0102).

Institutional Review Board Statement: Not Applicable to the study.

Informed Consent Statement: Not Applicable to the study.

Data Availability Statement: We would like to convey our gratitude to the CAM-CAN team (https://camcan-archive.mrc-cbu.cam.ac.uk/dataaccess/) for providing access to the dataset.

Acknowledgments: We acknowledge the contribution from the RIE2020 AME Programmatic Fund, Singapore (No. A20G8b0102) to our work. The work was also supported by the NTU-JHU grant from Nanyang Technological University, Singapore. J.D. received additional support from the NIH/NICHD grant P50 HD103538. R.K. and S.B. have support from the DBT Ramalingaswami Re-entry fellowship scheme (2021), sponsored by the Government of India.

Conflicts of Interest: The authors declare no conflict of interest.

References

1. Antal, A.; Alekseichuk, I.; Bikson, M.; Brockmöller, J.; Brunoni, A.R.; Chen, R.; Cohen, L.G.; Dowthwaite, G.; Ellrich, J.; Flöel, A. Low intensity transcranial electric stimulation: Safety, ethical, legal regulatory and application guidelines. *Clin. Neurophysiol.* **2017**, *128*, 1774–1809. [CrossRef]
2. Filmer, H.L.; Dux, P.E.; Mattingley, J.B. Applications of transcranial direct current stimulation for understanding brain function. *Trends Neurosci.* **2014**, *37*, 742–753. [CrossRef]
3. Razza, L.B.; Palumbo, P.; Moffa, A.H.; Carvalho, A.F.; Solmi, M.; Loo, C.K.; Brunoni, A.R. A systematic review and meta-analysis on the effects of transcranial direct current stimulation in depressive episodes. *Depress. Anxiety* **2020**, *37*, 594–608. [CrossRef] [PubMed]
4. Nitsche, M.A.; Doemkes, S.; Karakose, T.; Antal, A.; Liebetanz, D.; Lang, N.; Tergau, F.; Paulus, W. Shaping the effects of transcranial direct current stimulation of the human motor cortex. *J. Neurophysiol.* **2007**, *97*, 3109–3117. [CrossRef] [PubMed]
5. Nitsche, M.A.; Paulus, W. Excitability changes induced in the human motor cortex by weak transcranial direct current stimulation. *J. Physiol.* **2000**, *527*, 633–639. [CrossRef] [PubMed]
6. Datta, A.; Bansal, V.; Diaz, J.; Patel, J.; Reato, D.; Bikson, M. Gyri-precise head model of transcranial direct current stimulation: Improved spatial focality using a ring electrode versus conventional rectangular pad. *Brain Stimul.* **2009**, *2*, 201–207. [CrossRef] [PubMed]
7. Batsikadze, G.; Moliadze, V.; Paulus, W.; Kuo, M.-F.; Nitsche, M.A. Partially non-linear stimulation intensity-dependent effects of direct current stimulation on motor cortex excitability in humans. *J. Physiol.* **2013**, *591*, 1987–2000. [CrossRef] [PubMed]
8. Indahlastari, A.; Chauhan, M.; Sadleir, R. Benchmarking transcranial electrical stimulation finite element simulations: A comparison study. *J. Neural Eng.* **2019**, *16*, 026019. [CrossRef] [PubMed]
9. Huang, Y.; Liu, A.A.; Lafon, B.; Friedman, D.; Dayan, M.; Wang, X.; Bikson, M.; Doyle, W.K.; Devinsky, O.; Parra, L.C. Measurements and models of electric fields in the in vivo human brain during transcranial electric stimulation. *eLife* **2017**, *6*, e18834. [CrossRef] [PubMed]
10. Huang, Y.; Datta, A.; Bikson, M.; Parra, L.C. Realistic volumetric-approach to simulate transcranial electric stimulation—ROAST—a fully automated open-source pipeline. *J. Neural Eng.* **2019**, *16*, 056006. [CrossRef] [PubMed]
11. Bhattacharjee, S.; Kashyap, R.; Rapp, B.; Oishi, K.; Desmond, J.E.; Chen, S.A. Simulation Analyses of tDcS Montages for the investigation of Dorsal and Ventral pathways. *Sci. Rep.* **2019**, *9*, 1–17. [CrossRef]
12. Bikson, M.; Datta, A.; Rahman, A.; Scaturro, J. Electrode montages for tDCS and weak transcranial electrical stimulation: Role of "return" electrode's position and size. *Clin. Neurophysiol. Off. J. Int. Fed. Clin. Neurophysiol.* **2010**, *121*, 1976. [CrossRef]
13. Opitz, A.; Falchier, A.; Yan, C.-G.; Yeagle, E.M.; Linn, G.S.; Megevand, P.; Thielscher, A.; Milham, M.P.; Mehta, A.D.; Schroeder, C.E. Spatiotemporal structure of intracranial electric fields induced by transcranial electric stimulation in humans and nonhuman primates. *Sci. Rep.* **2016**, *6*, 1–11.
14. Laakso, I.; Mikkonen, M.; Koyama, S.; Hirata, A.; Tanaka, S. Can electric fields explain inter-individual variability in transcranial direct current stimulation of the motor cortex? *Sci. Rep.* **2019**, *9*, 1–10.
15. Caulfield, K.A.; Badran, B.W.; Li, X.; Bikson, M.; George, M.S. Can transcranial electrical stimulation motor threshold estimate individualized tDCS doses over the prefrontal cortex? Evidence from reverse-calculation electric field modeling. *Brain Stimul.* **2020**, *13*, 1150–1152. [CrossRef]
16. Caulfield, K.A.; Badran, B.W.; DeVries, W.H.; Summers, P.M.; Kofmehl, E.; Li, X.; Borckardt, J.J.; Bikson, M.; George, M.S. Transcranial electrical stimulation motor threshold can estimate individualized tDCS dosage from reverse-calculation electric-field modeling. *Brain Stimul.* **2020**, *13*, 961–969. [CrossRef] [PubMed]
17. Chew, T.; Ho, K.-A.; Loo, C.K. Inter-and intra-individual variability in response to transcranial direct current stimulation (tDCS) at varying current intensities. *Brain Stimul.* **2015**, *8*, 1130–1137. [CrossRef]
18. López-Alonso, V.; Fernández-del-Olmo, M.; Costantini, A.; Gonzalez-Henriquez, J.J.; Cheeran, B. Intra-individual variability in the response to anodal transcranial direct current stimulation. *Clin. Neurophysiol.* **2015**, *126*, 2342–2347. [CrossRef] [PubMed]
19. López-Alonso, V.; Cheeran, B.; Río-Rodríguez, D.; Fernández-del-Olmo, M. Inter-individual variability in response to non-invasive brain stimulation paradigms. *Brain Stimul.* **2014**, *7*, 372–380. [CrossRef] [PubMed]
20. Evans, C.; Bachmann, C.; Lee, J.S.A.; Gregoriou, E.; Ward, N.; Bestmann, S. Dose-controlled tDCS reduces electric field intensity variability at a cortical target site. *Brain Stimul.* **2020**, *13*, 125–136. [CrossRef]
21. Caulfield, K.A.; Indahlastari, A.; Nissim, N.R.; Lopez, J.W.; Fleischmann, H.H.; Woods, A.J.; George, M.S. Electric Field Strength From Prefrontal Transcranial Direct Current Stimulation Determines Degree of Working Memory Response: A Potential Application of Reverse-Calculation Modeling? *Neuromodulation* **2020**. [CrossRef]
22. Ammann, C.; Lindquist, M.A.; Celnik, P.A. Response variability of different anodal transcranial direct current stimulation intensities across multiple sessions. *Brain Stimul.* **2017**, *10*, 757–763. [CrossRef]
23. Esmaeilpour, Z.; Marangolo, P.; Hampstead, B.M.; Bestmann, S.; Galletta, E.; Knotkova, H.; Bikson, M. Incomplete evidence that increasing current intensity of tDCS boosts outcomes. *Brain Stimul.* **2018**, *11*, 310–321. [CrossRef]
24. Antal, A.; Polania, R.; Schmidt-Samoa, C.; Dechent, P.; Paulus, W. Transcranial direct current stimulation over the primary motor cortex during fMRI. *Neuroimage* **2011**, *55*, 590–596. [CrossRef] [PubMed]
25. Bai, S.; Dokos, S.; Ho, K.-A.; Loo, C. A computational modelling study of transcranial direct current stimulation montages used in depression. *Neuroimage* **2014**, *87*, 332–344. [CrossRef]

26. Wagner, T.; Fregni, F.; Fecteau, S.; Grodzinsky, A.; Zahn, M.; Pascual-Leone, A. Transcranial direct current stimulation: A computer-based human model study. *NeuroImage* **2007**, *35*, 1113–1124. [CrossRef] [PubMed]
27. Deurloo, K.E.I.; Holsheimer, J.; Bergveld, P. Nerve stimulation with a multi-contact cuff electrode: Validation of model predictions. *Arch. Physiol. Biochem.* **2000**, *108*, 349–359. [CrossRef] [PubMed]
28. Kosta, P.; Warren, D.J.; Lazzi, G. Selective stimulation of rat sciatic nerve using an array of mm-size magnetic coils: A simulation study. *Healthc. Technol. Lett.* **2019**, *6*, 70–75. [CrossRef]
29. Tigra, W.; Guiraud, D.; Andreu, D.; Coulet, B.; Gelis, A.; Fattal, C.; Maciejasz, P.; Picq, C.; Rossel, O.; Teissier, J. Exploring selective neural electrical stimulation for upper limb function restoration. *Eur. J. Transl. Myol.* **2016**, *26*, 6035. [CrossRef]
30. Kosta, P.; Mize, J.; Warren, D.J.; Lazzi, G. Simulation-Based Optimization of Figure-of-Eight Coil Designs and Orientations for Magnetic Stimulation of Peripheral Nerve. *IEEE Trans. Neural Syst. Rehabil. Eng.* **2020**, *28*, 2901–2913. [CrossRef]
31. Mikkonen, M.; Laakso, I.; Tanaka, S.; Hirata, A. Cost of focality in TDCS: Interindividual variability in electric fields. *Brain Stimul.* **2020**, *13*, 117–124. [CrossRef]
32. Opitz, A.; Yeagle, E.; Thielscher, A.; Schroeder, C.; Mehta, A.D.; Milham, M.P. On the importance of precise electrode placement for targeted transcranial electric stimulation. *Neuroimage* **2018**, *181*, 560–567. [CrossRef] [PubMed]
33. Fischer, D.B.; Fried, P.J.; Ruffini, G.; Ripolles, O.; Salvador, R.; Banus, J.; Ketchabaw, W.T.; Santarnecchi, E.; Pascual-Leone, A.; Fox, M.D. Multifocal tDCS targeting the resting state motor network increases cortical excitability beyond traditional tDCS targeting unilateral motor cortex. *Neuroimage* **2017**, *157*, 34–44. [CrossRef]
34. Bortoletto, M.; Rodella, C.; Salvador, R.; Miranda, P.C.; Miniussi, C. Reduced current spread by concentric electrodes in transcranial electrical stimulation (tES). *Brain Stimul.* **2016**, *9*, 525–528. [CrossRef]
35. Kashyap, R.; Bhattacharjee, S.; Arumugam, R.; Oishi, K.; Desmond, J.E.; Chen, S.A. i-SATA: A MATLAB based toolbox to estimate current density generated by transcranial direct current stimulation in an individual brain. *J. Neural Eng.* **2020**, *17*, 056034. [CrossRef]
36. Lancaster, J.L.; Woldorff, M.G.; Parsons, L.M.; Liotti, M.; Freitas, C.S.; Rainey, L.; Kochunov, P.V.; Nickerson, D.; Mikiten, S.A.; Fox, P.T. Automated Talairach Atlas labels for functional brain mapping. *Hum. Brain Mapp.* **2000**, *10*, 120–131. [CrossRef]
37. Talairach, J.; Tournoux, P. *Co-Planar Stereotaxic Atlas of the Human Brain 3-Dimensional Proportional System: An Approach to Cerebral Imaging*; Georg Thieme Verlag: Stuttgart, Germany; New York, NY, USA, 1988.
38. Collins, D.L.; Neelin, P.; Peters, T.M.; Evans, A.C. Automatic 3D intersubject registration of MR volumetric data in standardized Talairach space. *J. Comput. Assist. Tomogr.* **1994**, *18*, 192–205. [CrossRef]
39. Evans, A.C.; Marrett, S.; Neelin, P.; Collins, L.; Worsley, K.; Dai, W.; Milot, S.; Meyer, E.; Bub, D. Anatomical mapping of functional activation in stereotactic coordinate space. *Neuroimage* **1992**, *1*, 43–53. [CrossRef]
40. Holmes, C.J.; Hoge, R.; Collins, L.; Woods, R.; Toga, A.W.; Evans, A.C. Enhancement of MR images using registration for signal averaging. *J. Comput. Assist. Tomogr.* **1998**, *22*, 324–333. [CrossRef] [PubMed]
41. Amunts, K.; Zilles, K. Advances in cytoarchitectonic mapping of the human cerebral cortex. *Neuroimaging Clin. N. Am.* **2001**, *11*, 151–169.
42. Zilles, K.; Schleicher, A.; Palomero-Gallagher, N.; Amunts, K. Quantitative analysis of cyto-and receptor architecture of the human brain. In *Brain Mapping: The Methods*; Elsevier: Amsterdam, The Netherlands, 2002; pp. 573–602.
43. Eickhoff, S.B.; Stephan, K.E.; Mohlberg, H.; Grefkes, C.; Fink, G.R.; Amunts, K.; Zilles, K. A new SPM toolbox for combining probabilistic cytoarchitectonic maps and functional imaging data. *Neuroimage* **2005**, *25*, 1325–1335. [CrossRef] [PubMed]
44. Eickhoff, S.B.; Heim, S.; Zilles, K.; Amunts, K. Testing anatomically specified hypotheses in functional imaging using cytoarchitectonic maps. *Neuroimage* **2006**, *32*, 570–582. [CrossRef] [PubMed]
45. Eickhoff, S.B.; Paus, T.; Caspers, S.; Grosbras, M.-H.; Evans, A.C.; Zilles, K.; Amunts, K. Assignment of functional activations to probabilistic cytoarchitectonic areas revisited. *Neuroimage* **2007**, *36*, 511–521. [CrossRef]
46. Moffa, A.H.; Martin, D.; Alonzo, A.; Bennabi, D.; Blumberger, D.M.; Benseñor, I.M.; Daskalakis, Z.; Fregni, F.; Haffen, E.; Lisanby, S.H. Efficacy and acceptability of transcranial direct current stimulation (tDCS) for major depressive disorder: An individual patient data meta-analysis. *Prog. Neuro-Psychopharmacol. Biol. Psychiatry* **2020**, *99*, 109836. [CrossRef] [PubMed]
47. Nikolin, S.; Martin, D.; Loo, C.K.; Boonstra, T.W. Effects of TDCS dosage on working memory in healthy participants. *Brain Stimul.* **2018**, *11*, 518–527. [CrossRef] [PubMed]
48. Taylor, J.R.; Williams, N.; Cusack, R.; Auer, T.; Shafto, M.A.; Dixon, M.; Tyler, L.K.; Henson, R.N. The Cambridge Centre for Ageing and Neuroscience (Cam-CAN) data repository: Structural and functional MRI, MEG, and cognitive data from a cross-sectional adult lifespan sample. *Neuroimage* **2017**, *144*, 262–269. [CrossRef] [PubMed]
49. Shafto, M.A.; Tyler, L.K.; Dixon, M.; Taylor, J.R.; Rowe, J.B.; Cusack, R.; Calder, A.J.; Marslen-Wilson, W.D.; Duncan, J.; Dalgleish, T. The Cambridge Centre for Ageing and Neuroscience (Cam-CAN) study protocol: A cross-sectional, lifespan, multidisciplinary examination of healthy cognitive ageing. *BMC Neurol.* **2014**, *14*, 204. [CrossRef]
50. Ardekani, B.A.; Bachman, A.H. Model-based automatic detection of the anterior and posterior commissures on MRI scans. *Neuroimage* **2009**, *46*, 677–682. [CrossRef]
51. Oostenveld, R.; Fries, P.; Maris, E.; Schoffelen, J.-M. FieldTrip: Open Source Software for Advanced Analysis of MEG, EEG, and Invasive Electrophysiological Data. *Comput. Intell. Neurosci.* **2011**, *2011*, 156869. [CrossRef]

52. Bhattacharjee, S.; Kashyap, R.; O'Brien, B.A.; McCloskey, M.; Oishi, K.; Desmond, J.E.; Rapp, B.; Chen, S.H.A. Reading proficiency influences the effects of transcranial direct current stimulation: Evidence from selective modulation of dorsal and ventral pathways of reading in bilinguals. *Brain Lang.* **2020**, *210*, 104850. [CrossRef]
53. Tzourio-Mazoyer, N.; Landeau, B.; Papathanassiou, D.; Crivello, F.; Etard, O.; Delcroix, N.; Mazoyer, B.; Joliot, M. Automated anatomical labeling of activations in SPM using a macroscopic anatomical parcellation of the MNI MRI single-subject brain. *Neuroimage* **2002**, *15*, 273–289. [CrossRef]
54. Bikson, M.; Truong, D.Q.; Mourdoukoutas, A.P.; Aboseria, M.; Khadka, N.; Adair, D.; Rahman, A. Modeling sequence and quasi-uniform assumption in computational neurostimulation. *Prog. Brain Res.* **2015**, *222*, 1–23. [PubMed]
55. Bhattacharjee, S.; Chew, A.; Kashyap, R.; Wu, C.; Yeo, M.; O'Brien, B.; Rapp, B.; McCloskey, M.; Oishi, K.; Desmond, J.; et al. Could tDCS Modulate Bilingual Reading? *Brain Stimul.* **2019**, *12*, 569. [CrossRef]
56. Horvath, J.C.; Carter, O.; Forte, J.D. Transcranial direct current stimulation: Five important issues we aren't discussing (but probably should be). *Front. Syst. Neurosci.* **2014**, *8*, 2. [CrossRef] [PubMed]
57. Horvath, J.C.; Forte, J.D.; Carter, O. Quantitative review finds no evidence of cognitive effects in healthy populations from single-session transcranial direct current stimulation (tDCS). *Brain Stimul.* **2015**, *8*, 535–550. [CrossRef]
58. Horvath, J.C.; Carter, O.; Forte, J.D. No significant effect of transcranial direct current stimulation (tDCS) found on simple motor reaction time comparing 15 different simulation protocols. *Neuropsychologia* **2016**, *91*, 544–552. [CrossRef]
59. Goldsworthy, M.R.; Hordacre, B. Dose dependency of transcranial direct current stimulation: Implications for neuroplasticity induction in health and disease. *J. Physiol.* **2017**, *595*, 3265–3266. [CrossRef] [PubMed]
60. Jamil, A.; Batsikadze, G.; Kuo, H.-I.; Labruna, L.; Hasan, A.; Paulus, W.; Nitsche, M.A. Systematic evaluation of the impact of stimulation intensity on neuroplastic after-effects induced by transcranial direct current stimulation. *J. Physiol.* **2017**, *595*, 1273–1288. [CrossRef]
61. Labruna, L.; Jamil, A.; Fresnoza, S.; Batsikadze, G.; Kuo, M.-F.; Vanderschelden, B.; Ivry, R.B.; Nitsche, M.A. Efficacy of anodal transcranial direct current stimulation is related to sensitivity to transcranial magnetic stimulation. *Brain Stimul.* **2016**, *9*, 8–15. [CrossRef] [PubMed]
62. Kidgell, D.J.; Daly, R.M.; Young, K.; Lum, J.; Tooley, G.; Jaberzadeh, S.; Zoghi, M.; Pearce, A.J. Different current intensities of anodal transcranial direct current stimulation do not differentially modulate motor cortex plasticity. *Neural Plast.* **2013**, *2013*, 603502. [CrossRef]
63. Saleem, G.T.; Ewen, J.B.; Crasta, J.E.; Slomine, B.S.; Cantarero, G.L.; Suskauer, S.J. Single-arm, open-label, dose escalation phase I study to evaluate the safety and feasibility of transcranial direct current stimulation with electroencephalography biomarkers in paediatric disorders of consciousness: A study protocol. *BMJ Open* **2019**, *9*, e029967. [CrossRef]
64. Dmochowski, J.P.; Datta, A.; Huang, Y.; Richardson, J.D.; Bikson, M.; Fridriksson, J.; Parra, L.C. Targeted transcranial direct current stimulation for rehabilitation after stroke. *Neuroimage* **2013**, *75*, 12–19. [CrossRef] [PubMed]
65. Dmochowski, J.P.; Koessler, L.; Norcia, A.M.; Bikson, M.; Parra, L.C. Optimal use of EEG recordings to target active brain areas with transcranial electrical stimulation. *Neuroimage* **2017**, *157*, 69–80. [CrossRef] [PubMed]
66. Cancelli, A.; Cottone, C.; Tecchio, F.; Truong, D.Q.; Dmochowski, J.; Bikson, M. A simple method for EEG guided transcranial electrical stimulation without models. *J. Neural Eng.* **2016**, *13*, 036022. [CrossRef] [PubMed]
67. Shahid, S.S.; Bikson, M.; Salman, H.; Wen, P.; Ahfock, T. The value and cost of complexity in predictive modelling: Role of tissue anisotropic conductivity and fibre tracts in neuromodulation. *J. Neural Eng.* **2014**, *11*, 036002. [CrossRef] [PubMed]
68. Saturnino, G.B.; Antunes, A.; Thielscher, A. On the importance of electrode parameters for shaping electric field patterns generated by tDCS. *NeuroImage* **2015**, *120*, 25–35. [CrossRef]
69. Gomez-Tames, J.; Asai, A.; Hirata, A. Significant group-level hotspots found in deep brain regions during transcranial direct current stimulation (tDCS): A computational analysis of electric fields. *Clin. Neurophysiol.* **2020**, *131*, 755–765. [CrossRef]
70. Minjoli, S.; Saturnino, G.B.; Blicher, J.U.; Stagg, C.J.; Siebner, H.R.; Antunes, A.; Thielscher, A. The impact of large structural brain changes in chronic stroke patients on the electric field caused by transcranial brain stimulation. *NeuroImage Clin.* **2017**, *15*, 106–117. [CrossRef] [PubMed]
71. Habich, A.; Fehér, K.D.; Antonenko, D.; Boraxbekk, C.-J.; Flöel, A.; Nissen, C.; Siebner, H.R.; Thielscher, A.; Klöppel, S. Stimulating aged brains with transcranial direct current stimulation: Opportunities and challenges. *Psychiatry Res. Neuroimaging* **2020**, *306*, 111179. [CrossRef] [PubMed]
72. Hsu, W.-Y.; Ku, Y.; Zanto, T.P.; Gazzaley, A. Effects of noninvasive brain stimulation on cognitive function in healthy aging and Alzheimer's disease: A systematic review and meta-analysis. *Neurobiol. Aging* **2015**, *36*, 2348–2359. [CrossRef] [PubMed]
73. Brunoni, A.R.; Nitsche, M.A.; Bolognini, N.; Bikson, M.; Wagner, T.; Merabet, L.; Edwards, D.J.; Valero-Cabre, A.; Rotenberg, A.; Pascual-Leone, A.; et al. Clinical Research with Transcranial Direct Current Stimulation (tDCS): Challenges and Future Directions. *Brain Stimul.* **2012**, *5*, 175–195. [CrossRef]
74. Datta, A. Inter-individual variation during transcranial direct current stimulation and normalization of dose using MRI-derived computational models. *Front. Psychiatry* **2012**, *3*, 91. [CrossRef]
75. Rudroff, T.; Workman, C.D.; Fietsam, A.C.; Kamholz, J. Response variability in transcranial direct current stimulation: Why sex matters. *Front. Psychiatry* **2020**, *11*, 585. [CrossRef]

76. Thomas, C.; Ghodratitoostani, I.; Delbem, A.C.B.; Ali, A.; Datta, A. Influence of gender-related differences in transcranial direct current stimulation: A Computational Study. In Proceedings of the 2019 41st Annual International Conference of the IEEE Engineering in Medicine and Biology Society (EMBC), Berlin, Germany, 23–27 July 2019; pp. 5196–5199.
77. Russell, M.; Goodman, T.; Wang, Q.; Groshong, B.; Lyeth, B.G. Gender differences in current received during transcranial electrical stimulation. *Front. Psychiatry* **2014**, *5*, 104. [CrossRef] [PubMed]
78. Indahlastari, A.; Albizu, A.; O'Shea, A.; Forbes, M.A.; Nissim, N.R.; Kraft, J.N.; Evangelista, N.D.; Hausman, H.K.; Woods, A.J.; Initiative, A.D.N. Modeling Transcranial Electrical Stimulation in the Aging Brain. *Brain Stimul.* **2020**, *13*, 664–674. [CrossRef] [PubMed]
79. Wallace, D.; Cooper, N.R.; Paulmann, S.; Fitzgerald, P.B.; Russo, R. Perceived comfort and blinding efficacy in randomised sham-controlled transcranial direct current stimulation (tDCS) trials at 2 mA in young and older healthy adults. *PLoS ONE* **2016**, *11*, e0149703.
80. Chhatbar, P.Y.; Chen, R.; Deardorff, R.; Dellenbach, B.; Kautz, S.A.; George, M.S.; Feng, W. Safety and tolerability of transcranial direct current stimulation to stroke patients–A phase I current escalation study. *Brain Stimul.* **2017**, *10*, 553–559. [CrossRef] [PubMed]
81. Workman, C.D.; Kamholz, J.; Rudroff, T. The tolerability and efficacy of 4 mA transcranial direct current stimulation on leg muscle fatigability. *Brain Sci.* **2020**, *10*, 12. [CrossRef] [PubMed]
82. Uddin, L.Q.; Yeo, B.T.; Spreng, R.N. Towards a universal taxonomy of macro-scale functional human brain networks. *Brain Topogr.* **2019**, *32*, 926–942. [CrossRef] [PubMed]
83. Thomas Yeo, B.T.; Krienen, F.M.; Sepulcre, J.; Sabuncu, M.R.; Lashkari, D.; Hollinshead, M.; Roffman, J.L.; Smoller, J.W.; Zöllei, L.; Polimeni, J.R.; et al. The organization of the human cerebral cortex estimated by intrinsic functional connectivity. *J. Neurophysiol.* **2011**, *106*, 1125–1165. [CrossRef]
84. Kashyap, R.; Ouyang, G.; Sommer, W.; Zhou, C. Neuroanatomic localization of priming effects for famous faces with latency-corrected event-related potentials. *Brain Res.* **2016**, *1632*, 58–72. [CrossRef] [PubMed]
85. Kashyap, R.; Kong, R.; Bhattacharjee, S.; Li, J.; Zhou, J.; Yeo, B.T. Individual-specific fMRI-Subspaces improve functional connectivity prediction of behavior. *NeuroImage* **2019**, *189*, 804–812. [CrossRef] [PubMed]
86. Kashyap, R.; Bhattacharjee, S.; Sommer, W.; Zhou, C. Repetition priming effects for famous faces through dynamic causal modelling of latency-corrected event-related brain potentials. *Eur. J. Neurosci.* **2019**, *49*, 1330–1347. [CrossRef] [PubMed]
87. Kashyap, R.; Eng, G.K.; Bhattacharjee, S.; Gupta, B.; Ho, R.; Ho, C.S.; Zhang, M.; Mahendran, R.; Sim, K.; Chen, S.A. Individual-fMRI-approaches reveal cerebellum and visual communities to be functionally connected in obsessive compulsive disorder. *Sci. Rep.* **2021**, *11*, 1–15. [CrossRef]
88. Kashyap, R.; Bhattacharjee, S.; Yeo, B.T.; Chen, S.A. Maximizing dissimilarity in resting state detects heterogeneous subtypes in healthy population associated with high substance use and problems in antisocial personality. *Hum. Brain Mapp.* **2020**, *41*, 1261–1273. [CrossRef] [PubMed]
89. Csifcsák, G.; Boayue, N.M.; Puonti, O.; Thielscher, A.; Mittner, M. Effects of transcranial direct current stimulation for treating depression: A modeling study. *J. Affect. Disord.* **2018**, *234*, 164–173. [CrossRef]
90. Siddiqi, S.H.; Schaper, F.L.W.V.J.; Horn, A.; Hsu, J.; Padmanabhan, J.L.; Brodtmann, A.; Cash, R.F.H.; Corbetta, M.; Choi, K.S.; Dougherty, D.D.; et al. Brain stimulation and brain lesions converge on common causal circuits in neuropsychiatric disease. *Nat. Hum. Behav.* **2021**. [CrossRef] [PubMed]

Journal of *Personalized Medicine*

MDPI

Review

Application of Noninvasive Vagal Nerve Stimulation to Stress-Related Psychiatric Disorders

James Douglas Bremner [1,2,3,*], Nil Z. Gurel [4], Matthew T. Wittbrodt [1], Mobashir H. Shandhi [4], Mark H. Rapaport [1], Jonathon A. Nye [2], Bradley D. Pearce [5], Viola Vaccarino [5,6], Amit J. Shah [3,5,6], Jeanie Park [3,7], Marom Bikson [8] and Omer T. Inan [4,9]

1 Department of Psychiatry and Behavioral Sciences, Emory University School of Medicine, Atlanta, GA 30322, USA; mwittbr@emory.edu (M.T.W.); mark.h.rapaport@emory.edu (M.H.R.)
2 Department of Radiology, Emory University School of Medicine, Atlanta, GA 30322, USA; jnye@emory.edu
3 Atlanta VA Medical Center, Decatur, GA 30033, USA; ajshah3@emory.edu (A.J.S.); jeanie.park@va.gov (J.P.)
4 School of Electrical and Computer Engineering, Georgia Institute of Technology, Atlanta, GA 30332, USA; nil@gatech.edu (N.Z.G.); mobashir.shandhi@gatech.edu (M.H.S.); omer.inan@ece.gatech.edu (O.T.I.)
5 Department of Epidemiology, Rollins School of Public Health, Atlanta, GA 30322, USA; bpearce@emory.edu (B.D.P.); lvaccar@emory.edu (V.V.)
6 Department of Medicine, Cardiology, Emory University School of Medicine, Atlanta, GA 30322, USA
7 Department of Medicine, Renal Medicine, Emory University School of Medicine, Atlanta, GA 30322, USA
8 Department of Biomedical Engineering, City University of New York, New York, NY 10010, USA; bikson@ccny.cuny.edu
9 Coulter Department of Biomedical Engineering, Georgia Institute of Technology, Atlanta, GA 30332, USA
* Correspondence: jdbremn@emory.edu

Received: 18 June 2020; Accepted: 3 September 2020; Published: 9 September 2020

check for updates

Abstract: Background: Vagal Nerve Stimulation (VNS) has been shown to be efficacious for the treatment of depression, but to date, VNS devices have required surgical implantation, which has limited widespread implementation. Methods: New noninvasive VNS (nVNS) devices have been developed which allow external stimulation of the vagus nerve, and their effects on physiology in patients with stress-related psychiatric disorders can be measured with brain imaging, blood biomarkers, and wearable sensing devices. Advantages in terms of cost and convenience may lead to more widespread implementation in psychiatry, as well as facilitate research of the physiology of the vagus nerve in humans. nVNS has effects on autonomic tone, cardiovascular function, inflammatory responses, and central brain areas involved in modulation of emotion, all of which make it particularly applicable to patients with stress-related psychiatric disorders, including posttraumatic stress disorder (PTSD) and depression, since dysregulation of these circuits and systems underlies the symptomatology of these disorders. Results: This paper reviewed the physiology of the vagus nerve and its relevance to modulating the stress response in the context of application of nVNS to stress-related psychiatric disorders. Conclusions: nVNS has a favorable effect on stress physiology that is measurable using brain imaging, blood biomarkers of inflammation, and wearable sensing devices, and shows promise in the prevention and treatment of stress-related psychiatric disorders.

Keywords: PTSD; stress disorders; posttraumatic; depressive disorders; vagus nerve; VNS; sympathetic; inflammation; interleukin-6; vagal nerve stimulation; interferon; stress

1. Introduction

Stress-related psychiatric disorders, including depression and posttraumatic stress disorder (PTSD), are important public health problems. Early life stress increases the risk of development of depression in adulthood [1,2], and stressful life events are associated with an increased risk for depressive episodes [3], while PTSD requires exposure to a traumatic stressor as part of the diagnosis [4]. At any given time, 10% of the United States population meets the criteria for major depression or other mood disorders based on Diagnostic and Statistical Manual (DSM) criteria [5], with an annual cost of lost productivity of USD 44 billion [6]. Similarly, PTSD affects 6% of the population at some time in their lives [7]. The cost of treating PTSD and comorbid depression in soldiers returning from the wars in Iraq and Afghanistan has been estimated to be USD 6.2 billion [8], and since PTSD affects a larger total number of civilians in the United States than military personnel, the costs for society as a whole are likely much higher [9]. The most common cause of PTSD in women is sexual abuse and assault in childhood, while, for men, it is physical assault [10]. On average, women have higher occurrence of PTSD compared to men in the civilian population [11,12]. PTSD is characterized by intrusive thoughts, nightmares, avoidance, emotional blunting, negative cognitions, hypervigilance, and hyperarousal [13]. Depression is associated with depressed mood, loss of appetite, decreased psychomotor activity, and, in extreme cases, suicidal ideation. Other symptoms, such as poor sleep and concentration, negative cognitions, loss of interest in things, and anhedonia, are common to both conditions. In fact, there is a degree of comorbidity between the two conditions [14–19]. Furthermore, patients with comorbid disorders have a worse clinical course, with, for instance, a higher risk of suicidal ideation [20,21].

The standard of care for both PTSD and depression includes psychotherapy and/or medication [22,23]. Psychotherapy treatments for PTSD, however, have dropout rates as high as 50%, which limit their applicability [24,25]. First-line medication treatments for stress-related psychiatric disorders involves the Selective Serotonin Reuptake Inhibitor (SSRI) antidepressants [26,27]. However, as highlighted by a report from the Institute of Medicine, there is not sufficient evidence to conclude that they are effective for PTSD [28]. In fact, only one-third of those suffering from PTSD are able to achieve full remission with the current standard of care [26]. Similar limitations exist for treatment of major depression. As illustrated by the STAR*D study, only one-third of patients with major depression remitted to first-line therapy with antidepressants and only about two-thirds of patients met remission criteria after multiple algorithms that included psychotherapy, switching classes, and multiple heroic augmentation trials [29]. Given limitations of current treatment options, new paradigms are clearly needed for the management of stress-related psychiatric disorders.

2. Physiology of the Vagus Nerve

The vagus nerve represents a unique window between central functions of the brain and peripheral organ function that may be a promising target for treatment interventions for stress-related psychiatric disorders. The vagus has cell bodies in the brainstem and motor fibers that modulate peripheral organ function, as well as sensory fibers that relay information about peripheral organs to the brain (Figure 1). The efferent function of the vagus nerve primarily modulates parasympathetic nervous system function in the periphery and therefore acts as a counterbalance to the sympathetic nervous systems. Afferent vagal nerve fibers relay sensory activity of the visceral organs to the brain through the nucleus tractus solitarius (NTS) in the medulla oblongata and the locus coeruleus in the pons, with relays to areas of the brain involved in the modulation of emotion and the stress response, including the amygdala, insula, hippocampus, and anterior cingulate/prefrontal cortex [30].

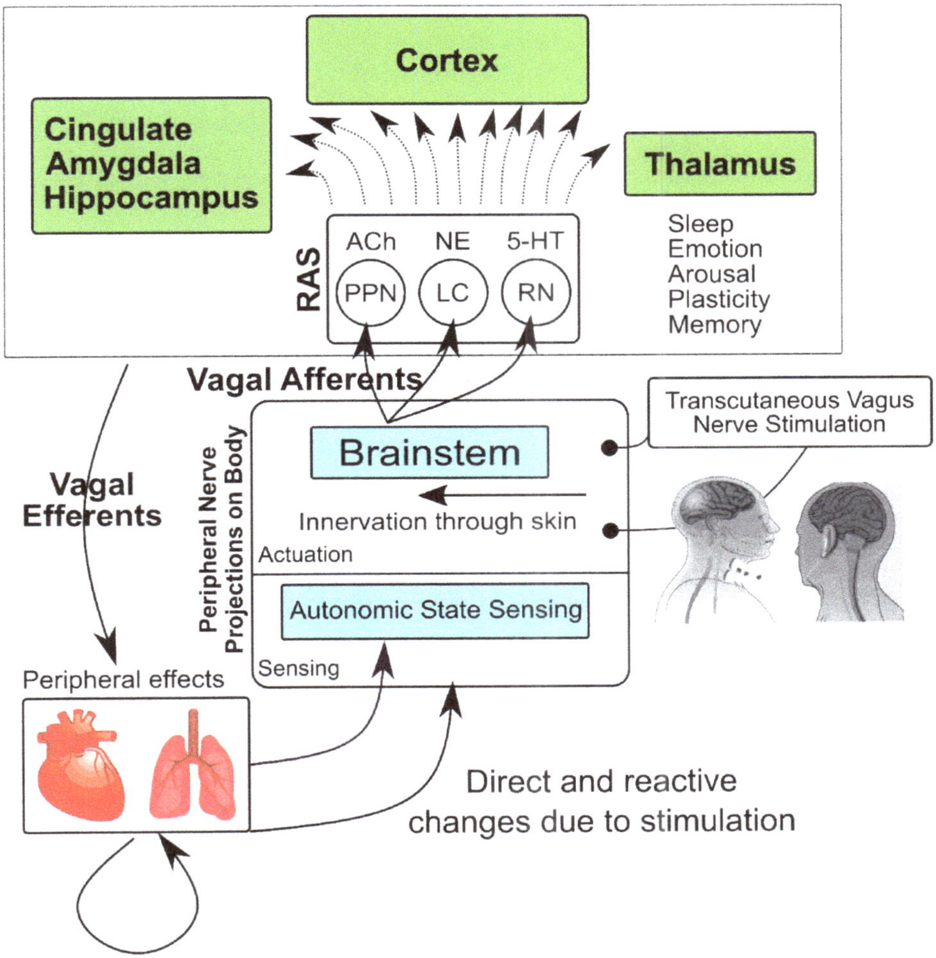

Figure 1. Model of effects of transcutaneous Vagal Nerve Stimulation (VNS) on physiological function. Stimulation of the vagus nerve in the neck as it passes through the carotid sheath (transcutaneous cervical VNS (tcVNS)) or in the ear (transcutaneous auricular VNS (taVNS)) activates the Nucleus Tractus Solitarius (NTS) in the brainstem, which has projections to other key brainstem nuclei containing cell bodies for neurotransmitters, including the locus coeruleus (LC), site of norepinephrine (NE), pedunculopontine nucleus (PPN) for acetylcholine (Ach), and raphe nucleus (RN) for serotonin (5-HT), and the reticular activating system (RAS). These regions, in turn, originate pathways to multiple brain areas involved in modulation of fear and emotion, as well as memory and neuroplasticity, including the anterior cingulate, hippocampus, amygdala, and cortex (including insula). Vagal efferents project to peripheral cardiovascular, autonomic, and inflammatory pathways. The vagus also projects information from the periphery back to the brain through afferents.

3. Neurobiology of Stress-Related Psychiatric Disorders

The vagus nerve modulates circuits and systems that underlie the symptoms of stress-related psychiatric disorders. The neurobiology of stress-related psychiatric disorders includes alterations in brain regions involved in memory and the stress response [31–34]. The hypothalamic–pituitary–adrenal (HPA) axis plays an important role in stress, and dysregulation of this system is associated with PTSD and depression [35–42] and is potentially modifiable by the vagus nerve [43–45]. Norepinephrine and sympathetic function are also involved in stress-related psychiatric disorders, with elevations typically seen in both patients with PTSD and depression, in addition to dysregulation of the peripheral autonomic nervous system [46–57].

Abnormalities of the inflammatory function are also associated with PTSD and depression [58,59]. Interleukin 1B (IL1B), IL-6, Tumor Necrosis Factor (TNF), Interferon gamma (IFN-γ), and C-Reactive Protein (CRP) are elevated in PTSD [60], and several of these immune mediators are increased after acute stress [61,62]. Patients with cardiovascular disease and the diagnosis of PTSD had an enhanced IL6 response to stressful tasks ("mental stress") compared patients without PTSD [63], with similar findings in individuals with early life stress, and vulnerability to depression [60,63,64]. Increased levels of proinflammatory cytokines and increased reactivity of the Nuclear Factor Kappa-light-chain-enhancer of activated B cells (NF-κB) system have been observed repeatedly in a subset of patients with depression [58,65]. Studies show that the stress-induced release of catecholamines acts through adrenergic receptors to activate NF-κB, and subsequently stimulates the release of cytokines, including IL-6 [66]. Interpersonal stress may have led to activation of inflammatory processes in response to imminent personal injury and therefore had survival value in evolution [58,67]. A recent meta-analysis showed that the statistically strongest findings in PTSD were for IL-6 and IFN-γ [68]. Elevations in IFN-γ and IL-6 are associated with decreases in tryptophan, the precursor of serotonin, a key neurotransmitter underlying the neurobiology of both depression and PTSD [69–71]. Increases in IL-6 also result in increases in kynurenine, which has been linked to suicide and depression [72], and quinolinic acid, which enhances glutamatergic transmission with associated decreases in brain derived neurotrophic factor (BDNF) in the hippocampus, which may be involved in symptoms of PTSD and depression and mechanisms of action of antidepressants [73–76]. These studies have shown the importance of intervention in the psychobiology of PTSD and depression, which potentially can be done with tcVNS.

Alterations in cell-mediated immunity in PTSD may be relevant to the mechanisms of action of tcVNS. Cell-mediated immunity utilizes T cells, including CD8+ cytotoxic cells that lyse cells harboring microbes and CD4+ cells that produce cytokines and activate phagocytes that engulf and kill microbes. These latter cells differentiate into Th1 and Th2 subsets, as well as Th17 subsets. T helper cell differentiation is partly controlled by cholinergic neurotransmission [77] and dysregulation of this system is associated with PTSD [78,79]. Glucocorticoids, including cortisol, inhibit immune function and lower concentrations of cortisol in patients with PTSD [41,80], and could result in enhancement of Th1 cell function [78,79] with an associated increase in IFN-γ. Studies have shown enhanced cell-mediated immunity in PTSD patients [81] and delayed-type hypersensitivity (DTH) reactions that are consistent with an enhancement of Th1 response and thus increased IFN-γ [82]. Other studies have linked DTH responses to elevated IFN-γ [83] and have shown increased IFN-γ in PTSD [68,84,85]. Vagus nerve stimulation activates T cells that produce acetylcholine, and by binding to the alpa-7 subunit of the cholinergic receptor, they inhibit NF-κB [86], and, based on our studies, IFN-γ [87]. VNS also inhibits High Mobility Group Box 1 protein (HMGB1), a proinflammatory master mediator, which is increased in PTSD and is modifiable by VNS [88,89]. These studies have shown several targets for modulation of immune function by vagal nerve stimulation in the treatment of stress-related psychiatric disorders.

Altered neuropeptidal function is another target for treatment intervention for stress-related psychiatric disorders [33]. Pituitary adenylate cyclase activating polypeptide (PACAP) is a neuropeptide that regulates and integrates adaptive responses to stress [90]. A growing body of literature has pointed to dysregulation of PACAP along with its selective PAC1 receptor in PTSD [90,91]. Elevated PACAP levels were associated with increased PTSD symptoms in females with PTSD [91]. In other studies, PAC1 receptor levels correlated with increased startle response [92,93], a marker of PTSD [94–96]. PACAP plays an important role in physiological stress responses, including those mediated by the sympathetic and parasympathetic nervous system [97]. PACAP distribution in brain areas involved in stress and emotion, including the hypothalamus, bed nucleus of the stria terminalis, and amygdala, suggests PACAP's involvement in limbic, autonomic, and neuroendocrine functions [98,99]. These systems are also regulated by the vagus nerve, an effect possibly mediated by PACAP.

4. Neuromodulation for Stress-Related Psychiatric Disorders

Neuromodulation represents a promising new paradigm for the treatment of stress-related psychiatric disorders [100]. Neuromodulation involves the use of electricity, magnetism, vibration, or ultrasound actuation to modulate neural function [101]. Forms of neuromodulation that have been applied to psychiatry include electroconvulsive therapy (ECT), transcranial magnetic stimulation (TMS), transcranial Direct Current Stimulation [102], and Vagal Nerve Stimulation (VNS) [103–107]. Electrical stimulation treatments show promise for the treatment of stress-related psychiatric disorders since they may act through effects on the underlying neurobiology of these disorders [103,104,106,108,109].

Electroconvulsive therapy (ECT) is one of the most effective treatments for patients with treatment-refractory major depression [110]. ECT involves the application of electrical currents to the skull while patients are under anesthesia with the goal of inducing a seizure with associated multiple firing of neurons felt to lead the therapeutic effect seen after multiple treatments [111]. ECT has an 80% response rate, which is a better response rate than for medications [110]. Some studies have suggested that ECT may be more effective in elderly depressed patients [112]. Predictors of good response include low Vitamin B-12 and folate levels and elevated homocysteine (all of which have been linked to depression) [113]. ECT may induce mechanisms which, as reviewed below, have been posited for VNS, and which are common to other successful antidepressant treatments, including modulation of excitatory amino acid transmission and promotion of neurogenesis in the hippocampus [75] and modulation of brain function in the medial prefrontal cortex [114]. ECT results in profound hemodynamic changes including bradycardia, followed by tachycardia and hypertension, as well as increased complication rates, can occur in patients with cardiovascular disease [111]. In spite of relative safety, many patients are hesitant to use ECT due to inconvenience and fear of side effects.

VNS is an electrical stimulation treatment that, in its implantable form, has been shown to be efficacious in the treatment of epilepsy [115–120] and treatment-refractory major depression [121–132], leading to approval by the Food and Drug Administration (FDA) for the treatment of these conditions [133]. VNS, which is currently approved for depression, involves surgical implantation with direct electrical stimulation of the vagus nerve [124,134,135].

VNS has a number of effects on brain circuits and systems that are likely beneficial for stress-related psychiatric disorders. In experimental models of PTSD, vagus nerve stimulation enhanced extinction of conditioned fear and reduced PTSD-like symptoms [136,137]. Thus, studies suggest that VNS is potentially useful for stress-related psychiatric disorders.

VNS has effects on autonomic nervous system function that are likely beneficial for stress-related psychiatric disorders [138,139]. VNS improves autonomic dysfunction, reducing sympathetic and enhancing parasympathetic tone [140–143]

VNS has other effects, including the modulation of fear circuits [137,144,145], induction of neural plasticity [140], enhancement of memory and cognition [130,146–156], and enhancement of central neurotransmitter function including norepinephrine [157,158]. VNS also reduces inflammatory function [159–165]. These findings suggest that VNS may be useful for stress-related psychiatric disorders characterized by central neurotransmitter and peripheral autonomic dysfunction, enhanced inflammation, and impairments in learning and memory [46,47,49–54,166].

5. Vagus Nerve and Neuroplasticity

In addition to efferent fibers, the vagus has afferent fibers that modulate central brain function. Effects of the vagus on neural function include both inhibition of cortical spreading depression [167], as well as effects on brain amino acids, neurotransmitters, and metabolites [168–170]. The vagus also has effects on neural plasticity, as evidenced by enhancement of recovery following cerebral hemorrhage with vagal nerve stimulation [171]. Pairing of vagal nerve stimulation with an auditory tone was beneficial in an animal model of tinnitus, a disorder involving ringing in the ears, an effect mediated through enhancement of neural plasticity in relevant areas of the brain [172–175]. The vagus enhances neural plasticity after stroke, with beneficial effects both for the recovery of cognitive function [176], as well as motor movement when paired with training in successful motor movements [177–180]. The enhancement of new learning and memory following stimulation of the vagus [149,181] probably occurs through enhancement of long term potentiation (LTP) in the hippocampus [182]. The vagus also modulates fear circuits in the brain in a way that promotes adaptive stress responses [46,136,137,144,183]. In addition to its effects on the brain, the vagus promotes recovery following cardiovascular events in animal models [139,184–186].

6. Neural Circuits in Stress-Related Psychiatric Disorders and Vagal Nerve Stimulation

Understanding neural circuits in stress-related psychiatric disorders is important for designing new treatments such as VNS that can target these underlying neurobiological disturbances [187,188]. A network of brain areas, including the hippocampus, amygdala, insula, and medial prefrontal cortex (including anterior cingulate), have been implicated by us and others in the pathophysiology of stress-related psychiatric disorders [34]. The hippocampus, which plays a critical role in declarative (or explicit) memory, is very sensitive to stress [75,189–192]. These effects are reversible with treatment with antidepressants or behavioral interventions like running [73,75,76]. Studies in patients with both PTSD and depression have shown alterations in memory function and reduction of hippocampal volume [193–197]. The amygdala is involved in the processing of emotional stimuli and emotional memory, and plays a critical role in the acquisition of fear responses [198]. The medial prefrontal cortex/anterior cingulate has been implicated in the appraisal and regulation of emotions, and inhibition of the amygdala function represents the mechanism of extinction [199]. Brain imaging studies have implicated the medial prefrontal cortex/anterior cingulate in PTSD [200–215] and depression [216–218]. An increase in function in PTSD is observed in insula [205,209,219] and increased amygdala function is associated with both PTSD [204,205,213,215,220–237] and depression [238–241]. Treatment is associated with changes in these brain regions for both PTSD [34,242–247] and depression [240,241,248–252]. As reviewed below, similar studies have been performed looking at neural circuits and systems response in depression [253–259], and our group has initiated studies using High-Resolution Positron Emission Tomography (HRPET) to assess neural correlates of treatment response in PTSD [260].

7. Noninvasive Vagal Nerve Stimulation: Safety and Reliability

Recently, devices have been developed for noninvasive stimulation of the vagus nerve [261]. Noninvasive Vagal Nerve Stimulation (nVNS) devices include transcutaneous auricular VNS (taVNS), which target the auricular branch of the vagus in the ear (with best results at the cymba conchae and tragus) [262], and transcutaneous cervical VNS (tcVNS), which act on the cervical branch as it passes through the carotid sheath in the neck [100]. These devices have been shown to be safe and effective and to reliably and predictably stimulate the vagus nerve in human subjects [263,264]. Vagal somatosensory evoked potentials associated with vagal afferent activation have been reported for both implanted VNS and noninvasive VNS devices used through the neck or ear [265]. Studies using evoked potentials have shown that nVNS reliably stimulates the vagus nerve in humans and anesthetized dogs [141,266–268]. Studies in humans using electroencephalography (EEG) measurements at scalp sites A1-Cz showed that tcVNS and taVNS both result in a predictable and reproducible P1 N1 P2 N2 pattern with biphasic peaks at 3 ms (P1, N1), followed by a large stimulation artifact and large biphasic peaks (P2, N2) at 10 ms that matches the pattern seen with implanted VNS [265,266,268]. Functional brain imaging studies of healthy human subjects with nVNS, including both taVNS [262,269,270] and tcVNS [271], showed the characteristic pattern of neural response of brain areas known to be connected to the Nucleus Tractus Solitarius (NTS), the primary relay point for vagal nerve fibers to the brain. These studies are all consistent with nVNS resulting in stimulation of the vagus nerve with resultant central effects in the brain. Other studies of neurobiology are also consistent with the role of nVNS in stimulating the vagus nerve.

NVNS has effects on a range of stress-related biological parameters. Studies using taVNS showed improved vagal activity [272,273], increased salivary alpha amylase, and decreased salivary cortisol [274]. Psychophysiology-focused studies have produced mixed outcomes. Whereas some studies noted no effect of taVNS on physiological markers of autonomic activity, such as pupil size, startle blink electromyography, and skin conductance responses [274–276], other studies noted improvements in psychophysiological indices of vagal activity with taVNS [272,273]. Our group recently studied tcVNS in physically healthy human subjects with a three-day stress paradigm, and found favorable results, indicating decreased physiological reactivity during stress and at rest for a wide range of biomarkers that could be obtained with wearable sensing devices [277,278]. We also explored computational methods to determine stimulation presence based on these continuous assessments of autonomic activity [279]. Anti-inflammatory effects of tcVNS based on serum cytokines have been noted in different healthy human studies and patients with Primary Sjögren's Syndrome [280–282].

8. Noninvasive Vagal Nerve Stimulation: Application to Stress-Related Psychiatric Disorders

The requirement for direct VNS to be surgically implanted has limited widespread implementation in stress-related psychiatric disorders to date due to cost and inconvenience [125,131]. These forms of VNS are also limited by the fact that true sham-controlled trials cannot be performed due to ethical reasons, which has led to questions about the true efficacy of these devices [261]. Since devices are only implanted in patients who have not responded to multiple antidepressants, the patient populations are also not necessarily representative of those typically seen in clinical psychiatry practices, which may explain why VNS, although yielding statistically significant improvements, did not lead to complete remission in all patients [283]. Additionally, treatments have not been reimbursed by Medicare or other insurance companies, which has further limited implementation [284]. Studies have shown the utility of both tcVNS and taVNS for various psychiatric disorders, including schizophrenia [285] and obsessive-compulsive disorder [286], as well as major depression [287]. Human studies also suggest that noninvasive VNS improves hyperarousal in PTSD patients with mild traumatic brain injury [288] and reduces symptoms in treatment-resistant anxiety disorders [289].

As proven by their cost and convenience, noninvasive VNS technologies have widespread applicability to patients with stress-related psychiatric disorders.

Neck-based tcVNS was recently approved by the FDA for the treatment of intractable cluster headache [264,290–292]. We have implemeneted this device in healthy human subjects with a history of exposure to traumatic stressful events since 2017, and have found it to be safe and feasible [277–279]. In our studies, we compared active tcVNS to a sham control in a randomized trial (Figure 2). Both were handheld devices that were applied to the left neck for stimulation with identical placement and operation (GammaCore, ElectroCore, Basking Ridge, New Jersey). nVNS or sham were applied using collar electrodes on the left side of the neck in order to permit placement while subjects were in the research-dedicated brain scanner, which had a small aperture. The treatment area on the neck was located by finding the carotid artery pulsation. An electrically conductive gel was applied on the stimulation surfaces and device is placed on the located treatment area. Active tcVNS devices produced a 5-kHz sine wave burst lasting for 1 millisecond (five sine waves, each lasting 200 microseconds), repeated one in every 40 milliseconds (25 Hz), generating 30-V peak voltage and 60-mA peak output current. The final stimulation intensity depended on the subject's verbal feedback: The researcher was instructed to increase the intensity gradually until the subject voiced discomfort, at which point the intensity was reduced slightly below that threshold. Sham devices produced a nearly direct voltage signal, whose polarity was slowly varied (0.2-Hz biphasic voltage), in contrast to the higher-frequency, alternating current used for the active nVNS (25 Hz with 5-kHz bursts). The sham device delivered a biphasic signal generating a 14-V peak voltage and 60-mA peak output current, consisting of pulses repeating every 5 s (0.2 Hz). High-frequency voltage signals (such as the active stimulus) pass through the skin with minimal power dissipation due to the low skin-electrode impedance at kHz frequencies. In contrast, lower-frequency signals (such as the sham stimulus) are mainly attenuated at the skin-electrode interface due to the high impedance [293]. Accordingly, the active tcVNS can deliver substantial energy to the vagus nerve to facilitate stimulation, while the voltage levels appearing at the vagus would be expected to be orders of magnitude lower for the sham device and thus vagal stimulation is unlikely. Nevertheless, since the sham device does deliver relatively high voltage and current levels directly to the skin, it activates skin nociceptors, causing a similar feeling to a pinch. This sensation is necessary for blinding of the participants and is thought as a critical detail by the investigators for the valuation of the potential treatment in psychiatric populations. Both active and sham interventions lasted for two minutes. The subject, research staff, and investigators were all blind to the device category, and the key was kept in a locked office by an individual not involved in the research in two locations. The specific details are summarized as follows: The manufacturer sent the active and sham devices to an individual who was not involved in research, and the individual randomized patients to the devices prior to patient recruitment. In addition, every subject was given a different, dedicated device, hence the number of patients was equal to the number of devices. Every week when a new patient arrived, the individual not involved in research delivered a different device to the research staff for use for that subject.

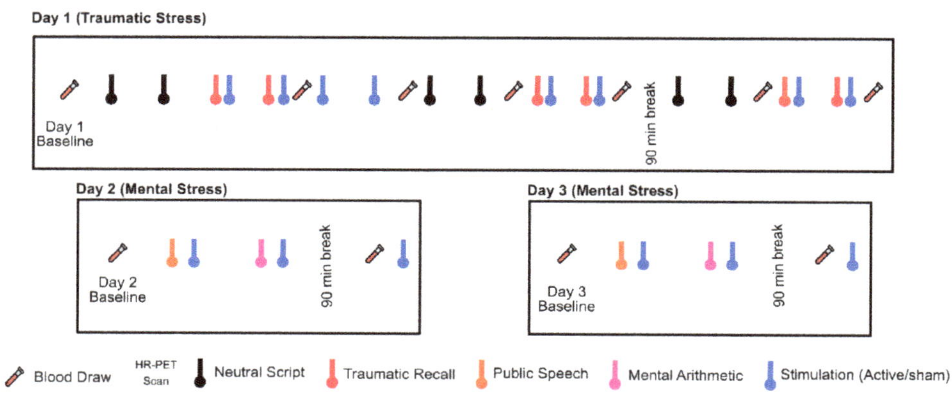

Figure 2. Study protocol undergoing since 2017. Physiological sensing data is collected continuously throughout three study days. The protocol timeline depicts neutral and trauma scripts, HR-PET scans (first day), mental stress tasks of public speech and mental arithmetic (second and third day), stimulation with active tcVNS or sham, and blood draws (all days).

In our study with physically healthy traumatized subjects and patients with PTSD, we constructed a multisignal dataset that include physiological signals related to cardiovascular and peripheral activity. The signals included electrocardiography (ECG), respiration (RSP), seismocardiography (SCG), photoplethysmography (PPG), electrodermal activity (EDA), and blood pressure (BP). Upon beat-by-beat signal processing, we extracted parameters related to autonomic tone with a beat-by-beat resolution. These parameters included both standard and nonstandard indices of psychophysiological reactivity, such as heart rate (HR), pre-ejection period of the heart (PEP), amplitude of the peripheral photoplethysmogram (PPG), pulse arrival time (PAT), properties of respiration signal (respiration rate, RR, width, RW, prominence, RP), frequency- and time- domain heart rate variability indices including low- and high-frequency heart rate variability (LF HRV, HF HRV), Poincare-based nonlinear heart rate variability (SD1, SD2), acceleration and deceleration capacity (AC, DC), and skin conductance level and response (SCL, SCR). In our healthy cohort, PEP, PPG amplitude, skin conductance, and respiratory indices resulted in marked differences between active and sham groups, indicating a blunted sympathetic response with tcVNS [277,294]. We later used this blunted physiological reactivity pattern to devise a machine learning based method that could indicate stimulation presence [278,279]. Brain imaging using High-Resolution Positron Emission Tomography (HR-PET) in traumatized participants without PTSD exposed to personalized traumatic scripts showed that tcVNS compared to sham stimulation blocked activations in the medial prefrontal cortex, parahippocampal gyrus, and insula, brain areas that play key roles in emotion and response to stress [295].

We also studied the effects of tcVNS on inflammatory markers in traumatized individuals with and without PTSD. We found that tcVNS paired with personalized traumatic scripts blocked stress-induced increases in proinflammatory biomarkers IL-6 and IFN-γ, and showed a pattern of decreased anger responses to scripts [87]. Increases in IL-6 and IFN-γ likely occur multiple times a day with minor stressors and triggers in PTSD patients, so tcVNS could result in a decrease in symptoms driven by inflammation and lead to improvements in clinical course. The reduction in subjective anger, in addition to improved mental health, also likely have beneficial health effects, for instance, in patients with comorbid PTSD and coronary artery disease (CAD), where we found not only an increase in mental stress-induced IL-6 in those with comorbid PTSD [63], but also that anger, PTSD, and other symptoms of psychological distress were associated with long-term adverse cardiovascular outcomes [296] and an increase in mental stress-induced myocardial ischemia [297,298].

Studies are ongoing with patients with PTSD, paired with assessment of the brain with High Resolution Positron Emission Tomography (HR-PET), and assessment of inflammatory and other blood biomarkers [278]. Due to low cost, increased convenience, limited side effects, feasibility for use at home or in the field for military medicine applications, and the ability to assess efficacy with true sham control comparison, tcVNS and taVNS show great promise in our opinion for the treatment of patients with stress-related psychiatric disorders and enhancement of human performance [261].

9. Conclusions

Current treatments for PTSD, major depression, and other stress-related psychiatric disorders, including medications and psychotherapy, have limitations and are not efficacious for all patients. Neuromodulation is an important alternative treatment, and noninvasive forms of VNS have the advantages of cost and noninvasiveness and can potentially be widely implemented for these patients. Both tcVNS and taVNS show promise for intervening at the level of the underlying neurobiology of these disorders.

PTSD is triggered by experiencing or witnessing exposure to traumatic events and leads to uncontrollable thoughts about the events. Our results from traumatized subjects without PTSD demonstrate decreased sympathetic and increased parasympathetic tone during tcVNS following acute traumatic stress, suggesting possible translation of this treatment to patients with PTSD, in the clinic or at home, as an acute treatment for these recurrent memories [277–279,299]. tcVNS has potential promise for enhancing recovery from acute traumatic stress by means of modulation of autonomic response in PTSD populations. As patients with PTSD show exaggerated responsivity to reminders of traumatic memories, the physiological changes induced by tcVNS observed in traumatized individuals without PTSD may be similarly observed in PTSD populations. Moreover, recent studies have shown that invasive VNS enhances the extinction of conditioned fear in rats [137]. Additionally, taVNS was shown to lead to improvement in vagal tone in patients with PTSD [288] and to inhibit long-term fear responses during extinction training in healthy human subjects [300]. Implanted VNS has already been approved by the FDA as a treatment for treatment resistant depression and epilepsy, but its cost and the intrusive nature of the surgery have limited its use. Noninvasive VNS technologies would be a significant addition to both facilitate further research into the circuitry of PTSD and treatment resistant depression, and would provide a new and highly acceptable treatment option for patients suffering from both severe and recurrent depression and PTSD [134,261].

Author Contributions: The following authors assisted with the design and execution of the research described in the article: J.D.B., N.Z.G., M.T.W., M.H.S., M.H.R., J.A.N., B.D.P., V.V., A.J.S., O.T.I. The following authors were involved in obtaining funding for the research: J.D.B., J.A.N., B.D.P., V.V., A.J.S., O.T.I. The following authors were involved in analysis of the data in the research: J.D.B., N.Z.G., M.T.W., M.H.S., J.A.N., B.D.P., O.T.I. The following authors drafted the initial article: J.D.B., N.Z.G., M.T.W., M.H.S., O.T.I. The following authors created the figures in the article: N.Z.G. The following authors added critical revisions to the article: J.D.B., N.Z.G., M.T.W., M.H.S., M.H.R., J.A.N., B.D.P., V.V., A.J.S., J.P., M.B., O.T.I. All authors have read and agreed to the published version of the manuscript.

Funding: The work reviewed here was supported by the Defense Advanced Research Projects Agency (DARPA), Arlington, VA, under Cooperative Agreement N66001-16-2-4054. Shah is sponsored by the National Institutes of Health, Award K23 HL127251.

Conflicts of Interest: J.D.B. has research funding support from ElectroCore LLC who also donated devices used in the research reviewed here.

References

1. Anda, R.F.; Felitti, V.J.; Walker, J.; Whitfield, C.; Bremner, J.D.; Perry, B.D.; Dube, S.R.; Giles, W.H. The enduring effects of childhood abuse and related experiences in childhood: A convergence of evidence from neurobiology and epidemiology. *Eur. Arch. Psychiatry Clin. Neurosci.* **2006**, *256*, 174–186. [CrossRef] [PubMed]
2. Kessler, R.C.; Magee, W.J. Childhood adversities and adult depression: Basic patterns of association in a US national survey. *Psychol. Med.* **1993**, *23*, 679–690. [CrossRef] [PubMed]
3. Kendler, K.S.; Thornton, L.M.; Gardner, C.O. Stressful life events and previous episodes in the etiology of major depression in women: An evaluation of the "kindling" hypothesis. *Am. J. Psychiatry* **2000**, *157*, 1243–1251. [CrossRef] [PubMed]
4. Weathers, F.W.; Bovin, M.J.; Lee, D.J.; Sloan, D.M.; Schnurr, P.P.; Kaloupek, D.G.; Keane, T.M.; Marx, B.P. The Clinician-Administered PTSD Scale for DSM-5 (CAPS-5): Development and initial psychometric evaluation in military veterans. *Psychol. Assess.* **2018**, *30*, 383–395. [CrossRef]
5. Kessler, R.C.; McGonagle, K.A.; Zhao, S.; Nelson, C.B.; Hughes, M.; Eschleman, S.; Wittchen, H.-U.; Kendler, K. Lifetime and 12-month prevalence of DSM-III-R psychiatric disorders in the United States: Results from the National Comorbidity Study. *Arch. Gen. Psychiatry* **1994**, *51*, 8–19. [CrossRef]
6. Stewart, W.F.; Ricci, J.A.; Chee, E.; Hahn, S.R.; Morganstein, D. Cost of lost productive work time among US workers with depression. *J. Am. Med. Assoc.* **2003**, *289*, 3135–3144. [CrossRef]
7. Pietrzak, R.H.; Goldstein, R.B.; Southwick, S.M.; Grant, B.F. Prevalence and Axis I comorbidity of full and partial posttraumatic stress disorder in the United States: Results from Wave 2 of the National Epidemiologic Survey on Alcohol and Related Conditions. *J. Anxiety Disord.* **2011**, *25*, 456–465. [CrossRef]
8. Eibner, C. *The Invisible Wounds of War: Quantifying the Societal Costs of Psychological and Cognitive Injuries*; RAND Corporation: Santa Monica, CA, USA, 2008.
9. McCauley, J.; Kern, D.E.; Kolodner, K.; Dill, L.; Schroeder, A.F.; DeChant, H.K.; Ryden, J.; Derogatis, L.R.; Bass, E.G. Clinical characteristics of women with a history of childhood abuse: Unhealed wounds. *J. Am. Med. Assoc.* **1997**, *277*, 1362–1368. [CrossRef]
10. MacMillan, H.L.; Fleming, J.E.; Trocme, N.; Boyle, M.H.; Wong, M.; Racine, Y.A.; Beardslee, W.R.; Offord, D.R. Prevalence of child physical and sexual abuse in the community: Results from the Ontario Health Supplement. *J. Am. Med. Assoc.* **1997**, *278*, 131–135. [CrossRef]
11. Kessler, R.C.; Sonnega, A.; Bromet, E.; Hughes, M.; Nelson, C.B. Posttraumatic stress disorder in the National Comorbidity Survey. *Arch. Gen. Psychiatry* **1995**, *52*, 1048–1060. [CrossRef]
12. Kessler, R.C.; Berglund, P.; Demler, O.; Jin, R.; Merikangas, K.R.; Walters, E.E. Lifetime prevalence and age-of-onset distributions of DSM-IV disorders in the National Comorbidity Survey Replication. *Arch. Gen. Psychiatry* **2005**, *62*, 593–602. [CrossRef] [PubMed]
13. Bremner, J.D. (Ed.) *Posttraumatic Stress Disorder: From Neurobiology to Treatment*, 1st ed.; John Wiley & Sons: Hoboken, NJ, USA, 2016.
14. Blanchard, E.B.; Buckley, T.C.; Hickling, E.J.; Taylor, A.E. Posttraumatic stress disorder and comorbid major depression: Is the correlation an illusion? *J. Anxiety Disord.* **1998**, *12*, 1–37. [CrossRef]
15. Franklin, C.L.; Zimmerman, M. Posttraumatic stress disorder and major depressive disorder: Investigating the role of overlapping symptoms in diagnostic comorbidity. *J. Nerv. Ment. Dis.* **2001**, *189*, 548–551. [CrossRef] [PubMed]

16. Flory, J.D.; Yehuda, R. Comorbidity between post-traumatic stress disorder and major depressive disorder: Alternative explanations and treatment considerations. *Dialogues Clin. Neurosci.* **2015**, *17*, 141–150.
17. Nijdam, M.J.; Gersons, B.P.R.; Olff, M. The role of major depression in neurocognitive functioning in patients with posttraumatic stress disorder. *Eur. J. Psychotraumatol.* **2013**, *4*, 19979. [CrossRef]
18. Shalev, A.Y.; Freedman, S.; Peri, T. Prospective study of post-traumatic stress disorder and depression following trauma. *Am. J. Psychiatry* **1988**, *155*, 630–637. [CrossRef]
19. Rytwinski, N.K.; Scur, M.D.; Feeny, N.C.; Youngstrom, E.A. The co-occurrence of major depressive disorder among individuals with posttraumatic stress disorder: A meta-analysis. *J. Trauma. Stress* **2013**, *26*, 299–309. [CrossRef]
20. Oquendo, M.; Brent, D.A.; Birmaher, B.; Greenhill, L.; Kolko, D.; Stanley, B.; Zelazny, J.; Burke, A.K.; Firinciogullari, S.; Ellis, S.P.; et al. Posttraumatic stress disorder comorbid with major depression: Factors mediating the association with suicidal behavior. *Am. J. Psychiatry* **2005**, *162*, 560–566. [CrossRef]
21. Ramsawh, H.J.; Fullerton, C.S.; Mash, H.B.H.; Ng, T.H.H.; Kessler, R.C.; Stein, M.B.; Ursano, R.J. Risk for suicidal behaviors associated with PTSD, depression, and their comorbidity in the U.S. Army. *J. Affect. Disord.* **2014**, *161*, 116–122. [CrossRef]
22. Ballenger, J.C.; Davidson, J.R.; Lecrubier, Y.; Nutt, D.J.; Foa, E.B.; Kessler, R.C.; McFarlane, A.C.; Shalev, A.Y. Consensus statement on posttraumatic stress disorder from the International Consensus Group on Depression and Anxiety. *J. Clin. Psychiatry* **2000**, *61*, 60–66.
23. Foa, E.B.; Davidson, J.R.T.; Frances, A.; Culpepper, L.; Ross, R.; Ross, D. The expert consensus guideline series: Treatment of posttraumatic stress disorder. *J. Clin. Psychiatry* **1999**, *60*, 4–76.
24. Schottenbauer, M.A.; Glass, C.R.; Arnkoff, D.B.; Tendick, V.; Gray, S.H. Nonresponse and dropout rates in outcome studies on PTSD: Review and methodological considerations. *Psychiatry* **2008**, *71*, 134–168. [CrossRef] [PubMed]
25. Hembree, E.A.; Foa, E.B.; Dorfan, N.M.; Street, G.P.; Kowalski, J.; Tu, X. Do patients drop out prematurely from exposure therapy for PTSD? *J. Trauma. Stress* **2003**, *16*, 555–562. [CrossRef] [PubMed]
26. Ballenger, J.C.; Davidson, J.R.; Lecrubier, Y.; Nutt, D.J.; Marshall, R.D.; Nemeroff, C.B.; Shalev, A.Y.; Yehuda, R. Consensus statement update on posttraumatic stress disorder from the international consensus group on depression and anxiety. *J. Clin. Psychiatry* **2004**, *65* (Suppl. 1), 55–62.
27. Davis, L.; Hamner, M.; Bremner, J.D. Pharmacotherapy for PTSD: Effects on PTSD symptoms and the brain. In *Posttraumatic Stress Disorder: From Neurobiology to Treatment*; Bremner, J.D., Ed.; John Wiley & Sons: Hoboken, NJ, USA, 2016; pp. 389–412.
28. Institute of Medicine of the National Academies. *Treatment for Posttraumatic Stress Disorder in Military and Veteran Populations: Final Assessment*; National Academies of Science, Engineering and Medicine, Health and Medicine Division: Washington, DC, USA, 2014.
29. Rush, A.J.; Trivedi, M.H.; Wisniewski, S.R.; Nierenberg, A.A.; Stewart, J.W.; Warden, D.; Niederehe, G.; Thase, M.E.; Lavori, P.W.; Lebowitz, B.D.; et al. Acute and longer-term outcomes in depressed outpatients requiring one or several treatment steps: A STAR*D report. *Am. J. Psychiatry* **2006**, *163*, 1905–1907. [CrossRef]
30. Komegae, E.N.; Farmer, D.G.S.; Brooks, V.L.; McKinley, M.J.; McAllen, R.M.; Martelli, D. Vagal afferent activation suppresses systemic inflammation via the splanchnic anti-inflammatory pathway. *Brain Behav. Immun.* **2018**, *73*, 441–449. [CrossRef]
31. Bremner, J.D.; Charney, D.S. Neural circuits in fear and anxiety. In *Textbook of Anxiety Disorders*, 2nd ed.; Stein, D.J., Hollander, E., Rothbaum, B.O., Eds.; American Psychiatric Publishing: Arlington, VA, USA, 2010; pp. 55–71.
32. Charney, D.S.; Bremner, J.D. The neurobiology of anxiety disorders. In *Neurobiology of Mental Illness*; Charney, D.S., Nestler, E.J., Bunney, S.S., Eds.; Oxford University Press: Oxford, UK, 1999; pp. 494–517.
33. Bremner, J.D.; Pearce, B. Neurotransmitter, neurohormonal, and neuropeptidal function in stress and PTSD. In *Posttraumatic Stress Disorder: From Neurobiology to Treatment*; Bremner, J.D., Ed.; John Wiley & Sons: Hoboken, NJ, USA, 2016; pp. 181–232.
34. Campanella, C.; Bremner, J.D. Neuroimaging of PTSD. In *Posttraumatic Stress Disorder: From Neurobiology to Treatment*; Bremner, J.D., Ed.; John Wiley & Sons: Hoboken, NJ, USA, 2016; pp. 291–320.
35. Yehuda, R. Post-traumatic stress disorder. *N. Engl. J. Med.* **2002**, *346*, 108–114. [CrossRef]
36. Vermetten, E. Epilogue: Neuroendocrinology of PTSD. *Prog. Brain Res.* **2008**, *167*, 311–313. [CrossRef]

37. De Kloet, C.S.; Vermetten, E.; Geuze, E.; Kavelaars, A.; Heijnen, C.J.; Westenberg, H.G. Assessment of HPA-axis function in posttraumatic stress disorder: Pharmacological and non-pharmacological challenge tests, a review. *J. Psychiatr. Res.* **2006**, *40*, 550–567. [CrossRef]
38. Van Zuiden, M.; Kavelaars, A.; Geuze, E.; Olff, M.; Heijnen, C.J. Predicting PTSD: Pre-existing vulnerabilities in glucocorticoid-signaling and implications for preventive interventions. *Brain Behav. Immun.* **2013**, *30*, 12–21. [CrossRef]
39. Yehuda, R.; Golier, J.A.; Yang, R.-K.; Tischler, L. Enhanced sensitivity to glucocorticoids in peripheral mononuclear leukocytes in posttraumatic stress disorder. *Biol. Psychiatry* **2004**, *55*, 1110–1116. [CrossRef] [PubMed]
40. Young, E.A.; Haskett, R.F.; Murphy-Weinberg, V.; Watson, S.J.; Akil, H. Loss of glucocorticoid fast feedback in depression. *Arch. Gen. Psychiatry* **1991**, *48*, 693–699. [CrossRef] [PubMed]
41. Yehuda, R.; Teicher, M.H.; Trestman, R.L.; Levengood, R.A.; Siever, L.J. Cortisol regulation in posttraumatic stress disorder and major depression: A chronobiological analysis. *Biol. Psychiatry* **1996**, *40*, 79–88. [CrossRef]
42. Carroll, B.J.; Curtis, G.C.; Davies, B.M.; Mendels, J.; Sugarman, A.A. Urinary free cortisol excretion in depression. *Psychol. Med.* **1976**, *6*, 43–50. [CrossRef]
43. Hosoi, T.; Okuma, Y.; Nomura, Y. Electrical stimulation of afferent vagus nerve induces IL-1β expression in the brain and activates HPA axis. *Am. J. Physiol. Regul. Integr. Comp. Physiol.* **2000**, *279*, R141–R147. [CrossRef]
44. Watkins, L.R.; Maier, S.F.; Goehler, L.E. Cytokine-to-brain communication: A review and analysis of alternative mechanisms. *Life Sci.* **1995**, *57*, 1011–1026. [CrossRef]
45. Thrivikraman, K.V.; Zejnelovic, F.; Bonsall, R.W.; Owens, M.J. Neuroendocrine homeostasis after vagus nerve stimulation in rats. *Psychoneuroendocrinology* **2013**, *38*, 1067–1077. [CrossRef]
46. Agorastos, A.; Boel, J.A.; Heppner, P.S.; Hager, T.; Moeller-Bertram, T.; Haji, U.; Motazedi, A.; Yanagi, M.A.; Baker, D.G.; Stiedl, O. Diminished vagal activity and blunted diurnal variation of heart rate dynamics in posttraumatic stress disorder. *Stress* **2013**, *16*, 300–310. [CrossRef]
47. Delgado, P.L.; Moreno, F.A. Role of norepinephrine in depression. *J. Clin. Psychiatry* **2000**, *61*, S5–S12.
48. Golden, R.N.; Markey, S.P.; Risby, E.D.; Rudorfer, M.V.; Cowdry, R.W.; Potter, W.Z. Antidepressants reduce whole-body norepinephrine turnover while enhancing 6-hydroxymelatonin output. *Arch. Gen. Psychiatry* **1988**, *45*, 150–154. [CrossRef]
49. Lake, C.R.; Pickar, D.; Ziegler, M.G.; Lipper, S.; Slater, S.; Murphy, D.L. High plasma NE levels in patients with major affective disorder. *Am. J. Psychiatry* **1982**, *139*, 1315–1318. [PubMed]
50. Veith, R.C.; Lewis, L.; Linares, O.A. Sympathetic nervous system activity in major depression: Basal and desipramine-induced alterations in plasma norepinephrine kinetics. *Arch. Gen. Psychiatry* **1994**, *51*, 411–422. [CrossRef] [PubMed]
51. Bremner, J.D.; Krystal, J.H.; Southwick, S.M.; Charney, D.S. Noradrenergic mechanisms in stress and anxiety: II. Clinical studies. *Synapse* **1996**, *23*, 39–51. [CrossRef]
52. Blanchard, E.B.; Kolb, L.C.; Prins, A.; Gates, S.; McCoy, G.C. Changes in plasma norepinephrine to combat-related stimuli among Vietnam veterans with posttraumatic stress disorder. *J. Nerv. Ment. Dis.* **1991**, *179*, 371–373. [CrossRef]
53. Geracioti, T.D.J.; Baker, D.G.; Ekhator, N.N.; West, S.A.; Hill, K.K.; Bruce, A.B.; Schmidt, D.; Rounds-Kugler, B.; Yehuda, R.; Keck, P.E.J.; et al. CSF norepinephrine concentrations in posttraumatic stress disorder. *Am. J. Psychiatry* **2001**, *158*, 1227–1230. [CrossRef]
54. Mason, J.W.; Giller, E.L.; Kosten, T.R. Elevation of urinary norepinephrine/cortisol ratio in posttraumatic stress disorder. *J. Nerv. Ment. Dis.* **1988**, *176*, 498–502. [CrossRef]
55. Zoladz, P.R.; Diamond, D.M. Current status on behavioral and biological markers of PTSD: A search for clarity in a conflicting literature. *Neurosci. Biobehav. Rev.* **2013**, *37*, 860–895. [CrossRef]
56. Bremner, J.D.; Krystal, J.H.; Southwick, S.M.; Charney, D.S. Noradrenergic mechanisms in stress and anxiety: I. Preclinical studies. *Synapse* **1996**, *23*, 28–38. [CrossRef]
57. Southwick, S.M.; Krystal, J.H.; Bremner, J.D.; Morgan, C.A.; Nicolaou, A.; Nagy, L.M.; Johnson, D.R.; Heninger, G.R.; Charney, D.S. Noradrenergic and serotonergic function in posttraumatic stress disorder. *Arch. Gen. Psychiatry* **1997**, *54*, 749–758. [CrossRef]
58. Miller, A.H.; Raison, C.L. The role of inflammation in depression: From evolutionary imperative to modern treatment target. *Nat. Rev. Immunol.* **2016**, *16*, 22–34. [CrossRef]

59. Pace, T.W.W.; Heim, C.M. A short review on the psychoneuroimmunology of posttraumatic stress disorder: From risk factors to medical comorbidities. *Brain Behav. Immun.* **2011**, *25*, 6–13. [CrossRef] [PubMed]
60. Marsland, A.L.; Walsh, C.; Lockwood, K.; John-Henderson, N.A. The effects of acute psychological stress on circulating and stimulated inflammatory markers: A systematic review and meta-analysis. *Brain Behav. Immun.* **2017**, *64*, 208–219. [CrossRef] [PubMed]
61. Steptoe, A.; Hamer, M.; Chida, Y. The effects of acute psychological stress on circulating inflammatory factors in humans: A review and meta-analysis. *Brain Behav. Immun.* **2007**, *21*, 901–912. [CrossRef] [PubMed]
62. Sugama, S.; Conti, B. Interleukin-18 and stress. *Brain Res. Rev.* **2008**, *58*, 85–95. [CrossRef]
63. Lima, B.B.; Hammadah, M.; Wilmot, K.; Pearce, B.D.; Shah, A.; Levantsevych, O.; Kaseer, B.; Obideen, M.; Gafeer, M.M.; Kim, J.H.; et al. Posttraumatic Stress Disorder is associated with enhanced interleukin-6 response to mental stress in subjects with a recent myocardial infarction. *Brain Behav. Immun.* **2019**, *75*, 26–33. [CrossRef]
64. Pace, T.W.W.; Mletzko, T.C.; Alagbe, O.; Musselman, D.L.; Nemeroff, C.B.; Miller, A.H.; Heim, C.M. Increased stress-induced inflammatory responses in male patients with major depression and increased early life stress. *Am. J. Psychiatry* **2006**, *163*, 1630–1633. [CrossRef]
65. Miller, A.H.; Maletic, V.; Raison, C.L. Inflammation and its discontents: The role of cytokines in the pathphysiology of depression. *Biol. Psychiatry* **2009**, *65*, 732–741. [CrossRef]
66. Bierhaus, A.; Wolf, J.; Andrassy, M.; Rohleder, N.; Humpert, P.M.; Petrov, D.; Ferstl, R.; von Eynatten, M.; Wendt, T.; Rudofsky, G.; et al. A mechanism converting psychosocial stress into mononuclear cell activation. *Proc. Natl. Acad. Sci. USA* **2003**, *100*, 1920–1925. [CrossRef]
67. Raison, C.L.; Miller, A.H. The evolutionary significance of depression in Pathogen Host Defense (PATHOS-D). *Mol. Psychiatry* **2013**, *18*, 15–37. [CrossRef]
68. Passos, C.I.; Vasconcelos-Moreno, M.P.; Costa, L.G.; Kunz, M.; Brietzke, E.; Quevedo, J.; Salum, G.; Magalhães, P.V.; Kapczinski, F.; Kauer-Sant'Anna, M. Inflammatory markers in post-traumatic stress disorder: A systematic review, meta-analysis, and meta-regression. *Lancet Psychiatry* **2015**, *2*, 1002–1012. [CrossRef]
69. Felger, J.C.; Li, L.; Marvar, P.J.; Woolwine, B.J.; Harrison, D.G.; Raison, C.L.; Miller, A.H. Tyrosine metabolism during interferon-α administration: Association with fatigue and CSF dopamine concentrations. *Brain Behav. Immun.* **2013**, *31*, 153–160. [CrossRef] [PubMed]
70. Raison, C.L.; Kelley, K.W.; Lawson, M.A.; Woolwine, B.J.; Vogt, G.; Spivey, J.R.; Saito, K.; Miller, A.H. CSF concentrations of brain tryptophan and kynurenines during immune stimulation with IFN-α: Relationship to CNS immune responses and depression. *Mol. Psychiatry* **2010**, *15*, 393–403. [CrossRef] [PubMed]
71. Delgado, P.L.; Price, L.H.; Miller, A.H.; Salomon, R.M.; Aghajanian, G.K.; Heninger, G.R.; Charney, D.S. Serotonin and the neurobiology of depression. Effects of tryptophan depletion in drug-free depressed patients. *Arch. Gen. Psychiatry* **1994**, *51*, 865–874. [CrossRef] [PubMed]
72. Myint, A.M. Kynurenines: From the perspective of major psychiatric disorders. *FEBS J.* **2012**, *279*, 1375–1385. [CrossRef]
73. Duman, R.S.; Malberg, J.E.; Nakagawa, S. Regulation of adult neurogenesis by psychotropic drugs and stress. *J. Pharmacol. Exp. Ther.* **2001**, *299*, 401–407.
74. Duman, R.S. Depression: A case of neuronal life and death? *Biol. Psychiatry* **2004**, *56*, 140–145. [CrossRef]
75. Nibuya, M.; Morinobu, S.; Duman, R.S. Regulation of BDNF and trkB mRNA in rat brain by chronic electroconvulsive seizure and antidepressant drug treatments. *J. Neurosci.* **1995**, *15*, 7539–7547. [CrossRef]
76. Santarelli, L.; Saxe, M.; Gross, C.; Surget, A.; Battaglia, F.; Dulawa, S.; Weisstaub, N.; Lee, J.; Duman, R.; Arancio, O.; et al. Requirement of hippocampal neurogenesis for the behavioral effects of antidepressants. *Science* **2003**, *301*, 805–809. [CrossRef]
77. Nizri, E.; Brenner, T. Modulation of inflammatory pathways by the immune cholinergic system. *Amino Acids* **2013**, *45*, 73–85. [CrossRef]
78. Griffin, G.D.; Charron, D.; Al-Daccak, R. Post-traumatic stress disorder: Revisiting adrenergics, glucocorticoids, immune system effects and homeostasis. *Clin. Transl. Immunol.* **2014**, *3*, e27. [CrossRef]
79. Zhou, J.; Nagarkatti, P.; Zhong, Y.; Ginsberg, J.P.; Singh, N.P.; Zhang, J.; Nagarkatti, M. Dysregulation in microRNA expression is associated with alterations in immune functions in combat veterans with post-traumatic stress disorder. *PLoS ONE* **2014**, *9*, e94075. [CrossRef] [PubMed]

80. Bremner, D.; Vermetten, E.; Kelley, M.E. Cortisol, dehydroepiandrosterone, and estradiol measured over 24 hours in women with childhood sexual abuse-related posttraumatic stress disorder. *J. Nerv. Ment. Dis.* **2007**, *195*, 919–927. [CrossRef] [PubMed]
81. Wilson, S.N.; van der Kolk, B.; Burbridge, J.; Fisler, R.; Kradin, R. Phenotype of blood lymphocytes in PTSD suggests chronic immune activation. *Psychosomatics* **1999**, *40*, 222–225. [CrossRef]
82. Altemus, M.; Cloitre, M.; Dhabhar, F.S. Enhanced cellular immune response in women with PTSD related to childhood abuse. *Am. J. Psychiatry* **2003**, *160*, 1705–1707. [CrossRef] [PubMed]
83. Barth, H.; Berg, P.A.; Klein, R. Method for the in vitro determination of an individual disposition towards Th1- or Th2-reactivity by the application of appropriate stimulatory antigens. *Clin. Exp. Immunol.* **2003**, *134*, 78–85. [CrossRef]
84. Woods, A.B.; Page, G.G.; O'Campo, P.; Pugh, L.C.; Ford, D.; Campbell, J.C. The mediation effect of posttraumatic stress disorder symptoms on the relationship of intimate partner violence and IFN-gamma levels. *Am. J. Community Psychol.* **2005**, *36*, 159–175. [CrossRef]
85. Lindqvist, D.; Wolkowitz, O.M.; Mellon, S.; Yehuda, R.; Flory, J.D.; Henn-Haase, C.; Bierer, L.M.; Abu-Amara, D.; Coy, M.; Neylan, T.C.; et al. Proinflammatory milieu in combat-related PTSD is independent of depression and early life stress. *Brain Behav. Immun.* **2014**, *42*, 81–88. [CrossRef] [PubMed]
86. Rosas-Ballina, M.; Olofsson, P.S.; Ochani, M.; Valdés-Ferrer, S.I.; Levine, Y.A.; Reardon, C.; Tusche, M.W.; Pavlov, V.A.; Andersson, U.; Chavan, S.; et al. Acetylcholine-synthesizing T cells relay neural signals in a vagus nerve circuit. *Science* **2011**, *334*, 98–101. [CrossRef]
87. Bremner, J.D.; Gurel, N.Z.; Jiao, Y.; Wittbrodt, M.T.; Levantsevych, O.M.; Huang, M.; Jung, H.; Shandhi, M.H.; Beckwith, J.; Herring, I.; et al. Transcutaneous vagal nerve stimulation blocks stress-induced activation of interleukin-6 and interferon-γ in posttraumatic stress disorder: A double-blind, randomized, sham-controlled trial. *Brain Behav. Immun. Health* **2020**, in press.
88. Huston, J.M.; Gallowitsch-Puerta, M.; Ochani, M.; Ochani, K.; Yuan, R.; Rosas-Ballina, M.; Ashok, M.; Goldstein, R.S.; Chavan, S.; Pavlov, V.A. Transcutaneous vagus nerve stimulation reduces serum high mobility group box 1 levels and improves survival in murine sepsis. *Crit. Care Med.* **2007**, *35*, 2762–2768. [CrossRef]
89. Wang, X.-W.; Karki, A.; Du, D.-Y.; Zhao, X.-J.; Xiang, X.-Y.; Lu, Z.-Q. Plasma levels of high mobility group box 1 increase in patients with posttraumatic stress disorder after severe blunt chest trauma: A prospective cohort study. *J. Surg. Res.* **2015**, *193*, 308–315. [CrossRef] [PubMed]
90. Gray, S.L.; Cline, D.L. PACAP: Regulator of the stress response. In *Stress: Physiology, Biochemistry, and Pathology*; Elsevier: Amsterdam, The Netherlands, 2019; pp. 279–291.
91. Ressler, K.J.; Mercer, K.B.; Bradley, B.; Jovanovic, T.; Mahan, A.; Kerley, K.; Norrholm, S.D.; Kilaru, V.; Smith, A.K.; Myers, A.J.; et al. Post-traumatic stress disorder is associated with PACAP and the PAC1 receptor. *Nature* **2011**, *470*, 492–497. [CrossRef] [PubMed]
92. Jovanovic, T.; Norrholm, S.D.; Davis, J.; Mercer, K.B.; Almli, L.; Nelson, A.; Cross, D.; Smith, A.; Ressler, K.J.; Bradley, B. PAC1 receptor (ADCYAP1R1) genotype is associated with dark-enhanced startle in children. *Mol. Psychiatry* **2013**, *18*, 742–743. [CrossRef] [PubMed]
93. Kamkwalala, A.; Norrholm, S.D.; Poole, J.M.; Brown, A.; Donley, S.; Duncan, E.; Bradley, B.; Ressler, K.J.; Jovanovic, T. Dark-enhanced startle responses and heart rate variability in a traumatized civilian sample: Putative sex-specific correlates of posttraumatic stress disorder. *Psychosom. Med.* **2012**, *74*, 153. [CrossRef] [PubMed]
94. Morgan, C.A.; Grillon, C.; Lubin, H.; Southwick, S.M. Startle reflex abnormalities in women with sexual assault-related posttraumatic stress disorder. *Am. J. Psychiatry* **1997**, *154*, 1076–1080. [PubMed]
95. Jovanovic, T.; Norrholm, S.D.; Blanding, N.Q.; Phifer, J.E.; Weiss, T.; Davis, M.; Duncan, E.; Bradley, B.; Ressler, K.J. Fear potentiation is associated with hypothalamic–pituitary–adrenal axis function in PTSD. *Psychoneuroendocrinology* **2010**, *35*, 846–857. [CrossRef] [PubMed]
96. Davis, M.; Walker, D.L.; Lee, Y.S. Roles of the amygdala and bed nucleus of the stria terminalis in fear and anxiety measured with the acoustic startle reflex: Possible relevance to PTSD. *Ann. N. Y. Acad. Sci.* **1997**, *821*, 305–331. [CrossRef]
97. Starr, E.R.; Margiotta, J.F. PACAP modulates distinct neuronal components to induce cell-specific plasticity at central and autonomic synapses. In *Pituitary Adenylate Cyclase Activating Polypeptide—PACAP*; Springer: Berlin/Heidelberg, Germany, 2016; pp. 83–107.

98. Cagampang, F.R.A.; Piggins, H.D.; Sheward, W.J.; Harmar, A.J.; Coen, C.W. Circadian changes in PACAP type 1 (PAC1) receptor mRNA in the rat suprachiasmatic and supraoptic nuclei. *Brain Res.* **1998**, *813*, 218–222. [CrossRef]
99. Piggins, H.D.; Stamp, J.A.; Burns, J.; Rusak, B.; Semba, K. Distribution of pituitary adenylate cyclase activating polypeptide (PACAP) immunoreactivity in the hypothalamus and extended amygdala of the rat. *J. Comp. Neurol.* **1996**, *376*, 278–294. [CrossRef]
100. Adair, D.; Truong, D.; Esmaeilpour, Z.; Gebodh, N.; Borges, H.; Ho, L.; Bremner, J.D.; Badran, B.W.; Napadow, V.; Clark, V.P.; et al. Electrical stimulation of cranial nerves in cognition and disease. *Brain Stimul.* **2020**, *13*, 713–720. [CrossRef]
101. Krames, E.; Peckham, P.H.; Rezai, A. *Neuromodulation: Comprehensive Textbook of Principles, Technologies, and Therapies*, 2nd ed.; Academic Press: London, UK, 2018.
102. Brunoni, A.R.; Moffa, A.H.; Sampaio-Junior, B.; Borrione, L.; Moreno, M.L.; Fernandes, R.A.; Veronezi, B.P.; Nogueira, B.S.; Aparicio, L.V.M.; Razza, L.B.; et al. Trial of electrical Direct-Current Therapy versus escitalopram for depression. *N. Engl. J. Med.* **2017**, *376*, 2523–2533. [CrossRef] [PubMed]
103. Bikson, M.; Unal, G.; Brunoni, A.; Loo, C. What psychiatrists need to know about transcranial direct current stimulation. *Psychiatr. Times* **2017**, *34*, 1–3.
104. Bikson, M.; Grossman, P.; Thomas, C.; Zannou, A.L.; Jiang, J.; Adnan, T.; Mourdoukoutas, A.P.; Kronberg, G.; Truong, D.; Boggio, P.; et al. Safety of transcranial Direct Current Stimulation: Evidence based update 2016. *Brain Stimul.* **2016**, *9*, 641–661. [CrossRef] [PubMed]
105. Bikson, M.; Bulow, P.; Stiller, J.W.; Datta, A.; Battaglia, F.; Karnup, S.V.; Postolache, T.T. Transcranial direct current stimulation for major depression: A general system for quantifying transcranial electrotherapy dosage. *Curr. Treat. Options Neurol.* **2008**, *10*, 377–385. [CrossRef] [PubMed]
106. Woods, A.J.; Antal, A.; Bikson, M.; Boggio, P.S.; Brunoni, A.R.; Celnik, P.; Cohen, L.G.; Fregni, F.; Herrmann, C.S.; Kappenman, E.S.; et al. A technical guide to tDCS, and related non-invasive brain stimulation tools. *Clin. Neurophysiol.* **2016**, *127*, 1031–1048. [CrossRef]
107. McCann, U.D.; Kimbrell, T.A.; Morgan, C.M.; Anderson, T.; Geraci, M.; Benson, B.E.; Wassermann, E.M.; Willis, M.W.; Post, R.M. Repetitive transcranial magnetic stimulation for posttraumatic stress disorder. *Arch. Gen. Psychiatry* **1998**, *55*, 276–279. [CrossRef]
108. Tortella, G.; Casati, R.; Aparicio, L.V.M.; Mantovani, A.; Senço, N.; D'Urso, G.; Brunelin, J.; Guarienti, F.; Lorencini Selingardi, P.M.; Muszkat, D.; et al. Transcranial direct current stimulation in psychiatric disorders. *World J. Psychiatry* **2015**, *5*, 88–102. [CrossRef]
109. Schachter, S.C.; Saper, C.B. Vagus nerve stimulation. *Epilepsia* **1998**, *39*, 677–686. [CrossRef]
110. Lisanby, S.H. Electroconvulsive therapy for depression. *N. Engl. J. Med.* **2007**, *357*, 1939–1945. [CrossRef]
111. Tess, A.V.; Smetana, G.W. Medical evaluation of patients undergoing electroconvulsive therapy. *N. Engl. J. Med.* **2009**, *360*, 1437–1444. [CrossRef]
112. Haq, A.U.; Sitzmann, A.F.; Goldman, M.L.; Maixner, D.F.; Mickey, B.J. Response of depression to electroconvulsive therapy: A meta-analysis of clinical predictors. *J. Clin. Psychiatry* **2015**, *76*, 1374–1384. [CrossRef] [PubMed]
113. Maier, H.; Helm, S.; Toto, S.; Moschny, N.; Sperling, W.; Hillemacher, T.; Kahl, K.G.; Jakubovski, E.; Bleich, S.; Frieling, H.; et al. S100B, homocysteine, vitamin B12, folic acid, and procalcitonin serum levels in remitters to electroconvulsive therapy: A pilot study. *Dis. Markers* **2018**. [CrossRef] [PubMed]
114. Scott, A.I.F.; Dougall, N.; Ross, M.; O'Carroll, R.E.; Riddle, W.; Ebmeier, K.P.; Goodwin, G.M. Short-term effects of electroconvulsive treatment on the uptake of [Tc-99m] exametazine into brain in major depression shown with single photon emission tomography. *J. Affect. Disord.* **1994**, *30*, 27–34. [CrossRef]
115. Ben-Menachem, E.; Hellström, K.; Waldton, C.; Augustinsson, L.E. Evaluation of refractory epilepsy treated with vagus nerve stimulation for up to 5 years. *Neurology* **1999**, *52*, 1265–1267. [CrossRef] [PubMed]
116. Ben-Menachem, E.; Manon-Espaillat, R.; Ristanovic, R.; Wilder, B.J.; Stefan, H.; Mirza, W.; Tarver, W.B.; Wernicke, J.F. Vagus nerve stimulation for treatment of partial seizures: 1. A controlled study of effect on seizures. *Epilepsia* **1994**, *35*, 616–626. [CrossRef] [PubMed]
117. George, R.; Salinsky, M.; Kuzniecky, R.; Rosenfeld, W.; Bergen, D.; Tarver, W.B.; Wernicke, J.F. Vagus nerve stimulation for treatment of partial seizures: 3. Long-term follow-up on the first 67 patients exiting a controlled study. *Epilepsia* **1994**, *35*, 637–643. [CrossRef]

118. Handforth, A.; DeGiorgio, C.M.; Schachter, S.C.; Uthman, B.M.; Naritoku, D.K.; Tecoma, E.S.; Henry, T.R.; Collins, S.D.; Vaughn, B.V.; Gilmartin, R.C.; et al. Vagus nerve stimulation therapy for partial-onset seizures: A randomized active-control trial. *Neurology* **1998**, *51*, 48–55. [CrossRef]
119. Salinsky, M.C.; Uthman, B.M.; Ristanovic, R.K.; Wernicke, J.F.; Tarver, W.B. Vagus nerve stimulation for the treatment of medically intractable seizures. Results of a 1-year open-extension trial. *Arch. Neurol.* **1999**, *53*, 1176–1180. [CrossRef]
120. The Vagus Nerve Stimulation Study Group. A randomized controlled trial of chronic vagus nerve stimulation for treatment of medically intractable seizures. *Neurology* **1995**, *45*, 224–230. [CrossRef]
121. Berry, S.M.; Broglio, K.; Bunker, M.; Jayewardene, A.; Olin, B.; Rush, A.J. A patient-level meta-analysis of studies evaluating vagus nerve stimulation therapy for treatment-resistant depression. *Med. Devices* **2013**, *6*, 17–35.
122. Dell-Osso, B.; Oldani, L.; Palazzo, M.C.; Balossi, I.; Ciabatti, M.; Altamura, A.C. Vagus nerve stimulation in treatment-resistant depression: Acute and follow-up results of an Italian case series. *J. ECT* **2013**, *29*, 41–44.
123. George, M.S.; Rush, A.J.; Marangell, L.B.; Sackeim, H.A.; Brannan, S.K.; Davis, S.M.; Howland, R.; Kling, M.A.; Moreno, F.; Rittberg, B.; et al. A one-year comparison of Vagus Nerve Stimulation with treatment as usual for treatment-resistant depression. *Biol. Psychiatry* **2005**, *58*, 364–373. [CrossRef]
124. George, M.S.; Rush, A.J.; Sackeim, H.A.; Marangell, L. Vagus Nerve Stimulation (VNS): Utility in neuropsychiatric disorders. *Int. J. Neuropsychopharmacol.* **2003**, *6*, 73–83. [CrossRef] [PubMed]
125. Marangell, L.B.; Rush, A.J.; George, M.S.; Sackeim, H.A.; Johnson, C.R.; Husain, M.M.; Nahas, Z.; Lisanby, S.H. Vagus Nerve Stimulation (VNS) for major depressive episodes: Longer-term outcome. *Biol. Psychiatry* **2002**, *51*, 280–287. [CrossRef]
126. Rush, A.J.; George, M.S.; Sackeim, H.A.; Marangell, L.B.; Husain, M.; Giller, C.; Nahas, Z.; Haines, S.; Simson, R.K.; Goodman, R.; et al. Vagus Nerve Stimulation (VNS) for treatment-resistant depression: A multicenter study. *Biol. Psychiatry* **2000**, *47*, 276–286. [CrossRef]
127. Rush, A.J.; Marangell, L.B.; Sackeim, H.A.; George, M.S.; Brannan, S.K.; Davis, S.M.; Howland, R.; Kling, M.A.; Rittberg, B.R.; Burke, W.J.; et al. Vagus Nerve Stimulation for treatment-resistant depression: A randomized, controlled acute phase trial. *Biol. Psychiatry* **2005**, *58*, 347–354. [CrossRef]
128. Rush, A.J.; Sackeim, H.A.; Marangell, L.B.; George, M.S.; Brannan, S.K.; Davis, S.M.; Lavori, P.; Howland, R.; Kling, M.A.; Rittberg, B.; et al. Effects of 12 Months of Vagus Nerve Stimulation in treatment-resistant depression: A naturalistic study. *Biol. Psychiatry* **2005**, *58*, 355–363. [CrossRef] [PubMed]
129. Sackeim, H.A.; Brannan, S.K.; Rush, A.J.; George, M.S.; Marangell, L.B.; Allen, J. Durability of antidepressant response to vagus nerve stimulation (VNS). *Int. J. Neuropsychopharmacol.* **2007**, *10*, 817–826. [CrossRef]
130. Sackeim, H.A.; Keilp, J.G.; Rush, A.J.; George, M.S.; Marangell, L.B.; Dormer, J.S.; Burt, T.; Lisanby, S.H.; Husain, M.; Collum, M.; et al. The effects of vagus nerve stimulation on cognitive performance in patients with treatment-resistant depression. *Neuropsychiatry Neuropsychol. Behav. Neurol.* **2001**, *14*, 53–62.
131. Sackeim, H.A.; Rush, A.J.; George, M.S.; Marangell, L.B.; Husain, M.M.; Nahas, Z.; Johnson, C.R.; Seidman, S.; Giller, C.; Haines, S.; et al. Vagus nerve stimulation (VNS) for treatment-resistant depression: Efficacy, side effects, and predictors of outcome. *Neuropsychopharmacology* **2001**, *25*, 713–728. [CrossRef]
132. Johnson, R.L.; Wilson, C.G. A review of vagus nerve stimulation as a therapeutic intervention. *J. Inflamm. Res.* **2018**, *11*, 203–211. [CrossRef] [PubMed]
133. George, M.S.; Sackeim, H.A.; Rush, A.J.; Marangell, L.B.; Nahas, Z.; Husain, M.M.; Lissanby, S.H.; Burt, T.; Goldman, J.; Ballenger, J.C. Vagus Nerve Stimulation: A new tool for brain research and therapy. *Biol. Psychiatry* **2000**, *47*, 287–295. [CrossRef]
134. Aaronson, S.T.; Sears, P.; Ruvuna, F.; Bunker, M.; Conway, C.R.; Dougherty, D.D.; Reimherr, F.W.; Schwartz, T.L.; Zajecka, J.M. A five-year observational study of patients with treatment-resistant depression treated with VNS therapy or treatment-as-usual: Comparison of response, remission, and suicidality. *Am. J. Psychiatry* **2017**, *174*, 640–648. [CrossRef] [PubMed]
135. Terry, R.S. Vagus Nerve Stimulation for Epilepsy. *Medicine* **2014**. [CrossRef]
136. Noble, I.J.; Gonzalez, I.J.; Meruva, V.B.; Callahan, K.A.; Belfort, B.D.; Ramanathan, K.R.; Meyers, E.; Kilgard, M.P.; Rennaker, R.L.; McIntyre, C.K. Effects of vagus nerve stimulation on extinction of conditioned fear and post-traumatic stress disorder symptoms in rats. *Transl. Psychiatry* **2017**, *7*, 1–8. [CrossRef] [PubMed]

137. Pena, D.F.; Childs, J.E.; Willett, S.; Vital, A.; McIntyre, C.K.; Kroener, S. Vagus nerve stimulation enhances extinction of conditioned fear and modulates plasticity in the pathway from the ventromedial prefrontal cortex to the amygdala. *Front. Behav. Neurosci.* **2014**, *8*, 1–8. [CrossRef]
138. Schomer, A.C.; Nearing, B.D.; Schachter, S.C.; Verrier, R.L. Vagus nerve stimulation reduces cardiac electrical instability assessed by quantitative T-wave alternans analysis in patients with drug-resistant focal epilepsy. *Epilepsia* **2014**, *55*, 1996–2002. [CrossRef] [PubMed]
139. Groves, D.A.; Brown, V.J. Vagal nerve stimulation: A review of its applications and potential mechanisms that mediate its clinical effects. *Neurosci. Biobehav. Rev.* **2005**, *29*, 493–500. [CrossRef]
140. Hays, S.A.; Rennaker, R.L.; Kilgard, M.P. Targeting plasticity with vagus nerve stimulation to treat neurological disease. *Prog. Brain Res.* **2013**, *207*, 275–299.
141. Polak, T.; Markulin, F.; Ehlis, A.-C.; Langer, J.B.M.; Ringel, T.M.; Fallgatter, A.J. Far field potentials from brain stem after transcutaneous vagus nerve stimulation: Optimization of stimulation and recording parameters. *J. Neural Transm.* **2009**, *116*, 1237–1242. [CrossRef]
142. Player, M.J.; Taylor, J.L.; Weickert, C.S.; Alonzo, A.; Sachdev, P.S.; Martin, D.; Mitchell, P.B.; Loo, C.K. Increase in PAS-induced neuroplasticity after a treatment course of transcranial direct current stimulation for depression. *J. Affect. Disord.* **2014**, *167*, 140–147. [CrossRef] [PubMed]
143. Zhang, Y.; Popovic, Z.B.; Bibevski, S.; Fakhry, I.; Sica, D.A.; Van Wagoner, D.R.; Mazgalev, T.N. Chronic vagus nerve stimulation improves autonomic control and attenuates systemic inflammation and heart failure progression in a canine high-rate pacing model. *Circ. Heart Fail.* **2009**, *2*, 692–699. [CrossRef] [PubMed]
144. Peña, D.F.; Engineer, N.D.; McIntyre, C.K. Rapid remission of conditioned fear expression with extinction training paired with vagus nerve stimulation. *Biol. Psychiatry* **2013**, *73*, 1071–1077. [CrossRef] [PubMed]
145. Souza, R.R.; Robertson, N.M.; Pruitt, D.T.; Gonzales, P.A.; Hays, S.A.; Rennaker, R.L.; Kilgard, M.P.; McIntyre, C.K. Vagus nerve stimulation reverses the extinction impairments in a model of PTSD with prolonged and repeated trauma. *Stress* **2019**, *22*, 509–520. [CrossRef] [PubMed]
146. Schacter, S.C. Vagus nerve stimulation: Mood and cognitive effects. *Epilepsy Behav.* **2004**, *5*, S56–S59. [CrossRef] [PubMed]
147. McIntire, L.; McKinley, A.; Goodyear, C. Peripheral nerve stimulation to augment human analyst performeance. *IEEE* **2019**. [CrossRef]
148. Clark, K.B.; Krahl, S.E.; Smith, D.C.; Jensen, R.A. Post-training unilateral vagal stimulation enhances retention performance in the rat. *Neurobiol. Learn. Mem.* **1995**, *63*, 213–216. [CrossRef]
149. Clark, K.B.; Naritoku, D.K.; Smith, D.C.; Browning, R.A.; Jensen, R.A. Enhanced recognition memory following vagus nerve stimulation in human subjects. *Nat. Neurosci.* **1999**, *2*, 94–98. [CrossRef]
150. Clark, K.B.; Smith, D.C.; Hassert, D.L.; Browning, R.A.; Naritoku, D.K.; Jensen, R.A. Posttraining electrical stimulation of vagal afferents with concomitant vagal efferent inactivation enhances memory storage processes in the rat. *Neurobiol. Learn. Mem.* **1998**, *70*, 364–373. [CrossRef]
151. Flood, J.F.; Smith, G.E.; Morley, J.E. Modulation of memory processing by cholecystokinin: Dependence on the vagus nerve. *Science* **1987**, *236*, 832–834. [CrossRef]
152. Ghacibeh, G.A.; Shenker, J.I.; Shenal, B.; Uthman, B.M.; Heilman, K.M. The influence of vagus nerve stimulation on memory. *Cogn. Behav. Neurol.* **2006**, *19*, 119–122. [CrossRef] [PubMed]
153. Ghacibeh, G.A.; Shenker, J.I.; Shenal, B.; Uthman, B.M.; Heilman, K.M. Effect of vagus nerve stimulation on creativity and cognitive flexibility. *Epilepsy Behav.* **2006**, *8*, 720–725. [CrossRef] [PubMed]
154. Jacobs, H.I.L.; Riphagen, J.M.; Razat, C.M.; Wiese, S.; Sack, A.T. Transcutaneous vagus nerve stimulation boosts associative memory in older individuals. *Neurobiol. Aging* **2015**, *36*, 1860–1867. [CrossRef] [PubMed]
155. Merrill, C.A.; Jonsson, M.A.; Minthon, L.; Ejnell, H.; Silander, H.C.; Blennow, K.; Karlsson, M.; Nordlund, A.; Rolstad, S.; Warkentin, S.; et al. Vagus nerve stimulation in patients with Alzheimer's disease: Additional follow-up results of a pilot study through 1 year. *J. Clin. Psychiatry* **2006**, *67*, 1171–1178. [CrossRef] [PubMed]
156. Vonck, K.; Raedt, R.; Naulaerts, J.; De Vogelaere, F.; Thiery, E.; Van Roost, D.; Aldenkamp, B.; Miatton, M.; Boon, P. Vagus nerve stimulation. 25 years later! What do we know about the effects on cognition? *Neurosci. Biobehav. Rev.* **2014**, *45*, 63–71. [CrossRef] [PubMed]
157. Follesa, P.; Biggio, F.; Gorini, G.; Caria, S.; Talani, G.; Dazzi, L.; Puligheddu, M.; Marrosu, F.; Biggio, G. Vagus nerve stimulation increases norepinephrine concentration and the gene expression of BDNF and bFGF in the rat brain. *Brain Res.* **2007**, *1179*, 28–34. [CrossRef]

158. Vida, G.; Pena, G.; Kanashiro, A.; Thompson-Bonilla, M.d.R.; Palange, D.; Deitch, E.A.; Ulloa, L. B2-Adrenoreceptors of regulatory lymphocytes are essential for vagal neuromodulation of the innate immune system. *FASEB J.* **2011**, *25*, 4476–4485. [CrossRef]
159. Bansal, V.; Ryu, S.Y.; Lopez, N.; Allexan, S.; Krzyzaniak, M.; Eliceiri, B.; Baird, A.; Coimbra, R. Vagal stimulation modulates inflammation through a ghrelin mediated mechanism in traumatic brain injury. *Inflammation* **2012**, *35*, 214–220. [CrossRef]
160. Borovikova, L.V.; Ivanova, S.; Zhang, M.; Yang, H.; Botchkina, G.I.; Watkins, L.R.; Wang, H.; Abumrad, N.; Eaton, J.W.; Tracey, K.J. Vagus nerve stimulation attenuates the systemic inflammatory response to endotoxin. *Nature* **2000**, *405*, 458–462. [CrossRef]
161. Corsi-Zuelli, F.M.G.; Brognara, F.; Quirino, G.F.S.; Hiroki, C.H.; Fais, R.S.; Del-Ben, C.M.; Ulloa, L.; Salgado, H.C.; Kanashiro, A. Neuroimmune interactions in schizophrenia: Focus on vagus nerve stimulation and activation of the alpha-7 nicotinic acetylcholine receptor. *Front. Immunol.* **2017**, *8*. [CrossRef]
162. Cunningham, J.T.; Mifflin, S.W.; Gould, G.G.; Frazer, A. Induction of c-Fos and delta-FosB immunoreactivity in rat brain by vagal nerve stimulation. *Neuropsychopharmacology* **2008**, *33*, 1884–1895. [CrossRef] [PubMed]
163. De Herdt, V.; Bogaert, S.; Bracke, K.R.; Raedt, R.; De Vos, M.; Vonck, K.; Boon, P. Effects of vagus nerve stimulation on pro- and anti-inflammatory cytokine induction in patients with refractory epilepsy. *J. Neuroimmunol.* **2009**, *214*, 104–108. [CrossRef] [PubMed]
164. Li, W.; Olshansky, B. Inflammatory cytokines and nitric oxide in heart failure and potential modulation by vagus nerve stimulation. *Heart Fail. Rev.* **2011**, *16*, 137–145. [CrossRef] [PubMed]
165. Majoie, H.J.M.; Rijkers, K.; Berfelo, M.W.; Hulsman, J.A.R.J.; Myint, A.; Schwarz, M.; Vles, J.S.H. Vagus nerve stimulation in refractory epilepsy: Effects on pro-and anti-inflammatory cytokines in peripheral blood. *Neuroimmunomodulation* **2011**, *18*, 52–56. [CrossRef]
166. Elzinga, B.M.; Bremner, J.D. Are the neural substrates of memory the final common pathway in posttraumatic stress disorder (PTSD)? *J. Affect. Disord.* **2002**, *70*, 1–17. [CrossRef]
167. Chen, S.-P.; Ayd, I.; de Moraisa, A.L.; Qina, T.; Zhenga, Y.; Sadeghiana, H.; Okaa, F.; Simon, B.; Eikermann-Haertera, K.; Ayataa, C. Vagus nerve stimulation inhibits cortical spreading depression. *Cephalagia* **2015**, *35*, 219–221. [CrossRef]
168. Ben-Menachem, E.; Hamberger, A.; Hedner, T.; Hammond, E.J.; Uthman, B.M.; Slater, J.; Treig, T.; Stefan, H.; Ramsay, R.E.; Wernicke, J.F.; et al. Effects of vagus nerve stimulation on amino acids and other metabolites in the CSF of patients with partial seizures. *Epilepsy Res.* **1995**, *20*, 221–227. [CrossRef]
169. Roosevelt, R.W.; Smith, D.C.; Clough, R.W.; Jensen, R.A.; Browning, R.A. Increased extracellular concentrations of norepinephrine in cortex and hippocampus following vagus nerve stimulation in the rat. *Brain* **2006**, *1119*, 124–132. [CrossRef]
170. Oshinsky, M.L.; Murphy, A.L.; Hekierski, H.; Cooper, M.; Simon, B.J. Noninvasive vagus nerve stimulation as treatment for trigeminal allodynia. *Pain* **2014**, *155*, 1042–2037. [CrossRef]
171. Hays, S.A.; Khodaparast, N.; Hulsey, D.R.; Ruiz, A.; Sloan, A.M.; Rennaker, R.L.; Kilgard, M.P. Vagus nerve stimulation during rehabilitative training improves functional recovery after intracerebral hemorrhage. *Stroke* **2014**, *45*, 3097–3100. [CrossRef]
172. Engineer, C.T.; Engineer, N.D.; Riley, J.R.; Seale, J.D.; Kilgard, M.P. Pairing speech sounds with vagus nerve stimulation drives stimulus-specific cortical plasticity. *Brain Stimul.* **2015**, *8*, 637–644. [CrossRef]
173. Engineer, N.D.; Riley, J.R.; Seale, J.D.; Vrana, W.A.; Shetake, J.A.; Sudanagunta, S.P.; Borland, M.S.; Kilgard, M.P. Reversing pathological neural activity using targeted plasticity. *Nature* **2011**, *470*, 101–104. [CrossRef] [PubMed]
174. Kim, H.J.; Shim, H.-J.; Kwak, M.Y.; An, Y.-H.; Kim, D.H.; Kim, Y.J. Feasibility and safety of transcutaneous vagus nerve stimulation paired with notched music therapy for the treatment of chronic tinnitus. *J. Audiol. Otol.* **2015**, *18*, 159–167.
175. Li, T.-T.; Wang, Z.-J.; Yang, S.-B.; Zhu, J.-H.; Zhang, S.-Z.; Cai, S.-J.; Ma, W.-H.; Zhang, D.-Q.; Mei, A.-G. Transcutaneous electrical stimulation at auricular acupoints innervated by auricular branch of vagus nerve pairing tone for tinnitus: Study protocol for a randomized controlled clinical trial. *Trials* **2015**, *16*, 1–9. [CrossRef] [PubMed]
176. Liu, A.; Zhao, F.-B.; Wang, J.; Lu, Y.F.; Tian, J.; Zhao, Y.; Gao, Y.; Hu, X.-J.; Liu, X.-Y.; Tan, J.; et al. Effects of vagus nerve stimulation on cognitive functioning in rats with cerebral ischemia reperfusion. *J. Transl. Med.* **2016**, *14*, 101. [CrossRef] [PubMed]

177. Hays, S.A. Enhancing rehabilitative therapies with vagus nerve stimulation. *Neurotherapeutics* **2016**, *13*, 382–394. [CrossRef]
178. Hays, S.A.; Ruiz, A.; Bethea, T.; Khodaparast, N.; Carmel, J.B.; Rennaker, R.L.; Kilgard, M.P. Vagus nerve stimulation during rehabilitative training enhances recovery of forelimb function after ischemic stroke in aged rats. *Neurobiol. Aging* **2016**, *43*, 111–118. [CrossRef]
179. Khodaparast, N.; Kilgard, M.P.; Casavant, R.; Ruiz, A.; Qureshi, I.; Ganzer, P.D.; Rennaker, R.L.; Hays, S.A. Vagus nerve stimulation during rehabilitative training improves forelimb recovery after chronic ischemic stroke in rats. *Neurorehabil. Neural Repair* **2015**, *30*, 676–684. [CrossRef]
180. Pruitt, D.T.; Schmid, A.N.; Kim, L.L.; Abe, C.M.; Trieu, J.L.; Choua, C. Vagus nerve stimulation delivered with motor training enhances recovery of function after traumatic brain injury. *J. Neurotrauma* **2016**, *33*, 871–879. [CrossRef]
181. Suthana, N.; Fried, I. Deep brain stimulation for enhancement of learning and memory. *Neuroimage* **2014**, *85*, 996–1002. [CrossRef]
182. Zuo, Y.; Smith, D.C.; Jensen, R.A. Vagus nerve stimulation potentiates hippocampal LTP in freely-moving rats. *Physiol. Behav.* **2007**, *90*, 583–589. [CrossRef] [PubMed]
183. McLaughlin, K.A.; Alves, S.; Sheridan, M.A. Vagal regulation and internalizing psychopathology among adolescents exposed to childhood adversity. *Dev. Psychobiol.* **2014**, *56*, 1036–1051. [CrossRef] [PubMed]
184. Li, M.; Zheng, C.; Sato, T.; Kawada, T.; Sugimachi, M.; Sunagawa, K. Vagal nerve stimulation markedly improves long-term survival after chronic heart failure in rats. *Circulation* **2004**, *109*, 120–124. [CrossRef] [PubMed]
185. Meyers, R.; Pearlman, A.; Hyman, R. Beneficial effects of vagal stimulation and bradycardia during experimental acute myocardial ischemia. *Circulation* **1974**, *49*, 943–947. [CrossRef]
186. Kent, K.M.; Smith, E.R.; Redwood, D.R.; Epstein, S.E. Electrical stability of acutely ischemic myocardium: Influences to heart rate and vagal stimulation. *Circulation* **1973**, *47*, 291–298. [CrossRef]
187. Bohning, D.E.; Lomarev, M.P.; Denslow, S.; Nahas, Z.; Shastri, A.; George, M.S. Vagus Nerve Stimulation (VNS) synchronized BOLD-fMRI. *Radiology* **2001**, *36*, 470–479.
188. Chae, J.H.; Nahas, Z.; Lomarev, M.; Denslow, S.; Lorberbaum, J.P.; Bohning, D.E.; George, M.S. A review of functional neuroimaging studies of Vagus Nerve Stimulation (VNS). *J. Psychiatr. Res.* **2003**, *37*, 443–455. [CrossRef]
189. Smith, M.A.; Makino, S.; Kvetnansky, R.; Post, R.M. Stress and glucocorticoids affect the expression of brain-derived neurotrophic factor and neurotrophin-3 mRNA in the hippocampus. *J. Neurosci.* **1995**, *15*, 1768–1777. [CrossRef]
190. Diamond, D.M.; Fleshner, M.; Ingersoll, N.; Rose, G.M. Psychological stress impairs spatial working memory: Relevance to electrophysiological studies of hippocampal function. *Behav. Neurosci.* **1996**, *110*, 661–672. [CrossRef]
191. Sapolsky, R.M.; Krey, L.; McEwen, B. Prolonged glucocorticoid exposure reduces hippocampal neuron number: Implications for aging. *J. Neurosci.* **1985**, *5*, 1221–1226. [CrossRef]
192. Woolley, C.S.; Gould, E.; McEwen, B.S. Exposure to excess glucocorticoids alters dendritic morphology of adult hippocampal pyramidal neurons. *Brain Res.* **1990**, *531*, 225–231. [CrossRef]
193. Elzinga, B.M.; Bermond, B.; van Dyck, R. The relationship between dissociative proneness and alexithymia. *Psychother. Psychosom.* **2002**, *71*, 104–111. [CrossRef]
194. Bremner, J.D.; Vermetten, E. The hippocampus and post-traumatic stress disorders. In *The Clinical Neurobiology of the Hippocampus: An Integrative View*; Bartsch, T., Ed.; Oxford University Press: Oxford, UK, 2012; pp. 262–272.
195. Bremner, J.D. Structural changes in the brain in depression and relationship to symptom recurrence. *CNS Spectr.* **2002**, *7*, 129–139. [CrossRef] [PubMed]
196. Bremner, J.D. Alterations in brain structure and function associated with posttraumatic stress disorder. *Semin. Clin. Neuropsychiatry* **1999**, *4*, 249–255.
197. Sheline, Y.I.; Wang, P.; Gado, M.; Csernansky, J.; Vannier, M. Hippocampal atrophy in recurrent major depression. *Proc. Natl. Acad. Sci. USA* **1996**, *93*, 3908–3913. [CrossRef]
198. LeDoux, J.E. *The Emotional Brain: The Mysterious Underpinnings of Emotional Life*; Simon & Schuster: New York, NY, USA, 1996.

199. Quirk, G.J. Memory for extinction of conditioned fear is long-lasting and persists following spontaneous recovery. *Learn. Mem.* **2002**, *9*, 402–407. [CrossRef] [PubMed]
200. Bremner, J.D.; Staib, L.; Kaloupek, D.; Southwick, S.M.; Soufer, R.; Charney, D.S. Neural correlates of exposure to traumatic pictures and sound in Vietnam combat veterans with and without posttraumatic stress disorder: A positron emission tomography study. *Biol. Psychiatry* **1999**, *45*, 806–816. [CrossRef]
201. Britton, J.C.; Phan, K.L.; Taylor, S.F.; Fig, L.M.; Liberzon, I. Corticolimbic blood flow in posttraumatic stress disorder during script-driven imagery. *Biol. Psychiatry* **2005**, *57*, 832–840. [CrossRef] [PubMed]
202. Shin, L.M.; McNally, R.J.; Kosslyn, S.M.; Thompson, W.L.; Rauch, S.L.; Alpert, N.M.; Metzger, L.J.; Lasko, N.B.; Orr, S.P.; Pitman, R.K. Regional cerebral blood flow during script-driven imagery in childhood sexual abuse-related PTSD: A PET investigation. *Am. J. Psychiatry* **1999**, *156*, 575–584. [PubMed]
203. Shin, L.M.; Kosslyn, S.M.; McNally, R.J.; Alpert, N.M.; Thompson, W.L.; Rauch, S.L.; Macklin, M.L.; Pitman, R.K. Visual imagery and perception in posttraumatic stress disorder: A positron emission tomographic investigation. *Arch. Gen. Psychiatry* **1997**, *54*, 233–237. [CrossRef]
204. Shin, L.M.; Orr, S.P.; Carson, M.A.; Rauch, S.L.; Macklin, M.L.; Lasko, N.B.; Peters, P.M.; Metzger, L.J.; Dougherty, D.D.; Cannistraro, P.A.; et al. Regional cerebral blood flow in the amygdala and medial prefrontal cortex during traumatic imagery in male and female Vietnam veterans with PTSD. *Arch. Gen. Psychiatry* **2004**, *61*, 168–176. [CrossRef] [PubMed]
205. Fonzo, G.A.; Simmons, A.N.; Thorp, S.R.; Norman, S.B.; Paulus, M.P.; Stein, M.B. Blood oxygenation level-dependent response to threat-related emotional faces in women with intimate-partner violence posttraumatic stress disorder. *Biol. Psychiatry* **2010**, *68*, 433–441. [CrossRef] [PubMed]
206. Phan, K.L.; Britton, J.C.; Taylor, S.F.; Fig, L.M.; Liberzon, I. Corticolimbic blood flow during nontraumatic emotional processing in posttraumatic stress disorder. *Arch. Gen. Psychiatry* **2006**, *63*, 184–192. [CrossRef] [PubMed]
207. Yang, P.; Wu, M.T.; Hsu, C.C.; Ker, J.H. Evidence of early neurobiological alternations in adolescents with posttraumatic stress disorder: A functional MRI study. *Neurosci. Lett.* **2004**, *370*, 13–18. [CrossRef] [PubMed]
208. Shin, L.M.; Whalen, P.J.; Pitman, R.K.; Bush, G.; Macklin, M.L.; Lasko, N.B.; Orr, S.P.; McInerney, S.C.; Rauch, S.L. An fMRI study of anterior cingulate function in posttraumatic stress disorder. *Biol. Psychiatry* **2001**, *50*, 932–942. [CrossRef]
209. Hopper, J.W.; Frewen, P.A.; van der Kolk, B.A.; Lanius, R.A. Neural correlates of reexperiencing, avoidance, and dissociation in PTSD: Symptom dimensions and emotion dysregulation in responses to script-driven trauma imagery. *J. Trauma. Stress* **2007**, *20*, 713–725. [CrossRef]
210. Hou, C.; Liu, J.; Wang, K.; Li, L.; Liang, M.; He, Z.; Liu, Y.; Zhang, Y.; Li, W.; Jiang, T. Brain responses to symptom provocation and trauma-related short-term memory recall in coal mining accident survivors with acute severe PTSD. *Brain Res.* **2007**, *1144*, 165–174. [CrossRef]
211. Lanius, R.A.; Williamson, P.C.; Hopper, J.; Densmore, M.; Boksman, K.; Gupta, M.A.; Neufeld, R.W.; Gati, J.S.; Menon, R.S. Recall of emotional states in posttraumatic stress disorder: An fMRI investigation. *Biol. Psychiatry* **2003**, *53*, 204–210. [CrossRef]
212. Lanius, R.A.; Williamson, P.C.; Densmore, M.; Boksman, K.; Gupta, M.A.; Neufeld, R.W.; Gati, J.S.; Menon, R.S. Neural correlates of traumatic memories in posttraumatic stress disorder: A functional MRI investigation. *Am. J. Psychiatry* **2001**, *158*, 1920–1922. [CrossRef]
213. Liberzon, I.; Taylor, S.F.; Amdur, R.; Jung, T.D.; Chamberlain, K.R.; Minoshima, S.; Koeppe, R.A.; Fig, L.M. Brain activation in PTSD in response to trauma-related stimuli. *Biol. Psychiatry* **1999**, *45*, 817–826. [CrossRef]
214. Liberzon, I.; Britton, J.C.; Phan, K.L. Neural correlates of traumatic recall in posttraumatic stress disorder. *Stress* **2003**, *6*, 151–156. [CrossRef] [PubMed]
215. Shin, L.M.; Wright, C.I.; Cannistraro, P.A.; Wedig, M.M.; McMullin, K.; Martis, B.; Macklin, M.L.; Lasko, N.B.; Cavanagh, S.R.; Krangel, T.S.; et al. A functional magnetic resonance imaging study of amygdala and medial prefrontal cortex responses to overtly presented fearful faces in posttraumatic stress disorder. *Arch. Gen. Psychiatry* **2005**, *62*, 273–281. [CrossRef] [PubMed]
216. Mayberg, H.S.; Liotti, M.; Brannan, S.K.; McGinnis, S.; Mahurin, R.K.; Jerabek, P.A.; Silva, J.A.; Tekell, J.L.; Martin, C.C.; Lancaster, J.L.; et al. Reciprocal limbic-cortical function and negative mood: Converging PET findings in depression and normal sadness. *Am. J. Psychiatry* **1999**, *156*, 675–682. [PubMed]

217. Sheline, Y.I.; Barcha, D.M.; Price, J.L.; Rundleb, M.M.; Vaishnavib, S.N.; Snyderb, A.Z.; Mintun, M.A.; Wanga, S.; Coalson, R.S.; Raichle, M.E. The default mode network and self-referential processes in depression. *Proc. Natl. Acad. Sci. USA* **2009**, *106*, 1942–1947. [CrossRef]
218. Drevets, W.C.; Price, J.L.; Simpson, J.R.J.; Todd, R.D.; Reich, T.; Vannier, M.; Raichle, M.E. Subgenual prefrontal cortex abnormalities in mood disorders. *Nature* **1997**, *386*, 824–827. [CrossRef]
219. Simmons, A.N.; Paulus, M.P.; Thorp, S.R.; Matthews, S.C.; Norman, S.B.; Stein, M.B. Functional activation and neural networks in women with posttraumatic stress disorder related to intimate partner violence. *Biol. Psychiatry* **2008**, *64*, 681–690. [CrossRef]
220. Rauch, S.L.; van der Kolk, B.A.; Fisler, R.E.; Alpert, N.M.; Orr, S.P.; Savage, C.R.; Fischman, A.J.; Jenike, M.A.; Pitman, R.K. A symptom provocation study of posttraumatic stress disorder using positron emission tomography and script-driven imagery. *Arch. Gen. Psychiatry* **1996**, *53*, 380–387. [CrossRef]
221. Admon, R.; Lubin, G.; Stern, O.; Rosenberg, K.; Sela, L.; Ben-Ami, H.; Hendler, T. Human vulnerability to stress depends on amygdala's predisposition and hippocampal plasticity. *Proc. Natl. Acad. Sci. USA* **2009**, *106*, 14120–14125. [CrossRef]
222. Bremner, J.D.; Vermetten, E.; Schmahl, C.; Vaccarino, V.; Vythilingam, M.; Afzal, N.; Grillon, C.; Charney, D.S. Positron emission tomographic imaging of neural correlates of a fear acquisition and extinction paradigm in women with childhood sexual abuse-related posttraumatic stress disorder. *Psychol. Med.* **2005**, *35*, 791–806. [CrossRef]
223. Rauch, S.L.; Shin, L.M.; Wright, C.I. Neuroimaging studies of amygdala function in anxiety disorders. *Ann. N. Y. Acad. Sci.* **2003**, *985*, 389–410. [CrossRef]
224. Protopopescu, X.; Pan, H.; Tuescher, O.; Cloitre, M.; Goldstein, M.; Engelien, W.; Epstein, J.; Yang, Y.; Gorman, J.; LeDoux, J.; et al. Differential time courses and specificity of amygdala activity in posttraumatic stress disorder subjects and normal control subjects. *Biol. Psychiatry* **2005**, *57*, 464–473. [CrossRef] [PubMed]
225. Chung, Y.A.; Kim, S.H.; Chung, S.K.; Chae, J.H.; Yang, D.W.; Sohn, H.S.; Jeong, J. Alterations in cerebral perfusion in posttraumatic stress disorder patients without re-exposure to accident-related stimuli. *Clin. Neurophysiol.* **2006**, *117*, 637–642. [CrossRef]
226. Felmingham, K.L.; Williams, L.M.; Kemp, A.H.; Rennie, C.; Gordon, E.; Bryant, R.A. Anterior cingulate activity to salient stimuli is modulated by autonomic arousal in posttraumatic stress disorder. *Psychiatry Res.* **2009**, *173*, 59–62. [CrossRef] [PubMed]
227. Semple, W.E.; Goyer, P.; McCormick, R.; Donovan, B.; Muzic, R.F.; Rugle, L.; McCutcheon, K.; Lewis, C.; Liebling, D.; Kowaliw, S.; et al. Higher brain blood flow at amygdala and lower frontal cortex blood flow in PTSD patients with comorbid cocaine and alcohol abuse compared to controls. *Psychiatry* **2000**, *63*, 65–74. [CrossRef] [PubMed]
228. Bryant, R.A.; Felmingham, K.L.; Kemp, A.H.; Barton, M.; Peduto, A.S.; Rennie, C.; Gordon, E.; Williams, L.M. Neural networks of information processing in posttraumatic stress disorder: A functional magnetic resonance imaging study. *Biol. Psychiatry* **2005**, *58*, 111–118. [CrossRef]
229. Armony, J.L.; Corbo, V.; Clement, M.H.; Brunet, A. Amygdala response in patients with acute PTSD to masked and unmasked emotional facial expressions. *Am. J. Psychiatry* **2005**, *162*, 1961–1963. [CrossRef]
230. Bryant, R.A.; Kemp, A.H.; Felmingham, K.L.; Liddell, B.; Olivieri, G.; Peduto, A.; Gordon, E.; Williams, L.M. Enhanced amygdala and medial prefrontal activation during nonconscious processing of fear in posttraumatic stress disorder: An fMRI study. *Hum. Brain Mapp.* **2008**, *29*, 517–523. [CrossRef]
231. Kemp, A.H.; Felmingham, K.; Das, P.; Hughes, G.; Peduto, A.S.; Bryant, R.A.; Williams, L.M. Influence of comorbid depression on fear in posttraumatic stress disorder: An fMRI study. *Psychiatry Res.* **2007**, *155*, 265–269. [CrossRef]
232. Kemp, A.H.; Felmingham, K.L.; Falconer, E.; Liddell, B.J.; Bryant, R.A.; Williams, L.M. Heterogeneity of non-conscious fear perception in posttraumatic stress disorder as a function of physiological arousal: An fMRI study. *Psychiatry Res.* **2009**, *174*, 158–161. [CrossRef]
233. Rauch, S.L.; Whalen, P.J.; Shin, L.M.; McInerney, S.C.; Macklin, M.L.; Lasko, N.B.; Orr, S.P.; Pitman, R.K. Exaggerated amygdala response to masked facial stimuli in posttraumatic stress disorder: A functional MRI study. *Biol. Psychiatry* **2000**, *47*, 769–776. [CrossRef]
234. Brohawn, K.H.; Offringa, R.; Pfaff, D.L.; Hughes, K.C.; Shin, L.M. The neural correlates of emotional memory in posttraumatic stress disorder. *Biol. Psychiatry* **2010**, *68*, 1023–1030. [CrossRef] [PubMed]

235. Brunetti, M.; Sepede, G.; Mingoia, G.; Catani, C.; Ferretti, A.; Merla, A.; Del Gratta, C.; Romani, G.L.; Babiloni, C. Elevated response of human amygdala to neutral stimuli in mild post traumatic stress disorder: Neural correlates of generalized emotional response. *Neuroscience* **2010**, *168*, 670–679. [CrossRef] [PubMed]
236. Pissiota, A.; Frans, O.; Fernandez, M.; Von Knorring, L.; Fischer, H.; Fredrikson, M. Neurofunctional correlates of posttraumatic stress disorder: A PET symptom provocation study. *Eur. Arch. Psychiatry Clin. Neurosci.* **2002**, *252*, 68–75. [CrossRef] [PubMed]
237. Milad, M.R.; Pitman, R.K.; Ellis, C.B.; Gold, A.L.; Shin, L.M.; Lasko, N.B.; Zeidan, M.A.; Handwerger, K.; Orr, S.P.; Rauch, S.L. Neurobiological basis of failure to recall extinction memory in posttraumatic stress disorder. *Biol. Psychiatry* **2009**, *66*, 1075–1082. [CrossRef]
238. Drevets, W.C.; Raichle, M.E. Neuroanatomical circuits in depression: Implications for treatment mechanisms. *Psychopharmacol. Bull.* **1992**, *28*, 261–274.
239. Drevets, W.C.; Price, J.L.; Bardgett, M.E.; Reich, T.; Todd, R.D.; Raichle, M.E. Glucose metabolism in the amygdala in depression: Relationship to diagnostic subtype and plasma cortisol levels. *Pharmacol. Biochem. Behav.* **2002**, *71*, 431–447. [CrossRef]
240. Saxena, S.; Brody, A.L.; Ho, M.L.; Zohrabi, N.; Maidment, K.M.; Baxter, L.R. Differential brain metabolic predictors of response to paroxetine in obsessive-compulsive disorder versus major depression. *Am. J. Psychiatry* **2003**, *160*, 522–532. [CrossRef]
241. Sheline, Y.I.; Barch, D.M.; Donnelly, J.M.; Ollinger, J.M.; Snyder, A.Z.; Mintun, M.A. Increased amygdala response to masked emotional faces in depressed subjects resolves with antidepressant treatment: An fMRI study. *Biol. Psychiatry* **2001**, *50*, 651–658. [CrossRef]
242. Bremner, J.D.; Campanella, C. Effects of psychotherapy for psychological trauma on PTSD symptoms and the brain. In *Posttraumatic Stress Disorder: From Neurobiology to Treatment*; Bremner, J.D., Ed.; John Wiley & Sons: Hoboken, NJ, USA, 2016; pp. 413–420.
243. Vermetten, E.; Vythilingam, M.; Southwick, S.M.; Charney, D.S.; Bremner, J.D. Long-term treatment with paroxetine increases verbal declarative memory and hippocampal volume in posttraumatic stress disorder. *Biol. Psychiatry* **2003**, *54*, 693–702. [CrossRef]
244. Letizia, B.; Andrea, F.; Paolo, C. Neuroanatomical changes after eye movement desensitization and reprocessing (EMDR) treatment in posttraumatic stress disorder. *J. Neuropsychiatry Clin. Neurosci.* **2007**, *19*, 475–476. [CrossRef]
245. Bremner, J.D.; Mletzko, T.; Welter, S.; Quinn, S.; Williams, C.; Brummer, M.; Siddiq, S.; Reed, L.; Heim, C.M.; Nemeroff, C.B. Effects of phenytoin on memory, cognition and brain structure in posttraumatic stress disorder: A pilot study. *J. Psychopharmacol.* **2005**, *19*, 159–165. [CrossRef] [PubMed]
246. Fani, N.; Kitayama, N.; Ashraf, A.; Reed, L.; Afzal, N.; Jawed, F.; Bremner, J.D. Neuropsychological functioning in patients with posttraumatic stress disorder following short-term paroxetine treatment. *Psychopharmacol. Bull.* **2009**, *42*, 53–68. [PubMed]
247. Fani, N.; Ashraf, A.; Afzal, N.; Jawed, F.; Kitayama, N.; Reed, L.; Bremner, J.D. Increased neural response to trauma scripts in posttraumatic stress disorder following paroxetine treatment: A pilot study. *Neurosci. Lett.* **2011**, *491*, 196–201. [CrossRef] [PubMed]
248. Brody, A.L.; Saxena, S.; Stoessel, P.; Gillies, L.A.; Fairbanks, L.A.; Alborzian, S.; Phelps, M.E.; Huang, S.C.; Wu, H.M.; Ho, M.L.; et al. Regional brain metabolic changes in patients with major depression treated with either paroxetine or interpersonal therapy: Preliminary findings. *Arch. Gen. Psychiatry* **2001**, *58*, 631–640. [CrossRef] [PubMed]
249. Bremner, J.D.; Vythilingam, M.; Vermetten, E.; Charney, D.S. Effects of antidepressant treatment on neural correlates of emotional and neutral declarative verbal memory in depression. *J. Affect. Disord.* **2007**, *101*, 99–111. [CrossRef]
250. Drevets, W.C.; Bogers, W.; Raichle, M.E. Functional anatomical correlates of antidepressant drug treatment assessed using PET measures of regional glucose metabolism. *Eur. Neuropsychopharmacol.* **2002**, *12*, 527–544. [CrossRef]
251. Kennedy, S.H.; Evans, K.R.; Kruger, S.; Mayberg, H.S.; Meyer, J.H.; McCann, S.; Arifuzzman, A.I.; Houle, S.; Vaccarino, F.J. Changes in regional brain glucose metabolism measured with positron emission tomography after paroxetine treatment of major depression. *Am. J. Psychiatry* **2001**, *158*, 899–905. [CrossRef]

252. Vythilingam, M.; Vermetten, E.; Anderson, G.M.; Luckenbaugh, D.; Anderson, E.R.; Snow, J.; Staib, L.H.; Charney, D.S.; Bremner, J.D. Hippocampal volume, memory and cortisol status in major depressive disorder: Effects of treatment. *Biol. Psychiatry* **2004**, *56*, 101–112. [CrossRef]
253. Henry, T.R. Therapeutic mechanisms of vagus nerve stimulation. *Neurology* **2002**, *59*, S3–S14. [CrossRef]
254. Henry, T.R.; Bakay, R.A.; Votaw, J.R.; Pennell, P.B.; Epstein, C.M.; Faber, T.L.; Grafton, S.T.; Hoffman, J.M. Brain blood flow alterations induced by therapeutic vagus nerve stimulation in partial epilepsy: I. Acute effects at high and low levels of stimulation. *Epilepsia* **1998**, *39*, 983–990. [CrossRef]
255. Conway, C.R.; Sheline, Y.I.; Chibnall, J.T.; Bucholz, R.D.; Price, J.L.; Gangwani, S.; Mintun, M.A. Brain blood-flow change with acute vagus nerve stimulation in treatment-refractory major depressive disorder. *Brain Stimul.* **2012**, *5*, 163–171. [CrossRef]
256. Fang, J.; Egorova, N.; Rong, P.; Liu, J.; Hong, Y.; Fan, Y.; Wang, X.; Wang, H.; Yu, Y.; Ma, Y.; et al. Early cortical biomarkers of longitudinal transcutaneous vagus nerve stimulation treatment success in depression. *Neuroimage Clin.* **2017**, *14*, 105–111. [CrossRef]
257. Liu, J.; Fang, J.; Wang, Z.; Rong, P.; Hong, Y.; Fan, Y.; Wang, X.; Park, J.; Jin, Y.; Liu, C.; et al. Transcutaneous vagus nerve stimulation modulates amygdala functional connectivity in patients with depression. *J. Affect. Disord.* **2016**, *205*, 319–326. [CrossRef]
258. Lomarev, M.; Denslow, S.; Nahas, Z.; Chae, J.-H.; George, M.S.; Bohning, D.E. Vagus nerve stimulation (VNS): Synchronized BOLD fMRI suggests that VNS in depressed adults has frequency and/or dose dependent effects at rest and during a simple task. *J. Psychiatr. Res.* **2002**, *36*, 219–227. [CrossRef]
259. Van Laere, K.; Vonck, K.; Boon, P.; Versijpt, J.; Dierckx, R. Perfusion SPECT changes after acute and chronic vagus nerve stimulation in relation to prestimulus condition and long-term efficacy. *J. Nucl. Med.* **2002**, *43*, 733–744. [PubMed]
260. Bremner, J.D.; Wittbrodt, M.T.; Gurel, N.Z.; Nye, J.; Alam, A.; Vaccarino, V.; Ladd, S.L.; Shallenberger, L.H.; Huang, M.; Ko, Y.-Y.; et al. Brain correlates of non-invasive Vagal Nerve Stimulation in stress. In Proceedings of the NYC Neuromodulation/NANS Conference, New York, NY, USA, 24–26 August 2018; p. 14.
261. Bremner, J.D.; Rapaport, M.H. Vagus Nerve Stimulation: Back to the future. *Am. J. Psychiatry* **2017**, *174*, 609–610. [CrossRef] [PubMed]
262. Yakunina, N.; Kim, S.S.; Nam, E.-C. Optimization of transcutaneous vagus nerve stimulation using functional MRI. *Neuromodulation* **2017**, *20*, 290–300. [CrossRef]
263. Redgrave, J.; Day, D.; Leung, H.; Ali, A.; Lindert, R.; Majid, A. Safety and tolerability of transcutaneous vagus nerve stimulation in humans: A systematic review. *Brain Stimul.* **2018**, *11*, 1225–1238. [CrossRef] [PubMed]
264. Ben-Menachem, E.; Revesz, D.; Simon, B.J.; Silberstein, S. Surgically implanted and non-invasive vagus nerve stimulation: A review of efficacy, safety and tolerability. *Eur. J. Neurol.* **2015**, *22*, 1260–1268. [CrossRef]
265. Nonis, R.; D'Ostilio, K.; Schoenen, J.; Magis, D. Evidence of activation of vagal afferents by non-invasive vagus nerve stimulation: An electrophysiological study in healthy volunteers. *Cephalagia* **2017**, *37*, 1285–1293. [CrossRef]
266. Usami, K.; Kawai, K.; Sonoo, M.; Saito, N. Scalp-recorded evoked potentials as a marker for afferent nerve impulse in clinical vagus nerve stimulation. *Brain Stimul.* **2013**, *6*, 615–623. [CrossRef] [PubMed]
267. Yoo, P.B.; Lubock, N.B.; Hincapie, J.G.; Ruble, S.B.; Hamann, J.J.; Grill, W.M. High-resolution measurement of electrically-evoked vagus nerve activity in the anesthetized dog. *J. Neural Eng.* **2013**, *10*. [CrossRef] [PubMed]
268. Fallgatter, A.J.; Neuhauser, B.; Herrmann, M.J.; Ehlis, A.-C.; Wagener, A.; Scheuerpflug, P.; Reiners, K.; Riederer, P. Far field potentials from the brain stem after transcutaneous vagus nerve stimulation. *J. Neural Transm.* **2003**, *110*, 1437–1443. [CrossRef] [PubMed]
269. Frangos, E.; Ellrich, E.; Komisaruk, B.R. Non-invasive access to the vagus nerve central projections via electrical stimulation of the external ear: fMRI evidence in humans. *Brain Stimul.* **2015**, *8*, 624–636. [CrossRef]
270. Badran, B.W.; Dowdle, L.T.; Mithoefer, O.J.; LaBate, N.T.; Coatsworth, J.; Brown, J.C.; DeVries, W.H.; Austelle, C.W.; McTeague, L.M.; George, M.S. Neurophysiologic effects of transcutaneous auricular vagus nerve stimulation (taVNS) via electrical stimulation of the tragus: A concurrent taVNS/fMRI study and review. *Brain Stimul.* **2018**, *11*, 492–500. [CrossRef]
271. Frangos, E.; Komisaruk, B.R. Access to vagal projections via cutaneous electrical stimulation of the neck: fMRI evidence in healthy humans. *Brain Stimul.* **2017**, *10*, 19–27. [CrossRef]

272. Clancy, J.A.; Mary, D.A.; Witte, K.K.; Greenwood, J.P.; Deuchars, S.A.; Deuchars, J. Non-invasive vagus nerve stimulation in healthy humans reduces sympathetic nerve activity. *Brain Stimul.* **2014**, *7*, 871–877. [CrossRef]
273. Badran, B.W.; Mithoefer, O.J.; Summer, C.E.; LaBate, N.T.; Glusman, C.E.; Badran, A.W.; DeVries, W.H.; Summers, P.M.; Austelle, C.W.; McTeague, L.M.; et al. Short trains of transcutaneous auricular vagus nerve stimulation (taVNS) have parameter-specific effects on heart rate. *Brain Stimul.* **2018**, *11*, 699–708. [CrossRef]
274. Warren, C.M.; Tona, K.D.; Ouwerkerk, L.; van Paridon, J.; Poletiek, F.; van Steenbergen, H.; Bosch, J.A.; Nieuwenhuis, S. The neuromodulatory and hormonal effects of transcutaneous vagus nerve stimulation as evidenced by salivary alpha amylase, salivary cortisol, pupil diameter, and the P3 event-related potential. *Brain Stimul.* **2019**, *12*, 635–642. [CrossRef]
275. Burger, A.M.; Verkuil, B.; Fenlon, H.; Thijs, L.; Cools, H.C.; Miller, I.; Vervliet, B.; Van Diest, I. Mixed evidence for the potential of non-invasive transcutaneous vagal nerve stimulation to improve the extinction and retention of fear. *Behav. Res. Ther.* **2017**, *97*, 64–74. [CrossRef]
276. Verkuil, B.; Burger, A.M. Transcutaneous vagus nerve stimulation does not affect attention to fearful faces in high worriers. *Behav. Res. Ther.* **2019**, *113*, 25–31. [CrossRef] [PubMed]
277. Gurel, N.Z.; Huang, M.; Wittbrodt, M.T.; Jung, H.; Ladd, S.L.; Shandhi, M.H.; Ko, Y.-A.; Shallenberger, L.; Nye, J.A.; Pearce, B.; et al. Quantifying acute physiological biomarkers of transcutaneous cervical vagal nerve stimulation in the context of psychological stress. *Brain Stimul.* **2020**, *13*, 47–59. [CrossRef] [PubMed]
278. Gurel, N.Z.; Gazi, A.H.; Scott, K.L.; Wittbrodt, M.T.; Shah, A.J.; Vaccarino, V.; Bremner, J.D.; Inan, O.T. Timing considerations for noninvasive Vagal Nerve Stimulation in clinical studies. *AMIA Annu. Symp. Proc.* **2020**, *2019*, 1061–1070. [PubMed]
279. Gurel, N.Z.; Wittbrodt, W.T.; Jung, H.; Ladd, S.L.; Shah, A.J.; Vaccarino, V.; Bremner, J.D.; Inan, O.T. Automatic detection of target engagement in transcutaneous cervical Vagal Nerve Stimulation for traumatic stress triggers. *IEEE J. Biomed. Health Inform.* **2020**, *24*, 1917–1925. [CrossRef] [PubMed]
280. Brock, C.; Brock, B.; Aziz, Q.; Møller, H.J.; Pfeiffer Jensen, M.; Drewes, A.M.; Farmer, A.D. Transcutaneous cervical vagal nerve stimulation modulates cardiac vagal tone and tumor necrosis factor-alpha. *Neurogastroenterol. Motil.* **2017**, *29*, e12999. [CrossRef]
281. Lerman, I.; Hauger, R.; Sorkin, L.; Proudfoot, J.; Davis, B.; Huang, A.; Lam, K.; Simon, B.; Baker, D.G. Noninvasive transcutaneous vagus nerve stimulation decreases whole blood culture-derived cytokines and chemokines: A randomized, blinded, healthy control pilot trial. *Neuromodulation* **2016**, *19*, 283–290. [CrossRef]
282. Tarn, J.; Legg, S.; Mitchell, S.; Simon, B.; Ng, W.-F. The effects of noninvasive vagus nerve stimulation on fatigue and immune responses in patients with primary Sjögren's Syndrome. *Neuromodulation* **2019**, *22*, 580–585. [CrossRef]
283. Milev, R.V.; Giacobbe, P.; Kennedy, S.H.; Blumberger, D.M.; Daskalakis, Z.J.; Downar, J.; Modirrousta, M.; Patry, S.; Vila-Rodriguez, F.; Lam, R.W.; et al. Canadian Network for Mood and Anxiety Treatments (CANMAT) 2016 clinical guidelines for the management of adults with major depressive disorder: Section 4. Neurostimulation Treatments. *Can. J. Psychiatry* **2016**, *61*, 561–575. [CrossRef]
284. Feldman, R.L.; Dunner, D.L.; Muller, J.S.; Stone, D.A. Medicare patient experience with vagus nerve stimulation for treatment-resistant depression. *J. Med. Econ.* **2013**, *16*, 63–74. [CrossRef]
285. Hasan, A.; Wolff-Menzler, C.; Pfeiffer, S.; Falkai, P.; Weidinger, E.; Jobst, A.; Hoell, I.; Malchow, B.; Yeganeh-Doost, P.; Strube, W.; et al. Transcutaneous noninvasive vagus nerve stimulation (tVNS) in the treatment of schizophrenia: A bicentric randomized controlled pilot study. *Eur. Arch. Psychiatry Clin. Neurosci.* **2015**, *256*, 589–600. [CrossRef]
286. D'Urso, G.; Brunoni, A.R.; Mazzaferro, M.P.; Anastasia, A.; de Bartolomeis, A.; Mantovani, A. Transcranial direct current stimulation for obsessive-compulsive disorder: A randomized, controlled, partial crossover trial. *Depress. Anxiety* **2016**, *33*, 1132–1140. [CrossRef] [PubMed]
287. Rong, P.; Liu, J.; Wang, L.; Liu, R.; Fang, J.; Zhao, J.; Zhao, Y.; Wang, H.; Vangel, M.; Sun, S.; et al. Effect of transcutaneous auricular vagus nerve stimulation on major depressive disorder: A nonrandomized controlled pilot study. *J. Affect. Disord.* **2016**, *195*, 172–179. [CrossRef] [PubMed]
288. Lamb, D.G.; Porges, E.C.; Lewis, G.F.; Williamson, J.B. Non-invasive Vagal Nerve Stimulation effects on hyperarousal and autonomic state in patients with posttraumatic stress disorder and history of mild traumatic brain injury: Preliminary evidence. *Front. Med.* **2017**, *4*, 124. [CrossRef] [PubMed]

289. George, M.S.; Ward, H.E.; Ninan, P.T.; Pollack, M.; Nahas, Z.; Anderson, B.; Kose, S.; Howland, R.H.; Goodman, W.K.; Ballenger, J.C. A pilot study of vagus nerve stimulation (VNS) for treatment-resistant anxiety disorders. *Brain Stimul.* **2008**, *1*, 112–121. [CrossRef] [PubMed]
290. Barbanti, P.; Grazzi, L.; Egeo, G.; Padovan, A.; Liebler, E.; Bussone, G. Non-invasive vagus nerve stimulation for acute treatment of high-frequency and chronic migraine: An open-label study. *J. Headache Pain* **2015**, *16*, 61. [CrossRef]
291. Nesbitt, A.D.; Marin, J.C.A.; Tomkins, E.; Ruttledge, M.H.; Goadsby, P.J. Non-invasive vagus nerve stimulation for the treatment of cluster headache: A case series. *J. Headache Pain* **2013**, *14*. [CrossRef]
292. Gaul, C.; Magis, D.; Liebler, E.J.; Straube, A. Effects of non-invasive vagus nerve stimulation on attack frequency over time and expanded response rates in patients with chronic cluster headache: A post hoc analysis of the randomized, controlled PREVA Study. *J. Headache Pain* **2017**, *18*, 22. [CrossRef]
293. Rosell, J.; Colominas, J.; Riu, P.; Pallas-Areny, R.; Webster, J.G. Skin impedance from 1 Hz to 1 MHz. *IEEE Trans. Biomed. Eng.* **1988**, *35*, 649–651. [CrossRef]
294. Gazi, A.H.; Gurel, N.Z.; Richardson, J.L.S.; Wittbrodt, M.T.; Shah, A.J.; Vaccarino, V.; Bremner, J.D.; Inan, O.T. Investigating digital cardiovascular biomarker responses to transcutaneous cervical vagus nerve stimulation: State-space modeling, prediction, and simulation. *JMIR hHealth uHealth* **2020**. [CrossRef]
295. Wittbrodt, M.T.; Gurel, N.Z.; Nye, J.A.; Ladd, S.; Shandhi, M.M.H.; Huang, M.; Shah, A.J.; Pearce, B.D.; Alam, Z.S.; Rapaport, M.H.; et al. Non-invasive vagal nerve stimulation decreases brain activity during trauma scripts. *Brain Stimul.* **2020**, *13*, 1333–1348. [CrossRef]
296. Pimple, P.; Lima, B.B.; Hammadah, M.; Wilmot, K.; Ramadan, R.; Levantsevych, O.; Sullivan, S.; Kim, J.H.; Kaseer, B.; Shah, A.J.; et al. Psychological distress and subsequent cardiovascular events in individuals with coronary artery disease. *J. Am. Hear. Assoc.* **2019**, *8*, e011866. [CrossRef] [PubMed]
297. Lima, B.B.; Hammadah, M.; Pearce, B.D.; Shah, A.; Moazzami, K.; Kim, J.H.; Sullivan, S.; Levantsevych, O.; Lewis, T.T.; Weng, L.; et al. Association of posttraumatic stress disorder with mental stress-induced myocardial ischemia in adults after myocardial infarction. *JAMA Netw. Open* **2020**, *3*, e202734. [CrossRef] [PubMed]
298. Pimple, P.; Shah, A.; Rooks, C.; Bremner, J.D.; Nye, J.; Ibeanu, I.; Murrah, N.; Shallenberger, L.; Kelley, M.; Raggi, P.; et al. Association between anger and mental stress-induced myocardial ischemia. *Am. Heart J.* **2015**, *169*, 115–121. [CrossRef] [PubMed]
299. Gurel, N.Z.; Mobashir, H.S.; Bremner, J.D.; Vaccarino, V.; Ladd, S.L.; Shah, A.; Inan, O.T. Toward closed-loop transcutaneous vagus nerve stimulation using peripheral cardiovascular physiological biomarkers: A proof-of-concept study. *IEEE Body Sens. Netw.* **2018**. [CrossRef]
300. Szeska, C.; Richter, J.; Wendt, J.; Weymar, M.; Hamm, A.O. Promoting long-term inhibition of human fear responses by non-invasive transcutaneous vagus nerve stimulation during extinction training. *Sci. Rep.* **2020**, *10*, 1529. [CrossRef] [PubMed]

Journal of *Personalized Medicine*

MDPI

Article

Lower Hippocampal Volume in Patients with Schizophrenia and Bipolar Disorder: A Quantitative MRI Study

Jinya Sato [1], Yoji Hirano [1,2,*], Noriaki Hirakawa [1], Junichi Takahashi [1], Naoya Oribe [1,3], Hironori Kuga [1,3], Itta Nakamura [1], Shogo Hirano [1], Takefumi Ueno [3], Osamu Togao [4], Akio Hiwatashi [5], Tomohiro Nakao [1] and Toshiaki Onitsuka [1,*]

1 Department of Neuropsychiatry, Graduate School of Medical Sciences, Kyushu University, Fukuoka 812-8582, Japan; jinya.sato56@gmail.com (J.S.); hirakawa34@gmail.com (N.H.); yoonil1977@gmail.com (J.T.); n.oribe@mac.com (N.O.); hirokuga.370@gmail.com (H.K.); nakamura.itta.352@m.kyushu-u.ac.jp (I.N.); hiranoshogo@gmail.com (S.H.); nakao.tomohiro.275@m.kyushu-u.ac.jp (T.N.)
2 Institute of Industrial Science, The University of Tokyo, Tokyo 153-8505, Japan
3 Hizen Psychiatric Medical Center, Division of Clinical Research, National Hospital Organization, Saga 842-0192, Japan; uenotk@gmail.com
4 Department of Molecular Imaging and Diagnosis, Graduate School of Medical Sciences, Kyushu University, Fukuoka 812-8582, Japan; togao@radiol.med.kyushu-u.ac.jp
5 Department of Clinical Radiology, Graduate School of Medical Sciences, Kyushu University, Fukuoka 812-8582, Japan; hiwatasi@radiol.med.kyushu-u.ac.jp
* Correspondence: yhouji@mac.com (Y.H.); onitsuka.toshiaki.939@m.kyushu-u.ac.jp (T.O.); Tel.: +81-92-642-5627 (Y.H. & T.O.)

Citation: Sato, J.; Hirano, Y.; Hirakawa, N.; Takahashi, J.; Oribe, N.; Kuga, H.; Nakamura, I.; Hirano, S.; Ueno, T.; Togao, O.; et al. Lower Hippocampal Volume in Patients with Schizophrenia and Bipolar Disorder: A Quantitative MRI Study. *J. Pers. Med.* **2021**, *11*, 121. https://doi.org/10.3390/jpm11020121

Academic Editor: Yoshihiro Noda

Received: 30 December 2020
Accepted: 9 February 2021
Published: 13 February 2021

Abstract: Since patients with schizophrenia (SZ) and bipolar disorder (BD) share many biological features, detecting biomarkers that differentiate SZ and BD patients is crucial for optimized treatments. High-resolution magnetic resonance imaging (MRI) is suitable for detecting subtle brain structural differences in patients with psychiatric disorders. In the present study, we adopted a neuroanatomically defined and manually delineated region of interest (ROI) method to evaluate the amygdalae, hippocampi, Heschl's gyrus (HG), and planum temporale (PT), because these regions are crucial in the development of SZ and BD. ROI volumes were measured using high resolution MRI in 31 healthy subjects (HS), 23 SZ patients, and 21 BD patients. Right hippocampal volumes differed significantly among groups (HS > BD > SZ), whereas left hippocampal volumes were lower in SZ patients than in HS and BD patients (HS = BD > SZ). Volumes of the amygdalae, HG, and PT did not differ among the three groups. For clinical correlations, there were no significant associations between ROI volumes and demographics/clinical symptoms. Our study revealed significant lower hippocampal volume in patients with SZ and BD, and we suggest that the right hippocampal volume is a potential biomarker for differentiation between SZ and BD.

Keywords: schizophrenia; bipolar disorder; MRI; hippocampus; volume reduction

1. Introduction

Patients with schizophrenia (SZ) and bipolar disorder (BD) share many biological features, including genetic architecture (e.g., [1,2]) and structural (e.g., [3]) and functional brain abnormalities (e.g., [4–10]). Clinically, it is an urgent issue to accurately diagnose and distinguish between the two diseases for providing appropriate treatment and improving patient outcome, as they sometimes present similar pathologies. Thus, the identification of anatomical and functional biomarkers is crucial for differentiating SZ and BD patients to optimize pharmacological and psychosocial treatments for each condition [11]. Subcortical and cortical abnormalities in psychoses have been reported extensively, and high-resolution magnetic resonance imaging (MRI) is well-suited for detecting subtle brain structural differences in these populations [12–15]. A gold standard approach in MRI research is the use of neuroanatomically defined and manually delineated regions of interest (ROIs). A voxel-based morphometric (VBM) method is useful to investigate the whole brain, but the anatomical warping and density-based methodology can lead to failure in detecting abnormalities that are identified using ROI analyses [16]. Furthermore, it has been suggested that the analytical flexibility and the complex and variable workflows have substantial effects on results [17]; therefore, simpler MRI analysis methods still carry value. In the present study, we adopted a neuroanatomically defined and manually delineated ROI method to evaluate the amygdalae, hippocampi, Heschl's gyrus (HG), and planum temporale (PT) as regions that have been shown to be crucial in the development of SZ and BD [18–21].

Medial temporal lobe changes are one of the most consistent findings in MRI studies of SZ and BD. The hippocampus is involved in memory and spatial learning [22]. Hippocampal volume reductions have been reported repeatedly in patients with SZ and BD [23]. The amygdala is an almond-shaped nucleus located deep within the medial temporal lobes and plays a primary role in the processing and memory of emotional reactions [24,25]. Both increases and decreases in amygdala volumes have been reported in patients with BD, although a recent meta-analysis found no significant amygdala volume changes in BD [26]. Conversely, an international collaboration for the study of BD, the Enhancing Neuroimaging Genetics through Meta-Analysis (ENIGMA) Consortium, reported significantly smaller amygdaloid volumes in BD compared with healthy subjects (HS) [27].

The HG includes the primary auditory cortex [28], and the left PT plays an important role in language processing [29]. Structural abnormalities of HG and PT [18,30], alongside auditory and language-related deficits [31,32], are observed frequently in patients with SZ. For example, patients with first-episode SZ showed lower left PT and bilateral HG gray matter volumes compared with HS and patients with BD [30]. In addition, Kasai et al. reported progressive volume reductions in the left HG and PT gray matter in first-episode SZ patients, which were not observed in first-episode affective psychosis patients or HS [18]. More recently, Hirano et al. investigated the association between neurophysiological and structural deficits in SZ patients and found spontaneous gamma oscillation deficits [33] and cortical volume deficits in HG [34]. In BD patients, Reite et al. reported alterations in structural/functional asymmetry in HG [18]. Moreover, Takahashi et al. reported that BD patients showed significantly lower left PT volumes compared with HS [35].

In the present study, we adopted a neuroanatomically defined and manually delineated ROI method to evaluate the amygdalae, hippocampi, HG, and PT. As noted before, functional or structural abnormalities have been reported in both SZ and BD in these four ROIs. We hypothesized that medial temporal lobe abnormalities (mainly hippocampus) may be common to both SZ and BD, and lateral temporal lobe abnormalities may be specific to SZ.

2. Materials and Methods

2.1. Participants

We analyzed magnetic resonance (MR) images of 23 patients with SZ, 21 patients with BD, and 31 HS. All subjects had normal hearing, were aged 20–63 years, and were right-handed [36]. After a detailed description of the study, all participants provided informed consent, according to the regulations of the Ethics Committee of the Graduate School of Medical Sciences, Kyushu University. Experimental procedures were approved by the Kyushu University Institutional Review Board for Clinical Trials (approval number: 26018, date: June 12, 2014), and conformed to the Declaration of Helsinki. The exclusion criteria were (1) neurological illness or major head trauma, (2) having received electroconvulsive therapy, (3) alcohol or drug dependence, (4) alcohol or drug abuse within the past 5 years, or (5) a verbal intelligence quotient below 75. HS were screened using the Structured Clinical Interview nonpatient edition. None of the HS or their first-degree relatives had an Axis-I psychiatric disorder. The socioeconomic status (SES) of the subjects and their parental SES were measured using the Hollingshead two-factor index [37]. For SZ, the Positive and Negative Syndrome Scale (PANSS) [38] was administered to assess the severity of psychiatric symptoms. The Young Mania Rating Scale (YMRS) [39] and the

Hamilton Depression Rating Scale (HAM-D) [40] were administered to assess the severity of mood symptoms in BD. Table 1 shows the demographic and clinical characteristics of the participants.

Table 1. Demographic and clinical characteristics of the participants.

	Healthy Subjects (HS)	Patients with Bipolar Disorder (BD)	Patients with Schizophrenia (SZ)	$\chi 2$ or F or t	df	p
Male/Female	11/20	11/10	8/15	1.66	2	0.44
Age (years)	49.2 ± 9.8	48.9 ± 9.1	44.3 ± 6.2	2.50	2, 73	0.09
Handedness [a]	92.0 ± 32.7	82.4 ± 51.0	96.7 ± 8.7	0.99	2, 73	0.38
SES [b]	2.4 ± 0.8	2.9 ± 1.0	3.6 ± 1.0	10.66	2, 45	<0.001
Parental SES	3.1 ± 0.9	2.9 ± 0.9	2.8 ± 0.9	1.10	2, 45	0.34
Education (years)	14.4 ± 2.6	14.2 ± 2.3	14.4 ± 2.0	0.95	2, 45	0.39
Symptom onset [#] (years)		37.8 ± 11.2	26.7 ± 6.7	31.95	42	<0.001
Medication dose (CPZ equiv., mg)		144.2 ± 183.9	599.8 ± 328.4	5.60	42	<0.001
PANSS positive			18.1 ± 7.9			
PANSS negative			22.5 ± 7.7			
PANSS general			42.9 ± 15.2			
YMRS		5.2 ± 5.7				
SIGH-D score		10.3 ± 5.9				

Values are means ± SD unless otherwise noted. [a] Edinburgh Handedness Inventory, [b] Hollingshead two factor Index of Social Position. SES = socioeconomic status, YMRS = Young Mania Rating Scale, SIGH-D = Structured Interview Guide for the Hamilton Depression Rating Scale. [#] Symptom onset is the age at which the symptoms appeared.

2.2. MRI Data Acquisition

T1-weighted MR images were acquired using a three-dimensional (3D) turbo field echo sequence on a 3 Tesla scanner (Achieva TX, Philips Healthcare, Best, The Netherlands) at the Department of Radiology, Kyushu University Hospital. The imaging variables were as follows: repetition time = 8.2 ms, echo time = 3.8 ms, flip angle = 8°, field of view = 24 × 24 cm, number of echoes = 1, matrix = 240 × 240, inversion time = 1025.9 ms, number of slices = 190, and slice thickness = 1 mm. Images were aligned using the anterior and posterior commissure line and the sagittal sulcus to correct head tilt.

Total gray matter, white matter, and cerebrospinal fluid (CSF) volumes were calculated using Statistical Parametric Mapping 12 (SPM12, http://www.fil.ion.ucl.ac.uk/spm (accessed on 7 October 2020)), and VBM was performed using SPM12, running in MATLAB R2014a (The Math Works Inc., Natick, MA, USA). T1-weighted images were first segmented into gray matter, white matter, and CSF sections using tissue probability maps based on the International Consortium of Brain Mapping template for East Asian brains. Subsequently, we performed diffeomorphic anatomical registration through exponentiated lie algebra in SPM12 for intersubject registration of gray matter images [41]. The registered images were then smoothed with a Gaussian kernel of 8 mm full-width half-maximum and transformed into Montreal Neurological Institute stereotactic space using affine and nonlinear spatial normalization, implemented in SPM12. Total gray matter, white matter, and CSF volumes were generated from the VBM analysis. Total intracranial volume (ICV) was calculated as the sum of the gray matter, white matter, and CSF volumes.

2.3. Regions of Interest and Volume Measurement

The gray matter of the HG and PT, hippocampi, and amygdalae were outlined manually on a PC without knowledge of diagnosis (Figure 1). We used 3D information to provide reliable measures of the ROIs using a software package for medical image analysis [3D slicer, http://www.slicer.org (accessed on 7 October 2020)].

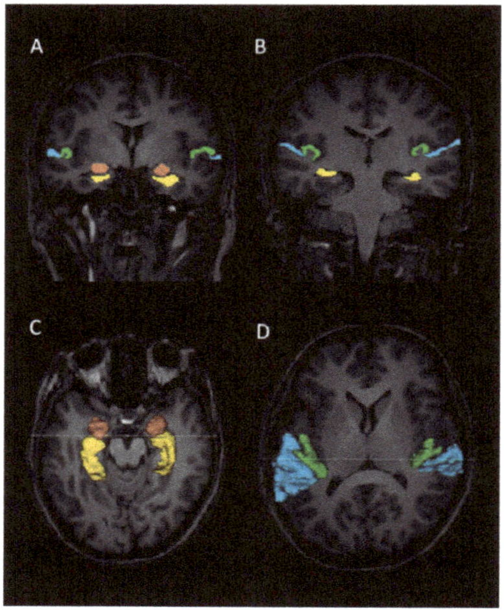

Figure 1. Delineation of Heschl's gyrus (HG), planum temporale (PT), hippocampi, and amygdalae on 3 Tesla magnetic resonance imaging slices in a healthy subject. The HG (green), PT (blue), hippocampus (yellow), and amygdala (brown) regions of interest are outlined. (**A**,**B**): Coronal view of the HG, PT, hippocampi, and amygdalae. (**C**): Three-dimensional (3D) reconstruction of the hippocampi and amygdalae superimposed onto an axial slice. (**D**): 3D reconstruction of HG and PT gray matter superimposed onto an axial slice. The lines on **C** and **D** correspond to the coronal slices of **A** and **B**, respectively.

We used similar criteria to the previous works of Kwon et al. and Barta et al. for delineating HG and PT [42,43]. Briefly, HG was first identified in the most posterior coronal slice. Investigators manually drew the gray matter of HG from the most posterior to the most anterior slice. The most anterior slice of HG was defined as the last slice that HG could be identified anteriorly. In most cases, HG represented a single transverse convolution. In cases of more than one transverse convolution, we followed the literature's definition [44–47]: when multiple convolutions originated medially from a common stem, these were all were defined as HG; however, when they originated separately from the retroinsular region, only the most anterior gyrus was labeled as HG, and the more posterior gyri were identified as PT. The anterior border of PT was defined by the posterior border of HG. Posteriorly, investigators traced the gray matter of the PT on the coronal images to the end of the Sylvian fissure. The amygdalae and hippocampi were also outlined manually. For the amygdala and hippocampus, the most anterior slice used for the amygdala was the slice in which the white matter tract linking the temporal lobe with the rest of the brain (temporal stem) could be seen. The most posterior slice of the hippocampus was the last appearance of fibers of the crux of the fornix. Once drawn, ROIs could be viewed in any plane as 3D objects for further editing. All editing was performed blind to diagnosis. Interrater reliability of the ROIs was evaluated by three independent raters (J.S., N.H., and J.T.), who were also blind to diagnosis. Five cases were selected at random, and every slice was edited by the raters. The intraclass correlations for interrater reliability were calculated.

2.4. Statistical Analysis

To correct for brain size differences, we used relative volumes, which were calculated using the following formula: relative volume (%) = (absolute ROI volume/ICV) × 100. For the ROI analysis of the subcortical structures, we used a mixed model repeated measures analysis of variance (ANCOVA) with group (SZ, BD, and HS) as the between-subjects factor, hemisphere (left or right) and region (amygdala or hippocampus) as the within-subjects factors, and age as a covariate. When significant interactions related to group were observed, we evaluated group differences separately for each region to identify the source of the interactions. We used follow-up ANCOVAs with group as the between-subjects factor, hemisphere as the within-subjects factor, and age as a covariate for each region. We performed one-way analyses of variance (ANOVAs) of the average volume across both hemispheres for each ROI. For the ROI analysis of the cortical structures, we used a mixed model ANCOVA with group (SZ, BD, and HS) as the between-subjects factor, hemisphere (left or right) and region (HG or PT) as the within-subjects factors, and age as a covariate. Post hoc tests were the same as the subcortical structure analyses. All statistical tests in ANCOVA and ANOVA were 2-tailed with *alpha* = 0.05. Exploratory analyses of the relationship between relative volumes of the ROIs and psychopathology scales were evaluated using *Spearman's rho*. Due to our analyses involving multiple correlations, we set alpha levels at a conservative $p < 0.001$.

When significant group differences were observed in a particular region, optimal sensitivity and specificity of the ROI for the diagnosis of HS, SZ, or BD were determined via receiver operating characteristic (ROC) curve analysis using a nonparametric approach. We calculated the Youden index for each cutoff value as corresponding ((sensitivity + specificity) − 1) to find the cutoff values that maximized discriminating power. We used IBM SPSS Statistics 26 for the analyses.

3. Results

3.1. Reliability

The intraclass correlations for interrater reliability were 0.95 for the left hippocampus, 0.92 for the right hippocampus, 0.91 for the left amygdala, 0.90 for the right amygdala, 0.91 for left HG, 0.93 for right HG, 0.91 for the left PT, and 0.95 for the right PT.

3.2. Relative Volumes of Each ROI

Table 2 shows the relative volumes of each ROI. For the amygdalae and hippocampi, the repeated measures ANCOVA showed significant hemisphere-by-region-by-group ($F[2,71] = 3.56$, $p = 0.03$) and region-by-group interactions ($F[2,71] = 8.72$, $p < 0.0001$) and significant main effects of group ($F[2,71] = 6.25$, $p = 0.003$) and region ($F[1,71] = 102.23$, $p < 0.0001$) but not hemisphere ($F[1,71] = 1.17$, $p = 0.28$). There was no significant hemisphere-by-group ($F[2,71] = 1.38$, $p = 0.26$) or hemisphere-by-region ($F[1,71] = 0.04$, $p = 0.84$) interactions. To delineate the significant hemisphere-by-region-by-group interactions, post hoc tests were performed for each ROI.

Table 2. Volume of each region of interest (ROI).

	Healthy Subjects (HS)	Patients with Bipolar Disorder (BD)	Patients with Schizophrenia (SZ)	*df*	*F*	*p*
Intracranial Volume (mL)	1380 ± 128	1422 ± 136	1418 ± 157	2, 72	0.79	0.46
Left Hippocampus						
Absolute (mL)	2.91 ± 0.22	2.92 ± 0.24	2.72 ± 0.24			
Relative (%)	0.211 ± 0.015	0.206 ± 0.022	0.193 ± 0.018	2, 72	7.47	0.001 *
Right Hippocampus						
Absolute (mL)	2.95 ± 0.29	2.86 ± 0.20	2.67 ± 0.28			
Relative (%)	0.214 ± 0.014	0.202 ± 0.020	0.189 ± 0.017	2, 72	15.06	<0.0001 †
Left Amygdala						
Absolute (mL)	1.26 ± 0.17	1.28 ± 0.14	1.24 ± 0.16			
Relative (%)	0.091 ± 0.009	0.091 ± 0.012	0.087 ± 0.009	2, 72	1.01	0.37
Right Amygdala						
Absolute (mL)	1.25 ± 0.20	1.31 ± 0.14	1.26 ± 0.17			
Relative (%)	0.091 ± 0.010	0.093 ± 0.012	0.089 ± 0.008	2, 72	0.78	0.46
Left Heschl's gyrus						
Absolute (mL)	2.03 ± 0.50	2.02 ± 0.53	1.95 ± 0.59			
Relative (%)	0.147 ± 0.032	0.148 ± 0.039	0.137 ± 0.035	2, 72	0.71	0.50
Right Heschl's gyrus						
Absolute (mL)	1.71 ± 0.48	1.77 ± 0.46	1.75 ± 0.55			
Relative (%)	0.123 ± 0.029	0.125 ± 0.034	0.123 ± 0.034	2, 72	0.03	0.97
Left Planum temporale						
Absolute (mL)	2.94 ± 0.60	2.88 ± 0.68	2.79 ± 0.56			
Relative (%)	0.213 ± 0.036	0.203 ± 0.046	0.197 ± 0.032	2, 72	1.20	0.31
Right Planum temporale						
Absolute (mL)	2.53 ± 0.76	2.56 ± 0.36	2.63 ± 0.65			
Relative (%)	0.183 ± 0.050	0.182 ± 0.032	0.186 ± 0.044	2, 72	0.06	0.94

* Post hoc tests indicated that schizophrenia (SZ) was significantly different from bipolar disorder (BD) and healthy subjects (HS) (Tukey's honestly significant difference test, $p < 0.05$). † Post hoc tests indicated that volumes were significantly different as follows; HS > BD > SZ (Tukey Honestly Significant Difference, $p < 0.05$).

For the amygdalae, the repeated-measures ANCOVA showed no significant main effects of group ($F[2,71] = 0.53$, $p = 0.59$) or hemisphere ($F[2,71] = 1.15$, $p = 0.29$), or a significant hemisphere-by-group interaction ($F[2,71] = 0.39$, $p = 0.68$). These results indicated that there were no significant group differences among the three groups in either hemisphere.

For the hippocampus, the repeated measures ANCOVA revealed a significant hemisphere-by-group interaction ($F[2,71] = 3.56$, $p = 0.03$) and a main effect of group ($F[2,71] = 9.21$, $p < 0.0001$) but not hemisphere ($F[1,71] = 0.32$, $p = 0.57$). In the right hemisphere, the one-way ANOVA showed a significant group difference ($F[2,72] = 15.06$, $p < 0.0001$), and post hoc Tukey's honestly significant difference (HSD) tests revealed BD < HS ($p = 0.04$), SZ < HS ($p < 0.0001$) and SZ < BD ($p = 0.03$) right hippocampal volumes. These results indicated that right hippocampal volumes were highest in HS, lower in the BD patients, and lowest in the SZ patients. In the left hemisphere, the one-way ANOVA showed a significant group difference ($F[2,72] = 7.47$, $p = 0.001$), and post hoc HSD tests revealed SZ < HS ($p = 0.001$) and SZ < BD ($p = 0.04$) hippocampal volumes. No significant difference was found for the left hippocampus between HS and BD patients ($p = 0.58$). These results revealed that SZ patients had a lower left hippocampal volume compared with HS and BD patients (see Figure 2).

For HG and PT, the repeated-measures ANCOVA showed a significant main effect of region ($F[1,71] = 20.85$, $p < 0.001$). There were no other significant main effects or interactions, which indicated no significant group differences in the HG or PT (see Figure 3).

We also performed repeated-measures ANCOVAs using age and sex as covariates for ROI analysis; statistical results were the same using both methods.

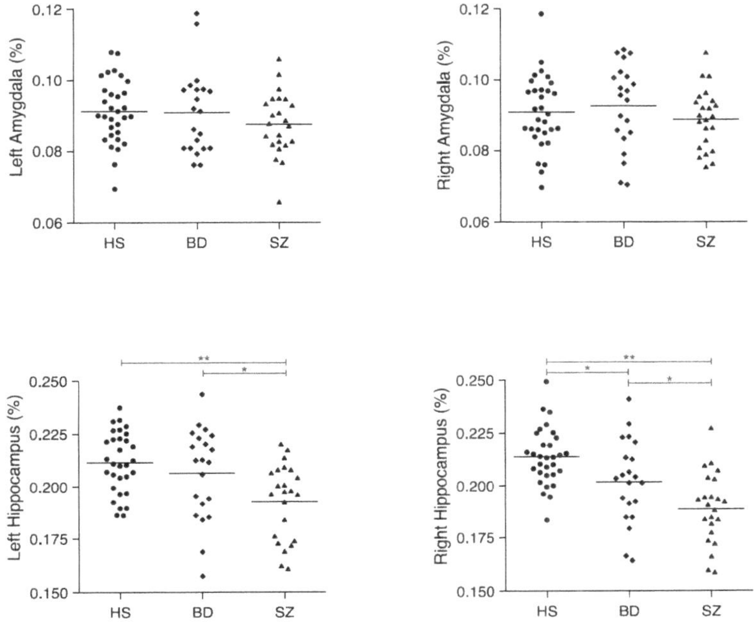

Figure 2. Relative volumes of the left and right amygdalae and hippocampi in healthy subjects (HS) ($n = 31$), patients with bipolar disorder (BD) ($n = 21$), and patients with schizophrenia (SZ) ($n = 23$). Horizontal lines indicate means. * $p < 0.05$, ** $p < 0.001$.

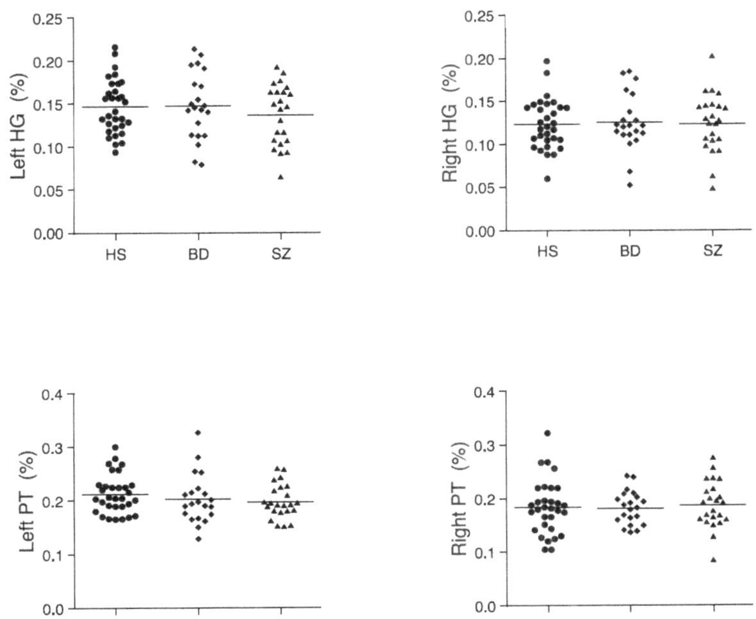

Figure 3. Relative volumes of the left and right HG and PT in HS ($n = 31$), BD ($n = 21$), and SZ ($n = 23$). Horizontal lines indicate means.

3.3. Correlations

Regarding the associations between ROI volume and demographic/clinical variables, we found no significant correlations in HS ($-0.34 \leq rho \leq 0.38$, $0.04 \leq p \leq 0.89$), SZ patients ($-0.34 \leq rho \leq 0.43$, $0.04 \leq p \leq 0.98$), or BD patients ($-0.40 \leq rho \leq 0.48$; $0.03 \leq p \leq 0.94$).

3.4. ROC Analysis

Since significant differences among three groups were observed in the right hippocampus, we used ROC curve analysis to explore the discriminatory value of the relative volumes. Figure 4 shows the ROC curve of relative volumes of the right hippocampus between HS and BD, HS and SZ, and BD and SZ. The area under the curve (AUC) of the ROC analysis in BD vs. SZ was maximal for the right hippocampal relative volume (AUC = 0.70, Standard error = 0.08, $p = 0.03$, 95% CI = 0.54–0.85), indicating that the right hippocampal volume could be used to differentiate between BD and SZ subjects with moderate accuracy. The Youden index indicated a favorable cutoff point of 0.20%, which resulted in 62% sensitivity and 74% specificity.

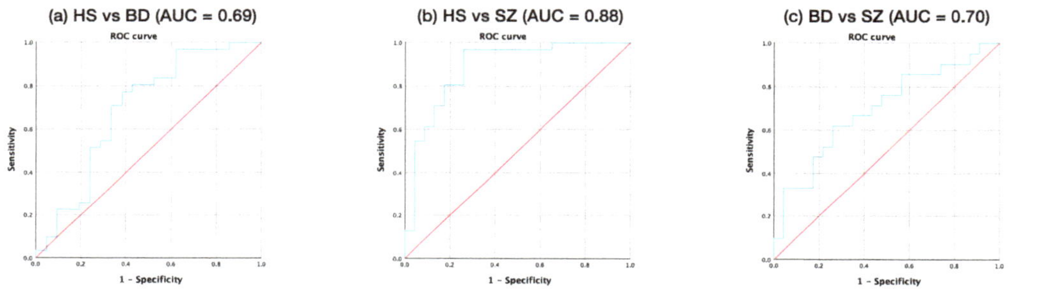

Figure 4. Receiver operating characteristic (ROC) curve of relative volumes of the right hippocampi between (**a**) HS and BD, (**b**) HS and SZ, and (**c**) BD and SZ. The area under the ROC curve was 0.69, 0.88, and 0.70, respectively.

4. Discussion

We investigated the volumes of the hippocampi, amygdalae, HG, and PT in SZ patients, BD patients, and HS. We found that right hippocampal volumes were lower in BD patients compared with controls, and further lower in SZ patients, whereas left hippocampal volumes were lower exclusively in SZ patients. There were no significant differences in either amygdala, HG, or PT among the three groups.

Our results are consistent with many previous studies (e.g., [27,48]) although the recent study [14] of the direct comparison found no significant volume differences between the two groups. Our findings suggest that the lateralized hippocampal volume abnormality is related to the development of SZ and BD. We also found that the lower left hippocampal volume was not observed in BD patients and was specific to SZ, which is in line with numerous studies that have reported left hemisphere dominant abnormalities in SZ [49].

Although the degree of lowered volume in BD patients was not to that observed in SZ patients, the volume of the right hippocampus was found to be significantly lower in BD compared with HS. The ENIGMA Consortium reported significant lower volumes in the hippocampus, thalamus, and amygdala in patients with BD [27]; however, they did not evaluate laterality. We revealed that lower right hippocampal volume may be associated with pathology of BD. We highlight that in addition to large sample automated analysis methods, alternative approaches, such as the manual ROI drawing method, are important and valuable.

In the present study, there were no significant differences in either amygdala among the three groups. Moreover, contrary to our hypotheses and findings of previous studies (e.g., [18]), we did not find significant group differences in HG or PT. Bryant et al. reported no differences in the volumes of temporal lobe structures between female SZ patients and

HS [50]. In addition, Bora et al. performed voxelwise meta-analysis and reported that gray matter reductions of SZ and BD were less severe in sex-balanced samples [15]. Therefore, sex effects should be considered in future studies in larger sample sizes. We did not find any significant associations between the volumes of the ROIs and demographics/clinical symptoms. Although hippocampal volume reductions may increase the risk of psychosis, they may not be directly related to the severity of symptoms. Given the function of the hippocampus, it will be important to investigate relationships between hippocampal volumes and cognitive functional domains in future studies.

Because SZ and BD share the biological basis of psychoses [1–11,51–57] and they sometimes present similar pathologies, detection of anatomical and functional biomarkers that differentiate SZ and BD patients is crucial for the optimization of pharmacological and psychosocial treatments for each condition. The results of our ROC analyses suggest that the right hippocampal volume is a potential marker for differentiation between SZ and BD. To this end, multimodal functional neuroimaging studies [26,51–61] that combine structural MRI [3,16,18–21,23,26–28,42–44,51,61–63], functional MRI [26,53–61,64,65], magnetic resonance spectroscopy [66–69], positron emission tomography [69–72], electroencephalography, and magnetoencephalography [4–9,59,73–85] may lead to a better understanding of the biological bases of SZ and BD and enable the development of optimized treatments (e.g., [53,54,58,61,86,87]).

We must note that this study has some limitations. First, we had a relatively small sample size owing to our type of dataset and manual drawing approach, which requires considerable time and labor. Therefore, weaker correlations that were hypothesized may have gone undetected. Second, as mentioned earlier, sex differences were not explored in our study but warrant investigation in a larger sample, as suggested by Bryant et al. [50], Egloff et al. [88], and Bora et al. [15]. Third, the effect of the duration of illness should be considered. The current sample of BD had higher age and lower duration of illness compared to SZ. Thus, in the present study, we could not exclude the effect of earlier disease-specific differences and late unspecific processes, including disease progress or effects of medications. Importantly, metaregression analysis by Fuar-Poli et al. [89] reported that the higher the cumulative exposure to antipsychotic treatment, the greater the gray matter decreases in the SZ group over follow-up time, while no significant effects were observed for duration of illness. Although there were no significant correlations between any ROI volumes and duration of illness in our study, associations between the effect of disease duration and the hippocampal volumes should be examined in a future study. Finally, we could not exclude the medication effects on hippocampal volumes in clinical groups, as pointed out by a previous study [90].

In summary, we showed that patients with SZ and BD have significantly lower hippocampal volumes compared with HS. Furthermore, we suggest that the right hippocampal volume is a potential biomarker for differentiation between SZ and BD.

Author Contributions: Conceptualization, T.O. and J.S.; methodology, T.O., J.S., N.H., and Y.H.; software, J.S., H.K., T.U., S.H., and N.H.; validation, J.S., N.H., J.T., I.N., N.O., Y.H., and T.O.; formal analysis, T.O. and J.S.; investigation, J.S., Y.H., and T.O.; resources, A.H. and O.T.; data curation, J.S., T.O., and Y.H.; writing—original draft preparation, J.S.; writing—review and editing, Y.H., T.N., and T.O.; visualization, J.S. and Y.H.; supervision, Y.H., and T.O.; project administration, Y.H., T.O., and T.N.; funding acquisition, Y.H. and T.O. All authors have read and agreed to the published version of the manuscript.

Funding: This research was supported, in part, by AMED (Japan Agency for Medical Research and Development) under Grant Number JP20dm0207069 (T.O.) and GAJJ020620 (JP19dm0107124h0004) (Y.H.); Grant-in-Aid for Young Scientists B JP22791129 (Y.H.), JP 15K19735 (N.O.), and JP 17K16385 (N.O.), a Grant-in-Aid for Scientific Research C: JP 16K10217 (T.O.), JP 19K08049 (N.O.), JP 15K09836 (YH), JP 18K07604 (YH), JP 19H03579 (Y.H.) and Fund for the Promotion of Joint International Research (Fostering Joint International Research B): JP20KK0193 (Y.H.) from the Japan Society for the Promotion of Science (JSPS); Medical Research Fund (Y.H.) from Takeda Science Foundation; SIRS Research Fund Award (Y.H.) from Schizophrenia International Research Society. The funding sources had no further role in study design; in the collection, analysis, and interpretation of data; in the writing report; and in the decision to submit the paper for publication.

Institutional Review Board Statement: The study was conducted according to the guidelines of the Declaration of Helsinki, and approved by the Institutional Review Board of Kyushu University Institutional Review Board for Clinical Trials (approval number: 26018, date: 12 June 2014).

Informed Consent Statement: Informed consent was obtained from all subjects involved in the study.

Data Availability Statement: The data that support the findings of this study are available on request from the corresponding authors upon reasonable request. The data are not publicly available due to privacy or ethical restrictions.

Acknowledgments: We thank the participants who took part in the study. We thank Sarina Iwabuchi, for editing a draft of this manuscript.

Conflicts of Interest: The authors declare no conflict of interest.

References

1. Anttila, V.; Bulik-Sullivan, B.; Finucane, H.K.; Walters, R.K.; Bras, J.; Duncan, L.; Neale, B.M. Analysis of shared heritability in common disorders of the brain. *Science* **2018**, *360*, eaap8757. [PubMed]
2. Lee, S.H.; Ripke, S.; Neale, B.M.; Faraone, S.V.; Purcell, S.M.; Perlis, R.H.; Wray, N.R. Genetic relationship between five psychiatric disorders estimated from genome-wide SNPs. *Nat. Genet.* **2013**, *45*, 984–994. [PubMed]
3. Ivleva, E.I.; Clementz, B.A.; Dutcher, A.M.; Arnold, S.J.; Jeon-Slaughter, H.; Aslan, S.; Tamminga, C.A. Brain structure biomarkers in the psychosis biotypes: Findings from the bipolar-schizophrenia network for intermediate phenotypes. *Biol. Psychiatry* **2017**, *82*, 26–39. [CrossRef]
4. Hirano, S.; Hirano, Y.; Maekawa, T.; Obayashi, C.; Oribe, N.; Kuroki, T.; Kanba, S.; Onitsuka, T. Abnormal neural oscillatory activity to speech sounds in schizophrenia: A magnetoencephalography study. *J. Neurosci.* **2008**, *28*, 4897–4903. [CrossRef] [PubMed]
5. Oribe, N.; Onitsuka, T.; Hirano, S.; Hirano, Y.; Maekawa, T.; Obayashi, C.; Ueno, T.; Kasai, K.; Kanba, S. Differentiation between bipolar disorder and schizophrenia revealed by neural oscillation to speech sounds: An MEG study. *Bipolar Disord.* **2010**, *12*, 804–812. [CrossRef]
6. Hirano, Y.; Hirano, S.; Maekawa, T.; Obayashi, C.; Oribe, N.; Monji, A.; Kasai, K.; Kanba, S.; Onitsuka, T. Auditory gating deficit to human voices in schizophrenia: A MEG study. *Schizophr. Res.* **2010**, *117*, 61–67. [CrossRef] [PubMed]
7. Tsuchimoto, R.; Kanba, S.; Hirano, S.; Oribe, N.; Ueno, T.; Hirano, Y.; Nakamura, I.; Oda, Y.; Miura, T.; Onitsuka, T. Reduced high and low frequency gamma synchronization in patients with chronic schizophrenia. *Schizophr. Res.* **2011**, *133*, 99–105. [CrossRef]
8. Isomura, S.; Onitsuka, T.; Tsuchimoto, R.; Nakamura, I.; Hirano, S.; Oda, Y.; Oribe, N.; Hirano, Y.; Ueno, T.; Kanba, S. Differentiation between major depressive disorder and bipolar disorder by auditory steady-state responses. *J. Affect. Disord.* **2016**, *190*, 800–806. [CrossRef]
9. Oribe, N.; Hirano, Y.; Del Re, E.; Mesholam-Gately, R.I.; Woodberry, K.A.; Ueno, T.; Kanba, S.; Onitsuka, T.; Shenton, M.E.; Spencer, K.M.; et al. Longitudinal evaluation of visual P300 amplitude in clinical high-risk subjects: An event-related potential study. *Psychiatry Clin. Neurosci.* **2020**, *74*, 527–534. [CrossRef]
10. Wolf, A.; Ueda, K.; Hirano, Y. Recent Updates of Eye-movement Abnormalities in Patients with Schizophrenia: A Scoping Review. *Psychiatry Clin. Neurosci.* **2020**. [CrossRef]
11. Kato, T. Current understanding of bipolar disorder: Toward integration of biological basis and treatment strategies. *Psychiatry Clin. Neurosci.* **2019**, *73*, 526–540. [CrossRef] [PubMed]
12. Brugger, S.P.; Howes, O.D. Group heterogeneity and homogeneity of regional brain structure in schizophrenia: A meta-analysis. *JAMA Psychiatry* **2017**, *74*, 1104–1111. [CrossRef]
13. Ellison-Wright, I.; Bullmore, E. Anatomy of bipolar disorder and schizophrenia: A meta-analysis. *Schizophr. Res.* **2010**, *117*, 1–12. [CrossRef]
14. Madeira, N.; Duarte, J.V.; Martins, R.; Costa, G.N.; Macedo, A.; Castelo-Branco, M. Morphometry and gyrification in bipolar disorder and schizophrenia: A comparative MRI study. *NeuroImage* **2020**, *26*, 102220. [CrossRef] [PubMed]
15. Bora, E.; Fornito, A.; Yucel, M.; Pantelis, C. The effects of gender on grey matter abnormalities in major psychoses: A comparative voxelwise meta-analysis of schizo- phrenia and bipolar disorder. *Psychol. Med.* **2012**, *42*, 295–307. [CrossRef]
16. Giuliani, N.R.; Calhoun, V.D.; Pearlson, G.D.; Francis, A.; Buchanan, R.W. Voxel-based morphometry versus region of interest: A comparison of two methods for analyzing gray matter differences in schizophrenia. *Schizophr. Res.* **2005**, *74*, 135–147. [CrossRef]
17. Botvinik-Nezer, R.; Holzmeister, F.; Camerer, C.F.; Dreber, A.; Huber, J.; Johannesson, M.; Kirchler, M.; Iwanir, R.; Mumford, J.A.; Adcock, R.A.; et al. Variability in the analysis of a single neuroimaging dataset by many teams. *Nature* **2020**, *582*, 84–88. [CrossRef]
18. Kasai, K.; Shenton, M.E.; Salisbury, D.F.; Hirayasu, Y.; Onitsuka, T.; Spencer, M.H.; Yurgelun-Todd, D.A.; Kikinis, R.; Jolesz, F.A.; McCarley, R.W. Progressive decrease of left Heschl gyrus and planum temporale gray matter volume in first-episode schizophrenia: A longitudinal magnetic resonance imaging study. *Arch. Gen. Psychiatry* **2003**, *60*, 766–775. [CrossRef]

19. Reite, M.; Teale, P.; Rojas, D.C.; Reite, E.; Asherin, R.; Hernandez, O. MEG auditory evoked fields suggest altered structural/functional asymmetry in primary but not secondary auditory cortex in bipolar disorder. *Bipolar Disord.* **2009**, *11*, 371–381. [CrossRef]
20. Frey, A.; Nery, M.; Quevedo, J.; Soares, K. The role of hippocampus in the pathophysiology of bipolar disorder. *Behav. Pharmacol.* **2007**, *18*, 419–430. [CrossRef] [PubMed]
21. Lieberman, J.A.; Girgis, R.R.; Brucato, G.; Moore, H.; Provenzano, F.; Kegeles, L.; Javitt, D.; Kantrowitz, J.; Wall, M.M.; Corcoran, C.M.; et al. Hippocampal dysfunction in the pathophysiology of schizophrenia: A selective review and hypothesis for early detection and intervention. *Mol. Psychiatry* **2018**, *23*, 1764–1772. [CrossRef]
22. Eichenbaum, H. Hippocampus: Cognitive processes and neural representations that underlie declarative memory. *Neuron* **2004**, *44*, 109–120. [CrossRef]
23. Haukvik, U.K.; Tamnes, C.K.; Soderman, E.; Agartz, I. Neuroimaging hippocampal subfields in schizophrenia and bipolar disorder: A systematic review and meta-analysis. *J. Psychiatr. Res.* **2018**, *104*, 217–226. [CrossRef]
24. Morris, J.S.; Ohman, A.; Dolan, R.J. Conscious and unconscious emotional learning in the human amygdala. *Nature* **1998**, *393*, 467–470. [CrossRef] [PubMed]
25. LaBar, K.S.; Gatenby, J.C.; Gore, J.C.; LeDoux, J.E.; Phelps, E.A. Human amygdala activation during conditioned fear acquisition and extinction: A mixed-trial fMRI study. *Neuron* **1998**, *20*, 937–945. [CrossRef]
26. Ho, N.F.; Li Hui Chong, P.; Lee, D.R.; Chew, Q.H.; Chen, G.; Sim, K. The Amygdala in Schizophrenia and Bipolar Disorder: A Synthesis of Structural MRI, Diffusion Tensor Imaging, and Resting-State Functional Connectivity Findings. *Harv. Rev. Psychiatry* **2019**, *27*, 150–164. [CrossRef]
27. Hibar, D.P.; Westlye, L.T.; van Erp, T.G.; Rasmussen, J.; Leonardo, C.D.; Faskowitz, J.; Haukvik, U.K.; Hartberg, C.B.; Doan, N.T.; Agartz, I.; et al. Subcortical volumetric abnormalities in bipolar disorder. *Mol. Psychiatry* **2016**, *21*, 1710–1716. [CrossRef]
28. Da Costa, S.; van der Zwaag, W.; Marques, J.P.; Frackowiak, R.S.; Clarke, S.; Saenz, M. Human primary auditory cortex follows the shape of Heschl's gyrus. *J. Neurosci.* **2011**, *31*, 14067–14075. [CrossRef]
29. Nakada, T.; Fujii, Y.; Yoneoka, Y.; Kwee, I.L. Planum temporale: Where spoken and written language meet. *Eur. Neurol.* **2001**, *46*, 121–125. [CrossRef] [PubMed]
30. Hirayasu, Y.; McCarley, R.W.; Salisbury, D.F.; Tanaka, S.; Kwon, J.S.; Frumin, M.; Snyderman, D.; Yurgelun-Todd, D.; Kikinis, R.; Jolesz, F.A.; et al. Planum temporale and Heschl gyrus volume reduction in schizophrenia: A magnetic resonance imaging study of first-episode patients. *Arch. Gen. Psychiatry* **2000**, *57*, 692–699. [CrossRef] [PubMed]
31. Javitt, D.C.; Sweet, R.A. Auditory dysfunction in schizophrenia: Integrating clinical and basic features. *Nat. Rev. Neurosci.* **2015**, *16*, 535–550. [CrossRef]
32. Hirano, S.; Spencer, K.M.; Onitsuka, T.; Hirano, Y. Language-Related Neurophysiological Deficits in Schizophrenia. *Clin. EEG Neurosci.* **2020**, *51*, 222–233. [CrossRef]
33. Hirano, Y.; Oribe, N.; Kanba, S.; Onitsuka, T.; Nestor, P.G.; Spencer, K.M. Spontaneous Gamma Activity in Schizophrenia. *JAMA Psychiatry* **2015**, *72*, 813–821. [CrossRef] [PubMed]
34. Hirano, Y.; Oribe, N.; Onitsuka, T.; Kanba, S.; Nestor, P.G.; Hosokawa, T.; Levin, M.; Shenton, M.E.; McCarley, R.W.; Spencer, K.M. Auditory Cortex Volume and Gamma Oscillation Abnormalities in Schizophrenia. *Clin. EEG Neurosci.* **2020**, *51*, 244–251. [CrossRef] [PubMed]
35. Takahashi, T.; Malhi, G.S.; Wood, S.J.; Yucel, M.; Walterfang, M.; Kawasaki, Y.; Suzuki, M.; Pantelis, C. Gray matter reduction of the superior temporal gyrus in patients with established bipolar I disorder. *J. Affect. Disord.* **2010**, *123*, 276–282. [CrossRef]
36. Oldfield, R.C. The assessment and analysis of handedness: The Edinburgh inventory. *Neuropsychologia* **1971**, *9*, 97–113. [CrossRef]
37. Hollingshead, A. *Two Factor Index of Social Position*; Yale University Press: New Haven, CT, USA, 1965.
38. Kay, S.R.; Fiszbein, A.; Opler, L.A. The positive and negative syndrome scale (PANSS) for schizophrenia. *Schizophr. Bull.* **1987**, *13*, 261–276. [CrossRef] [PubMed]
39. Young, R.C.; Biggs, J.T.; Ziegler, V.E.; Meyer, D.A. A rating scale for mania: Reliability, validity and sensitivity. *Br. J. Psychiatry* **1978**, *133*, 429–435. [CrossRef]
40. Williams, J.B. A structured interview guide for the Hamilton Depression Rating Scale. *Arch. Gen. Psychiatry* **1988**, *45*, 742–747. [CrossRef]
41. Ashburner, J.; Friston, K.J. Voxel-based morphometry-the methods. *Neuroimage* **2000**, *11*, 805–821. [CrossRef]
42. Kwon, J.S.; McCarley, R.W.; Hirayasu, Y.; Anderson, J.E.; Fischer, I.A.; Kikinis, R.; Jolesz, F.A.; Shenton, M.E. Left planum temporale volume reduction in schizophrenia. *Arch. Gen. Psychiatry* **1999**, *56*, 142–148. [CrossRef]
43. Barta, P.E.; Pearlson, G.D.; Brill, L.B.; Royall, R.; McGilchrist, I.K.; Pulver, A.E.; Powers, R.E.; Casanova, M.F.; Tien, A.Y.; Frangou, S.; et al. Planum temporale asymmetry reversal in schizophrenia: Replication and relationship to gray matter abnormalities. *Am. J. Psychiatry* **1997**, *154*, 661–667.
44. Shapleske, J.; Rossell, S.L.; Simmons, A.; David, A.S.; Woodruff, P.W. Are auditory hallucinations the consequence of abnormal cerebral lateralization? A morphometric MRI study of the sylvian fissure and planum temporale. *Biol. Psychiatry* **2001**, *49*, 685–693. [CrossRef]
45. Steinmetz, H.; Rademacher, J.; Huang, Y.X.; Hefter, H.; Zilles, K.; Thron, A.; Freund, H.J. Cerebral asymmetry: MR planimetry of the human planum temporale. *J. Comput. Assist. Tomogr.* **1989**, *13*, 996–1005. [CrossRef]
46. Barta, P.E.; Petty, R.G.; McGilchrist, I.; Lewis, R.W.; Jerram, M.; Casanova, M.F.; Powers, R.E.; Brill, L.B.; Pearlson, G.D. Asymmetry of the planum temporale: Methodological considerations and clinical associations. *Psychiatry Res.* **1995**, *61*, 137–150. [CrossRef]

47. Honeycutt, N.A.; Musick, A.; Barta, P.E.; Pearlson, G.D. Measurement of the planum temporale (PT) on magnetic resonance imaging scans: Temporal PT alone and with parietal extension. *Psychiatry Res.* **2000**, *98*, 103–116. [CrossRef]
48. van Erp, T.G.; Hibar, D.P.; Rasmussen, J.M.; Glahn, D.C.; Pearlson, G.D.; Andreassen, O.A.; Agartz, I.; Westlye, L.T.; Haukvik, U.K.; Dale, A.M.; et al. Subcortical brain volume abnormalities in 2028 individuals with schizophrenia and 2540 healthy controls via the ENIGMA consortium. *Mol. Psychiatry* **2016**, *21*, 547–553. [CrossRef] [PubMed]
49. Seidman, L.J.; Faraone, S.V.; Goldstein, J.M.; Kremen, W.S.; Horton, N.J.; Makris, N.; Toomey, R.; Kennedy, D.; Caviness, V.S.; Tsuang, M.T. Left hippocampal volume as a vulnerability indicator for schizophrenia: A magnetic resonance imaging morphometric study of nonpsychotic first-degree relatives. *Arch. Gen. Psychiatry* **2002**, *59*, 839–849. [CrossRef]
50. Bryant, N.L.; Buchanan, R.W.; Vladar, K.; Breier, A.; Rothman, M. Gender differences in temporal lobe structures of patients with schizophrenia: A volumetric MRI study. *Am. J. Psychiatry* **1999**, *156*, 603–609. [PubMed]
51. Karantonis, J.A.; Rossell, S.L.; Carruthers, S.P.; Sumner, P.; Hughes, M.; Green, M.J.; Pantelis, C.; Burdick, K.E.; Cropley, V.; Van Rheenen, T.E. Brain morphology does not clearly map to cognition in individuals on the bipolar-schizophrenia-spectrum: A cross-diagnostic study of cognitive subgroups. *J. Affect. Disord.* **2021**, *281*, 776–785. [CrossRef] [PubMed]
52. Dezhina, Z.; Ranlund, S.; Kyriakopoulos, M.; Williams, S.C.R.; Dima, D. A systematic review of associations between functional MRI activity and polygenic risk for schizophrenia and bipolar disorder. *Brain Imaging Behav.* **2019**, *13*, 862–877. [CrossRef]
53. Goodkind, M.; Eickhoff, S.B.; Oathes, D.J.; Jiang, Y.; Chang, A.; Jones-Hagata, L.B.; Ortega, B.N.; Zaiko, Y.V.; Roach, E.L.; Korgaonkar, M.S.; et al. Identification of a common neurobiological substrate for mental illness. *JAMA Psychiatry* **2015**, *72*, 305–315. [CrossRef] [PubMed]
54. Le, B.D.; Stein, J.L. Mapping causal pathways from genetics to neuropsychiatric disorders using genome-wide imaging genetics: Current status and future directions. *Psychiatry Clin. Neurosci.* **2019**, *73*, 357–369. [CrossRef] [PubMed]
55. Appaji, A.; Nagendra, B.; Chako, D.M.; Padmanabha, A.; Jacob, A.; Hiremath, C.V.; Varambally, S.; Kesavan, M.; Venkatasubramanian, G.; Rao, S.V.; et al. Examination of retinal vascular trajectory in schizophrenia and bipolar disorder. *Psychiatry Clin. Neurosci.* **2019**, *73*, 738–744. [CrossRef]
56. Omori, W.; Itagaki, K.; Kajitani, N.; Abe, H.; Okada-Tsuchioka, M.; Okamoto, Y.; Takebayashi, M. Shared preventive factors associated with relapse after a response to electroconvulsive therapy in four major psychiatric disorders. *Psychiatry Clin. Neurosci.* **2019**, *73*, 494–500. [CrossRef] [PubMed]
57. Kubo, K. Increased densities of white matter neurons as a cross-disease feature of neuropsychiatric disorders. *Psychiatry Clin. Neurosci.* **2020**, *74*, 166–175. [CrossRef]
58. Smucny, J.; Davidson, I.; Carter, C.S. Comparing machine and deep learning-based algorithms for prediction of clinical improvement in psychosis with functional magnetic resonance imaging. *Hum. Brain Mapp.* **2021**, *42*, 1197–1205. [CrossRef]
59. Knöchel, C.; Stäblein, M.; Storchak, H.; Reinke, B.; Jurcoane, A.; Prvulovic, D.; Linden, D.E.; van de Ven, V.; Ghinea, D.; Wenzler, S.; et al. Multimodal assessments of the hippocampal formation in schizophrenia and bipolar disorder: Evidences from neurobehavioral measures and functional and structural MRI. *Neuroimage* **2014**, *6*, 134–144. [CrossRef]
60. Hwang, H.C.; Kim, S.M.; Han, D.H. Different facial recognition patterns in schizophrenia and bipolar disorder assessed using a computerized emotional perception test and fMRI. *J. Affect. Disord.* **2021**, *279*, 83–88. [CrossRef]
61. Thompson, P.M.; Jahanshad, N.; Ching, C.R.; Salminen, L.E.; Thomopoulos, S.I.; Bright, J.; Baune, B.T.; Bertolín, S.; Bralten, J.; Bruin, W.B.; et al. ENIGMA and global neuroscience: A decade of large-scale studies of the brain in health and disease across more than 40 countries. *Transl. Psychiatry* **2020**, *10*, 100. [CrossRef]
62. Nogovitsyn, N.; Souza, R.; Muller, M.; Srajer, A.; Metzak, P.D.; Hassel, S.; Ismail, Z.; Protzner, A.; Bray, S.L.; Lebel, C.; et al. Aberrant limbic brain structures in young individuals at risk for mental illness. *Psychiatry Clin. Neurosci.* **2020**, *74*, 294–302. [CrossRef]
63. Nemoto, K.; Shimokawa, T.; Fukunaga, M.; Yamashita, F.; Tamura, M.; Yamamori, H.; Yasuda, Y.; Azechi, H.; Kudo, N.; Watanabe, Y.; et al. Differentiation of schizophrenia using structural MRI with consideration of scanner differences: A real-world multisite study. *Psychiatry Clin. Neurosci.* **2020**, *74*, 56–63. [CrossRef] [PubMed]
64. Roes, M.M.; Yin, J.; Taylor, L.; Metzak, P.D.; Lavigne, K.M.; Chinchani, A.; Tipper, C.M.; Woodward, T.S. Hallucination-Specific structure-function associations in schizophrenia. *Psychiatry Res. Neuroimaging* **2020**, *305*, 111171. [CrossRef]
65. van Dellen, E.; Börner, C.; Schutte, M.; van Montfort, S.; Abramovic, L.; Boks, M.P.; Cahn, W.; van Haren, N.; Mandl, R.; Stam, C.J.; et al. Functional brain networks in the schizophrenia spectrum and bipolar disorder with psychosis. *NPJ Schizophr.* **2020**, *6*, 22. [CrossRef]
66. Reddy-Thootkur, M.; Kraguljac, N.V.; Lahti, A.C. The role of glutamate and GABA in cognitive dysfunction in schizophrenia and mood disorders—A systematic review of magnetic resonance spectroscopy studies. *Schizophr. Res.* **2020**. [CrossRef]
67. Bustillo, J.R.; Jones, T.; Qualls, C.; Chavez, L.; Lin, D.; Lenroot, R.K.; Gasparovic, C. Proton magnetic resonance spectroscopic imaging of gray and white matter in bipolar-I and schizophrenia. *J. Affect. Disord.* **2019**, *246*, 745–753. [CrossRef] [PubMed]
68. Das, T.K.; Javadzadeh, A.; Dey, A.; Sabesan, P.; Théberge, J.; Radua, J.; Palaniyappan, L. Antioxidant defense in schizophrenia and bipolar disorder: A meta-analysis of MRS studies of anterior cingulate glutathione. *Prog. Neuropsychopharmacol. Biol. Psychiatry* **2019**, *91*, 94–102. [CrossRef] [PubMed]
69. Dogan, A.E.; Yuksel, C.; Du, F.; Chouinard, V.A.; Öngür, D. Brain lactate and pH in schizophrenia and bipolar disorder: A systematic review of findings from magnetic resonance studies. *Neuropsychopharmacology* **2018**, *43*, 1681–1690. [CrossRef]

70. Hellwig, S.; Domschke, K. Update on PET imaging biomarkers in the diagnosis of neuropsychiatric disorders. *Curr. Opin. Neurol.* **2019**, *32*, 539–547. [CrossRef]
71. Jauhar, S.; Nour, M.M.; Veronese, M.; Rogdaki, M.; Bonoldi, I.; Azis, M.; Turkheimer, F.; McGuire, P.; Young, A.H.; Howes, O.D. A Test of the Transdiagnostic Dopamine Hypothesis of Psychosis Using Positron Emission Tomographic Imaging in Bipolar Affective Disorder and Schizophrenia. *JAMA Psychiatry* **2017**, *74*, 1206–1213. [CrossRef]
72. Li, C.T.; Yang, K.C.; Lin, W.C. Glutamatergic Dysfunction and Glutamatergic Compounds for Major Psychiatric Disorders: Evidence from Clinical Neuroimaging Studies. *Front. Psychiatry* **2019**, *9*, 767. [CrossRef]
73. Molina, V.; Lubeiro, A.; de Luis Garcia, R.; Gomez-Pilar, J.; Martín-Santiago, O.; Iglesias-Tejedor, M.; Holgado-Madera, P.; Segarra-Echeverría, R.; Recio-Barbero, M.; Núñez, P.; et al. Deficits of entropy modulation of the EEG: A biomarker for altered function in schizophrenia and bipolar disorder? *J Psychiatry Neurosci.* **2020**, *45*, 322–333. [CrossRef]
74. Hudgens-Haney, M.E.; Clementz, B.A.; Ivleva, E.I.; Keshavan, M.S.; Pearlson, G.D.; Gershon, E.S.; Keedy, S.K.; Sweeney, J.A.; Gaudoux, F.; Bunouf, P.; et al. Cognitive Impairment and Diminished Neural Responses Constitute a Biomarker Signature of Negative Symptoms in Psychosis. *Schizophr. Bull.* **2020**, *46*, 1269–1281. [CrossRef]
75. Murphy, M.; Stickgold, R.; Öngür, D. Electroencephalogram Microstate Abnormalities in Early-Course Psychosis. *Biol. Psychiatry* **2020**, *5*, 35–44. [CrossRef]
76. Monaghan, C.K.; Brickman, S.; Huynh, P.; Öngür, D.; Hall, M.H. A longitudinal study of event related potentials and correlations with psychosocial functioning and clinical features in first episode psychosis patients. *Int. J. Psychophysiol.* **2019**, *145*, 48–56. [CrossRef] [PubMed]
77. Parker, D.A.; Hamm, J.P.; McDowell, J.E.; Keedy, S.K.; Gershon, E.S.; Ivleva, E.I.; Pearlson, G.D.; Keshavan, M.S.; Tamminga, C.A.; Sweeney, J.A.; et al. Auditory steady-state EEG response across the schizo-bipolar spectrum. *Schizophr. Res.* **2019**, *209*, 218–226. [CrossRef]
78. Spironelli, C.; Romeo, Z.; Maffei, A.; Angrilli, A. Comparison of automatic visual attention in schizophrenia, bipolar disorder, and major depression: Evidence from P1 event-related component. *Psychiatry Clin. Neurosci.* **2019**, *73*, 331–339. [CrossRef]
79. Newson, J.J.; Thiagarajan, T.C. EEG Frequency Bands in Psychiatric Disorders: A Review of Resting State Studies. *Front. Hum. Neurosci.* **2019**, *12*, 521. [CrossRef] [PubMed]
80. Zhou, T.H.; Mueller, N.E.; Spencer, K.M.; Mallya, S.G.; Lewandowski, K.E.; Norris, L.A.; Levy, D.L.; Cohen, B.M.; Öngür, D.; Hall, M.H. Auditory steady state response deficits are associated with symptom severity and poor functioning in patients with psychotic disorder. *Schizophr. Res.* **2018**, *201*, 278–286. [CrossRef] [PubMed]
81. Braeutigam, S.; Dima, D.; Frangou, S.; James, A. Dissociable auditory mismatch response and connectivity patterns in adolescents with schizophrenia and adolescents with bipolar disorder with psychosis: A magnetoencephalography study. *Schizophr. Res.* **2018**, *193*, 313–318. [CrossRef]
82. Ohara, N.; Hirano, Y.; Oribe, N.; Tamura, S.; Nakamura, I.; Hirano, S.; Tsuchimoto, R.; Ueno, T.; Togao, O.; Hiwatashi, A.; et al. Neurophysiological Face Processing Deficits in Patients with Chronic Schizophrenia: An MEG Study. *Front. Psychiatry* **2020**, *11*, 554844. [CrossRef] [PubMed]
83. Hirano, Y.; Nakamura, I.; Tamura, S.; Onitsuka, T. Long-Term Test-Retest Reliability of Auditory Gamma Oscillations Between Different Clinical EEG Systems. *Front. Psychiatry* **2020**, *11*, 876. [CrossRef]
84. Oribe, N.; Hirano, Y.; Del Re, E.; Seidman, L.J.; Mesholam-Gately, R.I.; Woodberry, K.A.; Wojcik, J.D.; Ueno, T.; Kanba, S.; Onitsuka, T.; et al. Progressive reduction of auditory evoked gamma in first episode schizophrenia but not clinical high risk individuals. *Schizophr. Res.* **2019**, *208*, 145–152. [CrossRef]
85. Hironaga, N.; Takei, Y.; Mitsudo, T.; Kimura, T.; Hirano, Y. Prospects for Future Methodological Development and Application of Magnetoencephalography Devices in Psychiatry. *Front. Psychiatry* **2020**, *11*, 863. [CrossRef]
86. Hirano, Y.; Tamura, S. Recent Findings on Neurofeedback Training for Auditory Hallucinations in Schizophrenia. *Curr. Opin. Psychiatry* **2021**. [CrossRef] [PubMed]
87. Habtewold, T.D.; Rodijk, L.H.; Liemburg, E.J.; Sidorenkov, G.; Boezen, H.M.; Bruggeman, R.; Alizadeh, B.Z. A systematic review and narrative synthesis of data-driven studies in schizophrenia symptoms and cognitive deficits. *Transl. Psychiatry* **2020**, *10*, 244. [CrossRef] [PubMed]
88. Egloff, L.; Lenz, C.; Studerus, E.; Harrisberger, F.; Smieskova, R.; Schmidt, A.; Huber, C.; Simon, A.; Lang, U.E.; Riecher-Rössler, A.; et al. Sexually dimorphic subcortical brain volumes in emerging psychosis. *Schizophr. Res.* **2018**, *199*, 257–265. [CrossRef] [PubMed]
89. Fusar-Poli, P.; Smieskova, R.; Kempton, M.J.; Ho, B.C.; Andreasen, N.C.; Borgwardt, S. Progressive brain changes in schizophrenia related to antipsychotic treatment? A meta-analysis of longitudinal MRI studies. *Neurosci. Biobehav. Rev.* **2013**, *37*, 1680–1691. [CrossRef] [PubMed]
90. Hashimoto, N.; Ito, Y.M.; Okada, N.; Yamamori, H.; Yasuda, Y.; Fujimoto, M.; Kudo, N.; Takemura, A.; Son, S.; Narita, H.; et al. The effect of duration of illness and antipsychotics on subcortical volumes in schi- zophrenia: Analysis of 778 subjects. *NeuroImage* **2018**, *17*, 563–569. [CrossRef]

MDPI
St. Alban-Anlage 66
4052 Basel
Switzerland
Tel. +41 61 683 77 34
Fax +41 61 302 89 18
www.mdpi.com

Journal of Personalized Medicine Editorial Office
E-mail: jpm@mdpi.com
www.mdpi.com/journal/jpm

www.ingramcontent.com/pod-product-compliance
Lightning Source LLC
Chambersburg PA
CBHW040806250926
51850CB00007BA/1092
* 9 7 8 3 0 3 6 5 3 1 3 1 1 *